Laurence Oliphant

Narrative of the Earl of Elgin's mission to China and Japan

in the years 1857, '58, '59.

Laurence Oliphant

Narrative of the Earl of Elgin's mission to China and Japan
in the years 1857, '58, '59.

ISBN/EAN: 9783742840257

Manufactured in Europe, USA, Canada, Australia, Japa

Cover: Foto ©Andreas Hilbeck / pixelio.de

Manufactured and distributed by brebook publishing software (www.brebook.com)

Laurence Oliphant

Narrative of the Earl of Elgin's mission to China and Japan

A WINTER SCENE IN JAPAN
FROM A JAPANESE DRAWING

NARRATIVE

OF

THE EARL OF ELGIN'S MISSION

TO

CHINA AND JAPAN

IN THE YEARS 1857, '58, '59.

BY

LAURENCE OLIPHANT, Esq.,

PRIVATE SECRETARY TO LORD ELGIN,

Author of the "Russian Shores of the Black Sea," etc.

"All sad the scene, a cheerless spot!
Ah! wo, I cry, an Envoy's lot—
Exiled, forlorn! How small his fame!
Peace, saith my muse; I'll aid thee bear
Thine honored toils. Away with care,
Nor murmur at thy country's claim."
HWASHANA'S COMPLAINT, p. 295.

NEW YORK:
HARPER & BROTHERS, PUBLISHERS,
FRANKLIN SQUARE.
1860.

PREFACE.

In the following pages I have endeavored to give a history of the proceedings of the Special Mission to China and Japan, which extended over a period of two years. It has been thrown into the shape of a personal narrative, in the hope that it would convey, in a more amusing and readable form, the record of our experiences in those empires.

Events have recently transpired in China which are deeply to be regretted, although they may possibly invest this work with an interest that it might not else have deserved. The untoward character of those events, and the serious consequences which they will probably entail, seemed to warrant my entering at greater length than I should otherwise have done into details more especially connected with the policy which Lord Elgin thought it expedient to adopt, and the difficulties with which he had to contend at the mouth of the Peiho.

The description I have given of Japan may very possibly be found to be somewhat at variance with the accounts which we may continue to receive from that empire. It is nevertheless in accordance with the results of our observation, and, I trust, conveys truthfully the impressions we were led to form of that country during our short residence in its capital. The circumstances under which we visited it were, perhaps, calculated to present to us the bright rather than the gloomy side of the picture. Our imaginations had not been excited by the glowing descriptions of former visitors, and our most sanguine anticipations consequently fell far short of the pleasing reality. We met with frankness and courtesy where we expected suspicion and reserve. In a country noted for its jealous distrust of foreigners, we enjoyed an entire immunity from all restrictions upon our personal liberty. We were prepared for a diplomatic contest with a government rigid in its adherence to a traditional policy of exclusiveness. A fortnight sufficed to enable us to conclude a treaty with it upon a most liberal basis. We had just passed a year in China, and all comparisons made with that empire were in favor of Japan.

That certain special reasons may have operated to render our reception at Yedo altogether exceptional; and to secure our diplomatic success, is very possible. It was only natural to suppose that, when those reasons had ceased to exist, those who followed us should experience a very different treatment.

In the accounts furnished by strangers of little-known countries, much depends upon the medium through which their observations are made—much also upon their capacity and knowledge of the world. Thus the diplomatist who expects to find the Japanese guided by the moral code of Western nations—desirous of giving effect to the stipulations of a treaty which they only accepted as an inevitable necessity, and anxious to increase their intercourse with a race which has been held for upward of two centuries in aversion and abhorrence—will probably describe them in a manner calculated to reflect less on their intelligence than his own. So the merchant, who expresses indignation and disgust at the reluctance of the government to assist him in his commercial enterprises —at its peculiar notions of political economy, and at the ignorance betrayed by his customers of all mercantile transactions on a grand scale, is certainly not likely to succeed in establishing a large "connection;" while a gentleman whose previous range of observation has been limited, on arriving in Japan from England, may be surprised at finding that it differs in some respects, in a social point of view, from his own country, and that the same articles of diet are not universally used by the human family in all quarters of the globe.

It is, however, most desirable that a new country should be presented in all its aspects; and it is only just to ourselves to state that the impressions we received during the brief period of our stay in Yedo are thoroughly borne out by the experiences of the Dutch, whose knowledge of the Japanese has extended over a period of two centuries and a half, as well as confirmed by those Americans who have resided for some years in the country. Meantime we may hope for the most beneficial results from the embassy which is about to be dispatched by the Japanese government to the nations of the West.

The very talented and truthful drawings, of which I have been permitted by Lord Elgin to avail myself, were presented to his lordship by Mr. Bedwell, R.N., who accompanied the mission to Japan in the yacht Emperor.

I am indebted to Mr. Jocelyn for several admirable photographs of the principal Chinese officials with whom we came in contact. My thanks are also due to Dr. Saunders for the Meteorological Register with which he kindly furnished me.

ATHENÆUM CLUB, 15*th Dec.*, 1859.

CONTENTS.

CHAPTER I.

The Origin of the War.—The "Arrow Case."—Policy of Sir John Bowring.—Hostilities at Canton.—Right of Entry into the City.—Bombardment of Yeh's Yamun.—The Results.—Insult to American Flag.—Destruction of the Factories.—Abandonment of the Factory Position.—Position of Affairs in February, 1857.—Effect of the foregoing Operations .... Page 17

CHAPTER II.

Appointment and Departure of special Mission.—Outbreak of the Mutiny in India.—Arrival at Singapore.—Its Chinese Population.—Causes of their Discontent.—Their Value as Colonists.—Trip to the main Land.—Residence of the Tumángong.—Wild Sports of the Malay Peninsula.—Gambier Plantations.—Luxuriant Forrest.—The Village of Tubrao.—Depredations of Tigers.—Great Increase of Cultivation.—Start on a Tiger-hunt.—Unsuccessful Result.—Arrival at Johore.—Malay Houses of Johore.—Historical Associations of Johore.—A picturesque Repast.—Return to Singapore.—Its rapid Progress.—Its Future 26

CHAPTER III.

Arrival at Hong Kong.—Trip up the Canton River.—A complicated international Question.—Chuenpee.—Monster Cannon.—Apathy of Population.—Macao Fort.—Unhealthiness of the River.—Spread of the Mutiny.—Its Influence on Lord Elgin's Policy.—Return to Singapore.—Address of mercantile Community.—Arrival at Calcutta.—Sensation created.—Moral Effect produced on the Natives 43

CHAPTER IV.

Condition of India in August, 1857.—State of Calcutta.—Organization of naval Brigade.—The Mohurrum.—Departure from Calcutta.—Policy adopted by Lord Elgin.—Residence at Hong Kong.—Its Absence of Attractions.—A Trip up the River.—Macao.—A Chinese Dinner 53

CHAPTER V.

Voyage to the Philippines.—Arrival at Manilla.—Appearance of the Town.—A varied Population.—Their Costumes.—Tobacco-manufactory.—The Price of Tobacco.—A Piña Shop.—Indolence of the Mestizoes.—Industry of the Chinese Population.—Chinese Emigration: its Advantages.—The Captain General of the Philippines.—Military Mass.—A Trip to Cavité.—A religious Procession.—Excursion to the Lago de Bai.—Los Baños.—The Romance of La Gironière.—The Island of Socolme.—A stormy Voyage.—The Trade of Manilla 60

CHAPTER VI.

Attempt of Count Poutiatine to reach Pekin.—Lawless Proceedings in the Canton River.—Singular native Proclamation.—The Hall of Peace and Patriotism.—

Preparations for War.—The Ultimatum.—Occupation of Honan.—Yeh's Answer.—Report of a Conversation between the Emperor Hien Fung and Ki Shuh-tsan.—Embarkation on board the Furious.—Disappearance of the floating Population.—Aspect of the river Face of Canton.—Expiry of the Delay.—Anchorage at Dane's Island.—Temper of the Inhabitants.—Delay of the Bombardment........ Page 75

CHAPTER VII.

Landing of the Troops.—Advance on Lin's Fort.—Treacherous Mode of Warfare.—Capture of Lin's Fort.—Attack of the Braves.—Position for the Night.—The Bombardment is continued.—Death of Captain Bate.—Skirmish with Braves.—Escalade of the Walls of Canton.—Aspect of the City.—Scene from Magazine Hill.—Capture of the City.—Capture of Gough's Fort.—Chinese Looting-parties.—Tartar Garrison of Canton.—Condition of the public Buildings.—Explosion of a Magazine 91

CHAPTER VIII.

New-Year's Day, 1858.—Exploration of the City by the Allies.—Capture of Yeh.—Yeh's Memorial to Pekin.—Behavior of Yeh in Captivity.—Conference relative to the Government of Canton.—Plans Proposed.—Scheme ultimately adopted.—Installation of Pihkwei.—Lord Elgin's Address to Pihkwei.—Pihkwei's Reply.—Institution of a civil Tribunal.—Moral and political Effects of the Occupation of Canton... 104

CHAPTER IX.

Withdrawal of the naval Force.—Yamun of the Tartar General.—"The Hall of State."—The ornamental Gardens.—Scenes at the Landing-place.—The Hall of Examination.—The "Avenue of Benevolence and Love."—Open-air Cookery.—Streets of Canton.—Joss-houses of Canton.—Future Punishments illustrated.—Allied police Corps.—Pihkwei's Proclamations.—A Luncheon at Howqua's.—Pihkwei's Dispatch on Trade.—Proposal to raise the Blockade 115

CHAPTER X.

Diplomacy in China.—Policy of the neutral Powers.—Proposed Expedition to the North.—Opinion of Count Poutiatine.—Proclamation raising Blockade.—Putinqua's Gardens.—River Scenes.—Lord Elgin's Visit to the Prisons.—State of the Prisoners.—Fate of Yeh.—Lord Elgin's Letter to Yu.—Departure for Shanghai.—Amoy.—Arrival at Shanghai.—Departure for Soo-chow.—Facilities of Water-communication.—Canal Scenes.—State of the Population.—Mr. Maclane's Visit to Soo-chow.—Boat-life on the Canals 125

CHAPTER XI.

The imperial Grand Canal.—Arrival at Soo-chow.—Entry of the City.—Curiosity of the Populace.—Reception by the Governor.—A complimentary Dialogue.—A Chinese official Repast.—Politeness of our Host.—Chinese Etiquette.—Political Effect of our Visit.—Reasons against exploring the City.—Exploration of the Water Suburb.—The Boat Population.—Manners and Customs of the People.—A nocturnal Visitation.—The Tai-hoo Lake.—A Gale of Wind.—Residence at Shanghai.—A Dinner with the Taoutai.—After-dinner Conversation.—Departure for Ningpo.—Ningpo.—The Shops and Joss-houses.—The old Pagoda 138

CHAPTER XII.

An Expedition to the Snowy Valley.—Mountain Scenery.—The Temple of the Snowy Crevice.—The Maou-kao-tae.—The "Thousand Fathom Precipice."—Sewe-kang-ha.—Our Fellow-lodgers.—The Dragon Waterfall.—Departure from the Snowy Valley.—Mountain Men.—A Voyage on bamboo Rafts.—Raft Navigation.—Arrival at Chusan.—A Roman Catholic Mission.—A Chinese country Residence.—Political Advantages of Chusan.—A British Grave-yard.—The sacred Island of Pootoo.—A degraded Priesthood.—The High-priest.—Picturesque Temples.—Pilgrims.—Magnificent View.—Chapoo .... Page 154

CHAPTER XIII.

Communication from the imperial Government.—Lord Elgin's Reply.—Sir John Bowring's Visit to the Peiho.—Course pursued on that Occasion.—Lord Elgin's Application for Gun-boats.—The Roman Catholic Mission of Siccaway.—System of Education.—Barren Results of Missionary Labors.—Superstitious Practices of Converts.—A "Feast of Tabernacles."—The Cathedral of Tonk-a-doo.—Difficulties attending Missionary Enterprise.—Non-arrival of the Admiral.—Departure of the Plenipotentiaries for the North.—The Miatou Straits.—Aground on a Sand-bank.—Arrival in the Gulf of Pechelee.—Dreary Weather.—An Expedition across the Bar.—Junk-hunting.—Arrival of the American Minister.—Difficulties of the Situation.—Unnecessary Delays.—Diplomatic Difficulties.—Aspect of the Forts.—Arrival of the Admiral.—The Dispatch-vessels cross the Bar.—Expiry of the Delay.—Postponement of Attack.—Political Consequences of the Delay 170

CHAPTER XIV.

Perilous Position of Dispatch Gun-boats.—Strengthening of the Forts.—Arrival of Chinese Re-enforcements.—The Question of full Powers.—Anglo-American Visit to the Peiho in 1854.—Intercourse on that Occasion.—Interview with Tsung and Tan.—Memorial of Commissioners in 1854.—Reference to Pekin.—Contemptuous Treatment by the Chinese Government.—Anxiety as to future Movements.—Memorandum of Sir M. Seymour.—Communication with Tan.—The final Summons.—Insolence of the Garrison.. 188

CHAPTER XV.

The Night before the Attack.—Delivery of the Ultimatum.—The Signal of Attack. —Advance of the Cormorant.—The Nimrod hotly engaged.—Chinese Artillery-practice.—The Batteries stormed.—"Sauve qui peut."—Terrific Explosion.—Aspect of the Fortifications.—Attack of the northern Forts.—Capture of the last Battery.—A Visit to Tan's Residence.—Imperial Edict.—Fate of Tan.—His Account of the Action.—Tan's Yamun.—A Poem "in Memoriam."—Return to the Furious 198

CHAPTER XVI.

Ascent of the River.—A Crowd of Junks.—Astonishment of Population.—Their submissive Behavior.—Brilliant Bonfires.—A Steppe Country.—Appearance of the Villages.—Difficulties of Navigation.—First View of Tientsin.—A Deputation of Merchants.—Appointment of imperial Commissioners.—The Plenipotentiaries ascend the Peiho.—Approach to Tientsin.—Dense Crowds.—"The Temple of Supreme Felicity."—View of the River.—Making ourselves comfortable.—Bedrooms in the Temple.—Farther Exploration of the Peiho.—Arrival of Russian and American Ministers.—Their Abodes.—Pean.—Arrival of the imperial Commissioners.—Full Powers at last.—Our official Procession.—" The Temple of the Oceanic Influences."—Interview with the Commissioners.—Exchange of full Powers.—Abrupt Termination of the Interview.—Arrival of the Kwang-Fang.—Kweiliang. Hwashana.—Success of Lord Elgin's Policy.—Its Bearing on Affairs at Canton.—Brighter Prospects .... Page 214

CHAPTER XVII.

The Chances of a Chinese political Career.—Arrival of Keying.—Interview with him.—Adverse Policy of Keying.—His Hostility to the Commissioners.—Proofs of his Insincerity.—Second Interview of Messrs. Wade and Lay.—Keying's Memorial.—Keying's Treatment of Barbarians.—A disagreeable Exposé.—Consequences of his Offense.—Lenient Sentence.—The Emperor's Decree.—Keying's Suicide 238

CHAPTER XVIII.

Insolence of the Mob.—A forcible Entry into Tientsin.—Making Reprisals.—Hostile Crowds.—Peaceful Proclamations.—Plan of the City of Tientsin.—Aspect of the City.—The Traffic in the Streets.—Declining Trade of Tientsin.—Notice concerning the Grain Supply.—Present State of the Grand Canal.—Official Expenditure of Grain.—Collection of the Grain-tribute.—State of the Yellow River.—Obstructions in its Navigation.—Grain Transport by Sea.—Report on the Grand Canal.—Price of Rice at Tientsin.—Table showing Proceeds of Grain-tax.—Trade of Tientsin.—Squalor of the Inhabitants.—Burial-places.—Total Allied Force at Tientsin.—Exploration of the surrounding Country.—The Harvest at Tientsin.—Kitchen-gardens.—Salt-pans.—Vetch-fields.—Locust-hunting 254

CHAPTER XIX.

Advantages gained by Russia and America.—A serious "Hitch."—The two important Demands.—The Right of a Resident Minister.—The Chinese System of Government: Mode of influencing it.—Principle of direct Communication.—The Concession gained.—The final Procession.—Signing of the Treaty.—An effective Illumination.—A Retrospect.—The new Ports.—The Transit-dues.—Climate of Tientsin.—Absence of Surveys.—Geography of the Country.—Abundance of Ice.—A Skittle-alley.—Curiosity-hunting 274

CHAPTER XX.

Duplicity of the Commissioners.—Arrival of the Emperor's Assent.—Arrival of Reenforcements.—Abandonment of Visit to Pekin.—Consequences of Delay.—State of Matters in the South.—Final Visit to Commissioners.—Death of the Prime Minister Yu.—Hwashana's Poems.—"Old" Chang: his poetical Effusions.—Departure from Tientsin.—The Great Wall.—State of Matters in the South.—Appointment of five Commissioners.—Military Government of Canton.—Lord Elgin's Dispatch to the General.—Departure for Japan 289

CHAPTER XXI.

First View of Japan.—Lovely Scenery.—Singular Boats.—Pappenberg.—Dungaree Forts.—Enchanting Scenery.—A philosophical Port-guardian.—Visit of Japanese

Officials.—Decima.—Removal of Restrictions.—Former Imprisonment of Dutch.—A smuggling Skipper.—Dutch Covetousness.—Strict Rules.—Recent Concessions.—Nagasaki.—Aspect of Houses.—Shops at Nagasaki.—The Streets.—Plan of the City.—Janitors of Decima..Page 301

CHAPTER XXII.

Missionary Success of Xavier.—Supernatural Gifts.—Heroism of Japanese Converts.—Theological Arguments of Converts: their Objections to eternal Punishment.—Louis Almeyda.—The Prince of Omura.—His Conversion.—Founding of Nagasaki.—Conversion of Princes.—Fate of Nagasaki.—Death of Sumitanda.—Constitution of the Japanese Government.—The two Emperors.—Taiko-sama.—Persecution of Christians.—Projects of Taiko-sama: his Invasion of the Corea.—Nagasaki annexed by the Ziogoon.—William Adams.—British Factory in Japan.—Japanese political Economists.—Intrigues of the Dutch.—Expulsion of the Portuguese.—Establishment of Decima 314

CHAPTER XXIII.

Surfeit of Sensations.—The Dutch and Russian Bazars.—Money-changers.—Tempting Investments.—Visit from the Vice-governor.—A Riding-school.—Surrounding Country.—A Visit to a Tea-garden.—Feasting and Music.—Productions of Fizen.—Coal Mines.—Prince of Satsuma.—Japanese Classes at Nagasaki.—Military Organization.—A Gale of Wind.—Volcanic Eruptions.—Places of future Punishment.—A stormy Night.—Arrival at Simoda.—Dangerous Harbor.... 331

CHAPTER XXIV.

Residence of the American Consul.—A Hermitage.—Visit to the American Consul.—His recent Success at Yedo.—Bazar at Simoda.—Torturing Indecision.—A Japanese Grave-yard.—Buddhist Temples.—The Sintoo Religion.—Household Gods.—A Japanese Temple.—Doctrines of the Sintoos.—Theological Speculations.—The Value of Sintooism.—A Visit from the Governor.—An expensive Form of Politeness.—General Appearance of Simoda.—Voyage up the Bay of Yedo.—Japanese Cottages.—Kanagawa.—Approach to Yedo 344

CHAPTER XXV.

Official Visitors.—We shift our Anchorage.—A Visit from Princes.—Object of the Interview.—A Japanese Man-of-war.—Visit to the Admiral.—Japanese Junks.—Imperial Uniform.—Inquisitive Water-parties.—Moriyama.—Visit of the Commissioners.—Landing-parties.—The Landing-place.—A Japanese Saddle.—The Procession through Yedo.—Excited Crowds.—The fair Sex.—Disfigurement of married Women.—Japanese Pleasure-parties.—Arrival at our future Residence 358

CHAPTER XXVI.

Residence of British Mission.—Plan of our House.—Soft Matting.—Japanese Spies.—Shingle Roofs.—The Princes' Quarter.—An obstructive Aristocracy.—Arguments on their side.—Evils of Civilization.—Restrictions on the Nobles.—Palaces of the Princes.—The Citadel.—Panorama of Yedo.—An imperial Banquet.—A shopping Expedition.—Fire-ladders.—We are mistaken for Chinese.—Bathing-houses.—Handsome Lacker-ware.—A Silk-mercer's.—An active Police.—Organization of the Police Department.—Street Dogs.—Wild Deer..................... 374

CONTENTS.

CHAPTER XXVII.

Constitution of Government.—"Nayboen."—The Spy System."—The Council of State.—A political Crisis.—The "Happy Dispatch."—Ruining a Politician.—The Japanese social Scale.—A Visit to the Citadel.—The Japanese Ministers.—Japanese Flunkies.—Tea and Sweetmeats.—Shopping in Yedo.—Dog Mania.—Official Visit of Commissioners.—Official Costume.—Ham and Champagne.—The first Day's Conference.—Jocosity of Higo-no-kami.—General Good-humor .... Page 391

CHAPTER XXVIII.

A Riding-party.—Beauty of the Suburbs.—A pleasant Tea-house. Tea-gardens at Hojee.—A picturesque Picnic.—Internal Arrangements of a Tea-house.—A Bathing-room.—Scenery of the Interior of Japan.—The Botanical Gardens.—A Visit to the Prime Ministers.—The Commissioners at Luncheon.—"The Scoundrel."—Schools at Yedo.—Linguistic Acquirements of the Japanese. System of national Education.—Japanese Literature.—The Postage System.—The Japanese Language: its Construction.—Universal use of Paper.—Ingenuity of the Japanese 407

CHAPTER XXIX.

A Japanese Funeral.—Mode of dressing Ladies' Hair.—Excellence of Japanese Steel.—Carvings in Ivory.—Musical Instruments.—Japanese War-fans.—An Expedition into the Country.—A Religious Festival.—Elaborate Tattooing.—The Logos River.—The Temple of Dai Cheenara.—The Interior of the Temple.—A singular Postscript.—Sumptuary Laws.—Sinagawa.—Taxation in Japan.—The Character of the Legislation.—Japanese Management of Children.—Results of our Experience.—Japanese Love of Pleasure.—Effect of Contact with Europeans 426

CHAPTER XXX.

Population of Yedo.—The Nipon Bas.—The Quanon Temple.—A Fair.—An Aviary.—A singular Tableau.—Theatrical Representations.—Toy-shops.—Astronomical System.—Mountain Pilgrims.—Japanese Wrestlers.—A conjuring Exhibition.—The Butterfly Trick.—The Commissioners at a Dinner-party.—After-dinner Enthusiasm.—Presents to the Mission.—Capacious Dressing-gowns.—Last Night in Yedo 442

CHAPTER XXXI.

Settling-day.—Japanese Currency.—Gold and silver Coins.—The Currency Difficulty.—Japanese Packing.—Signing of the Treaty.—Death of the Tycoon "Nayboen."—Probable Cause of his Death.—Profound Secrecy observed.—Evacuation of our Lodgings.—Presentation of the Yacht.—Parting Scenes 455

CHAPTER XXXII.

Future Prospects.—Civilization of Japan.—The Effect of the Treaty.—Dutch Subserviency.—Interviews of the Dutch with the Tycoon.—Policy to be pursued.—Necessity of mercantile Morality.—Resources of Japan.—Commercial Intercourse with China.—Government Interference.—Chow-chow Cargoes.—Competition with native Manufactures.—Probable Demand for woolen Manufactures, etc.—Vegetable Products.—Japan Wax.—Mineral Resources.—Commercial Prospects.—

Leave Japan.—The Port of Hiogo.—Ohosaka.—Kioto.—Caught in a Typhoon.—Arrival at Shanghai .... Page 463

CHAPTER XXXIII.

Effects of the Chinese Climate.—The Amenities of Shanghai.—Arrival of the Imperial Commissioners.—Correspondence relative to Canton.—Peace Proclamation.—Appointment of Sub-commission.—Our Chinese Colleagues.—Daily Conferences.—Rate of the new Tariff.—Transit Duties.—Collection of foreign Customs.—The Opium-trade.—Mr. Reed's Dispatch on Opium.—Reply of Lord Elgin.—Final Adjustment of the Question.—Visit of the Commissioners.—The jovial Ho.—A Dinner with the Commissioners.—The resident Minister at Pekin.—Proposed Expedition up the Yang-tse-kiang.—Signing the Trade Regulations.—Departure from Shanghai 477

CHAPTER XXXIV.

All the Ships aground.—The Delta of the Yang-tse.—Channel-hunting.—The Kiang-yin Bluffs.—Aspect of the River-banks.—Hard and fast.—Silver Island.—Yang-chow.—A Scene of Desolation.—Chinkiang.—Effects of Rebel Occupation.—Golden Island.—Magnificent View.—Off the Rock.—Tan-too.—Translation of Chinese Names.—Chinese Orthography.—Entrance to the Grand Canal.—Absence of Junk Traffic.—Approach to Nankin.—Action with the Rebels at Nankin.—Its Results 491

CHAPTER XXXV.

Renewal of the Action.—A sharp Bombardment.—The Batteries silenced.—An Action between Rebels and Imperialists.—Progress up Stream.—The Rebels receive a Lesson.—We land for Information.—Destitute Peasantry.—Request to aid the Rebels.—Notification in reply.—Enter the province Ngan-Hwui.—A military Procession.—The Eastern and Western Pillar Gates.—Arrival at Woohoo.—A Letter from the Rebel Chief.—We pay him a Visit.—A disorderly Mob.—Variegated Costumes.—An imperialist Spy.—Former Condition of Woohoo.—Its present State.—A Tai-ping Manifesto 505

CHAPTER XXXVI.

A Battle between Rebels and Imperialists.—An Exodus of the Population.—Arrival at Kew-hsien.—The Rebel Position.—Rebel Tactics.—Deserted State of the Country.—Tee-kiang.—Fine Scenery.—Recent Rebel Fortifications.—A wild-boar Hunt.—Description of the Country.—Our Pilot.—Cultivation.—Mandarin Visitors.—Character of the River-banks.—The Imperialist Fleet.—A Visit to the Commodore.—The Legend of the Hen Barrier.—Approach to Ngan-king.—We engage the Forts.—Attack of the Imperialist Troops.—The eight-storied Pagoda.—Tactics of the Imperialists.—Their Treatment of the Peasantry.—Toong-lew 525

CHAPTER XXXVII.

A foraging Expedition.—Our Pilot romances.—Grandeur of the Scenery.—The "Little Orphan Rock."—A windy Locality.—Entrance to the Poyang Lake.—Legend of the "Orphan Rocks."—Floods of the Yang-tse.—Method of accounting for them.—Rural Statistics.—Appearance of the Women.—Geographical Features of the Country.—The Valley of the Yang-tse.—Kew-kiang.—A Survey of its Resources.—Villages on the Banks.—Magnificent Scenery.—Depredations of the

Nee-fei.—We land at Hwang-shih-kang.—Its commercial Activity.—White Tortoise Island.—Enter the Province of Hoopeh.—The Philosopher Laoutz'.—The "White Tiger Mills."—An unsatisfactory Dialogue.—Approach Hankow .... Page 541

CHAPTER XXXVIII.

First Impressions of Han-kow.—Its Resemblance to Nijni Novgorod.—Our first Landing.—An orderly Crowd.—Plan of Han-kow.—View of Wo-chang and Han-yang.—Population of these Cities.—Manufacture of Bamboo Cables.—Price of Manchester Cottons.—Insect-wax.—The Mode of its Production.—Recent Demolition of Han-kow.—Its mixed Population.—Mandarinic Diplomacy.—Commercial Investigations.—Difficulty of obtaining Information.—A Dialogue.—Commerce of Han-kow.—The Tea-producing Districts.—A Visit to Han-yang.—Statements of Père Hue 558

CHAPTER XXXIX.

First Appearance of Strangers.—Snipe-shooting near Han-kow.—A Visit to the Governor General.—External Aspect of Wo-chang.—Reception by the Governor General.—A magnificent Repast.—The return Visit.—A brilliant Scene.—Inspection of Midshipmen.—The Brave Army.—Their singular Uniform.—Panoramic View of Wo-chang.—Reasons for our Return.—Subsidence of the River.—A "Squeeze."—Civility of the rural Population.—The Lee in Trouble.—Lime-quarries.—Wild Scenery.—Deep Water 572

CHAPTER XL.

Exploration of a Lake.—An educated Peasant.—Charging the Bar.—Intricate Navigation.—Good Sport.—We abandon the Furious.—Christmas-day.—Close Stowage in the Lee.—Approach Ngau-king.—Mr. Wade's Visit to the Rebels.—His Report of it.—Arrival at Woohoo.—A Rebel Communication.—We land at Nankin.—A Visit to a Rebel Chief.—Report of the Interview.—Our Interview with Le.—The real State of the Case.—Morals of the Rebels.—Strength of the Garrison.—The Rebel Theology 585

CHAPTER XLI.

The Yang-tse-Kiang commercially considered.—Sensation on our Arrival.—Sudden Appearance of the Furious.—The secret Edict.—Correspondence with the Commissioners.—The Affairs of Canton.—Result of the Correspondence.—Decree published in the "Pekin Gazette."—Departure from Shanghai.—Military Promenades near Canton.—Expedition to Fayuue.—A Voyage to Hainan.—Adieu to China.—Arrival at Malta 600

APPENDIX.

I. Treaty of Tientsin 611
II. Correspondence relative to a resident Minister at Pekin 622
III. The Treaty of Yedo 630
IV. Trade Returns between Shanghai and Japan 635
V. List of Articles generally sold, and of Staples found in the Shops at Hankow, when visited by H. M.'s Steam-ship "Furious," Dec., 1858 637
VI. Note on Prostitution 638
VII. Thermometrical Register kept by Dr. Saunders, R.N., from April 1, 1858, to March 31, 1859 640

LIST OF ILLUSTRATIONS.

	PAGE
A Winter Scene in Japan (*from a Native Drawing*)	Frontispiece.
Scene on the Tubrao River (Malay Peninsula)	35
Native House at Johore (Malay Peninsula)	38
Malay Sampan	40
Macao Fort (Canton River)	47
Mestizoes	62
Five-storied Pagoda	99
The Woosung River	133
Canal Scene near Soo-chow	146
Ningpo River	151
Tseen-chang-yen Waterfall	156
Sewe-kang-ha Waterfall	158
Our Bamboo Rafts	161
The Temple of Kwang-yin, Pootoo	165
Bonze at Pootoo	166
Bonze Praying	168
Capture of the Peiho Forts	203
Reception-Tent of the Imperial Commissioners, Takoo	206
The "Temple of the Sea-god" (Residence of Tan at Takoo)	212
A Bedroom at Tientsin	224
Sedan Chair	230
Kweiliang, First Imperial Commissioner (*from a Photograph*)	234
Hwashana, Second Imperial Commissioner (*from a Photograph*)	235
Signing of the Treaty of Tientsin	280
The Island of Pappenberg	303
Spire of a Japanese Temple (*from a Native Drawing*)	350
A Japanese Village (*from a Native Drawing*)	355
Yedo Forts	362
A Junk in the Bay of Yedo (*from a Native Drawing*)	364
The Landing-place, Yedo	368
A Japanese Horse-shoe and Saddle	369
Japanese Ladies and Children (*from a Native Drawing*)	372
Japanese Sandal	375
Plasterers at Work (*from a Native Drawing*)	377
A Fire-ladder (*from a Native Drawing*)	384
Pattern-designer (*from a Native Drawing*)	387
A Street in the Aristocratic Quarter of Yedo (*from a Native Drawing*)	389
Interview between the Earl of Elgin and the Prime Ministers of Japan	397
A Japanese Wig	402
Exchange of full Powers between the Earl of Elgin and the Japanese Commissioners	404

	PAGE
Tea-gardens near Yedo	410
Tea-gardens, Interior	414
Japanese Bath	415
Coopers at Work (*from a Native Drawing*)	421
Group of Horses (*from a Native Drawing*)	422
Japanese Artist (*from a Native Drawing*)	425
Japanese Funeral	427
Group from an Ivory Carving	430
Japanese Pipe, Case, and Pouch	431
A Samsie or Lute	431
A Japanese Divinity (*from a Native Drawing*)	435
Japanese Gymnasties (*from a Native Drawing*)	446
Astronomers (*from a Native Drawing*)	447
Pilgrims ascending a Mountain (*from a Native Drawing*)	448
Japanese Wrestlers (*from a Native Drawing*)	450
Travelers in a Snow-storm (*from a Native Drawing*)	454
Sieh, late Taoutai of Shanghai (*from a Photograph*)	481
The Seaou-koo-shan (Yang-tse-Kiang)	543
The Entrance to the Poyang Lake	545
View of Wo-chang	561
Kwan, Governor General of Hoo-Kwang, with his Suite (*from a Photograph*)	577

NARRATIVE

OF

LORD ELGIN'S MISSION

TO

CHINA AND JAPAN.

CHAPTER I.

The Origin of the War.—The "Arrow Case."—Policy of Sir John Bowring.—Hostilities at Canton.—Right of Entry into the City.—Bombardment of Yeh's Yamun.—The Results.—Insult to American Flag.—Destruction of the Factories.—Abandonment of the Factory Position.—Position of Affairs in February, 1857.—Effect of the foregoing Operations.

THE earlier incidents of the political rupture with the Chinese Commissioner Yeh, which occurred at Canton during the autumn of 1856, and which led to the appointment of a special mission to China for the purpose of settling existing differences, and, if possible, of placing our relations with that empire upon a new and enlarged basis, were too thoroughly canvassed at the time to render it necessary to renew here any discussion on their merits, or recall at length their details. As the "Arrow case" derived its interest, then, from the debates to which it gave rise, and its effects on parties at home, rather than from any intrinsic value of its own, so does it now mainly owe its importance to the accidental circumstance that it was the remote and insignificant cause which led to a total revolution in the foreign policy of the Celestial Empire, and to the demolition of most of those barriers which, while they were designed to restrict all intercourse from without, furnished the nations of the West with fruitful sources of quarrel and perpetual grievances.

But though, in this particular instance, the "alleged insult" itself claims but a brief notice, and that merely as a matter of history, the steps taken by our diplomatic and naval authorities on the spot to redress it are worthy of a fuller consideration, because there can be little doubt that it was in consequence of the results which these entailed, coupled with other causes which will be hereafter mentioned, that Lord Elgin was compelled to adopt a line of policy not altogether in accordance with his original instructions, as defined in the House of Commons by Lord Palmerston during the session of 1857. That this may be the more clearly apprehended, and a correct estimate formed of the embarrassing nature of the difficulties with which the high commissioner found himself surrounded at the outset, it will be necessary to narrate briefly the course of events which occurred in the Canton River previous to his arrival. Their consideration will enable us at once to perceive how humiliating was the attitude we were occupying in the eyes of the Chinese, and more especially of the Cantonese—how grave the injury which our national prestige was suffering in consequence, and how inconvenient were the complications arising out of the anomalous position in which Great Britain found herself placed with reference to other nations.

It will be remembered that on the 8th of October, 1856, a party of Chinese executives, in charge of an officer, boarded the lorcha Arrow, a vessel registered under an ordinance passed at Hong Kong eighteen months before, tore down the flag, and carried away the Chinese crew, refusing to listen either to the remonstrances of the master or of the consul, and insisting that the vessel was not British, but Chinese. Her papers were at the time in the consulate, but her register had expired more than a month before. Still Mr. Parkes maintained that she was entitled to protection under clause 10 of the ordinance, she not having been in the waters of the colony since the date of the expiry of the register. Mr. Parkes at once wrote to the imperial commissioner Yeh, complaining of the outrage, and offering to investigate any charge that might be brought against the persons seized. He also acquainted Sir J. Bowring and Commodore Elliot, the senior naval officer at hand, with the particulars of the circumstance. In the correspondence that ensued, Yeh refused to admit to Mr. Parkes that the lorcha was British, and maintained that some of the crew were pirates. He offered to return nine men. Mr. Parkes, however, was instructed to demand an apology in writing from Yeh— the return of the Chinese arrested to their ship—and their delivery to the authorities, if delivered, by and through the consul. Yeh persisted, in his reply, that the lorcha was not foreign property, had no flag flying, promised that Chinese officers should not seize foreign lorchas, and urged that foreigners should not sell registers to Chinese subjects building vessels. Meantime Sir John Bowring had threatened the commissioner with an application to the naval authorities; and a junk, supposed to be an imperial junk, but afterward found to be a merchant vessel, was seized by way of reprisal, and released. On the 15th of October Mr. Parkes informed Yeh of this seizure, also that a naval force was at the Barrier Forts. On the 21st inst., Mr. Parkes, under instructions, advised Yeh that, unless the requisition made was complied with within twenty-four hours, ulterior measures would be adopted.

In consequence of this threat, an hour before the expiry of the term, the twelve men were sent to the consulate, but without an officer of rank, or any letter of apology. Mr. Parkes wrote again to Yeh. Nothing resulting, he circulated among the foreign community the letter containing the ultimatum of the 21st. The same day Yeh had written, repeating his former arguments, and remonstrating against the seizure of the merchant junk. On the 22d Mr. Parkes replied to this as before, and in the evening warned the community by circular that the question was now in the hands of her majesty's senior naval officer. Correspondence to the same effect passed between Yeh and Sir John Bowring. It had in the mean time been decided by Sir John Bowring, in consultation with Admiral Seymour, that "the most judicious measure of compulsion" to be adopted would be "the seizure of the defenses of the city of Canton." In pursuance of this policy, on the 23d of October Admiral Seymour took possession of the four Barrier Forts, Blenheim Fort, and Macao Fort, without loss, and scarce a semblance of resistance, and, through the consul, advised Yeh of his arrival and intention to continue hostile proceedings against the defenses, public buildings, and government vessels, until reparation should be made for the wrong done. "His excellency's reply," says the admiral, "was very unsatisfactory." On the following day the Bird's Nest and Shameen forts were taken, without any attempt at opposition; and preparations were made for the defense of the factories, which were garrisoned; a body of

American officers, seamen, and marines provided for the interests of the American community.

On the 25th the island and fort of Dutch Folly were taken, and occupied without opposition. This act completed the series of operations, upon the efficacy of which the civil and military authorities had, to all appearance, confidently relied; but the result was as far from being attained as ever. The admiral writes: "*14th November*, 1856. All defense of the city being now in our hands, I considered the high commissioner would see the necessity of submission; and I directed Mr. Parkes to write and state that, when his excellency should be prepared to arrange the points in dispute in a satisfactory manner, I would desist from farther operations; but the reply did not answer my expectations." So far from any thing like submission, it appears that "an attack was made at 12.30 by a body of troops, supported by a much larger force, which occupied the streets in rear. Mr. Consul Parkes was on the spot at the time, and warned them to retire, but ineffectually. The guard of royal marines, in charge of Captain Penrose, then drove them back, with a loss, as we understand, of fourteen killed and wounded." The next day Yeh closed the Chinese Custom-house.

Such were the steps taken, and violent measures resorted to, in the vain attempt to induce the imperial commissioner to make the *amende honorable*. His power to resist even this trifling demand was now proved beyond a doubt. Our inability to enforce it had been no less unmistakably manifested; nevertheless, another letter to Yeh was dispatched on the 27th by the admiral, who thus alludes to it: "I concurred in opinion with Sir John Bowring that this was a fitting opportunity for requiring the fulfillment of long-evaded treaty obligations, and I therefore, in addition to the original demands, instructed Mr. Parkes to make the following communication." These additional demands involved the right for all foreign representatives of free access to the authorities and city of Canton. Hitherto the point at issue had been one simply of principle, and turned upon the right of the Chinese government to seize a lorcha under certain conditions. It is just possible that even this stubborn functionary may have had his doubts on the subject, and been disposed to purchase peace and quietness at the price of so immaterial a concession. But now any momentary weakness, if it ever existed, was passed forever. A grave question of policy had been raised—an old and much-vexed one, in the successful battling of which his predecessors had covered themselves with glory. Moreover, this sudden change of issue rouses the whole suspicious nature of the Chinaman, and he draws an inference somewhat discreditable to us, but not to be wondered at, which he thus expresses in a proclamation issued to the Cantonese:

"Whereas the English barbarians have commenced disturbances on a false pretense, their real object being admission into the city, the governor general, referring to the unanimous expression of objection to this measure on the part of the entire population of Canton in 1849, has flatly refused to concede this, and is determined not to grant their request, let them carry their feats and machinations to what length they will." Whereupon Yeh intrenches himself behind a triple mail of mandarinic pride and obstinacy, and retreats into the innermost recesses of his official dignity, from which we dug him out some fourteen months after. Meantime he does not condescend to answer the last letter, so at 1 P.M. his residence is bombarded. "The first shot was fired from the 10-inch pivot gun of the Encounter, and, at intervals of from five to ten minutes, the fire was kept up from that gun till sunset. The Barracouta, at the same time, shelled the troops on the hills behind Gough's Fort, in the rear of the city, from a position she had taken up in rear of Sulphur Creek." Under these circumstances, Yeh offered a reward of thirty dollars for the head of every Englishman.

The afternoon of the following day, from noon to sunset, was occupied in firing at slow time upon the houses opposite Dutch Folly, the inhabitants having been warned to evacuate them. The yamun of the imperial commissioner was distant about 150 yards from the river bank. By the afternoon of the 29th a breach had been effected to this spot, which was visited by the admiral with a force of marines and blue-jackets. The Chinese offered some resistance, killing three and wounding eleven of our men. For the three following days desultory firing was kept up on the town, and much of the suburb was destroyed by fire, but not intentionally. On the 1st of November the admiral again addresses Yeh, who answers, defending himself, without receding. He was nevertheless responded to by the admiral, and rejoined, in a letter, "recapitulating his former correspondence."

The admiral accordingly recommences operations, pulls down some Chinese houses to secure the factory position, and bombards the public buildings steadily, but slowly, for several days consecutively, during which French Folly is taken, and twenty-three war-junks are destroyed by the Barracouta, with a loss of one killed and four wounded. Another communication is also made to the commissioner, who seems to gain confidence from the frequency of these missives, for he answers curtly, and enters upon a vigorous course of retaliatory measures. Having neither armies or fleets to cope with ours, he makes war upon us in a desultory, irregular way, eminently harassing. Our ships in the river narrowly escape destruction from fire-rafts: night-attacks are made upon them; passenger steamers are fired upon, and foreign vessels, indiscriminately. An incidental result is an insult to the American flag, which is fired on from the Barrier Forts, which had been re-armed. As a measure of retaliation, these are taken and destroyed by Commodore Armstrong, of the United States Navy. Here the matter ends. Dr. Parker thinks the insult offered to the flag has been sufficiently avenged, and shortly afterward resumes correspondence with Yeh. The episode is interesting, as furnishing a contrast between our policy and that of the United States, under somewhat similar circumstances.

Meantime we demolish some of the Bogue Forts, and Howqua and other Canton notables address, and are answered by, Sir John Bowring and Admiral Seymour. On the 17th Sir John Bowring arrives at Canton, and puts himself into communication with the imperial commissioner on the 18th. The admiral (24th of November, 1856) states that he "reopened fire on the government buildings in the Tartar City from the guns in the Dutch Folly, but ceased at noon, to allow time for a reply to a note sent in by Sir John Bowring, proposing an interview with the high commissioner in the city; and his excellency added that, if it was granted, he was prepared to request me to cease hostilities. The reply was received the next day, declining the interview." The reward for barbarian heads was now raised from thirty to one hundred taels. On the 22d the French flag was struck at Canton.

On the 4th of December, French Folly, having been reoccupied and strengthened by the Chinese, was retaken, with a loss of two killed and several wounded. On the following day a seaman and marine are cut off. A few shells are still occasionally thrown into the city, and, on the 14th, the admiral states that he "feels a confident hope that the measures which have been taken will prove successful." The next day Chinese incendiaries burn down the whole of the foreign factories. The admiral writes (29th of December, 1856): "The great importance of holding our position at Canton being evident, and the church and barracks having been preserved, I determined to intrench a portion of the factory gardens." On the 17th the admiral commences to intrench himself accordingly, and garrisons the fortified position with a force of three hundred men.

Encouraged by this success, Yeh carries on the war, in his own peculiar fashion, with greater vigor than ever. On the 23d Mr. Cowper is kidnapped from Whampoa. On the 30th the Thistle postal steamer is seized by the Chinese on board; eleven persons murdered, and their heads carried off. The Chinese gentry of the district opposite Hong Kong interdict supplies being furnished to the colony. The magistrate of another district orders the servants to withdraw from foreign employ. Placards are issued interdicting trade, and promising rewards for heads. On the 4th of January the Chinese attack the ships about Macao Fort in force, and sink junks in one of the neighboring passages; also nearly succeed in blowing up one of our ships with explosive machines. On the 12th, our position in the factory gardens having been threatened, we burn the suburbs right and left of the factory site. During this operation, a party of the 59th, approaching the city-wall, is repulsed with loss. The admiral (14th of January, 1857) at once decides upon retreating from his position in the factory gardens and Dutch Folly, and, falling back upon Bird's-nest Fort and Macao Fort, applies to his excellency the Governor General of India for the assistance of 5000 troops. He subsequently finds himself compelled to abandon Bird's-nest Fort (30th of January, 1857), which he had intended to hold as his advanced post, and, withdrawing the garrison he had placed there, retains only Macao Fort. It was even at one time in contemplation to evacuate the river entirely, and this was a course strongly urged upon the admiral by some of his advisers. Fortunately, however, bolder counsels prevailed; and, although the Chinese kept up a series of pertinacious and harassing attacks upon our garrison in Macao Fort, commanded then by the gallant but lamented Captain Bate, we suffered no farther reverses at their hands. Meantime an attempt had just been made to poison the whole foreign community of Hong Kong.

From this condensed account, some idea may be formed of the stage which war and diplomacy had reached in the south of China at the beginning of February, 1857. But little change had taken place in either up to the time of our arrival there, about four months afterward. The diplomacy remained in abeyance; the war was apparently being kept up upon very much the same principles on which it had been begun. The Chinese continued to kidnap, assassinate, seize steamers, and annoy us in sundry cunningly-devised methods. We continued to hunt them down in creeks, burn villages where outrages had been committed, and otherwise pay them out to the best of our ability—not, it must be confessed, in a manner calculated to increase their terror for our arms, or their respect for our civilization. With the exception of the affair in the Fatshan Creek, no fighting of any consequence occurred.

It is not difficult to perceive how, under these circumstances, every month that passed by inspired Yeh with fresh confidence in his own resources, and, inasmuch as we never made a move in advance, with increased contempt for ours. Never before since the abolition of the old monopoly had Englishmen made so poor a figure in the eyes of the Chinese populace. If one went into a curiosity shop at Hong Kong, he was the object of the quiet irony of the sleek vendor of carved ivory behind the counter, who informed him that his choice collection was at Canton, and asked, "Why you no can come my shop Canton? allo same fore tim: my gotchie too muchee olo handser culio that side." The very urchins in the street considered a Briton a fit subject for "chaff," while their respectable parents took a mercenary view of his head. Hong Kong was neither a safe nor agreeable abode in those days.

It was too late then to consider whether the Arrow had in the first instance been British or Chinese, or whether the claim for redress made eight months previously was just or unjust; nor did it seem to avail now to discuss the wisdom of the policy which had superadded a second and infinitely more obnoxious demand, just at the period when it seemed most hopeless that we should obtain even the first. It was small consolation to be told that we ought never to have abandoned the factory position, and that a little sharp cannonading, instead of a shot every ten minutes, would have soon brought Yeh to his senses. These were professional questions on which it would have been presumptuous to offer an opinion; but there was one conviction arising out of it all which irresistibly impressed itself upon the mind of every new-comer, and which was, that a continuance of this state of matters would not only injure our colony, impair our prestige, embarrass us in our relations with neutral powers, and imperil our commerce at all the other ports of the empire, but enhance materially the difficulties in the way of any negotiations which might be attempted directly with the court of Pekin. It could hardly be expected or hoped that, while Yeh was waging a successful war with us in the Canton River, we could be treating upon favorable terms in the Peiho.

It so happened that other causes combined to give increased weight to these considerations: these will come to be noticed in their turn. Meantime I have thought it better, at the outset, to cast this brief retrospective glance over the events of the half year preceding our arrival in China, partly in the hope that it may enable the reader to form some idea of the actual posture of affairs at that juncture, and partly because it may be presumed that the insight which a review of these proceedings afforded, both as to the character of the people with whom he was about to deal, and the nature of the difficulties against which he would have to contend, was not lost upon Lord Elgin.

CHAPTER II.

Appointment and Departure of special Mission.—Outbreak of the Mutiny in India.—Arrival at Singapore.—Its Chinese Population.—Causes of their Discontent.—Their Value as Colonists.—Trip to the main Land.—Residence of the Tumángong.—Wild Sports of the Malay Peninsula.—Gambier Plantations.—Luxuriant Forrest.—The Village of Tubrao.—Depredations of Tigers.—Great Increase of Cultivation.—Start on a Tiger-hunt.—Unsuccessful Result.—Arrival at Johore.—Malay Houses of Johore.—Historical Associations of Johore.—A picturesque Repast.—Return to Singapore.—Its rapid Progress.—Its Future.

In consequence of the unsatisfactory progress of affairs in the south of China, described in the last chapter, that country was favored with a larger share of public interest in England during the spring of 1857 than had been accorded to it at any period for the last fifteen years. An expeditionary force of 5000 men, with a staff equipment calculated for a much larger army, and in every respect thoroughly complete, was on its way to the probable theatre of war. Generals and officers of high rank were leaving town by each successive mail. Not only had England determined to send out a special high commissioner, accredited as embassador to the court of Pekin, but France, Russia, and America had each declared their intention of improving the occasion, and dispatching plenipotentiaries extraordinary to China. Thus every thing conspired to induce the belief that the attention of the world was about to be concentrated on the Celestial Empire; and it was not to be wondered at that, though not present in London drawing-rooms, Yeh did in fact monopolize the honors of the earlier part of the season, or that the prospect of accompanying a special mission to the scene of his exploits, and, possibly, to the throne of his imperial master, possessed attractions of a novel and striking character.

More fortunate than former embassies, we were saved the long sea-voyage, which must have had a tendency to damp the ardor of exploration; and being consigned instead to the mercies of the Peninsular and Oriental Company, found ourselves, on the 9th of May, 1857, rushing across the desert in the first train which had ever carried passengers to the central station, enveloped in clouds of dust, and indulging in most sanguine anticipations of the future.*

How little could we imagine that a storm was at this moment bursting over the plains of Upper India which should rivet upon itself the concentrated and anxious gaze of the world, and which, in its swift and relentless course, seemed pregnant with consequences so disastrous and appalling, that all minor cares of state policy faded into insignificance, and became utterly absorbed in its one engrossing interest, just as passing squalls are overwhelmed and smothered in the impetuous fury of a typhoon.

It was not not until we reached Galle that we received from General Ashburnham, who had just arrived from Bombay, and was on his way to the commander-in-chief in China, the first intelligence of the serious aspect which matters had assumed in the northwest provinces of India, and of the spread of disaffection among the sepoy troops. Although the particulars of the dreadful tragedy which had taken place at Delhi and Meerut had not yet reached us, we heard enough to lead us to anticipate the probability of these occurrences affecting, in an important degree, the prospects of the mission to China.

General Ashburnham and his staff accompanied us to Singapore, whence they proceeded to China, while Lord Elgin disembarked here, and took up his residence with the governor, to await the Shannon, the frigate placed by the government at Lord Elgin's disposal, and the arrival of which was hourly expected. The importance of rendering the approach of an envoy invested with such extensive powers as imposing as possible in the eyes of a nation notorious for attaching the highest significance to external pomp and ceremony, seemed more than sufficient to justify

---

* The special mission was composed as follows: His Excellency the Earl of Elgin and Kincardine, K.T., High Commissioner; the Hon. F. W. A. Bruce, Secretary to the Mission; Messrs. Donald Cameron, George Fitz-Roy, H. B. Loch, and R. Morrison, Attachés; Mr. Laurence Oliphant, Private Secretary.

On the arrival of the mission in China, Mr. T. F. Wade was attached as Chinese secretary; and in August, Dr. M. K. Saunders, R.N., was attached as medical attendant. In March, 1858, Mr. H. N. Lay accompanied the mission to Tientsin as assistant Chinese secretary and interpreter. In July Mr. Bruce proceeded to England in charge of the treaty of Tientsin, and the Hon. N. Jocelyn arrived to replace Mr. Cameron, who was promoted to a post in Europe. Mr. Morrison also returned to England, and Mr. Oliphant succeeded Mr. Bruce as acting secretary to the mission. In September Mr. Loch went home on sick certificate, having also charge of the Japanese treaty.

the delay of three weeks which was thus unavoidably incurred. Nor, under the circumstances, was the time misspent. A confirmation of the news we heard at Galle, together with the representations of Lord Canning, induced Lord Elgin to take upon himself the serious responsibility of diverting from their destination the first installment of the troops which soon after arrived at Singapore from the Mauritius on their way to China.

Other circumstances were not wanting to render our stay at Singapore full of interest at this juncture, and these were closely connected with the objects of the mission. A few weeks had scarcely elapsed since occurrences had taken place among the Chinese population at Penang, Sarawak, and Singapore, which, from their simultaneity with one another, and with the treacherous attempt upon the lives of the British residents at Hong Kong, induced the suspicion of an extended concerted action—a suspicion which seemed to have amounted to certainty in the minds of the great majority of the English in these settlements, in whom a knowledge of the power and extent of the organization of the Chinese secret societies excited a not unnatural alarm, and whose minds were so deeply impressed, by old association and prejudice, with a fear of the cruelty and treachery of the Chinese, that they were apt to overlook other qualities in the character of that race which, to an impartial observer, seemed effectually to neutralize these attributes.

In each of the instances above alluded to local causes of irritation existed, apparently sufficient to account for the disturbances which ensued, without connecting them with the disputes at Canton. In Borneo, the immediate origin of the outbreak was a difference of opinion in a question of opium smuggling between Sir James Brooke and the Chinese, though for some time past these people had manifested an independent spirit, and a disposition to resist the laws which the rajah—who had treated them perhaps with too much kindness and indulgence—saw fit to impose. That their animosity was confined to himself and his executive only, and involved no general principle of hostility to the British, was proved by the fact that they requested the bishop to assume the reins of government. In the Straits settlement, the promulgation of some police regulations interfering with certain of their religious ceremonies and festivals, and the manner in which these were put into execution, roused their indignation, though it is questionable whether, had the object of these ever been explained to them, they would not have recognized their expediency.

At present there is a population of 70,000 Chinamen in Singapore, and not a single European who understands their language. The consequence is, that, in the absence of any competent interpreter, they are generally ignorant of the designs of government, and, regarding themselves still as Chinese subjects, are apt to place themselves in an antagonistic attitude whenever laws are passed affecting their peculiar customs. No effort is made to overcome a certain exclusiveness arising hence; and this is fostered by the secret societies, which exercise an important moral influence upon the minds of all, but more particularly the ignorant portion of the population. Were Chinese themselves put into positions of authority under government, and allowed to share to some extent in the duties and responsibilities of British citizens, which, intellectually speaking, they are quite competent to undertake, the barrier which now exists between the two races would be partially removed, and the mutual distrust and suspicion engendered by our present system would in all probability quickly disappear. Nor is this mere speculation. We have fortunately in their own empire a perpetual proof before our eyes of that reverence for authority *when judiciously enforced* which is one of their chief characteristics, and which has for so many centuries been the preservation of its union and one great source of its prosperity.

That the most active, industrious, and enterprising race in the Eastern world should be regarded as a source of weakness rather than of strength to a community, implies, *primâ facie*, a certain degree of mismanagement. The Chinese who have been attracted to Singapore by its freedom from commercial restrictions, and advantages of position, have contributed to make it what it is, the most prosperous settlement in the East; and when we consider their extraordinary acquisitiveness and love of gain, we can hardly suppose that their sympathies with their brethren in China would be sufficiently powerful to induce them wantonly to interrupt a commerce from which they derive enormous profits, and destroy a mercantile emporium which may be said to be in a great degree their own handiwork, and in which they possess a larger stake than any other class of its community.

To the stranger first arriving in Singapore nothing can be more striking than the busy aspect which the place presents. Every street swarms with long tails and loose trowsers; throughout whole sections of the town are red lintels of the door-posts covered with fantastic characters, which betoken a Chinese owner. At early dawn the incessant hammering, stitching, and cobleriug commences, which lasts until nearly midnight; when huge paper lanterns, covered with strange devices, throw a subdued light over rows of half-naked yellow figures, all eagerly engaged in the legitimate process of acquiring dollars by the sweat of their brow. It is impossible to overestimate the value of such a race, or to rate too highly the importance of placing them in such relations with the governing powers, by the cultivation of a more familiar intercourse, and a certain deference to their habits and prejudices, as should render them contented and trustworthy, as well as profitable members of society.

I was fortunate enough to have a farther opportunity of observing the energy and enterprise of these people in a short trip which I made to the main land, in company with Mr. Cameron and Captain Scott, at the invitation of the son of the Tumângong of Johore, who is now the ruler of that Malay state. The latter is the son of the man who claimed the independent rule of the territory in which, at the time of our purchase of Singapore, the island was situated. This claim was disputed by the then Sultan of Johore. The Tumângong, however, was supported by the British government, which entered into a treaty with him and the Sultan of Johore, by which it was agreed that the rights of the Tumângong to the government should be recognized upon payment by him to the sultan of a certain annual pension. Both these dignitaries now reside in Singapore, and the Tumângong or his son only occasionally visit their possessions on the main land. In the latter we found a most hospitable and amiable entertainer.

The protracted festivities consequent on a ball given in Lord Elgin's honor by the mercantile community rendered our departure rather later on the morning of the 13th of June than we had intended. At last, however, our host, to whom such gayety was unusual, appeared with a very roomy dog-cart, in which we packed away ourselves and our guns. Our roads intersected the island, here about fourteen miles across, first passing between well-trimmed hedges of graceful bamboo, through plantations of nutmegs, that clothe the numerous swelling knolls with which the country round the town is pleasantly diversified, and the summits of most of which are crowned with the handsome bungalows of the English and German residents. About half way we pass Bakit-timah, the highest hill in the island, and which, though only 500 feet above the sea-level, enjoys a climate so superior to that of the town of Singapore that it is talked of as a sanitarium for troops. The country generally is pretty well cultivated; there are two or three sugar plantations, but the cultivation is not sufficiently remunerative to induce extended speculation. Gambier (*uncaria gambir*) and pepper are more profitable; and we pass through occasional plantations of these on our way to Kranji, whence we were to cross the strait which separates the island from the main.

We had some difficulty in embarking on board the two sampans, or Malay boats, which we found waiting for us here, anchored at a distance from the sloping muddy bank, and which soon transported us to the opposite shore, whence we ascended to the comfortable bungalow of the Tumângong. Situated upon the summit of a cleared hill, it commands a beautiful view of the narrow straits and swelling shores, clothed in the richest verdure to the water's edge. At the foot of the hill the village of Sicudai, built and inhabited entirely by Chinese emigrants within the last few years, is perched on piles, which extend some yards from the shore.

We found a sumptuous repast prepared for us in European style in the bungalow, which answers the double purpose of a residence for the Tumângong and a court-house for his subjects. At this point the Sicudai River enters the straits, and upon its banks a large number of pepper and gambier plantations have been lately opened by the Chinese; it flows round the base of the mountain of Gunung Pulai, which rises to a height of about 3000 feet above the sea-level, and which the Tumângong has consented to allow the government to make use of as a sanitarium—an offer of which we have not as yet been sensible enough to avail ourselves. Easy of access, either by land or water, from Singapore, it would be a most agreeable resort for the European part of the population during the hottest months; and a road from hence might be cut across the country to Malacca, distant about seventy miles, which, while it would open up to Chinese enterprise an almost unknown district, would form a valuable means of communication between our own settlements.

At present the principal attraction which Gunung Pulai and its neighborhood offer are the wild animals which are found in those rarely-trodden forests. The sportsman who has exhausted every variety of game to be found in the jungles of India will derive a fresh excitement here in hunting the rhinoceros, or watching for the wary tapir; while on the muddy banks of sluggish rivers he may surprise the sâladang or wild ox, a species peculiar to the forests of the Malay peninsula, and which has not yet been described by naturalists. From the accounts we received, the elephant-shooting seems to be inferior to that in Ceylon; while, although the jungles literally swarm with tigers, a shickar, in the Indian sense of the term, is unknown. Our time, however, did not admit of any exploration in this direction; we therefore followed the advice of the host, who proposed visiting a large and prosperous village upon a neighboring river. Re-embarking in our sampans, we coasted for some miles along the northern shore of the straits. Generally they are not above a mile broad, and in some parts they narrow to little more than three furlongs, so that we could scarcely realize, as we glided between their wooded banks, that this was not a river, but the only passage which at one time was known into the China Seas, through which, for near two centuries, Portuguese and Dutch galleons had passed, freighted with the rich merchandise of the East.

In the afternoon we entered the mouth of a considerable river, which we ascended for two hours, when we left the boats and started on foot for the village of Tubrao, while our sampans proceeded to the same place, following the circuitous windings of the river. Our path led us through plantations of pepper and gambier, separated by broad belts of heavy jungle, winding between tall columns of leaves, where the pepper vine, trained like the hop, completely concealed with its rich luxuriance the slender poles that supported it. Sometimes we forced our way through thick bushes of the gambier, in the midst of which the thatched cottages of the cultivators are buried; if we observe a thick smoke issue from one of these, and enter to satisfy our curiosity, we find a group of Chinamen collected like witches round a caldron, in which are bubbling and boiling bushels of gambier leaves. As soon as the juice is inspissated and boiled to the consistence of a sirup, it is poured into moulds, and, when dry, cut into cakes, having very much the appearance of pieces of light-colored India-rubber. The refuse leaves are thrown into a large canoe-shaped trough, which projects over the caldron, and carried away to the pepper-plantations for manure. The leaves are pulled three or four times a year, and in fifteen years a plantation becomes exhausted. Mr. Crawford says: "Gambier contains from 40 to 50 per cent. of pure tannin, and hence it has been of late years largely imported into Europe, to be used in the purposes of dyeing and tanning, the quantity imported yearly into England being not less than 6000 tons."

It is a relief to escape from the slanting rays of the sinking sun, and dive into the dark recesses of the forest, where tall limbless trees rise to a gigantic height, and weave their topmost branches into an impenetrable shade, while orchids five or six feet in diameter, cling like huge excrescences to the leafy roof. It is singular that, though upward of two hundred species of timber have been collected, most of them of great height and growth, not above half a dozen are really valuable; among them are the ebony, sapan, and eagle-wood, but, more valuable than all, the gutta-percha. The Tumângong told us that he had prohibited the sale of this important article of commerce for the present, as the accessible parts of the forest had been cleared of nearly all the old trees. The price of the commodity has been recently very much increased in consequence. Among the palms we observed the nibung, nipa, and areka, while bamboos waved gracefully over us, rivaled only by the tree-fern; and conspicuous among the dense underwood, the ratan reared its tufted crown. Occasionally troops of monkeys noisily swung themselves from branch to branch overhead, and birds of gaudy plumage glanced across our path.

The village of Tubrao was situated on the banks of the river, and surrounded by plantations, and we no sooner made our appearance in the narrow street than the whole population turned out to inspect us, so unusual was the sight of a visitor to that sequestered spot. We held a sort of levee in the house of the old Chinaman who officiated in the capacity of Patriarch to the community. It was a quaint, rambling wooden tenement of one story, with a broad, deep veranda supported by carved pillars, and large empty apartments like audience halls, used as carpenters' shops, or bedrooms, or courts, as the occasion might arise, and hung over with the usual gigantic paper lanterns. We seated ourselves in the veranda, and were regaled with disagreeable

C

preparations of betel, in which I observed, as a principal ingredient, gambier, unknown as a condiment among the betel-chewers of Ceylon. Having done due honor to this mark of attention by filling our mouths with its crimson juice, we were glad to wash them out with some delicious tea, served to us in small China cups, together with divers descriptions of sweetmeats.

Meanwhile we were entertained by numerous eager narrators with wonderful accounts of the depredations which the tigers had recently committed in the neighboring plantations, and which surpassed all former experiences of a similar character. They pointed out to us among the crowd which surrounded us the occupants of no fewer than twenty plantations who had deserted their cottages through fear of these daring and ferocious animals, and taken refuge in the village. Out of the comparatively small population, upward of fifty Chinamen had been carried off during the preceding three weeks. On one day alone five had disappeared; and when we visited their burial-ground, and observed the number of graves with umbrellas over them, to mark that the bones of the occupants had been found and laid there after they had been picked by the tigers, we were convinced that this was no exaggerated statement. Upward of 10,000 piculs, or about £15,000 worth of pepper, had been, in consequence, left upon the trees, dread of the tigers predominating in the breasts of the owners over love of their property.

As we had brought some rifles with us, we informed our entertainers that we should be delighted to undertake a campaign against these savage enemies if they could hold out any prospect of success. The proposition was received with unanimous applause, but it was clear that no one had the slightest notion of how it was to be executed. We offered to wait until the following day, and have a regular battue, if they would beat the jungle with drums and fire-works. This, however, was a mode of procedure to which they entirely objected; and this I secretly did not regret, as a previous experience in India had taught me the danger of tiger-shooting on foot; so we then suggested that we should proceed, a little before the moon rose, to a deserted plantation, and watch a bait. This was more readily agreed to, and the whole crowd instantly dispersed, and instituted a vigorous crusade against the dogs of the village. The process of securing these was in the highest degree ludicrous; the screams of the

Chinamen mingled with the yells of their unfortunate victims, who seemed to have a presentiment of the fate which awaited them, and avenged themselves on the fat calves of their persecutors. At last, after a degree of noise and excitement sufficient to have secured as many wolves, two luckless curs were brought to us, and hung by the legs over a balustrade. We protested against this inhuman treatment, and they were in consequence transferred to an oblong basket.

We dined in a picturesque cottage, built upon piles over the river, and could see through the crevices of the floor the sampans moored beneath, and the current gently rippling past; a rustic foot-bridge spanned the stream, and massive foliage drooped into

Scene on the Tubrao River (Malay Peninsula).

the water. A few large trading-boats gave token of some mercantile activity even in this remote corner of Asia, and we were surprised to hear how recently the process of opening up the neighboring country, and the creation of commerce consequent upon it, had commenced. Ten years ago the banks of this river were almost unexplored; now the produce of 180 plantations was transported down its waters. Some notion of the extent of the Chinese population may be gathered from the consumption of opium. The Tumángong received $22\frac{1}{2}$ per cent. upon the monthly sales of opium from the farmer of the license. His monthly revenue derived from this source amounted to 13,000 rupees. He also received a ground rent of one dollar a month for every plantation of whatever description of cultivation, beginning from the commencement of the third year of its existence. There are now about 2000 plantations in the entire district of Johore paying this rent, and the number is steadily increasing. They are, almost without exception, the property of Chinese emigrants. It is to be regretted that the cultivators are not permanent occupants. Until, however, Chinamen can be induced to bring their wives into foreign countries, the community to which they migrate only derives half the advantage which would accrue were permanent ties created which should bind to the soil a race so eminently qualified for its development.

Our repast over, we sallied forth, an uncouth procession. A number of Malays led the way, and flourished their long spears, the handles of which were Malacca canes, with broad blades attached to them. Then we followed, surrounded by numerous torch-bearers, while the great part of the village population brought up the rear, the basket containing our canine victims being slung between two Chinamen. After stumbling in darkness through sundry plantations, we at last arrived at the cottage said to be deserted, in which we were to take up our station. To our disgust, we no sooner approached it than we were greeted with the barking of dogs and the shouts of men, who appeared as much astonished and dismayed at our nocturnal invasion as if we had been tigers ourselves. They informed us that ten days had elapsed since three of their number had been carried off. The two remaining had then left the plantation in a panic, but had lately returned, and had not been troubled with any new intimation of the proximity of their enemies. Nor could they tell us at which plantation our efforts would be most likely to meet with success, or even where we should be sure to find one deserted. As it now began to rain heavily, and the sky was so overcast as to render the prospect of a bright moon more than doubtful, we determined reluctantly to return to our boats, which we no sooner reached than we urged upon the Tumângong the expediency of proceeding at once upon our journey.

Meantime admirable beds were made up for us on the bottom of our boat under the pent-roof of palm leaves, which serves effectually to protect the voyager in a sampan against the midday sun or the dews of night; beneath this we stretched our weary limbs, while with sturdy stroke our Malay crew propelled our light craft rapidly down the stream.

Morning found us sailing with a light favorable breeze through the straits, and we soon reached the eastern outlet. Here, on the extreme point of the island, at a spot called Shangy, from whence a good road has been made to Singapore, we landed to breakfast. The straits at this point are divided by the island of Pulo Obin, upon which some valuable granite quarries are situated. Rounding this island, we shortly after entered a broad river, or rather frith, and sailed for about twenty miles between banks which were heavily timbered, and backed by an undulating country, but we looked in vain for some signs of life. The magnificent virgin forest has not yet been touched by the axes of men anxious to replace it by a profitable cultivation, nor has the broad bosom of the stream yet been plowed by the keels of native craft, freighted with all the varied produce which the soil is so well adapted to yield, and which possesses the additional advantage of being in close proximity, by water, to a large and ready market.

There can be little doubt, however, that ere long the face of nature here too will be changed by the industrious hand of the Chinese. Our host told us that higher up the river they had begun to open plantations, while he derived a considerable revenue from a tin mine some few miles above Johore. This town is situated upon the left bank of the river, here about four miles broad: a few Malay houses standing in the river upon piles, and a few more hidden in a thick grove of cocoanut-trees, are all that now represent the former capital of the state, and residence of its sultan. The desolation which surrounded it did not lead us to expect much in the town itself, but we were hardly prepared to find only a miserable village, containing scarce a thousand inhabitants. Still it was interesting to visit, as differing from those Chinese villages which are now dotting the coast and creeks of the main land. The houses looked more substantial, and had a more distinctive character. Some of them were three stories high, with windows usually in the gables, latticed and set in quaintly-carved frames, and out of these occasionally protruded the naked figures of wondering children, or the half-concealed countenances of inquisitive females. The thatch is made of a broad leaf called the jolong-jolong, screens of which also project over the windows.

Native House at Johore (Malay Peninsula).

The sides are sometimes formed of the same material; sometimes, in the better class of houses, of wooden panels. Whether on land or water the house is invariably built on piles some twelve feet high, and the first story is reached by a ladder. The only object of such an arrangement on land must be to serve as a protection from wild beasts.

There are no historical associations of any importance connected with Johore; indeed, it is a town of comparatively recent date, having only been founded by the Malays in 1512, after their expulsion from Malacca by the Portuguese in the previous year. According to Mr. Crawfurd, from that period until 1810 there reigned in Johore fourteen princes, giving an average duration of twenty-one years to each reign. The prince who died in the last of these years left two sons, who disputed the succession. It suited the policy of the English and Dutch governments to take each one of the rivals as its protegé, and hence the cession of Singapore to the first, and of the island of Bintang to the last. Both princes are now pensioners, the protegé of the English claiming sovereignty over the countries north of the straits of Singapore, and he of the Dutch, those to the south of it, as laid down by the Convention of London of 1824.

We strolled into the interior with our guns, in hopes of seeing game, but the jungle was impenetrable; and although the marks of large game were numerous, wood-pigeons and squirrels were the only signs of life visible. Then evening closed in, and the sun, ere it finally sank, polished the smooth surface of the river till it looked like a sheet of burnished copper; and numbers of flying foxes (*Pteropus Javanicus*) awoke to the duties of the night, and flapped lazily overhead on their way to the gardens of the village. We amused ourselves firing at them as they sailed overhead like giant and plethoric rooks going to roost; but they were usually too high up, and we only saw one tumbled headlong into a grove of cocoanut-trees, where, however, it was too dark to find him.

Meantime a busy group was assembled round a collection of pots and kettles, which began to possess a strong interest in our eyes. Our host had pointed out to us where the palace of his ancestors had once stood, but at the same time informed us that he possessed no habitation of his own at the former seat of his government, so he had determined to give us an *al fresco* dinner rather than invite us into a native house, an arrangement we thoroughly agreed in; and the growing darkness was soon illuminated with the glare of torches made of damar put into cocoanut husks, which flashed luridly upon the tall, limbless stems of the trees, and upon dark figures cowering over cooking fires, or hurrying about with water and the preparatives of dinner. A rude table of boards had been hastily improvised, and, in feeble rivalry to the surrounding blaze, was lighted by the subdued glimmer of a civilized reading-lamp. A handsome service of China, finger-glasses, damask napkins, and all the appurtenances of an elaborately appointed table, contrasted strangely with the rude figures and uncouth forms which waited on us; for a large portion of the population were in attendance, and added to the novel and picturesque effect of our picnic. Our well-cooked dinner was accompanied by draughts of deliciously cool cocoanut water fresh from the trees above us, whose branches were closely intertwined overhead,

> "A verdurous woof,
> A hanging dome of leaves, a canopy moon-proof."

We quitted with reluctance the scene of our rural festivities and once more in our sampans swept down the smooth current of the river in the calm moonlight, our crew beguiling the way with shrill unmelodious boat-songs, in which screaming choruses and sudden spasmodic refrains were strangely intermingled with long piercing whistles and yells. In spite, however, of their anti-soporific effect, these unearthly noises soon mingled in our dreams, and we only woke to consciousness to find ourselves in broad daylight, coasting along the southeastern shore of the island of Singapore, and, after a prosperous voyage of twelve hours, reached the town.

Malay Sampan.

Though our expedition had necessarily been limited, it had been sufficient to enable us to appreciate, on our return to Singapore, the strong contrast which the British settlement exhibits to the native territory. Forty years have not elapsed since the condition of our island was the same as that of the main land. It then contained only the huts of a few Malay fishermen. Already a hundred thousand souls occupy an area scarcely greater than that of the Isle of Wight; the forest is every where giving place to plantations of nutmeg and gambier; whole suburbs are springing up in the neighborhood of the town as if by magic; its capacious roads are filled with ships of every nation; its revenue, already exceeding 600,000 rupees, increased in 1856 by about a fifth of that sum, so that not only does it pay its own local expenses, but combines with the other Straits settlements to maintain a body of 3800 convicts, and to contribute nearly a lakh and a half of rupees toward the payment of the military force from Madras forming the garrison. Such progress—the natural growth of an American town, and surpassed even by some of our own colonies—is unprecedented in the annals of the East India Company's possessions, and is worthy, on that account, if on no other, of a higher consideration than it has received.

The future of Singapore is but faintly shadowed forth by its past history. That it is destined to hold the highest position among Eastern emporia seems inevitable; but the speedy arrival of so desirable a consummation depends upon its administration. Already its growth has been checked by a system which has, upon the continent of India, proved itself ill suited for the development of internal resources and the rapid extension of trade; but here are conditions differing from those of any other portion of the late Company's dominions. In addition to the large and daily-increasing Anglo-Saxon mercantile community, a continual influx of Chinese emigrants here compose the great majority of the inhabitants.

It may generally be said that, with few exceptions, whatever product of the Malay or Philippine archipelago demands skill and industry in its production is the result of Chinese labor. Without Chinese labor neither the Malay nor Philippine archipelago, nor Siam nor Cochin China, would have sugar or tin for their exportation. Of the first they are the sole producers; of the latter they produce about 8000 tons. Hence it will appear that at Singapore there is no apathetic population indigenous to the soil to be nursed, but one composed of the two most industrious and enterprising races in the world, and who are quite competent to appreciate the advantages of a more progressive system of government. When an altered state of commercial relations with China shall have opened that vast field to European enterprise—when the trade with Siam, created by the recent treaty, and already rapidly growing, has become more fully developed—when, under the skillful administration of its European rulers, the resources of a large portion of Borneo find their way into the English market—when the Malay peninsula, extensively peopled by industrious Chinese, furnishes its important and valuable produce—when, in fact, from these and other sources, the whole trade of the East has increased ten-fold, it will be found that the importance of Singapore has not been over-estimated. In the mean time we may be permitted to hope that those changes which have taken place in the administration of that Eastern empire, of which Singapore forms a portion, may exercise a beneficial influence upon this valuable commercial emporium.

CHAPTER III.

Arrival at Hong Kong.—Trip up the Canton River.—A complicated international Question.—Chuenpee.—Monster Cannon.—Apathy of Population.—Macao Fort.—Unhealthiness of the River.—Spread of the Mutiny.—Its Influence on Lord Elgin's Policy.—Return to Singapore.—Address of mercantile community.—Arrival at Calcutta.—Sensation created.—Moral Effect produced on the Natives.

WE had scarcely been a week at Singapore before our anxieties were relieved on the score of the speedy continuance of our journey by the arrival of the magnificent frigate which had been placed by the government at the disposal of Lord Elgin. The Shannon had made a remarkably quick passage from England, under the energetic command of the gallant Captain Peel, and we congratulated ourselves on the favorable auspices under which our first experiences of the Celestial Empire seemed destined to be made.

A farther delay of a few days was, however, involved, as Lord Elgin had determined not to leave Singapore until the most ample and complete arrangements had been made for the speedy transmission of the Chinese expeditionary force to India. With this view, vessels were sent to the Straits of Anjier to divert from that point the transports conveying the 90th and 82d regiments, so as to avoid the unnecessary detour through the Malacca Straits. Meantime the Simoon had arrived with the 5th Fusileers, and was immediately dispatched to Calcutta. On the 23d of June we bade adieu to Singapore, not without regret, as, in spite of the shortness of our visit, the community had contrived to render our stay there so agreeable, that the favorable impression we then formed was not afterward effaced by any of our subsequent experiences in the East.

The prevalence of the southwest monsoon, and the admirable sailing qualities of the Shannon, enabled us to dispense almost entirely with steam on our voyage up the China Sea; and on the evening of the ninth day after leaving Singapore, we thundered forth a noisy intimation of our arrival to the inhabitants of Hong Kong.

On the 6th of July Lord Elgin landed under a general salute, and proceeded to Government House for the purpose of holding a levee, and going through those official formalities incidental to his entry on the sphere of his future labors. As, however, in consequence of the Fatshan Creek affair, and other events which had recently occurred up the Canton River, the scene of our present operations there was invested with so much interest, Mr. Loch and I took advantage of the departure of H. M. S. Inflexible for Macao Fort on the day following for the purpose of collecting information with as little delay as possible. The scenery in the immediate neighborhood of Hong Kong, and for the first eight or ten miles after leaving it, is not unlike that of the Western Highlands of Scotland. We dexterously steered between high grassy islands, round sharp corners, past little hamlets at the end of secluded bays, and through narrow devious channels, till at last we might fancy ourselves threading the Kyles of Bute instead of the Capshui Moon, or straits which separate the island of Lantao from the main. From it we emerge upon the Bay of Lintin.

We can hardly consider ourselves upon the Pearl River (as the Canton River is properly called) until we reach Chuenpee, for here the opposite coast is not visible, and the white sails of innumerable junks dot the horizon—each high-sterned craft a matter of curious speculation to every naval officer who sees her, and who, in the condition in which our diplomatic relations with the empire then were, is thrown into a state of profound perplexity as to whether she is his lawful prize or not: he finds himself at once entangled in a maze of knotty points, involving intricate questions of international law, upon which he is called to decide on the spot. She may be a smuggler in British interests, in which case he is to let her pass; or a peaceful trader in American interests, taking up charcoal and saltpetre for gunpowder to be exploded against us, in which case he is not to let her pass; or a peaceful trader in purely Chinese interests, and as such to be respected; or a purely Chinese smuggler, when her capture is optional; or a regular out-and-out pirate, when it is advisable; or a merchantman, but suspiciously well-armed, when it is discretionary; or a mandarin (man-of-war) junk in the disguise of a merchantman, when it is imperative. Under these complicated circumstances, the simple plan of proceeding manifestly is to make a prize of the junk, and settle afterward whether she is pirate, trader, snake-boat, mandarin-boat, smuggler, or fast-boat, together with the law that applies to her.

Formerly boats had been allowed to go up armed, but not to come down; but recently a system of passes had been introduced, which only served to render matters more complicated. Meantime trifling affrays were daily occurring, reflecting but little glory on those engaged—injuring our prestige with the Chinese, but yet rendered inevitable by the anomalous condition in which our relations stood with reference not only to China, but to other nations engaged in carrying on commercial operations with her. Notwithstanding this species of constant irritation which was kept up on the river, our ships maintained the most amicable intercourse with the inhabitants on the banks, who supplied them with meat and vegetables; indeed, each ship had usually a bum-boat specially attached.

In about four hours we reached Chuenpee, and, in spite of the heat, scrambled to the top of the hill, from where we had a magnificent view of the surrounding country, out of which rise the naked hills, washed bare by violent tropical rains, so that the beauty of their slopes may be said to have been sacrificed by nature to fertilize the rich alluvial plains at their base. In the distance was the walled town of Hoomanchai, celebrated for the signing of the supplementary treaty. The creek by which it was approached was staked across as a means of defense.

Though of comparatively a trifling elevation, the little barrack at the top of the Chuenpee Hill answered the purpose of a sanitarium. The fort was held at this time by 130 men and one small gun. Some monstrous cast-iron Chinese cannon, weighing 5 tons each, measuring about 13 feet in length, and of a calibre larger than a 95 cwt., had been buried by the Chinese without ever having been fired, and were now being exhumed.

At Chuenpee we met Commodore Keppel and Sir Robert Maclure, and accompanied them to the Bogue, upon this occasion taking but a hurried view of those forts already so celebrated in the history of our Chinese wars, and with which we were destined to become much better acquainted. A little beyond them we passed a creek in which the Esk's boats had been engaged the day before, and had succeeded in capturing a snake-boat, which we saw, though with a loss of three men killed and seven wounded.

After passing the Bogue we are fairly in the river, and the navigation begins to be impeded by shoals. At the second of these is a pagoda, known as Second Bar Pagoda; then we turn off to the left into Blenheim Passage, along which, at the period of our visit, junks were not allowed to pass. Though these waters were exclusively traversed by our men-of-war, the agricultural population little heeded the puffing of the numerous steamers which were constantly engaged in keeping up the communication between Macao Fort and the other ships stationed on the river; and though rarely a day passed without the sound of a distant cannonade falling upon their ears, they had become accustomed to the strife by which they were surrounded, and worked as busily in their paddy-fields as though Fatshan were a myth, Canton in another world, and British gun-boats a necessary condition of their existence.

It was our first introduction to Chinese scenery: numerous villages dotted the river banks, some of them utterly destroyed and depopulated either by rebels or ourselves; others densely crowded among trees, the most conspicuous object being the high square tower, with massive loop-holed walls, rising in proud eminence above the surrounding roofs, indicative, not of some old feudal baron, who, secure in his strong-hold, holds the lives of his vassals in pawn for their good behavior, but—significant of the character of the race—of some old usurer who needs a fortress for the preservation of sundry goods and chattels which he holds in pawn for the credit of his victims. The number of these pawnbroking towers inspires one with rather a low estimate of the solvency of the community. Then there are tall red poles, scattered in pairs among the villages, betokening a joss-house, or the residence of a mandarin. The carved gables of the better class of houses project above the other roofs like gigantic grave-stones, while the graves themselves resemble the mouths of large wells.

Here and there a hill is crowned by a tall pagoda, while lesser pentagonal towers, four or five stories high, with pointed roofs, rise above the trees like those of churches. At the base of barren hills are charming wooded nooks, which look all the greener and fresher by the contrast, while an active population is swarming every where; men are fishing in tiny punts on the river: women are patching up the basket screens which retain the mud of the paddy-fields on the banks, or wading about in the mud looking for something; coolies are traversing with swinging gait the ridges of the fields, heavily loaded; while under the shade of the spreading branches of the giant *Ficus Indicus*, or at the doors of joss-houses, motley groups are collected, gazing at us as we sweep past.

We found the Fury and Highflyer the advanced ships, and, transferring ourselves here into a gun-boat, proceeded toward Macao Fort, past the boom which had been stretched across the river by the Chinese, close to the entry up the Fatshan Creek. The fort, so gallantly stormed by Commodore Elliot, was distinctly visible. Macao Fort is distant about three miles from Canton; situated on a little island nearly in mid-stream, it occupies a favorable position as an advanced post, though with a more active enemy the small garrison could never have maintained themselves there, as they did, for a year. The present force consisted of 160 men, and the fort mounted 14 guns. From the top of the tower, which was used as a hospital, we had a good view of Can-

Macao Fort (Canton river).

ton and the White Cloud Mountains in rear, on which sundry white tents betokened the presence of troops.

The garrison was composed of men from the Raleigh, and seemed to pass an existence in which the hardships of war were not altogether untempered by the refinements of civilization. The admirable band belonging to the "late" frigate played some elaborate pieces with great execution, while we discussed *patés de fois gras* and Champagne, seated, it is true, on upturned boxes and round a table of primitive manufacture, while our sideboard had apparently done duty at some former period as the altar of a joss-house. As habiliments were scarce, the costume of the sentry exhibited a pleasing mixture of John Chinaman and Jack Tar.

A good deal knocked up ourselves by our day's labors, we could not but sympathize with the naval forces stationed along the whole length of the river at so unhealthy a season of the year. The thermometer was standing at 102° under the shade of the awning on board the Esk; and it was not to be wondered at that, under the combined influence of sun and miasma, one vessel alone, out of a small complement of 130 men in perfect health, should have put 60 on the sick-list in the short space of three weeks. Under these circumstances, we were not tempted to linger up the river longer than was absolutely necessary, though the change to Hong Kong, which we reached on the following day, was only tolerable by contrast.

A few days after our return to Hong Kong news arrived, the serious nature of which increased, if possible, the already existing complications of the position in which Lord Elgin found himself placed on his arrival in China. The prolonged resistance at Delhi, the rapid spread of the rebellion into the lower provinces of Bengal, and the urgent representations of Lord Canning of the exigencies of the situation, not only deprived the embassador of any hope of saving any part of the China force from the vortex into which they were being swallowed by the inexorable necessities of India, but rendered it extremely improbable that they could ever be made available for the objects for which they were originally designed. His only consolation was that he had appreciated the true position of affairs in India at a sufficiently early date to enable him to divert the troops to that country at the most critical period of its fortunes; but the difficulties of the situation in China had been immeasurably enhanced by the sacrifice.

It was clear that any attempt to negotiate in the immediate neighborhood of the capital of the empire, unaccompanied by any force, must depend very much for success upon the moral effect created by the aspect of affairs in the south. The presence of an army at Hong Kong might have sufficed to produce this, but not only was our force there contemptible, but our naval operations had resulted in failure. Yeh had vindicated the policy of his treatment of the barbarians, and triumphal arches had been erected to commemorate his success; while, to import a new set of considerations into the question, Baron Gros was not expected to arrive in China for some months. Under these circumstances, only three other courses remained open—either to take Canton, to remain inactive at Hong Kong, or to leave the country until the diplomatic questions at issue there could be approached under different and more favorable auspices. The season of the year, and the weakness of the force to be employed, rendered the capture and occupation of Canton impossible in the opinion of the commanders-in-chief. A residence involving total inaction at Hong Kong was calculated to injure the prestige of the mission, while it was attended with no one single advantage.

On the other hand, this evil was avoided by an immediate departure, while in choosing Calcutta as his destination, and taking with him as many marines as could be spared from the river, Lord Elgin adopted a course which enabled him not only to satisfy himself as to the probable fate of the original China force, and to judge of the possibility and expediency of supplying their place, as was subsequently done, with quasi-mutinous Bengal regiments, but to bring a moral and material support to Lord Canning at a moment when it seemed probable that the safety of Calcutta itself was menaced. Indeed, so urgent appeared the exigencies of the case, that Lord Elgin even then determined to give up the Shannon to the Indian government, if Captain Peel considered that the organization of a naval brigade to operate in the provinces of Upper Bengal was a feasible scheme. That officer expressed no hesitation on the subject, and the high reputation which he had already earned in a similar service in the Crimea operated as an additional inducement with Lord Elgin to proceed with him to Calcutta. This resolution was no sooner formed than acted upon, and within thirty-six hours after the Indian intelligence was received the Shannon was once more plowing her way over the China Sea, accompanied by the Pearl, whose assistance was required for the conveyance of the troops.

D

SINGAPORE.—ADDRESS OF MERCANTILE COMMUNITY.

The following address, presented to Lord Elgin by the merchants of Singapore on his arrival there, was satisfactory to his excellency, as proving that the course he was then adopting carried with it the approbation of a community whose most important interests were at stake both in India and China:

"To his Excellency the Right Hon. the EARL of ELGIN and KINCARDINE, K.T., Her Majesty's High Commissioner and Plenipotentiary to the Court of Pekin.

"Singapore, July 20, 1857.

"MY LORD,—We, the undersigned mercantile firms and others interested in the trade of Singapore, are induced, by a consideration of the serious aspect of affairs in India, and of the important bearing which it must have upon those questions which it was the object of your excellency's mission to settle in China, to present this address to your lordship, believing that at this critical juncture, when complications have arisen involving such grave interests in both countries, it will be gratifying to your excellency to know that the mercantile community of Singapore, although closely connected in trade with China, and anxiously desirous for the speedy and satisfactory resumption of commercial relations with Canton, have nevertheless cordially concurred in the resolution which your excellency has taken of diverting the China expeditionary army from its destination to the assistance of the European force now engaged in the defense of our Indian possessions. The decided step which your lordship has so promptly taken of following that army yourself has afforded us the most lively satisfaction. Its absence from the sphere of its operations in China, and the uncertainty attending the period of its ultimate dispatch to that country, would, in our opinion, have rendered your stay there comparatively useless, more particularly as the extent of our naval force is amply sufficient for the protection of trade and the maintenance of the *status quo* until your lordship's return.

"On the other hand, we feel that the magnitude of the stake in India, and the fearful nature of the crisis which is now impending there, supersede all other considerations.

"We believe that the arrival of your lordship at Calcutta in this emergency will be of the greatest advantage in producing an important moral effect throughout India, and in affording the governor general most valuable support.

"At the same time, we sincerely trust that the progress of events in India may shortly assume such a character as will enable your lordship to return to the original field of your labors under more favorable auspices.

"We have, etc.,

(Signed), "A. L. JOHNSTON & Co.,
and twenty-seven others."

The awful intelligence of the massacre of Cawnpore reached us here, and we did not therefore remain longer than was absolutely necessary to take in 400 tons of coal—a feat which was performed in the almost incredibly short space of twenty-one hours—and to pick up 300 men of the troops wrecked in the ill-fated Transit. Distributing these between the Pearl and ourselves, we at once proceeded on our voyage, cheered by the news that the Himalaya had already passed, and that ships were on the watch at the Straits of Anjier for the diversion of the Assistance and Adventure, now daily expected. Our own decks were densely crowded with nearly a thousand souls, whose condition was not improved by an atmosphere in which the thermometer continually stood over 90°. Notwithstanding the utmost exertions of Captain Peel in "carrying on," in consequence of the prevalence of the southwest monsoon we had been a fortnight in beating down to Singapore; but we were favored up the Bay of Bengal by the gales which had been adverse to us in the China Sea, and reached the Sandheads in exactly three weeks from the date of our leaving Hong Kong.

The interest which we felt as we approached the theatre of the terrible drama which was then being enacted in India was converted into a still livelier emotion by the intelligence which we received when we reached Diamond Harbor of a rumor that a large body of mutineers were marching down from Berhampore upon Calcutta. The more ardent spirits among us at once imagined that we were fated to arrive there just in time to take an active share in the defense of the city; while Lord Elgin, who knew not what credit to attach to the report, at a time when every successive mail had so far surpassed our worst anticipations, immediately telegraphed to Lord Canning his proximity with 1700 men (the Pearl and blue-jackets included).

As we swept past Garden Reach on the afternoon of the 8th of August, the excitement on board was increased by early indications of the satisfaction with which our appearance was hailed on shore. First our stately ship suddenly burst upon the astonished gaze of two European gentlemen taking their evening walk, who, seeing her crowded with the eager faces of men ready for the fray, took off their hats and cheered wildly; then the respectable skipper of a merchantman worked himself into a state of phrensy, and made us a long speech, which we could not hear, but the violence of his gesticulations left us in little doubt as to its import; then his crew took up the cheer, which was passed on at intervals until the thunder of our 68-pounders drowned every other sound, shattered the windows of sundry of the "palaces," attracted a crowd of spectators to the Maidan, and brought the contents of Fort William on to the glacis.

As soon as the smoke cleared away, the soldiers of the garrison collected there sent up a series of hearty cheers; a moment more, and our men were clustered like ants upon the rigging, and, in the energy which they threw into their ringing response, they pledged themselves to the achievement of those deeds of valor which have since covered the naval brigade with glory. After the fort had saluted, Lord Elgin landed amid the cheers of the crowd assembled at the Ghaut to receive him, and proceeded to Government House, gratified to learn, not merely from the popular demonstrations, but from Lord Canning himself, that, though happily the physical force he had brought with him was not required to act in defense of the city, still that the presence of a man-of-war larger than any former ship that had ever anchored abreast of the Maidan, and whose guns commanded the city, was calculated to produce both upon the European and native population a most wholesome moral effect, more especially at a time when the near approach of the Mohurrum had created in men's minds an unusual degree of apprehension and excitement.

CHAPTER IV.

Condition of India in August, 1857.—State of Calcutta.—Organization of naval Brigade.—The Mohurrum.—Departure from Calcutta.—Policy adopted by Lord Elgin.—Residence at Hong Kong.—Its Absence of Attractions.—A Trip up the River.—Macao.—A Chinese Dinner.

WE spent August, 1857, in Calcutta. Of all the eventful months of that most terrible year in India's history, it was probably the one most pregnant with evil forebodings. At no former period had the crisis appeared so imminent. Two commanders-in-chief had already succumbed before Delhi; our army was dwindling away under its walls, and its leaders urgently demanding re-enforcements which did not exist. Agra was besieged by a mutinous army, and men feared for the unhappy garrison a repetition of the Cawnpore tragedy. This frightful catastrophe appeared to impend still more surely over the devoted band at Lucknow, whose deliverance at one time was considered hopeless. At Dinapore our troops had just met with a disaster. The gallant little army under General Havelock, despairing of re-enforcements, decimated by cholera, and worn out by battles and hardships, were compelled to retire on Cawnpore. Oude, Rohilcund, Bundelcund, were lost to us; the disaffection threatened to spread into the other presidencies; everywhere the mutineers seemed triumphant; station after station was being deserted and plundered; each week steamers full of fugitives arrived from up the country, with additional horrors to recount, and more disaffection to report. All communication was stopped with the northwest; from Burdwan to Delhi, the country was infested with mutineers; and every regiment but two in the Bengal army had either been disarmed, disbanded, or had mutinied. With the exception of the small China force, no European troops had arrived or were expected to arrive for two months. Meantime the hot weather was all against us, and all in favor of the rebels.

Under these painful circumstances, nothing struck me so forcibly on my arrival as the apparent calm which reigned in Calcutta; and yet, after the first few weeks, nothing appeared more reasonable than that this should be so. Those who are removed to a great distance from the scene of thrilling events, and experience at the receipt of periodical intelligence from it an intense degree of excitement, forget that if those on the spot were to be subjected to a similar strain upon the nervous system, continued over a length of time, it would give way altogether. Providentially, the very proximity of the danger, and constant familiarity with those horrible details, which, arriving by installments in England, acted on society like a series of electric shocks, produced a calmness almost amounting to apathy in India. So far as the outward aspect of society was concerned, Calcutta was just as I had left it seven years before. The Maidan was just as crowded by its beauty and fashion now as it used to be then; burra-cannas were nearly as numerous, considering it was the height of the hot weather; and there was even a wretched attempt at an opera, which, however, was very thinly attended. The only differences I observed were that constant reviews took place of volunteer corps; that the governor general's body-guard mounted sentry without swords; and that dining in Fort William involved the risk of being bayoneted by a series of Irish sentries, who would not admit your pronunciation of the parole to be correct, and were haunted by the suspicion that you were the King of Oude in disguise escaping in a buggy.

It would be in the highest degree unjust to attribute this apparent indifference to any want of appreciation of the real nature of the crisis, much less to any want of sympathy in behalf of those who had suffered, or of depth of feeling on the part of the sufferers themselves. It arose rather from that deliberate courage and steady determination to face the danger and support the trials which had so eminently distinguished our countrymen scattered throughout the upper provinces, and which had led to acts of unparalleled heroism. The public felt that, with the present deficiency of physical force, they must principally rely for safety upon that moral effect which an undaunted attitude would create in the minds of the natives. Nowhere was this conviction more decidedly entertained, or its results more conspicuously displayed than at Government House, and there can be little doubt that the example set by Lord Canning himself in this respect exercised a most wholesome and tranquillizing influence upon society at large.

Meantime the organization of the naval brigade proceeded rapidly; indeed, we had scarcely left the ship before our cabins were dismantled, and the preparations commenced for the equipment of very nearly the entire ship's company. Within a week after our arrival in Calcutta these were completed, and Lord Elgin went on board the Shannon to bid farewell to the men and officers in a parting address, which was received with hearty cheers. A few hours afterward they were on board the flats which were to convey them to the scene of their future triumphs.

We found Sir Patrick Grant at Calcutta, and a few days afterward Sir Colin Campbell unexpectedly arrived to assume the command-in-chief of the army in India, and to inspire fresh confidence into the minds of all. The most exciting period of our visit was during the last days of the Mohurrum, when predictions were rife of midnight attacks, and one or two ladies took refuge on board ships in the river. A 24-pound howitzer, hoisted up to the main-top of the Shannon, looked menacingly over the Maidan, while strong guards of soldiers and volunteers were posted all over the town. The last day, however, universally named as the day of attack, passed over quietly. I happened to meet the procession on their way to throw the Ziahs into the water. I have scarcely ever seen a Mohammedan religious procession less excited; indeed, the panic among the natives was much greater than among the Europeans, for the preparations made by the latter induced a dread on the part of the natives that they might be attacked by mistake.

Lord Elgin was detained at Calcutta until the arrival of the mail informing him that the force which he had diverted was to be replaced by 1500 marines. An offer made by General Hearsay for regiments to volunteer for China was only responded to by one, and it was evident, therefore, that no dependence could be placed upon extensive re-enforcements to be derived from this source. As for the original China force, it was owing to their opportune arrival that the tide of rebellion, which had been setting steadily down upon Calcutta, was already stemmed. The regiments diverted from Singapore had saved Dinapore, relieved Arrah, and were in full march to join Havelock: upon these timely re-enforcements not only was the relief of Lucknow, but the safety of Bengal depending. It was therefore clear to Lord Elgin that he need not expect to see again any one of the China regiments now employed in India, nor, while they were rendering such vital service, could he desire it. A consideration of these circumstances involved a very serious change in his policy in China, whither he was now desirous of returning for the purpose of conferring with Baron Gros immediately upon his arrival. In consequence of the Shannon having been made over for the service of the Indian government, the Peninsular and Oriental Company's steamer Ava was placed at Lord Elgin's disposal for his conveyance to China, and on the 3d of September we bade adieu to our hospitable hosts at Calcutta, and once more turned our faces toward the Celestial Empire.

General Van Straubenzee and his staff, who had arrived in Calcutta with Sir Colin Campbell, under the impression that the generals of the China force had proceeded with it to India, finding that they had not received orders to leave Hong Kong, accompanied us on our return voyage to that place.

On the 20th of September, after a prosperous passage, we once more found ourselves anchored under Victoria Peak in circumstances very little more encouraging than those which had forced us away from China two months before. An expedition to the mouth of the Peiho was more than ever to be deprecated. Two months more must elapse before the first installment of marines could be expected, at the most favorable computation. Baron Gros had not yet made his appearance.

In the mean time, during our absence at Calcutta, the complications and difficulties arising out of the anomalous state of things already described upon the Canton River had forced the admiral to establish a blockade, which gave a new complexion to the aspect of our diplomatic relations with the imperial government. To go to the mouth of the Peiho unsupported either by the representatives of other powers or a naval force of our own would be to insure an insult from the government at Pekin, while the prevalence of the northeast monsoon would retard our arrival in the Gulf of Pechelee until so late a period of the year that a departure would be forced upon us with a precipitancy in the highest degree encouraging to the systematic policy of the empire in dealing with barbarians, and injurious to our national prestige. The treatment which we received from the Chinese authorities upon the occasion of our subsequent visit to the Peiho fully confirmed the estimate then formed of the obstinacy of the government of Pekin. Under these circumstances, Lord Elgin determined patiently to await at Hong Kong the arrival of the force destined for the capture of Canton, and when that operation was concluded, to proceed northward as early as possible in the following year, retaining possession of the city as a material guarantee for the satisfaction of our demands.

In the mean time, the interval of inaction at Hong Kong, which this determination rendered inevitable, involved an existence under circumstances of a somewhat trying character. A steamer of the Peninsular and Oriental Company, however comfortable its accommodation, and obliging and amiable its commander (and in Captain Caldbeck we were particularly fortunate in this regard), is not exactly the residence which one would select in which to pass two summer months in one of the worst tropical climates in the world; nor, even if the attractions of Hong Kong were less than they are, which is scarcely possible, is it a pleasant thing to be anchored a mile at least from the shore. During the season of typhoons this distance was doubled. We then sought shelter under the Kowloon Promontory; and a dinner on shore was a serious undertaking, when it involved a midnight voyage in an open Tanka boat, possibly in a gale of wind or a pitiless storm of rain. This was an experience of common occurrence. Sometimes we were detained on shore from stress of weather; and on the occasion of a typhoon, which destroyed two hundred junks at Macao, but the full violence of which we escaped, the Ava was obliged to keep under steam all night.

When it was not blowing or raining, the heat was intolerable, and we all suffered more or less in health from its evil effects. Often for days together we remained sweltering on board from lack of energy or sufficient inducement to leave the ship. The charms of the Club or the excitement of a game of billiards failed to tempt us. Hong Kong boasts of only two walks for the conscientious valetudinarian—one along the sea-shore to the right, and the other to the left of the settlement: then there is a scramble to the top of Victoria Peak at the back of it; but this achievement involves an early start, and a probable attack of fever. The monotony of life is varied by this malady alternating with boils or dysentery, so that the proverbial hospitality of the merchants at Hong Kong can only be exercised under very adverse influences. It was not difficult to account for a certain depression of spirits and tone of general irritability which seemed to pervade the community. A large bachelors' dinner was the extreme limit of gayety.

It was provoking that a place possessing so many scenic attractions should have been so entirely devoid of other charms. Like a beautiful woman with a bad temper, Hong Kong claimed our admiration while it repelled our advances. We did, indeed, make one spasmodic effort to be "jolly under creditable circumstances." Lord Elgin gave a picnic at the Bogue Forts. As his invitations were responded to by nearly all the ladies in the place, as the day happened to be lovely, and the Ava admirably adapted for the excursion, the attempt was not altogether unsuccessful, and on our return at night we indulged in a little picturesque dissipation. The deck was turned into a ball-room. The band of the Calcutta supplied us with excellent music, while huge fantastic Chinese lanterns, swinging from the awning, threw a brilliant light upon the dancers.

On the 16th of October Baron Gros arrived in the Audacieuse, and, after conferring with Lord Elgin, took up his anchorage in Castle Peak Bay, Lantao Island, where Admirial Rigault de Genouilly, with the French fleet, were at anchor, about twelve miles distant from Hong Kong. As Lord Elgin was desirous of judging for himself on the state of matters in the river, he proceeded in the Ava to Macao Fort. With the exception of the withdrawal of the garrison from Chuenpee, the occupation of North Wantung Island, and the absence of any junks from the river in consequence of the blockade, the aspect of affairs seemed unchanged since my last visit. We cast longing glances from the top of the pagoda in Macao Fort upon the heights at the back of Canton, crowned by the five-storied pagoda and Gough's Fort, with which we hoped before long to make a closer acquaintance.

On our return voyage we passed through Elliot's Passage, which had not been traversed for months; we therefore took another gun-boat, towing an armed pinnace, so as to be prepared for the very improbable contingency of meeting mandarin junks. The scenery was extremely pretty; the people engaged in taking in the harvest stared at us with curiosity, but apparent confidence. We entered the Whampoa Channel at the town of Whampoa, formerly a place of as great bustle and activity as the port of Canton, the site of docks, and the anchorage of large merchant fleets, now partially deserted, and desolate-looking in the extreme.

On the following day we proceeded to Macao, and explored that interesting old Portuguese settlement, with which, however, we have been too long familiar in England to render description necessary. Its air of respectable antiquity was refreshing after the somewhat parvenu character with which its ostentatious magnificence invests Hong Kong. The narrow streets and grass-grown plazas, the handsome façade of the fine old Cathedral crumbling to decay, the shady walks and cool grottoes, once the haunt of the Portuguese poet; his tomb, and the view from it, all combined to produce a soothing and tranquillizing effect upon sensibilities irritated by our recent mode of life.

We strolled down to the harbor, and found it full of junks, most of them heavily armed with 6, 9, and 12-pound guns, bearing the well-known initials B., P., & Co., of this year's date, to be converted by Yeh to his own use when occasion required, for the crews did not conceal the fact that Canton was their destination— of course for trading purposes. Since the blockade of the river, the whole trade with Canton has been carried along the passage at the back of Macao, known as the Broadway.

We refreshed ourselves after the fatigues of our exploration at a Chinese restaurant, where I made my first experience in Chinese cookery, and, in spite of the novelty of the implements, managed, by the aid of chop-sticks, to make a very satisfactory repast off eggs a year old preserved in clay, sharks' fins and radishes pared and boiled into a thick soup, *bêche de mer* or sea-slugs, shrimps made into a paste with sea-chestnuts, bamboo roots, and garlic, rendered piquant by the addition of soy and sundry other pickles and condiments, and washed down with warm samshu in minute cups. Dishes and plates were all on the smallest possible scale, and pieces of square brown paper served the purpose of napkins.

On the 28th of October, the arrival of the Imperador, after a remarkably quick voyage, with the first batch of marines on board, imparted new life and hope to the breast of every one connected with the Chinese expedition. It was the first faint glimmering of daylight after the long night of despondency and inaction.

CHAPTER V.

Voyage to the Philippines.—Arrival at Manilla.—Appearance of the Town.—A varied Population.—Their Costumes.—Tobacco-manufactory.—The Price of Tobacco.—A Piña Shop.—Indolence of the Mestizoes.—Industry of the Chinese Population.—Chinese Emigration: its Advantages.—The Captain General of the Philippines.—Military Mass.—A Trip to Cavitè.—A religious Procession.—Excursion to the Lago de Bai.—Los Baños.—The Romance of La Gironière.—The Island of Socolme.—A stormy Voyage.—The Trade of Manilla.

It will easily be believed that the mode of existence described in the last chapter was one calculated to give one a very keen relish for any thing like a change, more especially when that change involved all the excitement of novelty and sight-seeing incidental to a visit to a new country. It was therefore with no little satisfaction that, on the 10th of November, I availed myself of permission to accompany Captain Sherard Osborn to Manilla in H. M. S. Furious, a ship with which I was destined afterward to become better acquainted, and in which he was then kind enough to offer me a passage. Mr. Wingrove Cooke, with whose graphic descriptions of the events which at this period transpired in China the public are familiar, was my fellow-passenger on this occasion. After a pleasant run of three days we sighted the high land of the island of Luzon, and coasted along its wooded shores, indented with deep bays, at the head of which small country towns were situated, and from which the country craft issued that carry on a brisk coasting trade with Manilla.

The Bay of Manilla is so capacious as to partake more of the character of an inland sea than of a harbor. It was nearly midnight when we made its narrow entrance, and three hours more ere we reached our anchorage. We were up early to take our first look of Manilla, but the view of the town from the sea presents nothing very imposing. A long row of red-tiled roofs, with here and there the dome of a church, appears over the walls of the fort, situated in the angle formed by the embouchure of the River Pasig, and separated from the sea by a strip of green esplanade. Two substantially-built moles or "murallons" confine the waters of the river for some distance after they have reached the sea; at the end of one is a light-house, and of the other a guard-house. We pull across the bar between walls of granite, and wend our way among the miscellaneous assemblage of shipping that crowds the river—Spanish feluccas and Malay proas, English merchantmen hauled up to refit, and gun-boats with long sweeps, and pontines, and galeras, and caraçoas, and every description of country craft and uncouth rig, and, by way of contrast, two small screw-steamers, which ply across the harbor to Cavité, of which the Spaniards are particularly proud, and to one of which they have given the significant name of the "Progresso." Small river-boats, full of vegetables or passengers, cut in and out; groups of women are collected on the steps bathing; and Custom-house guards lounge upon the river brink, but they have a proper respect for a British man-of-war's gig, and allow us to reach our landing-place unchallenged, and carry our portmanteaus to the hotel without manifesting the slightest curiosity to know whether they contain the two articles which are perhaps most commonly to be found in every traveler's luggage, but which are most strictly prohibited from being landed at Manilla, to wit, Bibles and revolvers.

In ascending the river, the fortified town, containing the garrison and residences of the officials, is on the right-hand side; on the other is a densely populated suburb, in which the shops, hotels, and foreigners' houses are situated. This is intersected by sundry canals running at right angles to the river, crowded with boats, and on the banks of one of these stood the hotel to which we were destined. It was patronized by what Americans would call "a mixed crowd," chiefly captains of merchantmen from every quarter of the globe, but whose polyglot conversation did not at all perplex our bustling hostess, as she spoke, during breakfast, English, French, Spanish, Malay, and Hindostanee, all with such perfect fluency that her own nationality remained a mystery.

In obedience to the first and most natural impulse of a visitor to Manilla, we lost no time in making our way to the principal cheroot manufactory, and as we drove through the streets there was plenty to engage our attention. Their whole aspect, as well as that of the population with which they are crowded, differs entirely from that of any other town I had ever visited in the East. The houses are two-storied, the upper half forming the dwelling-house and the lower the shop. Round the upper story runs a covered balcony, the sides and fronts composed of shutters divided into minute squares, which are filled with mother-of-pearl shells, the transparency of the nacre serving the purpose of glass. Beneath this balcony blue and white calico screens project, and fall beyond the side pavement in such a manner as to form a covered way for the passengers, sufficient not only to protect them from the sun, but to conceal them from the view of any body in the centre of the street. These screens are put up in accordance with a municipal regulation, and when they are new, and the colors are fresh, give a gay appearance to the streets.

A mixed multitude throng these shady sidewalks. Chinese and English, pure Spaniards and mestizoes, Malays and Tagala Indians, here jostle one another, and present every possible shade of color which could result from a combination of all these races in various proportions. The variety of costume is similarly graduated, its composition depending upon the composition of the wearer, and differing only in degree as it descends from the European to the Indian. The colored men are for the most part compelled by law to wear their shirts outside their trowsers.

Mestizoes.

These latter are often made of colored silk, while the shirt is composed of a transparent fabric called husè, for which Manilla is celebrated, woven from the fibre of the banana (*Musa textilis*), upon which gay patterns are generally worked. The women wear jackets of this material, which cover, but do not conceal, their figure to the waist, round which the saya or petticoat is bound. The coloring is always bright, and over it is sometimes worn, out of doors, a sort of wrapper, reaching from the waist to the knee, called a sapiz, and consisting of dark blue silk or cotton cloth. This is, however, more particularly an article of dress appertaining to the Chinese half-breeds as distinct from the Spanish. The slippers are an impossible-looking *chaussure*, the toes only being covered with cloth, gayly embroidered in gold and silver, but so scanty in quantity that it does not cover the little toe, which, projecting at the side, acts as a sort of movable clasp to keep on the slipper. For the proper performance of this function it must require a special education, and these slippers are consequently by no means a useful article of dress to present to any one out of Manilla. To all this gay coloring is contrasted the sober costume of the priests, whose numbers and bearing are significant of the extent of that ecclesiastical influence which is dominant in the Philippines.

The tobacco-manufactory is situated in a square, and, as we entered the archway, our ears were saluted with a din worthy of a Manchester cotton-mill. We go up stairs under the guidance of a cicerone told off to us, and walk through endless rooms full of women. The process of cigar-making, as practiced here, is simple, monotonous, and noisy. On each side of a passage or aisle leading down the centre of the long rooms are tables raised about a foot from the ground, round each of which are squatted twelve or fourteen women, who keep up an incessant chattering, hammering, and giggling. Each woman is provided with a mallet, with which she beats out the leaf preparatory to rolling within it a small handful of the broken tobacco, which she takes from a heap piled along the whole length of the table. Her fingers and mallet seem to move as mechanically as her tongue; but the combination of noises is deafening, and we are content to ask very few questions on the spot, and to get our information afterward.

I was surprised at the proportion of Havana-shaped cigars which were being manufactured. Formerly these were entirely reserved for local consumption. The present governor has, however, allowed them to come into competition in the markets of the world with the Havanas; and, whatever may be their success in that respect, they at all events bid fair to drive the old cheroot shape out of the market. The best tobacco is reserved for them, and more care is taken in their manufacture. They are, in consequence, very highly priced—the No. 1, Imperiales, a gigantic cigar, being thirty dollars a thousand; while the No. 2, Cortado, an ordinary-sized cheroot, is only eight. The Imperiales contain no broken tobacco, but consist simply of one leaf rolled into a cigar. As tobacco is a government monopoly, the prices are all fixed arbitrarily, and every body runs the same risk in making purchases. There is only one quality of each size, whether Havana or Manilla shaped; but the larger sizes may be said, as a rule, to be composed of the best description of tobacco. A certain amount of tobacco is served out to each table, out of which a given quantity of cigars are to be made. By these means a uniform size in the cigar is secured, and a check upon the consumption of tobacco imposed. Each woman is paid according to the quantity of cigars she makes; their earnings vary from six to ten dollars a month. There is a popular fallacy very common in England that cheroots contain opium. The value of the latter drug is quite a sufficient proof that they would not pay at their present price were that the case. I could scarcely credit, until I saw the returns, the fact that the consumption of tobacco in the Philippines themselves is about five times as great as the entire amount exported to foreign markets. The whole population, of both sexes and all ages, certainly appear to be constantly emitting clouds of tobacco-smoke, but their numbers scarcely seem to warrant this proportion of the entire consumption.

One of the most beautiful fabrics of Manilla, and for which it is justly celebrated, is the Piña cloth, woven from the fibre of the pine-apple. It is only used in the dress of the wealthy, being too costly for common use. Our curiosity on the subject of tobacco satisfied, we next proceeded, in search of some good specimens of Piña manufacture, to the house of an old lady celebrated for her varied assortment of this fabric. To my surprise, we were ushered through an imposing gateway into the court-yard of a no less imposing mansion. A handsome carriage, decorated with armorial bearings, was standing here, the property of the lady of the house. Ascending the massive staircase, we were shown into a well-furnished drawing-room, ornamented with pictures, flower-stands of Bohemian glass, mirrors, and other articles of taste or virtu. The presiding goddess of so much finery stood in the centre of it all, smoking a giant cigar, and looking like a retired old sick-nurse, with nothing on but a jacket of more than usually transparent texture, a dirty petticoat, and her bare feet thrust into faded slippers. I could scarcely persuade myself that so untidy an old female was the proprietress of the handsome carriage, and of the expensive-looking establishment to which it belonged. Her daughter, a young lady of some attractions, was sitting, similarly attired, in the next room, embroidering Piña pocket-handkerchiefs.

The Piña is more curious than useful to people who are in the habit of wearing something thicker than gauze; and accordingly a small outlay was sufficient to satisfy our wants, if not those of the old lady, who hospitably plied us with cigars while she spread before us articles of every variety and value. An elaborately embroidered Piña dress is often priced at £300 and upward.

Shopping at Manilla is an unsatisfactory pursuit. The principal streets are the Escolta and Rosario; but all the best shops are kept by Chinamen, who fairly beat the mestizoes out of the field as traders. The superior industry, intelligence, and economical habits of the pure Chinaman give him an immense advantage over the mestizo. The former despises feast-days, and cares little for personal comfort; he lives in the little shop which contains his stock in trade, and keeps his eyes open. The mestizo spends half his existence in a gala dress, does not condescend to live in his shop, and has no business habits when he is there. In the middle of the day he is generally asleep, and is excessively disgusted at being roused to serve a customer. It is not at all an uncommon thing to see a man coiled up snoring in one corner of his shop, and a mestizo girl stretched luxuriously at full length upon the counter, her beautiful black hair thrown back from her face, falling in wavy massive folds to the ground, and her bosom heaving so softly and regularly with the long-drawn breath of a profound slumber, that, rather than do violence to his æsthetic nature by disturbing sleeping beauty, the purchaser moves gently on to the next shop, and finds a grinning Chinaman, with his eyes so destitute of lids that he looks as if he could not wink,

E

much less sleep, but which sparkle with intelligence and cupidity, who is imbued with the firm determination, if he does not possess in his shop the article which you do want, to force you to buy from him something you do not.

Manilla, like Singapore, owes a great part of its prosperity to the Chinese portion of the population; and, in our management of this race in our own possessions, it might not be unprofitable to investigate the expediency of some of those measures which other nations, inferior to us in the art of colonization as a rule, have found it necessary to employ. All the Chinese arriving at Manilla are registered and taxed according to their occupations. They are divided into four classes—merchants, shopkeepers, artisans, and day-laborers. The entire Chinese population has been estimated as high as 30,000, but, according to a Spanish author, writing in 1842, "the number actually enrolled does not exceed 6000, and their capitation-tax is above 100,000 dollars a year, while that of all the native inhabitants, exceeding 3,000,000, does not equal eight times that amount." This taxation is manifestly excessive, and no good object could be obtained by drawing any distinction in our own possessions between the Chinese and the British subject; but the election of a capitan by themselves, whose office it is to collect the tribute, and arrange all internal differences, and who is, to a certain extent, responsible for the good conduct of his countrymen, is an excellent arrangement. At the same time that the capitan is elected, his lieutenant and head-constable are also chosen by the Chinese. Were we to establish a good system of responsible government among our Chinese populations, and employ a sufficient staff of interpreters, we should be relieved from apprehension on their account, and they from the dread of the consequences with which we are apt to visit them under the influence of that apprehension.

In all other respects, there is no comparison between the advantages held out to emigrants from the Celestial Empire by our possessions—with the exception of Australia—and those of other countries. Not only are they exempt from a poll-tax, but the rate of wage is higher than either in the Philippines or Java; while the freedom from commercial restrictions, and the bustling activity of an energetic Anglo-Saxon community, are congenial to that spirit of commercial enterprise which assimilates the Chinese to ourselves, and impels them instinctively to migrate to those localities best adapted to its development. This is most satisfactorily proved by the actual proportion which the Chinese bear to the whole population of different European settlements, and which Mr. Crawfurd computes as follows: "In Java the Chinese form the one hundredth part, and in the Philippines about the four hundredth part of the population. In the British possessions collectively the Chinese constitute about one third of the inhabitants, and in Singapore two thirds."

It would be a wise policy in us to encourage, to a greater extent than we do, Chinese emigration to other settlements besides those to which they have already found their way. Not only should we be able to retain Labuan as a colony from which we could exercise an important influence over Borneo, teeming with valuable productions, but we could make the little island itself profitable by the introduction of Chinese labor for the development of its mineral resources. It is not, however, merely in the settlements of the Malay archipelago to which Chinese emigration might be directed and encouraged by government with great advantage, but to many tropical colonies in other parts of the world, such as British Guiana, where there is an enormous capacity of production coupled with an utter inadequacy of means. We must be careful of judging of the results of Chinese immigration by the experiences of California, Australia, or any other colony where peculiar conditions, resulting from gold discoveries, exist, and where the climate admits of competition by whites. It is as undesirable that such a competition should be established in those countries adapted for European out-of-door labor, as that others should be deprived of the benefits of any such labor at all because the climate is fatal to the white man.

As we proposed a short trip into the interior, for which passports were necessary, we went to Government House to obtain them, and, at the same time, to pay a visit to the captain general. Two bridges, one of which is suspension, and the other a respectable structure of ten arches, span the Pasig, and connect the suburb with the fortified town. This suburb, or rather extramural city, contains a population of nearly 200,000 souls; the walled city contains about 10,000 people, almost entirely pure white, and consists of eight narrow streets running at right angles to one another, aristocratic and dull, and a square or plaza. In this the governor's residence is situated, and from the windows at the back a magnificent view of the harbor is obtained. The present governor is the most popular and enlightened man that has filled the office since Don Pascual Enrile, celebrated for having opened internal communication, and removed those restrictions on colonial shipping with which, with their usual infatuated policy, the Spanish government retarded the prosperity of one of its most valuable possessions. The advanced views of his predecessor have in many instances been improved upon and carried out by the present governor, who was peculiarly fitted for his post by the opportunities which were afforded him, during the years he spent in political exile at Manilla, of making himself acquainted with the wants of the colony at a time when he little thought he would ever be called on to govern it. It is fair to him to say that it does not follow that, because a man has been a *deportado* to Manilla, he should have been guilty of any act of treason against the existing government. It is simply the result of an electioneering "dodge," not unlike some that have been recently practiced in Kansas. The government, when it appeals to the country, begins by exiling a large number of the *probable* hostile voters — an effectual mode of counteracting the effects of the ballot, which might be suggested for adoption by ourselves should that measure ever be introduced.

The captain general had himself visited Calcutta, and was deeply interested in the intelligence which we gave him of the progress and prospects of the mutiny. In the evening we took a drive on the Calzada or public promenade. Unfortunately, it was too late for us to see as much as we wished of the fair or colored occupants of the numerous carriages, which form two long lines throughout the whole length of the drive, and which are kept upon their proper sides by mounted policemen stationed at intervals along the road, as solemn and pompous, if not so gorgeous, as the sentries at the Horse-Guards.

At Manilla, as in other Roman Catholic countries, the gayest day next to a feast-day is Sunday. It so happened that the Sunday we were there was also a saint's day—all the church-going taking place in the morning, and the dancing in the evening. The former begins almost with the day; and the ceremony of a military mass which we attended involved an effort of early rising. The Cathedral was undergoing repairs, and the churches we entered were none of them remarkable specimens of ecclesiastical architecture or ornament. The one in which military mass was held was poorly attended. When we first went in, a few pretty female figures, with dark complexions, lustrous eyes, and graceful mantillas falling over their shoulders, dotted about in kneeling attitudes, and old men mumbling in corners and crossing themselves, composed the whole congregation. Then the clang of martial music outside was followed by the entry of two or three regiments, the men uncovered, with their shakoes swinging between their shoulders. Six soldiers with drawn swords occupied the altar platform, and, as the priests entered, these presented arms, and the band opened the proceedings with a very pretty waltz. Indeed, the whole service, from beginning to end, was musical, the officiating priest, a very black man, confining himself to pantomime, and the band varying time according to his gestures. When he elevated the host they went down on their knees, and played an air very much resembling a polka, crossing themselves with great rapidity in time to the music. Then came tunes which the uninitiated might have supposed were galops or quadrilles. The whole performance was entirely devoid of any sacred character, and only lasted about half an hour. The soldiers were a handsome, well set-up body of men, in a neat white uniform, and red facings turned up with black. The officers have nearly all come out from Spain, as the service is a favorite one, and well paid. The Spanish army in the Philippines is maintained at about 12,000 strong. The last time they were employed on active service was in 1851, when a force of 4000 men was sent to chastise the Sooloo rajah: this they accomplished satisfactorily, with a loss of about 100 men. A contingent of 3000 men has recently been engaged, in alliance with the French forces in Cochin China, in an unsuccessful attempt to reduce the king of that country to submission.

We were rendered independent of any of the steamers which, decked with flags, were carrying crowds of gayly-dressed pleasure-seekers to the festa at Cavitè, as the Kestrel (Lieut Rason),* which had put into Manilla for repairs, carried us comfortably across the harbor in two hours. At Cavitè are situated the government docks; and the Spanish commodore came off to inspect the marvelous little craft which had just weathered the dangers of a passage round the Cape, and the minute dimensions of which

* This gallant young officer was killed in the recent attack upon the Peiho Forts.

struck him with astonishment. His residence was in the dock, through which we walked on our way to the town. It is small, and of no great pretensions to strength. Cavité contains about 15,000 inhabitants; and, as evening closed in, the main street presented a gay and brilliant aspect. The houses, although two-storied, were small and insignificant, but countless lights twinkled in every window, and drapery of gorgeous colors hung from the balconies, and, leaning over them, signoritas smoking cigarettes laughingly contemplated the crowd below, as it surged to and fro in anxious anticipation of the grand *spectacle*.

A general explosion of rockets, and the martial strains of a military band announced the start of the procession. Then came the usual struggle for places and loss of pocket-handkerchiefs; and through a lane in the crowd passed, first, the band, then a gentleman in black with a white tie, who looked like a master of ceremonies, and superintended the distribution of tapers to such of the crowd as were disposed to form part of the procession. These amateur taper-bearers formed two rows, and between them, in double file, toddled, rather than walked, a number of miniature nuns and monks, in full religious costume, the oldest of whom might have attained the age of five or six. The shaved crowns and sandaled feet of the tiny monks, as they led by the hand with great dignity and solemnity their still smaller sisters, produced a very grotesque effect, which was heightened, if possible, by the miscellaneous costume of a crowd of children that followed, in the most extravagant fancy dresses. Then came the Virgin, carried by men screened by drapery, on a wooden stage, a perfect mass of tinsel and wax-lights, followed by priests, while two or three regiments, with fixed bayonets, brought up the rear. As soon as this display is over, the revels of the night fairly begin. The taper-bearers, having escorted the Virgin home, plunge wildly into the delights of fandangoes and cachuchas; every house is open to the stranger, if he likes to take part in the amusement of the evening, and in almost every one dancing and gambling are carried on till the morning of the following day, which, not being dedicated to any saint, is dedicated to a rest from the fatigues of the debauchery committed on the one that is.

As we had determined to start the same night for the interior, we were not tempted to prolong our stay at Cavité. Indeed, having in the most orthodox way gone through the whole services of the day, we thought we might dispense with the sermon; and at midnight, instead of dancing fandangoes, we were snugly ensconced at the bottom of a canoe upon the River Pasig, lulled to sleep by the measured stroke of our boatmen's paddles, as they forced the little craft rapidly up stream. We were accompanied on our expedition by Mr. and Mrs. G——, to whose hospitality we were indebted during our stay at Manilla. Daylight found us in the Lago de Bai, under the lee of the island of Talim. Its high volcanic hills were wooded to the summit, and indented with charming little bays, fringed with drooping bamboos. The lake is somewhat in the shape of a horse's hoof—a peninsula, at the end of which is the island of Talim, forming the frog. From here we stretched across to the southern shore, the high and precipitous mountains of which looked comparatively near, but to the westward the waters of the lake formed the horizon. The Lago de Bai is the largest sheet of fresh water as yet discovered in the Eastern archipelago, being twenty-eight miles in length by twenty-two in breadth.

Our destination, which we reached in time for a late breakfast, is celebrated for some thermal springs, which, bubbling out of the ground almost at the water's edge, enable the weary traveler to refresh himself with a warm bath, though, as the temperature is sufficiently high to boil an egg in four minutes, he had better not make rash experiments. In consequence of these springs, which at one time enjoyed some celebrity, the village is called Los Baños. It consists only of a few Indian huts, in one of which, elevated on piles, and surrounded by a crowd of admiring natives, we restored exhausted nature preparatory to a trip to the island of Socolme. Fortunately, I had not seen the narrative of that amusing, but most audacious romancer, La Gironière, or our appetites might have been spoiled by the anticipation of the dangers to be encountered. His evidently was. The Indians had told him that the small lake in this island was infested with alligators, from whom—so great was their voracity—"escape in a canoe by rowing quickly was impossible." "There was much good sense," says La Gironière, "in what they said, but we were never deterred by dangers or difficulties," etc. So he and his friend, Mr. Lindsay, venture on the hazardous experiment of going in a canoe on a lake where there are reported to be alligators. "We had not proceeded many yards from the bank when we all experienced feelings of alarm, attributable, no doubt, to the expectation of danger being immediate, as well as the aspect of the place which presented itself to our view." Then comes a terrific charge of alligators—"the grand drama announced by the Indians is about to be realized," etc.—"when Lindsay, *running all risks*, fires his gun direct at the brute;" and so on, in a strain the accuracy of which may be judged of from the fact that he estimates the Lake of Socolme as having an elevation of 1500 feet above the Lago de Bai, when fifteen feet is really the outside; and says that it "does not receive the rays of the sun except when that luminary is at its zenith;" whereas, the banks in many parts being not above twenty feet high, and in only one place about 200, the lake, moreover, being at least two miles round, it rejoices to a very equitable extent in the blessed rays of that "luminary." We trust, for the sake of La Gironière's credit as a sportsman, that he displayed as much courage with his rifle as he certainly has with his pen.

We paddled round the margin of the lake enchanted with its loveliness, sheltering ourselves from the noon-day sun under the luxuriant vegetation which clothes its banks and droops into the water. Thousands of flying foxes had chosen for their retreat these leafy shades; their unsightly bodies were concealed by their expansive wings, as, clinging by their feet, they hung in dark festoons from the projecting branches. Disturbed by our approach, they flapped away over the lake, but we soon awoke its silent echoes with the reports of our guns, and two or three of these monstrous bats tumbled heavily into the water. If the alligators existed at all, they evidently had not recovered from the panic which must have been created by La Gironière's visit. Not one ventured to show the tip of his nose above the water.

We were loth to leave this fairy-like scene, and, looking back upon it as we dragged our canoes over the narrow strip of land, were reminded rather of a diamond set in emeralds than of the crater of an extinct volcano. As it was, the attractions of the island of Socolme had induced us to linger too long, for it was late ere we started on our return voyage, and a gale of wind had sprung up in the mean time of such violence that, to our dismay, the boatmen at first refused to venture on the traject. An attempt which we insisted on their making was not encouraging: our slight canoe was no sooner exposed to the full force of the wind and waves than she took in a sea which half filled and very nearly upset her, so that we were compelled ignominiously to put back to a little bay, where a government felucca was lying, with the padrone of which we hoped to come to terms. Unfortunately, though susceptible to the influence of dollars, his men were absent: so, as the lady of our party was undaunted by our former experience, we determined to effect some improvements upon our own little craft, and tempt the waves in her once more. First we took off the roof, which shut down on her sides so closely as to give her the ominous appearance of a gigantic coffin, and rendered it extremely probable that she would serve us in that capacity in the event of an upset. Then we added to and strengthened our outriggers, reefed our sail to its smallest dimensions, and once more pushed out into the lake. Throughout the twelve hours of a night that seemed interminable we battled with the waves; drenched to the skin, and seated in the water at the bottom of the boat, we chiefly employed ourselves baling, the hats of the boatmen rendering good service. Daylight found us hungry and rheumatic, gliding down the rapid current of the Pasig; but our condition rapidly improved under the genial influence of the morning sun, and an hour after our return to civilization we were so well satisfied with the adventures of our trip that we forgot its discomforts.

The little that we saw of the interior of Luzon only made us regret the more that our limited time did not admit of a more extended trip. The island affords magnificent scenery to the traveler in search of the picturesque, while its varied productions offer a wide and interesting field for observation. Government, however, is chary of gratifying the curiosity of foreigners in this respect; and the districts of Cayagan and Gupan, celebrated for their extensive growth of tobacco, are not to be visited without some difficulty. Sugar-cane is largely cultivated. The sugar, however, is only manufactured in small quantities at a time by the country people in a very primitive manner. It is remarkable that, in the absence of steam, it should form one of the largest articles of export. The markets to which it is almost exclusively sent are England and Australia. The United States, on the other hand, seem to monopolize the trade in hemp. The late Russian war had the effect of largely raising the value of this article in Manilla. Unmanufactured hemp is burdened with an export duty from which Manilla rope is free. In the Philippines, as in all other colonies of Continental European powers, the development of the magnificent resources of the country is cramped by the perpetuation of a system based on principles of political economy exploded among ourselves, and which we must hope can not long resist the pressure of the enlightened views and commercial progress of other countries.

Meantime our gun-boats have repaired the damages they have sustained during their long and hazardous voyage from England, and are again ready for sea; so we regretfully bid farewell to Manilla, and once more shape our course for the Celestial Empire, where events are in progress which will render our arrival there with one of these useful little craft in tow doubly acceptable.

CHAPTER VI.

Attempt of Count Poutiatine to reach Pekin.—Lawless Proceedings in the Canton River.—Singular native Proclamation.—The Hall of Peace and Patriotism.—Preparations for War.—The Ultimatum.—Occupation of Honan.—Yeh's Answer.—Report of a Conversation between the Emperor Hien Fung and Ki Shuh-tsan.—Embarkation on board the Furious.—Disappearance of the floating Population.—Aspect of the river Face of Canton.—Expiry of the Delay.—Anchorage at Dane's Island.—Temper of the Inhabitants.—Delay of the Bombardment.

THE principal event which had occurred at Hong Kong during our absence at Manilla was the departure of our commander-in-chief, General Ashburnham, for Calcutta, in the Ava, and the installment of Lord Elgin in the house vacated by him on shore. The increasing coolness of the temperature rendered this change doubly enjoyable. Early in November the American minister, Mr. Reed, arrived in a frigate of gigantic proportions, and the Russian minister, Count Poutiatine, in a paddle-wheel steamer of very minute dimensions. The latter had made the journey overland from St. Petersburg to the Amoor, not, however, without having applied for admission to Pekin by way of Kiahkta. On this being refused, he proceeded, on his own responsibility, to the mouth of the Peiho, where he was informed that no communication with the court of Pekin could be made on his behalf from that point. It was, however, after some time, conceded to him that a letter would be forwarded to Pekin, but that, if he wanted a reply, he must return to Kiahkta and wait there. Count Poutiatine refused to accede to these terms, and, in consequence, it was ultimately arranged that an answer should be sent to him at the mouth of the Peiho, whither he would return to receive it. When at last, after an interval of some weeks, Count Poutiatine once more appeared at the mouth of the Peiho, he received his answer, which consisted of a refusal to see him at Pekin, with an intimation that under no circumstances could the performance of the "Kotow" be dispensed with. The result of his experience had in fact been to confirm the opinion entertained by Lord Elgin from the commencement, that nothing could be done with the government of China except at the Peiho, and then only when a force sufficient to strike terror into the capital, and of a description calculated to navigate the shallow waters that lead to it, should be assembled there, to give irresistible force to the arguments of diplomacy.

About this time there occurred a curious illustration of the violent character of the more lawless portion of the population inhabiting the creeks and islands of the Canton River, as well as of their ingenuity in turning to good account the troubles in which their country was involved. The incident was also instructive, as tending to show how many and serious were the evils to which might be exposed the unfortunate well-disposed inhabitants, who found in our cruisers but a poor substitute for the mandarin and war junks which had formerly protected them, and which we had scared away. A petition was sent down to Lord Elgin, inclosing a copy of a notice stated to have been widely circulated among the people, to the following effect: "That, the British navy being now stationed from Shakok at the Bogue, up to Shekmun, it is hereby decreed that, in return for the protection the British vessels afford to the population against lawless persons who would otherwise cut grain without authority, 2 mace per acre (Chinese) shall be paid into the British office, called the Ning-i-Tong (Hall of Peace and Patriotism), near Nei-Tong; to which all agriculturists are directed to repair on the 30th or 31st of October, or 1st of November, with the money. On payment of this, they will receive a license to cut grain. If any person attempt to cut or carry grain without license, the vessels of the Ning-i-Tong of Great Britain will bring him to the said hall, with his vessels, which will be confiscated." Three regulations were appended to the above notice: "1. For every acre registered at the Hall of Great Britain, at Nei-Tong, license to reap shall be issued. 2. In any case where the brethren recognize the seal to be the seal of the hall, they will immediately release the person whom they may have detained. 3. Rice-junks, from any village or fort whatsoever, must give notice at the hall, where their papers or licenses will be viséd, for the prevention of delays." Mr. Wade, who translated the above, was requested by Lord Elgin to put himself at once into communication with the admiral, for the purpose of discovering, if possible, this Hall of British Peacemakers and Patriots, and visit with the punishment they deserved those who had foully wronged, if not our fair name, at least their own unfortunate countrymen. Mr. Wade proceeded with a force to a building indicated by some country people as the hall in question, where he found six persons in chains, and some papers, one of which stated that orders had been received from the captain of the ship of English barbarians to look after the grain, and menacing any of the brethren who should presume to cut grain on their own account. It was found difficult to bring home the charge to any of the persons in the neighborhood; a comprador, however (or man whose business it was to supply one of her majesty's ships in the river with provisions), was recognized and taken into custody in consequence. There is probably no other country in the world but China where an organization upon so large a scale could have been formed which would use for a protection the dreaded name of its country's enemy, display for its banners the symbols of peace and patriotism, and have for its object the plunder and spoliation of its neighbors.

Though there may be an absence of patriotism generally in China, patriots can always be found here by paying for them, as in other countries. Thus we discovered a spy located at Hong Kong, whose papers we seized, and who kept a daily record of events there, and, at some risk to himself, sent Howqua full information of all the plans and rumors of plans current in Hong Kong as to our movements. Nothing was too trivial for his report: the number of ships in harbor—the daily exercise of troops—Lord Elgin's personal appearance and reputed character—the extent of our losses in India, and the causes of the mutiny, all were minutely but frequently erroneously recorded, and forwarded by Howqua to Yeh. Some of the information was furnished by Americans resident at Hong Kong, and some by Chinese in our employ.

Meanwhile General Straubenzee had succeeded General Ashburnham in the command-in-chief, and the prospect of active service seemed to infuse new life and energy into the feeble and wasted garrison of Hong Kong. The one weak regiment of which it consisted was perpetually being inspected and reviewed, and exercised in camping and in rifle practice. The daily booming of artillery practice, added to the constant thundering of salutes from the ships, as admirals or plenipotentiaries paid or received visits of ceremony, began to prepare the Chinese mind at Hong Kong for something more serious than the "talkee pigeon" to which for so many years they had been accustomed. We were now only waiting for the last detachment of marines; their arrival early in December rendered farther delay unnecessary; and on the 10th of that month, Mr. Wade, accompanied by Mr. Marques, proceeded with a flag of truce to Canton, and delivered the ultimata of the French and English plenipotentiaries to a subordinate officer sent by Yeh to receive it.

In the communication which the British minister addressed to the imperial commissioner upon this occasion, he alluded to the exceptional attitude of hostility and dislike which had always been maintained by the authorities and people of Canton in their intercourse with foreigners, as compared with the other ports; to their determined refusal to fulfill treaty-rights; to the constant quarrels which had arisen out of this unsatisfactory state of things: and to the barbarous way in which hostilities on the last occasion had been carried on by the Cantonese. As a proof that these complaints were not ill founded, or confined to British subjects alone, his excellency adverted to the recent capture of the Barrier Forts which had been forced upon the Americans, and to the fact that the French were prepared to join us in the determination to procure reparation for past, and security against future wrongs.

The execution of treaty-engagements, and compensation for losses sustained by British subjects, were the only demands the fulfillment of which was required from the imperial commissioner, and a *delai fatal* of two days, to date from the 12th instant, was accorded: during this period, the island of Honan was to be occupied as a material guarantee, and at its expiry, in the event of non-compliance, Canton was to be taken. In consequence of the above intimation, Honan was successfully occupied on the 15th instant by 400 British marines and 150 French blue-jackets, no attempt at resistance having been made on the part of the inhabitants.

On the following day Yeh's answer reached Hong Kong. That functionary denied that there was any difference in their disposition toward foreigners between the inhabitants of Canton and those of the other ports—denied that any article existed in any treaty relative to the opening of Canton; though the question had been twice raised, he declared it to have been finally abandoned; then put in a plea in traverse to the effect that no treaty could force the people of Canton to do what they did not like;

and recommended Lord Elgin to adopt the policy pursued by Sir George Bonham, which might, as in his case, procure him the Order of the Bath. Yeh went on to recite the want of success which had attended the efforts of Sir George Bonham and Sir John Bowring to open a more direct communication with the capital as an instance of the impossibility of opposing the Emperor's will. He then discussed the merits of the "Arrow case," warned the embassador against the occupation of Honan as being likely to lead to hostilities, and concluded by assuring his excellency that all existing difficulties might be satisfactorily arranged through the medium of a little amicable correspondence.

The following report of a conversation between his Celestial Majesty and an ex-judge of the Quang-tung province will throw some light upon the policy of the emperor and his commissioner at Canton upon the extent of their acquaintance with barbarian affairs, and upon the sources from whence they derived their information. This most interesting and curious document was among the papers found in Yeh's yamun subsequently to his capture, and it has since been translated by Mr. Wade:

Report of a Conversation between the Emperor Hien Fung and Ki Shuh-tsan, ex-Judge of Kwang-tung, in 1851.

[The following is translated from a memorandum forwarded to Yeh by a late judge of Kwang-tung, named Ki Shuh-tsan, of his conversation with the Emperor Hien Fung, at the audience granted him, according to custom, on his return to Pekin at the end of his term of service.

In his "Chinese and their Rebellions" (page 123 to 136), Mr. Thomas Meadows gives a similar conversation between the late emperor and Pih-kwei, the present governor of Kwang-tung, and then judge of the province. This took place in 1849, and it is remarkable that, toward the close of that audience, the late emperor asks Pih-kwei if he is acquainted with the newly-appointed judge, Ki Shuh-tsan, and volunteers a very favorable opinion of him as an honest and unaffected man.

A great deal of his correspondence with Yeh was found in the papers of the latter, among the rest the memorandum here translated, and with it a note explaining that, besides the matter to which it relates, the emperor had put questions regarding the contumacy of the literati of the district of Tung-kwan, who had lately manifested their dissatisfaction with the authorities by refusing to attend the examinations for degree, regarding the alleged misconduct of a military officer who had been very backward against some Kwang-tung outlaws; and, lastly, regarding the publication of the "Sing-li Tsing-i," the "Essence of Moral Philosophy," and of another work, reprints of which had been ordered by his majesty, at the suggestion of a high official, for the regeneration of the age.

Ki Shuh-tsan was younger brother of Ki Tsiun-tsan, who died not long since, one of the four principal Secretaries of State.—T. F. W.]

(Translation.)

At my audience his majesty questioned me very particularly respecting my official career, my settlement, my family, and my life before and after I came to be employed. I submit no copy of these questions to your excellency, but confine myself to laying before you those which his majesty condescended to ask concerning Kwang-tung affairs. His majesty asked,

Q. Are the English barbarians quiet at the present time, or the reverse?

A. They are so far quiet.

Q. Will no trouble be caused by their trade at some future period?

A. In the nature of barbarians there is much to suspect. A communication received from them two or three months ago raised several questions in language of a menacing character.* Seu and Yeh perfectly understand their trickiness, and as it is only by being resolute and positive that they can deal with them, they employ no word in their replies either more or less than is sufficient fully to meet† what is said by the barbarians, and thus they are left without any thing to rejoin.

Q. Do you know what they wrote about?

A. In their administration of barbarian affairs Seu and Yeh hold it important to be secret. As governor general and governor they consult each other in confidence on all replies to be written (to barbarian letters). Neither your majesty's servant,

---

* Questions they had no right to raise; *lit.*, put forth shoots not from the joint: a figure from the bamboo-tree.

† To meet, to controvert, or to reprove.

nor his fellow-commissioners, nor the intendants, although residing in the same city (as their excellencies), are able to learn any thing beforehand. If, as is sometimes the case, reference has to be made to Pih-kwei, the Commissioner of Finance, the reply drafted by him has again to be considered and approved by them; and on such occasions, when the question has been disposed of, Seu and Yeh are sure to communicate it to your servant, and to the rest as well. In former times, when barbarian affairs were in process of administration, news has reached barbarian quarters even before the event; but, nowadays, not even those who are constantly about Seu and Yeh can obtain information of the measures they are considering, and so the barbarians can ascertain nothing; while we, on the other hand, are accurately informed of all that affects their countries.

Q. How are you informed of what passes in their countries?

A. In foreign parts (*lit.*, in the outer seas) there are newspapers. In these every thing that concerns any nation is minutely recorded, and these we have it in our power to procure. And as the barbarians can not dispense with our people in the work of interpretation, Seu and Yeh manage to make their employés furnish them privately every month with all particulars. We are thus enabled to know every thing that concerns them.

Q. How is it that persons in barbarian employ will, notwithstanding, furnish us with intelligence?

A. It merely costs a few hundred dollars more a year to bestow rewards upon them. For these they are well pleased to serve us. Then, again, if the news received from any one quarter appears unsatisfactory, there is more sent in from other quarters, and if the reports from different quarters agree, the information is of course entitled to full credit.

Q. Are their newspapers in their barbarian character or in our Chinese character?

A. They are translations into Chinese.*

Q. Have you seen those papers?

A. In the campaign in Tsing-yuen last winter Yeh† received some, which he gave me to look at.

Q. What did they say?

---

* That is, the papers he has seen, as will appear directly.

† Yeh was then Governor of Kwang-tung, and was absent from Canton four months, endeavoring to put down outlaws or rebels in Tsing-yuen and Ning-teh.

A. Your servant remembers one circumstance. The English were at war with Bengal.* A Bengal man-of-war wanted to pass through English territory to attack (*lit.*, trouble, have a row with) some other nation; the English authorities† refused her a passage. Both sides opened a fire, in which an English ship was sunk, and a large number of the managing heads (directors) killed. The sovereign of their state assembled the chief persons (*lit.*, the head eyes) in the chamber where business is discussed (*sc.*, the House of Parliament). It was there proposed (by some) to speak reason to (or argue the point with) Bengal, but by others to raise a force and take satisfaction. Your servant has also been told by Yeh that, in the different letters which have come from the sovereign of the state to Bonham, he has always been directed to trade with China in a friendly spirit, and not to be troublesome (or meddlesome). It is also said that, in reward for his administration of commercial intercourse, Bonham was presented by the sovereign of the state with a decoration called "O-tá-pá" (Order of the Bath), a thing somewhat of the same sort as the ancient red gold-fish purse.‡ Bonham is well pleased with this. He parades it with pride; it will prevent him from making any more difficulties.

Q. How did the barbarians put their alleged grievances in the letter received from them?

A. When your servant returned to Canton from the Tsing-yuen campaign to lay down his office, he was told by Seu and Yeh that in the third moon Bonham§ had written to say that, as there was no great market for goods at two of the five ports, namely, in Cheh-kiang and Fuh-kien, he wanted to exchange the two ports in question for two others. Hang-chow and Soo-chow would both answer the purpose; but, if this could not be, Chin-kiang would do. If Chin-kiang was also impossible, his ships of war would be obliged to go to Tien-tsin. Seu and Yeh replied that trade at the five ports having been long settled by treaty, no change could be made; that, besides this, there was a fixed quantity of goods sold in China every year, the amount of which did

---

* Birmah is probably meant.

† *Lit.*, those of the English barbarians who manage their affairs. This is very likely a translation of the term "Directors of the East India Company."

‡ An ornament or decoration of ancient date.

§ He alludes to Sir George Bonham's letters, under instructions from the Foreign Office, written April 19, 1851, in which an exchange of ports was proposed.

not depend on the number of ports, more or less. Take the trade, they said, as it was before the five ports were opened, and has been since that event, and a calculation of the profits and losses of different parties will convince you (of this). If, with a good understanding existing between our two nations, your men-of-war attempt to go up to Tien-tsin, it is on your side that the quarrel will have been commenced; no blame will attach to us. Since this reply was sent, no letter has been received from them.

Q. Who has charge of barbarian affairs besides Bonham?

A. Your servant has been told that Bonham is the governor-in-chief (*lit.*, general head of the troops). Besides him there are Gutzlaff and Meadows. Gutzlaff was a practiced machinator when he was in China before.* This time, it is said, the ruler of the state makes him confine his attention to commercial affairs, and does not allow him to meddle (with politics).

Q. Are the other trading nations on good terms with the English barbarians?

A. When the English barbarians gave trouble some time since (*sc.* 1839–42), different nations assisted them. In the sequel it is said the English barbarians became deeply indebted to other nations for shipping, the value of which they have been unable to recover from them; hence a good deal of misunderstanding. The other tribes, are jealous, too, of the English barbarians for having carried their point (*sc.* with China); and so, although so far as outward appearances go, they trade together amicably, each party is, in fact, considering his own interests, and no cordial understanding is possible.

Q. Are the French quiet in Kwang-tung?

A. The French continue to give no trouble in Kwang-tung. But it is said that, with the exception of trade, what they most prize is the teaching of their doctrine.

Q. What people practice their doctrine in general? Are there licentiates and graduates among them?

A. It is the common (*lit.*, the little people) who have no sense. All that they hear of the question is that, by the practice of virtue, they may look for happiness,† and so the chances are that they

---

* Mr. Gutzlaff, then Chinese Secretary, returned to China in January, 1851, and died in August.

† Confucianism does not teach men to be virtuous only in the hope of a reward. It is corrupt Buddhism, and other superstitions, which set the people propitiating good fortune.

are mystified by them. Licentiates and graduates, inasmuch as they have rather more reading and acquaintance with philosophy, which makes them respect themselves, are, of course, not to be so deluded. Your servant has never heard that such persons had embraced their doctrine.

Q. Have there been any prosecutions for the profession of the doctrine in Kwang-tung as well?*

A. Your servant has heard that some time ago there were some. There had been none from the time of his arrival last year until the fourth moon of the present, when Yeh wrote to him, confidentially, to the effect that, in the district of Ying-teh, Li San-wan was reported to be playing the Great King of the Red men,† and that in his behalf certain recreant graduates, already degraded with vagabonds and others, had privily leagued themselves with yamun followers and soldiers, most of whom were professing the doctrine; and he desired your servant to send a subordinate to make secret investigation. Your servant did send a subordinate, who went through the district from village to village in disguise, making inquiries for a month and more, but without any positive evidence of the fact. In the fifth moon your servant handed over his office to Tsui-tung, who again sent to make inquiry in every part of the Ung-yuen and Kiuh-kiang districts. When your servant left Canton the officer sent had not returned, and he can not say what steps were subsequently taken.

Q. Is not the doctrine of the Lord of Heaven‡ also preached in Shan Si?

A. It is. When your servant was a licentiate, and superintending instruction in the district of Hung-tung, in Ping-yang Fu, the outlaw, Tsáu Shun, and others, murdered the authorities in the city of Chau, and took the city itself. Hung-tung being but thirty li from Chau, we were on the alert night and day, and one day a confidential dispatch was received from the prefect of Ping-yang stating that in the street of the Shang-kia, in the city of Hung-tung, persons were propagating the doctrine, proselytizing, preach-

---

* His majesty probably means "as well" as in Kwang-si, although little if any notice had as yet been taken by the court of the troubles there. The word I translate "prosecution" includes the infliction of the penalty.

† The rebels have long been known as the "red head men," from their turbans. The "red" here used is, however, a different character.

‡ Here written "Tien tsu kiau," doctrine of the Grandfather of Heaven. "Tien chu kiau" is evidently meant. It is the style by which Christianity, as taught by the Romanist missionaries, is known.

ing observances, and reciting canonical books; and desiring that, as they were very probably in league with the bad characters of Chau, they should be secretly arrested. On this, the district magistrate, in co-operation with the military, seized a Chih-li man surnamed Wang, who was preaching the doctrine there, and on whose person was found a crucifix and some books of the doctrine of the Lord of Heaven, all in European characters (*lit.*, characters of the Western seas). After this, all persons teaching or professing the doctrine were proceeded against according to law.

Q. And what did their books say?

A. Your servant saw that, besides others, there were some books copied in our Chinese character, which were all about Jesus. Jesus was the person who was nailed on the cross. They purported to exhort people to be virtuous, to keep the heart good, and to do good actions. But there is great unanimity (or community of opinion) among the professors of the doctrine; and though, under ordinary circumstances, while people of no intelligence do no more than observe fasts in the hope of obtaining happiness, it can do no great harm, if, in the course of time, a single remarkable person should appear (among its professors), he would be almost certain to create trouble by inflaming and deluding (the public).

Q. Have you ever seen the barbarian buildings at Hong Kong?

A. Your servant has not seen them. Those in the foreign factories on the Canton River he has seen, but he has never been into them.

Q. Have you seen any barbarians or barbarian ships?

A. Your servant has seen a Flowery Flag (*sc.* American) steamer on the Canton River. There were barbarians on board the vessel, all dressed in white, both men and women. But she was too far off your servant's vessel for him to see them well.

Q. What nation is the Flowery Flag?

A. The American. The trade of the nation is very great; it is very rich and powerful, and yet not troublesome.

Q. How is it that America is rich and powerful, and yet not troublesome?

A. As a general rule, the outer barbarians trade, because their nature is so covetous. If one of them breaks the peace (makes trouble), the prosperity of the other's trade is marred. Thus the English are at this moment beggared;* but if they were to break

---

* And therefore, he means, not likely to go to war.

the peace, it is not on their own trade alone that injury would be inflicted: other nations are therefore certain to object to any outrageous proceeding on their part. Were they to commence a disturbance, the Americans would certainly be the last to assist them.

Q. Why would not the Americans assist them?

A. Your servant has been told that the Americans have business relations of great importance with Wu Sung-yau (How-qua), formerly a hong merchant of Quang-tung; indeed, that they have had money of Wu. Every movement of the English barbarians is certain to be privately communicated to the family of Wu by the Americans, and Wu Sung-yau therefore makes his private report to Seu and Yeh, who take precautionary measures accordingly. Thus, last year, it was by a communication from the Americans that it was known that a man-of-war of the English barbarians was coming to Tien-tsin (the Peiho). Not that this shows any sincere friendship for us on the part of the Americans: it was simply that their desire for gain is strong, and that they were afraid that their trade would be disturbed by (the act of) the English.*

In the absence of the Shannon, the Furious had been placed at Lord Elgin's disposal. Her very light draught of water rendered her a much more available ship for the purpose than the Shannon, while Captain Osborn spared no effort or personal sacrifice to fit her up as comfortably as possible for the accommodation of the mission. On the 17th we all embarked on board this good ship, which was destined to be our floating home for the following eighteen months, and proceeded up the river to Blenheim Reach, where Baron Gros with the French fleet were already assembled. It appeared that the communication of Yeh to the French embassador was couched in the same stubborn and unyielding tone as that which he had addressed to Lord Elgin; it was therefore determined, at a conference held on board the Audacieuse, that, in consequence of the unsatisfactory nature of the imperial commissioner's replies, the matter should be placed in the hands of the naval and military authorities, but that a few days' grace

---

* The remainder of this most curious and interesting document is to be found in the Blue Book. I have been induced to make this extract here, because it illustrates in a remarkable manner the position we held in the eyes of the Chinese authorities, and the views by which they were influenced in their dealings with us.

should be allowed after the expiry of the *delai fatal*, so as to afford some opportunity to the inhabitants of escaping.

I took advantage of the return of the admiral up the river to accompany him to Honan. Three miles after passing Macao Fort, the former limit of our explorations up the river, we rounded the point of Honan Island, and the scene became novel and interesting. The most striking feature in it was the entire absence on the part of the Chinese of any preparations to meet the attack which they must have been anticipating; much less did they offer any active resistance to the occupation of the pack-houses in Honan by our troops, or molest the men-of-war which had been quietly moored in front of the city wall, within 150 yards of the guns upon it. The instincts of self-preservation seemed to extend only to the floating population, which had simultaneously disappeared on the arrival of the ships, and taken refuge in the numerous creeks with which the country is intersected. Still, even these had not wholly vanished, and every now and then I was startled by seeing a two-storied mansion, with verandas and a tiled roof, which appeared to be the last house of a street, deliberately detach itself from its neighbors, and float complacently down the stream to some secure aquatic retreat. In this manner about half a million of people had moved to other waters; how they managed to subsist when they got there remains a mystery. Probably they adopted the Peace and Patriotic line.

The point of Honan Island was admirably adapted to the purpose for which it was designed. The pack-houses were spacious oblong buildings of solid construction, extending from the water's edge back to a narrow lane. On the opposite side of this was a row of mean cottages, and in rear of them an extensive mud flat separated our troops from a populous Chinese suburb. Many of these pack-houses contained tea, sweetmeats, and other articles of export, which were being rapidly transported by Chinese coolies, under the superintendence of their owners. The ginger, cumquots, and other preserves, often, however, proved too strong a temptation for our men, and their smeared faces and sticky fingers gave indisputable evidence that they had made the jars pay toll as they passed. In the evening, when the lofty warehouses were lit up by numerous large fires made upon the stone floor, round which were collected groups of hard-visaged men, the scene was animated and picturesque, and would have been by no means of a consolatory character to the Chinese authorities had they been there to witness it.

On the following day I visited a party of engineers engaged in erecting a mortar battery on the Dutch Folly. A large crowd were collected on the city bank of the river watching their operations, and men were stationed as look-outs on stages erected for the purpose above the roofs of the houses. I ascended one of the trees on the little island, and looked over the yamun of the imperial commissioner, not a hundred and fifty yards distant. Canton presents a most ragged appearance from this point: the river bank was strewn with the debris of houses, the result of the bombardment and fires of the previous year; the site of the foreign factory was covered with heaps of rubbish; half-demolished houses reared gaunt gables above their prostrate neighbors; and miserable hovels, which enterprising paupers had erected upon spots too exposed for the taste of the legitimate owner, only added to the dilapidated aspect of the town. Nevertheless, people passed briskly to and fro along the river margin, and were ferried across under the guns of our ships. I counted from one of these, the Cruiser, seven guns on the city wall, the muzzles of which were directed so as to cover her deck. In the afternoon Lord Elgin passed the town in a gun-boat, and was as much struck by the desolate appearance of the city as by the apathetic indifference of its inhabitants.

On the 21st, being the day before the expiry of the delay accorded in the ultimatum, a conference was held at Whampoa, by the plenipotentiaries and naval and military commanders-in-chief relative to the place of attack and the preliminary arrangements. On the 24th it was intimated to Yeh by the allied plenipotentiaries that, the delay having expired, they had called upon the naval and military commanders to act, and Lord Elgin stated that he "reserved to himself the right to make, on behalf of the British government, such additional demands as the altered condition of affairs, produced by the imperial commissioner's refusal to accede to terms of accommodation, may seem in his eyes to justify." At the same time Yeh also received a summons from the allied commanders-in-chief, stating that it was their intention to attack the town at the expiration of forty-eight hours if it was not surrendered within that time. In a communication addressed in reply to Lord Elgin's dispatch, the imperial commissioner recurred to the "Arrow case," and adverted at length to the points discussed in his former letter, without manifesting the slightest alteration in his tone, or in the tenor of his sentiments generally. Meanwhile, for many days past, Mr. Parkes had been occupied in posting up proclamations, both at Honan and along the river face of the city, at considerable personal risk, advising the inhabitants to leave the city during the approaching bombardment; but the very indifference with which they collected round the placards, and the contempt for them they occasionally manifested by tearing them down, only proved how insensible they were to the coming danger, and how hopeless it was to expect that these warnings would produce any effect.

Up to this time we had been anchored at Whampoa, close under Dane's Island, and our principal amusement was rambling over that picturesque spot; though not above five miles in circumference, the island was broken into hill, and dale, and fertile glens, where a rural population lived peaceably amid all the troubles, and seemed utterly indifferent as to the fate of their provincial city. Indeed, many of them who had suffered severely by the interruption of trade rather hoped for our success than otherwise; and in one of the villages we met a man who had formerly lived at Whampoa, and spoke a little English, who assured us that he expressed a sentiment very common among his countrymen when he said, "You takee Canton chop chop, my no gotchie money." He moreover told us that the army had not been paid for two months, and were very discontented, and that the authorities were really as well convinced as he was of our power to take the city. It was not, however, prudent to enter indiscriminately into villages. Although at Dane's Island we found the people well disposed, some members of the French embassy had not been so well received on Whampoa Island, and had not found it safe to extend their rambles very far from their ships; under all circumstances, it was desirable to take our evening walks armed with revolvers.

We celebrated Christmas day by taking up the position which the Furious was destined to occupy during the remainder of our stay in the river, with the view of getting as near Canton as her draught of water would admit. Captain Osborn pushed her past the Barrier Forts until her nose was buried in the mud; and from her main-top a panoramic view was obtained of the city, and that portion of the surrounding country which was shortly to be the scene of the military and naval operations. The Primauguet, in which Baron Gros had taken up his temporary habitation, was anchored immediately astern of us. Though by the terms of the summons the bombardment ought to have commenced on the 26th, preparations were not sufficiently completed until the 28th. It will thus be seen that every opportunity was afforded to the authorities to yield, and to the people to provide for their own safety and the security of their property.

CHAPTER VII.

Landing of the Troops.—Advance on Lin's Fort.—Treacherous Mode of Warfare.
—Capture of Lin's Fort.—Attack of the Braves.—Position for the Night.—The
Bombardment is continued.—Death of Captain Bate.—Skirmish with Braves.—
Escalade of the Walls of Canton.—Aspect of the City.—Scene from Magazine
Hill.—Capture of the City.—Capture of Gough's Fort.—Chinese Looting-parties.
—Tartar Garrison of Canton.—Condition of the public Buildings.—Explosion of
a Magazine.

ON the 27th we were able to perceive, from our post of observation, Major Clifford, Quartermaster General, landing with a party composed of two companies of the 59th, under Major Bannister, with the Engineers, to prepare stages for the disembarkation of the troops and guns on the following morning. The outposts, which were kept by the 59th, and extended for about half a mile into the interior, were unmolested during the night. In consequence of the shallowness of the water in the creek, the landing was fixed for nine o'clock on the following day, that being the earliest hour at which the tide would serve for our gun-boats. The French, however, being in ships' boats, reached the landing-stages first, and requested General Straubenzee to allow them to disembark, to which he acceded. Before their disembarkation was completed, the rest of the 59th and artillery arrived in the gun-boats, and as soon as the 59th were landed, they and the French naval brigade moved up toward Lin's Fort, the original party under Major Bannister being in advance. As I observe in the French papers that our gallant allies have claimed some credit for being the first to land on the 28th, it is only fair to state the amount of risk they incurred in landing at a spot which had been in our possession since the previous day.

From our exalted position we had a splendid view of the commencement of the bombardment, which began shortly after daylight, and continued without intermission for twenty-seven hours. Ten o'clock was fixed as the hour for the landing of the blue-jackets of the Furious under Captain Osborn; and I was glad to avail myself, by accompanying him, of the opportunity afforded of being an eye-witness, under the most favorable circumstances, of all the operations.

Thanks to the exertions of the Sappers, a very fair road had been made through the village near the landing-place. After passing through it, we met a wounded man of the 59th, and two wounded men of the French naval brigade—the first evidence of any active resistance having been offered to our progress. These men had been wounded in a slight skirmish which had resulted in the precipitate retreat of the Chinese. Meeting Loch, who was temporarily attached to the general's staff, in the village, I pushed on with him as quickly as possible to the front. As we proceeded, the country became very broken; small hillocks, covered with graves, were surrounded by dry paddy-fields, by which their slopes were sometimes terraced. It was just the country for skirmishing in; and, had not our enemy been contemptible, they might have harassed us seriously as we advanced. As it happened, what little danger there was arose rather from a species of treachery than from open warfare. Captain Hackett of the 59th, while carrying a message, was suddenly surrounded in the village above mentioned, only a short time after we had left it, and his head was cut off within sight of his own men, who succeeded in killing one of the assassins, and capturing the other. This man was brought up to head-quarters, and hung the same evening. The man of the 59th we had met told us he had been shot from behind a hedge after he had passed it. Indeed, it was very difficult to know whom to regard as enemies, and whom to ignore as such. The hills were crowded with spectators watching our proceedings; yet it was only natural to suppose that every villager was an enemy at heart, though they did not venture on open warfare, or seem to anticipate our considering them in the light of foes.

We found the front about a mile from the village, and, when we arrived, the French and English admirals and General Straubenzee were seated at luncheon in a grave. The advance had pushed on so rapidly in pursuit of the retreating Chinese that there was a pause in the operations in consequence of the guns and ammunition not having come up. Moreover, we were close to Lin's Fort, the capture of which it had been arranged should complete the first day's operations. As the French had a light field-piece with them, it was agreed that they should open upon Lin's Fort from a hillock within easy range, while the 59th should occupy a joss-house to the right, from which they could reach the embrasures of the fort with their Enfield rifles. To the joss-house, which was deserted, we accordingly repaired, and, screened by the wall, amused ourselves by trying to repress the harmless fire which the garrison kept up at intervals. When our field-piece came up, and a shell burst near them, these brave defenders unhesitatingly evacuated the fort—a fact as patent to our allies as it was to ourselves. When the banner of the last man had disappeared behind the rising ground beyond, the French rushed in, and it must be admitted that there was no reason why we should not have done the same. It was an operation entirely devoid of risk for either party, but to our allies is due the credit of their superior quickness of perception. Indeed, so little of this quality had some of our own men, that they rushed at the fort with loud shouts, apparently mistaking the tricolor which waved from its walls for a Chinese banner. As the French sailors often carry small tricolor flags in the pockets of their spacious trowsers, their conquests are rapidly proclaimed. Upon this occasion the leading marine, having been provident enough to supply himself with a national "pavilion," sprung upon the walls flag in hand, and shouting "Vive l'Amiral! l'Empereur! la France! l'Angleterre!" all in a breath, created an intense amount of enthusiasm, and was embraced by his admiral, and invested with the legion of honor on the spot.

The fort was a small circular building, fitted for the reception of about 200 men. We entered and inspected it, and from the parapet obtained a good view of the city walls, about 600 yards distant. As soon as the Chinese perceived us in possession, the guns from the city opened upon us, but without much effect. Meantime the naval brigade and marines had been coming up, and extending far to the right, over undulating ground covered with graves and clumps of wood. From Lin's Fort we had an excellent view of a skirmish in which they engaged with some braves, who now appeared for the first time in some force. These latter were soon driven back to the base of the hill on which Gough's Fort is situated, but only to advance again as our men retired. Indeed, as a considerable distance separated the combatants throughout, the Chinese seemed to gain confidence from this mode of warfare, and began to collect in great numbers behind a small village, from which they made a grand advance, with quantities of banners waving, and great yelling and vaporing, throwing forward skirmishers in pairs carrying gingalls, making contemptuous gestures at their enemies, and indulging in divers antics, for which their leader, a tall man in blue, who carried a huge sword, was especially conspicuous. He was followed by a standard-bearer, capering along ten yards in advance of the crowd. This brave army ultimately succeeded in occupying a straggling wood, and in ensconcing themselves in the horse-shoe graves with which the hill-sides abounded, and which formed natural rifle-pits. Above these, with their heads well under cover, they defiantly waved flags, and managed, with their gingalls, to wound some of our men as they dodged from one grave to another. The hill presented somewhat the appearance of an animated rabbit-warren. Two or three shells, however, judiciously dropped among them from Lin's Fort, soon started them from their hiding-places; and the gentleman in blue displayed even more agility in hopping back again at the head of his army than he had in his advance.

As this was the position we intended to occupy for the night, the remainder of the afternoon was spent either in replying to the guns from the city with our field-pieces, or in checking the advance of the braves whenever they ventured to attempt to reoccupy their old position. Our loss during the day's operations had been trifling. With the exception of poor Hackett, we had not a man killed, though, I believe, two or three afterward died of the wounds they had received from gingall balls. The scene had been one of considerable interest and novelty, if not of fighting. As none of the staff were mounted, and the distances were great, one or two of us, who were amateurs, were glad to find that we could be of use in carrying messages. Our head-quarters for the night was a joss-house in the rear of Lin's Fort, which was occupied by an allied force, while in the bamboo groves to the right the marines and naval brigade were encamped. Our slumbers were presided over by gods and godesses, but, unfortunately, were a good deal disturbed by the groans of some wounded men, who had been brought in to the veranda. Long before daylight the following day we were once more on the alert, and scrambled in the dark over the rough ground to Lin's Fort, the walls of which were lit up by the lurid glare of numerous fires of our men, who were encamped round it.

Meantime the bombardment was maintained with unabated

vigor, and as I listened to the whistle of the round-shot, and watched the meteor-like shells of our mortar-battery circling through the air, or the flaming track of the rushing rocket, the old nights of Sebastopol were forcibly recalled to my recollection.

As day broke the enemy once more opened fire upon us, and by this time the troops were on the move in all directions. The right wing was advancing upon a small hamlet, with a view of occupying a large building in it known as the Asylum of Indigent Females. The French, with the 59th, were taking up their position to the left, while we moved across the broken country to the Asylum. The enemy kept up as brisk a fire as they could, but apparently were incapable of directing their aim. They succeeded, however, in inflicting one irreparable loss upon us upon reaching the village. The general and his staff, accompanied by Captain Bate, proceeded to reconnoitre the walls preparatory to bringing up the scaling-ladders. As they approached to within thirty yards of the walls, they sought shelter from the sharp matchlock-fire which was opened upon them behind a mud house. It was necessary, however, that the ditch should be inspected, and it was in the performance of this dangerous service that Captain Bate, who undertook it in company with Captain Man, R.E., was killed.

Nine o'clock was the hour at which it had been arranged with the naval authorities that the firing should cease; it was not yet eight, and we were already under the walls. The shot and shell from our ships, which were at this time principally directed at the east gate, and that part of the wall opposite to which we then were, constantly fell near our own men: the angle of the Asylum was blown up by one shell; another burst among a party of the 59th, killing one man and wounding five.

The shot of the enemy was not apparently directed upon our men, or turned to any one point. It fell in distant cabbage-gardens to the right, whistled high over head to the left, seriously damaged unoffending trees in rear, and was very disagreeable for amateurs, for no one spot was safer than another; feeble rockets, barbed as arrows, thudded about, and fizzed for a moment in the grass, and the grasshopper buzz of a gingall ball was occasionally audible. Upon our occupying the village, the population, chiefly consisting of old men and "indigent" females with goat's feet, whose home ought to have been the Asylum, came tottering out, prostrating themselves on the ground and beating their breasts; dragging little children after them, they stumbled and hobbled over the rough ground among our men, by whom, of course, they were in no way molested.

All this time the Land Transport Corps, composed of Chinamen, were employed in bringing up ammunition to the front, to be used against their own countrymen, with a reckless disregard of gingall balls, and an absence of patriotism truly edifying.

Meantime, a large body of braves coming round the north angle, attacked our extreme right, and Colonel Holloway's brigade of marines was extended in skirmishing order to repel them. A pretty hot fire was also being kept up on the embrasures by the rifle company of a regiment of Madras native infantry, part of the 59th regiment, and by a rocket battery of the marine artillery, under Lieutenant Studdert. From the hillock upon which this battery was placed, an admirable view was obtained of the city wall and the scene of operations generally; and I took advantage of a few quiet moments in a grave, before the order for the assault was given, to make a sketch. Some heavy guns in the foreground, manned by blue-jackets under Lieutenant Beamish, were dropping shot and shell into Magazine Hill. As we had now been for some time exposed more or less to the fire of our own ships, and the French were apparently bent upon escalading before the time, the order was given for the French and the 59th to escalade, which they did simultaneously, Major Luard being the first man on the walls, closely followed by a French officer and Colonel Graham of the 59th: Lieutenant Stewart, Royal Engineers, however, would have disputed this honor with the foremost had not his ladder given way. Where so little honor was to be gained by any body, as at the siege of Canton, it is hardly fair for either party to appropriate the entire modicum. There can be no doubt that, had there been any body on the walls at the time and place at which they were scaled, the rivalry would not have been the less keen between our allies and ourselves; as it was, the enemy deserted the embrasures the moment the ladders were placed against them, and not a shot was fired at us from the time the walls were scaled to the capture of Magazine Hill, except from our own ships.

The scaling party on the right, not knowing that the left had assaulted before the time, were necessarily not upon the walls for some moments afterward. The ladders were soon swarming with marines and blue-jackets like bees clustering into a hive. Then we raced along the wall to Magazine Hill; Canton, silent as a city of the dead, lying at our feet, with here and there a corpse stretched in some narrow lane, to give a character of reality to the supposition. Whenever a luckless Chinaman was seen scampering over the country to the right, or the flutter of a bit of blue cloth indicated a human being in the streets to our left, dozens of Minie bullets showered round the devoted object—seldom, it must be admitted, striking it. I observed one man dodging about among the graves for at least a quarter of an hour, making short dashes from one grave to another, amid a storm of bullets, just as one runs from shelter to shelter in a shower of rain.

The city wall was about 25 feet in height and 20 feet broad; the guns were of small calibre, and wretched workmanship. A little beyond Magazine Hill the Chinese made a stand upon the walls, and a short and rather sharp combat took place at close quarters, in which Lord Gilford was wounded, and the general himself so hard pressed as to be compelled to shoot a man with his revolver. At the same time the enemy opened a fire upon us from some guns planted upon the walls about 200 yards distant, which were not immediately silenced.

The scene from Magazine Hill at this time was peculiar and exciting: 200 feet below lay the city, mapped out before us; a vast expanse of roofs, a labyrinth of intricate lanes, in a vain attempt to follow the windings of which the eye was bewildered—a pagoda here, there a many-storied temple, or the successive roofs of a yamun embowered in luxuriant foliage, above which towered a pair of mandarin poles—beyond all, the tapering masts of our own ships. Such were the principal features of the view in a southerly direction; but its striking element was that impressive silence, that absence of all movement on the part of a population of a million and a half, that lay as though entombed within the city walls, whose very pulsation seemed arrested by the terrors of the night before, and whose only desire, if they could think at all, appeared to be, that the bare fact of their existence should be forgotten by the conquerors.

This deathlike stillness upon one side was rendered all the more remarkable by the hubbub which was going on all round. On the right, **the Tartar troops on the** western walls were replying

G

with some vigor to the fire of a field-piece we had now brought to bear upon them; on the left the wall was still swarming with our men, who had just scaled and were crowding up. In rear the two blue-jacket forts were partially in flames, and we were completing the business with a few rockets from Magazine Hill, while from the same spot we had just opened a fire upon Gough's Fort, still occupied by the enemy. As it was not yet ten o'clock, a good morning's work had been already accomplished. The marines and French had turned to the right on surmounting the wall; but the 59th had been told off to take an opposite direction, and secure our position on the extreme left.

Having seen that Magazine Hill was satisfactorily in our possession, I accompanied General Straubenzee, who returned along the wall to the southern face. Here we found the 59th engaged in a little desultory rifle practice with the enemy, who were picking our men off the walls from the tops of their houses: while we were there, Lieutenant Bowen of the 59th received a wound, of which he afterward died, from a matchlock. General Straubenzee therefore, withdrew the men to an angle in the wall, which afforded good shelter, and where a building above a gateway offered some accommodation for the men. We found a wounded old Chinese warrior lying here, whom we revived with a little brandy and water, but from whom we could not obtain much information, though he was evidently puzzled at being humanely treated. This point was made the advanced post for the night.

As the capture of the city might now be said to be complete, I took advantage of the company of Captain Hall and Mr. Parkes, who, with a strong escort, were going to open up a new line of communication with the river, to return to the Furious. The east gate was barricaded on the inside; upon forcing it open we found an arc of wall in which was another gate, and which formed a sort of loop upon the main wall, inclosing a small collection of houses. On bursting these open, a number of frightened inhabitants, crouching in corners, immediately made their presence known by prayers and supplications for mercy. As one of these was an eating-house, with a large copper full of ready-made tea, we refreshed ourselves preparatory to new labors. Clearing these houses of inhabitants, we opened the next gate, and proceeded along the narrow streets of the suburbs, all of which were deserted, and the shops and houses shut. Still we could not be secure against a sudden attack from the numerous narrow lanes and dark corners in which the suburbs abound. Crossing the open parade-ground, we made our way unmolested to the river near French Folly, and I reached the Furious at one o'clock.

At three o'clock the same afternoon Gough's Fort was taken, and our right was advanced from Magazine Hill to the north gate. In performing this operation we met with some resistance; and throughout the night our advanced post, which was composed of blue-jackets under the command of Sir Robert Maclure and Captain Sherard Osborn, was a good deal harassed by the Tartar troops occupying this portion of the city. These soldiers had throughout exhibited considerably more courage than the Chinese braves. Mr. Parkes subsequently found the return of their killed and wounded, which was stated to be 450. The right and left advanced posts were held by our men. The French troops principally occupied the five-storied pagoda, a commodious and substantial building situated upon the wall: as a Chinese military position, it had suffered a good deal from our shot, but was nevertheless convertible into a most roomy and comfortable barrack. It is a very good specimen of Chinese architecture. The annexed wood-cut is taken from a photograph, for which I am indebted to Dr. Forbes, of the Cruiser.

Five-storied Pagoda.

On the following day Lord Elgin proceeded up the river to the Actæon, then lying off the Dutch Folly, and Mr. Wade and I started off for the front with a communication from his excellency for the general. We found the fighting over, and the city walls in complete possession of the allies. Thus a most important result had been achieved with a trifling loss to ourselves, and in a manner calculated to produce a deep impression upon a population whose habitual insolence to foreigners had rendered it extremely desirable that they should be made aware of the power we possessed of inflicting a severe punishment for insults, whether offered by the authorities or the people. The bombardment, which had lasted for twenty-seven hours, at the rate of nearly a hundred rounds per ship, was terrific in aspect and in its effects upon certain portions of the city, but by no means so destructive of human life as might have been expected. Directed principally against particular gates or angles of the wall, or against Magazine Hill, few shot or shell fell in the heart of the town, and the people soon found out the safe corners.

It was afterward reported by Chinamen that many women and children had been crushed to death by the crowds swaying to and fro under the influence of panic in the narrow streets; but we have no evidence of this. From the thin sprinkling of dead bodies I saw in the quarters most destroyed by our fire, and from the reports of others, I think Mr. Cooke's estimate of 200 (not including the Tartar garrison) is a very fair approximation as regards the whole number killed. At the same time, it may be remarked that, so far as the actual capture of the city was concerned, the bombardment for more than a day and a night was quite unnecessary: from the feeble resistance offered to us, it was evident that the walls might have been stormed as surely if our cannonade had only lasted for three hours instead of twenty-seven. Indeed, during the whole of this time, only two shots were fired upon our ships in the river from guns upon the walls. But the nature of the resistance may best be judged of by the list of killed and wounded, and the unusually small proportion which the former bears to the latter. In the entire British force, consisting of nearly 5000 men, the result of the two days' operations was eight killed and seventy-one wounded, including among the former one killed by our own shot, and one waylaid and murdered by villagers. The French, out of a force of 900, lost only two men killed and thirty wounded. Doubtless the mortality would have been greater had the attack been made from the west side, on which they were prepared for us, under the impression that we should adopt the plan of attack of 1842; but, under all circumstances, we should always have retained those advantages which result from such an immeasurable superiority of weapons, military skill, and *morale*, as would render failure in any military operation in China inexcusable, except under very peculiar and exceptional circumstances.

On our way to the city I observed in the suburb large looting-parties, composed of Chinese blackguards, ransacking the houses, and looking out for stragglers from our men, with whom they occasionally exchanged shots. They preferred, however, to be left alone, and kept as much out of sight as possible. At one place a pawnbroker's tower was being thoroughly gutted; a party on the top were engaged in overhauling the contents, and throwing over to their comrades below rich furs and brocaded silks; nor had we time, as we passed rapidly on, to interrupt them in their deeds of spoliation. It was already becoming evident that the work of administering the government of a large city containing a million and a half of inhabitants, so ready, upon the first opportunity, to prey upon each other, would be by no means an easy task for foreigners totally unused to, and comparatively unacquainted with, the system by which vast urban populations were governed and controlled, and only in one or two instances able to speak their language.

A great part of the suburb had been destroyed, so as not to afford shelter to thieves or assassins upon the immediate line of communication. The East Gate, at which we entered, was occupied by Colonel Graham and the 59th; and on our arrival at the front, we found that the general had just left Magazine Hill to make a circuit of the city walls. We therefore took advantage of a strong French escort to follow him. As we passed along the west wall flanking the Tartar quarter, the people were collected in groups gazing at us with interest, but with an air of profound respect and submission; when we warned them to disperse, they at once obeyed. At one guard we found a Tartar officer, whom we dislodged, and replaced with a small French guard. At the western gate we were informed by the English officer, who had been on guard there for some hours, that great crowds had been pouring out of the town, but that, when assured of our pacific intentions, they had ceased to manifest alarm or leave the town. The few persons with whom Mr. Wade conversed announced themselves to be Tartar soldiers, and presented a much finer appearance than the Chinese. The Tartar population of Canton has been established there for a century, and originally came from Kirin, in Manchouria. They were sent to this city to overawe and maintain order among the proverbially lawless population of the province. Numerous little white flags fluttered from sticks upon the wall and on the neighboring houses, to avert farther hostilities on the part of the barbarians. As we turned along the south wall we observed terrible evidence of the destructive effects of the bombardment. The south gate had been totally destroyed by fire, and a broad scar of burnt houses extended toward the centre of the city. Yeh's yamun was a heap of ruins; the wall behind it was battered and breached, and every house-roof was perforated with shot-holes.

Generally the habitations partook more of the nature of hovels than the residences of the respectable citizens of one of the most important and flourishing mercantile emporia in the empire. Decidedly the handsomest part of the town was in the neighborhood of the Confucian Hall, near the south gate. Here some gaudily-painted yamuns and joss-houses reared their fantastic gables among the massive foliage of the large trees which were planted in the court-yards.

The next day (the last of the year) Lord Elgin landed himself, and ascended, by means of a scaling-ladder, the southeast angle of the wall at the point where it was destined to be leveled so as to form the permanent line of communication. In the short piece of suburb intervening between it and the river sentries had been placed, and the houses were being demolished after the inhabitants had been allowed to remove their goods and chattels. A canal entered the city at this point, passing under the wall, in which there was a water-gate. Up to this time our military position was confined to the walls alone. No European had yet entered the city, but it looked calm and tranquil as ever. The alarm of the inhabitants appeared to have subsided. It was reported that the city authorities were still exercising their functions, and that Yeh had taken up his abode with one of them, and was in innocent expectation that fresh overtures touching our treaty right to enter the city were about to be made to him.

An unfortunate accident occurred to swell the list of killed and wounded in the course of the afternoon. Some blue-jackets, employed in clearing out a magazine, allowed a spark to fall among the powder, and an explosion ensued which caused the death of five men, and severely injured twelve more.

Thus closed the year 1857, so eventful in the history of British arms throughout the East, and thus closed with it the reign of the imperial commissioner Yeh.

CHAPTER VIII.

New-Year's Day, 1858.—Exploration of the City by the Allies.—Capture of Yeh.—Yeh's Memorial to Pekin.—Behavior of Yeh in Captivity.—Conference relative to the Government of Canton.—Plans Proposed.—Scheme ultimately adopted.—Installation of Pihkwei.—Lord Elgin's Address to Pihkwei.—Pihkwei's Reply.—Institution of a civil Tribunal.—Moral and political Effects of the Occupation of Canton.

NEW-YEAR'S DAY, 1858, was celebrated by a formal procession of the embassadors to Magazine Hill for the purpose of taking possession of the city; the ships in the river were all dressed out in flags, rainbow fashion; royal salutes startled the timid inhabitants into a belief that the bombardment was recommencing; and, indeed, the incessant booming of cannon was an appropriate introduction to the regime under which they were now to be governed.

For the next three days the troops were engaged in hutting themselves on the walls, a proceeding which was rendered the more necessary by the incessant rain to which they were subjected. In the course of certain interesting investigations into the personal property of the inhabitants, which are considered legitimate in the case of a captured city, some of the streets more immediately adjoining the walls were explored, and in most cases found deserted. Mr. Parkes, however, passed through the centre of the town with a strong guard, and met with no incivility from the people. In the mean time a memorial was sent in from the governor of the city, Pihkwei, and some of the other civic functionaries, stating their readiness to memorialize Pekin in any sense we might choose to dictate, protesting against the conduct of Yeh throughout, and assuring the ministers that they had never been consulted by the imperial commissioner upon those subjects which had involved the safety of their city.

On the 5th of January the seizure of the imperial commissioner was determined upon, and at half past 7 o'clock A.M. the city was entered at different points by three English and one French column; from the plans of the city in our possession, and information already received, the position of the principal yamuns was known. The French, proceeding along the great east and west street, known as the "Avenue of Benevolence and Love," from the westward, reached the large yamun belonging to the Tartar general, in which they captured that high functionary, and were shortly afterward joined by General Straubenzee; while Colonel Walsh's battalion of marines had been to the yamun of the governor, and made prisoner of Pihkwei, and thither the naval and military authorities proceeded. In the mean time Mr. Parkes had received information that Yeh was in a library not far distant, but on arriving there he found the house empty, with the exception of an old man who was reading in the garden. From this venerable student it was discovered that Yeh had been absent for five days; but the fact was at last extorted from him that the imperial commissioner had sought refuge in the house of the Tartar lieutenant general. Accompanied by an escort of a hundred bluejackets under Captain Key, Mr. Parkes at once repaired to this yamun, the doors of which they found closed; upon breaking them open, and rushing forward, an old man in a mandarin's coat and cap threw himself before them, stating that he was Yeh. This was the lieutenant general himself, who was at once thrust aside as an impostor; and as people were heard escaping through the back entrances, Captain Key hurried in that direction, and observing a stout man in a narrow passage, resembling a portrait he had seen of the imperial commissioner, threw his arms round the neck of the fugitive, and proclaimed him his prisoner.

A large collection of the archives of the imperial commissioner was seized here, and proved a most valuable and interesting assortment of papers. Some of the private correspondence which had passed between Canton and Pekin on barbarian affairs was extremely curious, while it proved that, even after more than a century's trade with China, a long and disastrous war concluded by a commercial treaty, and constant intercourse with the high authorities of the empire, the cabinet at Pekin were as far from appreciating our character and designs as they had been at the commencement. We found among these papers the English, French, and American treaties, which it is not certain had ever been sent to the capital. One of the most interesting specimens of a Chinese dispatch I insert in full, as it affords an amusing and curious illustration of the amount of information and intelligence which Yeh could bring to bear upon these barbarian affairs with the administration of which he was charged. The preliminary remarks are by our able Chinese secretary, Mr. Wade, who translated the document:

(*Memorandum*).—The following is translated from a draft in the same hand as that in which several of Yeh's draft memorials are corrected, and which I have other reasons for believing to be his own MS. It is the most unshapely specimen of Chinese writing I have ever seen, and has given a very competent native scholar considerable trouble to decipher. It was evidently a first draft, with much left to be filled in and corrected, and must have been written but a few days before the receipt of the plenipotentiaries' ultimatum of the 12th of December, 1857. We have no proof that it was sent to Pekin, though such was probably the case.

(*Translation*.)

(Yeh, etc.,) "presents a memorial to the effect that the English barbarians, troubled at home and pressed* with daily increasing urgency by other nations from without, will hardly attempt anything farther; that they are reported to have had several consultations upon the opening of trade, and earnestly desire the suggestion of some means to that end; that in consequence of the English chief† not returned to Canton. A respectful memorial (of which particulars) he forwards by courier, at the rate of 600 li a day, and looking upward, solicits the sacred glance thereon.

"On the 6th of the 9th moon (23d of October, 1857) your servant had the honor to forward to your majesty various particulars of his administration of barbarian affairs during the 7th and 8th moons (August and September), as it is recorded.

"Since the engagement of the 10th of the 5th moon (1st of June), a period of more than six months, the English barbarians have made no disturbance up the Canton River.‡ (It should be

---

* He may mean pressed by their solicitations or for money. His Hong Kong correspondents, as their seized letters prove, had been representing us deeply indebted to Russia, and in great difficulty as to the means of satisfying her claims.

† The preamble generally epitomizes the matter of the memorial. I take this part of it to be best explained by the last sentence of the memorial. There is evidently something to be filled up in the text.

‡ The affair of the 1st of June is the destruction of Heoang's fleet up Fatshan Creek, doubtless reported to Pekin as a victory. The manner in which the next

known), however, that in the defeat sustained by Elgin at Mang-ga-ta* in the 7th moon, he was pursued by the Mang-ga-la (Bengal) barbarian force to the sea-shore. A number of French men-of-war, which happened to be passing, fired several guns in succession, and the force of the Bengal barbarians falling back, the chief Elgin made his escape. The chief Elgin was very grateful to the French force for saving his life, and on the arrival of the French minister, Lo-so-lun,† who, in the beginning of the 9th moon, had also reached Quang-Tung, he the chief, Elgin, fêted the chief Gros at Hong Kong (*lit.*, merrily feasted and prayed him [to drink] wine), and consulted him upon the present position of affairs in China.

"The chief Gros said: I was not an eye-witness of last year's affair, but the story current among people of different nations who were by at the time has made me familiar with the whole question. You see,‡ when the forts were taken, the Chinese government made no retaliation; when the houses of the people were burned, it still declined to fight. Now, the uniform suppression, three years ago, of the Quang-Tung insurrection, in which some hundreds of thousands were engaged, shows the military power of China to be by no means insignificant. Will she take no notice of her injuries? (No.) She is certain to have some deep policy, which will enable her so to anticipate us that, before we can take up any ground, she will have left us without the means of finding fault with her, while she, on the other hand, will oblige the foreigners to admit themselves completely in the wrong. On the last occasion that your nation opened fire,§ it was but for some days, and people came forward (as mediators), but this time you did your utmost for three months. (You fired) 4000 rounds and more from great guns, as well as 3000 rockets. The high authorities of Canton, it is plain, have all along made their minds up (or

sentence is introduced shows that Lord Elgin's return had been already announced, but without full particulars.

* Mang-ga-ta is clearly a compromise between Mang-ga-la, Bengal and Calcutta.

† The French embassador's name is elsewhere given as Go-lo-so (Gros); his title of Baron is evidently taken to be his name, and is put in Chinese fashion after his surname—*lun* representing, doubtless, *pa-lun*, for *Baron*.

‡ The Chinese expression here used is generally rendered "for instance." Baron Gros is made to argue that he understands Yeh's policy, his opinion of which will be found at the end of the paragraph. We should have stated it at the beginning, and then have introduced the illustrations given.

§ This must be presumed to refer to Sir Hugh Gough's attack on Canton.

have seen their way). They understand the character of all classes, high and low, in our foreign states. This is the reason why they have been so firm and unswerving. When I was leaving home, the instructions my own sovereign gave me, with affectionate* earnestness, were these:

"'There is a quarrel with the English in Quang-Tung; when you go thither, confine yourself to the observance of the treaty and pacific communications. You are not to avail yourself of the opportunity to commit acts of aggression or spoliation. Do not make China hate the French as a band of hostile wretches† who violate their engagements. The circumstances, too, are so different (from those of the last war of the English with China), that it is essential you should judge‡ for yourself what course to pursue. There is no analogy, I apprehend, between the present case and the opium question of some ten years since, in which they had some wrongs to allege.'

"It appears that in the country of the five Indies appropriated by the English barbarians, they have established four tribal divisions—three along the coast, and one in the interior. One of the coast divisions is Mang-ga-la (Bengal), the country in the extreme east; one is Ma-ta-la-sa (Madras), southwest of Bengal; and one Mang-mai (Bombay), on the western limit of India. That in the interior is A-ka-la (Agra), lying midway between east and west. About the end of last summer, it is stated, twelve marts (or ports) in Bengal which had revolted were lost. Since the eighth moon the marts in Bombay have all been retaken (sc., from the English) by (Indian) chiefs; and since Elgin's return after his defeat, the leaders of the English barbarians have sustained a succession of serious defeats. The Indian chief drove a mine from bank to bank of a river, and by the introduction of infernal machines (lit., water-thunder) blew up several large vessels of war, killing above 1000 men. On shore they enticed (the English) far into the country, and murdered above 7000 of them, killing a distinguished soldier named Pu-ta-wei-ka-lut,§ and many more.

"Elgin passes day after day at Hong Kong, stamping his foot and sighing; his anxiety is increased by the non-arrival of dispatches from his government."

* The manner in which the Chinese mandarins address the people.
† Base, or low-caste persons.
‡ That is, you are not to accept the policy of England or any other nation as yours.
§ Possibly Brigadier Havelock.

I reached Magazine Hill shortly after the prisoners arrived there. Yeh, seated in a large room, surrounded by some of his immediate attendants, was answering in a loud, harsh voice, questions put to him by Sir Michael Seymour with reference to Englishmen who had been prisoners in his hands. Though he endeavored, by the assumption of a careless and insolent manner, to conceal his alarm, his glance was troubled, and his fingers trembled with suppressed agitation. His heavy sensual features, although relieved by a trembling vivacious eye, were not calculated to betray very keen emotional sensibility.

In another room, and more dignified in their bearing, perhaps because they had less cause for alarm, Pihkwei and the Tartar general philosophically awaited their fate—the former a quiet, gentleman-like old man, the latter of gigantic proportions and stolid countenance.

It was at once decided that the imperial commissioner should be deprived of all farther power for mischief, and kept as a prisoner on board the "Inflexible," whither he was conveyed forthwith. In the mean time, the two plenipotentiaries arrived at head-quarters, and at a conference with the naval and military authorities, discussed, for the remainder of the afternoon, the existing attitude of affairs, and the proper course to be adopted under the circumstances.

In the cause of humanity, the abandonment of the city to the refuse of its population was to be deprecated; while the restoration of confidence to the inhabitants generally was a result which, in a political point of view, was eminently to be desired. The necessity of organizing without delay a system of government was therefore apparent. The question for decision was what that system should be. The naval and military authorities had already confessed their inability to govern the city, and their conviction that the Chinese functionaries were alone competent to preserve order. In this opinion the plenipotentiaries thoroughly concurred. Indeed, every hour that passed was affording incontestable evidence of its accuracy. The Chinese rabble had already taken advantage of the defenseless condition of the city, and were daily furnishing us with proof of their skill as plunderers. Organized gangs were prowling about the suburbs, and venturing into the city, gaining courage by immunity, and numbers by success.

The temptation to loot was strong upon our own men, and the general professed himself unable, with the small force at his disposal, to patrol efficiently with police a town containing a million of inhabitants, with whom it was impossible to communicate, and hold six miles of wall at the same time, unless assisted by civil authority of a character which the people had been accustomed to respect. With a population imbued with a traditionary awe for their own authorities, and speaking an unknown tongue, at the same time containing a larger proportion of trained thieves and vagabonds than any in the world, with an imperfectly disciplined force in occupation, consisting of barely 5000 men, and composed of a heterogeneous assemblage of French and English, blue-jackets and marines, Madras sepoys and British infantry, and, to crown all, with only two gentlemen on the spot whose knowledge of the language enabled them to communicate directly with the people, it was manifestly absurd to think of replacing the local Chinese system of government by one of our own; any such attempt would assuredly lead to the plunder and destruction of the town, the demoralization of the troops, and to disappointment and failure on the part of those engaged in carrying out the experiment. Of this fact no persons were more thoroughly convinced than Mr. Wade and Mr. Parkes, upon whom would devolve the functions of all the mandarins in Canton.

The situation of affairs at this most critical juncture, and the difficulties by which they were surrounded, are very clearly defined in Lord Elgin's dispatch of the 9th of January, in which his excellency states: "Two plans for surmounting the difficulties of the situation in which we found ourselves were under the consideration of the commanders-in-chief when I reached the Magazine Hill. The one proposed that Pihkwei and the Tartar general should be permitted at once to return to their yamuns, on condition of their consenting to publish a proclamation, in which the military occupation of the city by the allied forces should be recognized. I thought it my duty to enter my protest against the adoption of an arrangement of this nature. Neither on the side of the Chinese was there, as it appeared to me, sufficient honesty, nor on our own sufficient means of acquiring information, and, perhaps I may add, sufficient forbearance, to afford a reasonable prospect of its working successfully. I felt confident that if Pihkwei returned to his yamun on the terms above mentioned, many days would not elapse before some act would be committed by him, or some proclamation issued, which would give rise to suspicions on our part; that on such suspicions, appeals to the commanders-in-chief, urging them to adopt measures of precaution or coercion, of increased stringency, would be grounded; and that in this way the irritation of the soldiery against the Cantonese would be kept up, and all the evils attending the occupation of a city by a hostile army perpetuated. The other plan which had been submitted for the consideration of the commanders-in-chief proceeded equally on the assumption that Pihkwei must be retained as governor of Canton. By way, however, of providing security for his upright behavior, and for the maintenance of a good understanding between the parties, it suggested that he should be detained as a prisoner of war, if necessary, on board one of her majesty's ships of war anchored in the river, and that he should exercise from thence the functions of his office. It is needless that I should here insist on the objections to which this proposition was open."

The course ultimately adopted was a compromise of these two extremes. It was decided that Pihkwei should be reinstated in his own yamun, in a manner calculated to increase rather than impair the prestige of that authority upon which the tranquillity, and, indeed, the very existence of the city, at that critical moment, depended; but, at the same time, that it should be impressed upon him that, inasmuch as the city remained under martial law, he was only administering its affairs subject to the approval of the general, who was the supreme authority; that he would be under a constant surveillance; and that the most serious consequences would result from any treachery on his part. This proposal was laid before Pihkwei, and, after twenty-four hours' deliberation, during which time he remained our prisoner, he accepted the new conditions under which he was to continue the government of Canton.

During his short confinement the governor and the Tartar general were occasionally visited by the Treasurer Howqua, and other of the principal merchants. The magistrate, prefect, and nearly all of the civic authorities, had already fled from the city; and, indeed, it was some time before they could be induced to return and resume their functions under Pihkwei.

The 9th of January was the day fixed for the installation of Pihkwei; and at two o'clock in the afternoon the two plenipotentiaries went in procession through the town, followed by a large body of troops, and preceded by military bands. The "Avenue of Benevolence and Love" was crowded with eager faces, gazing at us as we passed with respectful curiosity. The entry into the yamun of the governor was sufficiently imposing; and as the strains of martial music echoed through the several courts, the population outside can have had little doubt that both their city and its authorities were in our power, and that the latter only ruled by sufferance.

But while Lord Elgin was determined that it should be very clearly understood that Pihkwei held office only by the authority and at the will of the plenipotentiaries and commander-in-chief, he was by no means desirous that the prestige of that functionary should be impaired—this being, in point of fact, the instrument with which we were about to control the subordinate Chinese officials. He had, therefore, a double object in view in this ceremony of investiture, and at one moment it was apprehended that this double object might be in some degree compromised by certain mistakes which occurred in carrying the arrangements into effect. In the first place, no orders were given as to the time at which the prisoners who were to be converted into potentates were to be released from durance. This omission led to considerable delay, so that, in point of fact, the Tartar general and Pihkwei did not reach the yamun of the latter till long after the hour originally intended; and, secondly, when they did arrive, a dispute arose between them and the interpreters as to the seats which they ought to occupy. It was finally settled that they should be placed immediately below the embassadors; and Lord Elgin had barely time, while the shades of night were gathering, to address to them the following words, which were cordially seconded by Baron Gros: "We are assembled here to welcome your excellency on your return to your yamun, and on your resumption of the functions of your office, which have been momentarily interrupted. It is proper, however, that I should apprise your excellency, and, through your excellency, the inhabitants of Canton, that the plenipotentiaries of England and France, and the commanders-in-chief of the allied forces, are firmly resolved to retain military occupation of the city until all questions pending between our respective governments and that of China shall have been finally settled and determined between us, the high officers appointed by our governments for this service, and a plenipotentiary of equal rank and powers, whom his imperial majesty, the

Emperor of China, may see fit to appoint to treat with us. Any attempt, therefore, whether by force or fraud, whether by treachery or violence, to disturb us in our possession of the city, will not fail to bring down on its authors and abettors the most severe and signal punishment. I am, however, no less prepared to apprise your excellency that it is equally our determination, when the questions to which I have referred shall have been so settled, to withdraw from the military occupation of the city, and to restore it to the imperial authorities. Meanwhile, it is our sincere wish that, during the period of our military occupation, the feelings of the people be respected, life and property protected, the good rewarded, and offenders, whether native or foreign, punished. We are desirous to co-operate with your excellency for these objects; and, with this view, we have appointed a tribunal, composed of officers of high character and discretion, to act in concert with you. We hope that, through the agency of this tribunal, confidence may be restored to the people, and the foundation laid of a better understanding between foreigner and native, so that hereafter all may pursue their avocations in peace, and traffic together for their mutual advantage."

The substance of Pihkwei's reply to this address is as follows: "He begged his respects to his lordship. He acknowledged his lordship's consideration of the people of Canton. A state of tranquillity would be best secured by the exertion of authority on either side, native and foreign, to restrain those severally subject to it from doing what was offensive to the other. We promised to control our people; he would control his. This would be to the advantage of Canton. Lastly, he trusted that his lordship might soon meet an officer qualified to treat with him, and that the result of their negotiations would be the establishment of a good understanding."

The two mandarins were in full official costume, and retained throughout that charmed and delighted manner which a Chinaman always puts on when he is powerless and alarmed. The ceremony over, the plenipotentiaries returned to their ships, and left Pihkwei in possession of his own yamun: a cheerless residence it must be at the best of times, consisting of a series of buildings divided by court-yards, and each containing a large central hall, with two or three small rooms on either side, scantily furnished, and lighted by paper windows.

H

When I visited the yamun on the following day the outer courts were full of allied troops, and Pihkwei lived in the inner division, so that he could not keep up intercourse with the outer world without passing our sentries. In one compartment of the same yamun was established a commission, composed of Colonel Holloway, Captain Martineau, and Mr. Parkes. The object of this commission was ostensibly to adjudicate upon cases brought by the Chinese of robbery or violence committed by our men upon the population; but its principal function was to exercise a rigid surveillance over Pihkwei; to superintend the issuing of proclamations; and to collect information from private sources upon all matters affecting the disposition of the inhabitants, and the security of our tenure in the city. At the same time, the institution of a tribunal invested with judicial functions was not without a beneficial effect, as well upon the Chinese as upon our own troops. To the former it proved our desire to protect the private property and lives of the citizens; and to the latter it manifested the determination which existed on the part of their own authorities to repress those outrages which were unfortunately becoming too common, and which, while they struck at the root of all military discipline, impaired the influence it was desired to acquire over the inhabitants by the exercise of moderation and justice.

The number of complaints which were daily brought by the Chinese before this tribunal fully justified the estimate formed of its value.

Our occupation of Canton gave us an opportunity, which might never again occur, of endeavoring, by intercourse and daily contact, to overcome that antipathy and distrust toward Europeans which had always distinguished its population, and to the manifestation of which they were instigated by their own mandarins. Our former experience at Chusan gave us every reason to hope that a better acquaintance with us would remove their old existing prejudices, and that, in the end, the forcible occupation of their city would lead to a better understanding on both sides. Under the influence of terror, one step was already gained. The populace had lost their defiant and insulting manner, and substituted for it an air of profound submission and humility, always remaining in a standing position as a European passed, letting down their tails in accordance with their own customs when desirous of showing respect, and uncovering their heads out of deference to our prejudices upon the subject.

CHAPTER IX.

Withdrawal of the naval Force.—Yamun of the Tartar General.—"The Hall of State."—The ornamental Gardens.—Scenes at the Landing-place.—The Hall of Examination.—The "Avenue of Benevolence and Love."—Open-air Cookery.—Streets of Canton.—Joss-houses of Canton.—Future Punishments illustrated.—Allied police Corps.—Pihkwei's Proclamations.—A Luncheon at Howqua's.—Pihkwei's Dispatch on Trade.—Proposal to raise the Blockade.

THE city of Canton was now completely in the possession of the allied forces. Almost the whole of the British portion of the naval force was therefore withdrawn, the marines and 59th forming the army of occupation, together with a few hundred French sailors.

Our Jacks presented a most grotesque appearance as they returned to their ships, waving Chinese banners, their heads covered with mandarin caps, and their knapsacks filled with spoils of a miscellaneous description; though, to do them justice, we may fairly conjecture that these were rather ornamental than useful in their character. In this respect our simple tars presented a marked contrast in their looting propensities to their more prudent comrades among the allies. These latter possessed a wonderful instinct for securing portable articles of value; and, while honest Jack was flourishing down the street with a broad grin of triumph on his face, a bowl of gold-fish under one arm, and a cage of canary-birds under the other, honest Jean, with a demure countenance, and no external display, was conveying his well-lined pockets to the water-side.

All this time Pihkwei's yamun presented so much more the appearance of a barrack for French and English soldiers than the residence of a Chinese mandarin, that it was considered desirable that they should be removed to the more spacious yamun belonging to the Tartar general, but not at present occupied by him. Though in a dilapidated condition, it was a good specimen of the style of the best class of official residences in China. The first indication to the stranger of the existence of one of these buildings is the large masonry screen, upon which gigantic dragons are delineated, and which is often placed upon the side of the thoroughfare opposite the yamun, so that the street passes through the court-yard, of which it forms one face. Near it are the two lofty red poles, the invariable insignia of office. Walls inclose this square, on the fourth side of which is the entrance. Two carved lions guard a flight of granite steps, which ascend to the principal gateway. Upon the huge folding-doors are depicted gaudily-attired giants, who gaze contemplatively upon the crowd, holding with their left hands the points of their beards. Passing through this door, we enter a veranda, where once Tartar soldiers mounted guard, but of which all that remains are enormous tridents, spears, and cimeters stacked in a rack. Then down more steps, and across a paved yard, and through another painted gate, called the "Gate of Ceremony," on each side of which are circular slabs of granite, like millstones, carved with figures emblematic of eternity. Then across another grass-grown court, and up another flight of steps, to the "Hall of Audience," in the front of which is a raised paved yard, surrounded by an elaborately-carved granite balustrade.

Altogether there were five successive ranges of buildings, each separated from the other by a court-yard, each dedicated to some particular purpose, each surmounted by a tablet-like escutcheon, on which were inscribed in large characters the name of the general then occupying the yamun, to whom it was presented by the emperor, the date, and the character "Happiness." The fourth range of buildings contained the "Hall of State," where there was a stone screen, upon which were inscribed the merits which should distinguish the soldier, his necessary qualifications, and the position he should occupy with reference to them; in other words, that he should be "the right man in the right place;" and in the corner, in gigantic strokes, as appropriate to the profession in China at all events, the character "Longevity." The fifth was the innermost building of all: it possessed an upper story, and here were the apartments of the women. Each range was seventy or eighty yards long, the private apartments lighted by paper and occasional panes of glass, and ornamented with pictures.

There were detached buildings at the sides; a library with joss figures, but no books; a temple dedicated to the emperor's handwriting, where a slab was erected like those upon which the commandments are usually inscribed in our own churches, with writing in the Manchourian character in the emperor's own hand. Surrounding all were gardens, in which were tangled thickets, and shady walks, and little islands in the middle of ponds, approached by rustic bridges, and surrounded by ornamental rock-work; summer-houses and cool grottoes were pleasant retreats from the noonday heat. The grounds altogether were of that quaint character peculiar to Chinese taste, and which is not without a certain charm. The stone of which the caves and arches were composed comes from a district about a hundred miles distant; the fantastic shapes which are common to it render it especially suitable to ornamental purposes.

The whole of this establishment bore the marks of neglect and decay. Some of the rooms were tenanted by bats; the courts, which should have been shaded only by the spreading banyan or graceful bamboo, were overrun with noxious weeds, and the gardens were partly jungle. All this, however, was ultimately transformed by the allied civil and military officials, and a large body of troops, who entered into possession of these picturesque quarters shortly before we left Canton, and have remained in them ever since.

We had now been a fortnight in occupation of Canton, and found abundant employment, during the rest of our stay, in exploring the hitherto forbidden purlieus of that exclusive city. Lord Elgin seldom allowed a day to pass without visiting it, partly for the purpose of judging for himself of the temper of the people, partly from the pleasure he took in exploring its most hidden recesses, but principally to check, as far as possible, by his personal influence, those excesses on the part of the troops so detrimental to the policy he was determined to carry out. Nor, in this latter respect, were his efforts unavailing. The general thoroughly entered into the views of the plenipotentiaries, and, by his stringent orders, effectually restrained the somewhat natural tendencies of the men in the exercise of what they considered their legitimate privileges. It is only fair to state that, upon the whole, their conduct was in the highest degree creditable to the arm of the service to which they belonged.

A gun-boat, which the admiral had placed at Lord Elgin's disposition, conveyed us daily from our anchorage, about three miles from the landing-place, to and from the city. This landing-place ever presented a scene of picturesque confusion. At low water, a vast surface of deep mud was exposed to view, over which we were dragged in sampans by boatwomen, who kilted themselves for the occasion, and shoved and waded with immense energy and perseverance for a few coppers each. The boat population was indeed the first to regain confidence, and each gun-boat, as it arrived, was surrounded by a swarm of importunate sampan-owners, whose love of filthy lucre soon overcame any patriotic scruples they might have had. Parties of seamen and sappers were engaged in constructing a pier, stores were being landed for the garrison, and athletic Chinamen, who formed the land-transport corps, were collected in groups round the burdens they were destined to carry to the front. The services which these men had rendered from the commencement of operations can not be too highly estimated; their conduct under fire proved that, properly disciplined and supported, the Chinaman was not deficient in personal courage; while in their endurance and obedience they gave evidence of the most valuable qualities which go to make up the soldier.

The southeast angle of the wall was leveled, and a broad road made to it from the landing-place, so that an admirable line of communication conducted to every point occupied by our troops. Immediately within this angle the Hall of Examination, covering a great extent of ground, was the first striking object which met the eye. It consisted of a series of rows of cells on each side of a broad paved walk, not unlike the interior of a church, on a very large scale. Each row was separately tiled over, and divided into a quantity of stalls, about the size usually allotted to horses; each of these was supposed, during the period of the public examinations, to contain a student, the whole being calculated to accommodate 8000 with lodging. Certainly there was not much to distract their attention during the fortnight they were condemned to pass in these cells. A narrow passage separated them from the dead wall which formed the back of the next row, and thick partitions rendered communication with their neighbors on either side impossible. It is necessary to pass through this examination in order to obtain a master's degree; the only exception is made in favor of age; and after a man has passed threescore and ten years, he is considerately allowed to take out the degree of honorary master. At the period of our occupation the passages were overgrown with weeds, and it bore all the marks of disuse and neglect. The houses in the immediate neighborhood were wretched in the extreme, and had suffered a good deal from the fire of our ships.

The "Avenue of Benevolence and Love," or the great east and west street, was the principal thoroughfare of the city; here it was that the shops first began to open, and the population to resume those street habits which are the same in every Chinese town, and which were temporarily suspended by the capture of the city; one after the other shop-boards came down, and the owners stood smilingly behind their counters, thankful, doubtless, that the contents which they had not had time to remove, were there to tempt their barbarian customers. As the taste of these latter for curiosities became known, shops of this character multiplied with marvelous rapidity. "Olo bronzes, and too muchee olo crackly China," were lavishly displayed; and the crowds constantly collected at the doors of the shops proved that foreign purchasers were making rash investments within. At first it was not considered prudent to move about unaccompanied by an escort, but this was speedily discontinued, and, with a revolver and a companion, we used to venture into any part of the city or suburbs.

As the "Avenue of Benevolence and Love" was more frequented, it became a less agreeable lounge, and the already narrow streets were still farther diminished in breadth by large tubs full of live fish, baskets of greens, sea chestnuts, yams, and bamboo root. Cooking-stoves were erected, and elaborately cooked viands hissed and sputtered on the heated iron, titillating with their savory odor the nostril of the hungry passenger. Open coppers steamed and bubbled, and delicate morsels danced on the surface; round tables were daintily set out with pastry of divers patterns, and presided over by croupiers, who jerked reeds in a box, or spun a ball something after the fashion of roulette, thus enabling the dinner-seeker to combine the exhilarating excitement of the gambler with the epicurean enjoyment of the gourmand, the consideration that they had cost him nothing adding additional zest to his gastronomic pleasures. It might so happen, on the other hand, that one unkind turn of the wheel of fortune sent him supperless to bed.

Notwithstanding the apparent gradual restoration of confidence, people for some time continued to pour out of the West Gate, without, however, making any perceptible diminution in the amount of the population. It was singular to stand here and watch this exodus, to observe the miscellaneous property which was being conveyed by patient coolies, followed by anxious owners. Now a man passed with tables and chairs at one end of his stick, and two babies at the other; coffins balanced pots of manure; and men transported articles which we should consider worthless, as carefully as their wives; nor, considering the general aspect of the female part of the population, was this wonderful, when to their natural ugliness is added the deformity of feet and apparent entire absence of arms—for a Chinese woman seldom makes use of the sleeves of her jacket; any thing more unprepossessing than the lady part of the community could not be well conceived. In fact, after the first novelty has worn off, there is nothing to make a promenade in the streets of a Chinese town attractive. The foulest odors assail the olfactories. The most disgusting sights meet the eye—objects of disease, more loathsome than any thing to be seen in any other part of the world, jostle against you. Coolies staggering under coffins, or something worse, recklessly dash their loads against your shins; you suspect every man that touches you of a contagious disease; and the streets themselves are wet, slippery, narrow, tortuous, and crowded. The best streets were those in the suburbs, at the back of the site of the foreign factories, and which had formerly been frequented by foreigners. There the shops were gayer and more richly supplied; and the vertical shop-signs, gorgeously emblazoned in fantastic characters, were more numerous and striking to the stranger's eye.

The factories themselves were a heap of ruins; the only spot which could vie with their former site, as a scene of desolation, was Yeh's yamun, right in the line of the Cruiser's fire. The guns of that ship had effectually demolished the residence of the imperial commissioner. The street of triumphal arches, in a line beyond it, had also unfortunately suffered; many valuable bookshops had been destroyed, and four of the arches leveled. The same number, however, still remain; they are massively constructed of carved granite, and covered with inscriptions. Though of elegant design and workmanship, they are not comparable to those which span the streets of Ningpo. The joss-houses at Canton were not remarkable for beauty of architectural design or ornament. The handsomest was near the northeast angle of the wall; the exterior was elaborately adorned with carved groups in relief over the principal entrance, and under the quaint turned-up eaves the figures were gaudily colored, and reflected in looking-glasses let into the frame-work which supported them. Many of the larger figures in these joss-houses had been overturned, as a popular notion prevailed among the soldiers, which was not altogether without foundation, that within the portly persons of these deities treasure was often concealed.

Others of the joss-houses were more particularly dedicated to what is vulgarly known as "Sing-sing joss-pigeon." A favorite lounge of the idler part of the population was the spacious court of one of these, situated close to the treasurer's yamun. Here "*mendici, mimæ, balatrones, hoc genus omne,*" collected daily; gambling, fortune-telling, eating, and tom-toming went on perpetually; and public story-tellers kept gaping crowds entranced with the thrilling interest of their narrations, which were delivered with great volubility, accompanied by considerable play of feature, and with a loud, clear intonation. By way of a cheerful subject of contemplation for the public who frequented this haunt of excitement, the tortures of the damned were exhibited in recesses all round the court-yard. Clay figures, about three feet high, like those of terra-cotta to be seen in Italy, were represented in various attitudes inflicting or submitting to the most horrid penalties; men were being sewn up alive in raw bullock skins, women sawn asunder, and whole families were being stirred about as they simmered in huge caldrons. The tormentors invariably wore an expression of countenance indicative of placid enjoyment, while the faces of their victims, distorted with agony, were vividly portrayed. Altogether the tableaux were worthy of the most lively inquisitorial imagination.

During the first week of the occupation, bodies of men were marched through the different quarters of the city as patrols: it was found, however, that this served rather to alarm than to reassure the population; while a lawless rabble, following close in rear, took advantage of the confusion created to shoplift with a dexterity worthy of the swell-mob. An allied police was therefore substituted for these patrols, composed partly of Chinese and partly of English or French. Natives and foreigners were alike amused to observe a file of marines walking amicably side-by-side with a file of Chinamen, the one headed by a sergeant, and the other by a petty mandarin, gracefully fanning himself. This scheme proved eminently successful: European offenders were brought up and punished by the tribunal; while Pihkwei bastinadoed his own countrymen with an unsparing vehemence, to prove his desire of cordial co-operation. The experiment of a naval alliance for the suppression of piracy did not turn out so happily, the Mandarin junks taking the first opportunity, by escaping into the creeks, to dissolve the connection. As, in the course of his explorations, Mr. Parkes discovered some proclamations intended to inflame the population against foreigners, which evil-disposed persons were beginning to post up extensively, Pihkwei was ordered to issue notices to the head men of the districts, making them responsible for insulting or incendiary proclamations. The system of responsibility thus introduced is thoroughly in accordance with the Chinese plan of government. It was that pursued in the government of Canton with perfect success: it served the two-fold purpose of keeping Pihkwei constantly in check, and of proving to the inhabitants the absolute supremacy of our power.

Some of these proclamations were characteristic, and to the minds of the Chinese readers sufficiently novel and startling, after the inflammatory notices against foreigners to which they had been accustomed. In one the authorities call the people to account for calling names: "Whereas," they say, "the Canton people have a habit, whenever they see a foreigner, of shouting out 'Fan-kwei,' and otherwise committing themselves, in utter violation of all rules of proper demeanor, and of the conduct that is due from man to man, you forget that there is no distinction between natives and foreigners; that foreigners are but as the people of other provinces; and that there should be between you courteous intercourse and mutual concession; that you should not intentionally show contempt for them or stand aloof from them:" then it goes on to notice the practice of posting placards, and concludes by stating that, "This is to signify to all you, the people, that henceforth, when you meet foreigners in the streets, you must behave to them civilly; you must neither use the term 'fan-kwei,' nor any other opprobrious expression. You are not either to post placards containing any thing offensive to foreigners. We, the authorities above mentioned, spare not to reiterate this caution to you. We, at the same time, command all police and constables to keep strict watch, and to seize those who transgress. If you offend, you will be punished with the utmost severity. Do not, therefore, pursue a course which you will repent when it is too late. Do not disobey. A special notification." Another proclamation, concluding "Let every one tremble and obey," was from Pihkwei, commanding servants who had left the service of Europeans at Hong Kong in consequence of the pressure applied by the government, to return to their masters.

Among those most anxious for the re-establishment of a settled order of things was the celebrated Chinese merchant Howqua, who, in the fullness of his desire for conciliation, invited some of us to luncheon with him one afternoon. His house in the suburbs had remained uninjured during the troubles, and was tastefully but plainly furnished: he explained, however, that he possessed another handsomer residence. We met here a blue-button mandarin and an ex-judge from the province of Sz'chuen. The latter was an enlightened man, and said that Yeh had only received what he deserved. Howqua regaled us with some delicious tea, of course without milk or sugar, and we afterward sat down to a light repast of preserves and fruits, our host doing the honors with much courtesy and good-breeding.

But the Chinese merchants of Canton were not the only persons desirous of seeing commerce resumed. Most singular to state, Pihkwei wrote to Lord Elgin upon the same subject as follows:* "Still it is, without doubt, essential that, so far as trade is concerned, no time should be lost. By every day that the opening of the port is accelerated, by so much is the restoration of public confidence accelerated, not only in the minds of the Chinese, but in the minds of the merchants in every nation as well. The conditions of trade would probably be in accordance with the old regulations under which imports and exports were entered and inspected, and the duties on them paid. Your excellency is, of course, thoroughly conversant with these. I would add that, from the ninth moon of last year to the present time, a twelvemonth and more, the mercantile communities of both our nations have been subjected to loss. The eagerness with which merchants will devote themselves to gain, if the trade be now thrown well open, will increase manifold the good understanding between our nations, and the step will thus, at the same time, enhance your excellency's reputation."

Those who are familiar with the normal state of our relations with Chinese mandarins at Canton will appreciate the change which must have been operated upon them when the governor

* Blue-Book, 24th of January, 1858.

of the city approaches a British minister as a suppliant for the re-establishment of that trade, in the prosecution of which it has been the policy of England so often to humiliate itself before China.

The allied plenipotentiaries were not unwilling to respond to this appeal. It was indeed true that fifteen months had already elapsed since the unfortunate incident occurred wich led to an interruption of our commercial relations with Canton; the unsatisfactory state in which they had subsequently for some time remained ultimately resulted in the so-called blockade, which was established during Lord Elgin's absence in India. The embassadors were anxious to effect the speedy removal of this restriction, partly because, in the then state of our commercial relations with the other ports of China, its very existence was anomalous, and partly because the resumption of trade was the most effectual way of restoring that confidence to the population of Canton, on the establishment of which their policy in some measure depended.

The naval authorities thoroughly concurred with them in this desire, and were no less anxious to put an end to a blockade which, while it tended to exercise a demoralizing influence upon the class of vessels specially employed in enforcing it, had failed in the object it was designed to accomplish. Instead of preventing all trade with Canton, it had simply diverted it to the Broadway and other channels not guarded by our cruisers. Thus it was both ineffectual and illegal; a circumstance which fortunately it did not occur to any neutral power to complain of.

The accomplishment of so important a measure involved a new set of considerations, and it behooved the embassadors to prepare for the contingencies which were likely to arise under the altered conditions of the situation.

CHAPTER X.

Diplomacy in China.—Policy of the neutral Powers.—Proposed Expedition to the North.—Opinion of Count Poutiatine.—Proclamation raising Blockade.—Putinqua's Gardens.—River Scenes.—Lord Elgin's Visit to the Prisons.—State of the Prisoners.—Fate of Yeh.—Lord Elgin's Letter to Yu.—Departure for Shanghai.—Amoy.—Arrival at Shanghai.—Departure for Soo-chow.—Facilities of Water-communication.—Canal Scenes.—State of the Population.—Mr. Maclane's Visit to Soo-chow.—Boat-life on the Canals.

The position which the Chinese Empire has hitherto occupied with reference to the rest of the world has always invested the conduct of diplomatic relations in that country with peculiar difficulties. Not only are questions of the most exceptional character constantly arising with the imperial government, but out of them are often evolved complications in our intercourse with other European nations, which have no analogy elsewhere, and are unprovided for by any principle of international law.

Thus the capture of one city in an empire, while we were trading peaceably at others, was not a more abnormal proceeding than the reopening to the commerce of other nations a port of which we retained military possession, and governed under martial law. Yet it was manifestly a condition of things out of which international difficulties might easily spring, more especially if there should chance to be any disposition to create them. No doubt we confined ourselves to a strictly military occupation of the city; the custom duties were to be collected by Chinese officials, and paid into the Chinese treasury; still foreigners were not on the same footing here as at other towns in the empire, and, within certain limits, placed themselves within the somewhat arbitrary jurisdiction of martial law.

The suspension of diplomatic relations with the Imperial Commissioner Yeh, which had taken place in the autumn of 1856, had necessarily caused serious interruption to the commercial intercourse of other nations at Canton; but so unanimous was the desire on their part to take advantage of the opportunity then afforded of renewing relations with the Chinese government under other and more favorable conditions, that France, Russia, and

America sent out plenipotentiaries, whose very arrival in China, if it did not imply a tacit approval of our ground of quarrel, at all events evinced a determination to make it available for the attainment of the objects they desired.

So far as France was concerned, she had her own grievance, and her policy was laid down without any attempt at mystery. With Russia and America, however, the case was different. Not conceiving themselves entitled to the attitude of belligerents, they were driven, during the progress of hostilities, into a false position, from which the restoration of peace could alone relieve them. They were, however, so far fortunately placed that under no circumstances could they be losers by a quarrel in which they were not involved, while they might derive equal advantages from its results with those who were. As it had never been the policy of England to attempt to monopolize those advantages, and as a united pressure might more probably extort, without recourse to arms, those demands which the four nations were preferring in common, the time seemed to have come, in the opinion of Lord Elgin and Baron Gros, to invite the co-operation of the neutral powers, and thus not only to increase the moral pressure, but to avoid the chance of those difficulties, to which I have already alluded, being raised.

The plan of operations which Lord Elgin had proposed for himself, in the prosecution of his policy, was to proceed in the first instance to Shanghai, and to invite a properly accredited minister to meet him there for the settlement of all questions in dispute between the two countries. Shanghai being at a considerable distance from the capital, and being, moreover, the place where the relations between foreigners and Chinese were of the most friendly character, Lord Elgin considered this proposal the most conciliatory which it was in his power to make. In the event of his not being so met, his intention was to push northward without delay, for the purpose of approaching Pekin as nearly as was practicable, with gun-boats of the lightest draught. This scheme he had already discussed with Count Poutiatine, whose local knowledge was of great assistance (see Blue-Book, 14th of November, 1857, the Earl of Elgin to the Earl of Clarendon), in which his excellency says: "Count Poutiatine was very decided in the expression of his opinion that nothing could be done with the Chinese government unless pressure were brought to bear upon Pekin itself, and that the use of vessels drawing so little water that they could navigate the Peiho would be the best means of making such pressure effective. The mandarins on the spot, if I rightly understood him, had, in conversation with him, adverted with exultation to the fact that our ships of war could not perform this feat. I told him that we were pretty strong in craft of the description to which he referred; that we had, as he no doubt knew, a quarrel of our own in this neighborhood, but that, when that affair was concluded, we should be prepared to go northward in force, and very glad to be accompanied by the flags of other nations interested with us in extending commercial relations with China, and inducing that court to abate its absurd pretensions to superiority."

In furtherance of these views, Lord Elgin shortly afterward addressed a communication to the admiral, requesting him to dispatch the lightest draught gun-boats to the north for the purpose of "bringing pressure to bear at some point near the capital."*

Meantime, in answer to communications addressed to Mr. Reed and Count Poutiatine, those gentlemen at once cordially accepted the invitation to unite with France and England in the projected expedition to the north, and, either at Shanghai or at a point nearer the capital, press their common demands jointly on the cabinet of Pekin. It only remained now to issue a proclamation announcing the raising of the blockade, and to make the necessary arrangements for the reopening of trade. As Lord Elgin and Baron Gros did not participate in the general opinion that this measure was premature, or believe in the almost universal prediction that the raising of the blockade would not be the signal of the renewal of foreign trade, they determined to name the earliest day possible for the experiment. It was settled that the consular flags should be hoisted, and the customs levied by Chinese officers at Whampoa; while Canton itself, and its immediate suburbs, with the exception of Honan, should remain under martial law, and only be entered by Europeans under passports containing certain printed restrictions, to be granted by the allied naval and military authorities.

On the 6th of February a notification was published by the allied commanders-in-chief, announcing the raising of the blockade, and the nomination by them of the mixed commission already

* Blue-Book, the Earl of Elgin to Admiral Seymour, 2d of March, 1858.

mentioned, and consisting of Colonel Holloway, Captain Martineau, and Mr. Parkes, to preserve good order, and to inquire into infractions of their regulations, or of martial law, etc. And on the same day a farther notification was issued by the plenipotentiaries, declaring "that the city and suburbs will continue in military occupation, and under martial law, until farther notice, but that hostile operations against China, except such as the commanders-in-chief of the allied forces may consider it necessary to adopt for the security of their military position in Canton, are for the present suspended. With the exception of what was implied by the necessary clause announcing the suspension of our hostilities with China generally, no restriction whatever was placed upon the action of the allied commanders-in-chief, upon whom alone rested the responsibility of dealing with braves or disaffected populace as they should deem most expedient.

The 10th of February was the day fixed for the raising of the blockade; and although, in consequence of the Chinese New Year, and the festivities incidental to it, the reopening of trade was delayed for some weeks, the extent to which it increased within the next few months, and the fact that about one third of the exports were paid for in British goods, fully justified the plenipotentiaries in their view of the expediency of the measure.

We had now spent two months in the Canton River, and had exhausted the attractions of its banks and the resources of Canton. We had visited the Fatee Gardens, situated in a creek crowded with the boats which had taken refuge there on our occupation. Here box-trees were cut in the shapes of animals or dragons; young bamboos were fantastically twisted; gaudy and sweet-scented flowers bloomed in rows of pots; quaint little bridges led over pools, the water of which was hidden by broad-leaved languid lilies; and grotesque pavilions surmounted rocky islets. All Chinese gardens partake of much the same character. About four miles from Canton is the country house of Putinqua, deserted by its owner on the occasion of our visit, but very singular in its arrangement to European eyes. A tall white pagoda, situated on a rocky island, affords a bird's-eye view of several acres of water surrounded by a wall, with here and there islands and bridges, and pathways leading to them, paved and covered in with trellis-work, and overrun with creepers, and in the centre of all the mansion of the owner, built on piles in the water, with drawbridges communicating with the bedrooms, and canals instead of passages. It was the principle of Venice applied to a single residence.

As it was not safe to walk into the country for any distance, our explorations in the neighborhood of our anchorage were necessarily limited. Sometimes we visited the handsome nine-storied pagoda, which, from being slightly out of the perpendicular, is known as the inclined pagoda, about a mile distant; at others explored in a light boat the narrow creeks in the vicinity, where extensive villages of junks and sampans lay concealed between banks cultivated with rice and water-chestnuts. The very existence of a vast population within a short range of our ship was totally unsuspected; some of these creeks were already bridged by rows of houses built over them on piles, the whole presenting a quaint and novel appearance. As these villages contained a lawless and desperate population, who in a great measure depended for their livelihood upon river piracy, a distant walk involved a large party and revolvers. One day we captured a gang of eight of these plunderers rifling one of the Chinese bum-boats attached to the ships; they were kept in irons all night, and sent to Pihkwei next morning.

On another occasion we observed a portion of the population of a village turn out in pursuit of a gang who were escaping in a boat they had evidently stolen. The chase was a most exciting one, but, unfortunately, night closed in before we saw its results. Some of the gentlemen attached to the French embassy were attacked one evening in a sampan, and found it necessary to shoot one or two of their assailants with revolvers. Under these circumstances, expeditions, either afloat or ashore, were always invested with a tinge of excitement, which relieved the monotony of the occupation. For a few days we were employed in blowing up a monster brass gun, which had been left in one of the barrier forts taken by the Americans. They had endeavored to remove this prize in vain, so it became our perquisite. A remarkable specimen of Chinese workmanship, it measured twenty-five feet in length, and more than five feet across the breech.

One of the most interesting incidents which occurred about this time at Canton was the discovery, by Lord Elgin, of the public prisons, and the horrors which were disclosed induced him to remonstrate strongly with Pihkwei on the subject. The old mandarin was more roused by this act of interference on our part

I

than by the capture of the city, and, in a letter he addressed to Lord Elgin, makes an indignant appeal to his excellency's "enlightenment and rectitude," etc. "Would your excellency," he asks, "hold it correct, or not, were I, for instance, without giving you information, to desire any one to remove, by force, British prisoners confined in a British jail?" and he concludes pathetically, "I am not a man greedy of life, and, sooner than be thus unreasonably oppressed, I would gladly give my life to the state. The matter is of great importance; and I write that your excellency may, when you have considered it, inform me without loss of time of the course to be followed. I avail myself of the occasion to wish your excellency the blessings of the season."*

But old Pihkwei was not so unreasonably oppressed as the wretched victims of Chinese legislation. Their condition has been graphically described by Mr. Cooke, who was present at their discovery. Pihkwei was therefore informed that, in spite of his sensitive feelings on the point, he must take the unhappy beings into a room in his yamun, where I first saw them, wan and emaciated, but slowly recovering under medical treatment; in return for which, their countenances expressed gratitude more strongly than I had supposed possible in a Chinese physiognomy. One boy had been so tightly bound in a squatting position that he was unable to assume any other, while several of the men's legs and feet were a mass of bruises and ulcers, the effect of severe bastinadoing.

On the 7th of February the 70th native regiment of Bengal infantry landed. They were the first-fruits of our trip to Calcutta; but at Canton their arrival was inaugurated by an unfortunate accident which occurred the same day, partly owing to their ignorance of the regulations, and partly to the impetuosity of a French patrol, which fired upon some stragglers engaged in collecting firewood and looking for cooking utensils, and shot three men. The arrival of this regiment was most opportune; it was followed at a later period of the year by the 47th and 65th, also from Bengal, an accession of force which enabled the general to detach the 59th "Queen's" to the north at a critical point in the negotiations. Meantime, ever since his capture, Yeh had remained a prisoner on board the "Inflexible" at the Bogue Forts. As his presence so near the scene of his exploits was supposed to

* Blue-Book, 17th of January, Pihkwei to Earl of Elgin.

exercise a disturbing influence upon the minds of the Chinese population, and as a useful ship was kept unemployed while serving as his prison, it was decided that he should be sent to Calcutta, where government were in the habit of accommodating political state prisoners. Until he was informed of his fate he seemed never thoroughly to have realized the fact that he was our prisoner, and had constantly expressed his astonishment at Lord Elgin's absence, and the postponement of those negotiations to conduct which he professed was his object in living on board the "Inflexible." He manifested not the slightest emotion, however, on learning his destination, and expressed himself entirely satisfied with any arrangement that was come to in his regard.

Meantime the four powers, acting in concert, had decided on addressing a communication to Pekin, demanding a plenipotentiary possessing full powers to treat on the several points specified in their letters, to be sent to Shanghai, which was named as the place of negotiation in the first instance. In the event of an imperial commissioner not being sent there before the end of March, the allied embassadors declared it to be their intention to proceed to some point nearer the capital, with the view of placing themselves more directly in communication with the high officers of the Chinese government.

Lord Elgin's letter was addressed to Yu, the senior Secretary of State. It inclosed copies of the correspondence which had taken place with the imperial commissioner; explained the present position of affairs at Canton as resulting from the conduct of that functionary; announced the intention of the allied powers to continue the occupation until those demands which we had reserved to ourselves the right to make, under the altered attitude of affairs, had been satisfied; adverted in general terms to the nature of those demands, as having for their object the placing of our relations on a safer and more satisfactory basis. A resident minister at or near the court, a more extended intercourse throughout the country, were the principal points insisted upon in addition to those claims for indemnity, to which we already considered ourselves entitled. The letter concluded by stating that, in the event of no plenipotentiary presenting himself, or presenting himself without sufficient powers, or proving unwilling to accede to reasonable terms of accommodation, the British plenipotentiary "reserves to himself the right of having recourse, without farther announcement, delay, or declaration of hostilities, to such measures in vindication of the claims of his country on China as in his judgment it may appear advisable to adopt."

This letter was dated the 11th of February, or the day after the raising of the blockade; and on the following morning I left Canton in company with the Vicomte de Contades, the bearer of the French note, for Shanghai, for the purpose of having it forwarded with the least possible delay from that point to the capital. The American and Russian notes were dispatched by U. S. frigate Mississippi about the same time.

If the reader is only as tired of Canton and its neighborhood as we were, I shall have the less scruple in requesting him to accompany me to the north, more especially as no event of political interest occurred during the few weeks which formed the remainder of Lord Elgin's stay in the south, and my own journey terminated in a manner far more interesting than I could have anticipated.

We reached Amoy in the Peninsular and Oriental Company's steamer Formosa on the morning of the 16th. Though only here for a few hours, we saw enough of Amoy to reconcile us to a speedy departure. A walk to the British consulate led us through the centre of the town, along streets narrower and more filthy than those of Canton, crowded as it so happened with a gayly dressed population, engaged in feasting and visiting at one another's houses, and celebrating the new year. Children swaddled in finery were borne about like bambinos, their mothers resplendent in gaudy petticoats, glittering hoofs, faces powdered white, and hair bedizened with flowers of brilliant hues. Numerous toy-shops displayed, in tempting array, their fantastic contents, and the population seemed given over to merry-making. The British consulate is a handsome residence, situated under the walls of the citadel, through which we afterward walked, the Chinese guard betraying little interest or curiosity. The island of Amoy is a rocky barren spot, unattractive in a picturesque point of view, and owing its importance chiefly to the trade in tropical produce which it maintains with Singapore and the Straits. A good deal of sugar is also imported here from Formosa, and it has hitherto enjoyed the unenviable distinction of being the chief port of coolie emigration (so called) to Cuba and the West Indies.

At daylight on the morning of the 20th we found ourselves in the muddy waters of the Yang-tse-Kiang, though out of sight of land, and reached Woosung the same afternoon. This is simply an opium station, and the European population is composed of the occupants of receiving-ships. It is only twelve miles from here to Shanghai. The banks of the river are flat. Farm-houses

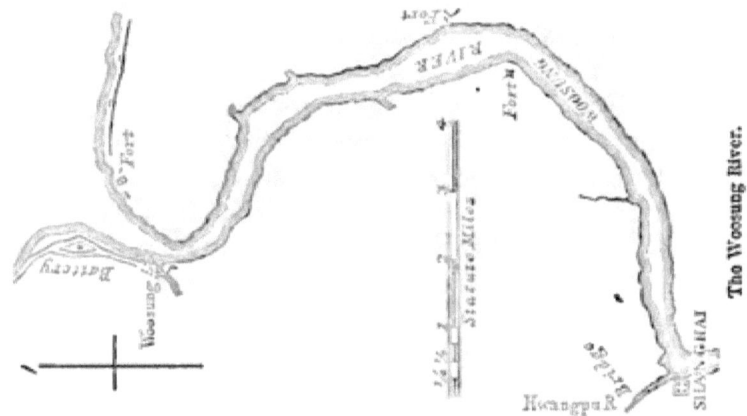

are situated in clumps of trees, leafless at this time of year, and surrounded by meadows; and the whole aspect of the country very much resembles some parts of Holland. The wind was bitterly cold; but the piercing blast, so far from being disagreeable, produced a most exhilarating effect upon systems more or less enervated by tropical heats.

That night we once more occupied the bedrooms of civilization, and reveled in the luxuries of carpets and curtains, crackling fires and warm blankets.

We found that the Taoutai or Intendant of Shanghai, the highest Chinese official in that place, was absent on his annual New-Year visit to his superior officers, the governor of the province and the governor general of the Two Kiangs. As in his absence there was no functionary of a sufficiently high rank to intrust with the transmission of letters of such grave importance to the capital, it became a matter for our consideration whether we ought not to deliver them in person to Chaou, the Governor of Kiangsu, to whom they were in the first instance addressed. This high functionary resided at the celebrated city of Soo-chow, which, since the occupation of Nankin by the rebels, has taken the rank of the provincial city.

The arrival of the Mississippi devolved upon us the charge of the Russian and American notes, and, upon consultation with Messrs. Robertson and Montigny, the English and French consuls, and the American Vice-consul, it was decided that we should proceed thither without delay, accompanied by those gentlemen and their respective interpreters. As Soo-chow had rarely been visited by Europeans, and these generally only when disguised as Chinamen, or concealed from observation in boats, the success of our experiment was very doubtful. Thus much, however, was certain, that if we were prevented from entering the city we should be met by the governor outside the walls, as in the case of the American commissioner, Mr. Maclane, on the occasion of his visit in 1854. Mr. Lay, the Inspector of Customs at Shanghai, whose knowledge of the language and local experience rendered him a most valuable addition to our party, also accompanied us.

We left Shanghai on the afternoon of the 24th. As the journey was to be performed by water, and our party was a large one, our seventeen boats formed quite a formidable fleet; and, as our destination was not a mystery, a number of Chinese were collected to see us start on so novel an expedition.

The whole delta of the Yang-tse-Kiang is intersected in every direction with water-communication, so that there were two ways of reaching Soo-chow: as some of our boats were of a large draught of water, we did not adopt the shortest and most common route, but continued for some distance up the River Wangpoo, on which Shanghai is situated. This accidental circumstance turned out the principal cause of our ultimate success. We anchored for the first night at a pagoda a few miles above Shanghai, and observed a mandarin boat immediately moor in significant proximity to us. We subsequently discovered that the suspicions we entertained at the time were correct, and that our every movement had been minutely recorded by a petty mandarin sent to watch us.

On the following morning we proceeded up the river, our progress being somewhat retarded by the difficulty we found in keeping our squadron together. The river was about a quarter of a mile broad, the character of its banks remaining unchanged. About midday we left it, and turned into a broad canal. Where nature has provided such abundant water-communication, it is sometimes difficult to distinguish what is artificial from what is natural; indeed, most of the channels are a combination of both. No doubt it is in a great measure owing to the extraordinary facility which exists for the conveyance of produce in every direction that the traffic does not appear so extensive as it really is, and as the density of the population would lead one to expect. Still, although the canal on which we journeyed was in no degree crowded, the sails of numbers of junks were visible above the level country, through which they seemed impelled by some mysterious and hidden influence. The population here is not so much collected into large villages as in the south, but is scattered over the country in farms and hamlets, imparting to the otherwise uninteresting scenery that air of domestic comfort and civilization which is more particularly the characteristic of Belgium and the Low Countries.

Every where the population were industriously engaged in agricultural pursuits; not an inch of ground seemed uncultivated, not a resource neglected for increasing the fertility of the soil. Men in boats were scooping the rich mud from the bottom of the canals with primitive dredges made of basket-work, which opened and shut on the principle of snuffers; and as they vomited their contents into the bottom of the boat, they opened their wide jaws like some river monster disgorging itself. This mud was discharged into a receptacle for it on a level with the water, where the bank had been excavated for the purpose. Half way up the bank, one on each side of this hole, stood two persons, each holding the end of a rope, to the middle of which was attached a bucket, which they ducked into the mud below, and then jerked to the top of the bank, where it was received in troughs and carried away to manure the fields. Such and many other novel and ingenious contrivances we observed employed by the laborers with whom the fields teemed, and who were so absorbed by their occupation that nothing less exciting than the appearance of a posse of barbarians would have interrupted their labors. One could not help making the unenlightened and antiquated political economical reflection that the introduction among them of European enterprise and discoveries would be a doubtful boon to persons who seemed to possess all the elements of material prosperity, and who so richly deserved whatever comforts they had obtained by their industry and ingenuity. Of course it was impossible for the mere passer to do more than guess how far they enjoyed substantial happiness, and how the system of government under which they lived might affect their domestic comfort. I have heard precisely opposite opinions expressed on the subject by persons whose long residence in the country, and knowledge of its language and government, entitled their authority to respect.

According to my own observation, however, the condition of the population varies as much in different parts of China as in the British dominions, and it would be as unfair to judge of the merits of the government, or of the general state of the population of the empire, by the people of Chili or Kiangsu, as it would be to form any like general theory in our own country, one way or the other, by the counties of Tipperary or Kent.

We passed numerous junks flying little yellow flags, to indicate that they were loaded with their annual tribute of rice. These junks were private, but pressed for the time into the service of the government. Toward evening we reached and crossed the Lake of Meaou, a shallow sheet of water, but of considerable extent. The opposite shore was not visible from the point at which we entered.

We continued our voyage during the greater part of the night, and observed strings of lanterns hoisted upon poles, which we supposed to be signals of our progress. Next morning I was told that a mandarin had been on board the boat of the American Vice-consul, and informed him that the governor Chaou was waiting for us at the village of Kwan-shan, upon the other route from Shanghai, where he had held his interview with Mr. Maclane, the plenipotentiary of the United States. This was a piece of information which we were determined to ignore, as it proved the existence of a strong desire on the part of the authorities to prevent our entering Soo-chow, and of binding us by the same precedent (which we had determined, if possible, to break through) on which they had insisted in the case of the American minister. Some light has been thrown on this event by the papers seized in Yeh's yamun at Canton. Among them is the memorial of Iliang, Governor General of the Two Kiangs, upon the subject of his interview with Mr. Maclane at Kwan-shan, in which that functionary states that, in reply to Mr. Maclane's request to be allowed to deliver a letter in person, he wrote as follows: "If the chief (Maclane) desired to present a letter from his government in person, he should follow the precedent furnished last year in the case of Marshall—hasten back to Shanghai, and there wait till Wu-kien-chang should bring him to Kwan-shan to introduce him. In obedient accordance with the above reply, the chief did presently turn back, and having transferred himself to a native vessel, was brought, on the 25th of the 5th moon, to Kwan-shan by Wu-kien-chang. Your slave, having with him Ping-han, the acting Prefect of Soo-chow, for long employed in that department, and thoroughly versed in business, had started from Soo-chow on the 24th, and also arriving at Kwan-shan on the 25th, on the following day assembled the officials present in the public hall of Kwan-shan, and summoned the chief to come forward and pay his respects. The chief's manner, it must be admitted, was reverential," etc., etc. Then follows a detailed account of the audience, and the arguments used by Iliang to dissuade Mr. Maclane from visiting the Peiho.

Having been favored by fair winds, we made good progress. Most of our boats sailed admirably, the tall masts giving our enormous flat sails such an elevation that we glided rapidly through the water under the influence of light airs. The weather was lovely. In the early morning a thick hoar-frost covered the fields; at midday it was pleasant to sit on the deck and bask in the sunshine; and at night, to retire into the snug cabin, stir the coal fire in the stove into a bright glow, and enjoy our cigars together after dinner, preparatory to separating for the night to our respective boats. We usually stopped for breakfast and dinner, and all met in a boat reserved expressly for a common dining-room. I was indebted to my kind host at Shanghai, Mr. Moncreiff, for a most comfortable boat. Indeed, the circumstances under which I made my first experiences of traveling in the interior of China were calculated to impress me most favorably; and, now that the whole of this vast continent is about to be thrown open by treaty to European exploration, there can be little doubt that the great facilities of transit which its net-work of water-communication affords will be duly appreciated. Seldom, indeed, does it fall to the lot of the adventurous traveler in an unknown country to pursue the work of discovery surrounded by so many of the appliances of comfort and civilization as he may enjoy when engaged in the "*exploitation*" of the Celestial Empire.

CHAPTER XI.

The imperial Grand Canal.—Arrival at Soo-chow.—Entry of the City.—Curiosity of the Populace.—Reception by the Governor.—A complimentary Dialogue.—A Chinese official Repast.—Politeness of our Host.—Chinese Etiquette.—Political Effect of our Visit.—Reasons against exploring the City.—Exploration of the Water Suburb.—The Boat Population.—Manners and Customs of the People.—A nocturnal Visitation.—The Tai-hoo Lake.—A Gale of Wind.—Residence at Shanghai.—A Dinner with the Taoutai.—After-dinner Conversation.—Departure for Ningpo.—Ningpo.—The Shops and Joss-houses.—The old Pagoda.

WHEN day broke on the morning of the 26th, it showed us the walls and pagodas of Soo-chow, distant about three miles. In order to deprive the governor of the power of saying, at any future time, that we had taken him by surprise, and slipped into the town in an undignified manner, M. de Contades concurred with me in deeming it prudent to write a joint letter to his excellency, informing him of our proximity to Soo-chow, which we followed in about two hours afterward.

We had entered the imperial grand canal during the night, and were now proceeding along that once celebrated channel of the internal commerce of the empire. Since the bursting of its banks by the Yellow River, and the destruction in consequence of a section of this canal, it has not been used for the last five years. The vast supplies of grain which were annually conveyed along it to the capital are now sent in sea-going junks from Shanghai, and other ports of the Yang-tse-Kiang, round the promontory of Shantung, and up the Peiho River. The expenses incidental to the rebellion have prevented the government from spending any money in repairing this magnificent work. The consequence is, that the enormous imperial grain-junks formerly employed now line the bank in a rotting condition. They are singular specimens of naval architecture, of immense solidity, and capable of transporting from two to three hundred tons of rice each. They look like so many stranded arks going to decay: this is their inevitable destiny, as the profane vulgar are not allowed to touch imperial property. Their valuable timbers were crumbling and worm-eaten, and, in some instances, their decks grass-grown.

We lowered our tapering masts to pass under a very handsome stone bridge, which spanned the canal in a single arch, and shortly after reached the southeast angle of the city wall. The view from this point was very remarkable. The city is built in the shape of a perfect square, each side four miles in length. On two sides the grand canal washes the walls, and on the other sides two smaller canals complete the square. We were at the junction of one of these with the grand canal, which extended before us, covered with boats and lined with houses, but at right angles to the left no suburb interrupted our view of the four miles of canal and wall which stretched in one unbroken line over the vast plain. Here a messenger arrived, saying that the governor was on his way to meet us, and suggesting that we should wait for him; but, anxious to get inside the city walls, we pressed on, threading our way in line along the densely thronged canal, and attracting to its banks and the roofs of the houses crowds of eager spectators, not accustomed to see British, French, and American flags flaunting impudently under their very windows.

We appeared so suddenly before the water-gate called "Foomun" that the officials, had they wished it, would scarcely have had time to shut it. However, they contented themselves with making the most frantic gesticulations and expressive signs to us to turn back; but we put on an air of the most obtuse stolidity, and pushed vehemently on; my boat, which happened to be leading, carrying away in the hurry some of the grille which formed part of the gate. Once in the city, we did not venture on an exploration of the lanes of water, which, like those of Venice, opened up in divers directions, but moored at once in a retired spot under the walls. We were not long, however, left in quiet. Almost immediately a dense crowd collected on both sides of the canal, deeply interested in the proceedings of the barbarians. Whenever any of us moved from one boat to another, a general titter of astonishment and curiosity was heard; but they manifested no semblance of dislike or hostility toward us, and were infinitely more respectable in their behavior than an English mob would have been under similar circumstances.

We had not been long moored here before the "Foo," a blue-button mandarin, came with a message from the governor to Mr. Lay, who was an old acquaintance of his, requesting to see him at the west gate. In about two hours this gentleman returned with the welcome intelligence that the governor would receive us at his yamun in the centre of the city, and would immediately send down chairs for us to a neighboring wharf. Accordingly, we proceeded, the same afternoon, to the appointed place, the whole party, with the exception of M. de Contades and myself, being in uniform. We were received at the wharf by a guard of soldiers, and were accompanied by them during our progress in chairs through the city. We thus traversed a distance of about two miles. The streets throughout were lined with spectators; the windows, housetops, and bridges were thronged with an eager and excited populace, who gazed with the most extraordinary earnestness at probably the first barbarians they had ever seen in their lives. So rapt in contemplation of these unknown specimens of humanity were they, that I did not even see them criticising us to one another, much less did they manifest any signs of hostility or contempt toward us. With mouths and eyes at utmost stretch, they stared in perfect silence. I observed many women among the crowd. Soo-chow is celebrated throughout China for the beauty of its women, and certainly those I saw did not belie its reputation. In no other part of the empire have I seen such fair complexions or regular features. In Canton the women are absolutely hideous; in the north they may be good-looking, but it is very difficult to catch a passing glimpse of them, so shy are they of barbarians; but in Soo-chow they love both to see and be seen, and with good reason. The Chinese proverb surely lacks wisdom which says, "To be happy on earth, one must be born in Soo-chow, live in Canton, and die in Liauchau;" which they explain by saying that those born in Soo-chow are remarkable for personal beauty, those who live in Canton enjoy the richest luxuries of life, and those who die in Liauchau easily obtain superior coffins from the excellent forest-trees which are there abundant.

We were received at the yamun by the usual Chinese salute of three guns, and passed through the several courts between rows of soldiers and attendants, drawn up in line and dressed in a species of livery. The governor met us with great politeness at the door of the audience-hall, and seated M. de Contades and myself on the raised estrade, which usually forms the centre of a semicircle of chairs on these occasions, and is considered the seat of honor. The governor himself took a seat to our right, which, in this land of ceremonies, was considered an additional compliment, inasmuch as the farther you are to the left of your host the more highly honored is your position. Then follows an elaborate interchange of compliments, when the visitor resigns himself entirely to the good offices of the interpreter, who in all probability throws them into somewhat the following shape.

English gentleman, who has never seen his Chinese host before, expresses his pleasure at meeting him.

Interpreter. "His excellency has long looked forward to this day."

Chinese Dignitary. "I meet him now as an old friend, and request to know his honorable age."

Int. "His excellency has profitlessly passed — years."

Chin. Dig. "The ears of his excellency are long, and betoken great ability."

Int. "Ah! oh! He is unworthy of the compliment."

Chin. Dig. "You have had an arduous journey?"

Int. "We deserved it."

Chin. Dig. "I trust your honorable health is good."

Int. "Relying on your happy auspices, his excellency's health is still robust."

Int. "The great emperor of your honorable nation, is he well?"

Chin. Dig. "He is well. The great sovereign of your honorable nation, is she well?"

Int. "She is well. Do the troublesome pests (rebels) still infest the country?"

Chin. Dig. "The insects are being speedily exterminated."

Such, I have little doubt, was the tone of conversation which Mr. Meadows and Chaou kept up for a few minutes, until we went on to inform his excellency that we were the bearers of notes for the prime minister Yu from the four powers, which were of the utmost importance, and which, we trusted, he would lose no time in forwarding, as delay in their transmission might seriously compromise the interests of the empire. The covering dispatch to himself he opened and read, a crowd of attendants collecting round him and making themselves acquainted with its contents over his shoulder. As we desired that the whole proceeding should be invested with as much publicity as possible, this mode of conducting business, though rather unusual in Western diplomacy, was quite in accordance with our wishes.

We were now conducted to a recess, and invited to partake of an extensive display of fruits, pastry, and preserves, first, however, being invited to uncover our heads by our host, who says, "Will you elevate the cap?" On which he is answered, "We are behaving in a scandalously outrageous manner; forgive our crime;" by which we mean elegantly to apologize for the liberty we are taking in sitting down bareheaded. Then we engage in general conversation, in the course of which Chaou makes sundry inquiries as to the condition of Canton, wishes to know whether we are going to kill Yeh, and when the embassadors are coming north. He also, in true Chinese style, indulges in a little quiet irony at the expense of us all, though ostensibly directed at our worthy consul, Mr. Robertson, who, he says, must be glad of having such a good opportunity of seeing the celebrated city of Soo-chow; but Mr. Robertson protests that Chaou himself is the only sight worth looking at. Certainly a man who is governor of a province containing thirty-eight millions of inhabitants, with a power of life and death, is not an every-day individual, and yet he is only the subordinate of the Governor General of the Two Kiangs, who, in his turn, is a responsible officer.

Chaou was the best specimen of a Chinese gentleman I had yet seen in China: nothing could be more dignified or courteous than his manner, and this at a time when a most disagreeable commission had been confided to him. But a Chinaman has wonderful command of feature; he generally looks most pleased when he has least reason to be so, and maintains an expression of imperturbable politeness and amiability when he is secretly regretting devoutly that he can not bastinado you to death. On this occasion our accomplished host overwhelmed us with civilities, constructed pyramids of delicacies on our plates, and insisted on our drinking a quantity of hot wine, obliging us to turn over our glasses each time as a security against heel-taps.

Chaou's yamun was a far handsomer residence than any similar official abode in Canton. The interior was invested with an air of comfort unusual in China, the walls nicely papered, and the floor carpeted. The whole establishment had been recently put into good order, and was altogether a fit residence for so elevated a functionary.

At last we "begged to take our leave," and began violently to "tsing-tsing," a ceremony which consists in clasping your hands before your breast, and making a crouching baboon-like gesture.

It is the equivalent of shaking hands, only one shakes one's own hands instead of another person's, which may or not have its advantages: in China the custom of the country is the preferable one. This is followed by a scene very like that which occurs on similar occasions among ourselves. Our host insists upon following us to our chairs. We remonstrate—"Stop, stop, stop, we are unworthy," say we. "What language is this?" he replies. "We really are unworthy," we reiterate. "You are in my house," he insists; and so we back to our chairs, perpetually imploring him not to trouble himself by accompanying us, which he vehemently resists, until at last, when we are in our chairs, he reluctantly consents to return, apologizing to the last for being so rude as to leave us even then. It is just possible that, under the circumstances, his satisfaction at getting quit of us had as much to do with this "empressement" as his sense of politeness.

It was dark when we returned to our boats; and so much had happened to excite and interest, that, even had it not been, I was not in a humor to engage in the work of accurate observation. Our expedition had terminated, after a good deal of anxiety, in complete success. For the first time in its history, barbarians had made an official entry into Soo-chow, and we hoped that this result would not be without an important political effect. In a country where every thing is established by precedent, a victory had been gained over Chinese exclusiveness, which, in the existing state of our relations with the empire, might be significant of a disposition to yield at last to that Western pressure which for so many years has been so successfully resisted. So wonderfully jealous are Chinese of foreigners entering their cities, that one of the first requests made to us by Chaou was that we should leave the city immediately after the interview, which we agreed to do.

Although it was late before we reached our boats, we determined to keep our faith, and shifted our berth to a wharf outside the west gate, opposite a yamun at which we had invited Chaou to breakfast with us on the following morning. This ceremony, and all the forms of etiquette which it involved, took place at the appointed hour; but there was an addition to the party in the person of the Taoutai of Shanghai, who had just returned from a fruitless expedition to Shanghai in search of us, by the short route, for the purpose of meeting us, and so preventing our reaching Soo-chow. We enjoyed a quiet laugh at his expense, and he no doubt was firmly convinced that we had designedly effected a very clever strategic manœuvre. We plied both our guests with quantities of Champagne in return for the hot wine we had imbibed, at the peril of our constitutions, on the previous evening.

After breakfast we expressed ourselves satisfied with the receipts Chaou had sent us for the dispatches we had delivered to him, and our guests got into their chairs amid a profusion of regrets and civil speeches.

Had we pressed the point, there can be little doubt that we should have been allowed to visit the principal objects in the city under favorable circumstances; but many reasons combined to render this inexpedient at the time, and among them the justification which it would have afforded to the governor's insinuation that we had taken advantage of a political mission to gratify an idle curiosity; so, to our great disappointment, we deemed it best to content ourselves with this transient glance of this interesting city, famed as the birthplace of beauty, and the cradle of all that is refined, elegant, and fashionable in the empire. We were even unable, as we passed through the streets, to judge of the shops, so dense was the crowd; and the only remarkable feature I could catch in passing was the numerous canals intersecting it in every direction, spanned, rialto fashion, by high single arches, and with houses rising out of the water as in Venice.

I observe that Mr. Fortune has added as little to our previous limited knowledge of Soo-chow as I have, but he is less excusable, as he seems to have resided there for some time in the disguise of a Chinaman. That there is much interesting information connected with this celebrated city may be inferred from the fact that a Chinese work, called the Soo-chow-foo-chi, in forty octavo volumes, is devoted to an account of its history, monuments, etc. Chaou told us that he estimated the population at about three millions.

As I was anxious to visit the large lake of Tai-hoo in the vicinity of Soo-chow, I parted from my companions shortly after breakfast. I regretted extremely that it was not in M. de Contades' power to accompany me, as I had found in that gentleman not only a most agreeable companion, but a colleague whose energy and tact largely contributed to the successful issue of our undertaking. He returned direct to Shanghai, while Mr. Lay and I proceeded, in the first instance, to explore the principal water-suburbs of the city. We followed the grand canal for about two miles. As far as I could judge, its average breadth was about 100 yards, but it is somewhat difficult to form a very accurate estimate on this subject, as the water is so concealed by boats, and the residences of the aquatic and terrestrial population so much resemble one another, that it is not always easy to tell where the water ends and the land begins. A narrow lane was kept clear for traffic, and along it passed innumerable craft of every description. There were as many different varieties of boats here as there are of vehicles in Fleet Street, and the water-way was as inconveniently crowded as that celebrated thoroughfare usually is. Ferry-boats plied as briskly and were as heavily loaded as omnibuses: heavy cargo-boats lumbered along and got in every body's way, just as brewers' drays do. Light tanka-boats, with one or two passengers, and deftly worked by a single oar astern, cut in and out like hansoms. And there were large passage-boats with accommodation for travelers on long journeys, that plied regularly between Soo-chow, Hang-chow, Chang-chow, and other distant cities, and that created the same sort of sensation as they passed as did the Brighton Age or Portsmouth Telegraph in days gone by. Gentlemen's private carriages were here represented by gorgeous mandarin junks, with the huge umbrella on the top, and a gong at the entrance to the cabin, beaten at intervals by calfless flunkies. Other junks there were, more gaudily painted even than these, from whence issued shrill voices, and sounds of noisy laughter and music. There was the costermonger in his humble substitute for a donkey-cart, a small covered canoe, which looked like a coffin, and in which he sat alone, forcing it speedily through the water with a pair of oars, one of which he worked astern with his hand, and the other at the side with his feet. The race of scavengers lived in flat punts, and, scooping up the mud and rubbish from the bottom of the canal, discharged it into them, where it was immediately examined by a number of ducks kept on board for the purpose, who picked out all that was worth eating, and what they rejected was then inspected by their owners for waifs and strays that had been lost from junks, and then taken to fatten the land. But the most curious appearance was presented by the boats which carried the fishing cormorants, solemnly perched in successive rows on stages projecting from the sides; they looked like a number of gentlemen in black on the platform at a meeting of a grave and serious character.

K

We had passed round three sides of the city, and yet I was no more tired of observing and watching the manners and customs of the inhabitants than they were of observing mine. Nor, unfortunately, can I be sure that I am giving a more accurate description of them than they would of me; in a country like China, the traveler can trust less to first impressions than in any other: when nothing is superficial, a superficial survey can not be depended upon. Every minute detail in their manners and habits of life bears the stamp of antiquity, has had its origin in some excellent reason, and possesses a special adaptability to the purpose for which it is designed, which is not at first sight appreciable by an utter stranger. One gazes at a party of Chinamen at work very much as one would at beavers or bees. Their results are startling, and their mode of arriving at them defies imitation by an ordinary mortal.

Turning sharp out of the grand canal, we passed down a narrower one, under high bridges, between tall houses with turned-up eaves, and balconies full of people, and quaint gates and archways covered with moral inscriptions, and so into the open country, where our men jumped out upon the paved towing-path, and dragged us rapidly between interminable green fields, stretching

Canal Scene near Soo-chow.

to the horizon, except in the direction we were going, where a range of low hills, purpled by the setting sun, gave promise of an approach to the picturesque. We met numbers of other boats being tracked in like manner, and passed under high single-arched bridges, like those the pictures of which first imbued our infantine minds with notions of Chinese quaintness in the willow-pattern plate. I only observed one which was of a different construction in a town through which the canal passed: it consisted of three arches, and on the middle one a building was erected with a twisted roof, and crowds of people gazed at us from beneath it. We observed here the commencement of those fields of mulberry-trees, which, extending throughout the departments of Kiashing and Hoo-chow, render these the most celebrated silk-producing districts in the province.

Just as we were going to bed we were aroused by shouts which called us on deck to witness a most romantic sight: a full moon was lighting up the silent water-ways of a picturesque old town, full of bridges and gaunt houses; the canal was so narrow that we had great difficulty in squeezing past the few boats already moored in it; from its edge rose houses three stories high, completely shutting in dark mysterious lanes, which turned off in every direction, allowing only here and there a gleam of silvery light to play upon the surface of the water. The inhabitants, unused to so late a visitation, peered curiously at us from their latticed windows, and bright rays shot across our gloomy paths as one after the other these were opened. The stream was strong against us, the street was a long one, and as there was no towing-path, it was some time before we had punted through it, and were clear of the long shadows of its lofty houses. We reached the edge of the lake shortly after this, and anchored for the night.

The morning was still and foggy, and the shores of the lake were concealed from us in almost every direction; we were five hours sailing slowly across to a high projecting promontory, called Tung-ting-shan. Ascending the hill—for the day had cleared—we had an extensive view: not far distant a high-wooded island seemed to float on the still surface of the lake, and beyond it the blue outline of the mountains that formed the opposite shore were dimly visible. At our feet, skirting the bay, lay the secluded little village at which we had landed, embowered in trees, above which curled wreaths of smoke; a spur of the promontory separated it from another village which seemed the twin brother of the first, so exactly did it resemble in situation and extent. We descended into it, and were, of course, immediately surrounded by the whole population. They were perfectly good-humored in manner, and when we threw handfuls of copper cash among them, the juvenile community indulged in a universal scramble, in which some of the elders even condescended to join. I would gladly have spent another day on the Tai-hoo, but was afraid of missing the mail from Shanghai; so we returned in time to pass through our old town of the night before by moonlight again, and here diverged from our former route.

In the middle of the night I was disturbed by a violent shock, to which I was indebted for a view of a famous bridge across an expansion of the grand canal, mentioned by Mr. Ellis, in his account of Lord Amherst's Embassy, as having ninety arches. I only counted fifty-three, and the moonlight was so bright that I do not think I was mistaken in the number. The next day we entered the Meaou Lake again, and crossed it with a fair wind, in company with a large and picturesque fleet, which must have been composed of some hundreds of junks. This breeze freshened into a gale the day after, and involved a tough beat down the river to Shanghai. My canal-boat, so delightful in calm weather, was by no means adapted for such an emergency: having no keel, she was extremely crank, and whenever she went about, every thing loose in the cabin fetched away; and, to crown all, when they were jumbled in picturesque confusion on the floor, my stove upset, and shot its contents of glowing coals into the middle of them. As this was close to Shanghai, I narrowly escaped signalizing my return to that place by a grand conflagration.

I remained for ten days at Shanghai, enjoying the hospitality of its merchant princes, and the invigorating effects of its bracing winter climate. Of all the spots upon the coast of the Celestial Empire at which Europeans have established themselves, it is certainly the pleasantest as a residence. With a society almost as numerous as Hong Kong, there is much agreeable social intercourse, owing, no doubt, in a great measure, to the fact that it is the Ultima Thule of civilization, and has not yet been forced into exclusiveness by miscellaneous hordes making it a house of call; while, as a foreign community in a distant land, it is not subject to those political dissensions which so often distract our own colonies. There is, moreover, an air of substantial prosperity about Shanghai, which occasionally expands into magnificence, and displays itself in palatial residences, and an expensive style of living; but there is also, unhappily, a gloomy side to the picture, and there are years when an unfortunately heavy venture in silk on the part of the community results in a corresponding reduction of crinoline.

Situated on the flat bank of the river, Shanghai owes none of its charms to the picturesque; but the handsome houses which line the shore for a distance of two miles give it an imposing appearance as approached from the sea. The English section of the town, though not confined exclusively to British subjects, is the largest. It lies between the French and American. Each of these different quarters is inhabited by subjects of other countries. The boundary of the French concession is the city wall. The city is about three miles in circumference, and contains a population of about 300,000. As all the Chinese towns of its class are so like each other as to be almost undistinguishable, and have been repeatedly described, I will only say of Shanghai that it is chiefly celebrated for old China, inlaid copper, and other objects of "virtu," which it imports from Soo-chow to meet the European demand. It has suffered a good deal from the occupation of the rebels, and its once famous tea-gardens are now a mass of grotesque rockwork and debris, but little frequented, and which, in their best days, must have been rather quaint than pretty.

I was glad to have an opportunity at Shanghai of renewing my acquaintance with the Taoutai, whom I found to be a person of considerable intelligence and enlightenment. One day I dined with him, and partook, not of a flimsy refection, such as those usually offered on such occasions, but of a good substantial repast, beginning with bird's-nest soup, followed by shark's fins, bêche de mer, and other indescribable delicacies, as *entrées*, then mutton and turkey, as *pièces de résistance*, carved at a side-table in a civilized manner, and handed round cut up into mouthfuls, so that the refined chopstick replaced throughout the rude knife and fork of the West. We may certainly adopt with advantage the more elegant custom of China in this respect; and as we have ceased to carve the joints in dishes, make the next step in advance, and no longer cut up slices of them in our plates. There, however, we might stop: the usage of stretching across the table, and collecting a heap of delicacies from every dish in your neighbor's plate, as a mark of politeness, is decidedly objectionable. Some of the dishes were so constructed as to admit of a small charcoal fire in the centre, so that the soup or viands surrounding it were kept constantly warm. There were wines of different qualities, but principally extracted from millet-seed, and always drunk warm; and after dinner some very strong but delicately flavored tea, called red, which answers the purpose of coffee as a digestive, and simply differs from the green in being subjected for a much longer time to the steaming process. The green tea, which is the least powerful and most refreshing, is a milder infusion, the leaf being slightly dried over a fire and still green. This was followed by some delicious almond tea. The guests upon the occasion were Mr. Robertson, Mr. John Meadows, and myself, the Haefanting or prefect, and the principal military mandarin in Shanghai. The conversation turned chiefly on a comparison of the different administrative systems of England and China, interspersed with the most fulsome compliments, with now and then a feeler thrown out by the Taoutai on the subject of existing troubles, when his endeavors to conceal his desire to gain as much information as possible on our probable policy were highly diverting.

I did not venture to broach a subject to his excellency on which I was no less anxious to be informed. Shanghai is the principal port for the export of the annual supply of rice to the north. Thousands of junks bound for the mouth of the Peiho leave the river in successive fleets during the spring months, and it was important that we should know the intentions of the Taoutai for the ensuing year, and discover, if possible, the quantity of grain to be exported, and the different ports at which it was to be collected, as well as the date of the earliest departure. In the event of our finding it necessary to operate in the north, one of the most important means of pressure which could be brought to bear upon the capital was by intercepting this supply, which it would be in our power to do, with a few gun-boats in the Gulf of Pechelee. At this time the river opposite the town was covered with a dense forest of the masts of junks, all waiting for clearances to Tientsin. We were afterward informed by the custom-house authorities that the amount of rice to be sent to the north from Shanghai alone was about 300,000 piculs.

As Lord Elgin was expected at Ningpo from the south about

this time, I proceeded thither in the dispatch gun-vessel Surprise to meet him. At midday on the 14th of March we reached the mouth of the Ningpo River, having run over in about twenty-four hours. After the dead level of the valley of the Yang-tse-Kiang, the approach to this river is sufficiently picturesque. To the right a bold promontory, about 200 feet in height, surmounted by a fort, overlooks the city of Chinhae, the walls of which extend along both the river-bank and sea-shore; numbers of junks block up the passage, and render great skill in steering necessary. Most of these are loaded with timber from Fokien, and their unsightly burdens extend on either side for some distance, almost concealing the junk itself, and giving it somewhat the appearance which a donkey presents when buried between two bundles of hay. Considerable ingenuity must have been exercised in loading these junks, by means, as I understood, of stays from the masts.

As we proceed up the river, the hills recede to some distance, and here and there picturesque valleys open up through them. The immediate banks are flat, and chiefly remarkable for a number of erections which look like enormous haystacks, but which are really ice-houses, for the preservation of fish. They are obliged by law to contain a three years' supply always in store. It is only about twelve miles to Ningpo, which we reached at sunset. The

Ningpo River.

following day was dedicated to an inspection of the city, which decidedly ranks first among those at present open to Europeans. It is situated at the confluence of two rivers, contains a population of about a quarter of a million, and is five miles in circumference. A bridge of boats, 200 hundred yards long, connects it with the principal suburb. But few Europeans reside here, and they live principally opposite the city, on the bank of the lesser of the two rivers. Ningpo is celebrated for having produced some of the ablest scholars in China, and numerous triumphal arches, in honor of those of her sons who have carried off the highest honors at competitive examinations, span the principal streets. They are constructed of granite, and ornamented with specimens of singularly clever carving; in some instances the slab has been cut through, and presents an open net-work of carving of the nicest delicacy. In others, the beauty of the workmanship is exhibited in the wonderful relief with which the most intricate patterns are made to stand out from the solid granite.

The book-shops of Ningpo are worthy its high literary reputation; and, indeed, the shops of every description were superior to those at any of the other ports. At that popularly known as Fortnum and Mason's, we used to sit down and drink exquisite tea, while various delicate conserves were being produced for trial, and smoke minute pipes full of mild tobacco at intervals.

In the best shops there is usually an outer and an inner shop, separated from each other by a glass-covered veranda. The inner room is generally a spacious apartment, fitted up with shelves, and pigeon-holes, and drawers, much as in England; and with extensive counters, behind which stand pale, studious-looking men with intelligent countenances, who measure out yards of silk, or display crapes and gauzes with the same insinuating grace which distinguishes their brotherhood in our own country.

Ningpo is noted for the excellence of its wood-carving and inlaying. The embroidery in silk and satin is often beautiful. Occasionally old China may be picked up, but the supply in this article is not equal to the demand. Soap-stone carving is abundant, but may be procured more cheaply at Foo-chow.

The joss-house dedicated to the goddess Ma Tsupu, and maintained by the Shantung guild, a flourishing corporation, was the handsomest building of the kind I had seen in China. The verandas and roofs were supported by freestone columns, carved into the forms of dragons and other unearthly monsters, while elaborate representations in gaudy colors and delicate tracery adorned the walls. Fishes, standing on their tails, and dragons with their mouths open, ornamented the ridges of the roofs, and terminated in grotesque turrets the projecting eaves. The city is intersected at intervals of two or three hundred yards by fire-walls, so as to confine the ravages of that destructive element within narrow limits.

The visitor is amply repaid for the trouble of ascending the old pagoda by the view which is obtained from the windy summit of its seven stories. The position of the city and the direction of the rivers lie mapped at his feet, with the blue mountains in the distance, which inclose the lakes and the snowy valley, and the picturesque sights of the neighborhood. This pagoda is 1100 years old and 160 feet in height.

I was fortunate enough, one day, to witness a "sing-sing joss" in one of the principal temples. The disagreeable necessity of being obliged to form one of a dense crowd of very odoriferous Chinamen prevented my staying very long, nor was the plot of so refined a nature as to render the performance attractive; but the acting was in some instances clever, and the female characters admirably sustained by men whose treble voices, and apparently distorted feet, rendered the disguise perfect. The audience seemed deeply interested; and the comic episodes, in which a good deal of rather coarse humor was displayed, elicited shouts of laughter.

The neighborhood of Ningpo was reported more worth seeing than the town itself; and as the scenery I had already visited in China possessed but small merit in a picturesque point of view, I was glad to accede to the proposal of Captain Saumarez, of H. M. S. Cormorant, that we should occupy the interval until the arrival of Lord Elgin by an expedition to the Snowy Valley.

CHAPTER XII.

An Expedition to the Snowy Valley.—Mountain Scenery.—The Temple of the Snowy Crevice.—The Maou-kao-tae.—The "Thousand Fathom Precipice."—Sewe-kang-ha.—Our Fellow-lodgers.—The Dragon Waterfall.—Departure from the Snowy Valley.—Mountain Men.—A Voyage on bamboo Rafts.—Raft Navigation.—Arrival at Chusan.—A Roman Catholic Mission.—A Chinese country Residence.—Political Advantages of Chusan.—A British Grave-yard.—The sacred Island of Pootoo.—A degraded Priesthood.—The High-priest.—Picturesque Temples.—Pilgrims.—Magnificent View.—Chapoo.

Mr. Thomas Meadows had been kind enough to furnish us not only with a guide, but with most accurate information as to the sights to be seen in the Snowy Valley, and the best way to see them. The first part of our journey was performed at night, in a covered boat of small dimensions, and which was propelled by a single oar astern. However, we had the tide with us, and daylight found us moored under a covered bridge, where we were to transfer ourselves to mountain chairs, and our baggage to the shoulders of stalwart porters. For the first three hours our way lay over the flat banks of the river, along the paved ridges which separated fields of beans, rice, wheat, cabbages, and all the varied assortment of Chinese cultivation. We only recrossed the river once by a bridge, where massive slabs of granite, about twenty-five feet in length each, were laid upon the wooden piles. The valley now began to narrow, and the hills, with an elevation of from 1200 to 1500 feet, to disclose rocky gorges and narrow valleys, where strips of wood and pine forest clothed the steep sides, and the navigation of the river, except for rafts of bamboo, had ceased altogether. Then we brace ourselves for the climb, and, discarding our light mountain chairs, we left them to follow, contented that they should form a picturesque feature of the procession as it wound up the steep rocky paths.

Our way led through young pine woods, the smaller branches of which had been lopped for firewood, and passed along the precipitous side of the hill in which it had been scarped. When we had attained an elevation of about 1000 feet, and looked back from a projecting spur in the range, a beautiful panoramic view met the eye. The valley we had traversed in the morning, dotted with scattered villages, and divided by the river winding away to the horizon like a silver thread, lay at our feet, while on our right pendulous woods of bamboo covered the steep slopes of the mountain: planted with perfect regularity, their feathery plumes, of varied hues and exquisite grace of form, waved gently in the breeze.

Taking a last look at this lovely scene, we reached in a few steps the summit of the pass, and, crossing it, found ourselves in an amphitheatre surrounded by partially wooded hills, in the midst of which the most prominent object was the group of quaint, gabled, upturned-cornered houses, which formed the "Temple of the Snowy Crevice:" this was to be our resting-place for the night. Here we were received by sundry bonzes, in black or gray serge, with shaven crowns, who were dispensing, at the charge of a few "cash," yellow tickets for the celestial regions to groups of female devotees, of whom we had already passed many on the hill-side, helping themselves along upon their little feet—so ill adapted to the mountains—by means of stout staves. A number of them, with ruddy countenances, by no means uncomely, and whose neat attire and comfortable embonpoint gave evidence of a domestic condition of ease and independence, knelt upon small circular mats or hassocks, and prostrated themselves before a row of gods and goddesses, the largest of which, in the centre, was about twenty-five feet in height. Huge black images, with ferocious countenances and drawn swords, guarded the sanctity of the temple; and near them was a handsome bell, where the officiating priest kept up a low monotonous chant, and tapped a little bell as the signal for genuflexion or prostration on the part of the congregation, who were in the mean time burning little pieces of yellow paper, lighting joss-sticks, or telling their rosaries. In another hall a number of persons were employed in manufacturing bamboo mats. We were compelled to pass through these holy places on our way to our bedroom, which was in a range of buildings at the back.

As we had yet a few hours of daylight, we procured at the temple a guide, by name Kim-bau, who should be immortalized in the first hand-book which Mr. Murray publishes of these regions. He had been initiated into the mysteries of ciceroneship by Mr. Meadows, and, although innocent of any language but his mother tongue, had learned his lesson, and took us to every point of view with scrupulous precision. First we went to the Maou-kao-tae, where a priest's little house is built upon a projecting ledge of rock that overhangs a precipice 1000 feet high by aneroid measurement, to the edge of which we crept cautiously and looked over broad fertile valleys intersected by rivers, which met lovingly and flowed away to water distant fields. The hill-sides were terraced with rice and other cultivation, in some places to their summits, at others the high lands were wooded, and strips of forest marked the course of impetuous torrents tumbling into the glistening streams beneath. A town lay peacefully sleeping in the midst of the principal valley, and tiny figures could be distinguished working in the fields, or following the winding paths.

Tseen-chang-yen Waterfall.

The scenery altogether reminded me of the Mahabuleshwar Hills, where, however, the precipices are higher. From here we scrambled along the edge of the precipice for a few hundred yards until we reached the waterfall called the "Thousand-fathom Precipice," where Kim-bau showed us the special pine-tree to which, as conscientious sight-seers, it was our duty to cling and crane over till we could see the pool beneath, and the rush of waters and the dizzy height made our brains spin. The waterfall itself is only 400 feet in height, but the stream tumbles and leaps down the valley after it has left the pool for at least as many hundred feet more, before it becomes a quiet, well-conducted river. We descended by steep slippery paths through pine-woods and groves of bamboo to the foot of the fall, and at a distance of thirty yards from the fall were drenched with the spray. From this point the scene was in the highest degree sublime and impressive; before us a smooth wall of precipitous rock, from four to five hundred feet high, intersected by a white line of foam, extended in the form of a semicircle on each side. Five hundred feet below lay the green valley, shut in by the lofty range beyond.

After returning to our temple, though it was nearly dark, and we had done a good day's work, we could not resist visiting a waterfall, the murmur of which was almost audible from our quarters. The hour of our visit was well timed; the last faint tints of daylight were fading away on the distant mountains; the only sound which broke the absolute stillness of the repose in which all nature was hushed was the continuous plash of the water, as it issued from the deep shadows of a dense mass of overhanging foliage at the head of the gorge, in a long white sheet of foam, like a ghost in the gloaming. Crossing a slab of granite which bridged the stream below the fall, we ascended a long flight of steps skirting a precipitous ledge overhanging the brook, and on reaching the top, followed the winding path through the gloomy recesses of the wood until it debouched upon a small amphitheatre, hemmed in on all sides by lofty hills, which rose abruptly from its circumference; here, buried in the mountains and far from the busy hum of men, lay the sequestered village Sewekang-ha, "remote," and, I should think, very "unfriended, melancholy, and slow" as a place of residence, but an excellent picture of tranquillity and picturesque seclusion. The only evidences of life were the blue wreaths which curled from the thatched roofs,

Sewe-kang-ba Waterfall.

and rested in a light cloud over the hamlet, as though it had put on a night-cap of smoke preparatory to "turning in." The hour was sufficiently late, at all events, to induce us to take the hint, so we scrambled by another path to the temple, where we found the kitchen crowded with pilgrims, who were going to spend the night here, and who were collected, as in a club dining-room, in groups round small square tables, vigorously plying chopsticks. The good fare they were enjoying made them quarrelsome. We heard the noise of their contending voices until long after we had retired to rest—indeed, until they were exchanged for snores. The whole establishment was full of lodgers; and overhead, in close proximity on either side of us, worshipers were slumbering.

Some disinterested American had been charitable enough to leave a stove in the temple for the benefit of future travelers, and it was grateful, when we rose in the morning, to warm our hands and drink our coffee by it previous to starting on farther explorations. First, however, we were called upon to settle sundry disputes between our coolies and certain devotees, who thought themselves entitled to a preference in the choice of food, accommodation, etc.; nor did our good friends the priests venture to interfere at the risk of offending their customers. The civility of these gentry to us was as unlimited as their curiosity; they perpetually plied us with tea and fingered our garments. I have generally found gloves and corduroy trowsers to be the most striking objects of dress to the uncivilized mind; shooting-boots are also curiosities. Our entertainers, however, were becoming accustomed to Europeans, and had evidently smoked a few cigars in their lives before; but they were particularly amused by my Madras servant, apparently a specimen of humanity heretofore unknown to them; they took him to look at the hideous black deities which guarded the entrance of the temple, a compliment to his personal appearance at which they chuckled hugely, but which he did not seem to appreciate.

An hour's walk over hill-sides cultivated with tea, and through pine woods, brought us to a pretty valley, divided by a stream fringed with wood, and spanned by a bridge of a single arch, concealed by creepers, their long twisted tendrils, like ladies' tresses, playing on the water. On the bank was the temple Lung-yin-tau, dedicated to the dragon god. After inspecting this grim divinity, we visited the romantic waterfall which bears the same name, where the stream after peacefully traversing the valley, plunges over a ledge of rock 120 feet high, into a cleft so narrow and precipitous that it is impossible to look into its full depth from above. It derives its name probably from the resemblance which the deep gorge, split into two sombre chasms, is supposed to bear to the jaws of a dragon. Although the waterfall is not so high as some of the others in the neighborhood, I thought this the most striking and characteristic in these mountains. From thence we proceeded to the Leshak-yong, a druidical-looking stone of great antiquity, but unknown origin, placed upon a projecting point which commands a panoramic view more beautiful and extensive than even the Maou-kao-tae. Immediately facing us, at the head of the valley, we had a splendid view of a waterfall, upward of 200 feet high, which falls in one perpendicular sheet to the bottom, the water dropping in curious snake-like jets, without ever touching the smooth surface of the rock, into the pool beneath. Our elevation above the sea at this point did not probably exceed 2000 feet.

We now returned to the temple, and, after a hearty meal, took an affectionate farewell of our holy hosts. We regretted that our time was so limited that we were unable to linger longer in the Snowy Valley, and explore more thoroughly its scenic attractions.

In any country they would be worthy of a visit, but in China especially, where the limited excursions of foreigners have disclosed so little of the picturesque, no traveler should visit Ningpo without taking a trip to the mountains; unless, indeed, the scenery they contain is eclipsed by wonders yet to be discovered by those who will explore the whole empire under conditions heretofore impossible. We had been fortunate in the time of year for our expedition; and though, while we were there, the Snowy Valley did not justify its name so far as the snow was concerned, in the early morning the water in the paddy-fields was coated with ice; and I observed a few days after at Ningpo that what fell as rain below had covered the mountains we had left with a snowy mantle.

The peasantry of this district, in spite of their nationality, possessed the *tout ensemble* of mountaineers in all parts of the world. Whether in the Highlands of Scotland, of Circassia, of the Tyrol, of the Himalayas, or of China, there is an indescribable air which I have observed distinguishes them all, while it in no way interferes with their national characteristics. Hot-tempered, good-humored, huge-calved, independent, hardy, and self-reliant—accustomed to solitude, but disposed to conviviality, I have always found hill-men the pleasantest companions, while the bracing mountain air and constant variety of scene exercises a corresponding influence upon one's own spirits. As we descended the hill, we passed long files of these sturdy mountain men, each staggering under a young pine-tree, and bearing his apparently superhuman load down to market, with a broad grin on his jocund countenance.

We determined to vary our mode of conveyance on our return journey, and on reaching the River Tsze-ke at the foot of the hill, instead of plodding wearily to our boats over miles of level plain, to perform a voyage in a bamboo raft, the river being too swift and shallow for any other description of craft. It was, indeed, little better than a trout stream. The population of a large village on the river bank, where we engaged the raft, turned out to witness our start, and, while the preparations were being made, we inspected a curious mill worked by water-power, by which a number of hammers or pounders were caused to fall with regular stroke into receptacles for grain formed like mortars. Our raft was composed of only ten bamboos, on a level with the water, which flowed freely through the interstices, so that we were obliged to lay some planks upon them to keep us dry. Still movement was impossible except at the price of being ankle-deep in water. The ends of the bamboos were turned up, like the corners of houses and every thing else in China. The object, no doubt, was to make a sort of bow, to prevent our being flooded. Upon this fragile construction we intrusted ourselves to the guidance of one man, sending our coolies and chairs overland, and dashed off in company with a number of other rafts, principally

Our Bamboo Rafts.

loaded with wood or charcoal, now grating over the pebbly bed of the stream, now whirled rapidly over a bubbling seething rapid, and then being brought sharp up by an eddy in some deep green pool, where the raftsman's pole could find no bottom, and salmon would have loved to lie. We were objects of great interest to other raftsmen, who ventured on jokes at our expense; so we retaliated by racing them, hoisted umbrellas to favoring gales, and hooked ourselves past our neighbors by holding on to them or poling against them, to the great merriment of the river population. The extreme bitterness of the wind, and the close of day, checked our energies at last, and we were pretty well knocked up by our day's work when we once more reached our boat, and, coiling ourselves at the bottom, indulged in undisturbed slumber until dawn once more found us alongside the good ship Cormorant, in the river off Ningpo.

I found that Lord Elgin had arrived, during my absence from Ningpo, after a cruise up the coast, in the course of which he had visited the ports of Swatow, Amoy, and Foo-chow. At the first of these, which is situated between Canton and Amoy, and is not one of those opened by the treaty of 1842, an illicit trade had sprung up, partly in sugar, which is exported from this point to other ports on the coast in foreign as well as in Chinese bottoms, partly in tea, which, from its greater proximity to the tea districts, and the recent troubles at Canton, had found this outlet to the foreign market, and partly in bean-cake, which is brought down in large quantities from Shanghai as an article of manure. Swatow occupies an important position in Chinese commerce; extensive banking operations are carried on here; a considerable junk trade radiates from it to the islands of Formosa and Hainan, and different ports on the coast. A good deal of opium is annually imported by our merchants, which is subjected to local duties.

On the 20th of March we left Ningpo in the Furious, on our way to Chusan, and, running over in six hours, dropped anchor in the beautiful land-locked harbor of Tinghae about sunset. On the following morning we landed to explore a locality rendered so notorious during the last war by the prolonged occupation of our forces, and by the terrible experiences through which they passed in this lovely isle, and which have given it a reputation which it has since been admitted it so little merited that we have never ceased to regret its ultimate abandonment. We no sooner stepped on shore than we obtained evidences of those associations connected with our occupation, which still linger among the inhabitants. Juvenile beggars crowded round us, beseeching cash from "mantalee," which was the nearest approach they could make to the honorable British title of "mandarin." The fort crowns an eminence overlooking the bay, and beneath, along the sea-shore, extends a long straggling suburb, which is connected with the town of Tinghae, situated about a mile and a half inland, by a paved causeway. It is a mean, dirty place, with inferior shops, surrounded by a wall, and containing at most 50,000 inhabitants. Passing through it, we entered the pleasant valley beyond; and observing a building in a wood surmounted by a cross, we decided that it was a Roman Catholic mission, and bent our steps thither accordingly.

A priest dressed in Chinese costume met us as we approached, and did the honors of the establishment with great simplicity and cordiality. He was the only European on the island, a Lazarist of the order of St. Vincent, and gave us some interesting details of his labors in Kiangsi, where he had resided for ten years. We inspected his industrial farm, cultivated by the boys of the school, a clean, chubby-looking set of little fellows, with happy, smiling countenances, very different in expression from that of Chinese youth generally. They evidently regarded their spiritual master with feelings of affection and gratitude. Many of them were waifs and strays whom he had picked out of byways and hedges, deserted by their parents on account of some physical infirmity. One was blind, another lame, another's arm and tongue were paralyzed. Generally, however, his pupils were the children of converts; the Roman Catholic system being rather to breed converts than to make them, an operation which is becoming daily more simple, as there are upward of half a million Roman Catholic Christians in the empire. Out of the entire population of Chusan, estimated at 200,000, the priest calculated that about 250 families were converts. Neither he nor his flock were in any way annoyed by the people, although jealously regarded by the authorities and literati. Still, no active hostility was exercised toward them; and, beyond being occasionally called upon to subscribe to pagodas, or take part in Buddhist ceremonies, they practiced their faith unmolested.

We afterward visited, with our reverend guide, a girl's hospital in the town, which did equal credit to his management with the rest of his establishment. He insisted upon acting as our cicerone over the island, and took us first to see the country residence of a rich Chinese proprietor. It was a good specimen of the ornamental taste of the country. Here were the usual summer-houses buried in rock-work, and approached by labyrinths tunneled through grottoes, or staircases winding through miniature mountains, and pavilions perched on islands in diminutive seas, connected with the main land by fragile bridges. Charming little baskets with mossy seats invited to repose in their cool shade, and gorgeous camellias and magnolias in full bloom flung a rich coloring of glowing tints over all.

After refreshing ourselves with numerous cups of tea of Chusan growth, which tasted a good deal like an infusion of straw, and the leaves of which looked as green as if they had been picked off the bushes the day before, we started off to the top of one of the highest hills in the neighborhood, so as to obtain as extensive a view as possible over the island before nightfall. From this elevated spot, at an elevation of 1200 or 1500 feet above the sea, we looked over fertile valleys teeming with life and rich in cultivation; and, throwing ourselves on the grass after our scramble, indulged in vain regrets, as our eyes wandered over the loveliness at our feet, at the infatuation which ever induced us to relinquish a spot not only so highly favored by nature in point of fertility and scenery, but possessing one of the finest harbors on the coast of China, a commercial position at the outlet of the Yang-tse-Kiang totally unrivaled, and political advantages of capabilities and situation such as no other spot upon the coast of China can boast.

The island is fifty-one miles in circumference. Fortunately, we had but little breath to expend in sighs; but, to judge from the headlong course we took to reach the bottom at the peril of our necks, the holy man who accompanied us must have suspected that despair was the cause of our recklessness; for on our arriving at the bottom, with impeded utterance and many compliments on Lord Elgin's activity, he went on to assure us that the population of Chusan preserved most flattering and agreeable reminiscences of British rule, and would receive us with open arms whenever we thought proper to resume possession; and then, to calm us, he led the way to a secluded nook in a deep valley, where a picturesque pagoda lay embowered in a dense grove of bamboo, impenetrable to noonday heats; and here we remained and drank more tea, supplied us by bonzes, till it was time to return on board, whither our kind guide accompanied us, and inspected for the first time in his life a few of the wonders of a British man-of-war.

Captain Osborn had sent on shore a party of men to examine the condition of the graves of those of our countrymen who lie buried in Chusan, and the following morning I went to see these melancholy records of this painful episode of the last war. A few hours had sufficed to clear away the rubbish which had been allowed to accumulate round them; the tomb-stones themselves were in good preservation, and the men were repainting those which had become partially effaced.

At midday we weighed from Tinghae, and, favored by lovely weather, passed through the intricate windings of the Chusan archipelago, past swelling islands indented with deep bays running back to rich fertile valleys terraced with cultivation, and through a narrow channel between beetling cliffs of gray weather-worn granite, where the sea surged into dark caverns, and murmured sullenly in deep fissures in the rocks. The scenery and climate reminded me of a former yachting experience among the sunny Grecian isles.

At sunset we dropped anchor in "the Sea of the Water-lilies," off the sacred island of Pootoo. We devoted a day to the examination of its holy mysteries. A broad paved causeway led us over the low shoulder of a hill into a lovely valley, where a pile of gray pagodas and temples, with upturned roofs of imperial yellow and walls of vermilion, were embosomed in foliage of the brightest green, and huge impending masses of rugged granite lay

The Temple of Kwang-yin, Pootoo.

scattered upon the steep hill-side above as though they had been glued upon it by some giant hand. A quaint gateway, covered with inscriptions, opened upon a maze of court-yards and a collection of sacred buildings, some especially erected to protect slabs of extreme antiquity inscribed with holy sentiments, others containing enormous bells, struck with a hammer swinging beside them instead of a clapper; others, and these were the largest and most numerous, filled with monster images of both sexes and all sizes, from the giant figure of Kwang-yin, the goddess of mercy, to whom the whole was dedicated, to a row of little gods three inches high. In the court-yards were sacred bronzes containing sacred fire, and overshadowed by sacred trees; and there was a sacred pond, full of sacred fishes, covered with the sacred lotus, and spanned by a single-arched bridge.

Every where groups of filthy bonzes were collected, basking half-naked in the sun, and inspecting their own tattered habiliments or those of their neighbors, chanting monotonous prayers, or wandering about telling their beads, crowding round me while I was sketching them, and staring vacantly through their blear eyes upon the strangers. Clad in ragged robes of gray serge, they infested the place like a description of vermin peculiar to it, wearing these ashy-colored vestments till they dropped off, appar-

Bonze at Pootoo.

ently ignorant of one use of water. Generally covered with cutaneous eruptions, they were, in all cases, pervaded by an atmosphere which rendered their proximity in the highest degree offensive. When we were entertained by the chief priest of the island on tea and preserves in a room of limited dimensions, crowded with these holy men, the odor of their sanctity became altogether unbearable. Our host himself was, however, an exception; he was a man cleanly in his appearance, of a mild and intelligent countenance, and robed in a stole of yellow. He told us that he was the spiritual superior of five hundred priests then on the island; that it was devoted entirely to religious purposes, no layman being allowed to reside upon it, but that a few nuns were numbered in the population. I should have been inclined to suppose that our authority considerably understated the number at five hundred, and, from the quantity of bonzes we saw, Mr. Williams' estimate of two thousand appeared more likely to be correct. That gentleman calculates the number of temples, shrines, and monasteries which are collected upon this little island at sixty. We were contented with rambling over the island, and entering five or six.

They all partook, more or less, of the same character, but varied in picturesqueness of situation: one perched upon a cliff, some 200 feet above the waves that broke at its base, contained shrines hewn out of the living rock, approached by narrow stairs which were tunneled through it; another was a massive pile of buildings built upon the hill-side, its spacious paved courts inclosed by carved balustrades, and reached by a series of broad flights of steps. In one temple, buried in a grove of camellia-trees, we surprised the whole priesthood in the refectory, sitting at long narrow tables, and shoveling rice into their capacious mouths with chopsticks. In another, a respectable-looking young man, who had made a pilgrimage of gratitude to the shrine of his choice, was having a private service for his special benefit, and was prostrating himself vehemently to the clashing of cymbals, the tooting of fifes, and the booming of tom-toms, while a venerable bonze chanted the thanks of the devotee to a wild-visaged deity with a protuberant gilt stomach. Every where the heavy perfume of incense mingled with the fouler odors of priests, and every where ponderous curtains and embroidered drapery concealed the same collection of burning joss-sticks and deformed divinities. Some of the temples were in a state of great decay, others were being repaired out of alms and subscriptions supplied by pious worshippers; for it is only fair to the holy men to say that if they neglect their own persons they are devoted in their attentions to the objects of their *culte*. It is said, however, that many of the members of the fraternity of Pootoo are criminals, who have sought refuge in this asylum, and atone for their past lives by a life of idleness and filth, superstition and celibacy.

Bonze Praying.

It was a relief to turn our backs upon these scenes, and, ascending to the highest point in the island, enjoy a sublimer worship in the grand temple of nature. On our way up the long flight of steps by which we reached a point 1200 feet above the sea-level, we passed numerous shrines where priests begged and pilgrims rested. In niches cut out of the bank devoted men passed their days in solitude, perpetually repeating the formula to which the whole island rings. Every building is covered with this one inscription, and every shaven inhabitant passes the greater part of each day in mumbling incessantly the pious invocation. All other ideas seemed merged into this one, which is embodied in a continuous sing-song chant of "Ometo Fuh, Ometo Buddhu." Men sit tapping little wooden bells, saying Ometo Fuh throughout the livelong day; and their particular haunt seemed to be the steps up the mountain. At last we passed them all, and standing on its highest peak, looked over the island-studded sea, with placid bays inclosed between long rocky promontories, and hamlets nestling in the woods on distant islands, and broad acres of cultivation extending far up the hill-sides, while our own little isle was carpeted with fields of flowering rape of the brightest yellow, dotted with groves and temples, intersected with broad stone causeways worn by the incessant tramp, for centuries past, of priest and pilgrim, and bearing marks of a venerable old age in its ruined shrines, gnarled old trees, hoary moss-grown rocks, and equally hoary occupants.

Leaving Pootoo, we crossed the muddy bay of Hang-chow to Chapoo, celebrated by a bloody but profitless victory during the last war. Once important as one of the termini of the grand canal (before that work was destroyed), it still retains some little mercantile position as the port of the populous and wealthy city of Hang-chow, and the only port on the coast open to trade from Japan. Four junks from those islands were now lying here. It is, however, worthless to us as a new port, partly because the harbor is exposed and shallow, and partly because Chapoo is connected with Shanghai by a canal, from which it is only about sixty miles distant. A low irregular range of hills border the alluvial plain on which the town is situated, and on their sides and summits forts have been erected. We landed and ascended one of these overlooking the compact walled city and the vast plain beyond, which extended in a blaze of variegated crops without an eminence higher than a pagoda, and with a land horizon stretching in one unbroken line for at least forty-five miles.

CHAPTER XIII.

Communication from the imperial Government.—Lord Elgin's Reply.—Sir John Bowring's Visit to the Peiho.—Course pursued on that Occasion.—Lord Elgin's Application for Gun-boats.—The Roman Catholic Mission of Siccaway.—System of Education.—Barren Results of Missionary Labors.—Superstitious Practices of Converts.—A "Feast of Tabernacles."—The Cathedral of Tonk-a-doo.—Difficulties attending Missionary Enterprise.—Non-arrival of the Admiral.—Departure of the Plenipotentiaries for the North.—The Miatou Straits.—Aground on a Sand-bank.—Arrival in the Gulf of Pechelee.—Dreary Weather.—An Expedition across the Bar.—Junk-hunting.—Arrival of the American Minister.—Difficulties of the Situation.—Unnecessary Delays.—Diplomatic Difficulties.—Aspect of the Forts.—Arrival of the Admiral.—The Dispatch-vessels cross the Bar.—Expiry of the Delay.—Postponement of Attack.—Political Consequences of the Delay.

The day after our arrival at Shanghai, Lord Elgin received from Pekin the reply of the imperial government to the dispatches which I had delivered for transmission at Soo-chow a month before. Although by the treaty of Nankin the right is secured to her majesty's representative in China to correspond direct with the highest imperial authority in the empire, the prime minister Yu, to whom the communications of his excellency had been addressed, did not condescend to respond, but instructed the authorities of the Two Kiangs to make a communication to the British plenipotentiary, in which, after adverting to the recent proceedings at Canton, it was stated that Yeh was in consequence degraded, and superseded by Hwang, who alone was authorized to manage the barbarian affairs at that city, whither we were enjoined to return, and at no other place. The prime minister went on to state that, "there being a particular sphere of duty allotted to every official on the establishment of the Celestial Empire, and the principle that between them and the foreigner there is no intercourse being one ever religiously adhered to by the servants of our government of China, it would not be proper for me to reply in person to the letter of the English minister. Let your excellency (the authorities of the Two Kiangs) therefore transmit to him all that I have said above, and his letter will no way be left unanswered."

This letter was returned to the authorities of the Two Kiangs as an unjustifiable disregard of that clause of the treaty of Nankin which states "that it is agreed that her Britannic majesty's chief high officer in China shall correspond with the Chinese high officers both in the capital and in the provinces, under the term 'communication.'"

Under these circumstances, Lord Elgin, after quoting the above clause in reply, states that it is his intention to "proceed at once to the north, in order that he may place himself in more direct communication with the high officers of the imperial government at the capital." As this was a measure which the embassador had always considered the most likely to be productive of successful results, so far as negotiation was concerned, he did not regret that the unwarrantable course taken by the prime minister rendered the step imperative. The French, Russian, and American ministers received communications more or less to the same effect, except that Count Poutiatine was directed to repair to the Amour instead of to Canton; and they all agreed with Lord Elgin that the proper, and, indeed, only course to be pursued was to appear with as little delay as possible with a sufficiently strong force at the mouth of the Peiho, to enforce that compliance with treaty obligations which the government so pertinaciously refused.

It was interesting, in connection with the determination thus arrived at by the allied plenipotentiaries, to refer to the document found in Yeh's yamun relating to the visit of Sir John Bowring, and Mr. Maclane, the United States Commissioner, to the Peiho in 1854. They too had endeavored, but with even less success, to communicate with the imperial government through the authorities of the Two Kiangs. Sir J. Bowring had been refused an audience altogether, and Mr. Maclane stopped at Kwan-shan, outside Soo-chow, as already described, and there remonstrated with on the impropriety of his proceeding to the north. At first Iliang, the governor general, seemed to think these remonstrances had proved effectual, but he afterward had misgivings on the subject; for, alluding to Sir John Bowring's complaint against Yeh for want of politeness, and the visit he threatens to the Peiho in consequence, he says: "It is, however, a standing device of the barbarians to make particular circumstances the plea of demands to be insisted on; whatever these chiefs may insinuate (or whisper) against Yeh-Ming-Chin, it is evident that Yeh-Ming-Chin is he whom they are used to fear. They say they are going to Tientsin. This may be, notwithstanding, an assertion made to compel acquiescence in their demands. Your slave has commanded them, with affectionate earnestness, to stay, and the ships of their chief have not as yet departed. Still, there is no certainty, so inconsistent and capricious is the barbarian character, that they will not after all sail north, and thereby attempt to constrain the imperial authority, and the high provincial authorities of the coast jurisdictions." To which the emperor replies that it is quite true that "it is the nature of barbarians to be cunning and malicious;" and he farther directs Iliang to inform them that "a force is assembled at Tientsin as the clouds in number"—all clearly showing how much the presence of foreigners was dreaded in the neighborhood of the capital, and how effectual, in all probability, any pressure applied there would be.

It was only to be regretted that this very expedition, to which the above papers refer, had gone to the north, and returned *re infecta*. This circumstance in itself was calculated to diminish the effect of another; and, indeed, as we afterward discovered, the same commissioners were sent to meet us at Takoo as had met the English and American commissioners on the former occasion, and no doubts seemed to have been entertained at head-quarters that they were endowed with a special faculty for dealing with barbarians, and that we should be as easily disposed of as our predecessors.

The decision in favor of an early move northward was arrived at on the 1st of April, the non-appearance of any imperial commissioner before the last day of March, the period appointed for the commencement of negotiations at Shanghai, having released the allied plenipotentiaries from their engagements upon this head. In view of this contingency, which Lord Elgin had before leaving Hong Kong anticipated as probable, he had, upon the 2d of March, addressed to the admiral a letter, stating that he was about to proceed to Shanghai, in the hope of meeting there a properly qualified plenipotentiary; but his lordship went on to say: "If I should be disappointed in this hope, it may be necessary, in pursuance of the policy prescribed by her majesty's government, to bring pressure to bear at some point near the capital. With a view to this contingency, I think it desirable that your excellency should collect at Shanghai, toward the end of March, or as soon after as may be convenient, as large a fleet, more especially of gun-boats drawing little water, as you can spare from service elsewhere."*

In reply to which communication the admiral states: " I beg to acquaint your excellency that for some time past my attention has been directed to this object. One of the gun-boats and one gun-vessel have already sailed for Shanghai, and arrangements are in progress for others to follow. It is my intention to sail for Shanghai in the 'Calcutta,' should nothing prevent, on or about the 16th instant." As a month had now elapsed since this letter was written, and every day was of importance, we were anxiously looking out for the first installment of gun-boats now due, as well as for the admiral himself, whose arrival was daily expected.

Meantime the weather at Shanghai was favorable for excursions, though the neighborhood presented few attractions of any interest. One day we took a walk of twelve miles to visit the Roman Catholic College and missionary establishment of Siccaway. The country is such a dead level that pedestrian exercise soon becomes wearisome. We followed narrow paths between fields of wheat, beans, and other cultivation reeking with high-flavored manure, but bearing, nevertheless, thin crops and abundance of weeds. The land in China, even in the elaborate cultivation of their kitchen-gardens, is never properly worked. The surface merely is scratched, and then deluged with strong manure. The consequence is that, though the young crops sometimes look green and promising, they seldom bear heavily.

The mission buildings are pleasantly situated on the banks of a small canal. We were received at the door by some priests, dressed, as usual, in Chinese costume, who conducted us over the establishment. We found the school-rooms full of noisy students, all swaying their bodies to and fro over their desks, and reciting their lessons to themselves in a loud monotonous chant, each apparently profoundly indifferent to the sharp tones which were ringing in his ears from his neighbor on either side. There were altogether eighty young men and boys in the several school-rooms, deep in the study of the classics and polite learning of the Chinese, for the system of the Roman Catholics consists not so much in imbuing the students with the dogmas of their own faith as in educating them to such a point in the literature of their

* Blue-Book, p. 223.

country as shall enable them to compete successfully with their fellows for the highest honors of the empire at the competitive examinations. By these means, if they do not gain converts, they secure to themselves protection in high places, and ever after have friends of the mammon of unrighteousness upon whom they can rely; for the tie formed between the student and his teacher at these establishments is not easily broken, and the kindness and toleration with which he has been treated by the Roman Catholics leaves, even in the mind of the stern Confucian, a strong impression in favor of that class to whom he owes his present greatness, and who, whatever their tenets, have, at all events in his own case, practiced some of the noblest maxims of the great philosopher. I was informed that the Roman Catholic missions could boast of converts even among the mandarins; while numerous instances of devotion and acts of private charity to the missionaries and their converts were related, both on the part of those Chinese who were members of the Church, and of those who had merely benefited from its institutions.

Notwithstanding, however, the system upon which Roman Catholic missionary enterprise is based in China, of conforming as much as possible to existing prejudices, and conciliating to the uttermost where it can not convince, I do not think that, even under the new treaty, or the most favorable conditions which can possibly be devised, its influence will ever be felt upon the governing classes. With the masses in almost all countries where it has been introduced at all, the Roman Catholic religion has been popular; but the emissaries of that plagiarist on their own philosopher, Mons. Auguste Comte, would have a greater chance of success among the literati of China than those of the Pope. I was informed by a high clerical Protestant authority that, out of the mass of Protestant converts hitherto made, there were only five whom he really believed to be sincere; and there is no reason to suppose that the proportion should be greater among the more intelligent of the Roman Catholics.

Among the ignorant and superstitious, doubtless many may possess a sort of mongrel belief; but their faith can not be worth much when it is obtained by conceding to them the permission to observe their own festivals, to worship at the graves of their ancestors, and go through all their own ceremonies of mourning, with the exception of burning joss-paper. At Chusan, indeed, our reverend friend told us that the converts often refused to take part in these ceremonies; but the fact that they should be permitted to do so, and still retain their Christian name and profession, is significant. The point is one which has caused a serious dissension between the Dominicans and Jesuits, the latter being in favor of the greatest latitude being given to the religious practices of the converts. The mission at Siccaway was almost entirely conducted by Jesuits. The best possible understanding evidently subsisted between them and their pupils, whose countenances all bore evidence of happiness and contentment. Notwithstanding the fact that twelve hours out of the twenty-four were devoted to work or religious exercises, the establishment was kept scrupulously clean; the dormitories were models of neatness; so that habits foreign to the Chinese domestic character were being instilled into the inmates. Some specimens of modeling in clay, by one of the elder students, gave promise of considerable talent as an artist.

The day of our visit to Siccaway happened to be a holiday in honor of the approach of spring—a Chinese "Feast of Tabernacles," and we met crowds in gala dresses, returning from the ceremonies which they had attended to propitiate the Ceres of the Celestial Empire. Numbers of bonzes in long gray robes were accompanied by soldiers in tall conical head-dresses, like red fool's-caps; and at one of the temples which we entered gongs were beating and worshipers prostrating themselves incessantly: perhaps some of them formed part of the crowd we saw no less reverently adoring the Virgin Mary on the following Sunday at the Cathedral at Tonk-a-doo. Here one side of the spacious area was filled by a large attendance of Chinese female converts, whose devout demeanor testified to their sincerity, and whose neat and occasionally handsome costume and pleasing countenances formed an agreeable contrast to the majority of the fair sex the stranger meets in a Chinese town, and of which, if he has no opportunity of seeing the better classes, he will probably form an unfavorable opinion.

The Cathedral is adorned with sacred pictures drawn in conformity with Chinese notions, though the shaven crowns and tails of the apostles, and small feet of the women, are startling to an Occidental eye; but the principal curiosity of the Cathedral is the organ, which has been constructed by Chinese mechanics, and the pipes of which are composed simply of the hollow bamboo of different sizes. The tones which it emitted, though powerful, were soft and melodious, except in some of the higher notes. There is a college attached to the Cathedral. The students here are all converts, and many of them were undergoing a course of preparation as native missionaries and catechists.

The efforts of the Protestant missionaries at Shanghai are devoted rather to the education of youth than the conversion of adults. Ningpo is regarded as the station at which their labors in this latter respect have been most satisfactory. At Shanghai, about 400 children are under Protestant instruction, but they are not, for the most part, taught English, and only the most rudimentary works in their own classics. Their education seems likely, therefore, to be of little service to them, either among their own countrymen or foreigners. It has been found at Hong Kong that a knowledge of English exposes youths to temptations, against which not even the principles they have, or ought to have imbibed, can protect them; and in too many instances the knowledge they have acquired only serves to increase their evil influence. In the American schools at Shanghai, however, English is taught; some of the girls in the schools of these latter missions, more especially, had attained a very extensive and sound knowledge of the language; and, so far as one could judge from their appearance, the most favorable results might be augured from the training they had undergone.

There is probably no country in which missionary enterprise is conducted under greater difficulties than in China, our isolated position, on the rim, as it were, of the empire, rendering it difficult for the missionaries to come into such close contact with the people as will enable them to acquire any lasting influence. A period of from two to three years after his arrival in the country is employed by the missionary in learning the language, which confines him to the particular districts in which the dialect is spoken, and which is not understood elsewhere. He is even then not able to settle away from those ports where the vices of the European population go far toward neutralizing his efforts. The Roman Catholic, on the other hand, does not remain above four or five months at a station before he is turned out upon the field of his labors and left to pick up the language as best he may, living with the Chinese, dressing as they do, and altogether identifying himself with those whom he seeks to influence. With the exception of Mr. Burn, comparatively few of our missionaries have followed this example. The opening of the country, however, by the new treaty, and the protection which it guarantees to Christian missionaries, will doubtless inaugurate a new era in evangelical enterprise.

On the 3d of April we received intelligence from the south that the admiral had postponed his departure for ten days. Though considerably embarrassed by this circumstance, Lord Elgin decided, in conjunction with Baron Gros, that it was expedient that the allied plenipotentiaries should proceed to the mouth of the Peiho, in accordance with the determination which had been so strongly expressed to the Chinese government, as any appearance of wavering at so critical a juncture would be liable to entail serious results. In order, however, as far as possible to carry out his original policy, his excellency took on himself the responsibility of requesting Sir Frederick Nicolson, then senior officer at Shanghai, to supply him with as large a naval force as could be spared from the station. The opportune arrival of the Highflyer, as relief of the Pique, enabled Sir F. Nicolson to accompany us himself to the north, and the Cormorant, dispatch gun-vessel, and Slaney, gun-boat, completed our little squadron. His excellency, before his departure, left a letter for the admiral, in which he states:* "I am most anxious for the arrival of the gun-boats drawing little water, which are referred to in your letter to me of the 2d ultimo, because I am confident that nothing will be so likely to bring the imperial government to terms as the appearance of vessels of war within the bar of the Peiho River. Such vessels will, moreover, be indispensable if it should be necessary to ascend that river to Tientsin."

At daylight on the morning of the 10th we left Shanghai with the Slaney in tow: the Russian steamer "Amerika," with Count Poutiatine on board, had left a day or two previously, and the Audacieuse and Minnesota were to follow immediately. Instructions were left with Captain Shadwell, of the Highflyer, to forward without delay any British man-of-war that might arrive at Shanghai.

We were favored with lovely weather up the Yellow Sea. The force of the northwest monsoon was apparently expended, and we were followed by light southerly gales. To these warm winds,

* Blue-Book, Earl of Elgin to Sir M. Seymour, 8th of April, 1858.

M

and the low temperature of the water in consequence of the melting of the winter snows, was doubtless to be attributed the haze that shrouded the horizon, and through which, on the morning of the 13th, loomed indistinctly the lofty promontory of Shantung, the easternmost point of China. After rounding the cape, we coasted along its northern shore, passing the port of Chee-foo, where we observed many junks at anchor in the distance. This town lies at the head of the bay of Ki-san-sen, and was entered by Lord Macartney by mistake for Teng-chow. A high rocky promontory, connected with the main land by a low sandy isthmus, terminates in a bold peak, rising to a height of 1130 feet above the sea; beyond this the shore is sandy, with a background of barren mountains. Altogether the scenery reminded me of some parts of the coast of Barbary, while the climate, on that day, was exactly that of the Mediterranean in early spring. Soon after, our experience destroyed any hope of this analogy lasting.

At 5 P.M. we sighted the large walled town of Teng-chow, one of the ports opened by the new treaty. The city is in the form of a parallelogram, and of considerable extent, the walls running along the sea-shore for upward of three miles. At the extreme right they terminate in a hill, crowned by a citadel and joss-house. The coast, however, does not afford any shelter at this point, nor did we see any junks at anchor off the town. The most available harbor for Teng-chow is situated in the Miatou group. These islands, immediately opposite the city, are separated from the main land by straits about four miles across; the largest and nearest is Chang-shan: it is seven miles long and three broad. Here, in all probability, will be established the future foreign settlement. It forms one side of a secure bay, in which we saw an enormous fleet of grain-junks at anchor. We were allowed some little leisure to make observations on the subject, as, while steaming rapidly through the straits, we suddenly grounded with considerable force upon a sand-bank at a spot where the chart gave nine fathoms of water. Our gun-boat in tow had acquired such impetus that she ran into our quarter, and lost her mizzen-mast before she could get clear of us. A tide running like a mill-race, and a strong northwest breeze, increased the difficulties of the situation; but by dint of getting all our heavy gear aft, going vigorously full speed astern, and making the men roll and jump the ship, at the expiration of an hour our exertions were rewarded with success. Although it was by this time dark, our indefatigable and skillful master, Mr. Court, carried us safely through the straits. As this gentleman had performed the northwest passage as the master of Sir Robert Maclure's ship "Investigator," his nerves had undergone a training which rendered them proof under all circumstances.

The province of Shantung, of which Teng-chow is the principal sea-board city, possesses the enviable notoriety in China of having produced its greatest philosopher, Confucius. Its most distinguishing feature is its lofty range of mountains, of which the highest, Tai-shan, is celebrated throughout the empire. Notwithstanding its mountainous character and barren aspect, Shantung alone contains a population equal to that of the United Kingdom, distributed over an area not exceeding that of England, Scotland, and Wales.

Daylight of the 14th of April found us plowing the muddy waters of the Gulf. Our soundings, which did not vary, gave us ten fathoms. In many respects the Gulf of Pechelee resembles the Sea of Azof, but its waters are not quite so green or thick. We observed numerous junks on their way to or from the mouth of the Peiho, and the varied character of their construction proved that many were from the ports of Manchouria, or perhaps even the Corea. Toward the afternoon it began to shoal, and this was the only indication that we had reached our destination. Nothing could be more dreary than the scene when the cry of four fathoms was followed by the order "Stop her!" which we were loth to construe into "Stop here." It was dreadful to contemplate the prospect of remaining permanently at anchor in so forlorn a spot. Not a sign of land broke the monotony of the dim hazy horizon. The turbid waters were lashed into foam by gales which spun round to every point on the compass with incredible velocity, and kept the gulf in the condition of a caldron of boiling pea-soup. Just as we were going to let go the anchor in despair, we descried through the misty atmosphere the little "Amerika" at anchor, and steamed off to her for consolation and company. Count Poutiatine had already communicated with the shore, and an opaque white-button mandarin had received a note which he had sent ashore notifying his arrival. The party had not landed, but a large crowd of spectators had collected on the shore to inspect them. Presents had afterward been sent off, which, however, the Russians had declined.

While communicating with the Amerika the Pique hove in sight; and as we found that, at the Amerika's anchorage, we should be aground at low-water, we weighed and anchored within half a mile of the frigate. At low tide we had twenty-two feet of water, the distance from the shore being somewhat over eight miles. As the coast of the province of Chili is very flat, the mud forts at the mouth of the Peiho were only visible from the deck of the Furious during brilliant sunsets, and on other rare occasions, which, however, for the first few days of our stay did not present themselves. Cutting northeast gales swept over the dreary waters of the Gulf, and whistled dolefully through the shrouds, ill preparing us to meet the sudden transition; blasts of hot air, charged with impalpable dust from the desert of Gobi, not only completely obscured the horizon, but cracked our lips, parched our throats, and insinuated itself into the innermost recesses of our clothing, or served as a general pepper to our food. Then would come another change of wind, and a pitiless rain; and the dust we had been anathematizing became visible as in muddy runnels it trickled down the rigging and sides of the funnels.

On the second day after our arrival in the Gulf the Cormorant made her appearance, and anchored near the bar. As Lord Elgin had not abandoned his intention of pushing up to Tientsin with as little delay as possible, the Slaney, Lieutenant Hoskins, was sent across the bar to capture a few empty junks, into which the Cormorant might discharge her coal and other dead-weight previous to trying the experiment of crossing.

I proceeded in the Slaney on this expedition, glad of the opportunity of obtaining a nearer view of the forts of which we had heard so much and knew so little. We found the bar to be about a mile wide, the channel marked by stakes, from which hung bunches of black net. At the top of high water (springs) there were upward of eleven feet of water at the shallowest part; and, as we afterward found, at dead neaps the depth was eighteen inches or two feet. There is, however, scarcely any inequality in the surface of the bottom. For a mile it is as flat as a billiard-table, and as hard.

Crowds of junks were entering the river like chickens running for shelter. Our appearance evidently caused no little sensation among them, which was not diminished when they saw one of their number suddenly boarded by a boat-load of barbarians, and her head put out to sea. Propelling the unwieldly craft with long poles, they accompanied their efforts to escape with a loud cry of alarm, which was taken up by each successive junk, until the sounds died away in the distance. However, we had no hostile intentions, and our wants were limited to four or five empty junks: two of these, capable of carrying a hundred or a hundred and fifty tons each, were dispatched to the Cormorant; the others were taken in tow by the Slaney, and were appropriated by the Pique and Furious, as likely to prove useful in our ascent of the river.

This expedition had led us right across the bar, and we pushed our reconnaissance to within a mile of the forts. We made out three forts on the south, and two on the north bank of the river. Innumerable banners fluttered from the parapets and embrasures, waving defiance; and an extensive crowd, probably of soldiers, were drawn up along the whole length of the batteries, watching, no doubt with no small wonderment, the evolutions of the little Slaney as she pounced upon her prey, and went puffing off over the bar in the wind's eye with a string of junks at her stern. Some of these junks were of a different construction from those we had been accustomed to see in the south; many of them had come across the Gulf from New-chwang with grain or beans, and some very possibly from the Corea. The crews at first were much alarmed, but upon discovering that our intentions were harmless, entirely recovered their equanimity; and when farther informed that they should be sent on shore, and receive a reasonable sum as the hire of their boats while they were employed, they seemed quite reconciled to the arrangement, and proved their confidence in us some time after by getting paid part of the junk-hire in advance, and then taking advantage of a dark night secretly to come and endeavor to abstract the junks from their moorings.

The next day two petty mandarins came on board, evidently on a tour of inspection, as they were not the bearers of any message; indeed, hitherto we had had no official communication with the shore. The arrival of the United States steamer Mississippi, with Mr. Reed on board, doubtless afforded these gentlemen fresh matter for speculation.

The Nimrod, Captain Dew, a dispatch gun-vessel of rather greater draught than the Cormorant, and which had been forwarded by Captain Shadwell, reached the anchorage on the 19th; but by this time the spring-tides had passed. It was considered impossible for the Nimrod, and a rash experiment for the Cormorant, to attempt the traject. Under these circumstances there was only one gun-boat available, and, although it was highly probable that at that period she might have passed the forts without being fired upon, still it was a risk which neither Lord Elgin nor Sir Frederick Nicolson felt justified in incurring. There was, therefore, no alternative but to await patiently the arrival of the admirals and a larger force—a necessity which ultimately compelled Lord Elgin to abandon entirely his original policy. It had been his hope, when he proceeded from Shanghai to the north, that at or about the time of his arrival in the Gulf of Pechelee, a force, especially of gun-boats drawing little water, would be collected there sufficiently large to enable him to approach the capital at once, and to conclude a peace at such a period of the year as would have admitted of his visiting Pekin before the hot season.

If this plan had been carried out, not only would many of the inconveniences I shall have to detail been avoided, but the difficult question of direct intercourse with the emperor would have been solved at a moment when there were unusual facilities for settling it satisfactorily. Unfortunately, this hope was not realized. In order to employ the time which elapsed before the arrival of the gun-boats, it was necessary to spend five weeks in temporizing at the mouth of the Peiho, during which time the Chinese authorities not unnaturally strengthened their defenses, and sent orders to the Braves in the neighborhood of Canton to harass us in our occupation of the city. A farther consequence of this delay was that, before the treaty of Tientsin was concluded, the thermometer was 96° in the shade—a state of things which, coupled with the urgent call from Hong Kong and Canton for the return of the force, rendered any advance on the capital highly inexpedient. Owing to this circumstance, it was left for the minister charged with the ratification of the treaty to solve the delicate questions involved in the reception of a British mission at Pekin.

Meanwhile our only excitement consisted in sounding and reconnoitring the mouth of the river. The result of our investigations only confirmed us in our original estimate of the insignificance of the forts, which were totally unprotected from attack from the rear, and, though formidable in their extent and display of banners, were little more than a line of mud batteries. During the five weeks which elapsed before they were attacked, hundreds of men were employed in strengthening and adding to them: we could observe guns of heavy calibre daily taking the places in the embrasures of the flaunting banners.

Sometimes sundry members of the mission would dispense with naval assistance upon these occasions, and one dark night, when three or four of us were navigating a very unseaworthy native craft, we were caught in a storm, and, more by good luck than good management, were picked up by the Slaney, and thus saved from prematurely making acquaintance with the forts of Takoo. It needed an occasional adventure of this sort to relieve the excessive monotony of our existence.

The arrival of Baron Gros on the 21st was the signal for renewed diplomatic action, and the four plenipotentiaries, being now assembled in the Gulf, decided on severally dispatching to the prime minister Yu, with whom they had already communicated through Soo-chow, another letter. Lord Elgin, in this dispatch to the prime minister, notified his arrival at the mouth of the Peiho, in pursuance of the intimation expressed in his letter from Shanghai of the 1st instant, of placing himself in more immediate communication with the high officers of the imperial government at the capital; and his excellency went on to say that he was "prepared to meet at Takoo, either on board of his own ship or on shore, a minister duly authorized by the Emperor of China to treat with him, and to settle by negotiation the several questions affecting the relations of Great Britain with China, which are detailed in a letter of the undersigned to the prime minister bearing date February 11.

"If, before the expiry of six days from the date of the present communication, a minister so accredited shall not have presented himself at Takoo, the undersigned will consider this pacific overture to have been rejected, and deem himself to be thenceforward at liberty to adopt such farther measures for enforcing the just claims of his government on that of China as he may think expedient."

Although Tientsin had been the point originally intended for negotiation, Lord Elgin was compelled, now that he found himself deprived of all certainty of ever reaching that place, to name Takoo.

On the 24th of April the Slaney towed in the boats of the four powers, their several flags floating gayly in the morning breeze. I accompanied Mr. Wade, who was charged with the delivery of the letter. As it was low water, we left the Slaney at the bar, and pulled into the river to a wooden causeway, which, crossing the mud flat from the centre fort, seemed to indicate the principal landing-place. Here we were received by a transparent blue-button mandarin, who apologized profusely for being obliged to refuse our request to land. So we received him into our boats, and delivered the letters to him. Meanwhile a large crowd, chiefly of soldiers, collected round us as spectators. They were fine-looking men, with a uniform consisting of an ample brown cape with a broad pink border, over long blue coats and trowsers. During the short while that the conference between Mr. Wade and the mandarin lasted in the boat, we were narrowly inspecting the "terrain" generally. Some of the brass pieces were of enormous calibre, but I could not count above fifty at this time. At the other end of the jetty to which we were moored a large blue tent had been pitched for the reception of sundry high officials who were expected. At that moment some of the Russians were on shore, having an audience with the treasurer of the province. We, however, had not insinuated ourselves so deeply into the good graces of the Chinese as our allies, whose neutral attitude naturally placed them on a different footing *vis-à-vis* the imperial government, which every day of delay enabled them to improve.

From this point the forts looked like a range of huge perigord pies, the flags rather aiding their resemblance to ornamented pastry. These banners were angular in shape, with a scalloped border, and white spots on a blue or yellow ground.

As we had at this time eighteen gun-boats in the China Seas, we were still sanguine enough to hope that, before the expiry of the term fixed in the above-mentioned letter to the prime minister, the two admirals would arrive in the Gulf, accompanied by a force of gun-boats sufficient, should that step prove necessary, to render the capture of the forts an easy operation. Great was our disappointment when, after beating back from our mission into the forts, we found the only accession to the squadron was the flag-ship Calcutta, but no gun-boat, or chance of any for some days. However, those energetic officers, Captains Dew and Saumarez, had satisfied themselves, after repeated inspections of the bar, that it would be possible to force the long-heeled craft they commanded across it. The Coromandel (admiral's tender), a paddle-wheel steamer, was also available for the same purpose; and the appearance, on the following day, of Admiral Rigault de Genouilly, accompanied by all his force, including three gun-boats, once more raised our hopes of getting speedily to Tientsin.

The arrival of these vessels convinced us that, so far as the monsoon was concerned, there existed no obstacle to the passage of our gun-boats along the coast. They had already weathered the Cape, and were now not surely incapable of following in the wake of the French. Indeed, had there been any chance of delay arising from this cause, it would probably have been mentioned when the gun-boats were first applied for. Inasmuch, however, as, notwithstanding their absence, the allied force had now become formidable, Lord Elgin lost no time in repeating to the admiral his opinion of the importance of a movement on Tientsin; and it was arranged that an attempt should be made at the first spring-tides to push the dispatch vessels over the bar; so that they might be in readiness, should the answer of the prime minister render necessary the capture of the forts on the 1st of May. On the 28th of April the first attempt was made, but the tide was not sufficiently high for our vessels, though some of the French gun-boats, which drew less water, succeeded in scraping over. On the following day, however, the Nimrod was forced over by her indefatigable commander, while the Cormorant ran past all the French gun-boats, and anchored within about 1500 yards of the forts. When this little squadron was joined by the Coromandel, we had seven men-of-war inside the bar.

On the 30th an extremely unsatisfactory communication was received from Tan, governor general of Chili, stating that he had, in conjunction with a mandarin named Tsung-lun, director general of granaries, and Wu, under secretary of the cabinet, been appointed commissioner to meet the foreign plenipotentiaries at Takoo, and enter upon negotiations. As he did not allude to the nature or extent of the powers with which he was invested, he was called upon to define them, and informed that, if they were not as full as those held by Lord Elgin, and specified in his former communications as required, he (the embassador) would regard his pacific overture for the appointment of a "duly qualified officer" as rejected. The reply to this letter was to the effect that the powers of Tan, Tsung, and Wu were limited to reporting our demands, etc., to the capital. The whole of this correspondence took place on the 30th. Under these circumstances, the only course left seemed to be to send in an ultimatum to Tan, stating that the plenipotentiaries had now placed the matter in the hands of the allied naval authorities.

As the 1st of May had been the day originally fixed as the expiry of the "*delai fatal*," the excitement became pretty general throughout the fleet on the 30th, more especially in consequence of a signal being made by the flag-ship for the small-arm men to hold themselves in readiness for landing. General orders were also issued by the admiral, containing the dispositions of attack. On the 1st, consequently, great were the preparations on board the Furious. Excited midshipmen, staggering under blankets, canteens, and havresacks, rushed frantically about the deck; the landing-parties had their rations served out, and were told off; the paddle-box-boats were lowered, and the guns put in them; and all were on the tiptoe of expectation until the afternoon, when it began to be whispered that a change had taken place in the views of the naval commander-in-chief, and that an attack on the forts was indefinitely postponed. This took all the world by surprise, as nothing had occurred which could explain this alteration of plan.

Thus a second time the policy which Lord Elgin had determined to carry out in his movement to the north sustained a check; on the first occasion, in consequence of the absence of gunboats to support him on his arrival in the Gulf, he had been compelled to invite a Chinese plenipotentiary to meet him at the mouth of the Peiho, instead of proceeding to some point nearer to the capital—a change of plan which was very injurious, because the mouth of the Peiho was the scene of the abortive negotiations of Sir John Bowring in 1854; and now again, when the Chinese plenipotentiaries had failed to produce their credentials within a fixed period, he was thwarted in his desire to foil their attempts at evasion by a rapid and immediate movement up the country. The consequences of these delays were serious in the extreme. In a military point of view they are graphically described in the admiral's dispatch of the 21st of May, upon the occasion of the taking of the forts three weeks afterward. "From the arrival of the embassadors on the 14th of April," says his excellency, "the Chinese have used every exertion to strengthen the forts at the entrance to the Peiho; earthworks, sand-bag batteries, and parapets for the heavy gingalls, have been erected on both sides for a distance of nearly a mile in length, upon which eighty-seven guns in position were visible; and the whole shore had been piled to oppose a landing." Politically they were even more disastrous, because, by obliging Lord Elgin to protract, at the mouth of the Peiho, negotiations which he clearly saw could lead to no good result, they gave to his proceedings a vacillating character, which was calculated to strengthen the self-confidence of the Chinese diplomatists.

CHAPTER XIV.

Perilous Position of Dispatch Gun-boats.—Strengthening of the Forts.—Arrival of Chinese Re-enforcements.—The Question of full Powers.—Anglo-American Visit to the Peiho in 1854.—Intercourse on that Occasion.—Interview with Tsung and Tan.—Memorial of Commissioners in 1854.—Reference to Pekin.—Contemptuous Treatment by the Chinese Government.—Anxiety as to future Movements.—Memorandum of Sir M. Seymour.—Communication with Tan.—The final Summons.—Insolence of the Garrison.

For the next three weeks our life in the Gulf was one of absolute inaction. This was the more trying, as the cool season was slipping rapidly past. The hot gusts came oftener, and in one week the thermometer rose from 42° to 74°. During all this time hundreds of grain-junks were passing into the mouth of the river, bearing the annual tribute of rice, on which Pekin is so entirely dependent. The interception of this grain-fleet had been one of Lord Elgin's principal objects in pushing northward early, and desiring to be accompanied by the gun-boats. It was impossible, however, to establish a blockade while negotiations ostensibly pacific were still in progress, and it was equally impossible to bring those negotiations to a close until the naval authorities announced that they were in a position to take the forts; because, if a state of hostilities had been produced before they were able to effect this object, the dispatch gun-boats, which were over the bar, and unable to recross it except at spring-tides, would obviously have been in a very perilous situation. Meanwhile Count Poutiatine had pushed his little steamer across the bar, and was living in the river and in daily communication with the Chinese. Mr. Reed, also, had frequent intercourse with the commissioners; and neither time nor opportunity were wanting to enable the neutral powers to exercise the blessed functions of the peacemaker.

There were now a sufficient number of ships inside the bar to induce us to pay them frequent visits, partly as a break to the monotony of our life, and partly to watch the progress of the fortifications and the arrival of Chinese re-enforcements. From the main-top of the Nimrod a most interesting bird's-eye view was obtained of the flat peninsula on which the forts were placed, and the steppe country stretching away to the horizon. Immediately beneath was the line of batteries, in which Chinamen were working like ants, happily thoughtless of throwing up any works in their rear, solely occupied in getting more guns into position, and strengthening the front face. These defenses were properly known as the forts of Tung-koo. Behind them the plain extended across the neck of the peninsula for about a mile, to the town of Takoo, situated on a bend of the river. Mandarins in state, officers on horseback, surrounded by their military retinue, Tartar couriers, soldiers, and camp-followers of all descriptions, were seen constantly passing across this plain; while here, for the first time in China, we saw carts drawn by horses or mules, generally tandem. In the town of Takoo, a pagoda or two marked the residence of the commissioners and the principal temples; while behind it, a line of trees denoted the course of the river, and furnished a green background refreshing to look upon.

On the north bank of the river, two square forts, built more in accordance with civilized ideas of fortification, were undergoing repair and armament, while in rear of them, upon the arid saltpans, a large camp, the tents scarcely distinguishable from the salt tumuli, betokened the arrival of an extensive body of troops from Pekin. A cavalry regiment forming part of this force was an attractive object of inspection. Near this camp another battery was in progress of erection, in a position which commanded a long reach of the river.

The masts of junks, forming a forest of dry sticks beyond Takoo, showed how thickly the river was packed with craft; while innumerable white sails dotted the horizon, and the clumsy hulls of others, which had reached their destination at low water, were imbedded in the vast expanse of mud which stretched out to seaward.

On the 6th of May the plenipotentiaries found themselves compelled to seek a new pretext for correspondence in order to gain time, and for that purpose reopened negotiations with Tan and Tsung. As the Chinese commissioners, when required to produce the proper credentials, were in the habit of declaring that it was not in accordance with the usages of the empire to grant to embassadors full powers similar to those conferred by European sovereigns on their representatives, Lord Elgin transmitted to them a copy of the full powers granted by the imperial government to Keying and Ilippo on the occasion of their treating with Sir Henry Pottinger, and intimated that he would be satisfied if they could procure from the emperor similar credentials for themselves. Their refusal to comply with this demand furnished additional evidence of the fact that they had not authority to settle the important questions pending between the two governments.

In order to a better appreciation of the peculiar conditions under which diplomatic relations in China are conducted, a perusal of the state papers discovered in Yeh's yamun, some of which have already appeared in the Blue-Book, and which are shortly to be published *in extenso*, by Mr. Wade, will be found very useful; those bearing upon the visit of Sir John Bowring and Mr. Maclane to the Peiho in 1854, and the circumstances incidental to it, were especially edifying and instructive to us, more particularly as the great bulk of the memorials were written by Tsung, the associate of Tan in the present commission. That functionary little dreamed that his most secret and confidential opinions upon the subject of the English barbarians were undergoing the closest scrutiny by those identical barbarians, at the period he was communicating with them in tones as conciliatory as was consistent with his hostile feelings. Certainly the circumstances under which we appeared off the Peiho were somewhat different to those under which it had been visited in 1854. Then the force was composed of one English and three American vessels, only one of which was inside the bar. Now there were upward of twenty men-of-war in the Gulf, of which nine were inside the bar; for an American steamer, as well as the Russian, had taken up her anchorage in the river. Then the foreign plenipotentiaries had manifested the strongest desire to be received in audience, and had visited the Chinese commissioners in the tent erected on shore for their accommodation. Now these latter had fixed two several days for interviews, and expressed their anxious readiness to receive the foreign plenipotentiaries; but their festive boards had been spread and their soldiers paraded in vain; instead of the plenipotentiaries they only saw Messrs. Wade, Lay, and some of the members of the staff, and so far forgot their dignity, in their anxiety to conciliate, that they entertained them officially. On the former occasion Drs. Medhurst and Parker had been received by two subordinates, Wan-kien and Shwanjin, whose memorials on the subject are in the highest degree amusing. This was pending the arrival of the imperial commissioner Tsung.

To judge from their account of the intractability of the barbarians, they must have undergone most trying experiences in their endeavors to carry out the emperor's injunctions "to discomfit their (the barbarians') deceit and arrogance, and foil their malicious sophistry." "There is no fathoming their (the barbarians') minds." They in one place despondingly remark, "Nor is it at all certain they are not covering a mischievous purpose, their real object being to find a pretext for misunderstanding with us." Most determined are the combats they seem to have had with the interpreters. "To judge by appearances, Medhurst is much the most crafty," they think; but elsewhere they exultingly exclaim, "your slaves lectured them upon the obligations of duty. Medhurst and Parker hung down their heads, having nothing to rejoin, and apologized for their error. They farther observed that, as a high officer was to be at Tientsin immediately, to look into the questions pending, there would now be peace between us, and (at this they were so delighted) that, though they should die, they should not care. They seemed greatly ashamed, and their language was most respectful."

Indeed considering how constantly Wan-kien and his colleague are " peremptorily enjoining" and "authoritatively commanding" the barbarians, they seem to produce but little effect; doubtless feeling the futility of their efforts, one of them, after suggesting that the governor general be sent to inquire into the matter, winds up in the following modest manner: "The opinion that is within the range of his stolidity, your slave, in the rashness of his ignorance, humbly declares; and, unequal to the excess of his trepidation, awaits your majesty's commands."

I had not the advantage of seeing Tsung. but those of our party who were received by that dignitary and Tan describe him as an ill-favored, suspicious-looking man, with a squint, who maintained a truculent silence throughout the short interview. Perhaps the following memorial which I have extracted from among Mr. Wade's translations of the same papers, will account for the evil eye with which he regarded us, while it is interesting, at the same time, as throwing much light upon the motives and modes of action of Chinese officials; it is supplementary to a long and very interesting memorial, in which he and his colleague describe their interviews with Sir John Bowring and Mr. Maclane, their peremptory refusal to listen to any of their demands, and the means by which, in their opinion, they can be induced to waive them. "Farther, they say, your slaves, having received your majesty's commands to administer barbarian business together, could they have so set the right before the barbarians as to prevent them going back from their engagements, would they have dared to trouble your sacred majesty with farther matter of thought, by the application which they respectfully make for a Celestial decision?

"The English barbarians are, however, full of insidious schemes, uncontrollably fierce and imperious. The American nation does no more than follow their direction. Every movement is the conception of the English. A perusal of the list of propositions presented by them shows that they are in general the views of a single self. They consist neither with right feeling nor principle. They have been mildly remonstrated with, but so crafty and slippery is their disposition that it is hard to set the right before them.

"Your slaves, having duly taken counsel together, have resolved to point out to them what articles in their paper admit of discussion; and for the discussion of these, whether important or otherwise, to refer them to one of the five open ports. The place to which they might prefer to proceed your slaves would report to the throne; high authorities in the province in which it lies receiving instructions from your majesty to consult together and make their disposition according to the particulars of the case, as ascertained by them on investigation, and to oblige the barbarians to return and abide the issue; to reject the rest of their propositions, one and all; and, on receipt of your majesty's approval of this course, to write them another letter for their instruction, and return them (*lit.*, throw back) their paper of articles. Should they be willfully perverse to take no notice of it, but to be more than ever active in preparing secretly for defense, and to wait spear in hand, with the right on our side and the wrong on theirs, it does not seem that they can have any thing to allege against us. It is the nature of the Mwan and I,* while they dread the strong, to

---

* *Note by Translator.*—The four barbarian races surrounding ancient China proper were the Mwan, the I, the Jung, and the Tih. The second is now almost generic for all races not Chinese.

insult the weak. Without some display of power, they will not, perhaps, be deterred from their purpose of prying and spying (*lit.*, their heart of spying will not be awed).

"It is proposed, in reply to them, to show a certain amount of indifference, thus to enhance the dignity of the state, and annihilate their treacherous projects. The barbarians are in no wise to be informed that the paper of propositions tendered by them has been laid before the throne. They were told, in the first instance, that it was taken away to be studied more carefully; that on any thing in it that might be of advantage to both sides, or in no way to the prejudice of either, your majesty's pleasure would, after due deliberation, be requested for them; that the remainder would be negatived, article by article, as being, from their offensiveness and impertinence, harmful and impracticable; and that the paper would be returned to them on the 18th. The barbarians have never been given to understand that a copy of it could have been submitted to your majesty for perusal. As in duty bound, they add this inclosure to the foregoing details."

There was no reason to suppose that Tsung, who adopted this tone with reference to barbarian affairs in 1854, had changed his mind in the interval, more especially as the policy he adopted on that occasion was eminently successful. He got rid of the barbarians, who were not more heard of until the "Arrow case" once more roused "these troublesome pests" into action.

Upon the above occasion the question of powers did not seem to arise, the commissioners untruthfully alleging not only that they were unable to entertain the demands of the barbarians, but even to refer them to Pekin. It appears, however, that they were so referred, and the emperor's decree on the subject was among our papers. Upon the occasion of our visit, they evidently wished it to be considered in the light of a concession that they offered to make reference to Pekin; but it was clear that this was a principle totally inadmissible, as being not merely inconsistent with the dignity of the powers represented on the occasion, but incompatible with the speedy or satisfactory progress of negotiations.

The practical inconvenience of treating with irresponsible functionaries is exemplified in a decree from the Council of State to Yeh, informing him of the proceedings of Sir John Bowring and Mr. Maclane in the north, in which they say: "They (the foreign plenipotentiaries) presented a number of requests; more than one of them objectionable, by reason of their unreasonableness and impertinence. We confidentially instructed Tsung-lun and his colleagues to disapprove and negative the whole of these, but to write a reply, promising, as it were of their own motion, that three of the questions—viz., the misunderstandings between the people and the barbarians, the arrears of duties at Shanghai, and the tea-duties in Kwang-tung, should, notwithstanding, be looked into and disposed of." This view of the subject was doubtless founded upon the opinion of Tsung-lun, as stated by him in one of his Memorials, in which he says: "Their (the foreign plenipotentiaries') object (was to obtain consideration of) the arrear of duties at Shanghai, the surcharge on the tea-duties at Canton, and trade up the Yang-tse-Kiang. The remaining articles were mere talk (or lies), to produce an effect." Our subsequent silence upon the subject for so long a period must have confirmed this opinion, while the Council of State, commenting upon the indignant departure of the squadron from the Gulf, sagaciously remarks, "They will go back to Kwang-tung—their averment that they will return home for instructions from their government being nothing more than another of their fictions." Then follow instructions to Yeh, that, when they get to Canton, he is to be as peremptory with them as Tsung-lun was. Above all, that "their proposition to trade up the Yang-tse-Kiang must be peremptorily negatived, nor must the barbarians be led to suppose that the idea was ever communicated to us."

With the advantage which these papers afforded him of an insight into the character of Chinese diplomacy, Lord Elgin was naturally desirous to avoid being entangled in this labyrinth of finesse and word-fencing; and the delays in the Gulf were doubly annoying to him, because they had a tendency to involve him in discussions of this nature.

Meantime the Chinese were daily gaining confidence; there was little doubt that they had now made up their minds to resist, and every day's delay was weakening our position morally. At one time it seemed probable that the whole force would leave the Gulf of Pechelee without accomplishing any object whatever.* The time was a most anxious one, for the plenipotentiaries considered that any such abandonment of the enterprise would tend

---

* The following men-of-war were at this time anchored in the Gulf:

to increase the arrogance of the court of Pekin, and perhaps compromise the safety of Europeans in other parts of the empire.

Finally, it was resolved that a movement up the Peiho, of a mixed hostile and diplomatic character, should take place, as described in the annexed memorandum of Sir M. Seymour, of the result of the conference held on board l'Audacieuse frigate, 18th of May, 1858.

"Proposed by the embassadors—

"To take the forts, and, in accordance with language held to

English.

	Guns.	Men.	
Calcutta	84	700	Anchored in Gulf of Pechelee.
Pique	40	270	do.
Furious, paddle steamer	8	220	do.
Nimrod, dispatch government vessel	6	120	Peiho.
Cormorant do.	6	98	do.
Surprise do.	6	98	Gulf of Pechelee.
Fury	8	160	do.
Slaney, gun-boat	5	48	
Leven, do.	5	48	
Bustard, do.	3	48	
Opossum	3	48	
Stanch	3	48	
Firm	3	48	
Coromandel, paddle steamer	5	44	Peiho.
Hesper, store-ship	0	54	
		2052	

French.

Nemesis, frigate	Gulf of Pechelee.
Audacieuse, frigate	do.
Primauguet, steam corvette	do.
Durance, store-ship	do.
Meurthe	do.
Phlegeton, steam corvette	do.
Mitraille, gun-boat	Peiho.
Fusée, gun-boat	do.
Avalanche, gun-boat	do.
Dragonne	do.
Renny, store-steamer	

American.

Minnesota, steam frigate	Gulf of Pechelee.
Mississippi, steam frigate	do.
Antelope, chartered steamer	Peiho.

Russian.

Amerika, paddle steamer	Peiho.

Tan, the Chinese high commissioner, to go nearer the capital to treat; to advance pacifically up the river with a view to meeting a plenipotentiary.

"It was remarked that the ministers of Russia and the United States would unite in this movement, after the capture of the forts.

"I stated that I was quite prepared to operate against the forts, and afterward advance the gun-boats in aid of the proposed movements up the river.

"The official authority requiring me to act is to be furnished by Lord Elgin."*

In keeping with this arrangement, a communication was addressed to Tan, in which the embassador stated that, the various delays accorded having expired without producing any satisfactory result, it had at last become necessary for him, in accordance with his expressed intention of "placing himself in more immediate communication with the high officers of the imperial government at the capital," to move "toward" Tientsin. "As a preliminary measure," his excellency goes on to state, "it will be requisite that the forts at the mouth of the Peiho be placed in the hands of the commanders-in-chief of the allied force. Their excellencies will signify the time within which the imperial troops will be called on to evacuate these works. The forts once in possession of the allied force, the undersigned will ascend the river, trusting that the imperial government will, without farther delay, admit the expediency of appointing a duly qualified representative to meet him."

On the 18th of May the plenipotentiaries and admirals met in conference, and it was finally arranged that the above summons should be sent in on the 20th; and that if the Chinese should decline accepting our offer of temporarily garrisoning their forts for them, force should be employed to obtain possession of them.

So at last, after five weeks of total inaction at anchor in one spot, there was some prospect of escape from a situation which was gradually becoming intolerable. During this period, which seemed an age, we had passed through every variety of temperature and every phase of sentiment. We had been hot and hopeful, cold and despondent, shrouded in fogs, beset with doubts, choked with sand and disgust, tempest and passion-tossed, becalm-

* *Vide* Blue-Book, page 306.

ed and torpid. We became wonderfully expert at games with rope quoits, and profoundly indifferent to sublunary affairs generally. News of the change of ministry at home, which arrived about this time, did not create nearly so much sensation as a present of fresh fish, for we were reduced to living on potted meats.

Information came from those in the river that the Chinese were working harder than ever in constructing stockades and abattis, that the camps were increasing in size, and the soldiers in bravado, insomuch that they hooted and waved flags at us jeeringly, wondering why we did not "come on:" all this was refreshing to the spirits of those who had become bloodthirsty, more especially the officers of the ships over the bar. The Nimrod and Cormorant had been quietly edged so close to the forts that, considering their escape was impossible, no other nation but the Chinese could have resisted the temptation of firing upon them; but in vain did their commanders watch for a little puff of white smoke which might have enabled them to cut the gordian knot which we in the Gulf had been so long endeavoring to unravel; in vain did parties of sportsmen look for snipe under the very guns of the batteries; the imperturbable garrison contented themselves with waving flags, well pleased to be allowed to play the part of the Earl of Chatham as long as we should continue to personify Sir-Richard Strachan.

CHAPTER XV.

The Night before the Attack.—Delivery of the Ultimatum.—The Signal of Attack.—Advance of the Cormorant.—The Nimrod hotly engaged.—Chinese Artillery-practice.—The Batteries stormed.—"Sauve qui peut."—Terrific Explosion.—Aspect of the Fortifications.—Attack of the northern Forts.—Capture of the last Battery.—A Visit to Tan's Residence.—Imperial Edict.—Fate of Tan.—His Account of the Action.—Tan's Yamun.—A Poem "in Memoriam."—Return to the Furious.

As if to compensate to us for all the delay and discomfort to which we had already been subjected during our stay in the Gulf, the climate for the last few days would have been a credit to the Mediterranean. The sky was cloudless, and fresh breezes from the seaward had driven the salt waves into the Gulf, and forced back the muddy waters of the Peiho, until that river indulged in the poetic license of "meandering level with its font."

On the 19th I crossed the bar at an early hour. The batteries maintained their usual aspect of repose. Here and there groups of soldiers were squatted round some big brass guns, or mandarins of rank with umbrella and banner bearers went their rounds; but as the day wore on they saw enough to rouse them to vigilance and activity. Six gun-boats came dancing merrily over the bar, each thronged with human beings, and forming a centre round which clustered a crowd of ships' boats, like chickens nestling under the maternal wing. Spasmodically puffing forth their six jets of white smoke, they steadily approached the awe-struck garrison, who, however, to do them justice, manifested no external signs of alarm. That even the hardy progeny of the soldiers of Genghis Khan should have felt some degree of trepidation at witnessing a phenomenon of this description for the first time was natural; but not only did they conceal their intimidation, but had the hardihood to send off a message through Count Poutiatine, inviting us to "come on." So we came on, and looked very pretty as we did so; the setting sun glancing on red coats and waving flags, and shedding its warm bright glow upon the devoted garrison, so many of whom were looking at it for the last time. These latter, however, probably not much given to sentiment at any time, were evidently more engrossed with the approaching foe than the departing day, and seemed to suspect that we were going to attack the same evening. Officers moved briskly about the batteries on horseback; the whole garrison stood to their guns, and turned out in a long and imposing line upon the glacis; but their prowess was not yet destined to be tried. The gun-boats came to an anchor at a long range from the forts; the garrison relapsed into quiet and security; the waves, so lately burnished gold, became polished silver as the rising moon tipped their crests, and the hoarse pant of the steam-engine was succeeded by the gruff chorus of the British sailor, who was too much excited by the prospect of "thrashing the fokees" on the morrow to go to sleep until he had exhausted his repertory of appropriate songs. At length the last barbarian strain died faintly away, and tar and Tartar were buried in profound repose.

At eight o'clock on the following morning, the English and French flag-captains, accompanied by Mr. Lay, landed under a flag of truce with the ultimatum, and an intimation that a delay of two hours would be accorded for the exchange of garrisons, as required in the ultimatum. These gentlemen were received by a petty mandarin near the blue tent, where a repast had every day been spread for the entertainment of any such barbarians of distinction as should honor the commissioners with a visit. To this official the ultimatum was handed, and the party retired. An interval of two hours then elapsed, at the expiry of which, as no farther communication was received from the forts, it was concluded that the authorities preferred their own garrison to the one proposed as a substitute, and had determined to abide by the consequences. At ten o'clock, therefore, the signal was hoisted for the ships to take up their respective positions.

The Cormorant, Mitraille, and Fusée had been told off to the attack of the two forts on the northern side, while the three forts on the southern bank, with their long connecting-line of sand-bag batteries, fell to the share of the Nimrod, Avalanche, and Dragonne. This apparently unequal distribution of French and English gun-boats, by which the former appeared to have monopolized an undue share in the operations was rendered necessary by the inefficiency of the French gun-boats for performing sundry functions for which our smaller class of gun-boats are alone adapted, and which we were compelled to do for them. Thus the Leven and Opossum were told off for French service throughout the day, and towed in their landing-parties. During the subsequent period of our residence at Tientsin our gun-boats were constantly employed on the French account, bringing up provisions, supplies, etc., and performing the entire river service for both squadrons.

To return to the signal of attack. Cameron and I had taken up our position for viewing the operations of the day on board the Nimrod. For a few moments before this signal was hoisted the river presented a most animated appearance. The advanced ship up the river was the Cormorant, letting off impatient puffs of steam, as she waited like a greyhound till the leash should be slipped, and she should be started to burst through the bamboo barrier which was stretched across the river, and run the gauntlet of the fire of forts to which she would be exposed before reaching her position. Immediately behind her lay the Nimrod, her decks cleared for action, the men at their guns, and every soul eagerly longing for the welcome order. Some distance astern of her were our own gun-boats, surrounded by their small fry, crowded with men, and the four large French gun-boats.

The signal flag had hardly reached the truck of the Slaney when the Cormorant darted off like an arrow; as her men were all lying flat on the deck, not a soul but her commander and two or three officers was to be seen on board. A moment had scarcely elapsed before Captain Saumarez had reason to congratulate himself on the wisdom of his precaution—puff, and a cloud of smoke like that of an exploded mine was followed by the whistle of a round-shot, then another, and another, till all three forts had opened on her in full chorus. But the Cormorant disdained reply; suddenly there was a shock, a tremor, and a start ahead—she had burst the barrier, composed of five seven-inch bamboo cables buoyed across the river. In a moment more she was in position, and, giving the batteries on the southern bank one gun by way of a recognition of the compliment they had paid her, she concentrated her tremendous fire on the northern forts, which were completely silenced in about eighteen minutes, at the expiry of which term the Fusée and Mitraille came up, too late, however, to participate in the bombardment.

Meantime the Nimrod had been no less alert, and, being already almost in position, opened incontinently a telling fire on the southern forts, thus diverting their attention from the Cormorant, and attracting their concentrated fire on herself. For about a quarter of an hour we held the distinguished post of engaging single-handed the whole three forts. Presently, however, the four French gun-boats, two of them on their way to support the Cormorant, and the other two (Avalanche and Dragonne) our supports, came slowly up; the strong tide and the narrow river considerably embarrassed the movements of these craft, which were of unwieldy construction and insufficient steam-power. However, when the Avalanche and Dragonne did get into position, just ahead of us, they did their work well, and for the next half hour we all three hammered away at the forts with great goodwill and pertinacity, the Tartars standing to their guns better than we anticipated. The shot for the most part passed over us, some of them flying as high as the top-gallant cross-tree. One went through the topsail yard, and we saw them bobbing in all directions into the river beyond us. The French gun-boats had poops; to this may no doubt be attributed the mortality among the officers; they lost no less than four killed, and only two men, if we exclude those killed afterward by an explosion.

The Nimrod was hulled in half a dozen places, but we had only one man killed and three wounded. The gingall fire was more telling than that of their large guns. The construction of a Chinese battery renders it a somewhat difficult matter to silence them effectually. Behind the gun is a bomb-proof chamber, containing the ammunition, and to which the men run for shelter. After the gun is discharged the gunners disappear into this retreat, and remain there until the enemy, having given the battery a benefit of shot and shell without reply, conclude it to be silenced; then the gunners stealthily emerge, and try, if possible, to load and fire the gun without being perceived, rushing back to their hiding-place immediately afterward. Of course, upon this system the firing can never be very rapid, but there is no reason why it should not last forever, unless the gun is disabled; to prevent this, they generally run it behind the solid earthwork after it is fired. By minute investigation with an opera-glass, we could often detect the gunners popping like rabbits out of a warren from the chamber into the battery, and then a shell, judiciously dropped among them, would shut up the gun for a quarter of an hour. As, however, there were 140 guns altogether in position, a good deal of firing went on notwithstanding.

A little before eleven, the admirals, followed by their fleet of gun-boats, passed up the river, receiving on their way a good many stray shots that passed over us. As the interest was now to be transferred to their operations, I went up with my companion to the main-top of the Nimrod, from whence we obtained a magnificent bird's-eye view of the scene. The batteries, with their active garrisons, lay immediately at our feet. We could see the gunners running in and out of their chambers, and working away like ants; and in the plain behind, a large crowd, probably a force in reserve, who, to their intense amazement, were favored with a shell or two immediately on our informing Captain Dew of their position and direction.

As the storming-parties landed within 300 yards of us, we could, from our elevated position, inspect their proceedings with great minuteness. The attention of the fort being concentrated upon the gun-boats in front of them, the garrison seemed unconscious of the fact that some hundreds of "barbarians" were landing just above them. Not knowing that our practice was to take batteries by assault, they were evidently taken completely by surprise: and as but a few yards of mud were to be traversed at that time of tide, the men were in the embrasures at once. In the late unfortunate attack, the distance of mud to be crossed was much greater, and the garrison doubtless fully expected that we should land and storm as we had done before, and were prepared accordingly. We saw the leading blue-jacket jump into the battery; an instantaneous panic spread itself like lightning along the line of batteries at our feet; and in the "sauve qui peut" which followed, some amusing scenes occurred, as Jack, at the top of his speed, dodged and chased the terrified soldiers, who, with outstretched arms and nimble legs, scattered in every direction. Here and there, one more courageous than his fellows would attempt to make a stand, or apparently disbelieve the report of a flying Tartar, who pointed to the rear and sped on with redoubled speed: but no sooner did the flash of the cutlass glance before his eye, than the bravest of them lost heart, and in ten minutes the whole garrison, together with the body in reserve, were scattered far and wide over the plain. Those who had a good start could afford to save their dignity, and walk composedly away; but the stragglers

Capture of the Peiho Forts.

Reception-tent of the Imperial Commissioners, Taku.

in rear fled as though demons were on their track, and for the most part fairly outran our gallant tars, whose wind was soon expended, and who were obliged at last to content themselves with stray shots at their light-heeled foe. After a race of this description their aim was somewhat wild, and I saw a marine aim with great deliberation at a man whom he had almost succeeded in running down, at a distance of about five yards, and miss him.

We now lost no time in landing ourselves, and were soon exploring the batteries and the plain behind. We met the marines and blue-jackets coming back from their chase, and the few corpses I observed on the field and in the batteries confirmed me in the impression that the Chinese loss had been comparatively trifling, probably not above 200 in all, including those killed on the north bank. There can be no doubt that, if it had been desired, we might, by sending a force round to the village of Takoo, have cut off their retreat, and caught the whole garrison in a trap from which they could not possibly have escaped.

We were the first to make an inroad upon the oranges and pomegranates which formed part of the repast spread out for our (pacific) entertainment in the blue tent, through the canvas of which two or three round-shot had let in daylight. Then we proceeded to pull down the Chinese banners, and demolishing-parties were set to work to upset the guns and dismantle the fortifications. We found them to be more solidly constructed than we had supposed, the three forts being composed of square blocks of stone masonry, the sea front faced with earth; they were about twelve feet in height, and ascended from the rear by a broad flight of stone steps.

While standing near the base of one of these, which we had just been investigating, and which was now filled with Frenchmen, we were startled by an explosion so close as to make us involuntarily retreat some yards, and inexpressibly shocked by the sight which met our eyes. A crowd of French sailors rushed wounded and panic-stricken out of the falling buildings; some of them, tortured beyond endurance by the horrible agony, threw themselves headlong over the glacis into the ditch at the base. One of these wretched sufferers I observed scramble out upon the opposite bank after rolling in the muddy pool, and, though blackened to a degree which gave him more the appearance of a cinder than a man, shout with characteristic vivacity, "Vive l'Empereur! Vive la France!" as he feebly waved his cap over his head. But those who first rushed out were only the less injured; the severely wounded were now being carried down from the fort by their comrades, and the objects were so painfully disfigured, and, as they writhed and groaned with agony, presented so heart-rending an appearance, that, as we were only in the way, we hurried from the spot; nor could I banish the scene from my memory for some time afterward. The French admiral was close by as this tragical event happened, and every assistance was instantly rendered to the sufferers, in spite of which, out of about forty who were more or less severely injured, the majority never recovered.

This incident cooled the ardor of our investigations into the fortifications. We had indeed been over the entire length of the works, and were amazed at the calibre and exquisite finish of some of the brass guns. The sand-bag battery which connected the forts had been well constructed, and had afforded sufficient shelter to enable the gunners to annoy us considerably. Numbers of beautifully-made rockets were piled up in different directions, and bags of powder lay scattered about. Some good canister-shot was lying about, as well as hollow 8-inch. There were also several English guns in the batteries. A battery of 200 gingalls, all laid close together in line, each about ten feet long, and carrying a pound ball, looked like a gigantic "infernal machine," and, properly worked, makes doubtless a formidable defense. Camps were situated behind the forts, and looting-parties rummaging out the tents for swords, etc., etc., every now and then unearthed a Chinaman. One of our own men, who had foolishly dressed himself in some of the clothes he had discovered, was unhappily shot by mistake for one of the enemy.

As it was not yet midday, and we still heard firing round the bend of the river, we were anxious to push up, if possible, to Takoo, and were glad to take advantage of the gun-boat Firm, which was dispatched to the front for the purpose of collecting wounded. On our way we observed some stranded fire-rafts, which were still burning, having been towed on shore. An attempt had also been made to send down some lighted junks, filled with straw, which fortunately proved abortive.

As we passed the northern forts, and saw the flanking fire to which they had been exposed from the Cormorant's heavy guns, we did not wonder at the rapidity with which they were evacuated—our landing-parties, under Captains Sir Frederick Nicolson, Sherard Osborn, and Commander Cresswell, together with the French landing-party, having entered them without opposition. After the usual amount of tricolors, etc., had been stuck up, the French crossed over to the left bank, and the men of the Pique. Furious, and Surprise followed the garrison of the forts, who were in full retreat upon two intrenched camps, one of which contained the cavalry force already alluded to. These camps were situated close to the river, and were protected in that direction by a formidable battery, which commanded the entire length of the reach. The shore-party, advancing over a flat salt plain, were covered on their left flank by the Bustard, Opossum, and Stanch, which were exposed to the whole fire of the battery as they advanced up the reach. A sharp engagement followed between these three little gun-boats and the battery, in which they lost two killed and five wounded; but upon the landing-party coming up at the double, and taking them in flank, the panic usual in such cases was followed by an utter rout, and the assailants, whose attention was particularly directed to the flying cavalry, only succeeded in knocking over a few of them as they fled across the open.

This episode had just terminated when we arrived. Each camp contained about twenty-five field-pieces, 6-pounders, four heavy brass guns throwing 68-pound shot, and a dozen iron guns of a new construction, on capital carriages, throwing an 18-pound ball. There was computed to have been about a thousand men in each battery, with abundance of admirable gingalls. We now moved up to Takoo, where a barrier of junks moored right across the river, debarred our farther progress. A battery of eighteen field-pieces, which was deserted as we approached, flanked this barrier, and so we immediately landed and took possession of it. Just behind this battery was the village of Takoo, the houses of one story, built of mud, and divided by narrow streets, and in every respect similar to a fellah village on the banks of the Nile. A crowd of people had collected about fifty yards distant, conscious, apparently, that we should not mistake them for soldiers, and watched our proceedings with great coolness and interest.

We were enabled to communicate with them through Mr. Wade, who now arrived, together with some others of our party. In answer to our inquiry, they informed us that the joss-house in the neighborhood had been the residence of the Imperial Commissioner Tan, so we immediately decided on paying it a visit. We were accompanied by several villagers, who appeared so perfectly friendly that three or four blue-jackets formed our only escort. On our way we found the headless trunk of a man lying across the path, who, the villagers informed us, had been beheaded in the morning for running away. We soon broke open the doors of the joss-house, proved to be the Hai-chin-Miao, or Temple of the Sea-God (the same at which Lord Macartney visited the Governor of the province), and were received by some priests, who not unnaturally betrayed a little nervous agitation. We assured them we only wished to ransack Tan's private room for papers. We discovered none, however, of any importance; though, from the confusion in which we found his apartments, he had evidently left in a hurry. A mandarin officer of some importance, who had committed suicide by cutting his throat, was also found in the house. We afterward discovered that this was Tehkwei, the acting commandant at the defense of the forts. The following extract from the *Pekin Gazette*, showing how the government of China deal with their officers who are guilty of failure, will prove that this unhappy mandarin only anticipated his destiny by a few months:

"The Prince of Hwui and others have, in concert with the Board of Punishments, presented a memorial setting forth the penalties they find the laws to award to the different officers whom we had directed them to try for the loss of the port of Tientsing. The following officers already degraded—namely, Chang Tien-yuen, commander-in-chief of the Chinese army of Chih-li, Tanien, acting as general-in-command of the Tien-tsing division of the same, and Tehkwei, acting commandant of Takoo, had been directed by T'an Ting-siang to occupy and defend the forts at Takoo, on the north and south banks of the river; Fulehtunt'ai, lieutenant general of Bannermen, had encamped at Chung-páu, in rear and in support of Chang Tien-yuen and the rest. When the barbarians opened fire they made every effort to keep them off, striking and wounding four barbarian ships, and killing several barbarian soldiers; notwithstanding which, all the forts and all the guns were taken. Certainly, their offense is without excuse! Let Fulehtunt'ai, Chang Tien-yuen, and Tanien, who, according to the award, should properly be decapitated, be imprisoned until after the autumn, and then put to death."

As our intercourse with Tan terminated shortly after, in a note from that fuctionary announcing the appointment of his successors, we may not inappropriately take leave of him, now that we have completed the search of his premises. In the same Pekin Gazette we find the following punishment awarded to him: "T'an Ting-siang, already degraded from the office of Governor General of Chih-li, has been found not guilty of cowardice and desertion; but, in that his operations were without plan or resource, his offense is no less without excuse. Let him be banished to the frontier,* there to redeem his guilt by his exertions."

Poor Tan was the victim of circumstances over which he certainly had no control, and it seems hard that his government should refuse him full powers in the first instance, and then punish him for the inevitable consequence of his being without them.

The tendency of which our own government has been accused —of rewarding incapacity—renders its service sufficiently discouraging to meritorious officers; but even it must be preferable to one which unrelentingly visits misfortune with disgrace.

Although we did not find any papers of political importance in the residence of Tan, the following account of the memorial he addressed to the emperor on the loss of Takoo, if true, furnishes an amusing illustration of the desperate falsehoods to which his unhappy servants are compelled to resort in hope of averting the imperial displeasure. The subjoined letter was received by Mr. Lay, on his arrival at Tientsin, from a Chinese correspondent in the city, who doubtless hoped to curry favor with the barbarians by sending them information; it must therefore be taken *cum grano:*

"Tan tells the emperor in his memorial respecting the loss of Takoo that he gained a great victory the day before" (by the day before is meant the 20th, or day of the capture), "and destroyed several barbarian ships. That the capture of the forts was attributable to a circumstance which it was not in his power to control. An unusually high tide on the day in question, and a sudden rush of water from the Gulf, swept away the southeast battery, and any defense of the place was rendered impossible. Long before your admiral reached Tientsin, Tan had fled, and with him every soldier and brave. The magistrate is the only one who remained in the city. Before the fight at Takoo the emperor issued two edicts to

* The confines of Siberia, on the far west of the Chinese dominions.

Tan, desiring him to accede to your demands so far as ports were concerned. Tan, however, did not dare to show these edicts, because they contained the word 'barbarian,' and he was afraid that the sight of the objectionable expression would only incense you. He therefore determined upon risking a trial of strength. The emperor is going to appoint Toh-mingah to treat with you. He does not appoint Sang-ko-lin-sin, because of his warlike disposition. Our high officers dread a personal meeting with your embassadors; they think they would be made prisoners, as was Yeh."

Such, according to popular gossip, was Tan's mode of accounting for his defeat at Takoo. It is highly probable that the imperial edicts above spoken of actually did exist, although Tan had evidently had time to carry off all his political documents. A

The "Temple of the Sea-God" (Residence of Tan at Takoo).

poem, however—translated, I believe, by one of the gentlemen attached to the American legation—was afterward discovered, which rouses our sympathies in behalf of the unhappy mandarin, and which I have thought worthy of insertion for the benefit of those who deny the existence in the Chinese bosom of the sentiment of domestic affection:

A POEM "IN MEMORIAM."—RETURN TO THE FURIOUS.

TRANSLATION OF A POEM in *Memoriam* of Tan's wife. Found in his room at Takoo. (The characters of black velvet, each on the representation of a Chinese fruit. In couplets of four characters each.)

Right hand.
"In the Mé* bowered window the spring is mild."

Left hand.
"In the lan† bordered pathway the breezes are fragrant."

[The following twe-lien, or scrolls, on blue and white silk, are funeral tributes to the virtues of a distinguished lady, presented by mourning relatives; blue and white being the appropriate colors of mourning.]

"Combining the qualities of Tan and Ki,‡ the Vermilion Pencil has honored her with a title.
Uniting the graces of Ha and Chang, the Scarlet Tube§ has published her excellence.
Possessing high rank of imperial bestowment, favor rested on her door-posts, and abundant grace upon her household.
Decorated with an imperial distinction, her virtues were published through her native district, and diffused the reputation of her worth.
With a stimulant made of bears' gall exciting the studies (of her son), her excellent example is worthy of imitation.
Clad in ivory-adorned vestments, she has gone to worship the True (one); and her benevolent countenance, where shall we look for it?
Having taught her son to respect her example and hold fast the classics, she saw him pluck with his own hand the sprig of the qué-hwá.∥
Having aided her husband to display his virtues, her gentle influence flowed over her kindred, and she long commanded the hearts of her relations."

Our search was soon concluded, and as the day was now advanced, and the enemy had become invisible, we thought it time to return to the Furious.

In the evening the second division moved up, embarked in our own gun-boats, supported by Captain Dew (of the Nimrod), to the line of junks moored abreast of the Takoo joss-house.

* Mé (pronounced *may*) is the name of a kind of plum indigenous to China.
† Lan is the designation of a bulbous flowering plant of ravishing sweetness. It is the *Aglaia odorata* of botanists.
‡ Tan and Ki were women famed for their virtues. Ha and Chang were ladies celebrated for their accomplishments.
§ Vermilion Pencil and Scarlet Tube are identical figures denoting the emperor.
∥ The qué-hwá, or què flower, is the *Olea fragrans*, the blossom of which yields a rich perfume. This plant is accepted as the emblem of the degree Kin-jin, equivalent to our M.A.; and plucking a sprig of the qué-hwá is, therefore, equivalent to attaining his second literary degree.

CHAPTER XVI.

Ascent of the River.—A Crowd of Junks.—Astonishment of Population.—Their submissive Behavior.—Brilliant Bonfires.—A Steppe Country.—Appearance of the Villages.—Difficulties of Navigation.—First View of Tientsin.—A Deputation of Merchants.—Appointment of imperial Commissioners.—The Plenipotentiaries ascend the Peiho.—Approach to Tientsin.—Dense Crowds.—"The Temple of Supreme Felicity."—View of the River.—Making ourselves comfortable.—Bedrooms in the Temple.—Farther Exploration of the Peiho.—Arrival of Russian and American Ministers.—Their Abodes.—Pean.—Arrival of the imperial Commissioners.—Full Powers at last.—Our official Procession.—"The Temple of the Oceanic Influences."—Interview with the Commissioners.—Exchange of full Powers.—Abrupt Termination of the Interview.—Arrival of the Kwang-Fang.—Kweiliang.—Hwashana.—Success of Lord Elgin's Policy.—Its Bearing on Affairs at Canton.—Brighter Prospects.

THE day following the capture of the forts was devoted to repose after our exertions. On the 22d, however, a report reached our distant anchorage, to which I had returned, that the allied admirals had decided on moving up the river. It had originally been arranged that they should be accompanied in the first instance by the plenipotentiaries; but, as it was now understood that the presence of the representatives of all four powers—two of whom were neutrals—might rather prove an encumbrance than otherwise, Lord Elgin expressed his readiness to await the admirals' pleasure on the subject, anxious to avoid any act which might embarrass the naval authorities in the unlikely event of their being induced, by a very active opposition, to exchange their pacific for a warlike attitude. I was, however, permitted to accompany the force upon this occasion, and found quarters on board the Opossum, with my old friend Commander Colin Campbell.

On my way I landed at the North Fort to inspect a gigantic brass gun captured by the Cormorant, and also to explore the scene of desolation for which her guns were responsible. These forts were even more substantially constructed than those on the south side, but upon no known principle of fortification. The consequence was a terrible slaughter to the exposed garrison, twenty-nine of whom had been counted lying round their guns in one battery. The commandant of the fort had not yet been buried, and was lying at the door of his room, a round-shot having struck him just as he was emerging from it. Every building was riddled, and shells, entering from the exposed rear, had burst inside the bomb-proof chambers, so that the garrison was little to be blamed for only waiting a quarter of an hour in so warm a locality. The Cormorant moved up, the next morning, to the barrier, through which an opening had been made to permit the egress of the junks, which were being cleared out of the river by the admirals' and advanced gun-boats.

The villagers of Takoo now came boldly down to the water's edge and communicated with us, and we amused ourselves and the populace by driving a donkey tandem through the narrow streets.

About midday the Opossum was ready to start for the front, but the passage through the junk barrier seemed an impossibility. Temple Bar on a wet day never looked more hopelessly crowded to a gentleman in a hansom anxious to catch a train, than did the junk barrier to us, anxious to overtake the admiral. At last we dashed at it in despair, and by a miracle of steering, which created a panic among the crews of the junks, who were all running into each other—crushing, jamming, and shouting at the same moment—succeeded in squeezing safely through. The breadth of the river at this point was not more than that of the Thames at Richmond. Its banks were thickly fringed by long reeds, behind the waving tops of which salt-pans extended as far as the eye could reach, covered with conical tumuli of varied dimensions. Borne onward by a strong flood tide, we swept round the sharp angles with which the river abounds throughout the whole length of its tortuous course from Tientsin, and soon found ourselves between banks of a more cheerful character. The gaunt reed had given place to the more profitable holcus, or Barbadoes millet, fields of which, bordered by willows, and neatly fenced in the neighborhood of the villages, imparted quite a civilized air to the country.

In two hours we arrived at the reach in which the admirals were at anchor with five gun-boats, and in company with them went quietly along, feeling our way with no little interest and curiosity, up waters for the first time plowed by a foreign keel. Toward evening the mud villages became more numerous: their entire populations turned out as the leading gun-boats passed, and saluted them with profound and reverential obeisances, then squatted in a long blue line upon the river's bank, and gazed in awestruck wonderment as our ardent little craft, defying wind and tide, puffed steadily along, a slight commotion under her stern being the only external evidence to the Celestial eye of the demon that was propelling her. Our progress was in some measure retarded by the necessity which existed of clearing all the junks out of the river as we advanced, lest, in so narrow a stream, the authorities might order them to be sunk behind us, with the view of catching us in a trap. Although, doubtless, this was a very proper precaution, it was perfectly evident, from the panic which our appearance created, that no real danger was to be apprehended on this score, and that, so far from wishing to entrap us, they would be only too glad to get rid of us. The villagers were clearly under the impression that we were on our way to upset the dynasty. I accompanied Captain Hall and Mr. Lay to the shore, when the latter gentleman had some communication with the people. It invariably commenced, however, with a request that we should come and reign over them. "Hail, O king!" they shouted, as we approached; "welcome, great king! be thou our emperor; come thou and reign over us!" Then they would protest with the greatest earnestness their intention immediately to comply with the order to clear out their junks, and offer provisions of all sorts, refusing to receive money; this latter piece of politeness arising from dread of their own authorities, and the rest of their civility being based upon the alarm inspired by ourselves, and a prudent desire to propitiate the incoming dynasty. When asked to procure beef or other provisions not easy to get, they would urgently plead the difficulty of obtaining any, but submissively conclude by saying, "However, since you, the great king, command, we must obey." Meantime, when the junks did not clear out fast enough, we cut their cables, sending whole fleets of them occasionally pell-mell down the river.

But we were not content with marking our track by these floating evidences of our progress; our advance was heralded by huge bonfires, which were made of stacks of millet straw, their position upon the margin of the river rendering them too available for fire-rafts to make it wise to leave them behind us, to be floated up with the flood tide on the first dark night. As night closed in, the lurid glare cast by these huge conflagrations over the sky doubtless carried terror into the hearts of mandarin and peasant, while upon ourselves the effect was no less solemn and impressive. A broad belt of light shed its glowing lustre upon a grove of large trees, illuminating its sombre recesses, but throwing into gloom yet deeper by contrast those which were still in shade. The thick foliage flushed for a moment, then crackled and withered up under the scorching heat, leaving the scarred and naked branch like a maimed limb extended toward the blaze. The river eddied and rippled in the ruddy light, and the gunboats, with every spar and rope vividly distinct, seemed anchored in a sheet of flame.

Our day's work was over. We had reached a point about twenty miles from the mouth of the river not only without molestation, but with every demonstration of good-will on the part of the inhabitants; and I went to bed, encouraged by the hope that, as this absence of hostilities seemed likely to continue, we might still succeed with our force of nine allied gun-boats, then anchored at or near the spot, in reaching Tientsin.

On the following morning we had another most convincing and satisfactory proof of the anxiety of the enemy (if such they could be called under the circumstances) to avoid us. On going up to the fore-top of the Opossum, I observed encamped on the plain, at a distance of about a mile and a half, a large body of cavalry, estimated at about a thousand by Captain Osborn, who, in company with Sir Frederick Nicolson, was in the Bustard and Stanch, leading gun-boats. They threw a round shot or two among them, on which they speedily decamped. They were, in all probability, the same cavalry which had retreated on the capture of the forts. We were detained a few hours this morning for the French Admiral, who had got aground a short distance astern of us; and, in the mean time, I inspected the surrounding country through a glass. It reminded me in many respects of the south of Russia. The only trees visible were those which marked the course of the Peiho; and, indeed, inasmuch as in whatever direction one turned, the river was always in sight, the trees which wooded it were sufficient to wood the landscape as well. Throughout its whole course to Tientsin I observed no stream or canal of any note entering it. The country stretched away to the horizon a dry brown steppe, and across it, in labyrinthine twists and most eccentric windings, the Peiho finds its way to the sea, watering at least twice the extent of country which it would traverse did it flow in a straight line. The banks are composed of clay and sand, and I scarcely remember to have seen a stone either at Tientsin or on the way there.

Not far from our anchorage there was a large village. On the dusty main road to it there passed a considerable traffic—covered carts and donkey tandems predominated. One large wagon drawn by six or eight horses, going at full trot, and crowded with passengers, appeared to be a stage-wagon. I also observed wheelbarrows—a man being in the shafts and a donkey leading. Sometimes these carry passengers, the occupants sitting back to back, as in an open Irish car, on each side of the single huge wheel which works in the middle, between them. I was particularly struck with the neatness of construction of the solid mud cottages of which the villages are composed. The angles are all sharply finished, the gables adorned with ornamental moulding, the overhanging eaves of an excellently thatched roof neatly trimmed, and rising out of it a respectable solid pair of chimneys. Circular brick-kilns, like watch-towers, here and there dotted the landscape, as bricks are occasionally used for joss-houses and the superior order of residences.

Hedges, fences, and mud walls divided the fields near the riverbank, but away from the possibility of navigation the country looked barren and uncultivated; primitive docks with mud dams contained junks undergoing repair or in process of construction; and the tapering masts of these craft were visible in all directions, as they were anchored in different bends of the river. Now we could make out the smoke of our leading gun-boats to the right, now to the left, now in front, now almost behind us, so interminable and intricate seemed the windings of the stream. Fortunately, our only difficulty lay in getting some of the larger craft round the sharp turns; of water there was always abundance in mid-channel, the soundings never giving less than two fathoms, and sometimes as much as seven. The French gun-boats especially were constantly sticking on the sharp angles, their length and want of power rendering it a difficult operation to steer them in a narrow river with a strong tide running. Occasionally the Coromandel shared the same fate; but, by getting out hawsers to the shore, she was hauled into the stream; and the villagers coming to the rescue in a strong body, and tugging away cheerfully at the ropes, facilitated the task considerably. Still we did not make so much progress as on the previous day, having accomplished probably ten or twelve miles.

Upon several occasions official messengers, with the buttons of petty mandarins, were observed waving on the shore, and making signs of their desire to communicate with us. Only once, however, was this attended to, and the messenger turned out to be the emissary of the magistrate of the district, who expressed a wish to hold intercourse with us; the admiral, however, very properly refused to incur any delay, or open communications with any one until he arrived at Tientsin.

The next day our advance was not more rapid; indeed we were left behind by the admiral and advanced gun-boats, in consequence of being attached to the Fusée, a heavy French craft that stood in need of much pulling and hauling at the corners. It is worthy of note that all our eighty and sixty horse-power gun-boats traversed the river without the slightest difficulty, subsequently making the passage in eight hours; and even the Cormorant dispatch gun-vessel got up to Tientsin from Takoo in about twelve hours.

We passed in the course of the day a barrier of junks, which, however, were soon sent floating down the stream, and offered no material impediment to our advance. On the 26th we reached a point within a mile and a half of Tientsin, the country as we advanced having become more thickly populated, the banks more richly cultivated, and the river itself more crowded with junks. From the mast-head of the Opossum the gates and pagodas of the city were distinctly visible. It was reported that the Bustard and Stanch had actually reached the suburb, and as the achievement had thus been successfully completed, the Opossum was sent back to the Gulf with the news, and I had the satisfaction of reporting to Lord Elgin, by midnight of the same day, the gratifying intelligence of the fortunate issue of the expedition.

The admirals did in effect reach Tientsin within a few hours afterward, and Admiral Seymour was immediately waited upon by a deputation of leading merchants and gentry. These people being impressed with the absurd notion that our real object, in pursuing a vigorous policy in China, was an extension of our commercial relations with it, immediately offered to trade with the gun-boats then at Tientsin, in spite, they themselves averred, of the opposition of their government, and requested the admiral to send in a list of the merchandise he wished to dispose of, together with their prices; and, in consideration of his finding a ready market, they went on to express a hope that he would spare the town. Mr. Lay informed these gentlemen that we desired not trade, but commissioners, and that, if these did not speedily make their appearance, he feared the town would be destroyed; upon which the deputation stated that they would themselves proceed to Pekin, and knock without ceasing at the imperial palace; and they guaranteed that by their importunity they would obtain commissioners, and hoped that in the mean time their august excellencies, then in the river, would be satisfied with abundance of beef and provisions, upon which numbers of oxen were incontinently brought to the bank and sacrificed as peace-offerings.

. . . .

During my absence the Sampson had arrived from Hong Kong with the Woodcock and Kestrel, forty-horse-power gun-boats, in tow, and having on board a company of Royal Engineers 105 strong.

On the following morning Mr. Bruce proceeded up the river to make arrangements for the reception of the embassador, and on the 29th news was received from him that these were completed, and that no obstacle remained to impede the immediate progress of the allied plenipotentiaries.

On the same day another and more important communication was received, the last with which we were favored from our old friends Tan, Tsung, and Wu. It inclosed, without comment, a copy of the following imperial decree: "We command Kweiliang, Chief Secretary of State, and Hwashana, President of the Board of Civil Office, to go by post-route to the port of Tientsin, for the investigation and dispatch of business. Respect this."

The fact that this document emanated from the court immediately on the report reaching Pekin of the arrival of our gun-boats at Tientsin not only thoroughly bore out the view of the plenipotentiaries in the estimate they had formed of the probable effects of the policy they had pursued hitherto, but served as a most complete justification of that policy, inasmuch as the imperial government, by at once superseding Tan & Company, tacitly acknowledged their mismanagement of affairs, and, by the appointment of two new commissioners, gave a fresh proof of their desire to settle matters amicably. With any other nation one would have supposed that the capture of the forts at the mouth of one of its rivers, and its subsequent ascent by a hostile force, would have called forth a warlike demonstration instead of a civil commission.

The Chinese differ, however, from other nations, and fortunately the plenipotentiaries appreciated the distinction. This news, of course, rendered their immediate departure for Tientsin more than ever imperative, and it was therefore arranged that Lord Elgin and Baron Gros should proceed up the river the same evening. As it was discovered at the last moment that the French gun-boat appropriated to Baron Gros's use was unable to ascend the river from defective machinery, his excellency and staff accompanied the English mission in the Slaney. A lovely moon lighted up the windings of our watery path, and tempted us to remain on deck till a late hour; and as we swept rapidly past grove and hamlet, we regarded with wonder, in the pale clear gleam of that midnight hour, all the evidences of a population as tranquil and unsuspecting of danger as though the thunder of barbarian guns had never fallen on their ears, or as if their countrymen flying before the barbarian bayonet was a sight devoid of all significance.

Yet scarce a week had elapsed since the fortifications these poor peasantry had gazed on wonderingly as impregnable fortresses had been leveled with the ground, and an army, in their eyes invincible, had been scattered to the winds. Now the pant of the steam-engine mingled with their dreams, but was powerless to keep them awake; and so thoroughly was this mutual confidence established, that a solitary gun-boat, in the dead of night, was fearlessly threading its way through an enemy's country, along the narrow and devious river which formed the high road to the capital, the mysteries of which, a week before, were unknown to the foreigner; and on board that lonely bark which now traversed it for almost the first time were the embassadors of the two greatest powers in the world, forcing their way into the heart of a country containing 300,000,000 inhabitants, in defiance of the will of the government, as expressed by an overt act of hostility only a few days before. Probably no British minister ever performed a journey in the country to which he was accredited under such anomalous circumstances as those which attended the one upon which Lord Elgin was now engaged; not even Lords Macartney and Amherst, when in the same capacity they ascended this same river in Chinese junks, and inscribed themselves as "tribute bearers" on the flags which floated from their mast-heads.

Daylight found us in the suburbs of Tientsin, the first aspect of which, as approached from the east, is most remarkable; enormous stacks of salt, numbering from two to three hundred, line the banks of the river for some hundreds of yards below the town; these stacks vary in length from two hundred to six hundred feet, and average about a hundred in breadth; they are twenty or thirty feet in height, shaped like the rounded top of a carrier's wagon, and covered with matting, or thatched with millet straw, the salt being stacked in bags. Passing these, we arrived at a bridge of boats, which connected one of the suburbs with the city, and which was opened to let us through. The river now flows between banks ten or twelve feet high, and densely populated; the mud houses were packed closely on either side, and their occupants still more compactly wedged, not only down to the water's edge, but into it up to their waists, in order to gaze at their ease on the phenomenon before them. Thus an oblique plane of upturned faces and bare heads extended almost from the surface of the water to the eaves of the houses; and up to the last day of our residence the banks were always more or less crowded with spectators watching the movements of the barbarians. A long straight reach extends from below the bridge of boats to the point of the junction of the river and the grand canal, which enters the Peiho at right angles from the southward, and here terminates its extended course of about 600 miles.

Directly facing us, as we steamed up this reach, past a line of our own gun-boats, which were anchored in it, was a picturesque line of buildings, abreast of which the allied admirals were moored. This fragile and somewhat fantastic construction suggested the notion of a summer palace. We were informed that as such it had, in fact, served the Emperor Kien-lung, in honor of which happy event it had been invested by imperial patent with the title of "The Temple of Supreme Felicity," under which auspicious designation it was now about to serve as our abode.

We were soon clambering up the steep bank, finding some difficulty in freeing ourselves from the services which were officiously pressed upon us by the Chinamen who crowded it, and who, thrusting forth helping hands, seemed anxious to show us every mark of civility. We found, when we stood within the walls which inclosed our future residence, that it was not belied by its external aspect. As is generally the case in China, it served the double purpose of a temple and a palace, though it had not been honored with the imperial presence since the Emperor Kien-lung had made it his temporary abode.

Upon the top of the wall, which was only separated from the edge of the river-bank by a narrow pathway, were two large apartments of light and graceful construction, surrounded by verandas elaborately carved, in which depended monster horn lanterns, gaudily painted, as transparent as ground glass, and decorated with innumerable tassels and silken hangings. The Chinese have carried the art of fabricating these lanterns to great perfection. They first soften the horn by the application of a very high degree of moist heat, and then extend it into thin laminæ of any shape, either flat or globular. The walls of these rooms were composed of paper pasted upon the wooden trellis-work; the sliding panels into which it was divided were made to answer the purpose of windows. When they were all shut, however, the paper was so transparent that there was plenty of light, and on a sunny day the glare was unpleasant. These two buildings were thirty or forty yards apart, and connected by a veranda which ran along the top of the wall, and terminated in two quaint little kiosks, their upturned roofs supported by carved posts. These apartments were appropriated by Baron Gros and Lord Elgin; that occupied by the latter being perched upon an artificial mound, laid out in true Chinese taste, and ascended by steps of ornamental rock-work. Overhanging the river, they commanded an extensive and ever-interesting view: below them, a dozen English and French gun-boats, some of them moored within pleasant conversational distance, imparted a satisfactory sense of security to the position.

Not a single native craft, except an occasional ferry-boat, rippled the surface of the stream or reposed upon its waters. What a metamorphosis had been wrought in a few hours by the magic devil-ships from the West! We were not able to appreciate it, but to the Chinese the change must have been startling and significant. We learn from the accounts of the embassies of Lords

Macartney and Amherst how active the river life at Tientsin was in their day. "We crossed a bridge over the river," says the historian of Lord Amherst's mission, "the surface of which was scarcely visible from junks;" and again, "I counted 200 spectators on one junk, and these vessels were innumerable." The spectators were as numerous as ever, but their posts of observation were no longer junks. People and houses completed the view from these windows—a part of the city wall, one of the gates, and some pagodas, appearing at no great distance to the right.

The *personnel* of the two missions were accommodated in the temple, and other buildings all inclosed within one outer wall. A partition wall, however, divided us from our allies. They occupied a number of detached summer-houses, dotted about a garden. We established ourselves in the innermost recesses of the temple, our bedrooms furnished with sacred pigs and bronzes, in which smouldered eternal fire (until we came and allowed it to go out); our slumbers presided over by grim deities with enormous stom-

A Bedroom at Tientsin.

achs, or many-armed goddesses, with heads encircled in a blaze of golden or rather brass flame. The perfume of incense still clung to these sacred purlieus. Would it had been the only odor to which our nostrils were subjected! Now began the process commonly known as "shaking down" into our quarters: altars were turned into wash-hand-stands; looking-glasses were supported against little gods; tables, chairs, and beds were indented for upon certain venerable citizens, who had been appointed by the authorities to attend to our wants. Doubtless they must have wondered much at many of our demands, and some of them—as, for instance, tubs—they never succeeded in satisfying.

Servants with a white badge, emblem of an armistice, attached to their coats, waited assiduously upon us, perpetually presenting us with little cups of tea; indeed, for the first few days a man was always walking about with a teapot, ready at the shortest notice to refresh the thirsty soul. The tables with which we were supplied were solidly constructed and well carved, square in shape, as Chinese tables always are. A red cloth, elaborately embroidered, served as a table-cloth, and, falling to the ground in front, concealed the legs of the table. The high-backed uncomfortable chairs were similarly decorated, gorgeous enough to look upon, but very disagreeable to use. Some of us erected our musquito-curtains over square wooden ottomans; others slept upon a brick platform, generally used in China, and which in cold weather is heated by fires from beneath, after the manner of an oven—an unhealthy style of bed-place at all times, it should seem, for in summer the damp is apt to strike through the bricks, and in winter, when they are not only dry, but heated, a semi-baking process must be more or less prejudicial.

In front of the temple was a square court-yard which was partially shaded by the spreading arms of a fine old tree; however, we thought nature required a little assistance; so the whole court was matted in, which not only added to the picturesque effect of our abode, and enabled those of us with vivid imaginations to fancy themselves in Italy, but was of a most practical utility in reducing the temperature, when mind and matter were both in danger of being melted entirely away. A raised flagged passage intersected this court, and on each side of it was a quaint little kiosk, the roof separated by four carved pillars, also elaborately carved, brilliantly colored, and surmounted with dragons' heads, rampant fish, and other devices. In one of these a marble slab was erected vertically upon an elevated stone platform, and was covered with

P

Chinese characters, alleged to have been traced by the hand of the Emperor Kien-lung, and to embody a high moral sentiment.

The building on the opposite side of the court-yard was formed into the guard-house, the guard being usually composed of engineers and marines, and numbering upward of a hundred men. Attached to this building were the servants' offices, and behind them the stables. Our establishment was thus very complete; and it was not without a feeling of regret that I saw it dismantled, preparatory to its restoration for the rites of paganism, when, after having occupied it for upward of a month, we looked back upon it for the last time.

As it had been deemed not impossible that it might be necessary to advance at some future period nearer to the capital, the admiral had been induced to push two of the gun-boats on an exploratory expedition still farther up the Peiho. One of these, the Kestrel, was of the smallest class, and, drawing only five feet water, was well adapted for the service. At a distance of about ten miles, however, above Tientsin, even this draught proved too much, and she was compelled to return, having solved the problem that, unless considerably lightened, and not with certainty even then, the ascent of the Peiho to Toong-chow would be impracticable for our gun-boats at that season of the year. From the high-water marks on the river-banks, however, there can be little doubt that at certain periods of the year the Peiho would be navigable for all classes of our gun-boats. She reported the character of the river-banks above Tientsin to be unchanged.

On the afternoon of the day of our arrival, Count Poutiatine and Mr. Reed arrived together in the Russian steamer "Amerika," and immediately issued a proclamation stating that their visit to Tientsin was altogether of a pacific character. The attitude they found themselves thus compelled to assume was not without its inconveniences as compared with ours; for, although exact in the payment of our just debts, we insisted upon all our reasonable wants being promptly and satisfactorily supplied. Thus we had at once appropriated the most convenient and respectable residence we could find; but our neutral allies had some difficulty in renting a house on shore: the proprietor (doubtless a good deal puzzled as to the relation of might and right in his view of the state of matters generally) made a novel proposition in the shape of an offer of 6000 dollars if they would *not rent* it. This, however, was declined, the difficulty somehow or other overcome and a handsome rent for the short space of one month was ultimately pressed upon the reluctant owner. To judge from the appearance of the mansion, he was a rich man. Mr. Reed lived in a charming retreat with a Levantine air about it; a court-yard with flowers and fountains, and ponds full of gold-fish was surrounded by cool, airy apartments with paper walls, and verandas and balconies overhanging the river. Count Poutiatine lived next door—a strip of intervening building which was impregnable from without, and consecrated to the use of the female portion of the Chinese owner's establishment, alone separating him from his colleague.

This residence was on the right bank of the river, and within view of our yamun, though distant from it about half a mile. Ere long the flags of our respective nations, waving proudly in the breeze, signified to the Chinese world of Tientsin the distinctive abodes of the chiefs of the four barbarian hordes who had thus boldly located themselves in their city.

In a country which abounded with horses and roads, it was not to be supposed that persons of an exploratory tendency were to be satisfied with pedestrian excursions; we therefore sent in a requisition for a certain number of steeds, and, after some delay, were furnished with what appeared the scum of the stables of Tientsin. These were indignantly rejected, and we ultimately obtained six very respectable ponies, and six very uncomfortable Chinese saddles, very hard and angular, and garnished with extensive drapery, and an awkward bolster-shaped protuberance in front. To these uncouth contrivances, however, we ultimately became accustomed; and I had minutely explored the country round Tientsin within a radius of about six miles before we left it.

Intelligence now reached us of the near approach of the commissioners, and Mr. Lay received a note from his friends who had formed the deputation on the day of the admiral's arrival, calling his attention to the fact of their prompt nomination as a proof that their promise had been fulfilled. This news was confirmed on the following day (2d of June) by the prefect of the city, Pean, who came to pay us a visit, ostensibly to see that our wants were supplied, and inform us of the proximity of the commissioners, but really to investigate the barbarian character, and acquire importance in the eyes of the commissioners by the fact of his having had personal intercourse with us—a proceeding the dangers of which he would no doubt discant upon, as also the wonderful talent he displayed in "soothing" our "uncontrollable fierceness."

In consequence, probably, of his own representations of his qualifications for the office, he was afterward appointed one of the subordinates in carrying on negotiations, and proved to be a self-sufficient ambitious "intriguant:" his dishonesty, however, was so transparent, and his general bearing so offensive, that he soon became as obnoxious to his own superiors as he was to us. Upon this occasion of his first interview his manner was one of fawning servility, while his aspect and gestures were so effeminate that the description of one of our party, who called him "a large flirt," was most appropriate. Notwithstanding an immense deal of insinuating giggle and coquetry, he failed in his principal object of seeing Lord Elgin, and returned very little wiser than when he came.

On the afternoon of the same day I was taking a ride with Fitz Roy, making trial of our ponies and of the road to Pekin for the first time, when a cortége, preceded by a cloud of dust, indicated the approach of some grand personages. Presently appeared runners with rods of office, corresponding to javelin-men: these cleared the way, and forced the people to the right and left; then followed two stately chairs, each borne by eight stalwart bearers, containing two of the most elevated dignitaries in the realm. The common people at once brought themselves up to the attitude "attention," the hands being pressed on the outside of the thigh, and the body maintained erect and motionless. We could scarcely make out the features of the inmates through the small window of the chair, across which was stretched fine gauze; but, though in all probability we were the first barbarians they had ever set eyes upon, they gazed, with all the imperturbability of Chinese dignity, impassively in front of them, their countenances manifesting neither curiosity, alarm, surprise, or any emotion whatever. Immediately behind was a dense and dusty crowd of footmen and horsemen, evidently coming off a journey, and, though many of them were handsomely appareled, and were doubtless officials of some rank, they looked worn and travel-stained. A number of excellent well-built covered baggage-wagons, drawn by four or six large fat mules, completed the procession, which was evidently one not of display, but of serious earnest.

On the following day, our conjecture that we had witnessed the entry of the commissioners was confirmed by the communication they addressed to Lord Elgin, in which, after styling themselves imperial commissioners and ministers, they announced their arrival with full powers, and fixed the day after for an interview. In answer to this communication the embassador informed the commissioners that, although the nature of their powers was not described in their letter, still, inasmuch as they appeared, according to the title by which they announced themselves, to be invested with authority corresponding to that conferred upon him as the plenipotentiary minister of his sovereign, he would make no objection to meet the commissioners at the hour they named, "to the end that, by an exchange of powers, all doubt may be removed as to the sincerity of an intention on both sides to terminate existing differences by peaceful negotiation."

It did, indeed, seem to augur favorably that the term "Minister bearing full powers" should have been used, as upon no former occasion had a Chinese functionary been invested with this title, and all previous demands for a commissioner so named had met with a decided refusal. It was consequently arranged that the interview should take place in a temple dedicated to the "Oceanic Influences." This building was situated in the middle of a plain at some distance from the town, and upward of three miles from our yamun. The midday sun had now become so powerful that it was considered expedient, for the sake of the soldiers forming the guard, that the ceremony should be postponed until late in the afternoon.

At 3 P.M. on the following day we left the yamun, the thermometer then standing at 133° in the sun. The procession was composed of the embassador and suite, in twelve chairs, accompanied by a guard of honor of 150 marines, preceded by the band of the Calcutta. Lord Elgin's chair was of the description usually employed by mandarins of the highest rank, much larger than the ordinary size, surmounted by a brass knob, and borne by eight bearers. To avoid a long detour, the chairs were sent round to meet us, and we crossed the river in boats. As usual, a dense crowd lined the river-banks, evincing the most eager interest and curiosity. Upon the guard presenting arms, the band striking up "God save the Queen," and the procession forming and commencing to move, this was converted into excitement; nor, indeed, was it to be wondered at that an event altogether unprecedented, and of so striking and novel a character, should create some sensation. A procession of 200 Chinamen marching down the Strand armed with spears, and bows and arrows, or gigantic matchlocks, with their own tails reaching to their heels, and squirrel tails adorning their conical caps, with dragon-emblazoned breasts, and trowsers and sleeves of equal dimensions—surrounding chairs of state containing obese dignitaries, with peacocks' feathers and red balls on their head, would probably attract a crowd; and should this crowd have become strongly impressed with the belief that in this outlandish procession they were gazing upon specimens of the race into whose hands the government of the country was about to pass, their countenance would betray a more than ordinary interest. But the effect, even then, upon an English mob would not be so great as that which our appearance was calculated to create, inasmuch as Chinamen do occasionally perambulate the streets of London, and this type of countenance and peculiarity of costume is familiar to every child who is fond of picture-books. But in a country where an "Illustrated Pekin News" does not exist, and the Chinese costume is popularly supposed to be the only dress known in the world at large, the appearance of our red-coated marines and cocked-hat diplomates must have been sufficiently startling.

Our way for nearly two miles led through the extensive suburb which surrounds Tientsin in almost every direction—the winding streets choked with people, who only allowed a narrow lane for the passage of the procession, and who bobbed as each successive chair passed down to the level of the window, so as to have a good view of the inmate.

Sedan Chair.

The most perfect order and silence was maintained throughout, and every sign of outward respect shown in the demeanor of the people, whose heads were uncovered and tails let down: the latter only, however, is the usual Chinese mark of respect. The shops were all shut; but our confined position in chairs, added to the intense heat, which rendered the task of observation irksome, and the dense crowd which confined its range, prevented our doing more on this occasion than obtaining a cursory impression of the surrounding scene. At last we emerged from the labyrinth of streets we had been threading, and found ourselves on a vast open plain, and in the distance observed the group of buildings, situated upon a slight eminence, and in an isolated position, which was our destination. The intervening distance was thickly dotted with human beings, reminding one of the Epsom Downs on a Derby day.

As we approached the building, the sounds of shrill pipe and tom-tom fell upon the ear, and mingled with the martial sounds of our band. A feeble intimation was made to Major Boyle, commanding the marines, that he was not to enter the gate of the court with the guard. This, however, he very properly disregarded, and soon the discordant music emitted by half a dozen blind performers, who stood at the door, and played probably the same air with which Lord Macartney had been honored, of "subjugation perfected," was completely drowned in a stentorian adieu to our "own Marianne." The group of buildings inclosed within the outer wall which we had now entered was composed of temples, audience halls, and priests' houses, separated by court-yards of different dimensions, in which were planted rows of trees and flowering plants, the whole covering a considerable area. The audience hall in which the commissioners were waiting had very much the appearance of a deep veranda, as it was entirely open to the court-yard on one side, from which it was approached by a flight of steps. Opposite to these the marines drew up. The commissioners came down the steps to meet Lord Elgin as he got out of his chair; the guard presented arms, and the band played the National Anthem. The effect of this mixture of European and Chinese ceremony was striking even to us, who were familiar with both; but to the commissioners, totally unacquainted with Europeans, the sudden appearance of 150 stalwart bearded soldiers, as they poured into the inmost court of the temple, must have been alarming; and as the hoarse word of command was given within a few yards of them, followed by the ringing clink of the muskets on the paved yard, and the roll of the big drum, they might be excused if a momentary suspicion flashed across their minds that the fate of Yeh might be in reserve for them.

Lord Elgin was now invited to a seat at a long table, covered with sundry descriptions of Chinese delicacies, the commissioners being seated upon either side of him. After the whole party had been accommodated with chairs round this table, and the usual preliminary compliments had passed, the embassador stated that the object of the meeting being, as is usual in such cases, an exchange of full powers, he had brought his, and they were forthwith produced and read.

The full powers of the commissioners were then handed to Kweiliang, upon a tray covered with a cloth of imperial yellow The venerable mandarin, after receiving them with every mark of respect, and holding them for a moment elevated above his head in a reverential attitude, handed them to Mr. Wade, who translated the document. Although the terms of the decree conferring full powers on the imperial commissioners were reasonably large, still Lord Elgin, on inquiry, ascertained that the commissioners had not been put in possession of a seal of office, termed the Kwang-fang. When he complained of this omission, he was informed by them that this seal was only given to officers holding permanent situations. Being apprehensive that some mystification might be involved in this explanation, he deemed the circumstance one which warranted him in manifesting some displeasure. Nor was he sorry to avail himself of the opportunity, knowing the importance which the Chinese attach to expression and manner, to make his dissatisfaction apparent. Among the Chinese the physiognomy and deportment of the individual are carefully noted, as indices of the spirit in which the affairs with the management of which he is intrusted are likely to be conducted; and in their dealings with foreigners especially, we have repeated evidence, from the accounts given in their official dispatches of the varied expression of the barbarian countenance, that the functionaries employed were much guided in the tone they held by the emotions they thought they could detect as portrayed in the physiognomy.

Lord Elgin had arrived at Tientsin as the representative of a nation whose dignity had been outraged. It had been necessary to have recourse to violence, and to force an entry into the country, to obtain satisfaction for insults: and any symptom of reluctance to grant it rendered a stern, uncompromising bearing doubly necessary. He accordingly declined the refreshment which was pressed upon him, and terminated the meeting abruptly, stating, as he did so, that he would reserve for a written communication any remarks he might have to make upon the subject of the full powers. As he descended the steps to his chair, the most undisguised dismay was depicted on the countenances of the commissioners and their satellites, the former hurrying after the embassador to his chair with a profusion of protestations and remonstrances.

This meeting was productive of the most salutary effect, and led precisely to the result desired by Lord Elgin. A communication from the commissioners arrived very shortly afterward, requesting that Mr. Lay might be allowed to visit them, and assist them with his advice in the difficult circumstances in which they found themselves placed. Mr. Lay's position at Shanghai, where he held the appointment under the Chinese government of Inspector of Customs, had brought him into close and intimate contact with their officials; and he possessed their confidence to an extent probably never accorded to a European. As Lord Elgin had the highest opinion of this gentleman's capacity and judgment, it was most desirable that the Chinese should place him in the position relatively to themselves in which Lord Elgin most wished to see him. From this period Mr. Lay was in daily communication with the Chinese commissioners, and affairs were thus early put into a train which enabled them to be brought to a speedy and satisfactory conclusion.

The mission of Mr. Lay, however, being somewhat of a confidential or non-official character, Lord Elgin kept up his official intercourse with the commissioners by insisting that the Kwang-fang should be obtained without delay. In this application he was quite successful; the Kwang-fang was sent down from Pekin, and the much vexed question of full powers set finally at rest.

Such was the nature and such the results of the first interview of Lord Elgin with the imperial commissioners. It did not last a quarter of an hour; nor did the embassador again visit the "Temple of the Oceanic Influences," or meet the commissioners, till he went there finally to sign the treaty. At the ceremony above described, the commissioners were dressed in the plain but handsome costume of the Chinese mandarin, the only mark denoting their high rank being the opaque red button and peacock's feather; a tippet of rich maroon silk covered their shoulders and arms; and, with the exception of one or two rings, their persons were devoid of all ornament. As is usual upon all occasions of ceremonial interviews, numbers of minor officials crowded the apartment, eagerly listening to the conversation, while four or five intelligent-looking secretaries took notes in writing of all that passed.

The senior commissioner, Kweiliang, was a venerable man, of placid and benevolent expression, with a countenance full of in-

Kweiliang, First Imperial Commissioner.

telligence, though his eye was somewhat dimmed, and his hand palsied from extreme age. His manners were polished and dignified, and his whole bearing that of a perfect gentleman. He is a Tartar, and has risen to his present high position after a long course of services. His brother Iliang was governor general of the Two Kiangs (in one of which Shanghai is situated), and his account of the visit of Mr. Maclane to the neighborhood of Soo-chow has been already alluded to. Kweiliang himself was governor general of the province of Chih-li at the period of Sir John Bowring's visit to the Gulf of Pechelee in 1854. He then ranked as second Manchu in the empire, Yu-ching, the senior chief secretary or prime minister, being the first. Yu-ching died during the negotiations. His full titles, under which he signed the treaty, were as follows: "Kweiliang, a senior Chief Secretary of State, styled of the East Cabinet, Captain General of the Palin White Banner of the Manchu Banner Force, and Superintendent General of the Administration of Criminal Law." His colleague, Hwashana, a mandarin of the same grade, was a much younger man, with a square, solid face, and a large nose. In general appearance he reminded one strongly of the pictures of Oliver Cromwell; and in the lines of the lower part of his countenance much firmness and decision of character were apparent. He styles himself "one of his imperial majesty's Expositors of the Classics, Manchu President of the Office for the Regulation of the Civil

Hwashana, Second Imperial Commissioner.

Establishment, Captain General of the Bordered Blue Banner of the Chinese Banner Force, and Visitor of the Office of Interpretation." The accompanying portraits are copied from photographs taken by the Hon. N. Jocelyn.

Within the two or three days following our meeting with the Chinese commissioners, Baron Gros, Count Poutiatine, and Mr. Reed had interviews with their excellencies, and expressed themselves respectively satisfied with the full powers which they produced.

It will thus appear, from the above narrative of events, that the allied plenipotentiaries had every reason to be satisfied with the results of the policy they had persevered in hitherto, in spite of the many obstacles which had been interposed. It was evident that the imperial cabinet was thoroughly alarmed, and that the plenipotentiary commissioners sent down to treat were prepared to make an extensive sacrifice of national prejudices in order to relieve the government from the standing menace which was presented by our appearance at Tientsin, and naval occupation of the Peiho to that point.

The opinion recorded by Lord Elgin on the occasion of his first arrival in China, that the only solution of the problem, as it then stood, was in the exercise of a moral pressure of this description in the neighborhood of the capital, was now in process of justification. By these means alone he conceived that, without in any way interfering with the flourishing trade which, in spite of our misunderstanding with the imperial authorities in the south, was being carried on at the ports, and any interruption to which would have been most disastrous to our commercial interests, the great object of the mission he had undertaken to China might be gained, and a lasting and satisfactory treaty effected. But it had seemed almost hopeless that, with the limited force at that early period at his disposal, any such measure could ever be successfully undertaken. Baron Gros not having arrived, the French support was hypothetical. An army of scarce 2500 men, still on their way from England, and the naval force then on the station, composed the entire resources upon which the embassador could depend in the attempt he was about to make to obtain satisfaction from the imperial government, and extort from it a treaty of a more extensive scope than that which was granted to Sir Henry Pottinger only after two thirds of the sea-board had been ravaged, the imperial troops repeatedly vanquished, and the principal cities of the empire stormed and captured. The expenditure of men alone upon that occasion, from sickness and other causes, was numerically as large as the whole force with which greater results were now to be achieved. But even then Lord Elgin might have adhered to his original intention of proceeding to the north as soon as the season permitted and the troops arrived, had not the conduct of affairs at Canton produced complications of so anomalous and intricate a nature that, upon his arrival at Hong Kong in September, he found himself compelled to abandon his idea of a northern expedition, and to devote to the capture and occupation of Canton the force which he had designed for Pekin.

He still clung to the hope, however, that a portion of it might yet prove available for this purpose, and the object of his visit to Calcutta was so far gained that he succeeded in obtaining a valuable re-enforcement of native regiments. He farther believed that form of government might be established at Canton which would facilitate the task of its military occupation, and enable the general to spare some of his troops for service in the north. In this expectation he was not disappointed: by the Sampson, which brought up the engineers, he received an intimation from General Straubenzee that, if more troops were required, they could be spared; and on the 4th of June, on the very day of the first interview with the commissioners above described, the Fury left the Gulf of Pechelee for the purpose of bringing to the scene of negotiations the 59th regiment. There can be little doubt that the timely arrival of this regiment removed from the imperial mind the last shadow of doubt as to the necessity of concluding the treaty. In a word, then, the policy of the allied plenipotentiaries, as so far developed, had in effect placed the emperor in their grasp, and the dynasty itself at their mercy, without in any way endangering the European communities at the ports, or even disturbing their trade. It was, indeed, matter for congratulation that they had at last succeeded in placing themselves in this favorable attitude with a force so limited and hampered, and under such adverse influences generally. It may be readily imagined that the five weeks we passed at Tientsin formed a most cheerful contrast to the same period spent in the Gulf of Pechelee. There we had more than once utterly despaired of ultimate success; now we felt that, though disappointed in our hopes of reaching Pekin, the doubts and anxieties we had experienced would probably be more than compensated for by a diplomatic triumph.

CHAPTER XVII.

The Chances of a Chinese political Career.—Arrival of Keying.—Interview with him.—Adverse Policy of Keying.—His Hostility to the Commissioners.—Proofs of his Insincerity.—Second Interview of Messrs. Wade and Lay.—Keying's Memorial.—Keying's Treatment of Barbarians.—A disagreeable Exposé.—Consequences of his Offense.—Lenient Sentence.—The Emperor's Decree.—Keying's Suicide.

A FEW days after the incidents recounted in the last chapter, an episode occurred singularly illustrative of the vicissitudes of Chinese official life, and of the dangers to which those are exposed in the Celestial Empire who are either "born to greatness or have greatness thrust upon them." The account which has been already given of the fortunes of Tan exhibits, in a striking manner, the dilemma in which the imperial government places its high functionaries when it forces them under the severest penalties to accept positions from which it is morally impossible for them to escape without incurring failure. There can be little doubt that the imperial government often appoints a man to an office with the express intention that he should serve as a scapegoat, and be sacrificed to its own folly or incompetency. The system of unscrupulously immolating innocent subordinates to screen guilty superiors extends through the whole Chinese official life; and so well recognized is this principle among them, that, in the numerous misunderstandings our authorities have had with the Chinese, the latter have invariably sought to lay the blame on one of our own inferior officers, with a view of enabling the superior to retreat with honor from a false position, should he desire to do so. If, however, the British official maintains his ground, as is commonly the case, the Chinese gets out of the scrape by a similar process.

When a high official position is attended with these inconveniences, it will readily be understood that intrigue among imperial officers often takes a precisely opposite direction to that which it commonly assumes in Europe, and that, so far from attempting the ruin of your greatest enemy by opposing his advancement, there are circumstances under which a Chinese politician can most surely gratify his revenge by procuring his nomination to an important and hazardous service, the refusal of which would entail the same extreme penalty which will be the result of his inevitable failure. Not only in the Chinese world of fact, but in their realms of fiction, is this practice used to point the moral and adorn the tale; and in many of their romances the interest of the plot is made to turn upon some crisis in which the virtuous hero is made the victim of a fatal promotion.

It is impossible for us to do more than speculate upon the secret motives which may have induced the imperial government to nominate Keying, in an independent capacity, to assist in the settlement of the barbarian business. That this appointment was more properly due to the able intrigues of his enemies than the ill-advised efforts of his friends may be inferred from the fact that the high officers who first moved the emperor to raise him from disgrace and employ him at Tientsin, were the first to denounce him as worthy of death in consequence of his conduct there; though it must be remembered that, in China, the only chance which the man who recommends an incompetent *employé* has of saving his own head is to be the first to denounce his nominee should he prove a failure.

Be that as it may, Lord Elgin was not a little surprised to receive an intimation from the old friend of Sir Henry Pottinger, whose name is most familiar to English ears as the negotiator of the last treaty, and who contrived, during the short period of his intercourse with Europeans, to create in their minds so high an estimate of his intelligence and good faith, announcing his arrival, but not stating that he held any official rank, while he at the same time requested an interview with the embassador.

Lord Elgin at first felt somewhat disposed to overlook this informality in favor of a man whose presence at the scene of negotiations might appear to indicate the existence of a strong desire on the part of the emperor to terminate existing difficulties amicably. The reputation which Keying had earned in his management of barbarian business had been founded on his conciliatory treatment of them; still, we were in possession of documents invalidating his sincerity, and we knew that his conciliatory policy had led to his disgrace. Messrs. Wade and Lay were therefore sent in to express Lord Elgin's regret at not being able to accord him an interview, and, at the same time, to observe the tendency manifested in his tone and sentiments.

They found an old, decrepit mandarin, half blind, and, to judge from his countenance, sinking into his dotage. He at first declared that he recognized Mr. Lay, and that gentleman had some difficulty in persuading him that he had mistaken him for his father. Then he burst into tears at the deplorable position of the Celestial Empire generally, and of himself in particular, stating that he was involved in a difficulty which must end in disaster to himself. Mr. Wade suspected that this was a mere theatrical effect. Mr. Lay giving him credit for sincerity, to test it, Mr. Wade assured him that he might be relieved from his situation, as he had no doubt Lord Elgin would write a letter peremptorily declining intercourse with him, which would be his justification to the imperial court. This, however, did not suit the crafty Keying, in whose senile brain some cunning still remained, and he complained that we were placing a knife to the throat of China and a pistol to its head; and gradually let it appear what his opinion was on this subject to an extent which convinced our envoys that his sentiments were distinctly hostile, so that he was requested in writing, the same evening, to postpone his visit for a few days. Notwithstanding this, however, on the day following (the 10th), Keying had the perseverance to appear at the gate of the yamun, and sent in his card, but was, of course, not admitted. I regretted not arriving in time to see more than the back of his chair as he was being carried away. As an historical personage, and one whose tragical end has since invested him with a deeper interest, Keying was a man worthy of having been noticed.

It may readily be supposed that the commissioners Kweiliang and Hwashana did not regard this interloper with any favorable eye. The only definite office he seemed to fill at first was that of spy, while the imperial commission which he managed subsequently to obtain only qualified him more fully to put in practice the resolution he at once manifested of thwarting the senior commissioners in every thing they proposed. We were informed, on tolerably good Chinese authority, that he totally dissented from the pacific policy by which they were actuated, and held the most pugnacious language with reference to the barbarians. To this he might have been impelled by two motives. In the first place, his independent appointment almost necessarily implied that he was expected to entertain independent views. As the views of his colleagues were "peace at any price," he felt bound to be warlike; and he the more readily adopted this tone, as he had himself, in his former dealings with us, adopted the "peace at any price" policy, and had remained in disgrace ever since. His second motive was, in fact, consequent upon this; he regarded the present as the only opportunity which was ever likely to be afforded him of retrieving his position, by becoming the vigorous advocate of a policy directly antagonistic to that which had already been his ruin: could he only show that Kweiliang and Hwashana were pursuing a course as weak and temporizing as that which, in the opinion of the imperial government, had characterized his own diplomacy, he might still hope to clothe the nakedness of his present disgrace with the miserable remnants of the robes of honor he had torn from the backs of his colleagues.

The commissioners finding him in this vein, and perceiving that their most earnest efforts to bring about a satisfactory adjustment of the existing difficulties were likely to be frustrated by the determination to thwart a conciliatory policy manifested by Keying, earnestly requested his removal. The emperor, however, as he himself states in his subsequent decree on the subject, knowing that he (Keying) must be aware of this, and lest he should feel embarrassed by the knowledge, again sent him orders to remain at Tientsin. But Keying, instead of taking this hint to pursue the independent policy which had been originally indicated to him, suddenly took the unexpected and indefensible course of deserting his post, thereby much delighting his enemies, and drawing upon himself the serious displeasure of his imperial master. In order, however, to comprehend the real motive which induced him to adopt this unusual and fatal line of conduct, it is necessary to explain the nature of the interference on our part, to which we were compelled to have recourse.

It no sooner became evident to the embassador that Keying was endeavoring to exert an influence which, if successful, would neutralize the good dispositions of the senior commissioners, and imperil the final and satisfactory issue of the negotiations already commenced, than he determined to remove from the scene one whose presence was calculated to prove a serious embarrassment, the more especially as he had been furnished with unmistakable evidence that the obstructive tendencies of Keying had not been exaggerated. Fortunately, among the papers discovered in Yeh's yamun was a memorial written by this very mandarin to the emperor upon the subject of barbarian affairs; and the tone in which that document was conceived furnished Lord Elgin with an instrument which, if properly used, would secure his removal from the present commission. It was considered that the most effective and certain way of accomplishing this desirable result would be for Messrs. Wade and Lay unexpectedly to produce in his presence his own memorial, and read it aloud for the benefit of himself and his colleagues. Accordingly, upon the 11th, or the day following the visit of Keying to the yamun, these gentlemen waited upon the commissioners. Their first object was to present a letter complaining of the unsatisfactory reply which the commissioners had returned to a confidential communication made to them by the embassador upon the subject of the propositions which were to form the base of the negotiations.

Upon entering the commissioners' room, Messrs. Wade and Lay found Keying present, apparently associated with them in the capacity of colleague. They adverted to the communication already received by Lord Elgin as differing altogether in tone and spirit from the document he had been led to expect, and as being one altogether impossible to be received by him as the base for future negotiations. The commissioners insinuated, as broadly as it was possible for them to do, in presence of Keying, that this gentleman was responsible for the letter in question, and for the tone in which it was couched. Messrs. Wade and Lay remarked that, while Lord Elgin did not conceive himself entitled to dictate to the emperor on the subject of the appointments he might be pleased to make to the imperial commission, it was clear that good faith on the part of the individuals likely to be engaged in the pending negotiations was a qualification of the first importance. It was evidently not in the interest of either party that a person discredited in this particular should be associated in the commission. It would be for the commissioners to make their own application of this principle with reference to the document which they now begged to produce, the authorship of which it was not necessary to particularize, as it was attached to the paper.

The circumstance of its having been found in Yeh's yamun at Canton among his private archives imparted an additional interest, doubtless, in the eyes of the commissioners, to this singular and interesting production of Keying. The following document was then handed to the senior commissioners, and read aloud by

Hwashana in a subdued tone, Keying being present, but keeping well in the background, conscious that the revelations it contained would put his command of countenance to the test should he seem to pay attention to its contents:

"*The Supplementary Memorial, detailing the peculiarities of the Receptions of the barbarian Envoys of different nations, and the Autograph* (lit., *Vermilion*) *approval of his Majesty the Emperor.*"

[The date of this Memorial was about the end of 1850.]

(*Translation.*)

"The slave Keying, upon his knees, presents a supplementary memorial to the throne. The particulars of his administration of the business of the barbarian states, and management* of barbarian envoys, according to circumstances, in his receptions† of them, have formed the subject of different memorials of your slave.

"The supplementary conditions of trade having been also negotiated by him, he has had the honor to submit the articles containing those to the sacred glance of your majesty, who has commissioned the Board of Revenue to examine and report upon them. All which is upon record. He calls to mind, however, that it was in the seventh moon of the twenty-second year (August, 1842) that the English barbarians were pacified. The Americans and French have successively followed in the summer and autumn of this year (1845). In this period of three years barbarian matters have been affected by many conditions of change, and in proportion as these have been various in character has it become necessary to shift ground, and to adopt alterations in the means by which they were to be conciliated and held within range.‡ They must be dealt with justly, of course, and their feelings thus appealed to; but, to keep them in hand, stratagem (or diplomacy) is requisite.

"In some instances a direction must be given them, but without explanation of the reason why; in some, their restlessness can only be neutralized by demonstrations which disarm (*lit.*, dissolve) their suspicions; in some, they have to be pleased, and moved to gratitude by concession of intercourse on a footing of equality;

---
* *Lit.*, riding and reining.   † Receptions of them as inferiors in rank.
‡ Conciliated—*lit.*, pacified, as a person or an animal that is wild, and comforted. Kept within range—*lit.*, tethered.

and in some, before a result can be brought about, their falsity has to be blinked, nor must an estimate (of their facts) be pressed too far.

"Bred and born in the foreign regions beyond (its boundary), there is much in the administration of the Celestial dynasty that is not perfectly comprehensible to the barbarians, and they are continually putting forced constructions on things, of which it is difficult to explain to them the real nature. Thus the promulgation of the imperial decree (*lit.*, silken sounds) devolves on the members of the great council, but the barbarians respect them as being the autograph reply of your majesty; and were they given to understand positively that (the decrees) are not in the handwriting of your majesty at all, (so far from respecting them), there would, on the contrary, be nothing in which their confidence would be secure.

"The meal which the barbarians eat together they call *ta-tsan* (dinner).* It is a practice they delight in to assemble a number of people at a great entertainment, at which they eat and drink together. When your slave has conferred honor upon (has given a dinner to) the barbarians at the Bogue or Macao, their chiefs and leaders have come together to the number of from ten to twenty or thirty; and when, in process of time, your slave has chanced to go to barbarian residences† or barbarian ships, they have, in their turn, seated themselves round in attendance upon him, striving who should be foremost in offering him meat and drink. To gain their good-will, he could not do otherwise than share their cup and spoon.

"Another point: It is the wont of the barbarians to make much of their women. Whenever their visitor is a person of distinction, the wife is sure to come out and receive him. In the case of the American barbarian Parker, and the French barbarian Lagrené, for instance, both of these have brought their foreign wives with them; and when your slave has gone to the barbarian residences on business, their foreign women have suddenly appeared and saluted him. Your slave was confounded‡ and ill at ease,

---

* The word used by our Canton servants for dinner: the great meal.

† The word *lau*, loft or story, is not that applied to the dwelling-houses of Chinese. The mandarins use it specially when speaking to their own people of our houses.

‡ Confounded, almost awe-stricken, as Confucius is described to have been in the presence of his ruler.

while they, on the contrary, were greatly delighted at the honor done them. The truth is, as this shows, that it is not possible to regulate the customs of the Western states by the ceremonial of China; and to break out in rebuke, while it would do nothing toward their enlightenment (*lit.*, to cleave their dullness), might chance to give rise to suspicion and ill-feeling.

"Again, ever since amicable relations with them commenced, the different barbarians have been received, on something of a footing of equality. One such interview is no longer a novelty; it becomes more than ever a duty to keep them off and to shut them out. To this end, on every occasion that a treaty has been negotiated with a barbarian state, your slave has directed Hwang Aw-tung, Commissioner of Finance, to desire its envoy to take notice that a high officer in China, administering foreign affairs, is never at liberty to give or receive any thing on his private account. That, as to presents, he would be obliged peremptorily to decline them; were they to be accepted, and the fact concealed, the ordinances of the Celestial dynasty on the subject are very stringent; and, to say nothing of the injury he would inflict on the dignity of his office, it would be hard (for the offender) to escape the penalty of the law. The barbarian envoys have had the sense to attend to this; but in their interviews with him they have sometimes offered your slave foreign wines, perfumery, and other like matters, of very small value. Their intention being more or less good, he could not well have rejected them altogether, and to their face; but he has confined himself to bestowing on them snuff-bottles, purses, and such things as are carried on the person, thereby putting in evidence the Chinese principle of giving much, although but little has been received.* Again, on the application of the Italians, English, Americans, and French, your slave has presented them with a copy of his insignificant portrait.

"To come to their government.† Though every state has one, there are rulers, male or female, holding office permanently for the time being. With the English barbarians, for instance, the ruler is a female, and with the French and Americans, a male. The English and French ruler reigns for life; the American is elected by his countrymen, and is changed once in four years, and

---

* Thus, according to the second of the Confucian books, should it be between the ruler and the nobles dependent on him.

† *Lit.*, their sovereign seniors.

when he retires from his throne he takes rank with the people (the non-official classes).

"Their official designations are also different in the case of each nation. To represent these, they for the most part appropriate (*lit.*, filch) Chinese characters, boastfully affecting a style to which they have no claim, and assuming the airs of a great power. That they should conceive that they thereby do honor to their rulers is no concern of ours; while, if the forms observed toward the dependencies (of China) were to be prescribed as the rule in their case, they would certainly not consent, as they neither accept the Chinese computation* of time, nor receive your majesty's patent (of royalty), to fall back to the rank of Cochin-China or Lewchew. And with people so uncivilized as they are, blindly unintelligent in styles and modes of address, a tenacity in forms of official correspondence, such as would duly place the superior above and the inferior below, would be the cause of a fierce altercation (*lit.*, a rising of the tongue and a blistering of the lips): the only course, in that case, would be to affect to be deaf to it (*lit.*, to be as though the earlap stopped the ear); personal intercourse would then become impossible; and not only this, but an incompatibility of relations would immediately follow, of any thing but advantage certainly to the essential question of conciliation.† Instead, therefore, of a contest about unsubstantial names, which can produce no tangible result, (it has been held) better to disregard these minor details, in order to the success of an important policy.

"Such are the expedients and modifications which, after close attention to the barbarian affairs, a calculation of the exigencies of the period, and a careful estimate of the merits of the question, as being trivial or of importance, admitting of delay or demanding dispatch, it has been found unavoidable to adopt. Your slave has not ventured to intrude them one by one upon the sacred intelligence, partly because they were of themselves of small significance, partly because there was no time‡ (so to report them). The barbarian business being now on the whole (*lit.*, in the rough) concluded, as in duty bound, he states them detailedly, one and

---

* *Lit.*, the first and last moons of the year, as computed by China, who issues her calendar to Corea, if not to her other dependencies. The sovereigns of Corea, Lewchew, and Cochin-China are invested by a Chinese envoy, and receive a patent from their emperor as their suzerain.

† As in note ‡, p. 243. ‡ He had to act at once.

all, in this supplementary dispatch, which he respectfully presents to your majesty."

"*Reply in the Vermilion Pencil.*"

"It was the only proper arrangement to have made. We understand the whole question."

While Hwashana was reading this production, his attention was more particularly directed to those passages which discuss so elaborately the various descriptions of "stratagem" which Keying was in the habit of resorting to in order "to keep the barbarians in hand."

So long as this controller of barbarians was associated with the commission, it was evident that it would be incumbent upon us to watch narrowly which mode of treatment he was applying; whether "a direction was being given to us without explanation of the reason why;" or whether "our restlessness was being neutralized by demonstrations which disarmed our suspicions;" or whether this was one of those occasions in which we were "to be pleased and moved to gratitude by concession of intercourse on a footing of equality;" or whether the crisis was so eminent that our "falsity was to be blinded, and the estimate of our facts not pressed too far." Whatever be the mode of treatment, he does not for a moment leave us in doubt as to its object. "Once such an intercourse (on a footing of equality) is established, it becomes more than ever a duty to keep them off and to shut them out." Nor was his chuckle upon our gullibility with reference to the imperial autograph lost upon us.

Hwashana and Kweiliang looked somewhat abashed when they had concluded this dissertation upon the "blindly unintelligent" race of barbarians with whom they were at that moment negotiating, and Keying requested to be allowed to see the paper, for the quiet perusal of which he retired into a corner. Meantime our envoys informed the imperial commissioners that the best way of establishing confidence in Lord Elgin's mind with reference to their good faith was to send in at once the letter containing the propositions originally agreed upon as the base of negotiations. They farther stated their intention of waiting in the yamun until it was signed and sealed, which they accordingly did, and it was not until 10 P.M. that they finally took leave, with the precious document, signed by Kweiliang, Hwashana, and Keying, in their possession. It was doubtless in allusion to this communication that Keying states, in the memorial to the emperor containing his defense, that when, after consultation with Kweiliang and Hwashana, it was agreed that a dispatch should be written, "they wept together beneath the window; they knew not in the morning that they should not die by night."

Two days after this it was that, finding himself discredited by us before his colleagues, to whom he was personally obnoxious, and who would gladly avail themselves of the weapon we had placed in their hands, and perceiving that it was impossible to pursue the obstructive and independent policy he was expected to adopt, Keying determined suddenly to return to Pekin, prefacing the step with a memorial to the emperor, stating only that he had "propositions of importance to submit." Before he reached the capital, however, he received an order to return to his post. Instead of obeying this command, he, to use the words of the emperor, "could not take himself out of the way fast enough." This was the head and front of Keying's offense. Thus conscience made a coward of him. Had the emperor read Shakspeare, he probably would not have asked, in passing sentence on him, "Had Keying any conscience, would the sweat have flowed down his back or not?" But so it happened that instead of bearing the ills he had, the unhappy mandarin fled to others that he knew not of.

Rumors were shortly after rife at Tientsin, first of the degradation, and then of the death of Keying; but the first authentic intimation we received of the severity of the punishment which was awarded him was from the following extract from the *Pekin Gazette*, which reached us on the 3d of July, or about three days prior to our leaving Tientsin.

Not previously aware of the circumstances under which he had been appointed to meet us, or supplied with every link in the chain of events detailed in the foregoing pages, we were much shocked at the tragical end of one who had so recently been among us, and whose conduct, though weak and vacillating, scarcely seemed to deserve death by suicide; nor, indeed, in so far as we are acquainted with the whole of his offending, does there seem any proportion between the guilt and the punishment. How little could we imagine that the objection taken to Keying as an imperial commissioner should even indirectly have been the cause of that fatal decree, the last sentence of which contains so painful a satire upon justice and mercy; for certain officers, having desired Keying to read the decree, are commanded to inform him "that it is our will that he put an end to himself, that our extreme desire to be at once just and gracious be made manifest." In a country where the highest attributes of divinity find such a manifestation, it is no very violent presumption to suppose that the fate of Keying was determined upon when he was first ordered to proceed to Tientsin, and that, whatever his conduct there might have been, it would always have furnished the excuse desired by his enemies of causing his public execution, a sentence which the emperor hypocritically modified by that parody upon leniency contained in the last clause, which commutes the public execution to private suicide.

"*Autograph Decree.*

"On receipt of a memorial by the Prince of Hwui* and others, praying that Keying's offense should be followed by instant punishment as under martial law, we commanded that he should be brought to the capital and subjected to rigorous examination. When put on his trial, he tendered his statement in defense, and we then directed the Prince of Kung† and others to decide and award with equity. They now find that, in not awaiting our commands, Keying acted with stupidity and precipitancy, and they sentenced him to be strangled after imprisonment until the Imperial Assize,‡ when his crime is to be entered among those not to be forgiven. Their award, certainly, is none other than a correct one. Still, as the terms in which they describe his transgression by no means define the criminality of his heart,§ it is incumbent on us to give full publicity [to the facts].

---

* Mien Yu, brother of the late Emperor Mien Ning, the style of whose reign was Táu Kwang.

† Yih Su, brother of the reigning emperor, who was associated with Yih Tsung, another brother, and the adopted son of the emperor's uncle, in the trial.

‡ A list of criminal cases is submitted once a year to the emperor. The prisoners whose names are without a certain mark made upon it by the emperor escape with life; those within the mark die. The term here rendered Imperial Assize is applied to this rehearing of cases tried in the capital; cases heard in the provinces are revised at the Autumnal Assize.

§ *Lit.*, are certainly not a description of it that cuts the heart open: a classical expression elsewhere paraphrased as the offense of "deceiving the sovereign, and so

"When Keying, being at the time an officer in disgrace, was again lifted up to be employed, it was our hope that he would exert himself to make a reputation in his declining years, and would competently perform the service needed in the matter [then before us]. When he had his audience to take leave, his words were, 'The powers of your slave are scarcely equal to his charge, but he will see what his fortune is;' language that betokened neither numbness of conscience* nor failing intelligence. On the 27th of the 4th moon (8th June), a letter from the council† followed him to Tientsin, by which he was instructed that he need not associate himself with Kweiliang and his colleague, nor be bound by forms in any way,‡ to the end that he might follow up any step of theirs by the measures his own policy might require. It can not be said that the position we gave him was other than independent, or that our gracious support of him was short of considerable. When Kweiliang and his colleague moved us to recall him, we assumed that he must be aware of this. Still, lest he might be somewhat§—a letter was sent from the council instructing him to remain at Tientsin, and take counsel for himself. Had Keying had any conscience, would the sweat have flowed down his back or not?‖ That officer, however, having dispatched¶ a memorial to us, takes on himself to return to the capital, his plea being that he has propositions of importance to submit to us. If so, why did he not address us a confidential memorial in his single name? He adds that there is matter that can not well appear in writing. Then why, when he [subsequently] received the decree to the effect that it was our pleasure he should stay at Tientsin, did he

causing damage to the state's interest;" treason, in short. One Chinese understands it, "their finding does not show him guilty of the treason he has committed."

* *Lit.*, dimness.

† These letters are what we call imperial decrees. They are drawn up under instruction of the emperor, and transmitted through the council to those whom they concern.

‡ *Lit.*, not to grasp the mud, stand on ceremony. Properly, as junior, he would have subscribed to the proposals of the senior commissioners, but he was authorized, "as exponent of his own policy, to take the second step," the other commissioners having taken the first.

§ There is an omission here of two characters, if not more.

‖ This is a classical expression, the parentage of which obliges it to indicate, not as we should have supposed, great exertion, but the sense of shame experienced when our little merits receive bounteous consideration.

¶ *Lit.*, having adored, prostrated himself before the memorial about to be sent.

hurriedly prepare another memorial? And what is there, after all, of moment, either in his memorials or in his defense? In all the irrelevancy which time after time he has obtruded upon us, his sole calculation is [the safety of] his own head. The total absence of available suggestions in the memorials and defense of this officer, again, might be held, had he not been deep in the secret, to be over-harshly visited by the law. But it is known that the measure he names had been long since considered by us with our servants. Besides, what might have come from another with propriety could not with propriety come from Keying. Why so? Because he was art and part of* the administration [of this question], and was free to carry out any views of his own. How was it, then, that, unprovided with measures suppeditative or remedial while acting with others, he was only ready with the right suggestion after the event?

"Had we but punished this officer as he humbly prayed we would, we had indeed fallen into [the snare of] his machinations. For [in that prayer] Keying has plainly declared himself. Not only [does he imply that] his former offense had been completely washed away, but he seeks to lay blame on others; an intention yet more to his disgrace.† He had fancied that, for unauthorizedly relinquishing his commission, dismissal from the service would be all the penalty awarded him, and, this end attained, he would have enjoyed himself at home. With the obligation laid upon him by long recognition of his little merit (*lit.*, dullness, sc., his employment in spite of it), should such a conception have been tolerable to him? Nor is this all, when his thoughts are unraveled.‡ When, after consultation with Kweiliang and Hwashana, it was agreed that a dispatch§ should be written, 'they wept together beneath the window;∥ they knew not in the morn-

---

* *Lit.*, in the game, in the plot, on the committee. He flies from Tientsin on the plea that he has an important suggestion to make which he dare not write; yet he writes, and his suggestion proves of no value; nor is it a novel one, as he well knew. This suggestion, say all Chinese expositors consulted, was war, which it must be inferred he was at liberty to resort to.

† *Lit.*, still less can his heart be inquired of. Man should be so that, "when he inquires of his heart, he finds nothing to be ashamed of."

‡ *Lit.*, [when we follow] the track, or footprints of his heart.

§ Dispatch or communication, probably one addressed to Lord Elgin two days before Keying disappeared from Tientsin.

∥ A common phrase applied to men consulting or studying together. It does not appear whether the emperor learned this from Keying's dispatches or elsewhere.

ing that they should **not die by night.'** But we do not learn that, in devout obedience to our will as earlier expressed, he then devised **any worthier expedient** of his own." By-and-by he observed to Hwashana that he feared his departure from Tientsin might disturb the population, and he would therefore pretend that he was moving thence for a while on business. But though, on arriving at Tung-chau, he received the later letter of the council [desiring him to return], we do not learn that he hastened back [to his post; on the contrary], he could not take himself out of the way fast enough. He treated our commands as a thing of course to be dispensed with.† Full of intrigue, bent on deceit, could a hundred voices excuse him from immediate annihilation?‡

"The [sentence proposed in the] original memorial of the Prince of Hwui and his colleagues was, nevertheless, too severe; neither was the memorial of [the Censor] Suhshun, again, proposing his immediate execution, as it should be. Our object in handing him over to our servants in the capital§ for trial was to have the circumstances of so grave an offense duly weighed by them, and a sentence deliberately pronounced, for the edification of all. If we were still to have approved his summary execution, what need was there for bringing him to the capital? What need, to go farther, for [the formality of] a finding and sentence? Then the remark [in one memorial], that 'if left for some months he might die a natural death, and so escape with his head,' is even more out of order.‖ Such words belong to sentences passed on malefactors (*lit.*, robbers). They could not, without serious impropriety, be applied to Keying.

"We have bestowed great attention [upon his case] for several days, seeking to spare his life; but, indeed, it is impossible; and were we to reserve him, as Yih Su and his colleagues¶ propose, for the Great Assize, then certainly to suffer, we feel that [when the time came] we could not endure to leave him in the market-

---

* *Lit.*, separately or distinctly, that is, from his colleagues.

† *Lit.*, as a cap-hair; the tuft of hair formerly thrown away when the cap of manhood was assumed; a thing to be rejected, and rejected of course.

‡ An expression that would include his family in the act of destruction.

§ That is to say, by the chief members of the administration.

‖ *Lit.*, then the remark—is a finding [in cases between which and the present there is] even less analogy. It could not wantonly, or at random, be applied to Keying. Colloquially, it would never do, etc.

¶ Yih Su, see note †, p. 249.

place.* In this dilemma, having given all our thought to a due appreciation of the facts and a just apportionment of the law, we command Jinshau, senior *tsung-ching*, and Mien Hiun, senior *tsung-jin*, of the imperial Clan Court,† with Linkwei, President of the Board of Punishments, to go at once to the Empty House of the Clan Court, and, having desired Keying to read [this] our autograph decree, to inform him that it is our will that he put an end to himself, that our extreme desire to be at once just and gracious be made manifest. Respect this!"

We were informed, upon good authority, before leaving Tientsin, that the punishment here awarded had been actually carried out, Keying having drunk a cup of poison in the presence of the imperial officers nominated to enforce it. Thus perished by his own hand this celebrated mandarin, whose signature, attached to the Treaty of Nankin exactly fifteen years before, had secured for him a political notoriety in Europe greater than had ever previously been accorded to a Chinaman, and the tragical termination of whose career must ever invest his name with a yet more significant and touching interest.

* Like a common criminal.
† The *tsung-jin-fu*, or imperial Clan Court, is an office charged specially with the registration, payment, and jurisdiction of the imperial family in all its branches. The Empty House mentioned just below is the prison of this establishment.

CHAPTER XVIII.

Insolence of the Mob.—A forcible Entry into Tientsin.—Making Reprisals.—Hostile Crowds.—Peaceful Proclamations.—Plan of the City of Tientsin.—Aspect of the City.—The Traffic in the Streets.—Declining Trade of Tientsin.—Notice concerning the Grain Supply.—Present State of the Grand Canal.—Official Expenditure of Grain.—Collection of the Grain-tribute.—State of the Yellow River.—Obstructions in its Navigation.—Grain Transport by Sea.—Report on the Grand Canal.—Price of Rice at Tientsin.—Table showing Proceeds of Grain-tax.—Trade of Tientsin.—Squalor of the Inhabitants.—Burial-places.—Total Allied Force at Tientsin.—Exploration of the surrounding Country.—The Harvest at Tientsin.—Kitchen-gardens.—Salt-pans.—Vetch-fields.—Locust-hunting.

Our suspicions of the hostile character of Keying's interference, alluded to in the last chapter, had received a somewhat singular confirmation in the altered demeanor manifested by the inhabitants within two or three days after his arrival. Up to that time nothing could exceed the respectful bearing of all classes with whom we had come in contact in the course of our rides and walks through the city and suburbs. Upon the very day, however, of the visit of Messrs. Wade and Lay to the commissioners' yamun, just described, the admiral, accompanied by two or three naval officers, was pelted and hooted at by the populace while walking in one of the suburbs. This was a course of proceeding on their part altogether unexpected; and our astonishment was increased on the following afternoon by the sudden appearance in our yamun of Captains Dew and Saumarez in a state of some excitement, the former hatless, and grasping a large stick, the battered condition of which gave evidence of some recent violent rencounter. It appeared that, while walking quietly inside the city, near one of the gates, they were pelted and hooted, and ultimately attacked by the mob, who, however, entertained too great a respect for barbarian prowess to press them very close, and they escaped with only the loss of a favorite dog of Captain Dew's, and the hat of that gallant officer. Immediately on the receipt of this news a message was sent to Major Boyle, commanding the marines, who were barracked only a hundred yards distant. As it was already late in the day, and no time was to be lost, that officer at once put himself at the head of a strong party of marines, and, accompanied by half a dozen blue-jackets of the Furious, and some of us as amateurs, proceeded, under the guidance of Captain Dew, toward that part of the city where the outrage was said to have occurred.

As, however, we had upward of half a mile of suburb to traverse before reaching the nearest city-gate, timely notice of our approach was received by the gate-keepers from scouts who ran on to warn them; and, in spite of our utmost endeavors to reach the gate before it was shut, we found, upon our arrival before it, that it was firmly barricaded against us, and, on looking through the chinks in the massive paneling, could discern a large crowd collected in the deep archway which passed under the wall at this point, some fifteen or twenty yards in breadth. We insisted upon a Chinaman ordering them to open the gate, who obeyed our commands in this wise: "Look out!" he cried; "here are a whole lot of barbarians wanting to come in! They have pressed me; I have nothing to do with it. Open the gate! open the gate! open the gate!" The first part of the sentence, intended only for his Chinese audience, was overheard by Mr. Lay; the latter part, intended for us, was shouted with the utmost vehemence.

Seeing that the people were determined not to admit us, and that it was hopeless to attempt to force the gate, I accompanied Captains Osborn and Dew in search of an available part of the wall for scaling. Some low houses were built against a crumbling angle at a likely place, and, scrambling on to the overhanging eaves, we were soon digging our fingers and toes into the crevices formed by the disintegration of the unburnt brick of which the wall was composed. In a moment more we were joined by three or four blue-jackets with muskets, and, running along the wall, jumped down into the street, and astonished the unsuspecting crowd in the archway as we took them in rear with a loud yell. They doubtless supposed that the whole British army was at our backs, for they tumbled about in all directions in their haste to escape, assisted by the application of a little judicious pressure upon sundry parts of their persons as they scampered away. Dew, seizing a hatchet from one of them, instantly cut through the bar of the gate, and in another moment the whole of the marines walked quietly in, the city having thus been stormed and taken in five minutes, without any more serious wound having been given or received than that which may be inflicted with the toe of a boot.

We marched tranquilly up the main street, then down to the South Gate, which Dew at first supposed to be the one at which he had been insulted. Finding out our mistake, however, we marched along the whole length of one face of the city, a distance of about a mile, upon the top of the wall, to the West Gate—a most striking procession to the admiring crowds, who were collected in astonishment to watch us make such free use of their mural defenses, considered the most sacred part of a Chinese city. Immediately on arriving at the West Gate Captain Dew's hat was presented to him, and we informed the mob that, in consequence of the impropriety of their behavior in that particular locality, it would be necessary to make prisoners of six respectable householders, as it was impossible to recognize the individual offenders. Thus the better class would come to see the necessity of treating foreigners civilly. So we laid hands on the captain of the Tartar Guard at the gate, and a few apparently well-to-do shopkeepers, and marched them solemnly off between two files of marines, Mr. Lay pointing the moral of the proceeding by making the Chinese, as we passed, say, "It is very wrong to insult an Englishman; I will never insult an Englishman." Any man who showed any reluctance to repeat this formula was at once brought forward, and compelled, in a distinct and grave voice, to give utterance to a variety of sentiments expressive of his regard and consideration for the English. The prisoners were only kept in confinement one night, and on the following morning were released, well satisfied with the treatment they had received, and full of promises to use their utmost influence to prevent a recurrence of a similar incident. Captain Dew's dog, a handsome retriever, swam off to the Cormorant, on board which ship his master was staying, during the night.

We were assured in different quarters that the behavior of the people was due to the instructions they had received from their mandarins, and that these instructions had only been issued subsequently to Keying's arrival. We had the greater reason to believe this assertion, as, in consequence of the representations made to the commissioners, no farther annoyance of the sort was experienced except upon the day following, and probably before any instructions upon the matter had been widely circulated, when Cameron and I were walking alone in a distant suburb, and were pelted by some of the younger part of the population, and surrounded by a hostile-looking crowd, who commenced hooting. Upon our turning round and facing them, with an appealing look to the most respectable individuals in the crowd, these latter restrained the more ardent spirits; and as we walked away, we could hear the voices of the advocates for and against insult in high altercation. After this, we could walk and ride to considerable distances with perfect impunity, though ever since our first arrival we had deemed it unwise to go about unarmed.

The appearance, a few days after this, of 120 marines and two guns from the fleet, who were marched with all possible military display to their quarters, did much to give effect to our remonstrances, and increased the civility of the people. Our force, until the arrival of this body and the engineers, had been very small, in consequence of most of the blue-jackets having been sent back to the fleet immediately upon our becoming installed in our quarters at Tientsin. Now, however, proclamations were posted up all over the city and suburbs, stating that foreigners were always to be attended by (Chinese) soldiers to preserve them from insult, and that persons insulting them would be severely punished. A news-room was discovered in the city, where placards containing the latest barbarian intelligence were posted up. Among other pieces of news, the public were informed that we had been induced to parade the town a few days previously in consequence of the auspiciousness of the day. We had certainly proved, upon that occasion, that, with even the comparatively small force now at our disposal, we might consider any day auspicious to take and occupy a city, the defenses of which were so feeble, and the garrison so weak and timorous.

The authorities were, moreover, extremely desirous of showing their sincerity by inflicting summary punishment upon any Chinaman against whom complaints were made. One cheerful-looking man used to appear daily at the gate of the yamun, and seat himself there with a cangue, or piece of board about three feet square, locked round his neck. The Chinese put their criminals' heads, instead of their legs, into the stocks, and the culprit is compelled to wear this cumbersome necklace for a given number of weeks, or sometimes months. Upon one occasion a man was brought into the yamun for smuggling samshu to the marines, and the petty official charged with ministering to our comforts, to show his zeal, instantly commenced slapping him violently with the open hand upon the back, as though impelled by an amiable desire to assist him in coughing up a fish-bone.

R

The city of Tientsin occupies the angle formed by the junction of the Grand Canal and River Peiho. It is built as nearly as possible in the form of a square, each face being, according to a rough estimate, a mile in length. Four massive gateways give entrance to the four roads which approach from the cardinal points of the compass. These roads, on entering the town, become the principal streets, and intersect it at right angles. At the point of intersection, in the centre of the town, is a pagoda-shaped building, supported upon four archways, which span the streets. From this point all four gates are visible. These streets differ entirely from those of a southern town. In the latter, two sedan-chairs meeting scarcely find room to scrape past each other; while at Tientsin wheeled vehicles traverse the streets, which are in places paved with large flag-stones, the foot-passengers being provided with a *trottoir*.

Nor was Tientsin superior to southern towns in the breadth of its streets alone. The visitor could pursue his exploratory investigations without having his nostrils assailed at every turn by the indescribably foul odors of the south; for, although the city and suburbs were by no means free from stenches, they existed but in a modified form. There was nothing, however, to tempt one to frequent its uninviting purlieus. The few shops that interested foreigners were in the suburbs; the shops and houses in the city containing the commonest articles of Chinese necessity, and the exterior was as mean as their interior was ill supplied. They were generally built of unburnt brick, sometimes of mud, often consisting of two very low stories, the ground floor open to the street.

Some fantastically-carved wooden arches, which spanned one of the streets, were the only ornaments of which the town could boast. The temples were poor in an architectural point of view, and the divinities they contained more than ordinarily shabby: the best was in the suburb. Two or three yamuns indicated the residences of the civic dignitaries. There was an absence of that life and bustle in the streets which usually characterize a Chinese town: this may have been partially owing to the panic created by our presence. Indeed, people were actually leaving the town, and many of the shops were shut from this cause; and in the suburbs this proof of their uncertainty with regard to our intentions was more general. They evidently did not wish to tempt our cupidity by the display of their wealth. Whether this wealth existed or not remained a matter of speculation. Most certainly the general impression created upon our minds was that, for a town which, with its suburbs, is said to contain half a million of inhabitants, Tientsin was the most squalid, impoverished-looking place we had ever been in.

The principal traffic in the streets seemed to be that of fuel and water. The fuel consisted of millet or wheat straw, carried on men's shoulders; the water was conveyed in the quaintly-constructed wheel-barrows already described: occasionally might be seen a man sitting upon one side of the wheel, to balance the two buckets of water poised upon the other. The water-way to the edge of the river was paved with flag-stones, cut down through the steep bank, the cutting being bridged over for the convenience of people passing along the river brink. As seen from the water, the groups of water-carriers, with their barrows and variously-shaped buckets, emerging from these subterranean avenues, or collected at their mouth, presented one of the few picturesque sights which greeted the eye of the traveler, if he had not become too much disgusted with the monotony around him to appreciate any thing.

Such was the internal aspect of the city of Tientsin. Its defenses consisted of the rickety walls above mentioned, which had crumbled away so much in places that it remained a mere shell. It was said that upon this wall were mounted eighty guns, being twenty to each face; but, even if that number was not exaggerated, they existed more in name than in reality. Instead of being mounted on carriages, they were, for the most part, imbedded in baskets of sand, and so corroded and decayed that the gunners would be in infinitely greater danger than the enemy. The gates are all surmounted by buildings which serve as barracks, of two stories, with pagoda roofs.

Upon the first occasion of our visiting the city, two or three days after our arrival at Tientsin, some slight reluctance to admit us was exhibited by the gate-keepers; but after our forcible entry, our visits were regarded as a matter of course.

I was informed by an old merchant of Tientsin, and his statement was corroborated by the present aspect of the place, that it had been decaying both in opulence and population since the overflowing of the Yellow River had broken down the banks of the Grand Canal, and the exigencies of the rebellion had swallowed up the funds which would otherwise have been devoted to the repairs of that great work. Produce of various descriptions, arriving from almost every province in China, formerly found its way by tributary canals into the main artery; much of the wealth of the empire thus flowed past Tientsin, which now reaches the capital by other channels of internal communication, or has ceased altogether. But the principal use of the Grand Canal was for the transport of the annual grain-supply. According to Sir George Staunton, a thousand grain-junks were passed by Lord Macartney's mission between Tientsin and Toongchow. It will be seen from the following interesting notice, compiled by Mr. Wade from various authentic Chinese sources, what, according to the most recent accounts, is the present state of the imperial canal, and under what conditions the grain-transport has been carried on in consequence:

"It is now several months since rumors reached us of the terror produced in the districts adjoining the lower part of the Yellow River by its disappearance from its ancient bed.* It seems beyond doubt established that, from a point which must be about as high up as Kai-fung Fu, this violent stream has forced a new, or, according to Chinese historians, has resumed an old channel, in a northeasterly direction, and now makes its way into the Gulf of Pechelee by superadding its waters to those of the Ta-tsing and other rivers of Shan-tung. Much of the intermediate country is described by a recent traveler as more lake than land, and the great artery of Northern China, the Grand Canal, clogged in some places and expanded out of all symmetry in others, lies useless for any of the greater purposes of trade or supply for which it was originally intended. From the statement of the crew of a Yang-chau junk, which had forced her way up to Tientsin early in 1857, the bed of the Yellow River had been filled with water from the canal reservoir by Hwai-ngan Fu to the depth of three feet, to enable vessels to cross. The junk in question drew but two feet. She found in many places up the canal but four inches water, and the greatest depth at any point did not exceed four feet. We have since learned that the bed of the Yellow River, if temporarily filled, as stated, at the point in question, is now, at all events, perfectly dry.

* See *North China Herald*, Nos. 336, 3d of January, 1857; 359, 13th of June, 1857; 407, 15th of May, 1858; 411, 12th of June, 1858.

"It is difficult to say from what depths of exigency the industry of China may not recover itself; but it is almost beyond a doubt that, for the present, the operation of one of her greatest works is in abeyance, and the north of her empire is consequently beholden for its commerce, and to a large extent for its subsistence, to the coast trade, which it has been the policy of the government, as regards the most important article of Chinese life, to restrict in favor of its inland traffic. The wants of Northern China naturally attract our attention at a moment when the ports of that region have been opened to a certain extent to our commerce, and the following particulars of what we were wont to describe as the Grain Tribute of China, and of the past and present methods of its transmission, may not be uninteresting.

"The code of the Board of Revenue of 1831, the latest edition, we believe, in print, showed that, exclusive of 13,340 tons for which a constant commutation tax, amounting to 246,570 taels, was levied at various rates in five of the contributing provinces, the whole Grain Tribute annually forwarded in kind used to be collected in the following proportions:

Rice	210,000 tons.
White rice for the court use	44,000 "
Wheat	4,000 "
Pulse	17,000 "

"The wheat and pulse were grown in Chih-li itself, in Shantung and in Honan; the black pulse in Manchuria. The wheat is stated to be the only sort destined for human consumption, but this is by no means certain.

"The subjoined table, drawn up from the same authority, declares the proportions in which, under ordinary circumstances, the producing districts would contribute. The wretched state of the canal communications and the rebellion, which, besides interrupting both the collection and transmission of the grain-supply, has for many years absorbed the funds otherwise applicable to the repairs of the canal and river, are causes which materially affect the original conditions of this branch of revenue. We will speak of it first as it was.

The official expenditure of grain in 1811 was some 113,000 tons, without reckoning the court's own demand; and, according to the Revenue Statistics of 1831, already quoted, there should always have been in store at Pekin 354,000 tons of rice, and at

Tung-chau, twelve miles off, 82,000 tons. None of this should be allowed to be unsold or unexpended longer than three years.

"The shipment of the grain was effected at forty-four major and nineteen minor stations in the eight provinces of

| Chih-li. | Kiang-su. | Kiang-si. | Hunan. |
| Shan-tung. | Ngan-hwui. | Cheh-kiang. | Hu-peh. |

"These, with all details of the establishment charged with its carriage and escort, are under a superintendent, with the title of governor general, whose head-quarters are at Hwai-ngan Fu. He has under him a force on a quasi-military footing, the total strength of which is about 64,000 men. The grain-junks used to leave the points of collection in fleets, departing at different periods, so as to avoid confusion, each vessel bearing 300 piculs on government account. The escort, known as *kiting*, carried a certain amount on private account, and were indeed rewarded for bringing in from 180 to 200 piculs in excess of the government cargo. Each junk was allowed a sum for her expenses ranging in amount from 160 to 200 taels.

"The collection of the grain tribute was supposed to commence on the 1st of the 10th moon, say in November, and all grain, no matter where collected, to be weighed and shipped for the canal two months later. The junks from the districts north of the Yang-tsz', in the neighborhood of the canal, by law should cross the Yellow River at Hwai-ngan Fu in the 12th moon, January or February; those from other parts of Kiang-su and Ngan-hwui, a month later; and those from Kiang-si, Cheh-kiang, Hu-peh, and Hunan, a month later than the last. After they are across, the law still allows them three months to ascend the canal to Tientsin, there to tranship their cargoes for Tung-chau, whence the chief part of them would be carried in carts to Pekin.

"The line of canal communication between the Yang-tsz' and the Yellow River has but two approaches officially recognized as available for the transmission of the Grain Tribute; one, the Kwa-chau mouth of the canal, opposite Chin-kiang Fu; the other at I-ching, a few miles higher up the stream. Punctuality has not been more remarkable in this than in any other branch of Chinese revenue, but the grand derangement of all calculations respecting the transmission of grain has ever been the capricious disposition of the Yellow River. The 20th term of the Chinese year, known as the "frost's descent," has always been watched with anxiety, and freedom from inundation during this period entitled the spirit of the stream to a special sacrifice in token of the emperor's gratitude. A glance at the map will show that from the points of its intersection by the Yellow River the canal takes a northwesterly direction, running for a considerable distance nearly parallel to the course of its turbulent neighbor. As it quits the border of Kiang-su it becomes principally beholden for its supply to various sheets of water, part lake, part reservoir, which, unless we misunderstand the *Pekin Gazette*, are of a construction precariously primitive. Vast earthworks are thrown up, and into the space they inclose water is worked from the adjacent streams, to the very great peril, as the *Gazette* admits, of the mud *enceinte*, which would be utterly destroyed were the body within it all water. To mitigate this danger, and at the same time to preserve the water-level necessary to the supply of the canal, the vast tanks are three fourths filled with mud.

"In 1851 a more than usually violent outbreak of the Yellow River swept away all the works of earth and masonry in the section of river-works known as the Fung-pch, in the north corner of Kiang-su. In August, 1852, the upward-bound grain-fleet was obliged to land its cargo in Shan-tung, some eighty miles below Tsi-ning, to a point in which department all the grain had to be carried by land for reshipment to Pekin. The emperor was shortly moved by various memorialists to consider some new means of supplying the capital with grain, the canal, it was urged, having become impracticable by mismanagement.

"Early in 1853 a censor recommends the transport of grain by sea. He puts the total consumption of the capital at four million piculs of superior, and two and a half million piculs of inferior descriptions of grain—say 430,000 tons. The provinces heretofore relied upon were all disturbed by rebels; but in Fuh-kien and Cheh-kiang, which were quiet, a sale of rank might be opened, and grain bought by the local government with the proceeds. The Formosa market was also spoken of. By the end of the year 333 junks of grain from the south had reached the Gulf of Peche-lee.

"In the spring of 1854 the capital was in sore distress. The rebels were on the borders of Tientsin, and Cheh-kiang was the only one of the supplying provinces not in disorder: even there floods had done damage. The emperor was accordingly prayed to give a general invitation to merchants to import grain from all parts. The river communication between Pekin and Tientsin had also been injured by inundation. Still, by the close of the year the grain-receipts at Tung-chau amounted to 1,424,946 piculs, nearly 100,000 tons. This is described as grain of 1853. It is classed under eight different denominations, and its carriage up from Tientsin, it is observable, employed 3892 river-junks from the 7th of June to the 3d of August.

"A decree of January, 1855, shows that the rendezvous of the junks bringing grain from Kiang-su or Cheh-kiang was the port of Liu-ho, a small customs station on the Yang-tsz', at no great distance from Shanghai. The emperor is in great want of rice, and lays an embargo right and left on flat-bottomed vessels along the whole coast, from the Gulf of Liau-tung down to Ningpo. Cheh-kiang furnished no less than 60,000 tons this year; but this appears all that Pekin received.

"In May, 1856, the governor of Cheh-kiang, in a somewhat self-complacent memorial, reports the shipment of about 60,000 tons in 721 junks, divided into six fleets. 'It is now four years,' he says, 'since the sea-transport was commenced on the recommendation of his predecessor, and the subsidy is increasing annually.' By the 5th of July, 1200 junks had discharged 100,000 tons at Tientsin and returned south. Some 6000 tons were still due. The insurrection being now to all appearance about to limit itself to the southern provinces, the canal was surveyed in the hope of again making it navigable for the grain-fleet. The report is long, and, from the use of certain technicalities, somewhat difficult of translation. The fact, however, is established that, owing to a series of inundations from 1851 to 1855, the artificial channels had sustained almost irreparable damage. The Weishan Hu, a principal reservoir, which should have in it fourteen feet of water, had but from two to eight feet; in many places mud banks stood out like islands, and along its whole western verge was a dry tract of varying width. A proposition to introduce more water and more deposit was rejected, as calculated to jeopardize the frail inclosure of the Hu. The year closes with disastrous notices. In Pekin rice was from nine to ten dollars a picul; the crop short in Kiang-su and Cheh-kiang, which were also suffering from locusts. There were locusts in Chih-li as well.

"In 1857 the authorities of the Two Kwangs are called on to find rice for the court. Some of the Kiang-su quota is detained for war supplies. That the abandonment of the canal transport is in contemplation, may be inferred from a proposal made by the Board of Revenue to dispose of the junks formerly employed upon the canal, many of which we know to be rotting at Hang-chau and elsewhere. The board also remarks, by the way, that an equivalent to their former tax in grain is now levied in coin on Hu-peh, Hunan, Kiang-si, and Ngan-hwui; another indication of the court's acceptance of the sea-transport as something more than a temporary measure. The authorities of Manchuria reported the shipment in June of some 3000 tons of grain, which they describe as rice. It was probably wheat.

"Supposing the censor's estimate, tendered in 1853, to be approximately correct, it follows that, in the last six years, the supply of the best grain has only twice equaled a third, and did not last year amount to a tenth of the Pekin demand. The supply of this year remains to be ascertained; but when the mission were at Tientsin, rice was selling at from five to six dollars a picul, and the resources of the province were threatened by locusts, which continued to arrive by myriads. These were sold dried as food at forty cash a catty. They did not seem in such request, nevertheless, as to cause future speculators in 'grain-stuffs' any serious apprehension."

TABLE SHOWING THE PROCEEDS OF THE GRAIN-TAX OF CHINA AS RETURNED IN 1831.

	Chih-li.	Shang-tung	Honan.	Ngan-hwui.	Kiang-su.	Cheh-kiang.	Kiang-si.	Hu-peh.	Hunan.	TOTALS.
	Piculs.	Piculs.	Piculs.	Piculs.	Piculs.	Piculs.	Piculs.	Piculs.	Piculs.	Piculs.
Rice, for Pekin.........	57,000	83,295	8,969	288,239	1,038,111	621,466	351,294	94,622	95,529	......
" surplus............	......	19,159	2,047	63,400	228,382	136,708	77,286	20,812	21,010	......
" for Tung-chau...	......	42,914	9,192	102,075	94,852	29,353	151,614	......	......	......
" surplus............	......	7,310	1,564	14,280	13,270	4,981	25,772	......	......	......
" for the court.....	......	......	......	......	69,025	29,975	......	......	......	......
" surplus............	......	......	......	......	20,700	13,482	......	......	......	......
Total rice......	57,000	152,678	21,772	467,994	1,464,340	835,965	606,066	115,434	116,539	3,837,788
Wheat, for Pekin......	......	9,015	23,652	......	......	......	......	......	......	......
" surplus...........	......	2,280	6,060	......	......	......	......	......	......	......
" for Tung-chau	......	9,891	12,746	......	......	......	......	......	......	......
" surplus..........	......	1,584	2,159	......	......	......	......	......	......	......
Total wheat...	......	23,167	46,257	......	......	......	......	......	......	69,404
Pulse, for Pekin......	......	82,114	67,189	......	......	......	......	......	......	......
" surplus...........	......	18,880	15,430	......	......	......	......	......	......	......
" for Tung-chau..	......	31,082	27,857	......	......	......	......	......	......	......
" surplus...........	......	5,270	4,726	......	......	......	......	......	......	......
Total pulse.....	......	137,346	115,202	......	......	......	......	......	......	252,548
Total grain.....	57,000	313,191	183,211	467,994	1,464,340	835,965	606,066	115,434	116,539	4,159,740
Commutation—										
In silver taels.......	......	12,000	12,000	4,322	74,543	......	......	22,764	3,647	......
At different rates...	......	40,000	40,000	17,829	......	......	......	......	......	......
	......	......	......	21,635	......	......	......	......	......	......
	......	52,000	52,000	43,786	74,543	......	......	22,764	3,647	......

The high price of rice at Tientsin was doubtless due to our occupation of the river and the presence of our ships in the Gulf. It had always been one of Lord Elgin's principal objects, in hurrying north at an early period of the year, to reach the mouth of the Peiho in time to intercept the fleet of grain-junks. That we should have been successful in carrying out this design, had not other circumstances intervened to prevent it, may be gathered from the fact that upward of nine hundred grain-junks were calculated actually to have passed within sight of the Furious on their way into the river, not counting those which sought the northern entrance in order to avoid our fleet. Thus, though Tientsin had lost in some respects in commercial importance, it was still, in a political point of view, the most favorable position for exerting a tremendous moral pressure on the capital. Every day was affording additional evidence of this, and the result proved it conclusively.

To return, however, to the statistics of Tientsin, it was extremely difficult to obtain any information on the subject. The only respectable Chinese merchant whom I had an opportunity of cross-examining on the matter was either very loth to impart his knowledge, or had no knowledge to impart. The theme upon which he dwelt most feelingly was the excessive poverty of the city of his abode. It exported absolutely nothing, he averred. Its only productions were salt, from the pans near it and the sea, and grain of various descriptions, but not more than sufficed for home consumption. Among its imports from the south are dried fruits, sugar, glass-ware, camlets, woolens, opium, etc., in small quantities. Numerous cargoes of beans and bean-cakes are brought over from Neu-chwang and the Manchurian coast. There can be little doubt that we shall find a considerable market in the north of China for our cotton and woolen manufactures. I observed in the bazar some Manchester calicoes, also English or German glass-ware, cutlery, lucifer matches, etc.

In contemplating the population of Tientsin with a practically commercial eye, the problem is not whether they want clothes, but whether they have money enough to buy them. Appearances certainly fully bore out the Chinese merchant's assertion as to the poverty of the town. In no part of the world have I ever witnessed a more squalid, diseased population than that which seemed rather to infest than inhabit the suburbs of the city.

Filth, nakedness, and itch were the prevailing characteristics. The banks of the river swarmed with men who lived entirely on the garbage and offal that were flung from the ships, or were swept up by the tide from the city. There was an eddy just in front of our yamun in which dead cats, etc., used to gyrate, and into which stark naked figures were constantly plunging in search of some delicate morsel. Their clothing generally consisted of a piece of mat or tattered sacking, which they wore, not round their waist, but thrown negligently over their shoulders—it was difficult to divine for what purpose, as decency was ignored, and in the month of June warmth was not a desideratum. Cutaneous diseases of the most loathsome character met the eye in the course of the shortest walk, and objects so frightful that their vitality seemed a mockery of existence shocked the coarsest sensibilities.

Upon several occasions I saw life ebbing from some wretched sufferer as he lay at his post of mendicancy. One old woman, in particular, attracted my attention. She used to lie motionless on a mat in the centre of the road, a diseased skeleton. She had just strength enough to clutch at cash that was flung at her. One day this strength seemed to have failed: I looked closer, and she was dead. A few hours after, I repassed; but her place knew her no more: she had been carried away and cast upon a dung-heap. I was riding on the outskirts of the city one day, and saw a man carrying another on his back. At first I thought the burden was a corpse; but, as I approached nearer, a certain flexibility of the legs, as they trailed in the dust behind, undeceived me. This was one of the city scavengers who prowl the streets for dying beggars, and when they find one in whom life is almost extinct, they bear him off to some suburban Aceldama, and fling him from their shoulders, a premature feast for crows and vultures. Certainly, if the imagination of the Chinaman who named this city Tientsin, "heavenly spot," could form no higher idea of an abode of bliss, it is difficult to conceive what must have been his notion of the opposite extreme.

As if in ironical allusion to the misery which the living seemed to endure, almost the only pretty spots near Tientsin were the burial-places. They were nearly the only localities honored with trees, and consisted generally of a square with an area of about a quarter of an acre, inclosed by a mud bank and ditch, so as to present exactly the appearance of a small earthwork or *tabia*. Each member of a family who reposes within this inclosure is placed beneath a conical mound of earth, about the size and shape of a bell-tent. A thick grove of trees, generally willow and cypress, surrounds the cemetery, and gives a cool and refreshing aspect to the place. One of these burial-places was of so great an extent, and contained so many graves, that in our ignorance we avoided it for some days, feeling certain it was an intrenched camp, as we had heard of the existence of one in the neighborhood. The absence of the usual trees confirmed the suspicion, until we mustered up courage to visit it one day, and found only a decrepit custodian, rapidly going to join those whose remains he was now guarding. The real camp we discovered a few days after from the summit of a species of martello tower, to the top of which we climbed for purposes of inspection.

It is not to be supposed, however, that the entire population of Tientsin and its neighborhood are invalids or beggars. There was a large class of respectable *bourgeoisie;* and the country people, though poor, looked cheerful and industrious as they worked in large gangs in the fields. The fair sex was almost invisible. It was by the rarest accident that a glimpse was caught of a woman not belonging to the lowest class. Even these latter all cramped their feet—a practice not so general among the same class in the south. Some of the little girls we saw were pretty; and, with their heads decorated with bright flowers, and their gaudy skirts fluttering in the wind, they looked piquant and graceful. But, as a rule, the women generally seen were hideous.

Ere very long we had explored the environs of Tientsin in every direction. Our yamun was situated on a peninsula, formed by a deep bend of the river, which doubled back so as almost to convert it into an island. Upon one side of us the mud houses of the suburb were built against the yamun wall, but to the left and rear were gardens, scattered houses, and waste land. The engineers occupied a temple within musket-shot, and next door to them, "Caserne Française," painted in large white letters, indicated the quarters of the "Marine Française." Just previous to our departure there was an allied force of nearly six hundred men quartered in different buildings upon this little peninsula, which was capable of being rendered defensible, if necessary, by an earthwork thrown across the narrow isthmus, so that we were fortunate both in respect to the accommodation and *locale* of our position.

Passing the isthmus, and riding parallel to the Grand Canal, we soon reach a bridge of boats, by which the Pekin road crosses to the city; turning sharp to the right, we follow this road, so interesting to us while we thought it possible we might have to traverse it. It soon emerges from the suburb, and crossing two canals, tributary to the Peiho, by substantial bridges, one of which is ornamented with a handsome balustrade of carved marble, reaches the Wenho, or salt river, a little above its junction with the Peiho. It is conveyed across this important stream by a bridge of boats, and, traversing the peninsula formed by the two, follows the right bank of the Peiho for as many miles as our explorations extended.

The farthest point I reached on horseback was the large village of Petsang, about seven miles from Tientsin by the road, and lately become interesting as the point at which Mr. Ward and his suite struck the Peiho on their way to the capital, from which, according to report, it was not above forty-five miles distant in a straight line. The country through which we passed presented all the appearance of being subject to annual inundations; deep ditches intersected it in various directions for the purpose of carrying off the water; and the Pekin road was raised fifteen or twenty feet above its level, the small country roads which crossed it being all bridged over. The high road was paved in places, and about twenty feet in breadth. The villages, which dotted the landscape in every direction, were also built upon raised mounds, which completed their resemblance to the mud towns of Egypt.

During the first portion of our stay at Tientsin, the flat country extending between the Grand Canal and the Peiho was one vast field of ripening wheat as far as eye could reach; and, uninterrupted by fence or inclosure, the yellow corn rose and fell to the breeze in gently rolling waves; while, dotted over its surface, the masts and sails of numerous junks were visible, looking as though they traversed a golden sea. These were navigating the minor canals. Only once, on an unusually clear day, could I distinguish in the dim distance the irregular outline of some far-off hills. Winding through this fertile plain, the courses of the Grand Canal and the Peiho were marked by the groves of trees which adorn their banks, and surround ancestral graves. Some of the villages also rejoiced in clumps of trees, but generally they looked like brown patches stuck upon a green ground.

Ere we left Tientsin the aspect of the country was entirely changed, for the harvest was over. Most of the corn was cut with the sickle, but I observed that grain of certain descriptions was plucked out by the roots; then it was collected into thrashing-grounds, to be tramped out by oxen, and winnowed upon breezy days, when carts, concealed by mountains of straw, and drawn by mixed teams of horses, mules, and oxen, creaked heavily over the soft land, and gleaners scattered themselves far and wide through the fields, and the whole population was out in the bright sunshine, looking cheerful and happy as they gathered in the blessed fruits of their labor and toil. In the mellow hour of evening, when the whole western sky was a blaze of red, and the scene was bathed in the glowing reflection of its fiery tints, it was pleasant to ride among the reapers of Tientsin, and forget, in the picture of content and plenty before us, the objects we had just witnessed of misery and starvation.

Although the country around Tientsin was a dead level, it was not destitute of variety. If the Pekin road led through nothing but a corn-field, that which followed the banks of the Grand Canal in a southerly direction conducted you for miles between kitchen-gardens so exquisitely tended that, in this respect, at all events, the environs of Tientsin are a pattern to those of London. Fences of the neatest and most tasteful construction inclosed little areas of ground, irrigated by a net-work of minute canals, divided into beds, devoid of weed or pebble. Greens of every description, gourds, egg-plants, leeks and onions, sweet potatoes, beans and peas, were planted out and manured, or trained, as the case might be, with the utmost care. Interspersed with the kitchen-gardens were vineyards, orchards, and fruit-gardens, containing apricots, apples, and pears of a coarse description, and vines trained on trellises, as in the north of Italy. This was one of the pleasantest rides, as it was for the most part shaded by trees, and the windings of the canal, with the river-life upon it, added to its picturesque interest. It was an immense relief, in all our rural rambles, not to be stifled at every turn with the filthy contrivances of the south. In this respect the horticulture and agriculture of the north are carried on under much pleasanter conditions. Our explorations in a westerly direction were uninteresting; the country was an immense grave-yard—not a collection of private cemeteries, such as I have described upon the banks of the Peiho and Grand Canal, but a plain crowded with conical tumuli, destitute of grass or trees, and extensive enough to have contained the whole defunct population of Tientsin since the original founding of that "heavenly spot."

There is only one more direction in which I will ask the reader to accompany me, if he be not already as tired of the environs of Tientsin as we were. A very considerable suburb, connected with the city by a bridge of boats, was situated upon the opposite side of the Peiho. Passing through it, we debouch upon a singular piece of landscape.

Here were salt-pans, with the salt stacked in large tumuli like gigantic graves. Interspersed with them were small tumuli, which really were graves; and there were deep pits, and ponds of water with narrow ridges between them, and more salt stacked in bags, and roofed in with millet straw; and huge stacks of wheat straw collected for purposes of fuel; and mud huts, like Irish cabins of the meanest description, inclosed by fences of millet straw, which is thick and strong enough for the purpose; and there were brick-kilns which looked like circular forts, and a circular fort which looked like a brick-kiln. Altogether, it was the oddest collection of big mounds and little mounds, and heaps and stacks, and pits, and stagnant ponds, and hovels, and forts, and brick-kilns, and fences, and waste land I ever saw. A high road led through it, and into a close, populous village beyond, and out of that into the illimitable steppe. There was no waving corn here: a weakly vetch and unhealthy-looking young plants of Indian corn were struggling to maintain a miserable existence in a soil so thin and friable that the united efforts of two men and a donkey, or two donkeys, were sufficient to drag a plow through it. It seemed to be of quite another character from that on the right bank of the river. Beyond the vetch-fields the steppe produced nothing but a short dry grass, across which we could scamper in every direction, with the chance of putting up a hare and riding after him across the country. It reminded me of some parts of the steppes of Southern Russia. Sometimes the monotony of this scene was unbroken by a living object; sometimes a cloud of dust would betoken the approach of country carts, and a succession of huge creaking vehicles would roll past, loaded with fuel, and drawn by a mixed team. I have counted a horse, a pony, a mule, a donkey, and two oxen in one cart. An ox and the horse served as wheelers; in front of them were the other ox, the mule, and the pony, while the donkey led the way in solitary dignity.

Toward the end of the month of June, fortunately just after the crops were taken in, a swarm of locusts invaded the country. You could gallop through miles of them in this plain as they whizzed and fluttered among the horses' legs; you could steam through acres of them as you traversed the river, and eat bushels of them fried, if so it pleased you, as they were hawked about in baskets by urchins in the streets. Locust-hunting was a favorite and profitable occupation among the juvenile part of the community. I had the curiosity to eat one, and thought it not unlike a periwinkle.

S

CHAPTER XIX.

Advantages gained by Russia and America.—A serious "Hitch."—The two important Demands.—The Right of a Resident Minister.—The Chinese System of Government: Mode of influencing it.—Principle of direct Communication.—The Concession gained.—The final Procession.—Signing of the Treaty.—An effective Illumination.—A Retrospect.—The new Ports.—The Transit-dues.—Climate of Tientsin.—Absence of Surveys.—Geography of the Country.—Abundance of Ice.—A Skittle-alley.—Curiosity-hunting.

MEANTIME the work of negotiation was progressing with the neutrals, whose task was less surrounded with difficulties than that of the quasi-belligerents, more rapidly than with ourselves.

On the 14th of June Count Poutiatine signed his treaty, in which the chief concessions gained were the right of correspondence upon an equal footing between the Russian minister of Foreign Affairs and the prime minister or first minister of the Council of State at Pekin; permission to send diplomatic agents to that city upon special occasions; liberty of circulation throughout the empire of missionaries only, under a system of passports; and the right to trade at ports at present open, and, in addition, at Swatow, at a port in Formosa, and another in Hainan.

Four days afterward the American treaty was signed by Mr. Reed, in which the same privilege of special missions to Pekin was accorded to the government of the United States, and the same additional ports opened to its trade.

These were by no means trifling concessions, and, eked out by "the most favored nation clause," were a great advance on the privileges formerly enjoyed by Russia and the United States in China. It would be a mistake, however, to suppose that they were willingly granted by the Chinese government. Much more moderate demands, when preferred the year before by the ministers of Russia and the United States respectively, had been peremptorily refused. Indeed, both Count Poutiatine and Mr. Reed, upon concluding these treaties, expressed, in the most frank and candid manner, the conviction they entertained that the concessions they had gained had been due to the pressure exercised at this juncture upon the imperial cabinet by the allied governments of France and England.

By the end of the week, after several pretty stormy discussions between the commissioners and Mr. Bruce and Messrs. Wade and Lay, who were acting on behalf of Lord Elgin, a general agreement had been arrived at as to the terms of the British treaty. It had been resolved that the clauses should be drawn up forthwith in English and Chinese, and the evening of the 26th had been fixed for the signature.

An incident, however, occurred on the evening of the 25th which threatened to lead to very serious embarrassments. Among the clauses in the British treaty which were not included in the other treaties, there were two which were most pertinaciously resisted by the Chinese commissioners. The one provided that the British minister in China should be entitled to reside permanently at Pekin, or to visit it occasionally at the option of the British government; and the other, that British subjects should have the right of traveling to all parts of the Empire of China for trading purposes. Having failed in their endeavors to induce Lord Elgin to recede from these demands, the commissioners had recourse to the Plenipotentiaries of the other powers then at Tientsin, and begged their intervention in conveying to Lord Elgin the important piece of intelligence that on the previous day an imperial decree had been received from Pekin to the effect that not merely degradation, but decapitation would be inflicted upon Kweiliang and Hwashana if they conceded these two points.

Whether or not any such decree had actually been received was problematical; but the appeal *ad misericordiam* was difficult to resist, more particularly as it was made just at the moment that the first rumors of Keying's death reached us. As the French plenipotentiary had not included in his treaty the specific demands now objected to, it would have been unreasonable to suppose that he would consent to enforce them by hostile measures. The circumstances of the case were obviously in the highest degree critical. To give way was perhaps to imperil all that was most valuable in the proposed treaty; for the commissioners, emboldened by success, would in all probability have proceeded to call in question other clauses, such as that for the settlement of the transit dues, which were peculiar to the English treaty, in the hope of indefinitely protracting negotiations. To persevere in the face of the representations which had been made was to run the risk of isolation, perhaps of a hostile advance on Pekin unaccompanied by allies. Nevertheless, Lord Elgin, after full consideration, resolved to adhere to his original demands; and upon the morning of the 26th he authorized Mr. Bruce to communicate his determination to the commissioners in peremptory terms, believing that language of a decided character would be the best protection to the commissioners against the imperial wrath, which, it was alleged, their acquiescence in his demands would provoke.

It is scarcely necessary to enlarge upon the motives which induced the embassador to exhibit so much persistence in so far as the second of these demands is concerned. The commercial advantages which England must derive from the vast extension of her import and export trade consequent upon the "*exploitation*" of the interior of the empire by her merchants are too manifest to require elucidation. With reference to the other point, however —viz., the power of appointing a resident minister at Pekin—as opinions are divided in England as to the expediency of taking advantage of this privilege, the concession of which cost the imperial government so sharp a pang, it is necessary to say a few words in explanation of the value which Lord Elgin attached to it.

Any person who has attentively observed the working of the anomalous and altogether unique system under which the vast Empire of China is governed will have perceived that, though ruling under altogether different conditions, supported, not by a physical force, but by a moral prestige unrivaled in power and extent, the Emperor of China can say with no less truth than Napoleon, "L'Empire c'est moi." Backed by no standing army worth the name, depending for the stability of his authority neither upon his military genius nor administrative capacity, he exercises a rule more absolute than any European despot, and is enabled to thrill with his touch the remotest provinces of the empire, deriving his ability to do so from that instinct of cohesion and love of order by which his subjects are supereminently characterized.

But while it happens that the wonderful endurance of a Chinaman will enable him to bear an amount of injustice from his government which would revolutionize a Western state, it is no less true that the limit may be passed when a popular movement ensues, assuming at times an almost constitutional character. When any *emeute* of this description takes place, as directed against a local official, the imperial government invariably espouses the popular cause, and the individual, whose guilt is inferred from the existence of disturbance, is at once degraded. Thus a certain sympathy or tacit understanding seems to exist between the emperor and his subjects as to how far each may push their prerogative; and, so long as neither exceed these limits, to use their own expression, "the wheels of the chariot of imperial government revolve smoothly on their axles." So it happens that disturbances of greater or less import are constantly occurring in various parts of the country. Sometimes they assume the most formidable dimensions, and spread like a running fire over the empire; but, if they are not founded on a real grievance, they are not supported by popular sympathy, and gradually die out, the smouldering embers kept alive, perhaps, for some time, by the exertions of the more lawless part of the community. But the last spark ultimately expires, and its blackened trace is in a few years utterly effaced.

The late rebellion is in this waning stage. Nor did the imperial government trust so much to its armies as to the inert mass of public opinion which had not yet decided in its favor. So long as the capital is not threatened, and the lives of "the powers that are" there are not in absolute danger, they contemplate with comparative calmness the vicissitudes through which remote cities and provinces pass, contented to wait until the agitation shall have subsided, and then resume the old despotic sway as though nothing had happened. It affects their repose but slightly at the capital whether rebel or foreigner occupy some distant city. The patriotism of the loyal part of the population is evoked by imperial decree; whether the people obediently respond, and are successful, or whether they are unsuccessful, or whether they disobediently refuse, is a matter which seems but little to disturb the philosophers at Pekin. Either the imperial authority exists absolutely, or it has been entirely extinguished. In the latter case, unprovided with adequate physical means to restore it, the emperor is forced into a fatalistic view of the subject.

A better illustration of the truth of the important principles above laid down could not be afforded than in the case of Canton. The instructions furnished by the emperor to Yeh furnish unmistakable evidence of the inefficacy of protracted diplomacy at a distance to influence the policy of the imperial government in its treatment of foreigners; while, so far from the capture of Canton

—which was the result of his acting in accordance with those instructions—humbling the court of Pekin, as it was prophesied at Hong Kong would be the case, the hauteur and obstinacy of the imperial government were increased by this event. The prime minister declined to communicate direct with Lord Elgin according to treaty, and refused to send commissioners to meet him at Shanghai. At a later period, when we were dallying in the Gulf, orders were sent down to Canton calling out the Braves, who immediately responded to them, and attacked the city. Shortly after the signing of the treaty, counter-orders were dispatched disbanding them, and commanding them to remain at peace with foreigners, and these were also ultimately obeyed. The popular impression among the British heretofore had been that the Canton question was purely local, and that authorities and Braves were alike acting independently of orders from Pekin.

But, if these incidents went to show how impossible it was to influence the court of Pekin by coercion applied at remote parts of the empire, still more hopeless was it to effect this object by diplomacy exercised at a distance from the seat of government. Yeh's stubbornness and Keying's shuffling alike proved that a provincial governor, charged with the conduct of foreign affairs, was approved of at court only so long as he could show that he was thwarting the barbarians, whether by obstinacy or craft. To bring conviction to the mind of a functionary so situated was of little avail, because it only made him an object of suspicion to his imperial master. Lord Elgin's observation had therefore led him to the conclusion that it was necessary to be at the heart to affect the extremities, and that it was impossible to affect the heart through the extremities. Conceiving this to be the knot of the situation, he determined to establish the principle of direct communication between the British embassador and the imperial ministers at the capital, and to secure, at all events, the right of the former to a permanent residence at Pekin. It would rest with the government whether to exercise the right or not, attended as it doubtless was with many objections of a practical character, such as difficulties of access, severity of climate, absence of accommodation in the first instance, and almost absolute isolation. But, whatever point might ultimately be fixed upon for the residence of the minister, the fact that he had a right to be at Pekin would be a source of influence in his hands scarcely less powerful than that

Signing of the Treaty of Tientsin.

which he might acquire by his actual presence there, and the dread of his exercising that right operate as a check not less effectual than if it was already in existence. It would still be *through* the heart, although not absolutely at it, that the extremities would be affected. It will be seen from Lord Elgin's dispatch from Shanghai of the 5th of November, which I have placed in the Appendix, upon what grounds he was ultimately induced to recommend non-residence at Pekin.

The decided tone held by Mr. Bruce having convinced the commissioners of the hopelessness of farther resistance upon these points, it was arranged that the treaty should be signed at the hour originally named. As it was deemed best that as much *eclat* as possible should be given to so important an event, the whole strength of the military force accompanied Lord Elgin as a guard of honor, while the admiral and most of the officers of the squadron also attended, a number of them having arrived from the ships in the Gulf for the purpose of being present.

The procession was one calculated to inspire the inhabitants of Tientsin with some respect—the military guard of 400 men, preceded by the band; the long array of chairs, and the body of spectators on foot, in full uniform, extending over a distance of nearly half a mile. The ships in the river were dressed out, and the crews manned the yards as the procession filed along the bank, which was lined with crowds of wondering Chinese.

In consequence of the heat of the weather, the hour fixed for the ceremony was somewhat late, and it was nearly dark before we had traversed the winding streets of the suburb, and crossed the plain in which the "Temple of the Oceanic Influences" was situated. We were received in the same hall which had been the scene of the former conference, but it was arranged in a more business-like manner. Instead of the long table covered with refreshments, three small square tables occupied the centre of the apartment. At the middle one of these Lord Elgin took his seat, flanked by a commissioner on either side. The admiral, together with some of the naval officers and members of the mission, were seated at the other tables, and the remaining space was densely crowded with European and Chinese spectators. Three large paper lanterns lighted the business-tables, upon which the various copies of the treaty were soon spread out, and the process of signing and sealing commenced, the interest of the ceremony being sufficient to retain in silence the miscellaneous throng who were watching it.

Thus expired, on its fifteenth birthday, the treaty negotiated by Sir Henry Pottinger in 1843; for, by a curious coincidence, the day of the signing of the Treaty of Tientsin was the anniversary of the day upon which the Treaty of Nankin was ratified.

After the treaty was signed, tea and refreshments were handed round, though the commissioners had scarcely provided for the reception of so many visitors. The Chinese attendants on the commissioners remained closely grouped round their chiefs; while the exploratory propensities of British naval officers, and the reckless enterprise with which the more juvenile portion of them attacked every species of unwholesome dish that was placed in their way, rendered it desirable, for their own sakes, not to prolong the ceremony unnecessarily. It was nevertheless quite dark before the procession started on its return to the yamun. As we passed along the brink of the river, the crews of both French and English ships sent up long and hearty cheers, and Admiral Rigault's band welcomed us with the national anthem.

On the following evening, when Baron Gros signed his treaty, there was an improvement in the programme; for, as the long procession of blue-coated and white-gaitered French marines were filing along the river's bank, the darkness was suddenly dispelled by the blaze of blue-lights, and the Chinese crowd found itself unexpectedly brought out in strong relief beneath their vivid glare; and with ears deafened with the shouts of hundreds of barbarian throats, and eyes dazzled by the unearthly brilliancy which illuminated the scene, they gazed in amazement on each other, and their own muddy river, and wondered, perhaps, whether the treaties, the signing of which was being thus vividly impressed upon their memory, would work as great a transformation in the empire as the process of obtaining them had effected in their own city.

On entering our yamun Lord Elgin received the congratulations of Baron Gros; and, indeed, it is scarcely possible to describe the feelings of satisfaction we experienced on this most successful termination to the doubts and anxieties of the past year. It wanted but a few days of the anniversary of our first arrival in the Celestial Empire; and, although much doubtless remained to be done before we could hope to turn our faces homeward, our future labors would be of a far more pleasing character than those which had just been concluded. Up to this point we had met with a series of disappointments; now we were sanguine enough to hope that an era of success was about to commence.

We could bear tranquilly to review the history of the events of the past year. We could recall the effect produced by the first staggering intelligence we received at Galle of the Indian mutinies, and the consequent diversion at Singapore of all our thoughts and energies from China to Bengal, and remember how our three weeks' stay there was devoted to the annihilation of all our hopes and plans, while Lord Elgin was solely employed in divesting himself of all his means for carrying out the objects of his mission. We thought of the time when it seemed so hopeless that these were ever to be achieved—that we went to India in sheer despair—and learned for our consolation that, though the China force had saved Bengal, the China mission had lost all claim to public interest in presence of the appalling events occurring in this quarter; we recollected with horror the dismal months we spent in the harbor of Hong Kong, living on board a Peninsular and Oriental Company's steamer during the hottest and stormiest season of the year, uncertain whether a force was ever coming to relieve us from our inaction.

There were other and more recent periods which afforded us very little satisfaction to look back upon, and when our anxieties were felt the more keenly because it seemed likely that the prize was to be snatched from us when it was within our very grasp; but we could afford to laugh now at these reminiscences, and the adverse influences which seemed to have beset our path from the commencement only served to enhance the pleasure of success. Hostilities with the Empire of China had terminated with a loss to the British arms of about twenty men killed in action (since our first arrival in the empire), and a treaty had been signed far more extensive in its scope, and more subversive of imperial prejudices than that concluded fifteen years before, after a bloody and expensive war, which had been protracted over a period of two years. The reflection that we should probably be compelled to return to the south without visiting Pekin would indeed force itself painfully upon us; but, for the moment, satisfaction predominated, and we endeavored to keep gloomy thoughts out of view.

As the result, then, of the process applied to the imperial government, we had obtained, first, the two points of a resident minister at Pekin, and permission to travel and trade in all parts of the empire already referred to. Next, besides Teng-chow in the province of Shantung, and the ports opened in the islands of Hainan and Formosa by the other treaties, we opened New-chwang in Manchouria. The political importance of this latter port will be evident from a glance at the map, in which will be seen that it is the nearest sea-port to the Soongary River, a tributary to the Amoor, and navigable for steamers as far as Petuné; it is also the port of Moukhden, the imperial capital of Manchouria. In addition to these ports we opened Chin-kiang, and secured the ports on the River Yang-tse-Kiang between that point and Hankow, a celebrated mercantile emporium in the heart of the empire. A condition was attached to this concession, declaring that it was not to come into effect until the rebels were expelled from its shores.

Lastly—and this, perhaps, in a commercial point of view, was the most important clause of the treaty—the much-vexed question of transit-dues was finally set at rest. A few words are necessary in explanation of this clause. Some misapprehension has prevailed in England as to the nature of these duties, and they were for some time regarded as applied only to foreign produce passing into the interior, and to native produce intended for exportation. It is, however, universally understood and admitted in China that the transit-dues are a tax in the form of an *octroi*, levied upon all produce indiscriminately which passes into the interior provinces of the empire, or from one to another. Inasmuch, then, as it is one of the permanent sources of revenue to the Chinese government, to demand the total abolition of these dues would have been a harsh and unjustifiable measure; nor was it likely that the imperial government would have consented to a domestic change involving such an enormous sacrifice of revenue. On the other hand, the Treaty of Nankin left the question in so unsatisfactory a state, that it has ever since proved a permanent source of complaint to the British merchant. That treaty simply provided that the transit-duty should not be increased beyond the then existing rates; but, as those rates were never ascertained, this provision proved, in effect, of no avail, and two evil consequences followed from the position in which the matter was left. In the first place, a number of articles—and more especially the important article of tea—were subjected occasionally to very heavy imposts under the name of Tea-duties, whereby, in point of fact, the provisions of the tariff were in a great measure rendered nugatory. In the second place, the power of indefinite taxation, thus left to the Chinese government, introduced an element of great uncertainty into mercantile transactions both in exports and imports.

In the various suggestions and communications which, at Lord Elgin's invitation, had been given to him by different mercantile bodies in China, this difficulty had been repeatedly referred to, but none of them contained any plan for its removal. It was met in the British treaty negotiated at Tientsin by an article enabling the British merchant to purchase, at the rate of 2½ per cent. *ad valorem*, in the case of imports at the port of entry, and in the case of exports at the first inland barrier through which his commodities would pass, a certificate enabling him to carry his goods duty free, in the latter case, to the port of shipment, and in the former to any place in the interior of China to which it may be destined.

In a separate clause the amount of indemnity claimed by us for losses sustained at Canton was stated at two millions of taels (about £650,000), and a farther sum of two million taels was claimed in compensation for the expenses of the war.

The above were the most important points in which the British Treaty of Tientsin differed from the other treaties signed at the same place and time. The first great step having been thus achieved toward the placing of our relations with the Celestial Empire upon a new and more substantial basis than had hitherto subsisted, it only remained for Lord Elgin to await the imperial assent to the treaty which had just been negotiated ere he finally bade adieu to Tientsin. Our experience of this "heavenly spot" had now extended over a period of a month, and we were not sorry to think that it was soon to be brought to a termination. During the last few days the temperature had been rapidly increasing. At first we had hot days, but the nights were cool, and the thermometer sometimes showed a variety of 20° in the twenty-four hours; now, however, the nights were beginning to be oppressive, and the thermometer ranged from 90° to 96° in the coolest part of the yamun. I am indebted to our medical attendant, Dr. Saunders, for the annexed register of the temperature during our stay at Tientsin. Although the thermometer showed so high a range, the heat was not accompanied by those debilitating effects which so often attend it in tropical latitudes. The air was dry and pure, and the general health of the squadron remained good. We had been threatened with a rainy season in June, but, with the exception of one or two heavy showers, the weather continued fine throughout the month.

It was, indeed, much to be regretted that—as, during the first portion of our occupation of the river and Gulf, the climate was so favorable to the health of the men—nothing should have been accomplished in surveying the unknown mouths of the Peiho and in exploring some of its tributaries. For a period of three months upward of twenty men-of-war lay idle in the Gulf, and during a number of weeks our gun-boats navigated the Peiho, yet we sailed away from those shores with our geographical knowledge as limited as when we first arrived there. Beyond pulling for about two miles up the Grand Canal, we know nothing more of the course or depth of water of that channel of communication than is furnished in the records of the former embassies. As far as we went, we found water enough for gun-boats, the banks being in places built up with wheat-straw and matting. The course is very winding, as indeed in this place it is, properly speaking, not a canal, but a river, into which the Grand Canal is led some miles above its junction with the Peiho. It is called by the Chinese the Grain-bearing River. About a mile higher up the Peiho, and debouching into it on the same side as the Grand Canal, is a smaller canal, which takes a southerly course across the wheat plain, and was reported to lead to Ho-kien and the Peh-hu lake, and so into the southern parts of the province of Shansee.

About half a mile beyond this canal the Peiho is entered by a river apparently exceeding it in size and volume, commonly known as the Yen-ho, or Great Salt River. It is spanned by a bridge of boats at its point of junction; and, to judge from the number and size of the junks with which the stream was crowded, must be an important channel of internal communication. Sir Frederick Nicolson pulled up it for a few hundred yards, and brought back a poor account of the depth of water; but I have ridden along its banks for some miles, and have seen junks navigating it whose draught of water must have equaled, if not exceeded, that of our smallest class of gun-boats. The direction which this river takes renders it important that we should know its capabilities, as it reaches a point to the west of Pekin as near to that city as the Peiho approaches it on the east.

The only channel of water-communication we observed to enter the Peiho on its left bank was a small canal which debouched opposite the peninsula upon which our yamun was situated. As far as I followed this canal, it pursued a northerly direction across the barren-looking steppe which I have already described. Its course was marked not so much by the usual line of trees as by large isolated mud villages, which doubtless it supplied with the means of intercommunication. It was navigated by very small junks, a number of which were often fastened in a long string to each other, and punted along till they came to a sharp turn or other impediment, when they would break up like a raft. This canal, I strongly suspect, connected the Peiho with the stream usually known as its northern mouth, and which enters the Gulf about ten miles to the north of Takoo; but this is mere conjecture, as I could not obtain any reliable information on the subject. From the different accounts one received in answer to geographical inquiries, it was evident how reluctant the people were to impart knowledge of their country to the barbarian.

If the climate of Tientsin was latterly somewhat oppressive, we could, at all events, luxuriate freely in that most powerful alleviation to the discomfort of intense heat—ice. The whole population could revel in it if they chose. Boat-loads of it traversed the river—coolies staggered under the refreshing burden along the broiling streets—beggars stood at corners and sold it for infinitesimal sums, and other beggars came and bought it. Food of all sorts was abundant, and our requisitions in this respect were promptly attended to; though it must be confessed that, in respect of beef, they were sometimes a little unreasonable, as all the cattle are used in these parts for draught purposes only, a fact which their well-shod hoofs undeniably attested. Coarse but not ill-flavored apricots, and coarser peaches, with small marsh-melons and apples and pears, furnished us with dessert, and the sailors in the river with the maladies incidental to an indiscriminate use of fruit in a hot climate.

The court-yard of the yamun, roofed over with matting, always afforded us a cool and agreeable lounge. In its grateful shade we played quoits and established a skittle-alley, a game which had the merit of being, at all events, as aristocratic in the eyes of the

Chinese as any other, and of giving us exercise when it was impossible to face the rays of the sun, even as it was sinking below the horizon. Unlike the sun of the tropics, merciful during the final hour of his existence, the sun at Tientsin darted fiery rays at you up to the last moment of the long summer day.

On Sundays this sheltered court was turned into a place of worship. The pulpit was on one of the raised platforms containing the emperor's handwriting, the roof adorned with dragons and the mystic signs of Confucian philosophy. Army, navy, and diplomacy seated themselves in the quoit-ground and skittle-alley, grouped themselves round the majestic old tree which stood in the centre, or took up a position beneath a collection of gods and goddesses, who gazed as imperturbably at the scene on one side as a group of Chinese did on the other. It was a picturesque, but, at the same time, an impressive ceremony, none the less suggestive in its simplicity because brought into such close and striking contrast with the mixed emblems of an obscure metaphysical system on the one hand, and a debasing superstition on the other.

After we had signed the treaty, and a proclamation had been issued by the commissioners informing the Chinese public that the foreigners now in the river might shortly be expected to evacuate it, the people began to regain their confidence; new shops were opening daily in the suburbs, and curiosity-hunting commenced with that energy which seems to distinguish the "barbarian" of every "outside nation" when he visits the "Central Flowery Land." The great inconvenience attending this amusement at Tientsin was in the medium of circulation. We had brought with us a quantity of sycee silver, but the weighing out of a mass of particles of silver for each purchase was a tiresome and uncertain operation. Mexican dollars were taken, but not very freely, and then for much less than their value, while the only small change current was copper cash, of which a dollar's worth weighs from ten to fifteen lbs. The simplest plan of dividing a dollar was to cut it in halves with a chopper, and redivide them if you wanted to purchase a shilling's worth of any thing; but it was as inconvenient to carry a chopper in one's purse as ten pounds' weight of copper, or a pair of scales, which were the other alternatives. Moreover, there was very little worth buying, and I saw no good old China, enamel, bronzes, or any of those articles which form the staple of Chinese works of "virtu."

CHAPTER XX.

Duplicity of the Commissioners.—Arrival of the Emperor's Assent.—Arrival of Reenforcements.—Abandonment of Visit to Pekin.—Consequences of Delay.—State of Matters in the South.—Final Visit to Commissioners.—Death of the Prime Minister Yu.—Hwashana's Poems.—"Old" Chang; his poetical Effusions.—Departure from Tientsin.—The Great Wall.—State of Matters in the South.—Appointment of five Commissioners.—Military Government of Canton.—Lord Elgin's Dispatch to the General.—Departure for Japan.

ALTHOUGH, in the ordinary course of diplomatic routine, it is considered unnecessary to procure, before ratification, the assent of the sovereign to a treaty negotiated between specially appointed plenipotentiaries, Lord Elgin decided upon adopting the course followed by Sir Henry Pottinger in the Treaty of Nankin, and obtaining the imperial assent to the treaty, the ratifications of which, it had been arranged, should be exchanged at Pekin within the period of a year from the date of its signature. His intention to this effect was expressed to the commissioners, who, accordingly, four days after it was signed, forwarded to his lordship a communication in which they stated that they had received an imperial autograph rescript to the following effect: "We have perused your memorial and know all. Respect this." As the fact of the emperor's cognizance of "all" did not by any means imply his assent to it, the embassador replied that he "was still awaiting his majesty's approval to the conditions of the treaty." In answer to which, the commissioners stated that, "as soon as we shall have in person presented the originals of the different nations' treaties, with the seals and signatures, to his majesty at the capital, and received the ratification of them in the imperial autograph, it shall be transmitted, with all speed, to Shanghai for the information of your excellency."

Lord Elgin, in reply to the above communication, states "that he can not consider peace to be re-established until he shall have been satisfied of the emperor's entire acceptance of the conditions agreed to by the commissioners as his majesty's plenipotentiaries. That the undersigned is neither acting nor insisting upon more than is justified by the usage of the empire, is shown by the decree of the late emperor, a copy of which he has the honor to inclose. Within a few days of its arrival at Nankin, Sir H. Pottinger began to move his fleet down the Yang-tse-Kiang. The undersigned is bound to require an assurance, similarly complete, of the purpose of his present majesty to abide by the engagements entered into on his behalf. Without such an assurance the undersigned can not quit Tientsin, and delay in procuring it will leave him no other alternative but to order up to that city the large body of troops which has arrived from Hong Kong, and is now lying in the Gulf of Pechelee."

This letter was followed up by a prompt requisition for barrack accommodation for the 59th regiment, which had recently arrived in the Gulf in the troop-ship Adventure. It produced an immediate effect, the commissioners replying the same day, and promising to procure the required assent, all difficulty on the subject being removed from their minds by the fact which had been brought to their notice of the existence of a precedent.

Accordingly, on the 4th of July, or only two days afterward, a letter was received from the commissioners with the following inclosure: "On the 23d day of the 5th moon of the 8th year of Hien Fung (3d of July), the great council had the honor to receive the following imperial decree:

"Kweiliang and his colleagues have submitted for our perusal copies of the treaties of the different nations. These have been negotiated and sealed by Kweiliang and his colleague. As Kweiliang and his colleague now represent that the different nations are desirous of having our autograph acknowledgment as evidence of their validity, we (hereby signify) our assent to all the propositions in the English and French, and in the Russian and American treaties, as submitted to us in their previous memorial by these ministers, and we command that the course pursued be in accordance therewith. Respect this."

With reference to this imperial decree, Mr. Wade states in his note on the above document that "these Shang-yu imperial decrees are never in autograph. They are prepared by the council, and go forth as the will of the emperor. It will be remembered with what ceremony Kweiliang produced that declaring the powers with which he and Hwashana were invested at their first conference with Lord Elgin." It will be observed that this decree, which was only forced out of the emperor by Lord Elgin's pertinacity, was in general terms, and applied to the treaties made by the other powers as well as ourselves.

The 59th were actually on their way up the river in gun-boats when this letter arrived. Their advance was at once countermanded, and they returned to Hong Kong without ever having reached Tientsin, but not without having done good service.

It was, indeed, with feelings of the deepest regret and disappointment that, in consequence of the news which now arrived from Canton, Lord Elgin found himself compelled to give this order, and to abandon his original intention of visiting Pekin in order to present to the emperor the letter with which he had been accredited by her majesty. The very success which had attended our operations hitherto, and the facility with which they had been carried out, only furnished a more unmistakable proof of the ease with which we might have reached Pekin, had we been at Tientsin two months earlier, when Canton and its neighborhood were still tranquil, when the Chinese were unprepared, and the climate was that of an English spring. The political importance of such an achievement it is impossible to overestimate. The much-vexed question of the reception of a British minister at the capital would have been set at rest forever, and under peculiarly favorable conditions.

Now, unfortunately, every thing combined to induce his excellency to abandon the idea. A Tartar force had collected in the neighborhood of the capital during the last two months, and, although a visit to Pekin after the signature of the treaty of peace would not have had a hostile character, yet it would have been distasteful to the emperor, and it must, in common prudence, have preceded the evacuation of Tientsin by the allied force. A state of affairs had, however, arisen in the south that made it imperative that neither the naval nor military force should be detained in the north any longer than was absolutely necessary. Moreover, the sun was in its most fatal month, and a march of fifty miles would be attended with serious consequences, while the *éclat* and prestige of any such movement would have been very much neutralized by the dilatory nature of the negotiations, and the apparent vacillation at the outset.

Thus every one of those evil results, as arising out of the delay, which had been anticipated by Lord Elgin at Shanghai more than three months before, and to avoid which he felt justified in proceeding to the north without waiting for the admiral, had been realized.*

On the 26th of May Lord Elgin had received a communication from General Straubenzee assuring him of the perfect tranquillity of Canton, and of his ability to spare a large share of his troops for operations in the north, should they become necessary. In consequence of this assurance, Lord Elgin did not hesitate, immediately on his arrival at Tientsin, to write to him requesting him to send up the force available for the purpose, and on the 30th of June these reached the Gulf. They brought with them, however, intelligence of a totally altered condition of affairs from that which had existed only a few weeks previously. Sufficient time had elapsed since our first appearance in the Gulf to enable the Chinese government to instigate the Braves to attack Canton. Their assaults on the city, the expedition of our troops to the White Cloud Mountains, and the increased audacity of the Braves in consequence of the unsuccessful issue of this operation, was news which imparted to the state of matters at Canton a more serious aspect than they had yet worn. Although, from our previous acquaintance with both the foreign and Chinese community, we were aware that the panic which existed in the south was probably to a great extent groundless, still the representations generally made of the nature of the crisis were too urgent to be disregarded. From the effect they produced in England some idea may be formed of the sensation they were calculated to create at Tientsin.

---

* *The Earl of Elgin to the Earl of Clarendon.*

"Shanghai, April 3, 1858.

"MY LORD,—The Coromandel, tender to Rear Admiral Sir Michael Seymour's flag-ship, has just arrived in this harbor, and reports that the admiral did not intend to leave Hong Kong before the 25th ult. He can not, therefore, be expected here before the middle of this month. If I were to postpone my departure for the north until after the admiral's arrival, I think, and I believe that my opinion on this point is shared by the plenipotentiaries of the other great powers who are acting in concert with us in this quarter, that the interests of the public service would suffer, for the following reasons: Firstly, because the Chinese would impute the delay to vacillation and weakness; secondly, because we should lose our hold on the rice-junks destined for Pekin, which are now proceeding toward the north, and may yet be arrested, if necessary, at the mouth of the Peiho; thirdly, because, if the information I have received from Count Poutiatine on this head be correct, the season for operations in the region to which we are proceeding terminates with the end of the month of May. I have, therefore, taken it upon myself, in the absence of Admiral Seymour, to address to the senior officers at Shanghai and Hong Kong letters, of which I herewith inclose copies, and which, I trust, will be approved by your lordship."—*Blue-Book*, p. 258.

To keep troops in the north after the treaty had received the emperor's assent, and when it was reported that the British community at Hong Kong were to be ruthlessly massacred, and the British garrison in Canton ignominiously expelled, for want of a sufficient military force to protect the one place and retain the other, would be clearly unjustifiable; and Lord Elgin at once returned the whole force to General Straubenzee, in the earnest hope that they might arrive in time to enable him to restore confidence by administering to the Braves that lesson, without which, according to the opinion generally entertained, they would never be imbued with a proper respect for British authority. With this view he reminded his excellency "that the power of resorting to such hostile operations as they might deem necessary for the security of their military position at Canton was reserved to the commanders-in-chief, in the most ample terms, in the communication addressed by the plenipotentiaries to the government of China, which formed the subject of my letter to yourself and Sir Michael Seymour, dated the 6th of February last."

Before leaving Tientsin Lord Elgin intimated his desire to meet the commissioners in a semi-official manner; and accordingly, on the morning of the 6th of July, we proceeded to the "Temple of the Winds, which was not so distant as that at which the former interviews were held, and there paid a friendly visit to the commissioners, in the course of which Lord Elgin alluded to the state of affairs in the south, and the conduct of the imperial commissioner Hwang. Had he insisted upon it, there is no doubt he might have procured this worthy's disgrace, instead of leaving this to be done on a future day. Lord Elgin was, however, unwilling to use language which might seem to imply that we were unable to cope with the Canton Braves, and he therefore contented himself with warning the commissioners that the conduct Hwang was pursuing in the south would lead to a recurrence of those scenes which they must deplore equally with himself. Kweiliang replied in the same spirit, and expressed his earnest hope that the troubles at Canton were now at an end, and that the treaty just concluded would inaugurate a more peaceful era in the relations of the Celestial Empire with foreigners. He promised to use his influence to put a stop to the proceedings of the Governor General Hwang.

Since our last interview with this venerable old man, news

have been received of the death of Yu, the first minister of the Council of State. This gave Kweiliang the highest rank in the empire.

The embassador adverted to the expediency of a Chinese officer of rank being sent to England as embassador, and asked the portly Hwashana whether he would like to go in that capacity; to which that sedate and imperturbable old aristocrat replied, "That if the emperor ordered him to go, he would go; but if the emperor did not order him to go, he would not go." Lord Elgin then complimented him on his eminence as a scholar and a poet, and referred to the distinction which was conferred upon him by his having taken the degree of Han, an allusion which caused him somewhat to relax as he acknowledged the compliment with an air of grim gratification. The allusion to his poetical compositions was met by an offer on his part to present Lord Elgin with a copy of some of them, and a goodly supply of volumes accordingly followed us on our return to the yamun, containing the metrical effusions of this accomplished "imperial expositor of the classics." As I am not aware that the poem of a Chinese cabinet minister has ever yet appeared in print, I take this opportunity of giving publicity to the following stanzas, as a specimen of those which have, during the intervals of his political labors, flowed from the pen of his excellency Hwashana. It is just possible that their merit is due rather to Mr. Wade's elegant translation than to the poetic talent of the composer.

Hwashana's Complaint when, on his second mission to Moukhden, the Capital of Manchouria, he finds himself once more at the Inn at Chalau.

I.

"On toward the sister capital once more,
 By duty called, I track my distant way;
 The watch-dog notes my wheel, as droops the night
 O'er the thatched cot, and slowly tramp my steeds
 Up the wild pass, in autumn's mourning sad,
 Joyless the moon. And now in chamber lone,
 Beneath his single lamp, the traveler dreams
 Of house and home, an hundred leagues behind.
 Where are his rhymes these panels bore of old?
 Vain search! o'er Lu-ho let him listless pore.

II.

Where herds and swine once lay, a hostel now.
 Chalau is won at last. My car is staid,
 As sunset, slanting, strikes its roof, and chill

> The widespread bars admit the evening's breath.
> Forlorn the scene—a very "Walk in Dew."*
> Envoy of majesty! so known to whom?
> Peace where the state hath need—no word of care;
> Turn to thy muse—let verse these walls adorn."

I leave to competent critics the task of discussing the merits of this production; but in justice to a humbler poet, who became well known to us during our trip to the north, and whose gentle and amiable character impressed us all in his favor, I venture to insert a composition which I think bears off the palm from his exalted competitor. Old Chang was one of those not very old men who have probably been known as "old Chang" all their lives. He was a not unfavorable specimen of the literary class of China—a good scholar, an efficient spy in behalf of his own government, a gentleman in his manners, a great humbug, and a confirmed opium-smoker. He did not speak a word of English, though he had lived with Mr. Wade as teacher for many years, and in that capacity accompanied us to Tientsin. The poem, also translated and versified by Mr. Wade, which was written on a fan in memory of the occasion, was thus headed:

"Two stanzas of verses, in five words each, presented by Chang-Tung-Yau to Wade his pupil, and literary acquaintance of nine years' standing, with whom he had been a shipmate to Taku, and at Tientsin, on finding himself several months on board the same vessel with him. Composed on the 5th moon of the year Wu Wu (June, 1854).

1.

> "So best, in lettered toil thine aim
> To aid the world—by one fair deed
> To earn a thousand autumns' fame.
> The day's capricious will why heed?
> Fitful as down upon the air
> A bubble that the waters bear,
> Is all our glory's fleeting pride.
> Thy pastime in the leisure hour
> The nicely-studied rhyme to pair;
> Nor titles win thy praise, nor power—
> And well, for all is change. Though fair
> The moon, yet dark the evening's doom:

---

* The "Walk in Dew" is a poem, allusion to which is made to convey to the reader the idea of shuddering or shivering horror with which the present poet gazes on the scene before him. The lines on the title-page of this volume are a rhythmical version of the last half stanza.

Changeful our lot, as light and gloom
Play o'er the blue stream's tide.

II.

Nine years since first we met are sped,
Thenceforth in friendly union bound;
Now six long moons one deck we tread.
Our night-lamp trimm'd, we chat the round
Of earth's affairs; the burning day
On weighty labors pours its ray;
We part inditing matters grave.
For me, my part fled vainly by,
And with what haste! No longer proud,
But free I stray, as floats on high,
Now clustering, now dispersed, the cloud.
Home to my books—I ask no more—
With age my limbs and travel sore;
Give me my hillside cave."

Hwashana's volume was not the only present Lord Elgin received from the commissioners; nine enormous earthen jars of wine, of dimensions sufficient for Morgiana to smother thieves in, made their appearance just as we were leaving the yamun.

The same afternoon we bade a final adieu to the "Temple of Supreme Felicity," and embarked on board the Firm gun-boat. A flowing tide swept us down to the Gulf in eight hours, and that night we had the satisfaction of once more finding ourselves on board the good ship Furious. As she had now remained without moving from her dismal anchorage for three months, our appearance was hailed with some pleasure, as the signal for a change to new and more lively scenes.

As we found that we should just have time, on our way back to Shanghai, to visit the Great Wall, we steered a northeasterly course after we had weighed anchor the following day. Before dark we saw the Sha-liu-tien, or "Sand-hill Fields," extensive sand-banks rising but a few feet above the water, remarkable only for being a favorite and profitable fishing-ground, and for a square joss-house painted white to serve as a beacon, and which, situated at one corner, is the only building visible.

The following morning found us off the high land of the department of Shuntien, in the province of Chih-li. Unfortunately, the weather was thick and lowering; the mountains were capped with clouds; and we could only judge of their height when we caught an occasional glimpse of a peak rising from two to three thousand feet above the sea-level. In fine weather there is no difficulty in finding the Great Wall, which is seen for miles scoring with an irregular line the sides of the steepest hills, and crossing their highest ridges. To-day, however, we looked in vain for any such indication of its existence; dense masses of cloud rolled along the base of the range; while misty drizzling rain rendered our search neither hopeful nor agreeable. About 9 A.M. we passed a large walled city, near which a mass of solid masonry abutted on the sea, with a tower or two in rear. This answered in some degree to Lord Jocelyn's description of the locality, but, according to the chart, the position was placed some miles farther on. We therefore followed the coast for two more hours, until we shoaled the water to five fathoms, without observing any sign of the Wall.

It was now evident that we had passed the object of our search, and that the walled town we had observed was Shan-hai, described as being situated at the point where the Great Wall abuts on the sea. The north shore of the Gulf of Leatung, along which we had since been steaming, was the most beautiful piece of coast scenery we had seen in China. Rich plains, covered with the brightest verdure, rose in swelling undulations from the sea to the magnificent range of peaked mountains in rear. Villages were scattered plentifully over them. Snug farm-houses nestled in clumps of wood, and innumerable cattle dotted the landscape, as though they had been sown upon it broadcast. Every thing indicated a prosperous rural population, occupying a champaign of much fertility and picturesque beauty.

We were sorry to turn our backs upon it without either prosecuting our voyage to the new port of Neu-chwang, from which we were scarce fifty miles distant, or returning to inspect more closely the far-famed Wall; but the heavy fogs would have decided the question against farther exploration, even had not our anxiety to reach Shanghai in time for the departure of the mail influenced Lord Elgin in avoiding any farther delay. A rapid and prosperous passage of four days to Shanghai from this point enabled us to secure this latter object.

Prior to leaving Tientsin Lord Elgin had acquainted the admiral with his intention of proceeding at an early date to Japan, at the same time adverting to the state of affairs at Canton, and informing his excellency that the conclusion of the treaty would release the naval forces from any farther service in the north of the empire. As the complexion of the news received from Canton on our arrival at Shanghai, however, was not in any degree improved, Lord Elgin determined to postpone his departure for Japan, in order to consult with the admiral upon the course to be pursued in that quarter.

The following fortnight we passed at Shanghai in a state of some anxiety, as the admiral did not appear, and the condition of Canton seemed to be getting worse by each successive mail: not until the 26th were we cheered by the arrival of the Coromandel in the river, the admiral having made a slow passage from the north in his flag-ship, which was then lying at the Rugged Islands. He had been more fortunate than ourselves in his trip to the Great Wall, which was visited both by his excellency and Baron Gros.

On the day previous to the arrival of the Admiral Lord Elgin received the intelligence from Pekin that five commissioners had been appointed to proceed to Shanghai for the settlement of the tariff, and the framing of those general trade-regulations which must necessarily be drawn up as a supplemental part of the treaty. Of these commissioners, two were our old friends Kweiliang and Hwashana, to whom was added the governor general of the Two Kiangs, Ho-Kwei-tsick, one of the most highly esteemed men in the empire for learning and administrative ability. Two other mandarins of less note completed the commission.

As no commissioners of the eminence of these mandarins had been demanded for the revision of the tariff, etc., their appointment to this function was a spontaneous act, on the part of the government, of some significance; and their position and character were such that, whatever idea Lord Elgin might at one time have entertained of proceeding to Canton instead of Japan was now abandoned, as he considered it above all things essential that he should not lose the opportunity which the visit of the commissioners would afford him of exerting that influence which personal intercourse would, he doubted not, enable him to acquire over them.

Though the Treaty of Tientsin effected the great object of revolutionizing the system under which our political and commercial relations with the empire were to be for the future conducted, there were many most important details to be considered in the altered conditions under which these latter were to be worked out, and the embassador perceived with no little satisfaction that these might now be arranged by himself in accordance with the spirit of the treaty, and with that deliberation and solemnity which they deserved; nor, indeed, however deeply interested he might feel in the state of affairs then existing at Canton, did he consider that their settlement fell within the province of a civilian. The city was under a purely military government. It is true, the Governor Pih-kwei was exercising certain functions as a Chinese authority, but he did so only with the sufferance of General Straubenzee, and as an assistance to that officer in preserving peace and order: should the general have found his presence an obstruction rather than an aid to his administration, it was in his power at any time to suspend him from his functions, and turn him out of the city or keep him in confinement, as, indeed, for some part of the time he did.

Lord Elgin was strongly impressed with the notion that the most thorough and satisfactory way of restoring quiet to Canton was to inflict a summary chastisement upon those who disturbed the peace there; and accordingly, in a letter to General Straubenzee, informing his excellency of the expected arrival of the commissioners above named, and of his intention to meet them at Shanghai, the embassador goes on to say: "It is not impossible that I may be able to induce these high officers to take some active steps to check the proceedings of the Braves at Canton; but, looking at the present state of affairs in that quarter as portrayed in your excellency's dispatch of the 22d instant, and in the reports I have received from Mr. Parkes, I can not help thinking that it would be very desirable that any such intimation by the Chinese authorities should be preceded by some vigorous decisive action on our part, showing our power to control and punish the Braves.

"It is for your excellency to determine how such a blow can be most effectually struck; but I trust you will excuse me for making a suggestion which is prompted by the expected arrival of the imperial commissioners, and the anomalous state of affairs at Canton."

Lord Elgin also wrote a letter to the admiral immediately on his arrival at Shanghai, calling his excellency's attention "to the continued existence in that quarter of a state of affairs to which it is most important an arrest should be put at the earliest period," and proceeding in terms almost identical with those I have quoted as already addressed to General Straubenzee. In reply to this communication, the admiral stated that it was his intention, prior to going south, to proceed to Nagasaki for the purpose of delivering over the yacht Emperor to the government of Japan, and watering the Calcutta.

During this period of our stay at Shanghai the climate was more oppressively hot than I ever remember to have felt it in any part of the world. The thermometer did not show a higher temperature than at Tientsin, but there was a stifling heaviness in the atmosphere which acted in a most depressing manner both on health and spirits. Cases of death by sun-stroke were of daily occurrence, chiefly among the sailors in the shipping which crowded the river. Upward of a hundred merchantmen, waiting hopelessly for cargoes, were lying at anchor under the broiling sun, their lists of sick daily increasing under the deleterious influence of the climate.

As two or three weeks must elapse before the arrival of the commissioners, Lord Elgin determined to escape for the interval to Japan, and return in time to meet their excellencies at Shanghai. In the mean time certain changes had taken place in the "personnel" of the mission. Mr. Bruce had proceeded to England with the treaty of Tientsin immediately on our return to Shanghai; Mr. Jocelyn had arrived to relieve Mr. Cameron, who went home on his promotion; and Mr. Morrison returned to England. With our party thus reduced, we embarked on board the Furious on the last day of July, 1858, delighted under any circumstances to escape from the summer heats of Shanghai, were it only for a few weeks, but our gratification increased by the anticipation of visiting scenes which have ever been veiled in the mystery of a jealous and rigid seclusion.

CHAPTER XXI.

First View of Japan.—Lovely Scenery.—Singular Boats.—Pappenberg.—Dungaree Forts.—Enchanting Scenery.—A philosophical Port-guardian.—Visit of Japanese Officials.—Decima.—Removal of Restrictions.—Former Imprisonment of Dutch.—A smuggling Skipper.—Dutch Covetousness.—Strict Rules.—Recent Concessions.—Nagasaki.—Aspect of Houses.—Shops at Nagasaki.—The Streets.—Plan of the City.—Janitors of Decima.

The distance from Shanghai to Nagasaki is not above 450 miles; but, if oceans rolled between the two empires, Japan could not be more thoroughly isolated than it is from the rest of the world. We steamed smoothly and rapidly over this narrow strip of sea, so rarely traversed by craft of any sort. There was not a speck of foam to ruffle its glassy surface, scarce a fleece of cloud to checker the deep blue overhead: well might we imagine ourselves gliding across these solitary waters to some dreamland, securely set in a quiet corner of another world, far away from the storms and troubles of this one. On the afternoon of the 2d of August we first saw symptoms of land, and passed close to some high pointed rocks of picturesque form, in places covered with verdure, but not affording standing-ground for an inhabitant. These bold landmarks are out of sight of the Japanese coast, and are called the Asses' Ears. Early on the following morning the highlands of Japan were in sight, the nearest land being the island of Iwosima. As we approached it, the first object visible was an evidence of civilization unknown among the Chinese; on its highest summit a flag-staff at once telegraphed our appearance to the main land. We did not then know that cannon, placed at intervals the whole way to the capital, were noisily repeating this signal, so that intelligence of our approach was even then reverberating almost from one end of the empire to the other; and his majesty the Tycoon at Yedo, six or seven hundred miles away, was informed that we had entered the Bay of Nagasaki by the time that we had dropped our anchor in it.

The high green islands of Iwosima conceal from view the entrance to the bay until you round their westernmost point: even then other islands and projecting promontories make it somewhat uncertain. Fortunately, the ship's pilotage does not rest with us, and we can bestow our attention unreservedly on the scenery, which is indeed of a character to rivet it, whether we will or no. The islands on our right rise abruptly out of the water. The overhanging promontory above us is crowned by a battery of guns, round which a few soldiers are grouped, gazing curiously: beyond it more batteries appear on sundry other projections of the shore, which is here and there indented with bays, from which deep-wooded valleys run up into the island. They seem thickly populated, for the cottages, with their high thatched roofs, cluster up the hill side, and peep out from under the dark foliage. In places the islands are precipitous, and masses of towering rock deny even to the hardiest shrubs holding-ground.

The scenery on the opposite shore is of the same character, but on a grander scale. It trends away in a series of deep bays and beetling cliffs, upon the rugged base of which the waves wage an incessant war, and surge and moan fretfully in deep caves and fissures, as though lamenting their fruitless efforts to undermine them. In charming contrast with these sterner features are grassy slopes and rice-fields rising in terraces on the green hill sides, and shady groves with blue smoke curling above them, denoting the existence of snug hamlets. Securely moored in secluded creeks, or hauled up on little patches of sandy beach, are quaint-shaped native craft; others are glancing about these calm inland waters, ferrying across from islands to the main passengers and cargo, or lying motionless as though asleep on the water, their sails "folded like thoughts in a dream," while the occupants are fishing. These sails are composed either of strips of matting or of cloth. These are generally black and white alternately, each strip not being above two feet wide, and hoisted perpendicularly. When it is necessary to reduce sail, one or more strips are taken in. When not sailing, they are sculled by ten or a dozen stalwart figures, their entire clothing consisting but of scanty waistcloths, and their light-bronze complexions giving them an unusually naked appearance. These men all work under substantial awnings of matting, or a light wooden frame-work, constructed in the afterpart of the boat. The bows are considered the more honorable position, and hence this is the portion of the boat set apart for passenger accommodation. The prows are sharp-pointed, and elevated high out of the water. Some of these passenger-boats passed close to us for the purpose of a closer inspection. Those within manifested no fear, but a good deal of interest and curiosity; numerous flags fluttered from small flag-staffs in the stern, each device having its appropriate signification, unknown to us. The colors were generally black and white, and the form square or angular. A black circle on a white ground, or black and white triangles were the commonest; but often they were complicated, and presented to the uninitiated the appearance of an elaborate collection of the emblems of free-masonry.

Steaming gently on, we presently open the mouth of the long narrow harbor, with the conical wooded island of Pappenberg guarding its entrance; beyond which, formerly, foreign ships were not allowed to penetrate, and which must ever hold an unenviable notoriety in the historical annals of Japan as the Tarpeian

The Island of Pappenberg.

rock, down the precipitous sides of which hundreds of Christians, during the fierce persecution which had for its object the utter extermination of all who professed the Creed, were hurled into the deep-blue waters which eddy round it. The moral of the sad story is written on the face of the steep hills which inclose the bay; tiers of cannon rise one above another; battery succeeds battery, as point after point is revealed to view. These guns are pointed not so much against the stranger as the Christian, who, while he is dreaded, is no less despised, and the principal result of whose intercourse with the Japanese has been to furnish them with weapons by which they can the more effectually resist his encroachments. Notwithstanding this, Japan is once again open to the Christian; it will remain to be proved how far the estimate which former experience led the authorities of that empire to form of his practice and his profession will be justified in the course of his renewed intercourse with its inhabitants.

The guns, which appeared of enormous calibre, were for the most part unprotected by embrasures; they stood under open sheds, generally surrounded by soldiers. In addition to those which were real, and apparently serviceable, were long lines of sham batteries, known to sailors as Dungaree forts, and which were made simply of coarse cloth or canvas, stretched and painted so as to represent batteries. It is possible that in many cases these concealed guns, and were purposely constructed in a manner calculated to mislead the beholder into supposing them a "solemn sham," and so hurrying him on to his own destruction. Whether that be so or not, these gaudily painted fortifications contributed a novel and characteristic feature to the scenery, which continued to be of the most enchanting description.

The harbor of Nagasaki is an inlet of the sea, four miles long, and with an average of about a mile in breadth. At its farther extremity lies the city, with a high range of hills in rear; the topmost summit, Kawarajama, attaining an elevation of about two thousand feet. The hills on either side of this sheet of water sometimes rise out of it in an abrupt wall of rock, at others swell gently back in wooded slopes, down which brawling streams leap into the sea; rock-cut steps ascend to airy pinnacles surmounted by guns or temples; dense foliage clusters wherever it can find holding-ground, flinging deep shadows over crag and fissure, subduing and toning down all the harsher elements—just as a soft eye and gentle smile give their own expression to a countenance rugged with lines and furrows.

Behind some Dungaree forts we observed substantial buildings, apparently barracks, and gardens beautifully kept, with terraces and walks, and carefully-trimmed borders—the bright colors of the dresses of those who frequented them imparting a gay and almost fairy-like aspect to the scene.

We had now reached the point at which, a few years ago, even Dutch ships were compelled to anchor, and the interval which elapsed until permission was given them to proceed to their anchorage was employed in secreting the Bibles. "On anchoring at the entrance of the harbor," says Thunberg, "all the Bibles and prayer-books belonging to the sailors were collected and put into a chest, which was nailed down. This chest was afterward left under the care of the Japanese till the time of our departure, when every one received his book again." They were also obliged to give up all their arms and ammunition. In spite, however, of the abhorrence in which the Japanese hold Bibles and revolvers, we retained our right to use the one and wear the other; and it is but fair to them to say that the spiritual weapon was the only one for which we found any need in their country.

Until quite recently, a cordon of boats, stretched across this part of the harbor, barred the farther progress of foreign ships. We found the obstruction represented only by one official boat, upon the deck, or rather roof of which a gentleman was seated, reading placidly, and gently fanning himself. On our approaching nearer he looked up and waved us benignly back with his fan. If he was the port-guardian, he was by no means a formidable janitor, for on our holding on our way, regardless of his signals, he fell to reading again, apparently satisfied that he had discharged his duty, and was henceforward relieved from all farther responsibility on our account. This man's conduct furnished us with a key in all our future intercourse with Japanese officials, who, in spite of the vehemence of their protestations so long as they believe it possible to carry out their instructions, possess a marvelous faculty of accepting whatever situation they find is inevitably to be forced upon them. In this instance we were the less disposed to heed the signals of the dignitary in the boat, as we could now perceive two or three ships at anchor off the town. These we discovered to be a Dutch merchant-ship and a Japanese man-of-war steamer, besides a small cutter; behind them were a few Japanese junks.

We were now soon at anchor, and ready to land under the Dutch flag, which betokened the factory of Decima, which, though an island, seems from the shipping as though it formed part of the city of Nagasaki. Before we had time to do so, however, we were boarded by a boat-load of Japanese officials, the novelty of

U

whose appearance and costume detained us. They came crowding on the deck in the most easy, unembarrassed manner imaginable, smiling blandly, and affably, and talking Dutch, which, however, nobody on board understood. Their gauzy overcoats, loose trowsers, gaiters, and "foot-gloves" combined to form an unusual costume; while the position of the two swords with which each man was furnished, as they projected behind, gave him the appearance, at a distance, of some new species of biped adorned with two tails. When our curiosity had been mutually satisfied, these gentry were signed to return to their boat; and as they were unable to extract any information from us, they at once complied, but only re-embarked to remain stationary, a short distance off, as a sort of guard-boat.

Some of us now went on shore to call on the Dutch officials in the factory. As we neared the land we observed some of the old posts standing out of the water, within a short distance of the factory, within which no Japanese boats were formerly allowed to pass, for fear of surreptitious communication being carried on with the Dutch. We landed at a rude quay, where some Dutch sailors were lounging under an open shed; and, passing through a wooden gate, found ourselves in a single street, about two hundred yards long, as clean and precise as a street in that paragon of neatness, the village of Brock. The houses were substantial little two-storied edifices, with green shutters and blinds, from behind which peeped sundry pretty-looking female Japanese faces; for the Dutch here are not allowed the companionship of their own countrywomen. Of the male inhabitants not half a dozen were visible, and these seemed all sailors. Asking one of them to point out the house of the chief superintendent, Mr. Donker Curtius, we were informed that he was absent on a visit to the capital, but that his secretary was in Decima.

We were most cordially and civilly received by this gentleman, and were delighted to learn from him that, by the latest arrangements entered into with the Japanese government, all former restrictions limiting the exploration of foreigners to the little island, or subjecting them to the most annoying formalities in case of their wishing to proceed beyond it, were removed, and that we were now at liberty to ramble unrestrained wheresoever we pleased. There can be little doubt that the government desires, by pursuing a very liberal policy at Nagasaki, and by offering greater facilities and conveniences to foreigners there than elsewhere, to attract them as much as possible to this port, to the prejudice and exclusion of others. Our host informed us, however, that the present governor was a man of by no means advanced or liberal views, and mentioned several instances in which he had manifested retrogressive tendencies. Under the regular system, the governors of the imperial cities are removed annually, but an exception is made in the case of Nagasaki, as a man is supposed to require time to learn the temper of foreigners, and a farther period is allowed him to turn the knowledge thus gained to account. On the whole, this is a convenient arrangement for foreigners, though, in the present instance, any change would in all probability have been for the better.

It appeared that Mr. Donker Curtius was now on his return journey from Yedo, where he had been residing for some time, unsuccessfully endeavoring to negotiate a new treaty. Mr. Harris, the American consul at Simoda, had, we learned, also returned to his post, after a residence in the capital attended with no immediate political results.

The houses of the Dutch officials in Decima are unpretending little abodes, generally constructed of wood, with verandas seaward; the lower story devoted to warehouse purposes, the upper containing three or four small, simply-furnished rooms. Up to quite a recent period Decima must have presented rather the aspect of a penal settlement than the abode of a community of merchants. So strict was the surveillance to which the members composing the factory here were subjected—so severe the restrictions by which they were bound—that one is tempted to believe that the gentlemen who chose the Dutch factory at Nagasaki as their habitation must have been the victims of that species of misanthropy which is supposed, in our own country, to induce men to apply for situations in light-houses. Until lately, the arrival of a Dutch ship in the harbor was the signal for a host of Japanese officials to flock to Decima. The interpreters occupied the abode assigned to them, and no one was allowed to pass from the shore to the ship unless furnished with a passport and accompanied by one of these gentry. Then a corps of "ottonas," or official spies, were quartered in the island, whose duty it was to watch the minutest proceedings of every member of the factory. They regularly mounted guard at the only gate through which access is to be had on foot into the town, as well as both the water-gates, and both by day and night went their rounds with religious punctuality and exactness.

The members of only one ecclesiastical sect, those of the Mountain of Koja, and the women of only one class, and that the most degraded, were permitted to enter Decima. At night the gates were shut, and no intercourse was allowed between the factory and the town after sunset. This was the case when we were there; but our passage to and from the ship was free and uninterrupted; nor were we exposed to that rigorous personal examination of which some of the old Dutch writers complain so bitterly. It must be admitted that their conduct provoked the annoyance. The captain of Thunberg's ship was in the habit of going on shore in breeches of enormous capacity even for a Dutchman, so heavily laden with secreted articles of contraband that he required the support of two sailors to enable him to walk. The Japanese, disposed, in the first instance, to believe well of strangers, are, on the other hand, when their suspicions are once awakened, vigilant in the extreme, and are not slow in enforcing preventive measures. Let the fate of the Dutch skipper be a warning to the British smuggler, who has been known occasionally to extend his operations eastward of the Cape: that dishonest navigator was obliged to reduce his trowsers to the dimensions of those worn by portly burgomasters, and was farther subject to the indignity of having his legs felt, and his pockets turned inside out, upon the rare occasions when, in compliance with the urgent representations of the Dutch superintendent, the governor allowed him to land and visit the factory. Henceforward no man was considered safe. One gentleman was betrayed by an indiscreet parrot talking in his pocket; another had sewn up dollars in his drawers; so that the Japanese researches became more curious than ever, even to the gauging of high-flavored cheeses and the breaking of suspected eggs. Thus has commercial dishonesty and political subserviency worked to the prejudice of the foreigner in the mind of the Japanese, whose confidence in us can only be restored by the adherence of the merchant to a high code of mercantile morality, and by the maintenance, on the part of those who represent our country, of its national dignity.

It will be well, in considering the present position and prospects of the Dutch in this empire, to observe how little they have gained by pursuing a course which has not merely discredited them in the eyes of the Japanese, but placed them on a moral footing inferior to that which it is now in the power of other foreign nations to adopt. Truly does old Kæmpfer remark, "So great was the covetousness of the Dutch, and so strong the alluring power of the Japanese gold, that, rather than quit the prospect of a trade (indeed most advantageous), they willingly underwent an almost perpetual imprisonment—for such, in fact, is our residence in Decima—and chose to suffer many hardships in a foreign and heathen country: to be remiss in performing Divine service on Sundays and solemn festivals—to leave off praying and singing of psalms—entirely to avoid the sign of the cross, the calling upon the name of Christ in presence of the natives, and all the outer signs of Christianity; and, lastly, patiently and submissively to bear the abusive and injurious behavior of these proud infidels toward us, than which nothing can be offered more shocking to a generous and noble mind."

So great was the horror and contempt of the foreigner with which their intercourse, first with the Portuguese and then with the Dutch, had inspired the government, that every Japanese connected in any way with the Decima Factory was obliged to take certain oaths, the infraction of which was visited upon the delinquent with the severest penalties. He was bound not to serve the Dutch but in the daytime; not to enter into any discourse or conversation whatever about the forbidden sect of the Christians; not to engage in any familiarity with the Dutch upon any subject whatever, besides numerous rigid rules having reference to complicity in contraband transactions. From the extreme reticence observed by all the officials with whom we came in contact during our stay in Japan, we had every reason to believe that they were bound by instructions, if not by oaths, of the same tenor, in their intercourse with us.

It will doubtless be a tedious and somewhat difficult task to dispel those unfavorable impressions, which the Japanese can scarcely be blamed for entertaining toward us. Still, their prejudices upon this point are not insuperable, and if we fail to remove them, it will only be because we have failed to prove by our practice that the civilization of the West does not contaminate those with whom it comes in contact.

Hitherto the Japanese have apparently regarded the fair sex of foreign countries as more dangerous guests than the males. A touching story is told of a certain Dutch President of Decima of thirty years since, one Herr Blomhoff, who brought his wife to Nagasaki, and, pending a reference to Yedo, obtained permission for her and her infant to land at Decima. Two months had scarcely elapsed, however, before a ruthless decree arrived, ordering the Vrouw Blomhoff to quit the Japanese shores, and condemning the unhappy husband to a long life of single-blessedness. The last rumor which reached us just before leaving Shanghai was to the effect that a wedding had been consummated at Nagasaki between a young English couple, who thus inaugurated in a most interesting manner the new and enlightened régime. In former times, not only a wedding, but a birth or death of a Japanese was prohibited at Decima. It was a more simple matter interfering with the operations of nature in the former than in the latter event. In the case of a sudden death, the body was secretly conveyed out of the factory. All children born of Japanese mothers were regarded as Japanese.

One of the most recent and important concessions which Mr. Donker Curtius had obtained from the Japanese government was permission for the children so born to be educated in Holland—on condition, however, that in the event of their ever revisiting Japan they should be treated as Dutch subjects. Letters arrived while we were at Decima from that gentleman stating that he was at Ohosaka, on his return journey from Yedo.

Returning on board the Furious with our report of Decima and its inmates, we landed again in the afternoon to explore the town of Nagasaki. As we neared the crowd of boats moored at the stone steps of the wharf, I experienced that feeling of pleasurable excitement, the keen edge of which becomes so blunted by the very necessity of the traveler's vocation, that he often despairs of ever again experiencing those delightful sensations incidental to strange and novel scenes which first lured him away from his fireside. Up to this moment the town itself had been only partially visible, for a sort of embankment runs along the shore at a distance of a few yards from the sea, and in the hollow behind it are situated the principal streets. There was no great crowd collected to watch our landing—foreigners were becoming a daily sight—and we were allowed to follow our inclinations in our choice of a line of exploration.

A flight of steps ascends the embankment, at the top of which is situated one of the official residences of the governor. This embankment, which is, in fact, a sort of raised parterre, is of considerable width, and a broad street runs along its whole length. Crossing this, we reach the head of the flight of steps that descend into the town, which now lies at our feet. The view is peculiarly striking, especially to the stranger who has just arrived from China. Instead of an indefinite congeries of houses built apparently on no settled plan, and so close together that the streets which divide them are completely concealed, we saw before us a wide, spacious street, about a mile in length, flanked by neat houses, generally of two stories, with tiled or wooden roofs, and broad eaves projecting over the lower story. A *pavé* ran down the centre of the street, on each side of which it was carefully graveled to the gutters. No wheeled vehicle or beast of burden was, however, visible, but, in default, a plentiful sprinkling of foot-passengers gave it an air of life and animation. It terminated in the distance in a flight of steps, which soon disappeared amid the foliage of the hill side, crowned with a temple or tea-house, or gleaming with the whitewashed walls of some fireproof store-house.

As we traversed its entire length, no foul odors assailed our nostrils, or hideous cutaneous objects offended our eyesight; nor did inconvenient walls or envious shutters debar us from inspecting, as we passed along, the internal economy of the shops and dwellings on each side. Light wooden screens, neatly papered, and running on slides, are for the most part pushed back in the daytime, and the passer looks through the house, to where the waving shrubs of a cool-looking back garden invite him to extend his investigations. Between the observer and this retreat there are probably one or two rooms, raised about two feet from the ground; and upon the scrupulously clean and well-wadded matting, which is stretched upon the wooden floor, semi-nude men and women loll and lounge, and their altogether nude progeny crawl and feast themselves luxuriously at ever-present fountains. The women seldom wear any thing above their waists, the men only a scanty loin-cloth. In the midday, during the summer, a general air of languor pervades the community: about sunset the world begins to wash, and the Japanese youth, like copper-colored Cupids, riot tumultuously.

The shops do not generally contain those articles in lacker and china ware for which Japan is so justly celebrated. To obtain them we must visit the Dutch or Russian bazars; but our interest is kept alive by the varied productions of native manufacture exhibited in the shops, which are as open to the street as stalls at a fancy-fair, and which contain all those articles which are in common request among the people. Umbrella, fan, and shoe shops abounded; bazars for toys and glass ornaments arrested us for a moment; but time was precious, and we could not do more than glance cursorily at the novelties displayed, and vainly endeavor to comprehend the object of various processes and manufactures which were being industriously carried on, but the result of which, in default of an interpreter, remained a mystery. Indeed, except from the Dutch gentlemen at Decima, we found it difficult, during our short stay at Nagasaki, to obtain any information, as only one Japanese had picked up a very few words of English. All the interpreters spoke Dutch, a language of which my knowledge was extremely limited; nor was it spoken by any of our party. Our rambles through Nagasaki, therefore, though in the highest degree amusing and attractive, possessed the one drawback of leaving the curiosity and interest they had excited at every turn unsatisfied. Nor could we gratify ourselves by making purchases of curiosities. As yet we had not been introduced to the government moneychangers, who sat in solemn conclave at the Russian bazar; and no consideration could induce a shopkeeper to accept the smallest or even the largest foreign coin. Well did he know that the eye of his neighbor was upon him, and that an official visit the next morning would remind him of his oblivion of that great national institution of universal espionage, which would with us be considered an intolerable tyranny, but which the Japanese regard as a necessary ingredient to the welfare and protection of society.

We pursued our peregrinations through the streets of Nagasaki unmolested, and almost unnoticed by the people, who did not crowd the thoroughfares with busy, noisy clamor, as in China, but strolled carelessly along, apparently little troubled with occupation, with an air of amiable contentment on their features, and an expression of kindly good-nature toward the curious, wondering strangers. Although Kæmpfer speaks of numerous beggars, I did not observe any, with the exception of one or two religious mendicants. A stream, about the size of an ordinary canal, intersects the town in a lateral direction, and is spanned by thirty or forty bridges, of which about fifteen are solidly constructed of stone, with handsome balustrades. Balconies, filled with women engaged in domestic avocations, overhang the water; small boats ply upon its surface; and here and there the quaint old buttresses of the bridges are partly concealed with creeping plants, and across them numerous passengers pass and repass. It is interesting to stand on one of these and watch the humors of the place, while we enjoy the picturesque view which it affords.

Nagasaki contains upward of eighty streets crossing each other at right angles, and from three quarters of a mile to a mile in length. Its population is estimated at about 60,000; but it presents a far more imposing appearance, and covers a much greater area of ground than a Chinese city of the same dimensions. Its outskirts run up into the secluded valleys formed by the surrounding hills, the spurs of which descend into the town, so that almost every street terminates in a flight of stone steps; and, indeed, some of them, which we visited afterward, climb the hill sides, the houses being built one above the other, as at Malta.

We terminated our first day's explorations of Nagasaki by a second visit to Decima, for the purpose of seeing the Dutch bazar. Crossing the moat which separates the factory from the town and makes an island of it, we pass through the gateway, under which, in a sanctum of their own, sit three or four officials, called by the Dutch "banjos," whose business it is to inspect narrowly every person seeking ingress and egress, and every article or package which is carried in or out. In former times these janitors were in a most responsible position, and their functions were regarded by the Japanese government as of the utmost importance. Now, however, the recent relaxations with reference to foreigners have diminished the cares of office; and these dreaded *custodii*, so long the bugbears of the Dutch *employés* at Decima, will soon cease to exist, or dwindle into respectable sinecurists.

It was late ere, utterly exhausted by the interest and excitement of our first day in Japan, we sought our floating home.

CHAPTER XXII.

Missionary Success of Xavier.—Supernatural Gifts.—Heroism of Japanese Converts.—Theological Arguments of Converts: their Objections to eternal Punishment.—Louis Almeyda.—The Prince of Omura.—His Conversion.—Founding of Nagasaki.—Conversion of Princes.—Fate of Nagasaki.—Death of Sumitanda.—Constitution of the Japanese Government.—The two Emperors.—Taiko-sama.—Persecution of Christians.—Projects of Taiko-sama: his Invasion of the Corea.—Nagasaki annexed by the Ziogoon.—William Adams.—British Factory in Japan.—Japanese political Economists.—Intrigues of the Dutch.—Expulsion of the Portuguese.—Establishment of Decima.

NAGASAKI was not in former times, as it is now, one of the imperial demesnes, or lands appertaining to the crown. It became so in consequence of a series of events over which it may not be uninteresting to cast a retrospective glance, as possessing some historical importance, and as illustrating the internal political condition of a portion of Japan to which the earliest associations of foreigners are attached, and which may convey some idea of the working of that system of government which still prevails in the empire.

The first intercourse which the Japanese held with foreigners was of a character which induced them to form the highest opinion of the advantages which were to be derived from the cultivation of relations with a race so far advanced in civilization, and under the influence of a religion of an elevating and apparently harmless tendency. The zeal and attainments of the sainted Xavier, and that band of devoted missionaries who immediately succeeded him, produced a revolution in the religious sentiments of a large and influential section of the community. The history of the acts of these first apostles of the Christian faith, as described in the works of Pères Bouhours, de Charlevoix, Marini, Froes, and others, though written, doubtless, under an inspiration not always to be depended upon, is a striking evidence of the influence which the Christian religion, under whatever form it is introduced, is calculated to produce upon minds which have been beforehand sufficiently cultivated and civilized to appreciate its merits. As in the Roman world, its ennobling doctrines seized hold of the minds of educated men, and gradually expelled the philosophies and creeds which had heretofore satisfied them; so did it commend itself to the refined and intellectual Japanese, spreading with a rapidity second only to that which marked its progress in the apostolic ages.

If we are to believe the records of these later fathers of the Church, who have recorded the history of the first missionary efforts in Japan, that supernatural aid was not withheld which contributed so largely to the success of the first propagators of Christianity in the West: Xavier is stated to have been endowed with the gift of tongues, and to have preached eloquently in Corean, Lewchew, Chinese, and Japanese, without ever having studied a word of those extremely complicated languages. His biographers record hundreds of miraculous conversions; and according to Père Charlevoix,* he restored a dead girl to life under circumstances which utterly confounded his enemies the bonzes, who, like the Pharisees of old, dogged his footsteps, and exerted all their energies in vain to counteract his daily increasing influence, and by secret intrigues and open arguments to destroy him and confute his doctrines.

Whatever may have been the means of proselytism which he employed, of the marvelous results there can be no doubt; and it is worthy of the attention of those interested in the conversion of the heathen to consider how far the success which attends their efforts may depend upon the nature and amount of the cultivation which the soil has received before the seed is sown. There can be no doubt that the imaginative Japanese, hearing of Christianity for the first time, would receive it in a very different spirit from an untamed New Zealander or a calmly-skeptical Chinaman. Nor was the faith thus implanted in the breasts of some hundreds of thousands of converts a mere nominal creed, to be swept away by the first wave of persecution. It not only furnished them with courage, but with arguments with which to meet their persecutors. The answer of a neophyte who was asked how he would respond to his sovereign if ordered to abjure Christianity, is thus recorded: "Sire, would you wish me to remain faithful, and ever to preserve that submission which it is seemly for a subject to feel toward his king? would you wish me to manifest zeal for your service on all occasions on which I can be of use, so that no private interest should cause me to forget what I owe you? would

---

* *Père de Charlevoix*, vol. ii., p. 42.

you wish me to be meek, temperate, and loving, full of charity toward my equals—that I should patiently suffer all the ill treatment to which I may be exposed? command me then to remain a Christian, for it is from a Christian alone that all this can be reasonably expected."

The early records of the Church do not afford instances of more unflinching heroism then is furnished in the narratives of those martyrdoms to which Japanese of all ranks were subjected when the day of trial came. Thousands were slaughtered at Simabarra, thousands more tormented and put to death in cold blood, or rolled down the Pappenberg; yet we have reason to believe that the last spark has never yet been extinguished, and that, smouldering secretly, the fire of François Xavier still burns in the bosoms of some of those who have received the traditions of his teaching. It is to be regretted that the inordinate love of political power which characterizes the disciples of Loyola should have led the successors of the first missionaries into intrigues which terminated so disastrously for themselves and their creed, for thereby they have closed Japan to those Protestant missionary efforts which the government of that empire are now firmly resolved on resisting.

Believing that Christianity, whether Catholic or Protestant, is but an excuse for the secret acquisition of political influence, they regard with equal dislike and suspicion the missionaries of either creed; nor does it seem probable at present, at all events, that opportunities will be afforded us of teaching them the difference. That they would have little difficulty in appreciating it, so far as their intelligence is concerned, were any exposition on the subject permitted, there can be no doubt.

We have the record of a treatise published by the Japanese neophytes proving the superiority of the Christian religion over that of the sects of Japan, while the arguments with which they met at the outset the teaching of Xavier prove how competent they were intellectually to detect the mysteries of the religion he promulgated. "One thing," says his biographer, "nevertheless arrested the progress of the evangelist. It was difficult to prove to the Japanese that those who, during their lives, had not worshiped the true God, would be consigned to everlasting fire in hell. They could not reconcile this article of faith with the infinite goodness of God. 'If the incarnate Word,' said they, 'died for all, why should not His death profit all? If He condemns to eternal punishment all those who are not obedient to His law, why has he delayed the announcement of it to us during more than 1500 years?' The bonzes did not fail to support these objections, and added 'that the priests of the Christians were good for nothing, since they had not the power of drawing one single soul out of hell, whereas this they themselves accomplished every day by the merit of their fasts and prayers; that this God must be either very cruel in not being willing to put an end to the punishment of the damned, or very impotent in not being *able* to do it.'"

"The Japanese love tenderly all who are related to them by ties of blood, and the memory of their ancestors is dear and precious to them. They could not be content to regard them as reprobates. 'What!' cried they, bursting into tears, 'our fathers, our children, our relations, our friends—must they remain during all eternity the unfortunate victims and the objects of vengeance of a God whom they would without doubt have adored if they had known Him? and this great God, who is represented to us as goodness and equity itself, will He have no regard to their ignorance?' They melted into tears while speaking thus; the whole place resounded with their sobs and with their cries, which so touching a thought made them send up to heaven; and the missionaries could not help mingling their tears with those of their neophytes."

The tears of their teachers must, however, have been but a poor consolation to these unhappy Japanese, who would at once have appreciated the practical distinction in favor of a creed which gave them the benefit of the doubt upon so momentous a subject.

It must not be supposed that the Jesuits confined themselves to the propagation of their faith alone: to the exertions of Louis Almeyda, a Portuguese gentleman of singular energy and tact, and who joined the order in Japan, is owing the successful establishment of the greater number of those Portuguese colonies of which Nagasaki became ultimately the most celebrated, and the political importance of which was the first indication that the emperor received of the growing ambition of the Portuguese.

When first Louis Almeyda paid a round of visits to the kings and princes of the island of Kiusiu, those high dignitaries almost quarreled for the honor of his acquaintance, and rivaled each other in their ardor to induce him to form establishments in their divers petty kingdoms. He succeeded even in persuading some of these princes to embrace Christianity: those who were indifferent or opposed to it he conciliated, and gained the friendship of the bonzes themselves, some of whom, upon one occasion, applied to be baptized, and were only refused upon the ground of the obligation under which they lay to take part in the funeral obsequies of their prince in the event of his death, in accordance with the religion of their country.

But the conversion which was fraught with the most serious consequences to Christianity in Japan, and the ultimate fate of the Portuguese colonies there, was that of the Prince of Omura, which was made in the year 1562. Though only a state of the province of Fizen, and in some sort in vassalage to his brother the King of Arima, Sumitanda, the Prince of Omura, who had never taken the title of king, was a man of great power and influence, and of an advanced and enlightened mind. His perusal of some of the Jesuit works, and his ready and instinctive appreciation of the advantages which might be derived from the introduction of the Portuguese into his principality, induced him to make overtures to Almeyda, who was then at Firando, inviting him to form an establishment in Omura. Notwithstanding the efforts made by the King of Firando to frustrate the project of his rival, Sumitanda had the satisfaction shortly after of welcoming Almeyda to his country, and establishing him in the port of Vocotsura, of which he made a concession to the Portuguese.

The Jesuit establishment proved an attraction to the Christians in the neighboring province, while the commencement of an active commerce soon raised the little collection of cottages, which originally formed the town, to the dignity of an active and bustling mercantile emporium. Meantime the ecclesiastical superiors of the establishment devoted themselves to the conversion of the prince, a task in which they apparently found no great difficulty. He is said to have met them with these words: "I am come here, my fathers, to hear your discourse on your religion. Consider, I beseech you, my heart as ground well prepared; do not fear to sow in it the seed of the Divine word. I trust that, under the blessing of Heaven, it may bring forth fruit. Moreover, my intention is not to limit its fruits to myself alone; I hope to extend them to all my subjects."

The result, as may be anticipated, of the teaching of the missionaries on a mind so disposed, was the declaration of his adhesion to the tenets of Christianity. One obstacle alone remained to the public profession of his faith. Sumitanda was childless, and he feared that so decided a step might involve his principality, so long as his throne was without a successor, in trouble. He therefore, for the present, contented himself with wearing a cross upon his bosom, and, thus attired, appeared at the court of his relative, the King of Arima, and announced his intention of becoming a Christian as soon as he should be blessed with a son and heir. The result of the visit was to induce the King of Arima to send for the ever-active Almeyda, who proceeded to form establishments at various points in his dominions. Meantime the Prince of Omura was zealously forwarding the cause of proselytism in his own states, and destroying the temples and idols with which they abounded.

It was not without serious opposition that Sumitanda thus warmly seconded the efforts of the missionaries. The Buddhist and Sintoo priesthood, finding their religion thus violently attacked by the highest authority, perceiving that their influence was daily lessening, and their office becoming discredited in the eyes of the people, entered into a conspiracy, at the head of which they placed the illegitimate son of the former prince. This was joined by many of the councilors of state, who still remained true to their heathen worship. Their first act was to destroy the palace and greater part of the town of Omura by fire, and to proclaim the usurper prince; they then marched upon the obnoxious Portuguese colony and Jesuit settlement of Vocotsura, and succeeded in reducing it also to ashes. Sumitanda, however, was not discouraged by these reverses, and, gathering about him those who still remained faithful to his cause, he marched on the insurgents, whom he utterly routed and defeated in a pitched battle with great slaughter, taking prisoner and decapitating their leader.

Shortly after this Sumitanda received a letter from the King of Portugal, congratulating him upon his conversion to Christianity, and swearing eternal friendship. In 1569 he formed the project of building a church at a spot in his dominions then called Fucaye, or Long Bay, now known as Nagasaki. This latter name is said to have been that by which the district was originally known, when the property of a family of Japanese nobility, to whom it belonged previous to its annexation to the principality of Omura. Be that as it may, Nagasaki soon rose into a thriving city: its advantages of situation, superior to those of any other port on the coast, attracted a large community of Portuguese, and it quickly became the centre of great commercial activity. Meantime the Prince of Omura, waxing stronger in the faith, and more learned in the doctrines of Christianity, believing that inasmuch as "he that provideth not for them of his own household hath denied the faith, and is worse than an infidel"— considering farther, that a prince ought to be to his subjects what a father is to his family, and that he would be responsible for the safety of those who died in unbelief—decided on all his subjects becoming Christian, and, collecting the chief families of his state, received with them the right of baptism.

Hitherto we have followed exclusively the fortunes of Sumitanda, Prince of Omura, not only as being the most interesting and enlightened of the royal converts who abounded in those days, but as the founder of the settlement destined to become celebrated on account of the singular position it has since held among the mercantile emporia of the world. It would be a tedious and somewhat unprofitable task to follow the Jesuit fathers in their prolix accounts of the progress of Christianity in all the different principalities into which it was introduced, to narrate the wars between the Princes of Bungo and Firando, to follow the tortuous policy of the King of Arima, or recount at length the extraordinary conversion of his highness of Gotto. Still more difficult would it be, but more interesting withal, to accompany the devoted Father Vilela on his mission into the interior, and become involved under his guidance, at Miako or Ximo, in those never-ending intrigues which characterized the imperial court in those days. Father Vilela, more ambitious than his predecessors and colleagues, devoted himself to the conversion of the highest dignitaries of the realm, and, engaging deeply in the political complications, which at that time were working out great changes in the government of the country, hoped to reap for the faith which he promulgated those temporal advantages upon the possession of which he relied for its ultimate triumph.

It may be necessary, before leaving Japan, to revert cursorily to some other of the more important episodes in its history; but, in the mean time, the fate of Nagasaki and its prince more immediately claims our attention. In 1579, the persecutions which overtook the Christians in some of the neighboring principalities, whose rulers were bitterly hostile to a faith the aggressive character of which they had begun to suspect, induced the Portuguese at Nagasaki to prepare for any contingency which might arise in the event of the death of the faithful Sumitanda, by fortifying the city. This was done, and batteries were erected, more especially for the purpose of securing the ships which might be in the harbor. The death of the Christian King of Gotto about this time, and the revolution which succeeded in his state, drove many of his converted subjects to seek a refuge at Nagasaki. About five years after this, the King of Bungo, who had become a convert, the King of Arima, and the Prince of Omura, decided on sending a mission to Rome, consisting of four Japanese of the highest rank, and related to the princes they went to represent. These envoys were most graciously received by his holiness, to whom they presented the letters of which they were the bearers, and which, as they were in all probability written for them by the fathers, are scarcely worth insertion. The heading of the King of Bungo's is as follows: "A celui qui doit être adoré, et qui tient la place du Roi du Ciel, le grand et très Saint Pape." That of the Prince of Omura, "Les mains élevés vers le Ciel, et dans les sentiments d'une veneration profonde j'adore le très Saint Pape, qui tient la place de Dieu sur la terre, et lui présente humblement cette lettre."

These epistles were cordially responded to by Pope Sixtus V., and, after making a tour of Italy and part of Spain, the Japanese embassadors returned to their country highly delighted with their Western experiences. In 1587, Sumitanda, Prince of Omura, died, to the great grief of all who had at heart the cause of Christianity. He was, however, consoled during his last moments by the reflection that in the long-wished-for son, whose tardy appearance in the world had, it may be remembered, deferred his baptism, he left behind him a worthy successor. Notwithstanding the good intentions of the young prince, and the zeal of his subjects, and many of the most influential among the neighboring princes, misfortunes now began to overtake the Christians; and the first of that series of events occurred which ultimately drove the Jesuits from Japan, and extinguished the faith they had labored so diligently to propagate. That we may, however, appreciate the position of the Christians at this epoch, it is necessary to explain in a few words the conditions under which the affairs of the empire were being administered.

X

In order to understand the system under which Japan is at present governed, it is scarcely needful to go back in our investigations to the reigns of the five god-men who between them ruled its destinies for 2,342,467 years, and whose successors were all more or less mythological or legendary characters. In the year 660 B.C., that theocratic form of government came into existence which still remains under altered conditions, and constitutes so singular a feature in the history of this people. Combined with an ecclesiastical hereditary authority of a very remarkable character, the Mikado in former times united theoretically in his own person an absolute and unlimited authority over those numerous feudal princes whose territories composed his empire. It could scarcely be expected that the prestige attending the sacred functions with which he was invested, and the despotic power which he exercised, would prove sufficient in themselves to check the ambitious designs of those feudal chiefs who, more enterprising and less submissive to spiritual despotism than their fellows, were tempted to make war upon each other, or even cope with the imperial forces. This state of affairs reached its climax about the middle of the twelfth century; and so serious had it become, that it was found necessary to intrust the entire command of the army to a generalissimo, who assumed the title of Ziogoon. The first ziogoon was a young man, by name Yoritomo, celebrated in the annals of Japan as the founder of that series of subordinate emperors, who, after dividing for a short time the temporal power with the Mikado or spiritual emperor, ultimately retained exclusive possession of it, and who are now, in their turn, being slowly squeezed out of this mundane sphere by the Council of State, who do virtually control the destinies of the country. As the two emperors are called by a variety of names, it may be as well, to avoid confusion, to specify them.

The proper appellation of the spiritual emperor is Mikado, but he is also frequently called Daïri, which means court or palace, and is an abbreviation of Daïri-Sama, or Lord of the Palace. In time of war the temporal emperor is called Ziogoon, or Generalissimo: in time of peace, Tycoon, or Koboe. The term emperor, as applied to this dignitary, is one to which the Japanese especially object, though they do not deny that in him is nominally vested the supreme temporal power.

One of the ziogoons of Japan, in the days of the early fathers, was a certain Nobanunga, originally King of Mino and Voari, and who, by his determined energy and daring, acquired the temporal dignity. Nominally the throne of the tycoons is hereditary; but the history of its occupants tells the usual story of violence, intrigue, and blood.

Under the influence of Fathers Vilela and Valegnani, the fierce and haughty Nobanunga was induced to regard with a tolerant, if not absolutely favorable eye, the religion of the West, and during his reign it attained its most flourishing condition. In his answer to the bonzes, as recorded by Don Rodrigo de Vivero y Velasco, who was shipwrecked there some years afterward, he displayed a freedom from religious bigotry rarely to be met with in civilized countries at that period. "The bonzes of all the sects having concurred in a request to the emperor that he would expel our monks from Japan, the prince, troubled with their importunities, inquired how many different religions there were in Japan? 'Thirty-five,' was the reply. 'Well,' said he, 'where thirty-five sects can be tolerated, we can easily bear with thirty-six: leave the strangers in peace.'" This prince fell a victim, in the year 1582, to one of his own generals, who, at the head of an army placed under his command by Nobanunga, besieged that monarch in his palace, and ultimately consumed it by fire, burying in its ashes the unfortunate Koboe and his eldest son.

His death was the signal for a struggle for the vacant throne. After five years of anarchy, during three of which it was held by Fide Noba, it was seized by the celebrated Faxiba, or Taiko-Sama, a man whose early occupation it had been to cut wood in the forest, and carry it on his shoulders to the town, but who, being originally introduced into the palace of Nobanunga in a menial capacity, was discovered by that penetrating commander to be the possessor of great qualities, rapidly advanced under his favor to the chief command of his army, and finally acquired his throne under the pretext of preserving it for the grandson of his benefactor.

Taiko-Sama (for this was the name which he subsequently adopted, and which means "most exalted and sovereign lord") was unquestionably the most remarkable man who ever filled the throne of the ziogoons. Of inordinate ambition, he combined great originality of conception with energy and skill in the execution of his daring projects. Fortifying himself by an alliance with the spiritual throne by his marriage with the daughter of the Mikado, whose indifference to sublunary affairs does not extend to his domestic relations, Taiko-Sama ruled the empire with a hand of iron. The condition of the empire at this time, and the change effected in it by this ziogoon, are thus noticed by Kæmpfer: "The ambition and insolence of the princes of the empire was successively grown to such a height, that at last it became almost impossible for the ecclesiastical emperors to restrain and control them. In vain did they, for four ages together, send the crown generals against them, at the head of numerous armies. And yet this great work was brought about by Taiko in about ten years' time, not so much, indeed, by force of arms, as by his prudent conduct and good management." At first he professed great regard for the missionaries and respect for their religion, but the result of his observations, made during a tour through the western and most Christian portion of his dominions, induced him to alter his opinion, and issue an edict for the expulsion of every missionary from the empire. This order was received with general dissatisfaction and remonstrance from the kings of Arima and Omura, which only increased the irritation of the emperor, who determined upon depriving the Prince of Omura of the port of Nagasaki, and taking possession of it for his own use.

The fortifications were consequently destroyed, some of the churches demolished, and the town itself only ransomed at a large price by the Prince of Omura, who was allowed to retain it. Meantime the missionaries concealed themselves in the palaces and cities of their converts, determined not to relinquish without a struggle a field in which their labors had been crowned with such an abundant measure of success. For some time Taiko appears to have been too much engaged with his various projects to care to enforce compliance with an edict which may possibly have been promulgated in a moment of irritation. His general success afterward may have rendered him amiable. Be that as it may, the missionaries speedily emerged from their hiding-places, and resumed their efforts with redoubled energy; while the arrival of the embassadors who had been to Rome, under the guidance of Father Valegnani, with the pontifical letters, was a most seasonable diversion in their favor. The journey to Miako was a sort of triumphal progress; their reception at the capital an ovation. At their audience with the Ziogoon it is recorded that they were dressed like Italians, in black velvet, and speedily succeeded in creating an interest in the narration of their adventures, and conciliating the good-will of their sovereign. Shortly after this these four Japanese nobles entered the Order of Jesus. Meantime the Governor of Nagasaki and his colleague occupied themselves, according to the Jesuit historian, in prejudicing the mind of the Ziogoon against the Christians, and so far succeeded as to induce him again to threaten them with expulsion. His answer to the letter brought to him by Father Valegnani from the Portuguese Viceroy of Goa is interesting and characteristic. After recapitulating at some length the success with which the execution of his projects had been uniformly attended, and the flourishing condition of the Empire of Japan in consequence, Taiko-Sama goes on to say:

"This vast monarchy is like an immovable rock, and all the efforts of its enemies will not be able to shake it. Thus not only am I at peace at home, but persons come even from the most distant countries to render me that homage which is my due. Just now I am projecting the subjugation of China; and as I have no doubt that I shall succeed in this design, I trust that we shall soon be much nearer to each other, and that communication will be much easier between us. As to that which regards religion, Japan is the kingdom of the Kamis, that is to say, of Xim, which is the principle of every thing. The welfare of the government, which has been established from the commencement, depends upon the careful observance of those laws upon which it is founded, and which have the Kamis themselves for their authors. We can not depart from them without perceiving the difference which subsists between sovereign and subjects disappear, as well as that subordination of women to their husbands, children to their parents, vassals to their lords, servants to their masters. In a word, these laws are necessary for the maintenance of order within and of tranquillity without. The fathers who are called of the company (of Jesus) are come into these islands to teach another religion; but as that of the Kamis is too well established to be abolished, this new law can only serve to introduce into Japan a diversity of religion prejudicial to the welfare of the state. That is why I have prohibited, by imperial edict, these foreign doctors from continuing to preach their doctrine. I have even ordered them to leave Japan, and I am resolved no longer to allow persons to come here to '*debiter*' new opinions. I desire, nevertheless, that our commercial relations shall remain upon the same footing between us. The Portuguese shall be allowed to communicate freely with my subjects, and I will permit no one to do them any injury."

In pursuance of his scheme for the subjugation of China, to which Taiko-Sama makes such an offhand allusion in the above epistle, he fitted out four armies, three of which he sent to the Corea, where they gained two victories, seized the capital, drove the king from his throne into China, of which empire he was a tributary, and spread consternation far and wide. A Chinese army was, however, speedily dispatched to the Corea, and after sundry bloody engagements the war was terminated by mutual consent, Corean embassadors being sent to treat with Taiko-Sama, who ultimately agreed to the following conditions: 1st. That of the eight provinces of which the Corea is composed, five should belong to the Japanese; 2d. That the Emperor of China should give one of his daughters in marriage to the Emperor of Japan; 3d. That the commerce which had been for so long interrupted between China and Japan should be re-established; 4th. That the Emperor of China should pay an annual tribute to the crown of Japan as a recognition of the superiority of the latter potentate.

According to Kæmpfer, it was about three years after this, or about 1596, that the emperor finally deprived the Prince of Omura of Nagasaki, and annexed it as an imperial city to his dominions. The Jesuit fathers are wonderfully silent upon his motive for this proceeding, but the Dutch historian states it to have been in consequence of the insolent behavior of a priest to one of the councilors of state whom he met in the street. Whatever may have been the immediate cause, there can be no doubt that the position of the Portuguese at Nagasaki was becoming so consolidated as somewhat to menace the integrity of the empire, a fact which sundry emissaries, who were sent at different times from the Philippines to maintain relations between the Spanish government and the Emperor of Japan, were not slow to point out to that high personage. Indeed, the intrigues of the Spaniards, in their efforts to dislodge their rivals, form a fertile and rather tiresome theme with the old Jesuit chroniclers.

The rivalry of the Spaniards and Portuguese was religious rather than commercial, and it was not until the year 1599 that the arrival of the Dutch in Japan imported into the foreign relations of that empire a new element. In the mean time hostilities had recommenced in the Corea, which had ultimately resulted in the withdrawal of the Japanese troops from that province, and the death of the redoubtable Taiko-Sama removed any farther cause of alarm from the breast of his Celestial majesty.

On the accession of his successor Ogosho-Sama to the throne, both Spaniards and Portuguese redoubled their intrigues against each other, and their combined machinations against the Dutch. They made little impression, however, upon the enlightened and liberal-minded monarch, who denied the right of any power to dictate the policy he should pursue in regard to strangers visiting his dominions, maintaining that all he cared for was the tranquillity of his country and the welfare of his people; and that, so long as strangers paid obedience to the laws, and by their fair and honorable dealings promoted the convenience and enjoyment of his subjects, it mattered not to him to what nation they belonged, or to what power in the West they were nominally subject. On the last occasion when a joint memorial was presented on the subject by the Spaniards and Portuguese, Ogosho seems to have lost all patience, and he drove the remonstrants ignominiously from his presence, vehemently declaring that if "devils from hell were to visit his realm, they should be treated like angels from heaven," so long as they conducted themselves conformably with the principles he had laid down.*

To Englishmen, the associations connected with this sovereign are particularly interesting; for our countryman William Adams, who had piloted the first Dutch ship to Japan, and who was the first Englishman who had reached that empire, attracted the favorable notice of Ogosho-Sama to so great an extent that he insisted upon his fairly entering his service—a fact which William Adams thus devoutly alludes to: "Now for my service, which I have doen and daily doe, being employed in the emperor's service, he hath given me a living like unto a lordship in England, with eightie or nintie husbandmen, that be as my slaves or servants; which or the like precedent was never here before given to any stranger. Thus God hath provided for mee after my great miserie, and to Him only be all honnor and praise, power and glory, both now and forever, worlde without ende."

Honest Adams proved that he was a Christian in practice as

* RUNDALL's *Memorials*.

well as in profession; for, in spite of the malignant aspersions which were thrown upon him and his country by Spaniards, Portuguese, and Dutch, who all yelled in common chorus at an interloper, he increased in influence and weight at court—" at which my former enemies did wonder, and at this time must entreat me to do them a friendship, which to both Spaniards and Portingals have I doen, recompensing them good for evill."

A few years after this, in 1613, Captain Saris arrived in Japan in command of the Clove, bearing a letter from King James the First to the Emperor of Japan, and, through the instrumentality of Adams, negotiated a most favorable treaty with Ogosho-Sama. We established a factory at Firando in consequence. It only existed for ten years, however; the bitter animosity of the Dutch, and the unscrupulous means they are said to have resorted to, to obstruct our trade, combined with the absence of any adequate demand for our productions, and our ignorance of the resources of the country with which we had opened relations, led to the abandonment of the enterprise after about £40,000 had been spent upon it.

Meantime both Portuguese and Dutch were driving a lucrative trade; the former especially had derived enormous profits from their exports of gold and silver from Japan—so much so that Kæmpfer remarks, "It is believed that, had the Portuguese enjoyed the trade to Japan but twenty years longer, upon the same foot as they did for some time, such riches would have been transported out of this Ophir to Macao, and there would have been such a plenty and flow of gold and silver in that town, as sacred writs mention there was at Jerusalem in the times of Solomon." One of their own political economists, writing subsequently, complains of this. "I compute," he says,* " the annual exportation of gold at 150,000 kobans, so that in ten years this empire is drained of fifteen hundred thousand kobans, equal to about £2,500,000. With the exception of medicines, we can dispense with every thing that is brought us from abroad. The stuffs and other foreign commodities are of no real benefit to us. All the gold, silver, and copper extracted from the mines during the reign of Ogosho-Sama, and since his time, is gone, and, what is still more to be regretted, for things we could do well without."

* From a treatise composed in 1708 by the prime minister of the Emperor Tsonna Yosi, quoted by Titzingh in the "Illustrations of Japan."

We have no reason, however, for supposing that considerations of political economy entered into the policy of the emperor when he determined on the expulsion of the Portuguese from his dominions, and the toleration of the Dutch only under restrictions of the most humiliating character.

We have had evidence sufficient of the liberal and tolerant disposition of successive Japanese monarchs upon the subject of foreigners to assume that, had the latter confined themselves to mercantile operations, that generous hospitality would still have been accorded to them which distinguished the Japanese in their earlier intercourse with strangers.

It is scarcely necessary to enter here upon a discussion of the immediate cause which led to the expulsion of the Portuguese and extermination of the Christians. It forms a subject of much vehement recrimination between the Jesuit fathers and early Dutch chroniclers. According to Kæmpfer, letters were intercepted by the Dutch, revealing a conspiracy in which the Japanese Christians had engaged, in conjunction with the Portuguese, against the emperor's life and throne. According to Père Charlevoix, these letters were forged by the Dutch for the purpose of giving color to the malicious libels which the latter were inventing against their rivals. However that may be, these two enlightened Western powers succeeded between them in causing the name of Christ to be hated and despised, and in hermetically sealing up for two centuries a rich and productive country, inhabited by one of the most amiable and civilized races in the world. The following proclamation was the result of the miserable triumph achieved by the Dutch over their competitors: "No Japanese ship or boat whatever, nor any native of Japan, shall presume to go out of the country; who acts contrary to this shall die, and the ship, with the crew and goods on board, shall be sequestered until farther orders. All Japanese who return from abroad shall be put to death. Whoever discovers a priest shall have a reward of from four to five hundred shuets (equal to the same number of pounds) of silver, and for every Christian in proportion. All persons who propagate the doctrine of the Christians, or bear this scandalous name, shall be imprisoned in the omera, or common jail of the town. The whole race of the Portuguese, with their mothers, nurses, and whatever belongs to them, shall be banished to Macao. Whoever presumes to bring a letter from abroad, or to return after he hath been banished, shall die, with all his family also: whoever presumes to intercede for them shall be put to death."

Then followed that frightful series of persecutions, not exceeded in horror or ingenuity of torment by those to which the early Christians were subjected; and in carrying out their ruthless policy against the Christians, the Japanese always found in the Dutch ready and willing assistants. These importunate traders lost no opportunity of insinuating themselves into the good graces of the islanders. They brought over the most exquisite objects of art and nature for annual presents, and demeaned themselves rather as willing slaves than as free burghers. When ordered to demolish their own warehouses and factories because they were built of finer blocks of hewn stone than the buildings of the country, and were inscribed with the date of the Christian era, they did so with seeming satisfaction, and finally put a climax to their obedience by bombarding, at the behest of the Japanese government, 37,000 Christians who were cooped up within the walls of Simabarra.

It was about this time, or in 1636, that Decima was founded. Since that period the Dutch have been confined to its limited area, and have consistently pursued the policy which had been inaugurated under such tragical circumstances. During these last two hundred years they have not even had the profits of a lucrative trade to console them for the ignominy with which they have been treated; on the contrary, it has steadily diminished in proportion as the indignities to which they have been exposed have increased, so that they have been glad, during these last few years, to make a merit of necessity, and profess an earnest desire to assist in promoting intercourse between the Japanese and other nations. Already their monopoly has disappeared. In the race which is about to ensue, their full-bosomed old craft will drop behind the horizon, and in ten years hence the Dutch trade with Japan will have become matter of history.

CHAPTER XXIII.

Surfeit of Sensations.—The Dutch and Russian Bazars.—Money-changers.—Tempting Investments.—Visit from the Vice-governor.—A Riding-school.—Surrounding Country.—A Visit to a Tea-garden.—Feasting and Music.—Productions of Fizen.—Coal Mines.—Prince of Satsuma.—Japanese Classes at Nagasaki.—Military Organization.—A Gale of Wind.—Volcanic Eruptions.—Places of future Punishment.—A stormy Night.—Arrival at Simoda.—Dangerous Harbor.

I FIND it difficult, in attempting to convey our first impressions of Japan, to avoid presenting a too highly-colored picture to the mind of the reader. The contrast with China was so striking, the evidences of a high state of civilization so unexpected, the circumstances of our visit were so full of novelty and interest, that we abandoned ourselves to the excitement and enthusiasm they produced. There exists not a single disagreeable association to cloud our reminiscences of that delightful country. Each day gave us fresh proofs of the amiable and generous character of the people among whom we were. Each moment of the day furnished us with some new fact worthy of notice. Our powers of observation were kept constantly on the stretch, but one felt they were overtaxed; the time was too short; sights and impressions crowded on each other with a painful rapidity and variety. It was like being compelled to eat a whole *paté de fois gras* at a sitting; the dish was too rich and highly charged with truffles for one's mental digestion. At the time it was delicious; it is only afterward, when you try to arrange the facts and describe the experiences, that the inconvenience attending a surfeit of sensations of this sort makes itself felt.

When we landed at the factory early next morning we found it crowded with British purchasers, both at the Dutch and Russian bazars; lackered and china ware, bronzes and delicate basketwork, were arranged in tempting display. The beauty and elegance of all we saw delighted and astonished us: it was only when we had "shopped" at Yedo that we came to hold Nagasaki workmanship at a proper estimation, and to appreciate the difference between those articles which are manufactured and exhibited there for the European market, and those which are made for the Japanese themselves. As a rule, Nagasaki lacker is of a most inferior description; the shapes and patterns are nearly all of Dutch suggestion, and the mother-of-pearl with which they are so abundantly and gorgeously inlaid is purely a Western invention. The egg-shell china is also manufactured for the European market: it is an exquisitely delicate fabric, made principally in the provinces of Fizen and Satsuma, and not used by the Japanese themselves. We were not able to obtain any of the thinnest description at Yedo.

In bronzes the Japanese far excel the Chinese, the design and workmanship being infinitely superior. At Nagasaki, the result of intercourse with Europeans for two centuries and a half is very apparent. There were to be seen admirable telescopes of native manufacture, clocks, magnifying-glasses, and glass-ware of various descriptions, besides many imitations of European fabrics. The Russian bazar, which was situated on the main land, is built like an Eastern caravanserai; it is a paved square, surrounded with small wooden houses and verandas, full of articles for sale. At the entrance gateway are a certain number of officials, who now take little heed of the visitor, and always appeared to me engaged in making servile obeisances to one another, and drinking very hot tea out of curiously-constructed steamers. The chief building in the square is devoted to the exchange of foreign money for Japanese paper currency.

In an up-stairs room, approached by a scrupulously clean staircase, on the upper step of which is a row of Japanese slippers, sit three or four grave two-sworded officials round a table on which are placed two boxes, one full of metallic, the other of paper currency. It is useless to endeavor to persuade a Japanese shopkeeper to take a foreign coin, however large and tempting it may be. The government has forbidden him to receive any thing from the foreigner but the little oblong pieces of card which bear the government stamp; so to this little room every foreigner is compelled to resort to obtain an available circulating medium. The currency between the foreigners and the tradespeople is taels, mace, can, and cash: in name the same as in China, but representing very different values, inasmuch as Japanese paper money is granted by the treasury in exchange for Spanish and Mexican dollars at the rate of four taels seven mace per dollar.

Meantime there is a great crush of naval officers round the small table, and the usual manifestation of impatience on the part of the Anglo-Saxon, but the Japanese lose neither "count" nor "countenance." They maintain the affable imperturbability of croupiers at German gambling-tables. They never make a mistake, nor cease to smile blandly; and if we are in a hurry, we had better make up our minds to sit quietly on a bench near the window which overlooks the canal till our turn comes. We can watch the boats plying with heavy loads along it, and observe the family arrangements of the houses, with balconies overhanging it; or we can look inward, and wonder at the extraordinary cleanliness of the padded mat under our feet, and the inexhaustible patience of the money-changers, and moralize over the difference in the civilization and national characters of Englishmen and Japanese, and try whether Mr. Buckle's theory will account for them; or we may look out of the opposite window into the yard, where an extensive and lucrative business is being carried on by the Japanese licensed by the government to trade with Europeans. They are struggling manfully with the English language; are inflexible as regards price, not to be beaten down, and are almost as importunate and insinuating in their manner to the foreign young gentlemen as if it was a fancy bazar for a charitable purpose, and they were English young ladies and had stalls. Then there are officious porters in readiness to carry away purchases; but their services are rejected by independent middies, who prefer staggering away under their own lacker, and all the while at the entrance-gate reverential greetings are continually going on, and the imbibing of hot tea.

But we must not linger too long here, for the vice-governor is coming on board to lunch, and it is time for us to return to the ship to receive him. He arrives seated in the bows of a stately barge, surrounded by a number of attendants, and with numerous black and white flags fluttering from the stern. He is a plebeian-looking man, with an extremely smiling countenance and very short legs. They are incased in loose trowsers, not unlike knickerbockers, of damask embroidery, of a pattern that would be considered rather too gaudy for curtains. He bows repeatedly and rapidly, and his two swords, like a double tail, cock up responsively. His legs, below the knee, are neatly gaitered, and his stockinged feet are thrust into straw sandals. Across his bosom are many folds of fine cotton, which compose his shirt, and over it a thin gauze tunic completes his costume. Luncheon has been prepared for him and some of his followers, and he is soon seated at Lord Elgin's right hand, drinking Champagne, and handling his knife and fork as if he usually lived in London. The other Japanese present seemed equally accustomed to Western manners. The vice-governor had been sent on the part of the governor to express his regret that illness prevented his seeing Lord Elgin, and at the same time to request that the yacht, which he understood had been brought over as a present to the emperor, should be made over to the Japanese governor at Nagasaki. As Lord Elgin depended chiefly for an excuse for proceeding to Yedo upon the necessity of delivering the yacht, if possible, to the emperor himself, he assured the governor that it was not in his power to part with the yacht except at the capital. Finding that no arguments were of any avail to divert Lord Elgin from this determination, the vice-governor gave up the matter as hopeless, and, after discoursing with considerable intelligence upon the recent treaty with China and other topics of interest, he took his leave.

As Lord Elgin had not yet seen much of the town, I accompanied him on shore on another tour of exploration. In the course of our walk we came to a large inclosure, and on entering it found fifteen or twenty men on horseback, galloping and curveting about a considerable area, apparently used as a riding-school. This we understood was the constant afternoon amusement of the "young bloods" of Nagasaki. They were all men of fortune and family, princes and nobles of the land, and this was their Rotten Row. They rode fiery little steeds, averaging about fourteen hands in height, and took a delight in riding full gallop and pulling up short, after the favorite manner of Arabs. The saddles were constructed on the same principle as they are in China, but with less padding. The stirrup-leathers were short, and the stirrups like huge slippers made of lacker. The bit was powerful, and the reins were of muslin, but strong notwithstanding. The most remarkable feature in the costume of the riders was their hats: these were like shields, almost perfectly flat, made of lacker, and fastened on the head by a variety of lashings. Two strings crossed each other at the back of the head, two crossed under the nose, and two more under the chin. It is as much trouble to tie on a Japanese hat as to put on a pair of skates; and when it is done, the face looks all laced over, as if there was something serious the matter with it. Still it is wonderful how effectual the lashing was, and how firmly the flat roof, or rather "tile," seemed fixed on their heads.

When we appeared, two or three good-looking young men pulled up near us, jumped off their horses, and most good-naturedly pressed them upon us. I took a short uncomfortable gallop upon one with a propensity to kick, and was glad soon to relinquish him to his smiling owner. We were much struck by the gentleman-like and unconstrained bearing of these young men, who evidently wished to show us all the civility in their power.

Before leaving Nagasaki we wished to extend our wanderings beyond the immediate limits of the streets. The city itself, like a lover at the feet of his mistress, nestles at the base of wooded hills of exquisite form, as though it did not venture to profane with its coarse touch those lovely slopes which are dedicated to the worship of Buddh and the Cytherean goddess, for these hill sides are dotted with the most enchanting sites, and every one of them is occupied with a temple or a tea-house.

In Japan, religion is not used, as in some countries, to conceal immorality, but rather to give it countenance and support, so that practically there is very little difference here between a temple and a tea-house. Both are situated in grounds beautifully laid out. In landscape-gardening the Japanese excel every other nation in the world. Both are resorted to as agreeable retreats from the turmoil and bustle of the city. The most delightful arbors, the choicest dishes, and the softest music, are provided equally at one and the other.

It is estimated that there are sixty-two temples (large and small) and seven hundred and fifty tea-houses on the hills round Nagasaki, all offering to the Japanese in search of repose delicious tea and extensive panoramic views. It is worth while climbing up to some of them, if only to enjoy the latter. Old moss-grown steps ascend the steep hill side, and you pass through venerable gateways and up more massive flights to a fairy-like wooden structure perched on a projecting point, and backed by terraced gardens and cool shady groves that lead to grottoes, where sparkling water gushes from the hill side. The building seems constructed with a view to the prospect it commands. The bare, softly-matted rooms are surrounded with deep verandas, and from every angle a fresh scene of beauty meets the eye. Behind us are wooded dells, and more temples and tea-houses. At our feet the city is mapped out, and we can inspect the back premises of the houses of families, who are all at this hour engaged in domestic ablutions. It is delightful to see papa, mamma, and all the children splashing so harmoniously in the back garden. Beyond the town are more terraced hills, and the beautiful winding harbor losing itself in deep creeks and bays, to all appearance a placid lake, for the ocean is nowhere visible.

Meantime the dinner, which has been ordered, has arrived. Spread out upon the floor in lackered bowls, it occupies the greater portion of the room. It has been quickly and deftly arranged by a train of neatly dressed maidens, who now seat themselves round it and invite us to partake. We have long since taken off our shoes, and now squat in a circle on the floor, and gaze with curiosity, not unmixed with alarm, at the display before us. There is raw fish thinly sliced, and salted ginger; there are prawns piled up with a substance which in taste and appearance very much resembles toffy; there are pickled eggs and rock-leeches, and pieces of gristle belonging to animals unknown, to be eaten with soy; and yams and pears, and various sorts of fruits and vegetables, prepared some of them palatably enough; but still the experiment is hazardous, and we are relieved at the sight of a bowl of rice as a safe *piece de resistance*.

The ministering spirits seem to delight in pressing upon us the nastiest things, apparently for the amusement which our wry faces afford them. Presently another troop of damsels with lutes and tom-toms come tripping in; but they elicit from their musical instruments the most discordant sounds to our non-Japanese ears, so that we are glad to take refuge in the balcony, and having once more feasted our eyes upon the fading prospect, we descend from our airy position to the streets, now rapidly subsiding into that early evening stillness which gives evidence that the good folks of Nagasaki do not allow either business or pleasure to steal from them the best hours of the night.

We should have regretted that our stay at Nagasaki was to be so short, had we not had Yedo in prospect. We had scarcely anticipated, on our departure from Shanghai, so brilliant a programme as the one which was gradually unfolding itself. The arrival of the admiral in the Calcutta set any doubt we had on the matter finally at rest. It had been his original intention to hand over the yacht himself. This, however, was now impossible, as his presence was urgently required at Canton, where the state of affairs was far from satisfactory. Under these circumstances, it was arranged that Lord Elgin should proceed with the yacht to Yedo, as it was evidently desirable that no time should be lost in proceeding upon this mission. It was therefore impossible for us to attempt to go upon any of those expeditions into the country in the neighborhood of Nagasaki, which Europeans have lately been allowed to make. I understood that the princes of the neighboring territories of Fizen and Tsikuzen were both favorably disposed toward Europeans. Fizen is indeed one of the most productive provinces in the empire, yielding a revenue to its prince amounting, it is said by Siebold, to £360,000 annually. Besides rice and various descriptions of gum, it produces tea, tobacco, and cotton, vegetable tallow, iron, sulphur, cinnabar, and marble.

There is a coal mine at a place called Wuku Moto, in the interior, which some of the Dutch mission have descended. They describe the mine as being well and judiciously worked, and the coal as bituminous in its nature, and made into coke for use.

Old Kæmpfer tells a story, by way of illustrating the volcanic nature of the country, of a coal mine in the province, which, through the carelessness of the miners, took fire, and has been burning ever since. A very excellent description of porcelain clay is found here, and the European demand for egg-shell china, which is sold in great quantities, is chiefly supplied by the provinces of Fizen and Satsuma. The prince of the former state is, so far as we could learn from our Dutch informants at Nagasaki, a man of tolerably advanced views; he does not seem, however, to have succeeded in thoroughly divesting himself of old prejudices. This was illustrated a short time prior to our visit by his refusal to allow the Dutch to enter his territory to put up a steam-engine which he himself had ordered out from Europe to pump the water out of one of his coal mines. It should be noticed as the most interesting feature connected with this province, that it is said to produce the most beautiful women in the empire.

But the Prince of Satsuma was the great hero of the Dutch residents at Nagasaki, he having at different times invited them to visit him. This prince, who has died since our visit, is said to have been the most enlightened, as he was one of the most powerful, of the independent princes. In close alliance with the late emperor, who had married his daughter, he possessed great influence at Yedo, where he owned no less than nine town-houses. His is one of the families from which, when a direct heir fails to the temporal throne, an heir-presumptive is selected. One of the ancestors of their great line was the conqueror of the Lewchew Islands. The province of Satsuma contains vast quantities of the sulphur which may form an item in our trade with Japan. At its southern extremity is situated the island of Ivogasima, or Sulphur Island, which is said to burn incessantly. The mines on this island yield the Prince of Satsuma an annual revenue of two hundred chests of silver. I was informed by Captain Katendyke, a Dutch gentleman at Nagasaki, that this prince had already established an electric telegraph, which was in successful operation between his palace and his capital city, Kagosima, a distance of about three miles. He has also extensive glass factories and cannon foundries, in which eight hundred workmen are employed.

Under Captain Katendyke's direction, the Japanese were at that time carrying out some extensive public works in the harbor. These principally consisted of a machine shop and foundry, with all the appurtenances necessary for the building and repairing of steamers, which the emperor had recently determined on establishing at Nagasaki. For the last six months prior to our arrival the Dutch engineers had been engaged collecting machinery; a large quantity had already arrived.

The spot selected for the erection of the various buildings is in a beautiful valley, sloping down to, and terminating at, the left bank of the harbor, entering from seaward opposite Nagasaki. We observed a boat-load of Dutch artificers and engineers cross to it daily, but had not time to inspect their progress ourselves. It was calculated that two years would elapse before the works could come into operation. A pier several hundred feet in length, and extending out sufficiently far to insure twenty feet at low water, was being built immediately in front, and as a part of the establishment. In the construction of this pier, the Japanese workmen, under Dutch direction, were making constant use of a diving-bell and Nasmyth's hammer.

Japanese are allowed to enter these works as apprentices, in order to perfect themselves in engineering and mechanics, and so strong are their acquisitive propensities, where knowledge is concerned, that several princes have sought and obtained permission from the emperor to place themselves under instruction, and are to be seen daily at the works, busily engaged at the lathe, the vice, or the forge, as the case may require, while others may be found in the drafting-room, preparing the necessary drawings for the various departments. Besides this, there has been for some years a naval school. By accounts we have received from Nagasaki, dated April last, we learn that an imperial decree has been received from Yedo, directing that the naval school be removed from Nagasaki to the capital, the government believing that their officers have attained such proficiency in navigation as to enable them to dispense with farther instruction in that department. This conclusion appears to have been arrived at from their screw steamer Yedo having lately made a successful passage from Nagasaki to Yedo in nine days, unaccompanied by any foreigner. The school of engineers, however, above alluded to, is still to be continued, as well as one of medicine and surgery, which has been for some time in existence, and very well attended.

Upon levies raised by the princes of Fizen and Tsikuzen would depend the defense of Nagasaki and the adjacent coast in the event of a war between Japan and any foreign country. Every independent prince throughout the country is bound to contribute a certain quota of troops to assist those of the imperial government. So large a proportion of the male population is considered available for this purpose, that the standing army of Japan ranks probably among the largest in the world, though totally deficient in that training or scientific knowledge of the military art which would render it formidable to a civilized people.

The occupation of a soldier is held in high estimation in the country. They belong to the fourth social grade, and are called Samlai, holding their lands by a nominal tenure of their feudal superiors, in consideration of their military service. The imperial troops, as distinguished from those of the feudal princes, have been estimated at 100,000 foot and 20,000 horse. I do not feel certain, however, that my authority for this is to be relied upon.

At three o'clock in the afternoon of the 5th of August we weighed anchor, and steamed out of Nagasaki harbor, the Retribution, yacht, and Lee gun-boat in company. Just as we did so a salvo of guns announced a foreign sail in sight, and as we cleared the Iwo-Sima Islands we discerned a large Dutch ship beating bravely up from the southward. We little guessed that at that moment a storm was brewing which should in a few hours strew the ribs of that goodly craft upon the rocks under our lee, and drive us for a shelter under the wild headland of Chichakoff. We went under easy sail, so as to get daylight for our passage through Van Diemen's Straits, and found ourselves next morning between two conical volcanic peaks, the apparent counterpart of each other, about 2500 feet in height, and situated some twenty miles apart. The wind now freshened to a gale; rocks and islands studded this little-known sea in every direction; and, as the weather thickened, it became evident that we must seek some friendly harbor in which to ride out the violence of the gale.

It was an anxious moment as we felt our way under the bluff cliffs of Cape Chichakoff, sounding in vain, and poking our nose into unpleasant proximity to breakers. Beyond the storm-beaten cape we need not hope for shelter. Our only chance was to push up the deep unsurveyed Bay of Kagosima until we found a safe anchorage. Fortunately we had not far to go—a slight indenture in the coast, with a few fishing cottages on the sandy beach, and a boat or two hauled up on it, gave promise of an anchorage, which we found about a mile distant from the shore. It was an iron-bound coast, the steep grassy hills terminating in rocky bluffs, at the base of which the sea broke heavily. Here, however, as long as the wind continued in one direction, we were secure, and accordingly, within a cable's length of us the Retribution and yacht were soon moored. Of the Lee, however, we had seen nothing since the previous evening, and were not a little anxious as to her fate. We almost regretted that fortune did not drive us up the bay to Kagosima, the capital of Satsuma, where we should have had an opportunity of visiting the residence of the prince, and of inspecting the progress of those foreign arts and inventions which he has introduced, and which have already contributed so largely to the prosperity of the chief city of his province.

The whole of this section of the coast of Japan is eminently volcanic; peaked mountains were observable far inland, while out to seaward peaked islands gave evidence of their fiery origin. In the island of Kiusiu alone, at the southernmost point of which we were now at anchor, there are no less than five active volcanoes: of these one is in Satsuma, but the most celebrated is the

Wunzen-take, or the "High Mountain of warm Springs," in Fizen. An account of one of its eruptions is contained in the Chinese Repository. In 1793 the summit of the mountain sank entirely down; torrents of boiling water issued from all parts of the deep cavity which was thus formed, and the vapor arose like thick smoke. In one of its eruptions it is recorded to have destroyed the ill-fated city of Sima Barra, when 35,000 persons are said to have perished. Old Father Froes, writing in 1586, tells a story of a strong castle in the kingdom of Mino, built at the top of a hill, which, after several violent shocks, sank down and disappeared of a sudden—"the earth gaping that not the least footstep remained, a lake quickly filling the place where the foundations of the castle had been. Another accident of this kind occurred in the province of Tkeja. Very many gaps and openings were observed up and down the empire, some of which were so wide and deep that, guns being fired into them, the balls could not be heard to reach the other end, and such a smoke and stench issued out of them that people would not venture to travel that way." Kæmpfer describes a small island near Firando which has been burning and trembling for centuries; while many hot and sulphurous springs bubble up all over the empire, and are much frequented for the healing qualities they are supposed to possess.

It is not to be wondered at, in such a country of fire and brimstone, that the inhabitants should speculate learnedly upon the infernal regions, and now and then choose some seething well or flaming mountain as the *descensus Averni*. They have, moreover, decided upon the various departments of punishment. To one spring, which is covered at the top with a white cream-like froth, are consigned pastry-cooks and confectioners who practiced adulteration while in this life; while deceitful brewers pass a miserable existence in a spring as thick and muddy as the beer or sakee they sold their customers.

To ride at anchor on wild, stormy nights off such an "uncanny" coast, was like being condemned to sleep in a haunted room. We were a prey to vague imaginary terrors, and never knew whether, in some convulsion of nature, the waters might not suddenly recede, and leave us, as they did the Russian frigate Diana, stranded on the bottom.

We remained at anchor in this dismal spot for about thirty-six hours, during which time the gale blew with such violence as to render it impossible to attempt a landing. About midnight on the 7th, however, it shifted suddenly. Captain Osborn, anticipating a quick change, had hove the cable short, and we were under weigh in a few minutes with a blinding wind and sea in our teeth, and our bows under at every heave. The huge pointed rocks off Chichakoff loomed black and threatening in the thick darkness, and we could hear the waves roaring against them as we struggled past this point—the Retribution, with the yacht in tow, doing her work manfully, and her light, like an *ignis fatuus*, dancing on the waves close to our quarter. We did not know until we met her at Yedo, just a week afterward, how nearly the Lee had left her bones to whiten on that inhospitable coast. Nailed to a lee shore for some hours, her life was despaired of by her gallant commander, Captain Grahame, whose skill and seamanship, ably seconded by Captain Colin Campbell, who was on board as a guest at the time, rescued her from her precarious predicament.

Though it blew very hard for the three following days, the wind was fair, and we made rapid progress. On the morning of the 10th we saw on the distant horizon the lofty cone of Fusiyama, a mountain of whose very existence I had heretofore been ignorant, and whose celebrity we did not even then suspect. At that great distance it was a striking object. Towering over all minor elevations, it reared its snow-streaked crest to a height of 12,000 feet above the sea, presenting in its form and outline very much the appearance of Mount Etna. According to Japanese accounts, it has not been active for upward of a century. Altering our course for this landmark, so worthy the great city of Yedo, we made out shortly on our starboard beam the "Isles Brisées," and near them the active volcano of Vries, with a puff of smoke resting above it as though a shell had burst upon its apex.

Our immediate destination was Simoda, but its narrow entrance on that bay-indented coast was somewhat difficult to find. As we neared the shore we observed numerous craft dodging in and out of harbors, and playing at "hide-and-seek" round bold green headlands, and behind rocky islets; and at last we opened the snug-looking bay of Simoda, and glided into its peaceful waters between shores heavily clothed with timber, and resplendent with brilliant foliage. Deep coves invited the tempest-tossed fisherman to calm security, the entrance guarded by rocks, the shores feathered to the water's edge, and the water itself clear as crystal, and alive with glancing fishes. We only gazed wistfully into these tempting retreats, too small for any thing but a fishing-boat, and steamed gently on into the tranquil harbor, in which two large rocks, rising from its centre, are a picturesque but most inconvenient feature. One of these, called Centre Island, is perforated with a cavern and crowned with trees. The water is deep all round it, and, as long as the wind is not blowing from the southeast, is perfectly smooth.

To the unwary visitor the harbor seems the perfection of security, so snugly embayed; while above it the hills rise in tumbled masses, surrounding the little town, and giving birth to the river that winds its sluggish course through a valley that might be in fairyland, to the sea. With a sullen plunge the anchor falls into the water deep and blue within a few yards of the shore, and sends a throb of fresh excitement through our veins as we gaze with ecstasy on the lovely scene around us, and prepare to explore its unknown charms.

CHAPTER XXIV.

Residence of the American Consul.—A Hermitage.—Visit to the American Consul.—His recent Success at Yedo.—Bazar at Simoda.—Torturing Indecision.—A Japanese Grave-yard.—Buddhist Temples.—The Sintoo Religion.—Household Gods.—A Japanese Temple.—Doctrines of the Sintoos.—Theological Speculations.—The Value of Sintooism.—A Visit from the Governor.—An expensive Form of Politeness.—General Appearance of Simoda.—Voyage up the Bay of Yedo.—Japanese Cottages.—Kanagawa.—Approach to Yedo.

At the head of the Bay of Simoda, and about a mile distant from the town, is situated a pleasant grove of trees. Its mysterious shades are dedicated, doubtless, to religious purposes, and conceal in their solemn recesses some picturesque old temple, in which, for an untold number of years, shriveled priests have performed their sacred functions. It is a spot eminently suggestive of repose and religious retirement; and we could scarcely believe our eyes when, on bringing our telescopes to bear, we distinguished, fluttering among the leaves of a sacred Bo-tree, the well-known combination of red, white, and blue which forms the national flag of our transatlantic cousins. Yet so it is; the stars and stripes wave proudly over the premises originally occupied by some recent incarnation of Buddh; and Mr. Harris, the American consul, has converted the shrine of that divinity into a four-poster. We learn all this from Mr. Hewsken, Mr. Harris's secretary, who comes off to visit us before we have had time to land, and who brings Lord Elgin an offer of services on the part of the American consul.

I landed with Lord Elgin to pay Mr. Harris a visit. The external aspect of his abode, as seen from the ship, did not belie its romantic character upon a closer acquaintance. Had one wished to retire altogether from the cares and anxieties of this troublesome world, it would be difficult to conceive a retreat more perfectly adapted for the purpose. When, however, entire and total seclusion is the result rather of necessity than choice, it is small consolation to feel that you are imprisoned in a corner admirably suited to a recluse. Often, in the course of his wanderings, the traveler is struck with the charms of some silent nook in this bustling universe. His first impression is, "What a delightful spot for a hermit!"—his next, "How I should pity the poor wretch!" For disciples of Zimmerman, notwithstanding, or lovers in a Petrarchian state, Japan offers greater attractions, probably, than any other country in the globe, but neither Mr. Harris nor Mr. Hewsken seemed altogether to appreciate them. A well-stored library, and a few rooms comfortably fitted up, gave an agreeable air of civilization to the establishment; but what can compensate for two years of almost entire isolation and banishment from communion with one's fellow-men? Except upon the rare occasions of Simoda being visited by some foreign vessel, these two gentlemen had not seen a creature with whom they could exchange an idea. They had been for eighteen months without receiving a letter or a newspaper, and two years without tasting mutton—sheep being an animal unknown in Japan. Still, this exile had not the effect of disgusting them with the country of their banishment. Mr. Harris spoke in terms even more eulogistic than those universally employed by the Dutch of the Japanese people. His residence among them, under circumstances which compelled him to form intimate relations with them—for they were his only companions—only served to increase his high opinion of their amiable qualities and charming natural dispositions. He told us numerous anecdotes illustrative of this, more especially of the extraordinary attention shown him by the emperor and empress on the occasion of a serious illness which he had suffered. The emperor insisted on sending his own medical man to attend upon him, while her majesty delighted in providing him with culinary delicacies, prepared by herself, and suited to his state of health.

Mr. Harris had only recently returned from Yedo, where he had just succeeded in negotiating a more favorable treaty with the Japanese government than had been made since the days of Captain Saris. He had passed some months in that city, during which time both he and Mr. Donker Curtius had been engaged in fruitless efforts to induce the government to accede to their terms. In 1855 the latter gentleman had concluded a mercantile arrangement, by which certain concessions were allowed to foreigners; but the cumbersome machinery of the Geldkammer was still retained, and the monopoly of the trade was reserved to the Japanese government, under conditions which rendered the concessions worthless to nations engaged in commerce upon enlightened principles. Mr. Harris, however, was determined to make a treaty worthy the progressive people whom he represented; and Mr. Donker Curtius, finding him so engaged, repaired to Yedo, determined, if possible, not to be outdone. It so happened that his precautions were unavailing.

Finding the Japanese government inexorable, both gentlemen left in despair—Mr. Donker Curtius upon a long overland journey of two months to Nagasaki, Mr. Harris to return to Simoda. He had scarcely reached it, however, before the Powhattan arrived with intelligence of the Treaty of Tientsin. Mr. Harris then lost not a moment in himself carrying the news of this to the capital; and while Mr. Donker Curtius was journeying laboriously to Nagasaki, ignorant of the great events which had taken place, his rival had signed his treaty, and was back again at Simoda reposing on his laurels.

We walked along the edge of the bay from Mr. Harris's temple-abode to the town. Simoda is a mean place compared with Nagasaki, and it is difficult to conceive why Commodore Perry should have fixed upon it as a port. Even in those days it was little more than a fishing village, and since then it has been visited by an earthquake, from the effects of which neither town nor harbor has yet recovered. Always exposed, even where the anchorage was tolerable, there is now no holding-ground in the event of a storm, so completely did that terrible convulsion of nature change the surface of the bottom.

The town, which is situated at the debouching of the small river into the sea, is composed of a few mean streets, running at right angles to each other, and contains, probably, from three to four thousand inhabitants. At one corner of it is a bazar established for the benefit of foreigners, containing lacker of a superior description to that exhibited at Nagasaki, and sundry articles of native manufacture I had observed before. Among others, I bought some water-proof great-coats for eighteen pence apiece, made of wax paper, and as completely effectual in a storm of rain as the best mackintosh that ever was manufactured. They are very light and portable, the only drawback being a liability to tear; but then they are half the price of a pair of white kid gloves.

These bazars are the most tantalizing of resorts. There is so much displayed, and it is all so beautiful and new, that one walks through avenues of brilliant novelties in a stupefied condition of mind, and with a strong sensation of overwhelming responsibility. If any body would only come and tell one which to choose, and what was most likely to be admired at home. Alas! every body else is buying furiously; nobody seems to have a doubt upon the subject; all the best things are being bought up under your nose, and there you stand bewildered and dismayed; so you finally determine to buy recklessly and indiscriminately until your pocket is emptied of its contents. The process is simple. As soon as the article is determined upon, the Japanese vendor hands you a slip of paper and a fine hair brush dipped in ink. On this you write your name and the price, after which you convey the simplest expression of which your name will admit to the Japanese, who writes in his own language the nearest approximation which his ear retains of the uncouth sound. At the end of the day you proceed to a sort of bureau, where all the purchases are piled up, duly labeled, and their prices attached. These are added up by the officials employed, and the foreign coin which is tendered taken by weight. There is no haggling in the first instance, or disputes afterward; every thing is managed with perfect order and system.

Another inconvenience attending these bazars is the waste of time which they involve. One is a martyr to one's conscience all the while. What business have you to stand and stare at lacker all day, when the town and its neighborhood are to be explored, and numerous interesting and important facts are to be observed and noted? It is less expensive and more instructive to turn one's back upon this scene of extravagance, and start off in search of the novel and the picturesque. We have not far to go. Just behind the bazar rises a densely-wooded hill, and of course it is adorned with temples and shrines, which we reach by clambering up long flights of steps, and find little figures standing behind strips of colored paper, and inscriptions, and the ashes of a sacred fire. We look down over the town and bay, and then follow a romantic path which winds through the damp impenetrable shade formed by dense foliage, and suddenly opens upon an extensive grave-yard, where quaintly-carved tomb-stones are planted thick under the tall trees. The graves, of which these monuments indicate the position, are said to be of circular form, plastered with lime to prevent the infiltration of water. According to old Arnoldus Montanus, the women are placed in these in a sitting posture, with their hands separated, and their faces turned as though looking over the shoulder; the men are seated in a devotional attitude, with their hands clasped. The tomb-stones are called sisek, and some of them are elaborately carved, and adorned with representations of warriors fighting, or, in the case of women's graves, with drawings of flowers. The inscriptions are carved in the stone, and left in that condition until the owner of the grave becomes its occupant, when they are gilt.

Altogether, a Japanese grave-yard, abundantly supplied with tall sculptured monumental stones, many of them hoary and moss-grown, embowered amid dense foliage, and overshadowed by the twisted gables of some sacred edifice, is an object of interest and tranquil beauty, calculated to produce in the mind of the stranger from the Western world a strong impression in favor of a people whose taste and sentiments upon so solemn a subject seem to be in accordance with his own.

We passed from the grave-yard into the temple. The interior was a spacious hall, matted and hung with large lanterns; a centre space, inclosing sacred tapers, and images of different sizes, was railed off, as is usual in Buddhist temples. To those not deeply versed in the mysteries of the religion, neither the principal idol nor the general aspect of the building seemed to differ very much from temples dedicated elsewhere to the same worship; but, inasmuch as there are thirty-five sects in Japan, or, at any rate, were in the days of Nobanunga, there was doubtless much that was not orthodox in the temple in question. The priest, a venerable old man in a long gray robe, was remarkably civil to us; but, as it was impossible to exchange an idea with him, we contented ourselves by looking as pleased and interested as we could.

The numerous temples in the neighborhood of Simoda form the most attractive feature in its environs. They are more easily approached than those at Nagasaki: there is less climbing, and the walks are prettier. Under almost every hill is hidden a yasiro or miya: the entrance gateway is probably composed of two monoliths, and resting upon them a long block of stone, upturned at the ends, and perhaps curved in the centre; from this a broad paved avenue leads to a flight of steps, at the top of which sits enshrined a many-armed divinity. Dense groves of bamboos and other trees offer a delicious and refreshing shade to the pedestrian, who can lounge upon the hottest day along shady walks from one temple to another, and smoke innumerable cigars on the steps of them. Most of these temples bore a strong resemblance to each other; one, however, which we visited, differed entirely from the rest, and this we discovered to be Sintoo.

A Japanese on a visit to this country, who should endeavor to impart to his friends in Japan some idea of the varied shades of religious opinion which obtain in it, would find but little light thrown on the subject by the comparison and inspection of any number of cathedrals, churches, or chapels; and if his time was limited, and his interpreter imperfect and not versed in theology, his account of the religious denominations of the British empire would be somewhat confused. So, of our own knowledge, we can say but little of the religions of Japan; that one, however, which is entitled to be called the national religion, and which dates from the earliest period, is the religion of Sinsyn, or "Faith of the Gods." The votaries are called Sintoos, and its temporal head is the Mikado, or Spiritual Emperor. The divinity who is the chief object of adoration is the goddess Ten-sio-dai-zin, or patron deity of Japan. She was the daughter of the first god who ever married, and who created the world, which then consisted of Japan: prior to him there extends a mythological history scarcely necessary to follow. This goddess with the long name was succeeded by four terrestrial gods, the last of whom married a mortal wife, and left a mortal son upon earth, the immediate predecessor of the mikados.

This mikado, besides being the spiritual emperor of Japan, is a species of intercessory mediator between his subjects in this world and the spirits and canonized beings of the next. In many respects his functions seem very similar to those of the Pope. In him rests the power of canonization, a much-coveted honor among the kamis and great men of the empire. When canonized, they retain the name of kami in the next world, and are chiefly useful in interceding with the goddess Ten-sio-dai-zin, who can not be approached directly; so every Sintoo Japanese has his patron kami, who are enshrined in his house, and constitute his Lares and Penates. The kamis are divided into superior and inferior, 492 being born gods, and 2640 being deified or canonized men.

The temple we visited contained numbers of these little shrines, with representations of kami, together with models of ships and other curiosities called Jemma, which, however, are only placed there as donations by grateful worshipers, to furnish amusement to persons frequenting the temple. The building itself was devoid of all architectural pretension, and of a slate-color, the interior remarkable for its simplicity as compared with Buddhist temples. Its chief external peculiarity consisted in a curious ornamented spire, of which the annexed Japanese drawing will con-

Spire of a Japanese Temple (from a native drawing).

vey a better idea than any description. The popular mountain of Fusi-yama appears in the background covered with snow. The distinguishing feature of Sintoo temples is a looking-glass, as emblematic of the soul's purity. On the right-hand side, on entering, was a sort of font containing water, and opposite to it a large bell. An oblong open box, laced across the top with wire, is a conspicuous object to remind the worshipers of their duties as almsgivers. The form of worship is very simple. Church-goers commence by washing themselves in the font; they then pray opposite the looking-glass, asking for their necessities as we do; then chink a few coppers into the wire-covered box, strike the bell thrice as a signal that it is all over, and retire. Some, with a metaphysical turn of mind, suppose that God sees into their hearts as plainly as they do into the looking-glass, and therefore do not pray at all.

I observed many strips of white paper, called by Siebold "Gohei," and on which Japanese characters were inscribed. Kæmpfer states that the Sintoo believes in Elysian or sub-celestial fields as the abode of disembodied spirits, but that he is a universalist in the matter of future punishment, and can form no idea of a devil except as represented by a fox. Siebold, however, says that "the Sintooist has a vague notion of the soul's immortality—of an eternal state of future happiness and misery, as the reward respectively of virtue or vice—of separate places whither the soul goes after death. Heavenly judges call each to account: to the good is allotted Paradise, and they enter the realm of the kami; the wicked are condemned, and thrust into hell." Certainly the famous dispute about the color of the devil would go to show that they believe in one, and disprove Kæmpfer's assertion. The following is a translation of a text from one of their sacred books given by that author: "In the beginning of the opening of all things, a chaos floated, as fishes swim in the water for pleasure: out of this chaos arose a thing like a prickle, movable and transformable. This thing became a soul or spirit, and this spirit is called Kunitoko Datsuo Mikotto."

The numerous sects which exist in Japan seem to be modifications, in divers degrees, of Buddhism and Sintooism. Buddhism was not introduced in Japan until the year A.D. 552, and, after some struggle to obtain a footing, finally took root about the end of the century, and became gradually infused into the religion of the country. After all, it differed in no great degree from the existing worship. They both inculcated a high moral standard: purity of heart and life was the great feature of Sintooism; purity of body was enforced by ceremonial ordinances, almost Levitical in their character. Certainly, in that vague condition of future bliss which the Buddhist looks forward to in Nirvana, he does not approximate to the Sintoo notion of Paradise; but then, supposing Siebold to be correct, he escapes the infernal regions of the latter by his doctrine of Metempsychosis. On the other hand, Sintoo priests are a more favored race than those of Buddha; for marriage is permitted them, the Mikado setting the example.

This spiritual functionary dwells theoretically in heaven, but he is doubtless occasionally reminded of his propinquity to this vale of tears by some of the twelve wives to which by law he is entitled.

Buddhist priests invariably shave the head, which they leave uncovered. The Sintoo priesthood allow their hair to grow, and wear a remarkable head-dress, resembling an inverted boat lackered, and often of a most brilliant color.

In addition to the religions of Sinsyn and Buddha, with their various shades of intermixture, is the philosophic creed of Sutoo, or "the Way of Life," apparently a modification of Confucianism, which is here, as in China, sufficiently "broad" and elastic to consist with any form of superstition. Properly speaking, it recognizes no gods, temples, or places of worship; acknowledges a universal pervading spirit; denies any future state of rewards and punishments, holding that happiness consists in a righteous life, and that, when the five cardinal virtues are practiced, the man is perfect. These are, to live virtuously, to do right, to be courteous, to govern wisely, and to obey the conscience.

We may assume that in Japan, as in all countries where Buddhism exists, those elevated and somewhat mystic tenets which are developed in its sacred books commend themselves to the understandings of the more enlightened and refined classes of society; while the humbler portion of the population take refuge in the idolatry of that gross material form which can alone satisfy their coarse, sensuous requirements. It seems a question whether the vulgar mind is really the crucible in which to test the power and value of a theology; how often does it degrade the noblest faith to its own level, and the hasty observer judges the religion by its coarsest development! If, however, we are to consider the character of the Japanese with reference to their religious training alone, Buddhism is certainly not the religion which has exercised the most favorable influence upon their minds and dispositions. Buddhism is said to be the religion of three hundred and fifteen millions of the human race, who are all morally and intellectually inferior to the Japanese. If, therefore, we ignore all physical causes, and those theories by which it has recently been sought to account for civilization and social progress, and reduce it to a question of religion alone, we are forced to admit that the Sintoo religion has produced results which entitle it to a very high rank among the religions of the world.

Having arrived at which conclusion, we descend from the steps of the temple of Sinsyn, upon which we have seated ourselves while speculating upon the value of the creed; and the sun being by this time concealed behind the peaked hills of the valley, we can stroll along the rice-fields by the river's brink, and enjoy the balmy air of evening, or stop in answer to an invitation, and indulge in delicious tea without paying for it. In its present unsophisticated state, Japan is a cheap as well as a pleasant residence, foreign coin being forbidden, and the inhabitants being either very conscientious, or very much afraid of being reported to government. We smoke pipes, drink tea in delightful summer-houses, cross ferries, and in various manners incur pecuniary liabilities which we have no means of liquidating, for our money is resolutely declined, and with an air of politeness which quite makes us regret that we ever made the tender; so we are compelled to reconcile ourselves to our fate, and by an interchange of tobacco endeavor to convey a reciprocity of cordial sentiments.

The day following our arrival at Simoda, Lord Elgin received a visit from the governor. He had learned that we proposed going up the Bay of Yedo, and his object now was to exert all his powers of persuasion to induce Lord Elgin to forego this intention. He brought a large suite on board with him, all of whom seemed to appreciate an English luncheon. I was rather startled to hear one of them refuse Curaçoa, and ask for Maraschino instead. The governor himself was a man of a most jovial temperament. He indulged in constant chuckles, and rather reminded one of Mr. Weller senior. He seemed to consider every thing a capital joke—even Lord Elgin's positive refusal to comply with his request to hand over the yacht at Simoda and remain at that place. He used every possible argument to carry his point, but without avail. He said he dreaded the consequences to himself, and chuckled; still more did he dread the consequences to us, and chuckled again; and when at last he found that we were neither to be frightened or cajoled, he seemed perfectly contented, and proceeded to wrap up in square pieces of paper any articles of food which particularly struck his fancy, which he carried in the folds of his shirt, saying, as he did so, that he had a number of children at home of an age to appreciate the culinary curiosities of foreign parts. Many of his suite seemed to have families also, for they followed his example. I rather think one attempted to

Z

carry away some strawberry jam in his bosom, or in the sleeve of his coat, which was made full and baggy for the purpose. These square pieces of paper are not used exclusively for wrapping up food in; upon them inquisitive Japanese take notes, and in them they blow their noses. It is a mark of politeness to carry away a quantity of food from a dinner-table; so much so, that a very civil guest sometimes brings a servant and a basket to carry away those remnants which a good English housekeeper would appropriate to luncheon next day. This is a somewhat expensive mode of showing approval of one's friend's dinner, but not so disagreeable as the gradations which a man of good-breeding indulges in with the same object.

The governor told us that he was allowed to have his wife with him at Simoda, but this, as we understood, was only because his rank was not sufficiently high to bring him within the category of those obliged to leave their wives at Yedo. There are two governors of Simoda, who relieve each other every six months, the object being that each should serve as a check upon his colleague. The governor, having now apparently satisfied his conscience, prepared to take leave. He subsequently preferred a request in writing that two Japanese officials should be allowed a passage in the Furious up the harbor. This, however, was declined, upon the plea that it was contrary to the rules of the service to take on board passengers.

Under the new treaty Kanagawa is substituted for Simoda, which ceases to be an open port. It is indeed valueless as such: the harbor is unsafe, the population is small and of the poorest description, consisting chiefly of fishermen. The means of communication with the interior are bad, as the town is situated on a peninsula, to pass from which into the country it is necessary to cross a mountain range about six thousand feet in height.

The houses are all built of wood, many of them only of one story. The shops are poor and thinly supplied. Here, as at Nagasaki, the poorer classes are but lightly clad, the men having little on besides a loin-cloth, and the women being generally uncovered above the waist. They manifested but little curiosity at us as we strolled about the streets, but I was amused to observe a crowd collected round a dog belonging to one of our party, of the Shantung terrier breed, and which, though a purely Chinese dog, is scarcely to be distinguished from a Skye terrier. This long-haired specimen of the canine race created immense excitement and interest, both among Japanese dogs and men, as he trotted complacently along the streets of Simoda.

We experienced great civility and kindness from Mr. Harris during our short stay at Simoda, but were more especially indebted to him for the liberality with which he supplied a most important deficiency, in placing at Lord Elgin's disposal the services of his excellent Dutch interpreter, Mr. Hewsken. This gentleman proved, during our stay at Yedo, a very obliging and agreeable companion, as well as a most able assistant. Having spent two years in the country, he had picked up a good deal of the language, and I am indebted to him for much interesting information. In all official transactions a Japanese interpreter was employed to interpret from Dutch into Japanese.

We got under weigh from Simoda at daylight on the morning of the 12th of August, and with a fair wind proceeded rapidly up the bay, passing on our left a mountain range of about 6000 feet in height. The shores now begin to close in, and at the Straits of Uraga, which we reached in about five hours from Simoda, they are not above ten miles apart. At this point the scenery was very

A Japanese Village (from a native drawing).

pretty; wooded hills rise from the water's edge, sloping gently back, here and there deeply furrowed with a charming glen, in which cottages with steep-thatched roofs and overhanging eaves are snugly ensconced. The western shore resembles some parts of the coast of the Isle of Wight. The town of Uraga itself is the most important-looking place on the coast. It is considered a sort of barrier to Yedo, and even country craft should stop here to give an account of themselves. Two boat-loads of two-sworded officials pushed off in haste as we steamed up, and by gesticulations and gestures of entreaty invited us to stop; but we passed on, utterly indifferent to their signals; and as we left them far behind, we could still discern them tugging hopelessly after us, in the vain attempt to overtake a steamer of 400 horse-power going at full speed.

We could scarcely believe our eyes when, at anchor, the same night, we observed these identical boats pull alongside, they having never relinquished the pursuit.

Meantime we steamed steadily on through waters traversed for the first time by Commodore Perry's squadron a few years ago, and consequently but little surveyed. Passing the Perry and Webster islands, prettily wooded, and of a picturesque form, we came within sight of the Russian squadron, anchored at Kanagawa, at about midday. This place is situated at a distance of eighteen miles from Yedo. It affords good anchorage about half a mile from the shore; it is a town of considerable importance, and has been selected as one of the new ports. Count Poutiatine, who had proceeded to Japan direct from the Gulf of Pechelee, had arrived here about a fortnight previously, and been engaged during that period in making arrangements for his proper reception at the capital. Lord Elgin, however, instead of stopping at Kanagawa, determined to adopt the unprecedented course of sailing straight up to the capital, believing that, if the achievement were feasible, it would not only save valuable time, but that the presence of our ships there would produce a most salutary effect upon the government, and in all probability tend to facilitate our negotiations. It was eminently fortunate that on occasions of this sort he had in Captain Sherard Osborn a commander upon whose zeal and professional skill he could always place the most perfect reliance.

Our unexpected appearance must have somewhat astonished

our Muscovite friends, more especially as we passed on at full speed up the bay, where no Western ship had ever before ventured. Up to this point, the western shore under which we had been coasting was uniformly high, and broken with projecting promontories; now, however, it sank to a level with the waters of the bay. The soundings in Perry's chart cease just before reaching Kawasaki Point—a long sandy spit which runs far out into the bay, and off which the Japanese have placed a beacon.

The water now became shallow, and the channel somewhat intricate. We were just doubting whether the undertaking was practicable, when we saw in the distance some large square-rigged ships, of a tonnage which satisfied us that their anchorage would do for us; but for a moment we felt bitterly disappointed at the discovery of European-built ships, betokening, as we supposed, the presence of some foreign flag more enterprising than our own. It was only when we approached nearer that we perceived that these Western-looking craft were in reality Japanese, and observed the white flag with the red ball floating from the peak of a dapper little steamer, and marking it "Imperial."

Gradually behind these vessels the island forts, and then the houses of the city of Yedo, rose into view. Gently, with two leads going, we crept up to the long-desired haven, closely followed by the Retribution and yacht; and by two o'clock the same afternoon, after a most prosperous passage from Simoda, we anchored not far from the Japanese fleet, at a distance of about three miles from the shore, and five from the capital of the empire.

CHAPTER XXV.

Official Visitors.—We shift our Anchorage.—A Visit from Princes.—Object of the Interview.—A Japanese Man-of-war.—Visit to the Admiral.—Japanese Junks.—Imperial Uniform.—Inquisitive Water-parties.—Moriyama.—Visit of the Commissioners.—Landing-parties.—The Landing-place.—A Japanese Saddle.—The Procession through Yedo.—Excited Crowds.—The fair Sex.—Disfigurement of married Women.—Japanese Pleasure-parties.—Arrival at our future Residence.

We had not been long at anchor before we were boarded by those ever-vigilant and active two-sworded gentry, who seem to swarm upon the shores of Japan, and who pounce upon the stranger as if he was their peculiar property. They always come tumbling up the ladder full of smiles and impetuosity, not the least afraid of boarding the foreign ship; then they bow and look amiable, and talk with excessive volubility in Dutch and Japanese, jerking out now and then a word of English. They want to know who we are, how many guns we mount, how many men there are on board, what our object is in coming, whether more ships are following. Suddenly they recognize Mr. Hewsken; he is an old friend, and there is Mr. Harris's palanquin (he had kindly lent it to Lord Elgin). Our visitors are much puzzled. It is evident Mr. Harris is secreted somewhere on board, or else how comes it that here are both his secretary and his palanquin? But then Mr. Harris sails under the "stars and stripes," and the Japanese know that the flag waving above them is the British ensign. They bombard Mr. Hewsken with questions, which they do not give him time to answer, and, at all events, are perfectly clear upon one point—whether Mr. Harris is on board or not, we must instantly return to Kanagawa. We explain that the British minister is on board, though not visible to their vulgar gaze, and that we can not venture to broach such a proposition to him. Meantime more official boats arrive, and we learn that Count Poutiatine has that day arrived from Kanagawa, and made his official entry by land into Yedo, where he has taken up his residence. It was evident that none of our visitors were men of rank; they came rather with the view of collecting information than as official messengers; but the burden of the song always was, "Go back to Kanagawa." Lord Elgin sent a letter on shore the same afternoon to the prime minister, stating that he had come to make a treaty, and to present the yacht to the emperor, and requesting that he might be furnished with a suitable residence on shore.

On the following morning, finding by our boats that we could get nearer the shore, we ran on into three-fathom water, and anchored about a mile and a half from it, and in the midst of the Japanese fleet. This consisted of two large, square-rigged ships, a pretty little paddle-wheel steamer, which had been purchased from the Dutch government, and a three-masted schooner. From our present anchorage we could follow the houses of the city lining the shores of the bay from the suburb of Sinagawa, off which we were lying, to a long bridge just visible in the extreme distance. This view was intercepted by five island forts, which rose from the shallow waters of the bay about half way between us and the centre of the city. Low hills prettily wooded, and crowned with temples, formed a background to Sinagawa and the western portion of the city, while a wooded eminence in the centre, gleaming here and there with a patch of white wall, and distinguished by the roofs of a pagoda, marked the citadel, or residence of the Tycoon.

Towering over all in the western distance, but too often concealed by clouds, the majestic Fusi-yama reared its conical summit. The princes came off to luncheon about midday, bringing with them an answer to the letter of yesterday. These dignitaries are only Saimios, or titular princes, and are of an inferior rank to the Daimios, or hereditary princes. One of them, Sinanono-kami, was the alternate Governor of Simoda, the colleague of our jovial friend of yesterday. They were plainly dressed, and accompanied by the usual retinue, the use of which we now began to perceive. Most of them were engaged during the whole period of their interview with Lord Elgin in reporting in note-books precisely every word that passed. I even caught one fellow, as I glanced over his shoulder, making a sketch of his excellency.

When no conversation was actually taking place, they noted down observations of surrounding objects. Most inquisitive were they in their inquiries about every thing, and ready in booking the answer. The people who had no note-books were spies, whose business it was to see whether those who had did their duty properly; also to keep an eye on the princes, and report any indiscretion of which they might be guilty. So, when every body was watching every body else, it was only natural that the Japanese should wonder who was watching us. They solved this difficulty in an amusing way. Finding that there was only one British minister on board, but observing also that his letter had been signed Elgin and Kincardine, they gave us to understand, in the least offensive way possible, that Kincardine, who was nowhere visible, they supposed to be engaged in keeping his eye on Elgin. It was some time before we made them understand how two titles could be vested in one and the same person.

Meantime they did not forget the main object of their visit: this was to endeavor to persuade Lord Elgin to return to Kanagawa, at which point, they assured us, arrangements could much more easily be made for his reception at Yedo. This was by no means evident. Lord Elgin objected that going eighteen miles farther could not facilitate his coming to the capital; then they said that the anchorage was very dangerous. They were recommended, in that case, to remove their own fleet to a place of greater safety. Farther, they urged it would be impossible to send supplies to the ship; but they were assured that we were quite independent, having a sufficient stock of supplies on board. In fact, each prince severally made a remonstrance, doubtless for the benefit of his spy; and when they had fulfilled this duty, they received with smiles Lord Elgin's assurance that any movement from his present anchorage was impossible until he had fulfilled the object of his visit, and handed over the yacht to the imperial government. This decision, they said, they would report to their superiors, and for the remainder of their visit they devoted themselves to *pate de fois gras* and Champagne. They ultimately departed, promising to return with an answer on the morrow. The next day, however, was so wet that we could hardly blame them for not braving the elements; and, to relieve the monotony, a party of us went on a voyage of exploration to the largest ship in the fleet, and then on to the forts.

Both the square-rigged ships looked like those cumbrous arks in which our ancestors used to circumnavigate the globe, and were, in fact, built upon old Dutch models, although of recent construction. The one we boarded was painted a bright red: her masts were of ponderous size, built and ribbed with iron hoops; the rigging bleached white, and ragged from the action

Yedo Forts.

of the weather and the absence of tar. We ascended the heavy ladder to a large square hole, which admitted us to the main deck. We were most civilly received by an individual who may be supposed to have been the officer of the watch, and shown over the ship. Two or three 32-pound Paixhan guns were lying about, but there was not a vestige of a carriage, or any bolts for side-tackles. The scantling was of enormous thickness, and the port-holes were closed with clumsily-built shutters. There was an appearance of comfort, nevertheless, about the main deck generally, which was inhabited by the crew, whose mats were all neatly arranged round it. The lower deck was empty, with the exception of a few stores and water-casks.

Under a high poop astern was the captain's cabin. We entered it, and found two or three naval dignitaries squatted upon the floor drinking tea; one of these we afterward discovered to be the admiral-in-chief of the imperial navy. He was appointed one of the commissioners to treat with Lord Elgin, and proved to be a most intelligent person. We had no idea that the plain-looking group before us contained so important a personage; and, in answer to a polite invitation to join their party, we twisted our legs under us, received from them pipes containing homœopathic doses of tobacco in exchange for our cigars, and refreshed ourselves with some delicious tea. Unfortunately, we were compelled to confine our observations to smacking our lips and puffing out smoke, for we were without an interpreter. We did, indeed, ultimately, by the exercise of great intelligence on both sides, get so far as to learn the Japanese numerals up to ten, and teach them the English; but the intellectual effort was too great to be sustained; and we parted with feelings of mutual relief, and the warmest expressions of good-will, as conveyed in our mother tongue. The cabin in which we had been entertained was devoid of furniture, as rooms in Japan always are; but the mats were soft, and there was an air of comfort and cleanliness about the apartment. It was built apparently of fir-wood, the carpentering of perfect workmanship.

We now made for the left-hand point of the left-hand fort, taking advantage of the opportunity to sound as we sailed slowly along. We found the forts constructed of huge blocks of stone, surmounted by guns of large calibre, and staked round with piles. Considerable knowledge of fortification has been displayed both in their construction and situation. They extend in a parallel line with the coast for some distance. Between some of them the water is so shallow as not even to admit of the passage of boats; between the two westernmost, however, it is comparatively deep. We were in the deepest channel, to judge from the size of the native craft which chose it, and found at half flood eight feet of water at our farthest sounding. At this point numbers of junks were anchored, and some small schooners built from European models. The largest of these junks may have been of 150 tons burden, high-sterned, heavily-masted, quaint-looking craft; the masts are not composed of a single spar, but built and ribbed with iron, rising from the deck like some gigantic forest-tree to a height of forty or fifty feet: the top of the mast was slightly bent, and from it depended a vast expanse of a coarse cotton fabric, attached to a yard on the same scale as the mast, so massive, that to hoist it must be as laborious an operation as weighing anchor. The rudder projects far astern, and is moved by a huge tiller ex-

A Junk in the Bay of Yedo (from a native drawing).

tending half the length of the craft. An extensive assortment of anchors garnish the bow, and on deck there is frequently a thatched shed for the crew. Altogether the rig is clumsy to the nautical eye; but we met several of their junks making good weather of it when it was blowing freshly. It is said, however, that a government rule exists, compelling them to be built on a principle which renders it dangerous for them to venture far from shore, so as to prevent their visiting foreign countries. The annexed Japanese drawing conveys a very good idea of a scene in the Bay of Yedo, with Fusi-yama in the distance.

On our return to the ship we found a message had arrived apologizing for the non-appearance of the commissioners, and inclosing a copy of the American treaty. We were always able to recognize government messengers from afar. Generally they came in a boat painted red, about the size of a pinnace, and rigged with two lug-sails. The crews were always in uniform—either in blue or black, with white stripes. Black and white are the imperial colors, but the national flag is a red ball on a white ground. The Japanese seem to hold the sun in almost as great respect as the Parsees. Their patron divinity, Ten-sio-dai-zin, is the sun-goddess, and they have adopted the luminary as their national emblem.

While the costume of the government boatmen was uniform and respectable, the same can not be said of the crews of the numerous other boats which used constantly to surround us. A pocket-handkerchief would have supplied material for a full suit; but even then it must be torn in half, and while one piece crosses the loins, the other is drawn tightly over the nose. It is not, as may be supposed, from any feeling of modesty that this feature is concealed: the idea is, that it is sensitive to cold; but the general effect of a man with nothing on but two scanty strips of cotton—one round the middle of his body, and the other round the middle of his face—is in the highest degree ludicrous.

In the afternoon, pleasure parties from the shore used to come and inspect us; boat-loads of ladies, with a great deal of white powder on their cheeks, and lips painted a brilliant vermilion, gazed on us with the utmost interest and delight, making witty remarks at our expense, and then laughing immoderately. Some of the gentlemen ventured on board, and one of them mistook Lord Elgin's Chinese chair for a shrine, and, being evidently of a tolerant and liberal spirit in religious matters, did us the honor of prostrating himself before what he supposed was one of our divinities; but his fair companions contented themselves with gyrating round us, and looking in at our port-holes with that curiosity which doubtless characterizes the sex even here. We had not much opportunity of judging of the extent to which this propensity is indulged; but, considering that the most inquisitive men in the world are certainly Japanese men, it is difficult to form a conception of what the women must be.

On the following day five commissioners came off to complete the arrangements for our taking up our residence on shore. In addition to the three whom we had already seen was our naval friend of yesterday, Admiral Nangai Gembano-kami, and a cheerful colleague, by name Higono-kami, who turned out the most agreeable and intelligent person I met in Japan. These gentlemen were accompanied by an individual who played a very important part throughout the negotiations, and whose real value was indeed very little below his own very high estimate of it. He was the interpreter Moriyama, for some time resident at Nagasaki, he wrote and spoke Dutch with almost as much facility as Japanese, and was the means of communication between Mr. Hewsken and the commissioners.

Beneath a ludicrous affectation of manner Moriyama concealed an infinite amount of practical, shrewd common sense. He was, in fact, a diplomate of the Talleyrand school, always silky and smiling, anxious to impress upon you that he was a mere humble interpreter, while through his bland diffidence it was easy to distinguish a latent ambition to have every thing his own way, and a perfect confidence in his own powers. When we jokingly called him a humbug, and tried to explain to him the meaning of the term, he evidently regarded it as a compliment, while he deprecated it in his usual air of insinuating self-satisfaction.

I was fortunate enough to sit next Higono-kami at lunch, and we employed ourselves in making a vocabulary on his fan. Though he had never seen a foreigner, until within the last few months, in his life, he could write in the English character, and was very quick in picking up and retaining the correct pronunciation of every vowel I told him. He informed me that he was qualifying himself to be appointed one of the embassadors to be sent to Europe, and anxious, in consequence, to lose no opportunity of learning English. I saw him almost every day during the remainder of my stay in Yedo, and he generally used to repeat without a mistake the lesson of the day before. He was infinitely more interested in studying English than in watching the progress of the negotiations, and carried perpetually about in his bosom a stock of fans, which contained his vocabulary. At luncheon, however, he generally contrived to combine duty with inclination, and having carefully noted the name of each dish, forthwith proceeded to partake of it.

Our guests informed us that a choice of two houses was at our disposal, but that they regretted that the emperor's illness would prevent his giving Lord Elgin the audience he desired. In the mean time, it was arranged that some of our party should go on shore to examine our future abode. After luncheon the admiral went over the ship, inspecting her thoroughly, when he took occasion to discuss the merits of oscillating cylinders, and show himself well versed in machinery.

Upon our visitors taking their departure, the humbler members of their retinue, who were all ranged upon the deck, prostrated themselves as their lords and kamis passed.

In consequence of the unfavorable state of the weather, our landing was postponed until the 17th of August. On the morning of that day great preparations were made, in order that the event might take place with due éclat. It had been arranged that some Japanese officials should come off to accompany his excellency on shore. They were evidently under the impression that we were going to land in their boats, and were not a little startled to find themselves on board the Lee, in company with the greater part of the officers of the squadron, all in full dress, and with thirteen ships' boats in tow, looking spruce and gay, with their neat crews, and ensigns flying. The Retribution, Furious, and yacht were all dressed out; and as the little Lee steamed boldly on past the forts, and threaded her way among the junks beyond, the faces of our Japanese friends elongated at finding our entire indifference to shallow water and sandbanks.

At last soundings in seven feet reminded us that even the Lee had a bottom, and we dropped anchor and got into our boats. As we did so the ships thundered forth a salute, the band of the Retribution, in a paddle-box boat, struck up "Rule, Britannia," the rest of the boats formed in procession, Lord Elgin's barge in the centre between four paddle-box boats, each with a brass gun in the bow, and in this order we pulled along the shore for about three miles, a spectacle such as Japanese eyes had never before witnessed, and the novelty of which induced numerous boats to push off and take a nearer view of us as we moved steadily and rapidly along. The landing-place was about the centre of the city, which is here protected along the sea-face by green batteries: the grassy slopes, dotted with handsome trees, would rather lead us to suppose that we were approaching a park than the most populous part of a densely-crowded city. We turned off from the waters of the bay into a little creek, spanned by a bridge. So shallow, however, was the water, that we had some difficulty in

The Landing-place, Yedo.

forcing even the smaller boats to the foot of the stairs; we were consoled for the inconvenience by being informed that this was the landing-place reserved for the exclusive use of the highest officers of state.

At this point there was comparatively no crowd, the batteries being inclosed, and not open to the general public. Had the Japanese been as civilized as we are, they would have admitted a select few with tickets, to obtain which it would have been necessary to make immense interest with our friend Admiral Nangai Gembano-kami. As it was, all who were there seemed in some way officially connected with the day's proceedings. We were supplied with tea while the norimons and horses were getting ready. Norimons are the palanquins of Japan; they differ, however, from the ordinary palanquin in being square instead of oblong, so that a reclining posture is impossible. The occupant sits cross-legged, and is very near the ground, the pole on which the norimon is supported passing over the roof. Four men carry this somewhat uncomfortable contrivance, which is by no means well adapted to the stranger desirous of looking about him; under these circumstances, I always avoided a norimon when it was possible to get a horse. Upon this occasion we had our choice; they were all standing outside the gate, where an immense crowd was already collected.

I soon found myself upon a fiery galloway, perched on a very hard saddle, my feet in stirrups almost big enough to go to sea in, and something between a catamaran and a Turkish slipper in shape. They are pointed at one end so as to serve the purpose of a spur; and if the horse is fresh, the great business of life is to keep the stirrup from touching him; but it is impossible to devote one's whole attention to this; for, as the stirrup-leathers are full of knots, and the saddle full of knobs, and most of us have left China martyrs to that scourge of the country, boils—our minds are fully occupied with a variety of weighty considerations. Still I found time to observe that my horse's tail was carefully tied up in a long bag which almost reached the ground; that his feet were swaddled in straw shoes, an abundant supply of which I carried

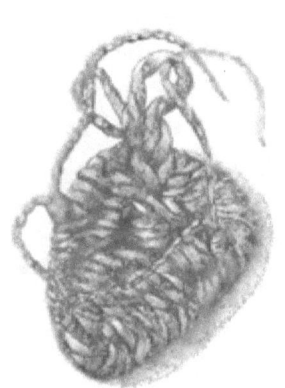 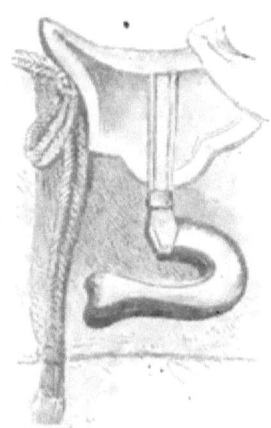

A Japanese Horse-shoe and Saddle.

hanging under my stirrups. These were carefully fastened on with lashings of twisted straw, and whenever one shoe was worn out or kicked off, another was immediately tied on; hence arises the custom in Japan of measuring distances by horses' shoes.

Here you ask in how many horse-shoes will I reach the residence of the spiritual emperor? which, after all, does not differ very much from the old problem of how many cows' tails will reach the moon.

Fortunately, each horse was attended by two grooms, it being a great point with a Japanese that the public should suppose him riding an animal so spirited that the combined exertions of two men are scarcely sufficient to restrain his ardor. These men tugged incessantly at the mouth of my poor steed, shouting to him constantly "Chai, chai," which means "Gently, gently," and making an immense fuss whenever we came to a gutter; but I was too glad to be relieved of the responsibility of guiding him to interfere, and the muslin reins hung listlessly between my fingers.

Meantime the procession was formed, and was by no means unpicturesque. In front marched a pompous official, accompanied by a man carrying a spear, the badge of authority; he was closely followed by a knot of officials in a neat costume of a coarse-looking black gauze, like thick musquito-curtains. On their backs or shoulders was stamped the imperial trefoil, or the private arms of the owner. Some were dressed exactly alike, others wore blue and white dresses; but every individual was evidently in a uniform befitting his rank and position. All these men, however, were probably servants, or quite subordinate officials; some carried aloft umbrellas covered with large water-proof bags, and others lackered portmanteaus on poles over their shoulders. This was supposititious baggage. On each side of the procession walked policemen in a sort of harlequin costume, composed of as many colors as if their dress was made from a patchwork counterpane: each of these men carried iron rods six or seven feet long, from the top of which depended a quantity of iron rings. Every time that this rod was brought to the ground with the jerk of authority, it emitted a loud jingle, which was heard far and wide through the crowd, and was, I am bound to say, respected by them accordingly. Behind this vanguard we came, some on horseback and some in norimons; and more men in black gauze, and umbrella-carriers, and variegated policemen, brought up the rear.

As for the crowd, it was wild with excitement; the inhabitants of every cross street and lane poured out to see us pass. The excitement of maid-servants in our own country, where the strains of martial music fall upon their ears, was nothing to it. There were mothers with small babies hanging over their shoulders, reckless of their progeny, hastening to swell the crowd; children dodging under old people's legs, and old people tottering after children, and bathers of both sexes, regardless of the fact that they had nothing on but soap, or the Japanese substitute for it, crowding the doorways. The clatter of pattens was quite remarkable: as all the women wear high wooden pattens, which are very inconvenient to run in, and as women in Japan, as in England, formed the largest proportion of the mob, the scuffling they made added to the tumult. Not that the people were the least disorderly: they laughed, and stared, and ran parallel with us, till stopped by a barrier, for the Japanese are perfect in the management of crowds. In the principal street there are wooden gates about every two hundred yards, with a gatekeeper seated in a little house like a turnpike. The moment we pass this the gate is shut, and the old crowd is left behind to crane through the bars, and watch with envious eyes the new crowd forming. All the cross streets entering the main street are shut off from it by ropes stretched across them, under or over which the people never attempt to pass.

The crowd was, to all appearance, entirely composed of the shopkeepers and lower classes. The men were decently clothed, and the women wore a sort of jacket above their skirt, which was, however, constructed upon a rather *negligé* principle. The first impression of the fair sex which the traveler receives in a Japanese crowd is in the highest degree unfavorable: the ghastly appearance of the faces and bosoms, thickly coated with powder, the absence of eyebrows, and the blackened teeth, produce a most painful and disagreeable effect. Were it not for this abominable custom, Japanese women would probably rank high among Eastern beauties, certainly far before Chinese. All Japanese writers whom I have read upon the subject affirm that to have no eyebrows and black teeth is considered a beauty in Japan, and that the object of the process is to add to the charms of the fair one. The result of my inquiry and observation, however, rather led me to form an opposite conclusion.

In the first place, young ladies do not, as a rule, neglect any means of improving their looks; but no Japanese young ladies, even after they are "out," think of taking this method of increasing their powers of fascination; they color their cheeks and lips, and deck their hair, but it is not until they have made a conquest of some lucky swain, that, to prove their devotion to him, they begin to blacken their teeth and pull out their eyebrows. He, privileged being, is called upon to exhibit no such test of his affection; on the contrary, his lawful wife having so far disfigured herself as to render it impossible that she should be attractive to any one else, seems to lose her charms for her husband as well; so he places her at the head of his establishment, and adds to it an indefinite number of handmaidens, who neither pull out their eyebrows nor blacken their teeth; hence it seems not difficult to account for the phenomenon which is universally admitted, that while Japanese wives are celebrated for their virtue, their husbands are no less notorious for their licentiousness.

It is only fair to state that, in addition to black teeth and bare brows, a Japanese Lothario has the avenging dagger to deter him from intrigue, adultery in Japan being punished by the death of both the guilty parties. But it must not be supposed that the ladies of Japan consider themselves a more ill-used race than those in other parts of the world; so far from it, there is probably no Eastern country in which the women have so much liberty or such great social enjoyment. Polygamy is not permitted, and, from all we could learn, the position of the ladies corresponds more nearly to that which they occupy in the West than in the East. They are respected in society as lawful wives, and their children inherit whatever titles or property appertain to the family. To them be-

Japanese Ladies and Children (from a native drawing).

long all the privileges of legitimacy in a country where "family" is much esteemed: a matrimonial alliance is, consequently, a matter of serious consideration to parents, and a good match much to be desired. Then these ladies are subject to no seclusion, but go to theatres, breakfasts, picnics, and even flower-shows, conducted after their own fashion. They are very fond of pleasure-parties on the water, and are skilled in the guitar, so that it is quite possible to be sentimental in Japan even with black teeth. The ladies are also said to be adepts at dancing, but the gentlemen look on instead of offering themselves as partners. We had, unfortunately, no opportunity of seeing any Japanese ladies, our time was so fully occupied; and when I did at last obtain a promise from Moriyama to take me to his abode, we could not find a spare hour.

Fortunately, we did not digress so much from the main street of Yedo as I have from this account of our progress along it. For at least two miles did we pass between two rows of human beings six or eight deep, until at last, turning down a short lane, and passing between a pair of heavy wooden gates, which closed behind us, we entered a court-yard formed by a temple and its adjacent buildings, at one corner of which a number of servants were standing on the steps of a veranda waiting to receive us.

Here we dismounted, and exultingly took possession of our future residence in Yedo.

CHAPTER XXVI.

Residence of British Mission.—Plan of our House.—Soft Matting.—Japanese Spies.—Shingle Roofs.—The Princes' Quarter.—An obstructive Aristocracy.—Arguments on their side.—Evils of Civilization.—Restrictions on the Nobles.—Palaces of the Princes.—The Citadel.—Panorama of Yedo.—An imperial Banquet.—A shopping Expedition.—Fire-ladders.—We are mistaken for Chinese.—Bathing-houses.—Handsome Lacker-ware.—A Silk-mercer's.—An active Police.—Organization of the Police Department.—Street Dogs.—Wild Deer.

The apartments appropriated to the use of the British mission were connected with a Buddhist temple, in which some description of service seemed constantly to be going on. Before landing, Lord Elgin had been requested to send in an exact list of the number of Europeans, including servants, by whom he was to be accompanied, and he accordingly furnished a requisition for accommodation for eighteen. This included a certain number of officers from the squadron. Some of these occupied rooms usually inhabited by priests, immediately to the right on entering the outer yard. Our rooms formed one side of an inner court, or rather garden, consisting of a lawn, in the centre of which was a pond covered with lotus, and containing a tiny island, approached by a rustic bridge. Very large gold-fish floated lazily about under the broad lotus-leaves.

This agreeable retreat was shut in from the outer world by the temple on one side, and in all other directions by a high artificial bank, covered with shrubbery and pine trees, from between the lower branches of which, nevertheless, curious eyes might frequently be detected watching the movements of the mysterious strangers. The lower rooms were all divided from each other by paper screens running on slides, and movable at pleasure, so that they could be subdivided as circumstances required. By these means we procured a large dining-room, besides Lord Elgin's sitting-room; and a spacious loft up stairs, in addition to the rooms below, furnished sleeping accommodation for the whole party.

Considering how short a time had been allowed our hosts to make preparations for our reception, it was quite wonderful how carefully they had forestalled our wants. They had first been made acquainted with the requirements of Europeans in the matter of furniture through Mr. Harris. Prior to that gentleman's visit, the government had sent privately to Simoda to have exact copies made of his furniture, so that, on reaching Yedo, he found, to his astonishment, chairs, tables, and beds, in a city where all such articles had been previously unknown. So we were delighted to find not only beds, but mattresses, and musquito curtains, and comfortable dressing-gowns, of rather too thick a texture, however, for the time of year.

On my dressing-table was a black lacker jug and basin, but on a purely Japanese model, the jug like a small bucket, the basin like a miniature tub; besides this there was a black lackered tobacco-stand, furnished with pipes and tobacco. These stands are like small trays, and contain two compartments for tobacco; one for fire, which is preserved in a glowing cake under ashes, and one for the discharged remains of the pipes: these lie like pens in their own division. I had, moreover, a little window overlooking the residence of a Japanese family of moderate means. From this post of observation I could see the children playing games, the mamma sewing, or busy with household cares, and listen to a young lady who used to be rather too fond of playing the lute.

All our rooms were matted in the usual way with wadded mats, so scrupulously clean that we began by walking about in our own or Japanese socks, for fear of dirtying them; but it was so exceedingly troublesome to be perpetually putting on and kicking off our shoes, that we ultimately sacrificed cleanliness to convenience. We found, moreover, that a Japanese sandal was

A Japanese Sandal.

by no means adapted to the tender toes of the West. These mats were all exactly the same size, so that there is never a difficulty about getting them to fit the apartment. Each mat was six feet three inches long, three feet two inches wide, and four inches thick; they were made of rice or wheat straw plaited tightly. A mat has thus come to be regarded as a standard measure in Japan; and inasmuch as the rooms are capable of expansion or retraction at pleasure by sliding the screens, and the mats are conveniently small and movable, the internal fitting of a house is not a very elaborate process.

The bathing arrangements were perhaps the most complete part of the establishment. There were three bathing-rooms, each containing two large new wooden tubs, one of which was kept constantly supplied with hot, the other with cold water. There were buckets of all sizes for convenient douching and splashing.

As the Lieutenant Governor of Yedo was the high official responsible for our good behavior, and for all contingencies which might arise out of our sojourn in the capital, it was only natural that he should adopt the necessary precautionary measures. The large anteroom adjoining our apartments was accordingly filled with a numerous body of Japanese, told off ostensibly to wait upon us, but really to watch and report our hourly proceedings as well. These men swore allegiance to one Tainoske, an interpreter of an inferior grade to the distinguished Moriyama, but a most civil and obliging person; nevertheless, he made up for a scanty knowledge of Dutch by an anxious willingness, and an imperturbable temper, under sometimes rather trying circumstances. It is due to his satellites to say that they were equally amiable, and when caught poking their heads above the stairs to watch the process of the Briton going to bed, and ordered by him peremptorily to decamp, they always did so with smiles and bows, only, however, to peep at him again when the first opportunity offered. The excuse which naturally occurs to a Japanese when he visits your apartment is that he has come to clean something.

Some of our party inhabiting the rooms near the entrance gateway were more highly honored. They were separated from an adjoining house only by a paper screen. One morning, while dressing, their attention was arrested by a scratching upon the paper, followed by a suppressed tittering. Upon investigating the cause, a pair of sparkling eyes were visible at two little peepholes expressly constructed: it was evident that a toilet, as performed by an English gentleman, was a spectacle which afforded intense amusement to the young ladies of the family next door.

The outer court-yard was a constant scene of bustle and confusion; here were norimans and horses always in readiness, and a row of impromptu stables was run up during our stay with wonderful rapidity. I watched with astonishment the process of roofing them with shingles. A man crawled along with a basket under his arm full of shingles about three inches square, and a little thicker than wafers, and his mouth full of wooden tacks: these he disgorged, and tapped in with a small mallet with extraordinary skill and quickness, completing a water-proof roof in a very short time, but so fragile in appearance that it seemed as though a puff of wind would blow it away. The Japanese are very skillful builders. The annexed wood-cut is a representation, by a native artist, of the mode of plastering a house.

Plasterers at Work (from a native drawing).

Altogether we were well pleased with our abode, and, having seen ourselves fairly installed in it, the appetite for more novelty began again to make itself felt, and we were glad of the excuse which a visit to Count Poutiatine afforded us to sally forth once more into the streets of Yedo.

This time we soon turned out of the main street, and, leaving the dense crowd behind us, dived into the Princes' or aristocratic quarter. We were amazed at the different aspect which the streets here presented from those we had just left; the party-colored policemen did not think it worth while to accompany us, so small was the crowd that gathered as we went. Belgravia in September does not look more deserted than did these fashionable thoroughfares, so dull, clean, and respectable. On each side of the street, which was twenty or thirty yards wide, was an open paved drain, about four feet in depth and as many in breadth; an abundant stream of running water carried off any impurities which might be thrown into it. These conduits looked moats in miniature to the princely habitations under the walls of which they passed. The lower parts of these walls were built of huge blocks of rough stone, above which they were raised to the height of about twenty feet, constructed of masonry, but carefully whitewashed, and ornamented with raised groinings. In the centre was a gateway painted red or some bright color, with a pent roof, and ornaments in lacker upon it. Beyond this there was no sort of architectural pretension about these palaces. They evidently covered a large area of ground, as four or five were sufficient to compose a whole street, the walls of one residence extending for two or three hundred yards, and here and there perforated with windows, from between the bars of which peered female faces.

We had no opportunity of inspecting the internal economy of any of these sumptuous abodes. They belong to a class who are for the most part unfavorable to the introduction of foreigners into Japan. With few exceptions, the old aristocracy of Japan dread the foreign element as possibly subversive of that influence which they at present exercise in the government of the country.

Knowing that these sentiments prevailed largely, and were to some extent gaining ground in consequence of the concessions made in the treaty recently concluded with Mr. Harris, it was with some dismay that we heard that the enlightened prime minister, Bitsuno-kami, with whom that treaty had been negotiated, had been turned out of office a few days before our arrival, and was succeeded by men known as prominent members of what might be called the Tory party of Japan. In fact, we arrived immediately after a political crisis which had turned upon the foreign question, and in which the government of the day had been beaten.

As we rode past the palaces of these obstructive grandees, we could scarcely wonder at their opposition to the introduction of any disturbing element into the country. Had they known as much of the civilization of the West as we did, they might, perhaps, have doubted about the propriety of excluding it. Not being so well informed, they argue probably in this way: "Our country supplies every want which is felt by the population that inhabits it. Abundantly favored by Providence, we are dependent for no one single article upon our neighbors, and are still deprived of none of the necessities or luxuries of life. Our large population, estimated at thirty-five millions, has, nevertheless, space enough in the area furnished by these fertile islands. With the exception of a few orders of religious mendicants, abject poverty is unknown among us. The government is conducted upon a system which supervises all classes of the community, from the greatest man in the realm to the humblest individual in it; while, in order to the due protection of society, it requires a strict adherence to the criminal code, which punishes severely those who infringe it. Thus the great mass of the people are happy and contented, while we, the nobles of the land, are by no means disposed to imperil the privileges attaching to our exalted position. We see no change by which either we or those beneath us can possibly be benefited. We desire nothing which we have not got. It has not been proved to us that railroads or electric telegraphs make people happier. We tried the Christian religion, and it led to the destruction of thousands of our countrymen. We do not think our civilization would be increased by a knowledge of the latest improvement in gunnery, or the newest invention for the destruction of our fellow-creatures. We are contented with sakee, and desire neither brandy, rum, gin, whisky, nor any other spirituous production of progressive countries. We can bear to be deprived of opium, a luxury the charms of which are as yet unknown to us. There are also a few diseases which do not exist among us, and the importation of which we do not think would increase our general happiness. At present our subjects are peaceable and well-conducted, of an honest and simple nature, not given to brawling and quarreling; but from what we have seen of the Europeans who man the ships coming to our country, we do not think this simplicity and tranquillity in our sea-ports would be likely to continue.* For these reasons we, the pig-headed aris-

* The following extract from a late Hong Kong paper will confirm the statement

tocracy of Japan, do not desire to see that happy and favored empire opened to the civilization of the West."

If such be their mode of reasoning, we can only pity their ignorance and blindness, and refer them to the other side of the Atlantic for a definition of the term " manifest destiny." It must not, however, be supposed that, because these princes are contented with their condition, it is such as would suit the aristocracy of other countries, except, perhaps, that of Russia. It has been, doubtless, the result of their own turbulence and insubordination that they are now so narrowly watched by the government, and treated as though they were the natural enemies of the state. In former times Japan was divided into sixty-eight separate principalities. In consequence, as I understood, of the difficulty of keeping in order some of these minor potentates, it was found expedient, when the opportunity offered, to subdivide their territories with a view of lessening their power, so that there are now three hundred and sixty feudal princes of greater or less importance, each of whom is compelled to have a residence in Yedo, to live in the capital during six months of the year, and during the remaining six months to retire in solitude to his principality, leaving his wife and family at Yedo as hostages for his good behavior.

Besides these, there are about three hundred smaller divisions of territory, so that the empire is altogether divided into upward of six hundred fiefs. I could not exactly discover the nature of the tenure by which these were severally held. The original sixty-eight doubtless owed allegiance to the Mikado alone. Others hold of the Tycoon, or temporal emperor; while others appear to be vassals to the larger princes, or, if not holding directly of them, at any rate recognize their ascendency, and are considered so far beneath them in rank as to be deprived even of the priv-

<sub>of the Japanese in this regard: "The sooner the consuls are at their posts in Japan, and the treaties ratified, the better. The sailors from the ships are bringing sad disgrace on the foreign name. At the fire which occurred at Decima a few weeks back, they behaved most shamefully, and it was known that they had plundered dollars to a considerable amount. These they of course desired to spend after the Jack-on-shore fashion. They accordingly go on shore in quest of drink, and commit all those excesses for which their class, under such circumstances, is notorious. Some of these sailors had armed themselves, and had taken refuge in the mountains, but had been apprehended and sent back to their ships. The Japanese government were naturally much incensed at this, and the foreign community greatly grieved."
—*Daily Press*, Hong Kong, 21st of April, 1859.</sub>

ilege of having a wife and family permanently resident in the capital. Doubtless some of these princes are, practically, absolute in their own dominions, and set even the council of state at defiance. Kangono-kami, who is the first prince in the empire; Satsuma, whose daughter is married to the temporal emperor; Achino-kami, and others, are not to be trifled with, and do not allow governmental interference in the internal management of their affairs. It is a hazardous office to play the spy in the capital of one of these magnates. Others, however, are less fortunate; they are compelled to submit to the supervision of two government secretaries, who take it in turn to administer the affairs of their territories.

The Prince of Satsuma was reported to have no less than nine town-houses in Yedo, and he pays his annual visit to the capital accompanied by an army of very respectable dimensions. It is an ordinary thing for one of these princes to parade the country with a force of some thousands of men. When we remember that all these followers have to be lodged on the premises of their chief, and that there are three hundred and sixty of these dignitaries, we can not wonder that their residences are necessarily capacious, and cover a very great extent of ground. To judge from the noble trees we observed rising above the walls, spacious pleasure-grounds must be inclosed within them. The handsomest palace I observed in Yedo was that belonging to Prince Achi. Situated on the steep side of a hill, the gates were tastefully ornamented, the walls surmounted with trellis-work, and numerous magnificent plane and other trees drooped over them into the street, tempting one to effect a burglarious entrance, and explore, if possible, the sacred precincts. Occasionally, in the course of our explorations of the city, we met men of rank riding along one of those silent streets, their retinue taking up almost its entire length, consisting, as usual, of men carrying badges on long poles, the insignia of the rank of their lord, umbrellas in bags, and lackered portmanteaus. When a great man wishes to move about "nayboen," or incognito, his retinue is not decreased, but these badges of his rank are packed up in the aforesaid portmanteaus.

If the residence of Count Poutiatine, which we at last reached, was in a more fashionable quarter than ours, it was neither so commodious nor so picturesque. His excellency was having his audience with the prime minister, so we prolonged our ride toward the citadel. Crossing a species of canal which forms the outer moat, we continued to pass through a quarter still occupied by the residences of the nobility, until we burst suddenly upon a view so unexpected and so remarkable in its character, that we could scarcely believe that we were still in the centre of a huge city, and that city the capital of an empire supposed to be in a state of barbarism. Standing on a broad terrace, we looked down some seventy or eighty feet upon a moat fifty or sixty yards in width, but expanding to a small lake, covered with lotus, as it approached the precipitous causeway by which it was traversed. A steep slope of grassy turf rose from the opposite edge of the water to an even greater elevation than that at which we were standing. Groups of trees fringed the water, and drooped their boughs into it; while a massive wall, constructed of blocks of stone almost Cyclopean in their proportions, crowned the high bank. This wall was in its turn surmounted by a wooden palisade—the spreading branches of gigantic cedars, and the leafy crowns of numerous tall trees appearing above it, gave evidence of gardens and pleasure-grounds within.

Following along the margin of this gigantic ditch, the largest artificial work of the sort I ever saw, we reached the narrow causeway which affords ingress to this *rus in urbe*, for from this point we were emphatically reminded that we were indeed in the centre of a vast city. We had now attained a considerable elevation, and, except where the prospect was interrupted by the citadel itself, obtained an extensive panoramic view over the greater part of Yedo, extending in an endless series of house-tops in a southerly direction, and fully confirming the impression which was rapidly gaining upon us, that the capital of Japan must take a first-class position, in point of extent and population, among the cities of the world. The citadel alone is said to measure eight miles in circumference, and to afford shelter to forty thousand souls, which it may well do, and yet leave room for spacious palaces, and scenes of rural retirement and rustic beauty. As its imperial occupant is too great a person ever to be permitted to pass into the vulgar world outside its walls, he is, poor man, entitled to as much space as can reasonably be afforded to him within them.

Reluctantly turning our backs upon the entrance to these forbidden precincts, we jogged homeward back through the quiet streets to where policemen again waited to take us in charge,

AN IMPERIAL BANQUET.

and crowds again pressed and scrambled to stare at us; and so, thoroughly exhausted by our first day in Yedo, to seek repose in the cloisters of our temple. We found, however, that another ordeal was to be passed before we could flatter ourselves that we should be left alone. The emperor had sent a Japanese dinner to his excellency, and when we arrived the floor of our dining-room was strewn with delicacies. Each person was provided with a little repast of his own, the exact ditto to that in which all his friends were indulging; and when any body made a gastronomic discovery of any value, he announced it to the company; so, at the recommendation of one, we all plunged into the red lacker cups on the right, or, at the invitation of another, dashed recklessly at what seemed to be pickled slugs on the left. We found it difficult even then to describe to each other the exact dishes we meant, how much more hopeless to attempt it now? There was a good deal of sea-weed about it, and we each had a capital broiled fish. With that, and an immense bowl of rice, it was impossible to starve; but my curiosity triumphed over my discretion, and I tasted of every pickle and condiment, and each animal and vegetable delicacy, of every variety of color, consistency, and flavor: an experience from which I would recommend any future visitor to Japan to abstain.

As the Japanese have neither pigs nor sheep, poultry, venison, and fish are the staples. Many of the religious sects in the country forbid the consumption of animal food. Meanwhile our lacker cups were abundantly replenished with hot sakee, a spirit extracted from rice, and of a pale-sherry color. It is by no means of a disagreeable flavor, though, when imbibed very hot, it is somewhat intoxicating. We were thankful at last to get to bed after so much excitement; and if our rest was somewhat troubled, we had no right to complain.

On the following morning we started immediately after breakfast on a shopping expedition. Turning to the left on entering the main street, we followed it for upward of an hour. As our horses stepped out well, I should judge the distance traversed to have been about four miles. Throughout its entire length, we passed between crowded lines of spectators, and through a long series of barriers. I observed that we were preceded by runners, who went in advance to inform the ward-keepers of our approach. At most of the barriers a ladder was erected with a bell at the top

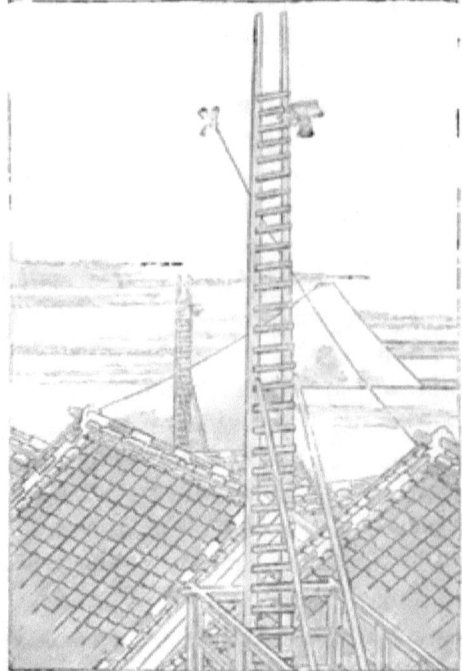

A Fire-ladder (from a native drawing).

of it, to be rung in case of fire. These ladders present a singular appearance as you pass along the street, and look as if they formed part of a show, and only waited for "the donkey." The houses were most of them built of wood, but tiled, and of two stories. The architecture of Japan, however, is so unpretending, that, although the streets are broad and clean, and thronged with passengers in the business quarter, they are by no means imposing. Here and there we pass a building higher than the rest, built of unburnt brick, with iron shutters. This is a fire-proof store, in which property can be stowed away in safety at the first tinkle of the fire-bell. Some of the houses are supplied with large tubs, kept constantly full of water, in anticipation of the same much-dreaded element.

As the only foreigners of whom the untraveled inhabitants of Yedo have ever heard are the Chinese, we had the very high compliment paid us of being supposed to belong to that favored nation; so that, as in China you are called, as you ride along the streets, a barbarian or a "foreign devil," in Japan the gamins run after you and say, "Look at the Chinamen!" "There go the

Chinamen!" while their commercial instinct is betrayed by the shout, "Chinamen, Chinamen! have you any thing to sell?"

This trifling circumstance enables us forcibly to realize the extent of that entire exclusion of strangers which has been for so long so jealously and successfully maintained. As we approached the heart of the city the shops improved in appearance. They are open to the street, the wares displayed for the most part upon a counter facing it. We passed over three wooden bridges on piles, crossing branches of the Todagawa. Many of the shops have sign-boards on single posts, like those of public houses in England, inscribed with both Chinese and Japanese characters; others have them written on pieces of cotton. The bathing-houses are all distinguished by a dark blue or black strip of cotton, like a banner, waving over the doorway. These establishments are always full of occupants, and I consequently observed no bathing in the streets as at Nagasaki. They differ slightly from those at Simoda. In that primitive town there was only one room for both sexes; but at Yedo there was sometimes a partition about breast high to divide the ladies from the gentlemen. Over the bathing-rooms there are generally tea-rooms, to which the bathers resort when in that soothed and relaxed state which is produced by the abundant use of hot water, and, without troubling themselves about their personal appearance, refresh themselves with that most popular beverage.

At last, after a progress which seemed interminable, we arrived at a celebrated lacker-shop, and were soon ushered up stairs to the show-rooms. Here we found specimens of that manufacture far superior to any thing we had seen either at Nagasaki or Simoda, the excellence consisting in the extent to which the design is raised upon the wood.

The varnish itself is extracted from a shrub called the Orrosinoki, or *Rhus vernix:* it is said to be procured from incisions made on stems that are three years old, from which it oozes like the milk of the India-rubber-tree. It is tinted in a great variety of colors with coloring matter, which is rubbed into it upon a copper plate: it is then laid on in successive coats, and heavily embossed in gold or silver.

The most common designs are the three emblems of longevity, the tortoise, the stork, and the pine-tree. The Japanese are very fond of chimerical animals. Thus the tortoise is often represent-

B B

ed with a large bushy tail; in this form he is called Mooki. They are also fond of a fabulous monster with the head of a dragon, the body of a horse, and the hoofs of a deer. In addition to which Fusi-yama, junks under full sail, or fishes lashing the waves furiously with their tails, are very favorite subjects.

The charm of every thing we saw at Yedo lay in the fact of its being purely for Japanese use. Every article was illustrative of the customs of the country. There were luncheon-trays, ladies' toilet-stands, arrangements for carrying fire, writing-cases, cabinets to be presented on the occasion of weddings; in fact, a host of patterns and contrivances, strange to our Western eyes, but exquisitely finished, and most elaborately ornamented with quaint and beautiful devices.

Having ticketed our purchases here, to be paid for in all due form through the government money-changers afterward, we proceeded to an extensive silk-shop upon the scale of Howell & James's. The whole of the lower story was open to the street, and looked like a vast hall fifty or sixty yards long by twenty in width, intersected with counters nicely matted, and surrounded by shelves and drawers containing goods; but the largest show-rooms were up stairs. Following obsequious shopmen to the upper story, we were soon seated on a low divan, covered with red cloth, where a train of boys, carrying tea and pipes, made their entry, and presented them to us on their knees. As sugar is considered a great luxury in Japan, and is one of the few articles imported into the country, it is considered a mark of refinement to furnish *eau sucré* on these occasions; but the most sentimental description of beverage is hot water poured over rose-leaves. It requires a highly æsthetic frame of mind to relish a rosebud cocktail.

While we are sipping our tea, the whole floor has become strewn with silks, crapes, and embroideries of every description of texture, shade of color, and brilliancy of pattern. The silks in Japan are said to be inferior to those of China, though to our inexperienced eyes they looked quite equal to them. The gauzes and crapes would create a furor in England, particularly the former, as the stuff is made of so stiff a material that it would answer the double purpose of a cage and a dress. The embroideries were infinitely superior to any thing that China can produce: they are usually worked on satin, and remind one rather of the Gobelin tapestry than of any modern embroidery. Many of the patterns and combinations of color show great taste. The Japanese are remarkable for the simplicity and elegance of their taste in matters of dress or ornament, as a general rule avoiding gaudy patterns, or any thing which, in the vernacular of the day, is known as "loud." Here is an old gentleman with spectacles on nose, whom a native artist, with some humor, has represented as engaged in designing patterns.

Pattern-designer (from a native drawing).

We quite regretted that all these curiosities of dress and material should be displayed before persons so little able to appreciate them. There can be no doubt that the contents of a Japanese silk-mercer's shop, transported to England, and exhibited to the female public of our metropolis, would draw large and fashionable crowds. While we were in despair about what to buy, and lost in perplexed speculation as to what would do for dresses, I was amused in watching the humors of the crowd collected in the street below, waiting for our appearance. They were kept from pressing near the doorway by a cord drawn in a semicircle round it. But a good deal of badinage went on; and one man was so much laughed at that he got excited, and was about to resort to violent measures, when he was at once collared by the ever-vigilant police, his hands were fastened behind him, and he was walked off in double-quick time, to the great amusement of the bystanders.

I also observed, for the first time, one or two carts of a very rude construction, and drawn by bullocks: but they are apparently very little used in Japan. The lower orders, whose rank does not entitle them either to ride on horseback or to go in norimons, are carried by two men in a most uncomfortable sort of basket, which doubles their knees up to their chins, so that it almost gives one the cramp to look at them.

The whole system of municipal government in the cities in Japan seems very perfect. There is a mayor or governor, some of whose emissaries lived in our ante-chamber; and there are a certain number of deputies to assist him, and a class of officials who seem to be the intermediaries between the people and those in authority, and whose business it is to receive and present petitions, and to forward complaints to the governors, and plead the cause of the aggrieved memorialists. Then every street has its magistrate, who is expected to settle all disputes, to know the most minute details of the private and public affairs of every creature within his jurisdiction, as reported to him by spies, and to keep an accurate record of births, deaths, and marriages. He is responsible for all broils and disturbances, and for the good conduct of the street generally. This functionary is also provided with deputies, and is elected by the popular voice of the inhabitants of the street. To render the task easier, the male householders are divided into small companies of four or five each, the head of which is responsible to the magistrate for all the proceedings of the members. This complete organization is furnished with a secretary, a treasurer, a certain number of messengers, etc. Besides the regular constables, it is patrolled at night by the inhabitants themselves, in parties of two or three. From all which it will appear that "our streets," in a Japanese city, must be a source of considerable interest and occupation to its inhabitants.

The streets of Yedo are infested with dogs—not the wretched mangy curs of Constantinople or the pariahs of India, but sleek, well-fed, audacious animals, who own no masters, but who seem to thrive on the community, and bid it defiance. They trot proudly about, with ears and tail erect, and are most formidable to meet in a by-lane. These animals are held in as high veneration and respect as they were in former times in Egypt; the most ancient traditions attach to them, and it is a capital crime to put one to death. There are even guardians appointed for their protection, and hospitals to which they are carried in case of illness. Certainly a long experience has taught them to profit by the immunity from persecution which they enjoy. It is only due to them to say that, as a race, they are the handsomest street-dogs I ever saw. The only large animals in Japan are horses, oxen and cows, and buffaloes; but milk, butter, and cheese are unknown as articles of consumption. There are no asses or mules, and scarcely any pigs. The largest wild animals are deer, of which, however, there are very few.

As the audience with the two chief ministers of state was fixed for the afternoon, we were obliged to hurry home to prepare for that important ceremony.

A Street in the aristocratic Quarter of Yedo. (From a native book-m.)

CHAPTER XXVII.

Constitution of Government.—"Nayboen."—The Spy System."—The Council of State.—A political Crisis.—The "Happy Dispatch."—Ruining a Politician.—The Japanese social Scale.—A Visit to the Citadel.—The Japanese Ministers.—Japanese Flunkies.—Tea and Sweetmeats.—Shopping in Yedo.—Dog Mania.—Official Visit of Commissioners.—Official Costume.—Ham and Champagne.—The first Day's Conference.—Jocosity of Higo-no-kami.—General Good-humor.

BEFORE proceeding to describe our audience with the ministers of state, it will be necessary to give a brief sketch of the system of government of Japan, although gathered from somewhat imperfect sources; for the communicative Moriyama was generally too busy to enter upon any detailed account of Japanese institutions; and, although he professed the utmost frankness in his intercourse with us, there can be no doubt that he shared the prejudices and obeyed the instructions of his government in withholding from us all the information in his power. It was rather from incidental circumstances, in the course of our negotiations, that we gathered some idea of the true source of authority in Japan.

Although nominally consulted in temporal matters, and jealously distinguished from his temporal rival by the term emperor, the Mikado, or spiritual emperor, is in fact a mere puppet. He occasionally receives visits of ceremony from the Tycoon, and gives a formal sanction to matters of state, but generally votes the spiritual crown a bore before he has worn it very long, and, abdicating in favor of a son, descends from the realms above, and passes a peaceful old age in this sublunary sphere.

The Tycoon, on the other hand, is ostensibly the administrator of the empire; but he, too, has been exalted to so high a pitch of temporal dignity that his lofty station has been robbed of all its substantial advantages, and he passes the life of a state prisoner, shut up in his magnificent citadel, except when he pays a state visit to Miako. It was a cruel satire upon this unhappy potentate to present him with a yacht; one might as well request the Pope's acceptance of a wife. There is, indeed, a practice which exists in Japan, and which may have extended to other countries, of doing improper things "nayboen," as it is called here; in other words, in a recognized incognito. Whether, under this happy arrangement, the emperor sometimes slips out of his back door, I was not informed; but it is certain that the nobles of the land avail themselves extensively of the latitude which it permits.

In a country governed by etiquette, and in which every individual is a slave to conventional rules of the most precise and rigid description, it is necessary to have a loop-hole which enables them to sink to the level of ordinary mortals; in other words, to indulge their natural appetites for pleasure or vice. Under the convenient system of "nayboen," a noble may do any thing which is not forbidden to the meanest subject. If the emperor can not take advantage of "nayboen" while he is alive, he can, as we afterward discovered, die "nayboen." This is a common practice among grandees, their death being kept secret until the next heir is firmly installed in the possession of the family dignity and honors.

The time of the emperor seems to be occupied with audiences, receiving reports, and other official formalities, and he is nominally consulted, and his ratification obtained to every measure decided upon by his council of state. It is said that he is as narrowly watched by spies as any of his subjects. In fact, the more we investigate the extraordinary system under which Japan is governed, the more evident does it become that the great principle upon which the whole fabric rests is the absolute extinction of individual freedom: to arrive at this result, resort is had to a complicated machinery so nicely balanced that, as every body watches every body, so no individual can escape paying the penalty to society of any injury he may attempt to inflict upon it. One most beneficial result arising from this universal system of espionage—for it extends through all classes of society—is the entire probity of every government employé. So far as we could learn or see, they were incorruptible. When men can neither offer nor receive bribes; when it is almost impossible, even indirectly, to exercise corrupt influences, there is little fear of the demoralization of public departments of the state. In this respect Japan affords a brilliant contrast to China, and even to some European countries. So long as this purity exists, even though purchased at the cost of secret espial, there can be little cause to fear the decadence of the empire. Nominally not a constitution, but a despotism, the government of Japan is practically an oligarchy; but every noble is watched by the spies and enthralled by the public opinion of his class, which he dares not venture to outrage. There is, indeed, a council of state, composed of five of the highest grade of the aristocracy, who are chosen by the Tycoon himself, and a minor council, consisting of eight of the titular princes. All these are under the strict surveillance of private spies, who report to their own masters; and from the evident difficulty the commissioners found in conceding certain points to which the kamis or princes were avowedly hostile, the government probably stand in awe of that influential body. It was doubtless owing to the pressure which the latter brought to bear upon the government of Bitsu-no-kami, the late prime minister, that he was compelled to resign his office. It is a singular fact, that in Japan, where the individual is sacrificed to the community, he should seem perfectly happy and contented; while in America, where exactly the opposite result takes place, and the community is sacrificed to the individual, the latter is in a perpetual state of uproarious clamor for his rights.

It is this council, then, influenced by the public opinion of the aristocracy, which governs Japan. To it all official spies report; they appoint all governors and secretaries for the administration of the affairs of provinces belonging to the crown and many of the princes, and are supposed to act as a check upon these latter, who are, however, in all probability, kept in better order by rival jealousies than direct governmental influence. There is another body of men who possess great influence in the state; these are the princes of the blood. Should the Tycoon and his council differ upon any weighty matter of state government, the question is referred for arbitration to a tribunal composed of three of these royal princes. Should they confirm the opinion of the council, the Tycoon, to whom is denied the privilege of hara-kiri, or the "happy dispatch," has no alternative but to abdicate incontinently in favor of his nearest heir. Should, on the other hand, the umpires agree with their royal relative, which in all probability they do, unless public opinion is too strongly against them, then the whole of the council are bound, without farther ceremony, at once to dispatch themselves, in the happy manner peculiar to Japan, to those Elysian fields, where they will probably become distinguished as canonized kamis, and the patron saints of many a Japanese household.

This notorious method of suicide, the only Japanese custom

with which the Western world has long been familiar, has of late years assumed a somewhat modified form, and no longer consists in that unpleasant process of abdomen ripping, which must have been almost as disagreeable an operation to witness as to perform. My friend Higo-no-kami presented me with a knife proper to be used under the old system—an exceedingly business-like weapon about ten inches long, sharp as a razor, and made of steel of the highest temper. Now this knife is only used to make a slight incision, significant of the intention of the victim to put an end to himself. He has collected his wife and family to see how a hero can die; his dearest friend, he who in our own country would have been his best-man at his wedding—stands over him with a drawn sword, and when he commences to make the aforesaid incision, the sword descends, and the head rolls at the feet of his disconsolate family.

Whether this mode of suicide is really common at the present day, I could not ascertain; no instance of it came to our knowledge during our stay; and I imagine it is too serious a step to be taken except on very weighty grounds. These may arise either from failure or neglect in a public trust, or in consequence of the commission of some private injury. In some instances it seems to answer the purpose of a duel; it is the reduction of that practice to its logical conclusion, and terminates in the death of both parties by the hands of their friends; but more commonly it is resorted to as the means of preserving from disgrace a whole family, one member of which has in some way dishonored his name: it is a certificate which whitewashes all the survivors. A man who fears to face his destiny in this form, when the claims of honor demand it, places his entire family without the social pale. I am not aware wherein the Japanese points of honor consist, but we may assume that where the preservation of it in the individual requires so great a sacrifice, the standard is proportionably high—far more so, probably, than would suit our views in England, where it would be an exceedingly unpopular way of solving a constitutional difficulty. A ministry would always prefer a dissolution of Parliament to a personal dissolution of this nature. It is pleasanter to go to the country than out of it. A mere change of government, even in Japan, however, does not involve these consequences, unless the Tycoon is implicated. Witness the still-living Bitsu-no-kami.

Perhaps it is because the "happy dispatch" is found to be an inconvenient way of settling personal or political difficulties that another mode exists of removing a dangerous person much more refined in its character. When a man becomes an object of distrust or suspicion to the government, either from his great influence or wealth, he is promoted to some office generally at Miako, which he is compelled to accept, and which entails such a vast expenditure that he is inevitably ruined. Even if his means stand the first shock, one visit from the Tycoon, when he goes to pay his respects to the Mikado, completes the work.

Such is an imperfect outline of the system of government and of the constitution of the upper ranks in society. Although the commissioners were called kamis, it did not necessarily follow that they were of princely rank, or belonged to the first class of nobles. Kami seems to be a generic appendage to the names of men of a certain rank, just as, in England, all noblemen between the ranks of marquess and baron are styled lord. It is a title which can not be used except by those of gentle blood. Next in order to the Saimios, or second class of nobles, come the priests, who are in their turn followed by the first and second classes of officials, who are for the most part men belonging to the military grade, and have achieved their rank, and the privilege of wearing two swords, by their merit. They are followed by the professional class—merchants, traders, and peasantry. In addition to these social distinctions, there is a pariah or despised caste, consisting of tanners and others.

To return, however, to the council of state, each of the five ministers of which it is composed are appointed by the Tycoon, and preside over separate departments; they rank in regular order, and, among their other functions, to the two senior is committed the control of foreign affairs. There were two gentlemen, Otto Bungo-no-kami and another, whose acquaintance we were now about to make. Our morning had been so much occupied in the lacker and silk shops that it was late in the afternoon before we started on a five-mile journey to the official residence of these dignitaries, which was just inside the farther gate of the citadel.

Our way, as usual, led us down the main street. I made my first experience of a norimon on this occasion, and obtained a view of the crowd in a squatting posture; for, while the train of ten norimons was passing, the people sat on their heels to obtain a view of the occupants. As some of these were naval officers in full uniform, they exhibited signs of unusual satisfaction.

In order not to dirty the mats of our hosts, we were each provided with a pair of slippers in which to scuffle across the yard, for it is not etiquette in Japan for any but the owner of the house to go beyond the outer threshold in his norimon. At that point all guests are put down, and walk to the next entrance.

Passing over a bridge which spanned the moat, and under a gateway of massive proportions, we found ourselves within the walls of the citadel at the opposite side from that on which we had visited it in our ride of the day before.

Unluckily we had not far to go, so that we saw scarcely any thing of the interior of this interesting spot. A broad street, similar to those in the Princes' quarter, led us to a handsome gateway; this, on one account, at all events, we were not a little relieved to find, was our journey's end, as the posture during an hour and a half had been a trying one for British legs. Emerging from our box-like conveyances, we shuffled after Moriyama, who was always at his post. Ascending some steps, at the top of which we relinquished our slippers, we passed through a series of ante-chambers, with walls of paper screens, until we were ushered finally into an oblong apartment, at the farther end of which, on the left-hand side, stood the two ministers behind two low square tables and six wax candles on single stands, for it was by this time 7 P.M. Exactly facing them were three tables and six more candles, behind which we took up our position. For some time we all remained standing, and the usual complimentary expressions were interchanged. Then, all having left the room except Lord Elgin, Mr. Hewsken, and myself, we sat down on chairs (an unexpected luxury), and proceeded to business. Moriyama, during all this time, was in a prostrate attitude on the floor between Lord Elgin and the ministers, touching the ground reverentially with his forehead whenever he was called upon to interpret. Lower down, and remaining standing, were our friends the commissioners; while in a sort of passage formed by a hanging screen behind the ministers were a row of people who ostensibly took no part in the ceremony, but some of whom were no doubt spies, while others I observed occasionally prompting the ministers. These latter personages seemed somewhat embarrassed by the novelty of their situation, and gave one the impression of being very new to office.

Interview between the Earl of Elgin and the Prime Ministers of Japan.

Otto Bungo-no-kami was a thin, spare man, with a shriveled face, indicating shrewdness, and I should have guessed parsimony. His colleague was heavier-looking, and without any marked expression. They opened the conversation by manifesting some anxiety about the yacht, and wished to know at what period his excellency intended to make it over to the Japanese government. Lord Elgin assured them that its delivery should take place immediately on the signing of the treaty. After a somewhat prolonged discussion on the subject of full powers, so difficult of comprehension to the Eastern mind, it was arranged that the interchange should take place on the following day.

While this was going on, a train of youths entered, bearing pipes and tea. They were all dressed simply and uniformly; indeed, so exactly did they resemble one another, that they must have been selected as good matches. They entered with an air of profound respect, the head slightly bent, the eyes fixed on the ground, and moved with a shuffling gait, as though afraid to lift their feet from the floor.

During the period of our visit these young men were constantly coming in with refreshments, and as they never looked up, it was always a matter of wonder to me how they found their way, while the monotonous regularity of their movements was quite painful. Notwithstanding which, it must be admitted that the manners of flunkies in Japan are infinitely more agreeable than those of the same race in our own country.

After the ordinary tea, we were supplied with a beverage peculiar to the upper classes of Japan: this consists of a sort of *purée* made of the tea-leaves themselves. They are first stewed, then dried and ground in a hand-mill into a powder; this is mixed with hot water and whipped with a split bamboo until it creams. It is served up hot, and looks like physic. Altogether, I thought it more palatable than senna. This delicacy is called koitscha, or thick tea; it was succeeded by a number of small square wooden boxes on little stands; they were rather like toy-boxes, and might be supposed to contain some description of game. We each had one of these to ourselves. When the lids were removed, we discovered a very tempting assortment of barley-sugar, sponge-cakes, Gibraltar rock, and other confectionery, not to be distinguished in taste from the manufactures of our own country, except by school-boys or those really versed in the subject. We were not only supposed to nibble at these sweetmeats during the visit, but the boxes, with all that remained in them, were sent after us to our abode, so that we were enabled, for some days afterward, to retire to the privacy of our chambers whenever we felt moved, and feast in secrecy upon their luscious contents. Our audience having at last come to an end, we took leave with many profound bows and polite speeches, and returned to our norimons, our companions having in the mean time been feasted with tea and sweetmeats in an adjoining room.

I was not sorry for the opportunity of passing through the streets of Yedo by night. The effect of our procession was very picturesque. In addition to the jingling police, we were accompanied by men bearing on high huge lanterns attached to poles.

Pretty lamps, painted in bright colors and covered with quaint devices, hung in clusters over the shops, illuminated the bathhouses, flared over street-stalls, or depended from ropes slung across the side-streets. As the crowd seemed even more dense than in the daytime, the brilliant glare lit up their eager, curious faces and half-clad figures, and imparted a wild, uncouth aspect to the scene. It was nearly ten o'clock at night before we reached home, and we had as yet no reason to reproach ourselves with idleness or inactivity.

The representations which we had frequently made to our friend and guardian Tainoske, and the avidity which we manifested in the purchase of all Japanese articles of manufacture, induced that worthy to collect for our benefit, every morning, a number of vendors of lacker, china, and embroidery, who used to spread their wares in our verandas; so that, during the earlier part of the day, they assumed somewhat the appearance of a bazar. In the enjoyment of this extravagant amusement, our mornings used to fly rapidly. Each box contained some specimen we had not yet seen. The china, in particular, was an endless source of interest, from the variety of patterns and devices which it presented. On some of the cups were raised lacker representations of pleasure-boats, with tiny windows, on opening which a party of ladies and gentlemen drinking tea were discovered within, all on the minutest possible scale. At the bottom of other cups, a tortoise, beautifully executed in china, might be observed placidly reposing, until the tea was poured in, when he rose to the surface a most animated reptile.

But the taste for China and the rage for lacker were nothing as compared to the mania for dogs. The dog peculiar to Japan, and which is supposed to have been the origin of the King Charles spaniel, does indeed bear a considerable resemblance to that breed: the ears are not so long and silky, and the nose is more of a pug; but the size, shape, and color of the body are almost identical. The face is by no means attractive: the eyes are usually very prominent, as though starting from the head; the forehead is overhanging, and the nose so minute that it forms rather a depression than a projection on the face; the jaw is somewhat prominent, and is frequently so much underhung that the mouth can not be shut, in consequence of which the tongue protrudes in a waggish manner, at variance with the staring eye, which should, for the sake of consistency, be slightly closed, with a tendency to wink.

When the great majority of our party had furnished themselves with three or four of these prepossessing animals each, which were confined in kennels formed of paper screens up in our loft, the consequences to an unhappy victim like myself, who had resisted their charms, were most trying. They used to demolish their paper kennels with their teeth, quarrel with each other, howl dismally during the still hours of the night, or have spasms. They were subject to weakness and violent cramp in the loins and hind legs, and then their owners used to devote the small hours of the morning to fomenting them with hot water, and wrapping them in warm flannels. In spite of all their efforts, some of these delicate little creatures died, to the inexpressible grief of those who had listened so often to their nocturnal whinings. Even in Yedo, the price of a handsome pair of these dogs is as much as fifty or sixty dollars, so that it is worth while to sit up at night to alleviate their sufferings.

In accordance with the arrangement arrived at on the preceding day, the six commissioners appeared a little before luncheon, in order to exhibit their full powers, and enter upon the preliminaries of the treaty. They were dressed in the official costume used upon state occasions, and which was remarkable for its simplicity. The fashion and color of their garments are all prescribed by a rigid code of official etiquette. A pale straw-color is considered full dress; this, combined with pale or dark blue and black, are the orthodox colors on state occasions. On gala-days their costume is somewhat more gaudy and fantastic. We had an opportunity, before leaving, of seeing them thus attired: on their ordinary official visits, however, they wore a sort of undress or riding costume. This differs from full dress in the cut of the trowsers, which admit of the legs being widely separated, an impossible achievement in their best clothes. They also, in riding, dispense with the light gauze sort of habit shirt, which is thrown over the rest of the costume, and, projecting at the shoulder like wings, falls in long bands in front. In formal salutations, it is the correct thing to stoop until the ends of these bands touch the ground.

The Japanese seldom wear any thing on their heads except when riding. The head is shaved on the crown, and the side and back hair brought forward in a roll about the thickness of a small sausage to the top of the forehead; here it is firmly gummed down with a species of bandoline, in the manufacture of which the Japanese are very proficient. Wigs are common in the shops, but are only worn as a part of a masquerade dress. Not a particle of hair is ever allowed to appear on their faces. The winter costume consists in robes cut like dressing-gowns, padded throughout with silk wadding. These unwieldy articles of attire are also used upon state occasions, and are a standing item in the list of imperial presents to a foreign mission. But the most singular portion of their apparel are the trowsers which they wear at their audiences with the Tycoon; they seem to be cut upon a principle precisely the opposite to that which regulates our court-dress. We consider that when we have brought our nether garments down to the knee, we have not only satisfied decency, but reached the highest pitch of refinement and elegance. The great object of the Japanese is to create an entire misconception in the mind of the spectator as to the situation of that important joint; he wishes it to be supposed that he shuffles into the royal presence on his knees; but, finding that process attended with much practical inconvenience, he compromises the matter by having his

A Japanese Wig.

Exchange of full Powers between the Earl of Elgin and the Japanese Commissioners.

trowsers made about eighteen inches longer than his legs; by these means his feet are made to represent his knees, and he is enabled to walk upon them comfortably with his sham legs dragging after him.

The commissioners brought us the intelligence that, the Tycoon being childless, he had within the last few days adopted a son. This lad was to be his successor; and in the event of his subsequently having a son of his own, he would be compelled to give him away rather than dispossess the adopted one. The choice of adoption is confined to the sons of six of the princes of the blood. What amount of truth there was in this information we had not at the time any opportunity of judging.

Before proceeding to work, our guests sat down with great readiness to luncheon, and made formidable inroads upon the ham, the dish of all others which they most highly appreciate. They also indulged freely in Champagne; indeed, so conscious were they of the risk attending these libations preparatory to entering upon business, that Iligo facetiously expressed a hope that the Treaty would not taste of ham and Champagne.

After luncheon we adjourned to Lord Elgin's sitting-room, where his excellency and the commissioners seated themselves round the table and mutually exhibited their full powers. While some necessary details involved in this process were being transacted, Mr. Bedwell took the opportunity of making the accompanying characteristic and truthful drawing—a fact which Iligo no sooner remarked than, seizing a pencil and paper, he proceeded to caricature the artist, and suddenly interrupted the proceedings by triumphantly producing a very fair attempt at a likeness.

Now that we had really settled down to work, every body lighted a pipe or a cigar, and although, as regarded from a red-tape point of view, the general aspect of the scene may have been somewhat informal, a great deal of business was accomplished. It was necessary, however, to get over a difficulty in the first instance, arising from the necessity which the commissioners felt of being watched. It was an unnatural thing for them to transact business except in the presence of government and private spies, so they formally requested that a certain number of these gentry should be allowed to be present during the conferences. This was of course objected to by Lord Elgin, his excellency remarking that there were already six Japanese commissioners to one English minister, and that any farther accession of force on the other side would be manifestly quite unfair. On which the commissioners neatly enough replied "that it did indeed take six Japanese heads to cope with such an English head as they saw before them, and that, in fact, they felt quite unequal to the task." The matter was ultimately compromised by the presence of one secretary being allowed in addition to the indispensable Moriyama.

We were now able to enter upon the body of the treaty, and very soon discovered that the commissioners manifested the greatest acumen in the discussion of points of detail, never resting satisfied until they thoroughly comprehended the *rationale* of every question raised. Once, indeed, so serious a difficulty arose that, to create a diversion, some one proposed that we should have some cha (tea), upon which Lord Elgin suggested cha-*pagne*, an amendment which caused infinite merriment, and which was carried by acclamation. The Japanese have a keen appreciation of the ludicrous, and many a knotty point was solved by *bon mot*; indeed, to judge by the perpetual laughter in which they indulge, they are forever making jokes. Higo was the wit of the party, and was often, in consequence, not only inattentive himself, but apt to distract the attention of the others. It was evident in the twinkle of his eye when he was meditating a pun. His observations, nevertheless, upon business matters, whenever he condescended to make them, were always shrewd and to the point. The following are the names of the six commissioners, as written down by him in the English character upon a fan which he presented to me. The spelling is his own.

1. Midjmats-ko-goni-kami (formerly Governor of Nagasaki).
2. Nagai Gembono-kami (the admiral).
3. Inogge Sinanono-kami (Governor of Simoda).
4. Iwase Higo-no-kami.
5. Holi Olibeno-kami.
6. Tsuda-handzoboro.

The admiral was the most intelligent and active member of the party; and when he and the ex-Governor of Nagasaki were agreed the rest seldom failed to follow their lead.

Altogether we had every reason to be satisfied with the result of our first day's conference; it inaugurated a series of meetings invariably characterized by the utmost harmony and good-humor, and which must recall to the memory of those who participated in them many agreeable associations and pleasant reminiscences.

CHAPTER XXVIII.

A Riding-party.—Beauty of the Suburbs.—A pleasant Tea-house. Tea-gardens at Hojee.—A picturesque Picnic.—Internal Arrangements of a Tea-house.—A Bathing-room.—Scenery of the Interior of Japan.—The Botanical Gardens.—A Visit to the Prime Ministers.—The Commissioners at Luncheon.—" The Scoundrel."—Schools at Yedo.—Linguistic Acquirements of the Japanese. System of national Education.—Japanese Literature.—The Postage System.—The Japanese Language: its Construction.—Universal use of Paper.—Ingenuity of the Japanese.

It had been arranged with the commissioners that Lord Elgin should make a trip into the country upon the day following the exchange of full powers. Our destination was a summer resort about ten miles distant, called Hojee, where pretty scenery, botanical gardens, and well-appointed tea-houses were the attractions. Accordingly, immediately after breakfast our steeds appeared at the door, and we started off, a party of eight or ten, in that enjoyable frame of mind which is produced by pleasurable anticipations. For the first four or five miles our way led us through the town, along the castle moat, past the point at which we again obtained a panoramic view of the city, and on through more winding streets, which we had not before explored, and which seemed interminable. At last we got clear of the more crowded thoroughfares, and found ourselves traversing pleasant suburban lanes, passing the spacious palace of the most powerful prince in the empire, Kagano-kami. The outer walls of this establishment inclose an immense area of ground, and contain buildings which are said to afford accommodation to ten thousand men. The groves of lofty trees which towered above the walls gave token of the beauty of the gardens within them. Many of the streets and roads which we traversed were lined with peach and plum trees; at the period of the year when these are in full blossom, they must form a most charming and fragrant avenue.

We were filled with astonishment and delight at the exquisite taste displayed in the gardens and cottages upon the roadside. No model estate in England can produce "cottages ornées" comparable to those which adorn the suburbs of Yedo. We always fail in our detail; there is a want of that minuteness which the Chinaman glories in until he becomes grotesque. The Japanese have hit the happy medium. With an elaborate delicacy of detail, they combine the art of generalization in design, so that the relation of the parts with the whole is maintained throughout, and the general effect is not sacrificed to minor beauties. These charming little cottages, raising their thatched roofs amid the fruit-trees and creepers which threatened to smother them in their embraces, were surrounded by flower-beds tastefully laid out, resplendent with brilliant hues, and approached by walks between carefully-clipped hedges. Yew-trees, cut into fantastic shapes, and dwarfed trees, extending their deformed arms as if for assistance and support, are favorite garden ornaments. Here and there, at the end of a long avenue, we could discern a temple embowered amid trees; and ancient priests in gauzy and transparent costume, with broad embroidered belts and sashes, and enormous lackered hats, would hurry to the entrance to see the strangers pass. The beauty of the cemeteries was in keeping with the taste displayed in every thing else; here walks wound amid flowering shrubs and drooping cypresses.

We could always judge of the respectability of the quarter through which we passed by the size and character of the crowd which accompanied us. In some parts of the suburb we were followed by a noisy mob, who pressed upon us cheering and laughing—not, however, showing any signs of ill-will. Some of our party, on the previous day, not attended by a sufficiently large body of policemen to inspire awe, passing through some of the less reputable parts of the town, had been hooted, and even pelted, the crowd calling out, "Chinamen, Chinamen! have you any thing to sell?" a circumstance for which the commissioners never ceased apologizing, while they took occasion to impress upon us the necessity, which we were always anxious to forget, of never moving about unless accompanied by a proper staff of police. Upon this occasion we were attended by twenty officials, in a black gauze uniform, who marched in front of us. As we were desirous not to lose time, and our steeds were willing, some of the elder members of this party were knocked up before we got to the half-way tea-house, where we changed our escort.

As we got farther from town the cottages became more scattered, but the country did not lose its air of civilization. Groves of

Tea-garden near Yedo.

tall trees overshadowed the road, apparently bordering some ornamental grounds, for they were inclosed by palings exactly resembling those of our own parks.

The tea-house at which we stopped to rest was situated in a garden where sparkling water gushed out of mossy grottoes, and quilted mats invited to repose. Here pipes and tea were served by fair damsels, who also pressed upon our acceptance unripe pears. Beyond this tea-house we found ourselves fairly in the country; we had exchanged the suburbs of London for the lanes of Devonshire.

Although the country was undulating, the road was neither too steep nor too narrow for wheeled vehicles. Sometimes it passed between high banks crowned with hedgerows and shrubs, among which I observed the holly. With the exception of groves of trees, left doubtless for a special purpose, and which served to diversify the prospect, every acre of ground seemed cultivated. This is probably partly in consequence of a law compelling every man to cultivate his land within the year, upon pain of forfeiting it. Fields of yams and egg-plant or brinjall, of beans and Indian-corn, millet and onions, alternated with each other in rapid succession. At every clump of trees through which the road passed were resting-places for all classes of travelers—simple benches under the gnarled branches of some venerable oak or plane tree for humble wayfarers, and little tables with fruit and tea set out in the cool shade; or summer-houses, composed of a single hut, with the same invariable beverage hot and ready to refresh the thirst of the weary pedestrian; or an establishment of greater pretensions, where men of rank might stay and rest.

At last we suddenly descended into a dell where a charming village lay embosomed in a wood. It consisted of a few cottages, and a tea-house on a grand scale. At the entrance to this establishment we dismounted, much to the edification of the whole population of the village, who assembled to stare and wonder at us. We found the tea-house situated on the edge of a brawling stream, the balconies of the upper rooms overhanging the water. Hanging woods and gardens, tastefully laid out with rock-work, and yew-trees cut into quaint shapes, fringed the bank of the river, to the point at which it entered the grounds in a picturesque cascade. Taking possession of a summer-house perched on a projecting point, and which commanded a charming view of the surrounding objects, we signified to a group of young ladies, who came to look at us under the pretext of waiting for orders, our desire to be furnished with some luncheon.

We were not kept long in waiting for our meal, which consisted of some excellent vegetable soup, and some rice and fish. By way of dessert we had marshmelons, apricots, and pears, so that we had no difficulty in satisfying the cravings of hunger. We found that these gardens were a favorite resort of pleasure-parties from Yedo of the highest rank. When any grandee wishes to enjoy a domestic treat of this sort, accompanied by his wife and family, he gives a previous notice of his intention to the keeper of the tea-house, so that a dignified privacy may be secured to him. There, screened from the vulgar gaze, he and his companions give themselves up to the enjoyment which this species of recreation affords. Their wives play, dance, or sing for their benefit; in fact, so far as I could gather, they behave very much as we do when we are working off the fag-end of the season in picnics to the Star and Garter, or Hampton Court. I was not able to discover, however, under what conditions the unmarried members of society were allowed to partake of these amusements.

If any aristocratic picnic was going on during our visit to Hojee, we were not fortunate enough to get a glimpse of it. We did, nevertheless, explore the internal economy of the establishment. Unfortunately, it not being the custom for the guests to go into the kitchen, I was ignominiously expelled from that department just as I was commencing my investigations into the arrangements by which so large a number of guests were kept constantly supplied with every description of Japanese delicacy, and tea in rivers. I had only time to find myself encompassed by a bevy of active, bustling waitresses, and to catch sight of huge steaming caldrons, when a strong-minded old woman showed me the door with a soup-ladle. The accompanying illustration, taken on the spot by Mr. Bedwell, will convey a better idea than any description of the interior of the public rooms, and of the costume of the attendants. The complexions of many of these girls were quite as fair as those of our own countrywomen. In waiting, their manners are graceful and respectful. Almost every thing is served in lacker, and is presented in a reverential attitude. The guests sit dotted about on the mat till they have done dinner, when they lie down to smoke, sip tea, and digest. According to

Interior of Tea-garden.

Golownin, the varnish with which the lacker is composed is poison. Not only is it perfectly free from any injurious effect on this account, but, although the hottest tea may be served in lacker cups, it is impossible to detect the slightest flavor of the varnish.

Whether the tea of Japan is actually superior to that of China, or only prepared in a different way, I had no opportunity of judging; but the flavor struck me as much more delicate. According to Siebold, the plant is manured with dried anchovies, and a liquor pressed out of mustard-seed.

One method of preparing the tea is by keeping it constantly boiling. Enough of tea leaves are put into the kettle for the day's consumption, and the decoction is never taken off the fire. This is, however, generally only used at wayside refreshment-houses.

We did not observe any of it growing, as it is said that the plantations are generally remote from the habitations of men, lest they should be injured by smoke, or any other deleterious emanations.

A Japanese Bath.

Attached to the tea-house was a bathing-room containing a singular oval depression in the floor, to which the bathers confine themselves during their ablutions, as outlets are constructed for the escape of the water. Hot water is abundantly provided, while the cold flowed in a perpetual cascade from a green grotto in the wall.

Leaving Hojee, we rode up to the brow of the hill behind the village. To do so it was necessary to diverge from the high road, and gallop across a greensward dotted with handsome park-like trees. Our attendants, not prepared for this sudden escapade, ran breathlessly after us, vehemently remonstrating, and passing their hand across their throats, as an indication that our transgression would be visited upon them with summary punishment; but our curiosity to obtain a view from our elevated position overcame our scruples on their account, and we were well repaid for our want of humanity. The prospect upon which we feasted our gaze more nearly resembled that from Richmond Hill than any other with which I am acquainted. Beneath us was a winding river, now hidden among thick woods, now shining in the broad light of day as it emerged upon grassy fields. Beyond, as far as the eye could reach, the country was richly cultivated and charmingly diversified, while here and there the smoke of a town or hamlet imparted an air of animation to the view. It was a most tantalizing sight, and we longed to explore the unknown scenes which lie still unvisited in the heart of this magnificent country.

It is some consolation to know that the interior of Japan will in all probability, ere long, be laid open. By the late treaty it is reserved to the consul general and his immediate staff, and to them alone, to travel to any part of the empire. We know, from the accounts of the Jesuits and the Dutch missions, how many objects of interest there are at Miako, and other places upon the main route to Nagasaki, but our curiosity has been chiefly stimulated by the illustrations contained in the Japanese picture-books of the most striking features in their scenery. The Japanese are one of the few so-called uncivilized nations who really seem to have an intuitive appreciation of the picturesque. Even the Chinese, who occasionally venture upon representations of scenery, choose some uninteresting subject, and invariably make it subservient to a scene of domestic or military life in the foreground, displaying, moreover, an entire ignorance of perspective; but the Japanese portray the grandest scenic features of their country evidently for their own sake alone. Waterfalls and precipices, picturesque villages perched on overhanging cliffs, or rocky ledges running out into the sea, are favorite subjects, and executed with a much more correct notion of art than has been attained in the sister empire. From the views which many of these books contain, there must be scenery in Japan worth a pilgrimage to that distant island, were it for no other purpose but to visit it. Even our followers seemed to think it natural that we should wish to linger on the green edge of the hill, to take a long last look at the widespread prospect before us, but they were evidently relieved when we slowly turned our horses' heads into the narrow path which was to lead us to the botanical gardens.

A thick grove of overhanging trees afforded a grateful shade from the rays of the August sun, while little wicket-gates opened off it into gardens that formed a setting of flowers to the cottages in their midst. The botanical gardens themselves did not exactly correspond to our notions on the subject. There were neither fine old trees in great variety, nor a large and curious collection of all descriptions of plants. The rage of horticulturists in this country seemed to be grasses, mosses, and ferns of all sorts, added to which there was an extensive assortment of dwarfed trees. Instead of glass green-houses, there were long mat-sheds for the more delicate specimens; while ranged upon stands, as in England, were quantities of porcelain pots of various shapes and colors, but generally blue, with a piece of rock in the centre, and a root of grass or moss growing round it. But a Japanese gardener chiefly prides himself upon his skill in dwarfing. The most venerable forest-trees may here be seen in flower-pots, their old stems, gnarled and twisted as if writhing under the torture of distortion, perhaps scarce two feet high, while their unnatural branches spread out laterally like the fingers of a deformed hand. One of the Dutch factory told a story of a box three inches long by two broad, containing a fir-tree, a bamboo, and a plum-tree in full blossom, which was sold for a sum equal to twelve hundred dollars. There was a pine wood behind the gardens, with some pleasant retreats in it, and artificial hillocks crowned with summer-houses. These gardens are also a very favorite resort for picnics from Yedo.

Once more swinging ourselves into our uncomfortable saddles, we jogged home, a weary three hours' ride; but we had been amply repaid for our fatigue by the novelty and interest of the day's experiences.

On the following morning we paid another visit to the chief ministers of state, as Lord Elgin wished to make farther arrangements with reference to the delivery of the yacht, and to introduce Captains Barker and Osborn, and Commander Ward, in whose charge she had come out from England. The ceremony differed in no respect from that of the previous occasion, except that it took place in the daytime. The ministers were anxious to know the difference between a man-of-war and a yacht; and then there was some discussion as to the salute which should be fired by the Japanese, they having never, upon any previous occasion, saluted a foreign flag. The ministers took the opportunity of expressing, on behalf of the Tycoon, his regret at not being able to see Lord Elgin, but it was suggested that his excellency might have an audience with his son, a lad of thirteen years of age. This proposal Lord Elgin did not deem it expedient to accept.

We reached home just in time to receive the commissioners for luncheon. They expressed themselves extremely embarrassed at always arriving at our luncheon hour—"they really could not think of partaking of any to-day—it would seem so very much as if they had come for ham and Champagne." Lord Elgin, however, answered them that no such suspicion had ever entered his head; and that, unless the proper amount of ham and Champagne had been consumed, it would be impossible to proceed with the treaty. This argument seemed at once to decide them; and they had evidently fasted carefully, in order to a more thorough appreciation of the meal they pretended to repudiate. After luncheon we had no difficulty in getting through fifteen articles, by which Moriyama was the only sufferer, for he was engaged in making duplicate copies in Japanese and Dutch. One day Lord Elgin asked him whether he had nearly finished copying the treaty; but Moriyama was too good an interpreter to give a direct answer to any question in the presence of his superiors; so, turning to the commissioners, he asked them, "Has Moriyama nearly finished copying the treaty?" Upon which they gravely replied, after consultation with him, "No, Moriyama has not yet finished copying the treaty, but he is getting on with it as fast as he can." When an inferior in Japan is in conversation with a superior, the correct posture for the former is to rest his hands upon his knees and remain slightly stooping—practically, this is abbreviated into a rapid slipping of the hand down the thigh to the knee, a gesture which Moriyama used constantly to perform, accompanying it with a noisy inhalation of the breath, as if he had just sucked a sherry-cobbler through a quill, and was relishing it still.

But we made another acquaintance at Yedo even more noteworthy than Moriyama. He was popularly known as "the Scoundrel," but his real name was Tanjeram. This man appeared in our garden one evening, and astonished us all by speaking English without any perceptible accent, using very long words, and informed us that he was in the habit of taking lunar observations. He farther asserted that he had never been out of Japan in his life, and that he acquired his knowledge of the English language at a school at Yedo. This school he described as being attended by Japanese desirous of learning foreign languages, which they were taught by professors, who had qualified themselves by study for the purpose. With all our respect for the intelligence and advancement of the Japanese, this was rather more than we could accept, and we could gain no corroborative testimony on the subject, so that I have no doubt it was a pure piece of invention on the part of Tanjeram, who had evidently, by some accident or other, passed some years of his life in the United States. He stoutly denied that such was the case, and he spoke with a slight nasal twang, making use of expressions which he certainly must have acquired from a professor who had studied the "American" and not the English language. The expression of his face was totally different from that of any other Japanese I ever saw. There was a mixture of cunning and insolence in his manner foreign to the nature of his countrymen, and which indisputably proved that he had lived long enough abroad to substitute the manners of Western civilization for those of Japanese barbarism.

But, although we took leave to doubt the existence of professors of European languages at Yedo, there is no question about the advanced state of education, and its wide diffusion throughout the empire. Dutch is certainly taught at Yedo as well as at Nagasaki; and pupils who have studied the latest mechanical and scientific inventions at the latter place under the Dutch, come to the capital as teachers. Thus they are competent to manage their own steam-engines, and to navigate their own ships, working their course by observation. They are extremely sensitive at being supposed incapable of acquiring any branch of knowledge which is possessed by others, and have a very high estimate of their powers in this respect. This was amusingly illustrated in a discussion which took place as to the language which should hereafter be the medium of official correspondence. "Oh," said one of the commissioners, "you had better make English the official language; there is no telling how long it will be before you will be able to write a dispatch in Japanese; but give us five years, and we shall be quite competent to correspond with you in English." This affords a striking contrast to our experience at Tientsin, where we found such difficulty in inducing the Chinese to accept the English as the official language, even as a prospective arrangement—one, indeed, which I have little hope of ever seeing carried out; for, even if a Chinaman could be induced to study a foreign language, he is so utterly destitute by nature of the faculty of acquiring any tongue but his own that a lifetime would be spent in the vain attempt. During the whole period of my stay in China I did not meet a single native who could speak, read, and write English correctly.

In Japan, on the other hand, there is a rage for the acquisition of every description of knowledge. A Chinaman thinks that any study but that of the Confucian books is degrading, and treats every modern invention with an air of calm contempt. Probably he contends that the art has long been known in China; so that if you were to show him a railway, he would most likely say, "Hab got alo same that Pekin side, only two tim more chop chop can go."* A Japanese, on the other hand, is full of zeal and curiosity. He examines and asks questions about every thing within his reach, carefully noting the answers.

Père Charlevoix says that in the time of Xavier there were in the neighborhood of Miako four academies, at each of which education was afforded to between three and four thousand pupils, adding that, considerable as these numbers were, they were quite insignificant in comparison with the numbers instructed near the city of Bandone, and that such institutions were universal throughout the empire. Mr. Macfarlane, quoting from M. Meylan, a more recent authority, states that children of both sexes and of all ranks are invariably sent to rudimentary schools, where they learn to read and write, and are initiated into some knowledge of the history of their own country. To this extent, at least, it is considered necessary that the meanest peasant should be educated.

* *Anglicè*—We have got the same at Pekin, only it goes twice as quickly.

From this account, which was corroborated by all I could gather upon the subject, it will appear that a more widely-diffused system of national education exists in Japan than in our own country, and that in that respect, at all events, if in no other, they are decidedly in advance of us. Often in passing along the streets I heard the pleasant babble of children learning their lessons.

Closely connected with this subject is that of the literature of the country; but upon this head it was difficult to collect information—still more so to obtain books. Although book-stalls were numerous, and their contents were temptingly displayed toward the street, whenever we approached one a general scramble invariably took place to secure the contents. It was evident that a government order had been issued not to sell books to the strangers; and although our attendants used to pretend to assist us in procuring them, we used to discover them secretly abetting the shop-keepers. Once when I seized a great prize—a map of a province in the empire—it was snatched from me by an old lady who had the fear of government very vividly before her eyes, so that I only carried off a small fragment. Still, by soft speeches and perseverance, we managed to pick up a good many picture-

Coopers at Work (from a native drawing.)

books. One of these, illustrative of various trades in Japan, was a most interesting study. The preceding wood-cut gives some idea of the graphic character of the drawings. Most of the books which I obtained, written in Japanese, were of little use, as nobody could read them; but I procured one or two bulky volumes in the Chinese character. According to the Dutch authors, Japanese literature generally comprises works of science, history, biography, geography, travels, moral philosophy, natural history, poetry, the drama, and encyclopedias—a very goodly catalogue, if it be a correct one.

Besides the books containing nothing but pictures are works of fiction illustrated with wood-cuts, the engravings being made upon the same blocks with the type. It is said that recently the art of engraving on copper has been introduced.

Though ignorant of the art of painting in oils, the Japanese are skillful in the management of water-colors, and some of their col-

Group of Horses (from a native drawing).

ored prints are life-like and characteristic. They are generally in a regular sequence, and the thread of a story is to be followed throughout. I procured one book containing a series of sketches of groups of horses, in crayon, drawn with much spirit and artistic talent.

We may fairly presume that the Japanese are a reading people; and from all I could learn, the fair sex were not behind their lords in the improvement of their minds. Golownin bears testimony to this fact. "The Japanese," he says, "are extremely fond of reading. Even the common soldiers, when on duty, were continually engaged with books. This passion for literature, however, proved somewhat inconvenient to us, as they always read aloud in a tone of voice resembling singing." They are also almost as fond of writing notes to each other as if they rejoiced in the luxury of a penny-post. Although they have not made that important discovery, an organization does exist for the transmission of letters from one end of the empire to the other, of the most perfect description. The letter-carrier is always attended by a companion, to guard against the chances of sickness or accident delaying the regular postman. These men are constantly relieved, each stage being performed at their utmost speed. I once met one of these carrying his packet and dashing along with a vehemence which induced me to inquire what his errand could be. He was, however, alone: probably it is not considered necessary for town postmen to run in couples.

The Japanese write, like the Chinese, in columns, from the top to the bottom of the paper, beginning at the right-hand side. The character is less fantastic and far more running than the Chinese. There is, indeed, not the slightest similarity between the languages, the one being monosyllabic and the other polysyllabic. The Japanese words are often of unconscionable length, but the sounds are musical, and not difficult to imitate; whereas the Chinese words, though of one syllable, consist generally of a gulp or a grunt, not attainable by those whose ears have not become thoroughly demoralized by a long residence in the country. We learned more Japanese words in a week than we had of Chinese in a year; and in making a small, rough vocabulary, I found no difficulty in so allocating the letters of the English alphabet as to convey to my memory a fair representation of the sound I wished to recollect. In Chinese this is quite impossible. Klaproth says, in his *Asia Polyglotta*, that the Japanese language is so dissimilar from all known languages in structure, grammar, and every characteristic, that the nation who speak it must be a distinct race. It is impossible to see them and not to arrive at this conclusion, on other grounds besides the construction of their language. That they originally sprang from the same Mongol stock, the descendants of which now form a large proportion of the population of China, seems to be generally admitted; but the peopling of Japan was, in all probability, an event prior to the first Mongol invasion. Their features differ essentially from the Chinese type. Their noses are not so broad and flat, and their eyes are more prominent and not so oblique. Altogether, the cast of countenance is far more agreeable. Those of our party who had visited the South Sea Islands found in the Japanese many points of resemblance with the natives of that archipelago. It would be interesting to discover whether any similarity existed also in their language.

The student of Japanese will possess one great advantage over the victim condemned to the acquirement of the tongue of the Celestials, inasmuch as he starts with the benefit of an alphabet, or rather a syllabarium—an appendage to his language which a Chinaman despises. The Chinese character is, nevertheless, constantly to be seen on sign-boards and the walls of buildings. It is read by educated Japanese, but with a pronunciation which a Chinaman would find it difficult to understand. Nor does the character always represent to the Japanese mind the idea which it would convey to the natives of the Celestial Empire. The difference in pronunciation may be accounted for by the fact that the Japanese also attempt to render the Chinese sounds by means of their own alphabetic symbols. It would, indeed, appear that there are two distinct languages in vogue in Japan, called the Yomi and Kaye, of which the former is the national and popular tongue, and the latter Chinese, with a Japanese pronunciation. This is a subject, however, upon which our information is scanty; but with our present establishment of students at the new ports, we shall, ere long, have abundant light thrown upon this most interesting field of investigation. The student would do well to follow the example of the Japanese in one respect, and carry about with him a note-book. Every Japanese wears on a string round his waist a little portable inkstand: this is usually neatly lackered, and contains one pen, or rather brush, and a little water-tight compartment for ink: in his bosom are many sheets of paper, either separately or made into the form of a note-book. Our metallic note-books were always subjects of envy and curiosity, and the merits of India-rubber bands were duly appreciated.

We found, on the other hand, no less interest in examining the various uses to which they apply that most essential item in their wants—paper. It constituted the walls of our rooms and the fans that were in universal vogue; it was the wrapping of every purchase, and furnished the string with which it was afterward tied. In square pieces it was used as pocket-handkerchiefs, and, pressed together and lackered, it was worn as hats: it was of every consistency, thick, and coarse, and full of impurities, or thinner and more transparent than the finest tissue paper, but always wonderfully tough. As it is prepared from the bark of the mulberry-tree, this is not to be wondered at. The younger branches furnish the whitest paper. The process consists in boiling down the bark and straining it through a sieve, when it is mixed with rice, and the water is gradually drawn off. The pap-like substance is then spread carefully out into sheets, pressed between boards, and laid out in the sun to harden and dry. It is impossible to tear this paper against the grain; thin strips of it torn in the opposite direction, and rolled up, make tough and convenient pieces of string.

The more we saw of this singular and attractive people, the more we felt that though we, on our side, had much to exhibit which astonished and delighted them, we were the greatest gainers, for the investigation of their manufactures and appliances, at once so original and ingenious, proved a never-failing source of interest and amusement.

Japanese Artist (from a native drawing).

CHAPTER XXIX.

A Japanese Funeral.—Mode of dressing Ladies' Hair.—Excellence of Japanese Steel.—Carvings in Ivory.—Musical Instruments.—Japanese War-fans.—An Expedition into the Country.—A Religious Festival.—Elaborate Tattooing.—The Logos River.—The Temple of Dai Cheenara.—The Interior of the Temple.—A singular Postscript.—Sumptuary Laws.—Sinagawa.—Taxation in Japan.—The Character of the Legislation.—Japanese Management of Children.—Results of our Experience.—Japanese Love of Pleasure.—Effect of Contact with Europeans.

For the two or three days following our excursion to Hojee our time was fully occupied with the commissioners. Some of our guests, however, were enabled to employ themselves agreeably and profitably in riding about the town. Not far from our residence was a most tempting-looking temple, entered by a massive gateway at the end of an avenue which led to the base of a wooded hill on the summit of which the gables of the building appeared amid the foliage. Some enterprising explorers made an ineffectual attempt to visit this attractive-looking spot, but were refused admittance in a manner rather too peremptory and abrupt to be consistent with the uniform courtesy of the people generally. Upon this circumstance being mentioned to the commissioners, they were, as usual, profuse in their apologies, but begged us not to press the point, as the temple in question was sacred to the manes of defunct tycoons. This fact only stimulated our curiosity still farther, but we refrained from urging a request which seemed distasteful. On another occasion, some of our party were fortunate enough to witness a Japanese funeral. In consequence of the corpse being placed in a sitting posture, the shape of the coffin is more that of a sedan chair than an oblong case. It is preceded by servants and members of the establishment, and followed by priests and mourners in white, with norimons for the ladies, and policemen, as usual, to keep off the crowd. According to Siebold, the corpse is interred to funeral music, produced by striking copper basins.

We were so fortunate as to discover, not far from our abode, a small back street, which was an unfailing resource when time did not permit of an expedition into that part of the city which corresponds to the borough of London. Here were a quantity of

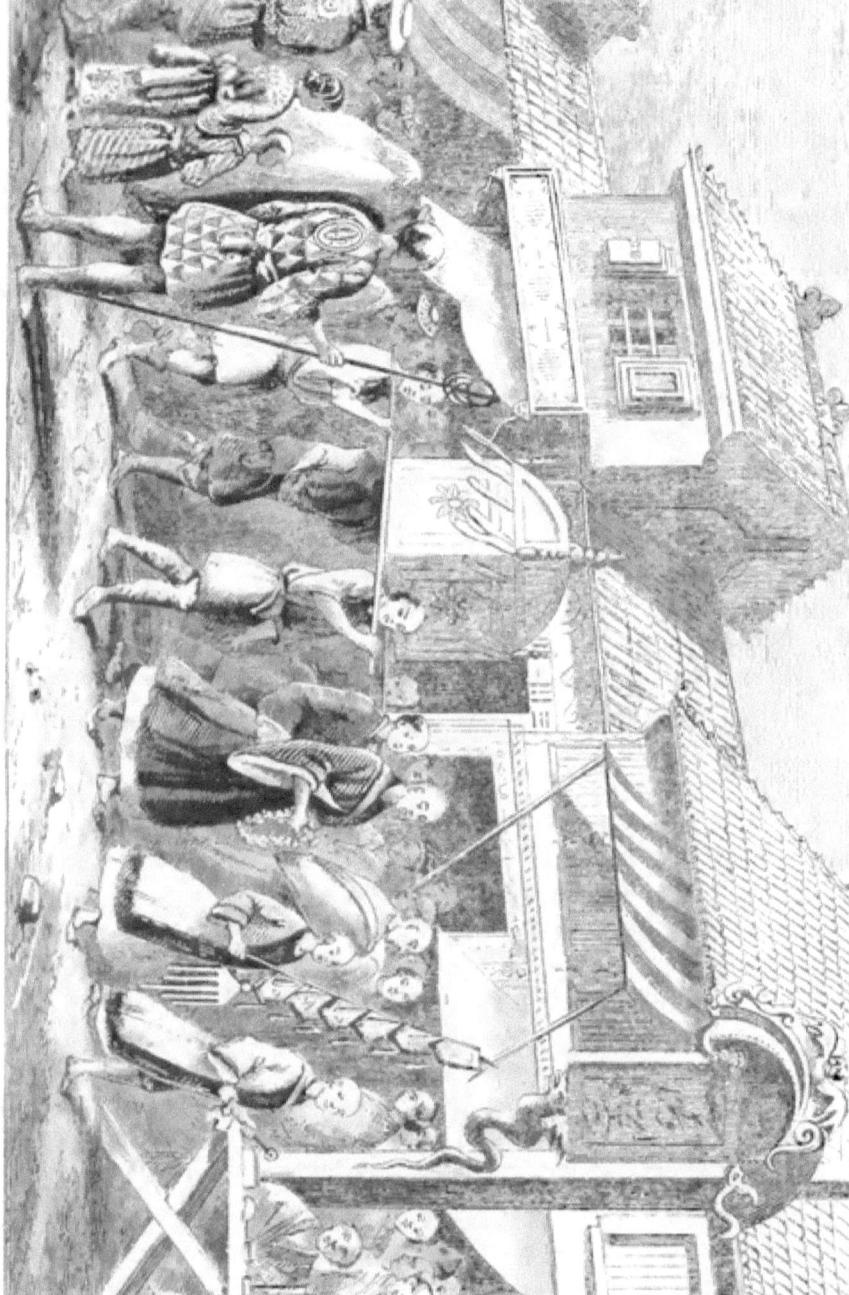

Japanese Funeral.

book-stalls, some shops containing very curious China, and a great variety of the peculiar manufactures of the country. The Japanese are a people plain and simple in their tastes, and, as a rule, eschewing ornaments. Those, however, in which the ladies indulge most freely are made of glass, in the fabrication of which into quaint devices the manufacturers are peculiarly expert. A favorite trick is to fill glass tubes of various shapes and patterns with colored fluids. These are frequently used as hair-pins. Sometimes there is a globe at the end, in which the liquid may be detected by the air-bubble as it glances in the raven tresses of a Japanese belle. Most of the women wear their hair somewhat in the style which was in vogue among ourselves forty or fifty years ago—the back-hair being massively arranged, and skewered in various directions with glass ornaments. The female attendants in the establishments of princes are alone allowed to wear their hair *à l'impératrice*. It is singular that while the Japanese have brought the manufacture of glass to such perfection in certain forms—as, for instance, the most exquisitely-shaped bottles, so light and fragile that they seem as though they were mere bubbles, of every shade of color, and beautifully enameled with devices—plate-glass is unknown among them. Their looking-glasses are circular pieces of steel, polished so highly as to answer all the purposes of a mirror, and usually elaborately ornamented on the back.

The ornaments worn by the men are almost exclusively confined to the handles of their swords. These are generally gold, or of a composite metal called syakfdo, consisting of gold and copper mixed with other metals, the effect of which is very beautiful. The device is generally the representation of some bird or animal, executed in the most perfect and finished style. In most cases the handles of the swords are covered with shagreen, upon which these ornaments are bound with silk cord. The scabbards are either of leather or wood, beautifully lackered, and the blades of steel of the rarest temper. I procured a pair for thirty dollars, which bore the edge of a razor; but the price was considered paltry; and a really good sword, such as, according to Fischer, can cut through a European sword without turning its edge, is of fabulous value. I afterward learned that Baron Gros had obtained some of the finest swords which were to be procured at Yedo, and had paid in proportion.

There can be no doubt that they have attained to the highest pitch of excellence in the art of tempering steel. Old Struys says of the manufacturers of swords in Japan: "They are grown famous in all the East for expert armorers, and temper steel better than the Chineezes, which far exceed the Europeans. Their swords are so well tempered that I have struck with one through an iron pin, of half an inch thick, without the least token of damage to the edge." At first we found great difficulty in persuading our attendants to procure us some swords to purchase; they even exhibited some reluctance to draw those they had on when informed that we wished to inspect them. There is some superstition connected with their sale to foreigners, as the exportation has heretofore been rigorously prohibited. Latterly, however, we completely overcame these scruples.

The same prohibition is laid upon the sale of gold, and this we did not find it so easy to remove. Indeed, ornaments of pure gold were excessively rare; but we were consoled by the charming little wood and ivory carvings, which are extensively used by the dandies of Japan as appendages to their pipes, just as those of this country tie bundles of charms or chatelaines to their watch-chains. Some of these combine, with the utmost delicacy of execution, a keen sense of the ludicrous, and often represent objects highly characteristic of the people and their manners. The carvings in ivory I preferred to any thing of the same description in China; they were the most expensive trifles which we discovered at Yedo. The pipes, to which these are attached by a silk cord, are worn buttoned on to the dress near the waist. The stem is generally composed of a reed, with a mouth-piece of brass or composite metal elaborately chased, and a bowl of the same material, but absurdly small to our Western notions. A pipe contains merely a whiff; a pinch of tobacco is rolled up to the size of a pea, and one long soothing inhalation completes the process: as in the East generally, the smoke is retained for some time in the lungs. The apparatus being constantly at hand, a Japanese

Croup from an Ivory Carving.

will smoke fifty such pipes in a morning. The tobacco is of a pale yellow color, not unlike Turkish, except in being cut more finely, and having a more delicate flavor. The best tobacco is grown in the territories of the Prince of Satsuma, and the neighborhood of Nagasaki. The plant was first introduced by the early Portuguese traders.

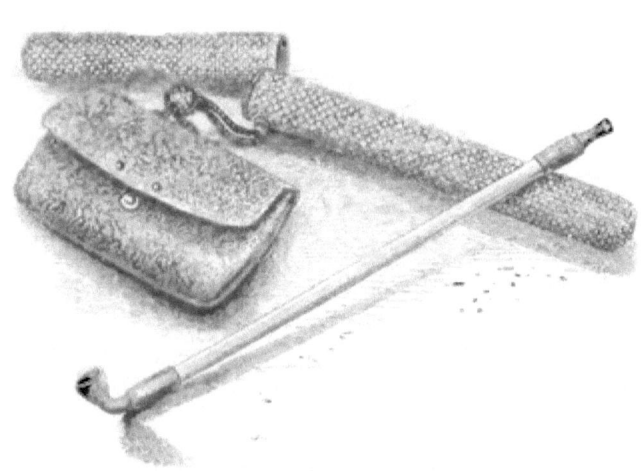

Japanese Pipe, Case, and Pouch.

Some of these shops were devoted to the sale of musical instruments, but they were somewhat cumbersome as curiosities. The most popular is the samsie or lute. It is played with a thin slip of wood, and is as necessary an accomplishment among the fair sex as the piano-forte is with us. Reed pipes, tomtoms, and flutes are also among the instruments we observed exhibited. Next door lived an old man, whose occupation consisted in the manufacture of bows and arrows, which are still used as offensive weapons in war. Some of the bows were prettily lackered.

A Samsie or Lute.

Perhaps, however, the most singular arm which the Japanese employ in the battle-field is the war-fan. This is a paper fan of a larger size than usual, the sheaths of which are made of iron, so that if, fatigued by a violent personal encounter, a warrior sits down for a moment to rest and cool himself, and is unexpectedly attacked, he immediately hits his enemy over the head with his fan. I endeavored to obtain one of these; but they were only made to order, and were not completed when we left Yedo. The pattern on the fan is the national emblem, a red sun on a black ground; but the process of fanning one's self with an iron fan can not be cooling. In strong contrast to these is a description of fan made of a substance so thin and transparent that it resembles gold-beater's skin; nothing can be conceived lighter or pleasanter to use. The fan is an inseparable part of a Japanese dress. It is his shelter from the sun, his note-book, and his plaything if it does not happen to be hot. Without it he is as much at a loss to know what to do with his hands as an Englishman is at an evening party without his hat. There is so great a variety that it would be quite an interesting occupation to take up the subject seriously and make a collection.

On the 24th of August we started on another riding expedition to the celebrated temple of Dai Cheenara, situated about ten miles from Yedo, toward Kanagawa. Our road, therefore, led in the opposite direction from that which we had followed upon the former occasion, and took us through the long western suburb that skirts the bay for a distance of five or six miles, first through the notorious quarter called Sinagawa which we saw to greater advantage on our return journey, then for half a league through Omogawa, and past a spot which was celebrated as the place for public executions; it was just on the outskirts of the town, in an aceldama where the grass was long and rank, and a monolith, eight or ten feet high, was surrounded by a stone bench, the victim's last seat. Generally criminals who have committed crimes worthy of death forestall the public executioner, and save themselves the disgrace by hara-kiri. The ordinary mode of execution is decapitation. Titsingh, however, says that in some cases the torture is prolonged as much as possible, and the skill of the executioner is tested by the number of wounds he can inflict without causing death.

A little beyond this disagreeable locality we come out upon

pleasant rice-fields and wide areas of cultivation, divided by rows of trees, which are occasionally grouped in clumps. The country is perfectly level, the road broad and good, and lined with trees; wayfarers are abundant, generally on foot, but sometimes in the basket-chairs peculiar to the middle classes. Even after the town has ceased houses are thickly dotted along the road. But our journey to-day is doubly interesting, because it happens to be a religious festival. The Japanese celebrate these about twice a month, upon each occasion to do honor to some special divinity or saint. One, indeed, is in honor of the devil, and originated in a dispute which for some time agitated the religious world in Japan as to the color of his satanic majesty. One sect maintained it was black, another white, another red, and another green. The Mikado, deprived of the assistance of an ecclesiastical court, determined the matter in a manner worthy his infallible pretensions. He declared that the devil was of all these four colors at will—a decision which carried conviction to the minds of all. This is a story told by Meylan. Siebold, as I have before said, denies that the Japanese believe in a devil at all, while, according to Kæmpfer, their only idea of him is in the likeness of a fox. It did not occur to me to make inquiries upon the subject.

Another celebrated festival is the Feast of Lamps. When this takes place, processions of boats, brilliantly illuminated, move about the harbor, and produce a striking effect. I have forgotten the name of the saint in whose honor the whole world was basking in the sun, doing nothing, when we went to Dai Cheenara, but the streets had never before seemed so crowded; flags waved from balconies, and strips of bright-colored cotton, covered with characters, fluttered from poles; the women wore flowers in their hair, and the men had more on than usual. Some, however, denied themselves the benefit of dress, apparently for the purpose of exhibiting the brilliant patterns in which their skins were tattooed. One man had a monster crab in the small of his back, and a pretty cottage on his chest. It is rather fashionable to have scarlet fishes playing sportively between your shoulders. The scarlet tattooing presents a very disgusting appearance. The skin looks as if it had been carefully peeled off into the required pattern. On a really well tattooed man there is not an inch of the body which does not form part of a pictorial representation. If the general effect is not agreeable, it is perfectly decent, for the skin

E E

ceases to look bare, or like skin at all; it rather resembles a harlequin's costume. It must be dreadful to feel that one can never undress again. Yet what anguish does the victim undergo in order to put himself into a permanent suit of red dye and gunpowder!

Of course, after we had completed a little more than half our journey, we stopped at a tea-house. The day was scorchingly hot. Riding in the sun on a lacker-saddle, without an umbrella, in the middle of August, is a process which makes one appreciate the merits of a tea-house. We find the coolest corner, stretch ourselves full-length on the soft mats, drink tea, eat fruit, smoke infinitesimal pipes, and get ourselves fanned into a comatose state by fair damsels, until the inexorable Tainoske tells us that the time is up, and that, if we are to see the temple, we must once more brave the rays of the Japanese sun. So we are again *en route*, and jog on till we reach the Logos River, a deep stream about fifty yards broad, and which is chiefly noteworthy because it is named by the treaty as the future limits of the rambles of the European community in this direction. Round every one of the new ports is a line of demarcation, beyond which it will not be permitted to Europeans to penetrate. This, as a general rule, comprises a radius of about twenty miles.

We were ferried across the Logos River, and found ourselves in the village of Kawasaki; after traversing which we are once more in the open fields, but our road has narrowed to a bridle-path, and it leads between neatly-clipped hedges, along the margin of purling streams; past more cottages with steep thatched roofs: sometimes these are double; a sort of hood is constructed above the regular roof, which has deep overhanging eaves that are formed into verandas. Here, as on the road to Hojee, the people love to bury themselves beneath creepers and flowering shrubs, but they do not neglect the essentials altogether. There are kitchen-gardens attached to every establishment, with vegetables, and fruit-trees, and orchards, where the pears are trained on trellises like grapes. At last we reach a spacious pile of building, which is surrounded by a ditch, and a massive wall surmounted by a paling, which is in its turn overshadowed by lofty trees.

The single street which composed the village was gay with flags and crowded with people; it led us straight up to the principal entrance to the temple, and the crowd thronged us as we pushed on, so that we were glad to get inside the gates, which were at once closed after us. But we were little better off here. The spacious court was filled with a dense crowd, who clustered on the broad flight of steps leading up to the temple.

In this court was a ponderous bell, swinging in a handsome belfry of carved wood, on a massive pedestal. In Japan the bells never have tongues or clappers, but are always struck from without by a piece of wood conveniently suspended. Near the principal flight of steps hung a large gong, while in the outer veranda were swinging paper lanterns, some of an oval shape, ten or twelve feet in length by about six in breadth, and others like truncated columns.

The building itself was in the form of a shed, with very deep verandas, slightly twisted gables, a steep roof, and substantial walls. The columns which supported the veranda were of wood, sheathed in copper at the base, while the capital was ornamented with carved representations of lions.

Within the building were more similar columns. The wooden panels which formed the ceiling were elaborately carved, and abundantly ornamented with colored lacker, covered with pretty landscapes. In the space, inclosed by a railing, at the farther end of which was the tiny image, were magnificent brass candelabras, elegantly shaped, so as to represent the sacred lotus. A profusion of brazen and tinsel ornaments almost concealed the minute god, seated on his table in the dim distance, in the centre of a screen which bore the imperial arms. In the middle of the apartment a priest in green robes was performing service; assisting him was another in yellow; while some more in red were present as by-standers.

A Japanese Divinity (from a native drawing).

The chief priest soon took an opportunity of coming up to Lord Elgin with the polite intention of doing the honors of the establishment, but our means of communication were too limited to enable us to extract very much information from him. He was a man of mild, amiable countenance, which did not, however, betoken a very high order of intellect.

Meantime the news had spread that beings of strange aspect were in the temple, and when we emerged from it the crowd had increased so much that we had some difficulty in remounting our steeds. By the time we reached Kawasaki the fatigues of the day were beginning to tell upon us, and we felt that a meal was necessary to the restoration of our prostrate energies; so we took possession of the upper story of a tea-house, from the balcony of which we could look over the garden, with its ponds, and ornamental rock-work, and artificial islands, and awaited the repast which it might please the cook to send us. We had faith in the never-failing rice and fish, and were not disappointed. To crown all, a breathless messenger appeared bearing a huge dish of pears—a present from the priest of the temple we had just left to Lord Elgin—a fact which was intimated in a note, which contained, by way of an inclosure, a piece of dried salt fish. This singular accompaniment forms a recognized part of Japanese correspondence. It is the postscript to the letter, and the burden of it is, "Happy those who never depart from the wisdom of their ancestors." In other words, "Remember we were originally a nation of fishermen; let us not now become effeminate and luxurious, but recognize in the inclosed slice of fish the emblem of our former occupation, and let it recall to us the necessity of abstinence and frugality." Nor is the moral thus intended to be conveyed a mere piece of barren sentiment. It is the embodiment of an active principle in Japan, and accounts for that Spartan simplicity and absence of display which characterizes the natives. The aristocracy, in their domestic arrangements, are said to practice the utmost economy, and, except in obedience to official requirements or the claims of conventional etiquette, to avoid as much as possible all ostentation or personal extravagance.

Alluding to this striking feature in the national character, Thunberg says: "It is in Japan, above all, that I have found that wise and useful economy, which must not be confounded with avarice, and to which I do not hesitate to accord the name of virtue, because the opposite is one of the most disgusting of vices. This virtue is practiced equally in the palace of the emperor and in the hut of the pauper. The latter knows how to content himself with the little he possesses, while the rich man does not dissipate his wealth in a profusion at once hurtful to the poor man and fatal to the general well-being of society. Hence arises a happy ignorance of those two scourges so common among our wise European nations, scarcity and high prices, words for which it would be difficult to find synonyms in the Japanese language."

The rigid code of sumptuary laws which obtains in Japan, proscribing certain luxuries, and defining minutely the style of dress to be worn by each grade in the social scale, singularly illustrates the powerful influence which this marked national characteristic exercises over the community at large.

It was late in the afternoon ere we re-entered Sinagawa, and the streets seemed more crowded than ever; but the most singular feature in this suburb is the houses of which it is composed, and the purpose to which they are dedicated. For at least a mile we rode between establishments organized on a most extensive scale. Deep verandas, approached by flights of steps, seemed literally packed with the unfortunate victims of a system which is one of the most singular characteristics of the country.* While, however, it is impossible either to extenuate or to justify the toleration by society, or the countenance by government, of an evil which must exercise so pernicious an influence upon all classes of the community, it is only fair to estimate at its true value the extent of that influence. It is impossible to compare the general social well-being of Japan with that of any other country, and not admit that, notwithstanding the existence of this peculiar development of immorality, it will gain by the contrast.

Universal testimony assures us that in their domestic relations the men are gentle and forbearing, the women obedient and virtuous. I will venture to assert that it is unknown in Japan for a man to knock down his wife and then stamp upon her, having previously driven her teeth down her throat with an iron bolt; perhaps because his wife has never, either by her intemperate habits, frail conduct, or abusive language, given him cause to do so; and so, in every department of crime, we have reason to believe that the amount of grave offenses committed against society is less in proportion to the population than that of other countries.

It is true that their criminal code is severe; but the best authorities on the subject state that there is an absolute impartiality in the infliction of punishment. The great principle upon which

* See Appendix.

their legal system is based is the administration of equal justice, and the punishment which comes home to the rich as well as to the poor man, with equal force, is death. This, then, is the penalty in most cases; but imprisonment and corporal punishment are also resorted to.

But it would appear from Rundall's notes* that the Japanese not only enjoy the advantage of a just and impartial administration of justice; they are still more highly privileged by exemption from taxation in the strict sense of that term. The territory of which the empire consists is vested entirely in the crown. The revenues are derived solely from the rents of the land, which vary according to the crops. There are assessors annually appointed, whose business it is to make the necessary valuation and adjust the respective rights of landlord and tenant. The land is held either directly under the crown, or under the princes or nobles who have been invested by the crown with territorial rights, and who, in return, pay rent, accompanied by the performance of certain feudal services. Tenants holding direct from the crown pay to the emperor's stewards four parts out of ten of the produce of the soil, whether of rice, corn, or pulse, reserving the residue for their own use. Such as hold under the princes pay six parts out of ten.

In cities a house-tax is levied. Houses, however, under ninety feet in length, are exempt from this impost. The same authority also states that, though sanguinary in principle, the laws are greatly modified in practice. All the Dutch writers unite in extolling the excellence of the native tribunals, and their competence to deal with criminal, and give satisfaction in civil causes. Kæmpfer says: "I would not have the reader suppose that the Japanese live entirely without laws; far from it; their laws and constitutions are excellent, and strictly observed." Our information upon this subject is, however, not sufficiently ample to enable us to decide upon the extent of influence exercised by the administration of justice in the prevention of crime. Macfarlane, quoting Dutch authorities, after describing the safety of the roads, states: "This result is not all produced by legislations, severe laws, and municipal and police regulations; the Japanese, as a proud people, have a contempt or abhorrence of cheating, pilfering, stealing, or robbing." There are doubtless many causes operating to produce

* RUNDALL'S *Kingdome of Japonica* (NOTES).

the same effect, but it would require a closer insight into the constitution of society and character of the people than we were able to obtain to specify what they are. We could only judge by the result. As locks and keys did not exist, our rooms were open to the incursions of any of the numerous attendants who swarmed about our lodgings, and, though we left the most tempting English curiosities constantly displayed, yet we never had to complain of a single article missing, even of the most trifling value.

I thought it singular that, during the whole period of our stay in Yedo, I should never have heard a scolding woman, or seen a disturbance in the streets, although, whenever I passed through them, they were densely crowded. Upon no single occasion, though children were numerous, did I ever see a child struck or otherwise maltreated. Thunberg, who passed many years in Japan, mentions the same fact; and in a description of the empire in the sixteenth century, from "The Firste Booke of Relations of Moderne States," Harleian MS. 6249, the following passage occurs: "They chastice their children with wordes onlye, and the' admonishe theire children when they are five yeares oulde, as yf the' weare oulde men." To our own knowledge, this mode of educating youth has been in existence for more than three centuries, and the result, according to universal testimony, is in the highest degree satisfactory. Kæmpfer, Charlevoix, and Titsingh agree in saying that the love, obedience, and reverence manifested by children toward their parents is unbounded; while the confidence placed by parents in their children is represented to be without limit. Parents select their children to be arbitrators in their disputes with others, and submit implicitly to their decisions; it is also a constant practice for parents to resign their state and property to a son when he shall have attained a suitable age, remaining for the rest of life dependent on him for support; and abuse of this trust is said to be unknown.

With the exception of one or two religious mendicants, I did not observe in this vast and populous city any beggars. Kæmpfer, however, records having seen them on the country roads. Deformed objects rarely met the eye; not a drunkard crossed our path, though from recent accounts revelers occasionally parade the streets of an evening. From the numbers of people marked with small-pox, that disease must rage with virulence in Japan, but the appalling sights so familiar in China are unknown there.

So, in our daily intercourse with the commissioners and our attendants, no instance occurred of any Japanese losing his temper, though it is impossible to suppose that, belonging to a race naturally proud and haughty, they were never tried. These were our experiences, but it does not by any means follow that those who live longer in the country may not have reason to change them. We left Japan thoroughly agreeing with old Kæmpfer, who, after a residence of many years there, thus sums up his estimate of the character of the people: "United and peaceable, taught to give due worship to the gods, due obedience to the laws, due submission to their superiors, due love and regard to their neighbors, civil, obliging, virtuous; in art and industry excelling all other nations; possessed of an excellent country, enriched by mutual trade and commerce among themselves; courageous, abundantly supplied with all the necessaries of life, and, withal, enjoying the fruits of peace and tranquillity." Xavier says as the result of his long missionary experience: "The Japanese, so far as I have been able to judge, surpass in virtue and in probity all other nations hitherto discovered. They are of a mild disposition, opposed to chicanery, covetous of honors, which they prefer to every thing. Poverty is very common among them, but in no way discreditable, although they endure it with difficulty."

It can not be denied that their good qualities are dimmed by sundry weaknesses, without which they would be more than human. They are notoriously vindictive, superstitious, haughty, exceedingly tenacious of their honor, and often cruel and unsparing in their mode of protecting or revenging it.

From what we saw of the habits of the people, we should be disposed to agree with those who charge them with being a somewhat frivolous and pleasure-loving race; but this has by no means the effect of rendering them effeminate. "The Japaneezes," says Struys, "are in general a very hardy people, and can endure any extremity of heat or cold, hunger or thirst, to a miracle. This they seem to come to by a hardy usage when young, for they always bathe their infants in cold water in rivers, and sometimes plunge them over head and ears in snow."

It would seem that, while physically robust, their minds are of a cultivated and dilettante order. They love not idleness, but occupations which are refined and congenial to their tastes. Commerce is considered by them a degrading pursuit; while literature and the fine arts, and scientific acquirements, are held in high estimation. It is a question whether that activity of mind and energy of character which finds expression in pleasure-parties and gala-days is not far preferable to the apathetic indifference of a Chinese mandarin, who thinks gayety undignified, active exercise a penance, and who only desires to be left alone with his pipes and women, rapt in contemplation of the Taoli, and the red tape peculiar to the Board of Rites. One result of this difference between the habits and mode of feeling of the two nations is undoubtedly this, that whereas the Chinese are steadily retrograding, and will, in all probability, continue to do so until the empire fall to pieces, the Japanese, if not actually in a state of progressive advancement, are in a condition to profit by the flood of light that is about to be poured in upon them, and to take advantage of those improvements and inventions which the Chinese regard with contemptuous scorn, but which the Japanese will, in all probability, when they come to know us better, be both able and anxious to adopt.

It will be a happy thing for Japan if this light is not followed by a very thick darkness. In the mean time, it would be contrary to all our experience of human nature to expect that the inauguration of our intercourse with a nation wedded to the habits and traditions of centuries, coming for the first time into contact with a civilization so different from its own, will be unattended with difficulty.

CHAPTER XXX.

Population of Yedo.—The Nipon Bas.—The Quanon Temple.—A Fair.—An Aviary.—A singular Tableau.—Theatrical Representations.—Toy-shops.—Astronomical System.—Mountain Pilgrims.—Japanese Wrestlers.—A conjuring Exhibition.—The Butterfly Trick.—The Commissioners at a Dinner-party.—After-dinner Enthusiasm.—Presents to the Mission.—Capacious Dressing-gowns.—Last Night in Yedo.

THERE remained yet one section of the city unvisited. The whole of the eastern quarter, as distant from our abode as Blackwall is from Chelsea, was still a *terra incognita*. There was a celebrated temple to be seen here, and the far-famed Nipon Bas to be traversed in reaching it. This ride, taken in connection with our previously acquired knowledge of the extent of the town in the opposite direction, gave us some idea of the vastness of this gigantic city. It is difficult to form an estimate of the population it contains, as the people are more closely packed in some parts than in Western cities; while in the large area occupied by the princes' quarter, the population must be comparatively thin. Upon this occasion we rode at a fast walk for two consecutive hours between dense masses of people. We had done so the day before along the continuation of the same street in the opposite direction. Kæmpfer, who visited Yedo during the early part of the last century, confirms our impressions upon the subject. "Yedo," he says, "properly the capital of the whole empire, and the seat of the secular monarch, is so large that I may venture to say that it is the biggest town known. Thus much I can affirm from my own certain knowledge, that we were one whole day riding a moderate pace from Sinagawa, where the suburb begins, along the chief street, which goes across, a little irregularly indeed, to the end of the town."

Golownin has made a rather wild estimate of the population at 8,000,000. This is a statement worthy of Père Huc. Don Rodrigo de Vivero y Velasco, on the other hand, puts it at 700,000: but two hundred and fifty years have elapsed since the visit of the Spaniard. The present population would, in all probability, be found to exceed two millions. Yedo is built upon the banks of the Todagawa, at the point where that river debouches into the head of the Bay of Yedo. The principal part of the city is situated on the right bank. The river, expanding as it nears the sea, is, at a point at which it has attained a considerable breadth, spanned by the Nipon Bas, a bridge of enormous length, built on piles. It is notorious as the Hyde Park Corner of Japan—the point from which all the mile-stones throughout the empire are numbered. Crossing it, we gradually emerged from the more densely crowded streets, and found ourselves at last in a lane which presented all the appearance of a fair. Booths on each side displayed an infinite variety of toys, women's ornaments, prints, and playthings of every description. Crowds of idle loungers thronged the thoroughfare, at the end of which we could discern the massive proportions of the temple rising among the trees, and towering above them and the peaked roofs of a five-storied pagoda. It was dedicated to Quanon, a popular divinity in Japan, though of Buddhist extraction, and imported from China. The most celebrated temple in honor of this deity is at Miako.

Passing under an entrance archway, the shops on each side were replaced by an avenue of handsome trees. This terminated in an open space which was densely crowded, as was the broad flight of steps leading up to the veranda. We heard a good deal of hooting and yelling, but it was not accompanied by pelting or other marks of ill-will, and was probably the result of excitement and exuberant spirits on the part of the more juvenile and least reputable part of the mob. They were always sufficiently civil to leave a small vacant space immediately round us. As we stood at the top of the steps, and looked down upon the sea of upturned faces gazing at us, I doubted whether the spectacle which we presented was as striking to them as their appearance was to us.

The interior of this temple did not differ materially from those we had already visited. It was the oldest and most cobwebby, and therefore, in an ecclesiastical point of view, the most respectable. The paper lanterns were more monstrous—some of them were at least twenty feet in height—I should think double that in circumference, and covered with characters. The temple was decorated with numerous pictorial representations; among others were depicted scenes of by no means a religious character, the originals of which were to be found in a neighboring quarter, to which I have already alluded as the least-reputable part of the city. We failed to perceive the connection between them and the holy rites to which the temple was dedicated.

In the gardens surrounding the building we had a still more striking illustration of this blending of the sacred with the profane. In all the grosser forms of superstition, it seems essential to the very existence of the religion that it should contain a strong infusion of the carnal and material element. So, while the priest inside was propitiating the many-armed deity in whose image he saw but the representation of a divine being, the congregation without were paying their devotions to peep-shows and pleasure-booths, which had been erected for their benefit in the temple-grounds.

These we now proceeded to explore. As we approached them, the tapping of tom-toms and shrill whistle of pipes gave token of gayety and merry-making. The scene did not differ materially from an English fair. Aunt Sally, under divers modifications, seems to be a relative of the universe. It is worthy of remark, however, that gambling is not allowed by the government, or even games of cards. Here were people throwing sticks at marks, shooting arrows at so much a shot, looking into peep-shows through small slits in the canvas, or lounging through flower-booths. There was, indeed, a better show of flowers here, and more curious specimens of plants, than we had seen at Hojee; the gardens were more extensive and tastefully laid out, particular localities being set apart for grandees, from which the vulgar herd are excluded by cords stretched across the entrance.

To one of these we retired for rest and tea; then we proceeded to inspect an aviary which contained an extensive collection of birds interesting to the ornithologist. Unfortunately, my knowledge of the subject does not warrant my venturing to describe them. There were pheasants, green pigeons, rice-birds, and tiny little flutterers, somewhat resembling avadavats. But the greater part were species with which I was not familiar.

One young bird, apparently moulting, and the most hideous specimen of the feathered tribe I had ever seen, I in vain endeavored to purchase. It made a noise corresponding to its disgusting personal appearance—a wheezing, spasmodic choke, as if it was in the last stage of suffocation, or subject to violent asthmatic attacks. They assured me it grew to a monstrous size, and would not hear of selling it for less than thirty dollars. It seemed scarcely worth while to pay so much for the privilege of having an asthmathic companion saddled upon one for the remainder of the voyage. Lord Elgin, however, purchased a pair of very beautiful green pigeons, both of which arrived safely in this country. We now went to examine the shows in the fair. The discordant jangle of musical instruments is resorted to in Japan, as in England, to entice the passers-by into entering the mysterious precincts. We could not resist the inducement, the ever-ready Tainoske, as usual, settling all our pecuniary liabilities.

Immediately on entering, a gorgeously decorated junk, almost the size of nature, gayly freighted with a pleasure-party, was sailing over an ocean so violently agitated that only one result could be anticipated in real life; but the junk was merely a sort of scene to conceal the exhibition behind it. This consisted of a series of groups of figures carved in wood the size of life, and as cleverly colored as Madame Tussaud's wax-works. No. 1 was a group of old men, in which decrepitude and senility of countenance were admirably portrayed. No. 2, a group of young Japanese Hebes dressing, and a country clodhopper rooted to the spot in ecstasy at the contemplation of their charms. The humor of this tableau consisted in an appearance of unconsciousness on the part of the ladies. No. 3 was a princess in magnificent array, seated on a dais, watching her maids of honor going through divers gymnastic performances: one of them was in a position more agile than graceful, her occupation being, while extended on her back, to keep a ball dancing in the air on the soles of her feet. The attitudes, which were extremely difficult to represent correctly in wood-carving, were executed with wonderful spirit and truth to nature. No. 4 was a group of men quarreling over sakee; the fragments of the cups, dashed to pieces in their anger, lay strewn about. Upon the countenances of two of the men the expression of ungovernable rage was well depicted. The other was leaning back and laughing immoderately. No. 5 was a group of women bathing in the sea: one of them had been caught in the folds of a cuttle-fish; the others, in alarm, were escaping, leaving their companion to her fate. The cuttle-fish was represented on a huge scale, its eyes, eyelids, and mouth being made to move simultaneously by a man inside the head.

I have given a somewhat detailed account of this "show," as it displayed a good deal of artistic talent. The subjects were characteristic, and it is a fair sample of the perfection at which the Japanese have arrived even in the lowest walks of art.

We had made arrangements to go some night "nayboen" to witness some of their theatrical performances: unfortunately, with many other projects, we were compelled to abandon this one for want of time. From all we could learn, however, we did not miss much. The theatres differ from those in China in being more commodiously arranged, as the spectators are all seated, and there is some attempt at stage scenery. Boys perform the part of women, and, according to Thunberg, there are seldom more than two actors on the stage at the same time. He states the subjects of their representations to be generally deeds of heroism, the loves of their gods and of their heroes, expressed in verse. There is a drop-scene as with us.

Japanese Gymnastics (from a native drawing).

We examined the toy-shops on our way back, and bought wonderful Jacks-in-the-box; representations of animals, beautifully executed in straw; models of norimons and Japanese houses, as neatly finished as Swiss models; figures, some of them more humorous than decent, carved in wood; little porcelain figures, whose heads wagged and tongues shot out unexpectedly; tortoises, whose head, legs, and tail were in perpetual motion; ludicrous picture-books, grotesque masks and sham head-dresses of both sexes. Enough absurd contrivances were here exhibited to create a revolution in the nurseries of England. When we got back into the business part of the town, we stopped at a watchmaker's to buy jewelry and clocks: the former consisted chiefly of the sword ornaments already described, but the latter were of various descriptions, some constructed on European models, others fashioned upon a principle peculiar to Japan, and supposed to be more convenient for the registration of the singular division of their time.

The twenty-four hours are divided in Japan into twelve periods

Japanese Astronomers (from a native drawing).

of time, six of which are appropriated to darkness and six to the light. The day being calculated from sunrise to sunset, there is a necessary variation in the length of the six day and six night hours, the latter being the longest in winter, the former in summer. The clocks are altered periodically to suit the seasons of the year. As I never succeeded in comprehending the system by which these hours are numbered, I shall not venture upon any attempt at explanation. Some of the old Dutchmen have, however, mastered the mystery, and the reader, curious in the Japanese division of time, can consult Kæmpfer or Siebold. Their whole chronological system is in the highest degree complicated; one set of cycles is fixed arbitrarily by the mikado, another depends upon the length of his reign; while a third, called the astronomical cycle, is a wonderful combination of the "ten elements" with the twelve signs of the zodiac.

We returned home by a different route, passing one quarter, dedicated to the sale of china, at which we would fain have stopped. The shops were upon a more extensive scale, and more abundantly supplied than any we had yet seen. Unfortunately, the commissioners were waiting for us, so we pushed on, passing into the outer inclosure of the citadel through an archway, the buttresses of which were composed of gigantic blocks of stone.

We returned home highly gratified by our visit to the Quanon temple; altogether, had we been Japanese, we could scarcely have been more assiduous in making pilgrimages to holy places. Among them such journeys are acts of the highest merit. There is the pilgrimage which it is incumbent upon every Japanese to perform once in his life, while the pious perform it annually. I

Pilgrims ascending a Mountain (from a native drawing).

regretted that the undertaking must fall to the lot of some future explorer. It is to the shrine of the sun-goddess, Ten-sio-dai-zin, the patron divinity of Japan, and is situated at Isye, her supposed birthplace. Another very favorite act of devotion, and one in which some enterprising Englishman will doubtless, ere long, participate, is the ascent of the celebrated Fusi-yama, the "Matchless Mountain," the Mount Meru of Japan. The ascent is said to occupy three days. Its rugged sides are always inhabited by a sect of mountain priests, called Jemmabos. Their daughters, according to Kæmpfer, a beautiful race, are among the few beggars to be met with in the country. Their occupation is unhappily not confined to begging, and their parents are supported on the contributions of the licentious, as well as on the alms of the pious.

Another mendicant sect are the Fekis, an order of the blind, so named after their founder, a rebel prince. But, while Fusi-yama is regarded as the object of religious veneration, it is no less admired for its scenic beauty, its striking form, great elevation, and volcanic character, and has made a deep impression on the artistic mind of Japan. It forms the background of almost every picture, and is a favorite device on lacker and china; sometimes covered with snow, at others in a state of eruption, its appearance during that terrific natural convulsion having been handed down by tradition.

From an account given in the Chinese Repository, it would appear that the last eruption took place in 1707, on the night of the 23d day of the 11th moon, when "two violent shocks of an earthquake were felt. Mount Fusi opened, vomited flames, and hurled cinders to the distance of ten leagues. Next day the eruption ceased, but it was revived with greater violence on the 25th and 26th. Enormous masses of rock, sand reddened by heat, and an immense quantity of ashes, covered all the neighboring plateau. The ashes were driven to a great distance, and fell several inches thick at Yedo."

As Lord Elgin was desirous of seeing some of the national sports and amusements, it had been arranged with the commissioners that they should come to dine with us, and that previous to the entertainment some wrestlers, top-spinners, and jugglers should exhibit for the benefit of our own party, and a number of officers who were to come on shore expressly to witness the performances. Unfortunately, through some mistake, neither the top-spinners nor wrestlers made their appearance. Mr. Hewsken, who had seen both, pronounced the exhibition of the latter to be somewhat disgusting. From the detailed description contained in the account of the American expedition to Japan, the sight must resemble a human bull-fight. The wrestlers are described

Japanese Wrestlers (from a native drawing).

as "so immense in flesh that they appeared to have lost their distinctive features, and seemed only masses of fat. Their eyes were barely visible through a long perspective of socket; the prominence of their noses was lost in the puffiness of their bloated cheeks, and their heads were almost directly set upon their bodies, with only folds of flesh where the neck and chin are usually formed. Their great size, however, was more owing to the development of muscle than to the mere deposition of fat; for, although they were evidently well fed, they were not the less well exercised, and capable of great feats of strength."

Under these circumstances it was perhaps scarcely to be regretted that we were not favored with these gentlemen's company. The top-spinners Mr. Hewsken described as most dexterous in their management of this popular plaything, one great achievement being to spin it along a string as though it were dancing a tight-rope.

We were, however, not disappointed by the juggler; he arrived late in the afternoon with attendants, wearing the apparatus indicative of his calling, and proceeded to convert Lord Elgin's sitting-room into a theatre for his operations. The spectators were ranged on seats in the garden. The conjuror was a venerable old man with a keen eye, a handsome intelligent face, and a long gray beard, the only instance I saw in the country of a countenance so adorned. His dress was very similar to that usually worn by the magicians of Egypt, and was well calculated to increase his imposing aspect. Its ample folds and flowing sleeves, moreover, afforded him many facilities in the exercise of his sleights of hand. Those tricks which were dependent merely on prestidigitation were certainly not superior to the ordinary tricks of conjurors in other countries. He produced inexhaustible substances out of very shallow boxes, which became unaccountably full and empty, and magically converted a small quantity of cotton which he had tapped into an egg upon his fan into a number of very substantial umbrellas; but these were the mere tricks of the trade, the excellence of which could best be appreciated by professional artists. That about which there was no trick, but which struck us as exhibiting the most singular display of skill, was the famous performance with artificial butterflies. These were made in the simplest manner. A sheet of paper torn into slips supplied all the materials. By tearing these again into small oblong pieces, and twisting them in the centre, they were made roughly to represent the body and two wings. Two of these impromptu butterflies were then puffed into the air, and kept in suspense there by the action of the fan beneath them. This required to be most carefully and scientifically applied, so as not only to prevent their separating, but to guide their motions in any required direction. Now they would flutter aloft as though chasing each other in playful dalliance, at one moment twine together, at another so far apart that it seemed a mystery how the same fan could act upon both. Then they would settle together upon the leaf of a neighboring shrub, or, more curious still, alight gently on the edge of the fan itself. The intense attention which this performance required on the part of the operator proved that, though to the spectators the matter seemed easy enough, it called forth the exercise of all the faculties, and involved, no doubt, a long course of practice before proficiency could be attained.

During the whole period of his performances, the wizard, after the manner of that fraternity, never ceased talking; and, to judge by the merriment he excited among the commissioners, and the extent to which Higo was tickled, his remarks must have been of a highly facetious character, though he maintained himself the most imperturbable gravity throughout.

When the entertainment was over we adjourned to dinner. As this was a more formidable meal than those luncheons at which the commissioners had been in the habit of assisting, they addressed themselves to it with becoming solemnity, partaking steadily of every thing that was offered to them, and mixing up the most incongruous articles of food in a manner which was somewhat distressing, but difficult always to prevent. On the whole, they fed more like Christians than any other unchristian nation I have ever seen, constantly glancing at us slyly out of the corners of their eyes to see what we were eating, and how we were doing it. At last the final act was concluded, and Lord Elgin informed the commissioners that, it being the habit among loyal Englishmen to drink the health of their sovereign, he was now about to propose that toast. This was evidently a custom entirely new to them; and they had scarcely had time to comprehend its meaning before their ears were startled by the noisy "honors" with which it was immediately followed. Quickly taking their cue, however, the three times three had not been rung out before it was lustily joined in by our guests. The next toast was the health of his majesty the Tycoon, which was no less uproariously responded to, the commissioners by this time having arrived at a pitch of enthusiasm and Champagne which made them enter warmly into the proceedings of the evening. "When you in the West want to honor a person especially, you roar and shout after your meals. It was a curious custom, but they understood it now." Indeed, to prove it, Sina-nono-kami, a very grave old man, during a dead pause in the conversation, suddenly started to his feet and emitted a stentorian cheer, after which he sat solemnly down, the effect on the rest of the company being to produce an irresistible shout of laughter.

But, though Sina-nono made a slight mistake upon this occasion, it was worthy of remark how easily our guests seemed to fall into our ways, and how quickly they adapted themselves to them. It very soon occurred to them that some sort of acknowledgment was due from them, which they begged to express; and then Lord

Elgin's health was drunk, and their own healths, and, by the time dinner was over, they had evidently come to the conclusion that the dinners and customs of the English were not devoid of merit.

As the period of our departure from Yedo was approaching, the emperor had sent Lord Elgin and the members of the mission a number of presents. These were all displayed in a room at the back of the temple, and thither we repaired after dinner to inspect them. The handsomest article was a group of storks, beautifully worked in silver, about eighteen inches in height, and of exquisite design. This was presented to his excellency. To each of us was given a number of rolls of silk. These were all spread out upon trays, and differed only in pattern. They were in strips about three yards in length and one in width, useless, therefore, for any practical purpose.

Their chief merit consisted in the associations connected with their manufacture. In Japan, distinguished culprits are not sent to a reformatory to make mats, but are banished to an island by themselves, where they fabricate silks. To enjoy this privilege, they must, however, be nobles—exiled probably for political offenses—as, according to the criminal code, it is affirmed that justice is meted out equally to the prince and the peasant.

However that may be, these silks were woven by nobles banished to the island of Fatsizio. No man below a certain rank is, in consequence, allowed to wear them, or even to have them in their houses, so that they are not to be purchased in shops. Some of the patterns were remarkably neat and tasteful; others were somewhat gaudy. The texture of the silk itself was most substantial, and, from its appearance, I should imagine, durable.

Commander Ward, who brought out the yacht, was presented with a very handsome china bowl, curiously lackered inside, and a lackered cabinet very highly finished. But the most singular item in the list of presents was the dressing-gowns or robes of state, for they seemed indiscriminately applied to both purposes. Lord Elgin was overwhelmed with about thirty of these, each one occupying as much space as a large German duvet, and containing an equal amount of warmth. We found the deck of the Furious piled with these most inconvenient articles of attire when we subsequently went on board of her, the sight of which, with the thermometer at 80°, was the reverse of refreshing; while their enormous dimensions occupied half the quarter-deck, and threatened to produce serious effects upon the mind of the first lieutenant. The lining consisted of silk wadding, a discovery we made in ripping them open to take it out, as in no other way was it possible to stow away such bulky additions to one's wardrobe. The wadding proved most serviceable in packing egg-shell china.

Lord Elgin, not having been supplied with any suitable presents to bestow in return for this manifestation of good-will on the part of his majesty, was compelled to make a selection from the ship's stores of the Furious, of which he requested the acceptance of the commissioners. They seemed perfectly satisfied with the flannel, blue cloth, soap, and chocolate, which was abundantly pressed upon them, and more especially appreciated the addition of some rifles and carbines.

It was with no little reluctance that we parted late in the evening; it was our last night in Yedo. We looked forward with horror to a return to that empire, the reverse of celestial, with which so many disagreeable associations were connected, and looked back with regret on the few but happy days we had passed in the capital of Japan. The life of a traveler is a succession of such experiences; he has long since ceased to growl at them, for they point the moral of his *metier*, and furnish him with a philosophy which should avail him at all times and in all lands, even in that retirement to which he will probably be doomed on his return to his own country.

Travelers in a Snow-storm (from a native drawing).

CHAPTER XXXI.

Settling-day.—Japanese Currency.—Gold and silver Coins.—The Currency Difficulty.—Japanese Packing.—Signing of the Treaty.—Death of the Tycoon "Nayboen."—Probable Cause of his Death.—Profound Secrecy observed.—Evacuation of our Lodgings.—Presentation of the Yacht.—Parting Scenes.

The 26th of August was the day fixed for the signing of the treaty. On that day two months before, the Treaty of Tientsin had been signed under very different circumstances.

From the earliest hour of the morning our abode was a scene of turmoil and bustle. The day's programme was so extensive, it seemed quite hopeless to get through it. The hubbub in the apartment assigned to our Japanese retinue was so constant that I went to investigate the cause. Here were collected tradesmen who had all come to have their "little bills" settled under government auspices; visitors who came to take a last look at the English strangers; many faces familiar to us as attendants on sundry expeditions; our old servants and spies; and presiding over all, a functionary appointed by the lieutenant governor to superintend arrangements, settle disputes should any arise, and report upon all matters connected with the foreigners.

An amount of tea and tobacco was being consumed sufficient to fumigate a seventy-four, and float her afterward. Piled up in corners were Japanese costumes ordered by one gentleman; tethered opposite were two little Japanese dogs ordered by another. Stacked against the wall were a number of swords, heaped near them a quantity of books, articles which it was impossible to get the first day, but which were coming in readily enough now.

Unfortunately all these had to be paid for. The settling of these formidable accounts loomed in prospect, all the more dreadful from the solemnity of the process. Two old Japanese, senior wranglers probably of their year, with corrugated foreheads and countenances betokening unlimited sagacity, stalked gravely in, with attendants carrying balances, scales, weights, pens, ink, and paper, and seated themselves in the centre of the dining-room. Then approached tremblingly the shop-keeper and the victim who was to pay him. The latter had a strong presentiment that all the dollars in his possession, nay, even the entire amount of the handsome annual income he enjoyed, in consideration of the valuable services he was rendering his country in these distant regions, would be insufficient to meet the terrific expenditure he had been induced to incur in this seductive city. Anxiously he emptied his bag of dollars into one scale of the balance. The silver itzibus in the other kicked the beam. Moment of intense relief! he remained the happy possessor of two dollars, having, it must be premised, previously borrowed as much from all his neighbors as they could possibly spare. There was very little discussion over the settlement. The officials came provided with an exact list furnished by the shopkeepers; they knew how much each of us owed the moment we gave our names. The amount had been added up. There was no discrepancy in our accounts; the right number of itzibus were in the balance; nothing remained but to weigh our dollars against them. Then the itzibus were handed to the shopkeepers, and the dollars retained by the government.

The currency of the country consists of a great variety of gold, silver, and copper coins. These are all specified at great length in Thunberg, but our observation does not quite agree with his information on the subject. The largest gold coin known is the obang, a most inconvenient circulating medium, as it is nearly six inches in length and three inches and a half in breadth. I did not see a specimen of this unwieldy piece of gold. It is estimated in value at £20 sterling, but is not in common use. The gold coin in ordinary circulation is the cobang: it is about two inches and a half in length, and an inch and a quarter wide. Its extreme thinness, however, diminishes its value; it is intrinsically worth £1 10s. Although I saw this coin, I was unfortunate in not being able to procure one. We found the greatest difficulty in obtaining specimens of the currency of the country, and I came away at last the possessor of a solitary itzibu. These are either of gold or silver: the gold itzibu is a small oblong piece of money, intrinsically worth about seven and sixpence. The intrinsic value of the gold half-itzibu, which is not too large to convert into a shirt-stud, is about one and tenpence.

I have spoken of the intrinsic value of these coins, because by the treaty our gold should pass in Japan for its corresponding weight in Japanese gold; but inasmuch as it is not nearly so pure as that of Japan, there must always be a difference between its actual and intrinsic value. The value of silver in Japan is as nearly as possible the same as it is with us. The silver itzibus, against which our dollars were weighed, were worth rather more than a shilling apiece. These are divided into half and quarter itzibus, and at last we descend to the lowest medium, copper and iron cash. Most of these coins have the stamp of the mint upon them, consisting of some Japanese characters, as well as the print of flowers, like *fleurs-de-lis* and other devices.

The dollars which we paid in lieu of this money, together with all the foreign coin that has entered the government treasury since the signing of the treaty, have been melted down and coined into a new currency, the circulation of which, I regret to observe by the last accounts from Japan, the government, in opposition to the spirit of the treaty, has endeavored to confine to commercial transactions with foreigners. It was to avoid the inconveniences arising out of the former system that the currency clause was inserted in the treaty, by which it is stipulated that "all foreign coin shall be current in Japan, and shall pass for its corresponding weight in Japanese coin of the same description. British and Japanese subjects may freely use foreign or Japanese coin in making payment to each other." By the term Japanese coin was intended the then existing currency of the empire. Instead of accepting this as the meaning of the clause, however, the Japanese government has issued a new coin called a nichon, which is intrinsically worth about, and is declared current at, half a dollar: it is not allowed, however, to pass current among the people, and the Japanese merchant is consequently compelled to take them to the government treasury, where he is obliged to receive one old itzibu, worth about one shilling and twopence, in exchange for two nichons, worth four and twopence. It is evident that this arrangement must operate as an actual bar to trade. The motives which may have induced the government to adopt it I shall consider presently. Meantime we may be thankful that our own account is settled, and it only now behooves us to pack up our purchases.

We have had gigantic deal cases ordered some days back, and the skill of Japanese carpenters has been displayed in the finish and solid workmanship of our boxes; but it is a serious question whether that mountain of lacker and those pyramids of china can be disposed of in their recesses. We have dreadful visions of unpacking them at some future day, and finding all that delicate egg-shell, those charming devices, which are to be the wonder and delight of our friends at home, crushed into infinitesimal atoms. Fortunately, every piece of china has a little box to itself, the lid of which fits to perfection, and the contents have been so carefully swathed in cotton by the shopkeeper that we don't venture to open them. Every piece of lacker has been similarly cared for, and we put a blind trust in the Japanese packers, and stow away our fragile purchases hopefully amid a universal hammering, and bargaining, and settling, and packing, until at last we know that the luncheon hour has stolen upon us by the opportune arrival of the commissioners, who are much amused at the apparent confusion which reigns every where.

The signing of the treaty was a most solemn and serious operation, inasmuch as there were copies made in Dutch, Japanese, and English, of which each were in triplicate, and each required the signatures of Lord Elgin and the six commissioners, besides sundry additional clauses to be signed separately; no fewer than eighty-four signatures had to be appended. Some of the commissioners were, moreover, very particular in making pretty signatures, and painted away at the hieroglyphics which represented their names with evident care and anxiety. Others, friend Higo, for instance, dashed away with his brush, perfectly regardless of the opinion which people in England might form of his handwriting. The process of sealing, unknown to them, created a good deal of interest and curiosity; and afterward, when Lord Elgin proposed an interchange of pens, he having purposely made use of six different ones, the admiral appropriately remarked that he gladly availed himself of this opportunity of inaugurating the interchange of the products of the two countries, which he trusted might ever be marked with that interchange of good feeling which had characterized our mutual interchange hitherto.

Then came Moriyama's turn to receive those compliments which his skill and ability amply justified. He had made a copy of the treaty in Dutch, the caligraphy of which would have been a credit to a Dutch writing-master; and he smirked and smiled like a bashful young lady on having his performance eulogized. By this time the ceremony was concluded, and the treaty had been ratified in a loving cup, in anticipation of that future day when it should be more formally recognized by our respective sovereigns. We found that a grand banquet had been provided for us by the emperor, who sent Lord Elgin a great many civil speeches, expressed in the warmest terms his regret at never having been able to receive him, and wished him a brilliant career, and future success and prosperity.

Fortunately we were spared, at the time, that shock which the nerves of the susceptible reader will sustain, when he learns that his majesty the Tycoon had taken his departure "nayboen" from the domestic and political troubles of this weary world about the period of our arrival in Yedo, and was now in the realm of the kamis, little heedful, probably, of the affairs of his late temporal kingdom, and rapt in the contemplation of "Xim which is the principle of every thing."

We were not informed of this melancholy event until the return of the French mission from Yedo to Shanghai, about two months afterward. The fact had then been made public, and the whole city was in mourning. Our only consolation was that every body else had been taken in as well as ourselves. The deceit which had been practiced was in no way referable to the presence of foreigners. The custom of the country is, that for six weeks after the death of a tycoon it shall be kept profoundly secret, until the successor is firmly seated on the vacant throne, and all possibility of any disputes with reference to it is removed. Of whom consist the favored few whose office it is to gull every body else, I was not informed; doubtless the crown princes, and probably the council, so that it is just possible that our friends the commissioners were themselves ignorant of the fact. If they were not, they had certainly attained a high proficiency in the art of living a lie, for the conversation frequently turned upon the emperor's health, and they sometimes volunteered the information that it was so much improved that, after all, an audience might be practicable.

It was a still more gratuitous piece of false intelligence on their part to tell us the story of his adopting a son; nor can one clearly perceive the object of the fable.

We never exactly learned the date of his death. The Dutch, who are perhaps a little jealous at the rapidity of our success, declare that he put an end to himself during our stay in Yedo, in consequence of the difficulties in which the policy of his government with regard to foreigners was involving him. The French, on the other hand, assert that he died shortly after Mr. Harris's treaty was signed, overcome, possibly, by that event; while Mr. Harris himself, who had an audience with his majesty, described him to us as a wretchedly delicate-looking man, and a victim to epilepsy. It is therefore most probable that his death was the result of natural causes, and occurred about the time of our arrival. This is taking the French account, and calculating upon an interval of six weeks intervening between the occurrence of the event and its being made public.

Under all circumstances, it is a striking illustration of the perfect organization which pervades all classes of society, and of the system to which all possible contingencies and events are by law reduced. Many retainers and servants in the palace must have been aware of the circumstance. A burial of some sort probably took place. It is difficult to conceive, even if it did not, how such absolute and entire secrecy could have been maintained, or to imagine it possible that the female part of the establishment, some of whom must have been cognizant of so important an event, should have been able to preserve a discreet silence upon it.

Certain it is that the world at large were as little conscious of it as we were, when, doing justice to the dinner of our defunct entertainer, we drank his health in hot sakee.

The most important part of the day's work was yet to come. The yacht was still flying the British ensign, and the ceremony of handing her over to her new owners was to be the occupation of the afternoon. The commissioners had already started off to attire themselves in the robes appropriate to the occasion. It happened to be Prince Albert's birthday, and the usual salutes had already been fired, the ships remaining dressed out all day In one of the Japanese forts no small amount of excitement reigned. For the first time in the annals of Japan a salute was to be fired in honor of a foreign flag. This was a concession which had never before been made to any nation, and we were curious to observe how the performance would be executed. Meantime our sacred lodgings were beginning to assume a melancholy and deserted appearance; servants and baggage were moving about the yard, sturdy Japanese porters pervaded our sleeping apartments. We took a lingering look at our quaint abode, so comfortable, and yet so unlike any house that any body had ever lived in before, and with a sigh of regret mounted our steeds for the last time. The sensation is not unlike that which is felt if, when very hot and thirsty, one is stopped in the middle of a delicious draught of beer, having only had time to swallow two mouthfuls. However, we were not destined to have "more;" so we rode again down the main street, through crowds as dense as those which had greeted us on our first arrival, and, seating ourselves once again in the barge, pushed off from that shore on which we had spent nine such interesting and exciting days.

We found the commissioners had preceded us, and were now strutting about the deck of the yacht in all the bravery of their resplendent costumes. I had no notion that it entered into Japanese customs to wear such dresses. They are only donned on festive occasions, such as this was supposed to be.

Higo was literally covered with crabs, some of them large enough to be an honor to an English sea-port. The dress was embroidered silk, with these crabs in raised silver, standing out in high relief. Another of the commissioners flaunted about with a robe ornamented with the cheerful device of a skull. Each had his peculiar emblem, worked on a large scale, on his breast and back. Though somewhat gaudy and fantastic in detail, the general effect was striking and imposing.

Lord Elgin now formally addressed the commissioners, handing over to them, on behalf of her majesty, the yacht which she had presented to the Tycoon as a token of friendship and goodwill. Then down came the English ensign, and up went the red balls on the white ground, the signal for the forts to salute; and the puff curling over the blue waters of the bay, and followed by a dull roar, proved how well the Japanese signal-man had kept his watch.

With perfect precision, the native gunners fired twenty-one guns with an interval of ten seconds between each. The weather was lovely, the bay was alive with pleasure-boats—the wonder-struck Japanese listening to their own forts conducting themselves in this totally unprecedented manner. Then came the sharp, ringing response from the 68-pounders of the Retribution and Furious, and the yacht got slowly under weigh, commanded by a Japanese captain, manned by Japanese sailors, and her machinery worked by Japanese engineers. Notwithstanding the horizontal cylinders and other latest improvements with which her engines were fitted, the men had learned their lesson well, and were confident in their powers. We steamed gallantly through the fleets, the admiration of all beholders, whether British or Japanese. A brilliant sunset added its glories to this lively and attractive scene. The shores of the bay were lined with people; in places green wooded banks came down to the water, and the smoke from their guns still rested upon the island forts. Many-colored flags fluttered in the breeze, hundreds of boats flitted to and fro on the still waters of the bay; while, rearing its conical summit far into the blue sky, old Fusi-yama formed a noble background to a picture such as had never before been witnessed in the course of all the many centuries during which this majestic peak has presided over the capital of Dai Nipon. Captain Barker had prepared a feast for the commissioners on board the Retribution, and they examined the fittings of this handsome vessel with much interest. At last the moment of parting arrived, and, amid many demonstrations of affection on both sides, they bade us a final farewell.

As night closed in, the golden sun was followed by a moon which had borrowed a lustre from the reflected rays of the luminary it rivaled. Then rockets shot into the heavens, and blue-lights burned at the yard-arms, and the rows of forts were illuminated in quick reply. The long day was over at last, and with it we felt that our Japanese experiences had finally terminated. They had been marked by an interest and a novelty not to be surpassed, and by a success, in a political point of view, scarcely to have been anticipated. The 26th of August, 1858, will be a date long to be remembered by all of us who shared in the singular and interesting proceedings of that day; but it will be an epoch in the history of the Japanese empire, and, in centuries to come, natives and foreigners will alike record with interest the anniversary of an event pregnant with such important results to commerce and civilization.

CHAPTER XXXII.

Future Prospects.—Civilization of Japan.—The Effect of the Treaty.—Dutch Subserviency.—Interviews of the Dutch with the Tycoon.—Policy to be pursued.—Necessity of mercantile Morality.—Resources of Japan.—Commercial Intercourse with China.—Government Interference.—Chow-chow Cargoes.—Competition with native Manufactures.—Probable Demand for woolen Manufactures, etc.—Vegetable Products.—Japan Wax.—Mineral Resources.—Commercial Prospects.—Leave Japan.—The Port of Hiogo.—Ohosaka.—Kioto.—Caught in a Typhoon.—Arrival at Shanghai.

BEFORE bidding a final adieu to Japan, it may be interesting to cast a brief glance at the present state and future prospects of our political and commercial relations with that empire. In the account which I have given of our intercourse with its officials and people generally, I have endeavored to convey honestly the impression produced upon our minds during our brief experience among them. These impressions coincided thoroughly with the accounts we received from Dutch and American gentlemen, whose acquaintance with the country had dated from a longer period: but it is more than probable that, as our relations with the Japanese become more extended, the character they will receive at our hands will be less favorable. This may arise from two causes. In the first place, they will very probably be provoked and irritated into an antagonism to us by the overbearing and insolent behavior, common, unhappily, to a certain class of our countrymen when brought into contact with semi-civilized races; and, in the second, even those among us who are superior to any such imputation rarely make allowances for different moral standards, and altogether dissimilar habits and modes of thought from those to which they are themselves accustomed. They forget, for instance, that *truth* is a virtue unknown except to a mere fraction of the human family—that, as a general rule, a strict adherence to truth is to be met with only in countries peopled by races among whom chivalry has existed as an institution. To the east of Europe I have ever found it regarded rather as a weakness than a virtue—a fact which in no way militates against Asiatics being in some respects superior to Europeans.

It is nevertheless possible that many persons will go to Japan, and, because they do not find a code of honor corresponding to our own, complain that the moral qualities of the people have been overstated.

The civilization of Japan differs entirely from that of any other country, and if we expect them to meet us half way in the spirit of advancement and progression common to the West, we shall be grievously disappointed. There are, it is true, among the aristocracy of Japan men who are said to be really desirous of admitting foreigners into the empire, and of deriving for their countrymen all the advantages which may be gained by a liberal and progressive policy. Some nobles of this party were in power at the time of our arrival there, and violent discussions were reported to have taken place as to the policy to be pursued; for, with the majority of the aristocracy, the prejudices even of two centuries could not be removed at a bound.

With them that exclusive system, which originated in the discovery of the ambitious designs and treacherous machinations of the first Europeans with whom they came in contact, was at last abandoned only under the influence of fear. The cordiality of our reception at Yedo was, in certain quarters, the mask which a somewhat shallow diplomacy led them to assume, in order to avert a danger they deemed imminent, and which they dared not meet. They fancied they saw impending over them the fate of India, and they believed that the only alternative was to grant us concessions such as we had already wrung from China. It is only fair to ourselves to say that they were entirely mistaken in this assumption. The treaty with America had already been made, and ours followed as a matter of course; but it is scarcely to be wondered at that, when this fear was removed, the liberals should be at a discount, and their opponents should endeavor, even at the expense of good faith, to retreat from engagements they would never willingly have entered into, more especially when encouraged by the intelligence that the Chinese government had already commenced to pursue the same policy with success.

With a crude knowledge of the sacredness of treaty obligations, and an instinctive dread of the aggressive tendencies of people from the West, the old Japanese party seem now inclined to ignore stipulations actually ratified by the government. If we hope to conduct relations with Japan upon a satisfactory footing, our true policy is to intimate distinctly to the government that we intend to enforce every one of our rights to the uttermost letter. The subserviency of the Dutch for upward of two centuries will doubtless render it more difficult for us to maintain our relations upon that footing of equality, without which the evil results of a false position must necessarily ensue, than if no intercourse had hitherto existed between Japan and European countries.

In order to appreciate the pitch to which the Dutch carried their compliance with the humiliating code of court etiquette forced upon them by the Japanese government, it is worth while glancing at the account which we have received from the veracious Kæmpfer of the ceremonies of the audience at Yedo between the resident of the Dutch factory and the temporal emperor. "As soon as the resident entered the hall of audience," says the old German physician, "they cried out 'Holanda captain,' which was the signal for him to draw near and make his obeisances. Accordingly, he *crawled* on his hands and knees to a place shown him, between the presents ranged in due order on one side, and the place where the emperor sat on the other; and there kneeling, he bowed his forehead quite down to the ground, and so crawled backward, like a crab, without uttering a single word. So mean and short a thing is the audience we have with this mighty monarch."

This was the form of the audience of ceremony, but now let us see what took place on the next occasion, when his Japanese majesty condescended to unbend. After the members of the Dutch mission had, to use the word of the same writer, crept into the audience chamber, " the emperor sat himself on our right behind the lattices, as near as he possibly could. Then he ordered us to take off our cappa or cloak, being our garment of ceremony; then to stand upright, that he might have a full view of us; again to walk, to stand still, to compliment each other, to dance, to jump, to play the drunkard, to speak broken Japanese, to read Dutch, to paint, to sing, to put our cloaks on and off. Meanwhile we obeyed the emperor's commands in the best manner we could. I joined to my dance a love-song in High German. In this manner, and with numerous other such apish tricks, we must suffer ourselves to contribute to the emperor's and the court's diversion."

In the present state of our political relations, not only with Japan, but with China, it is most important that we should recall the history of the earlier intercourse which Europeans maintained with those countries, as tending to encourage in these semi-civilized courts that assumption of superiority which must sooner or later be resisted, and to which may be traced all the political complications which have arisen, or are likely to arise, with those empires.

We are at this moment suffering in China from the false position which we assumed during those years when our trade was confined to Canton and governed by a monopoly of Hong merchants, and when we submitted to restrictions and indignities, not so insulting, indeed, as those offered to the Dutch in Japan, but sufficiently so to establish in the Celestial mind our position of inferiority, of which we have never yet succeeded in disabusing it.

In Japan, fortunately, we have not as yet thus committed ourselves, but there can be no doubt that we suffer to a certain extent from the low moral position which the Dutch took up at the outset, and which must more or less affect all foreigners. Assuredly, if our political agents in Japan inaugurate our intercourse with that court by crawling about on their hands and knees, playing the drunkard and singing love-songs, we shall very soon have a Japanese war on our hands. Happily, in our consul general at Yedo we have a sagacious and experienced man, who is not likely to give way upon points of national dignity; but, unless our diplomacy is conducted upon principles calculated to make us respected as a nation at the outset, it will be impossible for us, in the long run, to maintain satisfactory relations with the Japanese government. It is no doubt true that the influence of the governments both of China and Japan, and, indeed, their stability, depend in a great measure upon the prestige which attaches to them in the eyes of the people at large; but if that prestige is to be purchased at the price of the humiliation of Great Britain as a nation, we had better leave to more mercenary countries the privilege of trading with those empires. So far as Japan is concerned, there is no reason to suppose that the application of force will be necessary to inculcate the principal lessons of reciprocal international obligations. With so quick-sighted and intelligent a people, moral influences may be made to operate more effectually than physical force, and with far happier results.

But if it is so essential to the maintenance of an amicable intercourse with Japan that our diplomatists in that country carry out a policy of combined firmness and forbearance, it is no less vital to the success of commercial enterprise, in this new and comparatively unexplored field, that our merchants set an example, to a people totally inexperienced in transactions of this nature, of a rigid adherence to treaty obligations. Where these are sought to be evaded, and advantage is taken of the ignorance or stupidity of native officials to infringe even in the smallest degree the strict letter of the law, the consequences of such a course are certain to recoil upon the mercantile community generally. Sooner or later the government becomes aware of the abuse, and either resents the wrong by creating out of it a cause of international difficulty, or perhaps, unable to remedy the mischief, recognizes the principle, and thus introduces an element of dishonesty which can not fail in the end to exercise a most demoralizing influence upon all persons engaged in the trade.

There are so many most tempting occasions for stretching the provisions of a treaty which, in the case of a country like Japan, must necessarily be somewhat vague, that it is by the spirit rather than by the letter that foreigners should be guided. By observing this principle we shall the more rapidly and successfully develop the resources which yet lie hidden in Japan.

It would be somewhat rash for a visitor whose experience of the country has been limited to a residence of a fortnight in its capital to attempt to detail with any certainty what those resources are. That they are very varied we know, from the circumstance that they suffice for every want of a civilized and cultivated people. That they are very extensive we can not doubt, because between thirty and forty millions of people are dependent on them alone. How far they are yet capable of expansion we shall only learn from those who have extended opportunities of judging.

We may, however, venture to predict that, in the first instance, the great preponderance of the trade of Japan will be with China. Formerly the intercourse between these two countries was limited to ten Chinese junks a year—Chapoo, near Shanghai, being the only port in China to or from which junks were permitted to trade. No Japanese junk was allowed to engage in this trade, their construction, indeed, involving a coasting voyage; and this construction results not from their ignorance of a better model, but from the stringent regulations forbidding them to build on a principle which would enable them to enter upon distant voyages. The cargoes of the Chinese junks consisted principally of sugar, besides spices, dyes, and drugs of various descriptions. In return, a certain quantity of bar copper was allotted to each junk, the remainder of the cargoes consisting of lackered ware, dried fish, whale oil, etc.

According to Thunberg, the crew were always brought on shore, and all charge of the vessel taken from them till such time as every thing was ready for their departure; consequently, the Japanese unloaded it entirely, and afterward brought the vessel on shore, where, at low water, it was quite dry. The next year it was loaded with other goods. They were, in fact, treated with even greater indignity than the Dutch, while, as a larger percentage was deducted from their merchandise, their profits were even less.

So complete has been the control which the government has uniformly exercised over all commercial transactions in which its subjects have engaged, that we shall doubtless find considerable difficulty in emancipating trade from its undue interference. I have already remarked that, even in the last treaty negotiated by the Dutch in 1855, the old machinery of the Geld Kammer was preserved, by which government reserved to itself the control over the sale of every cargo arriving at Nagasaki. With a government still laboring under the traditions of a commercial policy, the essential principle of which is a minute investigation into every act of the trader, and an immediate supervision of his every mercantile transaction, we must be prepared for difficulties in our commercial intercourse at every turn. A Japanese has no more idea of individual freedom than a child of three years old, and is about as learned in matters of trade. He has always been in the nursery, and is contented to remain there.

His paternal, or rather maternal government, tells him the price at which he is to purchase his goods, the description of money he is to pay for them in, and what he is to sell in return. When the Englishman, with his notions of personal liberty and his habits of free trade, comes into business contact with a slave instead of a free man, and finds himself hampered by regulations which apply to his customer in such a manner as to act most injuriously on himself, it requires no prophet to foretell the results. We shall have a considerable and very natural irritation produced, and bitter complaints made against the Japanese government, who must learn to conform to the usages of civilized nations in this respect, and be taught that, beyond a certain point, no isolated community has a right to dictate to the rest of the world upon a matter in which mankind are universally interested.

The appointment of a Japanese embassy to this country would do more than any thing else to convey this necessary and wholesome truth to the minds of the council at Yedo.

The trade between China and Japan, to which I have already alluded, and of which foreign ships would always retain the monopoly, consists principally in the interchange of articles of diet peculiar to those countries. Thus one of the most expensive luxuries in China is the root called ginseng; it is used medicinally, or by the rich as an agreeable tonic; but the price at which it is sold in the bazars in China is something fabulous. Already great quantities of ginseng have been exported from Japan, where it grows abundantly. Dried fish, sharks' fins, and sea-slugs are also enumerated among the imports into China from Japan, while the Chinese have been supplying their neighbors, in return, with preserved eggs, birds' nests, and various spices and drugs used as medicines, too numerous to mention. The generic name for a cargo composed of miscellanies of this nature is chow-chow.

As Japan does not produce sugar, when the taste for that article becomes more universal there will probably be a large demand for it. The most convenient source of supply is Formosa; but the taste for sugar is only one among numerous wants which we have yet to create in order to provide ourselves with a market in Japan. Hitherto they have lived in blissful ignorance of the comfort of a cotton pocket-handkerchief, and have satisfied themselves with square pieces of whity-brown paper. The mysteries of long ells and Spanish stripes have not yet been made known to them, nor could they distinguish between broad-cloths and velveteens. Printed cottons, American domestics, drills, and all varieties of piece-goods, have been supplied hitherto by articles of native manufacture. It will be for the manufacturer of this country to substitute for them goods which can answer the same purpose, of a more suitable material and at a lower figure.

In China we have hitherto failed in producing that great revolution in the fabric of which the dress of the people is composed, which was predicted on the conclusion of the Pottinger treaty. Chinese cottons, manufactured by the hand, still compete successfully with the productions of the machinery of this country, although it is fair to say that a gradual improvement is taking place in this respect, and the new regulation affecting the transit-dues will materially facilitate the introduction of foreign produce into the country. So far as we are aware, no such obstructions to the free internal traffic of the country exist in Japan. When once the goods are disposed of, their circulation is unrestricted. Of course, the extent of that circulation will depend in a great measure on the facilities of internal communication which the empire affords. Its volcanic and mountainous character renders the transport of goods by land expensive, although the roads are often broad enough for wheeled vehicles; but very few of these are used, and then almost exclusively for agricultural purposes. On the other hand, the great extent of the Japanese sea-board, and the large population to which easy access may thus be obtained, will render the task of supplying their wants comparatively easy.

There is one material, in particular, for which there ought certainly to be a large demand in Japan when its merits become known. Old William Adams, who sailed for South America with a cargo of woolens three hundred years ago, thus describes the result of a conference held on board the Dutch ship Erasmus, when they had failed in disposing of her cargo: "At last it was resolved to go to Japan, for by report of one Derrick Geritson, which had been there with the Portugals, woolen cloth was in great estimation in that island, and we gathered by reason that the Malaccas, and most part of the East Indies, were hot countries, where woolen cloths would not be much accepted; therefore it was we agreed to go for Japan."

At present the Japanese wear in winter garments thickly padded either with cotton or silk wool. In the latter case warm clothing is somewhat expensive, and there can be little doubt that our woolen fabrics would answer the purpose better, and be far cheaper. In China, sheepskins and coarse furs are used by the lower orders, but I did not observe any fur-shops in Yedo. By the treaty both cottons and woolens are admitted into Japan at a duty of five per cent. The remaining articles included in the five per cent. list are all articles used for the purpose of building, rigging, repairing, or fitting out of ships; whaling gear of all kinds; salted provisions of all kinds; bread and bread-stuffs; living animals of all kinds; coals, timber for building houses, rice, paddy, steam-machinery, zinc, lead, tin, and raw silk. A duty of thirty-five per cent. is placed upon all intoxicating liquors. Gold and silver, coined or uncoined, are admitted duty free. All other articles pay a duty of twenty per cent.

The exportation of rice and wheat, gold and silver coin, and copper in bars, is prohibited. The Japanese government, however, engages to sell from time to time, at public auction, any surplus quantity of copper that may be produced. This, together with all other articles of Japanese production which are exported as cargo, is liable to a duty of five per cent. One of the most important clauses in these regulations is the right reserved of revision of the tariff at the end of five years.

Silk, camphor, vegetable oil, and vegetable wax are among the principal products which are likely to be exported to this country; the tea and tobacco are both of a very superior quality; while, among manufactured articles, lacker and china in small quantities will always find a market in the West. Hitherto the most successful cargo brought to this country from Japan has been one of Japanese wax. Mr. Simmonds, in the *China Telegraph*, gives the following account of Japan wax: "Rhus succedanea, the species which furnishes the Japan wax, has long been grown in our green-houses, having been introduced from China nearly a century ago.

"It might be raised, we should suppose, in the Cape and Australian colonies, in the Mauritius and India, and would be far preferable as an oleaginous plant to the species of candleberry myrtles from which wax is obtained. It will grow in any common soil, and may be readily increased by cuttings. We shall probably soon learn what is the ordinary mode of culture in the plantations of Japan, and whether any attention is paid to pruning, manuring, etc. The wax is of medium quality, between beeswax and the ordinary vegetable tallows, such as Bassia butter, Borneo vegetable tallows, Cocum butter, etc. Though there are shades of difference, several of these varieties of wax possess the essential properties of that formed by bees; indeed, it was formerly supposed that bees merely collected the wax already formed by the vegetable, but Huber's experiments show that the insect has the power of transmuting sugar into wax, and that it is, in fact, a secretion. Japan wax is softer, more brittle and fatty than beeswax, easily kneaded, and melts between 40° and 42° C. It contains twice as much oxygen as beeswax, and has a different composition, consisting of palmitic acid united with oxyde of glyceryle. The small parcels which formerly reached this country have been used in Price's Patent Candleworks in substitution for wax, and for hard neutral fat, and, after conversion into the acid state, both for candles and night-lights. If the wholesale price can be reduced, this wax will find its way into extensive consumption on the Continent for various purposes."

The seeds of another tree, called the Rhus vernicefera, also contain a tallow-like oil which is used in the making of candles.

But, so far as our present limited knowledge of the resources of Japan will enable us to form an opinion, its mineral are more likely to form a profitable source of commerce than its vegetable productions. At present there is every probability of the government placing obstacles in the way of European enterprise in this direction. They have reserved to themselves the monopoly of that most abundant mineral in Japan, copper, which is used for mechanical and other purposes there almost as we should use iron. Iron, however, also abounds in various parts of Japan, and the mines appear to be extensively worked. Judging from articles of casting of their own construction, the ores must be of excellent quality. Specimens of wrought iron, cast and blister steel, have been examined with very satisfactory results. The wrought iron is usually hammered, and in small flat bars varying from twelve to twenty lbs. each. This is probably to be attributed to a want of proper machinery for heavier bars, and its being better suited to their purposes.

Coal, as well as copper, is a government monopoly. Hitherto the coal brought for sale since the opening of trade has been surface coal, and consequently inferior in quality: it is described as small. It burns slaty, leaving considerable ash, and is very light. The price at the first opening of trade was 3½ Mexican dollars a ton, but it has probably risen since then. There can be little doubt that good coal will be found in the islands when the mines begin to be properly worked, but whether or not the government will permit English engineers to enter the country to assist in developing them is highly problematical.

However much we may regret the difficulties which oppose themselves to the commercial exploration of so fertile and productive a country as Japan, the result of our experience leads us to believe that we must wait for many years before trade can be carried on with it upon an extensive and really profitable scale. Still we need not despair of a prosperous era ultimately arriving. We have already succeeded in demolishing that external rampart of exclusiveness which had successfully resisted the assaults of Western nations for upward of two centuries. We must now apply ourselves steadily to undermine the inner barriers which have been constructed during that period, under the influence of long-standing prejudices and bitter memories of the past. We shall most successfully achieve this important result by the exercise of forbearance and integrity on the part of our merchants, and by the maintenance of a dignified but conciliatory policy on the part of our government.

It will be a source of legitimate pride and gratification to this country if, on some future day, a Japanese, looking back through the history of the empire, can point to the pages which record our first intercourse with it as being those which mark the dawn of a brighter and purer civilization.

. . . .

When the day broke on the following morning we were no longer visible to the good people at Yedo. Early in the afternoon we were abreast of Simoda, and bade adieu to our invaluable interpreter and friend Mr. Hewsken, consigning him the less reluctantly to his hermitage on shore because the days of his solitary confinement were drawing to an end, and intercourse with China would henceforward be a matter of common occurrence.

We had hoped, on our return voyage to Shanghai, to explore the Suwonada Sea and those interesting waters which lie between the islands of Kiu-siu, Sikok, and Nipon, and which have not as yet been traversed by foreign keel, and which must afford a most interesting field for surveys of a scientific character, as also for general observation. The Suwonada Sea is thickly covered with islands, and was reported to us by the Japanese as navigable for ships of large draught. The large and important island of Sikok intervenes between it and the North Pacific Ocean, with which this sea is connected by the Straits of Bungo on the west, and the narrow Channel of Kino on the east. Sikok is, as its name implies, divided into four provinces; as, however, we did not even sight its shores, we had no opportunity of obtaining any information about it. It is about 150 miles long, with an average breadth of 70 miles, and is computed to contain about 20,000 square miles.

With the Suwonada Sea, however, we are more closely interested, for upon its margin is the port of Hiogo, opened by the treaty to the commerce of the West.

This port is situated in the Bay of Ohosaka, opposite to the celebrated city of that name, from which it is ten or twelve miles distant. The Japanese government have expended vast sums in their engineering efforts to improve its once dangerous anchorage. A breakwater, which was erected at a prodigious expense, and which cost the lives of numbers of workmen, has proved sufficient for the object for which it was designed. There is a tradition that a superstition existed in connection with this dike, to the effect that it would never be finished unless an individual could be found sufficiently patriotic to suffer himself to be buried in it. A Japanese Curtius was not long in forthcoming, to whom a debt of gratitude will be due in all time to come, from every British ship that rides securely at her anchor behind the breakwater.

Hiogo has now become the port of Ohosaka and Miako, and will, in all probability, be the principal port of European trade in the empire. The city is described as equal in size to Nagasaki. When Kæmpfer visited it, he found three hundred junks at anchor in its bay.

The Dutch describe Ohosaka as a more attractive resort than even Yedo. While this latter city may be regarded as the London of Japan, Ohosaka seems to be its Paris. Here are the most celebrated theatres, the most sumptuous tea-houses, the most extensive pleasure-gardens. It is the abode of luxury and wealth, the favorite resort of fashionable Japanese, who come here to spend their time in gayety and pleasure. Ohosaka is one of the five imperial cities, and contains a vast population. It is situated on the left bank of the Jedogawa, a stream which rises in the Lake of Oity, situated a day and a half's journey in the interior. It is navigable for boats of large tonnage as far as Miako, and is spanned by numerous handsome bridges.

The port of Hiogo and city of Ohosaka will not be opened to Europeans until the 1st of January, 1863. The foreign residents will then be allowed to explore the country in any direction for a distance of twenty-five miles, except toward Miako, or, as it is more properly called, Kioto. They will not be allowed to approach nearer than twenty-five miles to this far-famed city.

As the Dutch have constantly been in the habit of passing through Kioto, it is probable that before very long this restriction will be removed, and Europeans will be permitted to visit what is, without question, the most interesting spot in the empire. If Yedo is the London, and Ohosaka the Paris, Kioto is certainly the Rome of Japan. It is here that the spiritual emperor resides, and that enormous ecclesiastical court by which he is surrounded, and which is called the Dairi, is permanently fixed. It is here that the celebrated tomb of the great Taiko-Sama, the most famous of Japanese temporal emperors, is situated; and here are to be seen the most magnificent and imposing temples of which the empire can boast. The population of Kioto is said to be half a million, and it has had the reputation of being the principal manufacturing town in the empire. Had we then known how little our presence was needed at Shanghai, we might have been the first foreign ship to visit the new port of Hiogo. Unfortunately, however, the period fixed upon by the commissioners for their arrival from Pekin was already passed, and Lord Elgin felt bound to push on with all speed to meet them at the appointed rendezvous. We afterward found that any anxiety in this respect was misplaced, for, with true Chinese indifference, they had postponed their journey for many weeks. Meanwhile we were plowing the rough seas of Japan in hot haste, a gale of wind astern driving us more rapidly than we cared for to the unloved shores of China. Cape Chichakoff, our old enemy, though we had reason to be thankful to him for friendly shelter, looked more inhospitable than ever as we swept past him. Heavy storms, strong currents, and numerous rocks, with probably many more undiscovered, combine to render navigation on the shores of Japan a somewhat anxious undertaking. Fortunately, we had passed the Straits of Van Diemen before the tail of a typhoon caught us suddenly, carrying away every thing that was set, and rendering an immediate reference to the law of storms necessary. There can be little doubt that the application of this law saved us some heavy weather; for, instead of holding on our course, we fairly turned tail, and fled from the circle of its influence.

Count Poutiatine, in the large frigate to which he had now transferred his flag, was less fortunate. She suffered so severely in the same storm that she was compelled to put into Nagasaki to refit. We were perfectly contented with our allowance, nevertheless, and spent a period of much anxiety, in consequence of the risks to which our lacker was exposed. Captain Osborn had most good-naturedly permitted us to stow it away on the main deck, for our cabins were incapable of containing a fourth part of our purchases; but, as the main deck was often ankle-deep in water, the fate of our Japanese curiosities caused us serious misgivings.

There was, moreover, that constant struggle between a desire for air and light, and a dread of shipping seas, so familiar to those who have made voyages in hot latitudes. Once only was I tempted to trice up my port, and had hardly done so before I paid dearly for my indiscretion. Five thousand cheroots, a small Japanese dog that was accidentally visiting me, all my boots, and a considerable part of my wardrobe, were swimming together in hopeless confusion, and the weather continued so bad that two or three days elapsed before I could dry them. The dog was ever after a martyr to cramp in his loins.

In spite of all these misadventures we made the passage from Yedo to Shanghai in a week, and had the satisfaction of announcing to our friends there, whom we had left scarce a month before, that this short interval had sufficed to enable Lord Elgin to open a new market to the British merchant, and one from which those residing at this port would most immediately benefit.

CHAPTER XXXIII.

Effects of the Chinese Climate.—The Amenities of Shanghai.—Arrival of the Imperial Commissioners.—Correspondence relative to Canton.—Peace Proclamation.—Appointment of Sub-commission.—Our Chinese Colleagues.—Daily Conferences.—Rate of the new Tariff.—Transit Duties.—Collection of foreign Customs.—The Opium-trade.—Mr. Reed's Dispatch on Opium.—Reply of Lord Elgin.—Final Adjustment of the Question.—Visit of the Commissioners.—The jovial Ho.—A Dinner with the Commissioners.—The resident Minister at Pekin.—Proposed Expedition up the Yang-tse-kiang.—Signing the Trade Regulations.—Departure from Shanghai.

The first intelligence which we received upon our return to Shanghai was not of a nature calculated to console us for our hurried flight from Japan. It appeared that the departure of the imperial commissioners from Pekin had been postponed for some weeks, an interval which we might have spent with pleasure and profit in making excursions in the neighborhood of Yedo, or exploring the Suwonada Sea. In default of any such excitement, we found ourselves thrown upon our own resources at Shanghai at a period of the year when the climate seems to be most trying to European constitutions, though the temperature was not so high as it had been six weeks previously.

We had now been for nearly eighteen months knocking about on the coast of China, and the results were beginning to manifest themselves. Mr. Loch went home on sick certificate, taking with him the Japanese treaty. Of those that remained, all of us more or less suffered from the effects of climate; and the hot days, chilly evenings, and malarious exhalations of Shanghai were not calculated to remove a tendency to ague, where such existed. Our own experience enabled us, without any difficulty, to credit the fact which is established by the official returns, that the China station is the most unhealthy to which our ships are sent, the sickness and mortality being greater here than even on the west coast of Africa.

Meantime the period of our return home seemed more remote than ever. We were reminded of a Japanese fable which seemed not altogether inappropriate to our condition. A moth is said to exist in Japan so beautiful that all the night-flies fall in love with it. To get rid of their importunity, she sends them to bring her fire; and her rash admirers, in their ardent attempts to do her bidding, are consumed in a flame, fatal alike to themselves and their aspirations. Moral: Beware how you allow yourself to become a night-fly in the service of your country.

As Shanghai is situated in a flat and highly-cultivated country, intersected by canals and ditches, and traversed by narrow foot-paths, driving is impossible, and riding attended with discomfort, if not actual risk, the pleasure of crawling at a foot-pace in Indian file being varied only by the excitement of crossing a single-log bridge. The enterprising community of Shanghai, to compensate for these drawbacks, have constructed a race-course, round which equestrians gyrate daily, as though they were being lounged. Those who prefer gossip to exercise frequent the bund, a broad quay which extends along the whole length of the settlement, and which is crowded with Chinese porters all the morning, and sprinkled with European ladies and gentlemen in the afternoon.

Sportsmen who do not mind foul odors may plod through cotton-fields all day, and return home well satisfied with their luck if they bag a brace of pheasants to each gun. And pedestrians have been known to sacrifice their noses to their livers, and take long walks into the wearisome country for the good of their health. Rackets, American bowls, and billiards afford relaxation to a large section of society; and now and then a ball, at which the proportion of gentlemen to ladies is ten to one, or an amateur theatrical entertainment, infuses a little animation into the world.

As the utmost harmony and hospitality characterized the community during our stay at Shanghai, we found it infinitely the most agreeable place of residence in China, and the month which elapsed prior to the arrival of the commissioners slipped rapidly by. We occupied the handsome residence of the British consul, and experienced some relief, after our long confinement on shipboard, in the comfort of its spacious apartments.

On the 3d of October the four commissioners, Kweiliang and Hwashana, Ming and Twan, arrived at Shanghai. As Lord Elgin had been disappointed in his desire to see the Canton braves summarily chastised, it became incumbent upon him to accomplish by moral pressure what had better have been achieved by physical force; before, therefore, consenting to an interview with the commissioners, his excellency addressed certain inquiries to them with reference to the conduct of Hwang, the successor to Yeh, as governor general of the province of Kwang-tung, and to the appointment of a war committee, which had been instrumental in raising braves for the purpose of harassing our garrison in Canton. Until a satisfactory reply was made to these inquiries, his excellency declined to enter upon any business with the imperial commissioners.

The committee for the organization of militia, or braves, was principally under the direction of these political adventurers, well known for their turbulent character, and who were now seeking to win promotion by making themselves prominent as the leaders of that patriotic party who had sworn to devote themselves to the extermination of the barbarians. The names of these men were Lung, Lo, and Su.

We had good reason to suppose, and we were afterward confirmed in the belief, that these men were acting in accordance with secret instructions from Pekin, directly opposed to protestations of amity which the commissioners were at this moment making in behalf of the emperor.

With reference to the subjects referred to in Lord Elgin's dispatch, the imperial commissioners stated that the news of the treaty had not yet reached Canton, nor the treaty itself been officially promulgated; that Hwang had therefore not changed his policy; and that, as to the "high officers, Lung, Lo, and Su, they are gentlemen and literates, who have had the honor to receive the emperor's commands to superintend the organization of the militia. This is so in every province; it is not in Kwang-tung alone. Wherever the country is unsettled, it is the business of the gentry who superintend the organization of the militia to be the first informed."

They proposed, however, to order Hwang to issue the following proclamation, and to publish it extensively themselves:

"*Draft Proclamation.*

"The commissioners hereby give notice that a treaty of peace to endure forever, between China and England, France, and America, has been concluded by them at Tientsin; and as they are indeed apprehensive that the same may not be generally known to the gentry, merchants, and population at large of the different ports, they deem it right to issue a proclamation to that effect.

"They accordingly proclaim to the merchants, and all other persons of the different ports, that a good understanding is evermore to endure and increase between the Chinese and the foreigners of all nations, and that they are together to share the enjoyment of comfort and advantage. Such is the earnest hope of the commissioners. Let none disobey.

"Attend!
"Attend!
"A special proclamation."

So far from accepting this communication as a satisfactory answer to his demands, Lord Elgin announced to the commissioners in reply that, "after all that has happened, he can not accept any measure short of the removal of the governor general, and the withdrawal of the special powers with which the gentry are invested, as proof of the sincerity of the imperial government in its desire for the establishment and maintenance of peaceful relations between the two countries."

In reply, the commissioners promised to obtain the removal of Hwang, and the withdrawal of their powers from the War Committee.

This matter being so far satisfactorily arranged, the commissioners express their readiness to enter upon the consideration of the revision of the tariff and the settlement of trade regulations, this being the ostensible object of their journey from Pekin. In the mean time, the Governor General of the Two Kiangs, Hokwei-tsick, joins them as imperial commissioners, and is reputed to bring to their councils the most subtle intellect as well as the most liberal mind. The population over which his supreme administrative functions extend is about equal to that of Great Britain and Ireland.

In order to discuss the details of the tariff and trade regulations, a commission was appointed, consisting, on the part of the Chinese government, of Wang, the provincial treasurer, and Sieh, the provincial judge; and on the part of the English, of Mr. Wade and myself. It was arranged that Mr. Lay should also be present, though not as one of the commission. In his dispatch to the commissioners upon the subject, Lord Elgin states "that the peculiar nature of Mr. Lay's relation to the Chinese authorities has alone prevented the undersigned from officially attaching that gentleman to the commission above nominated. As, however, it is most important that, in a matter involving such grave interests on both sides, neither party should be deprived of the experience and information which Mr. Lay can bring to bear upon the subject, it is his wish that that gentleman should be present at the meetings of the commission."

These meetings took place at a building called the Ye-shi Yuen, situated at the farther extremity of the city, nearly four miles distant from the consulate: the daily journey thither in chairs, through the narrow, reeking streets of Shanghai, was certainly, if not the most arduous, the least pleasant part of our duties. Our Chinese colleagues were both agreeable, intelligent men. The treasurer, Wang, though superior in rank to the judge, took little part in the discussions. His experience of barbarians had been limited, and his principal recommendation lay in his gentle,

Sieh, late Taoutai of Shanghai.

conciliatory manner, and the absence of any marked antipathy toward foreigners. It was in Sieh that the imperial commissioners reposed all their confidence. For many years taoutai or intendant at Shanghai, there is certainly no Chinese mandarin in the empire whose intercourse with foreigners has been so extensive, or whose views upon foreign policy are so enlightened. There can be little doubt that, had the advice of Sieh been attended to, the Chinese government would not recently have committed an act which now calls for a heavy retribution.

At that time his opinion carried great weight in the councils of the imperial commissioners, while he was to a large extent influenced by his colleague in the service of the Chinese government, Mr. Lay. As our approach was always signified by a runner in advance, we invariably found these high functionaries standing at the door, waiting to receive us with a profusion of ctsin-ctsins. Then we ascended to a cool upper chamber, commanding an extensive view of upturned house-tops, and here, with due solemnity, assisted by a consumption of tobacco which would have quickened the intellect of a Wouter Van Twiller, and refreshed by copious relays of almond and ordinary tea, we transacted the business of the day. When it was over, we were regularly pressed to partake of a repast which was laid out for us in a lower room. This part of the ceremony we usually found a pretext for escaping. It would have been a breach of politeness, however, to have invariably declined to be thus entertained after our labors, though it involved the consumption of much grease and many unknown viands, and usually terminated in a drinking-match of hot samshu with the judge, he being naturally of a jovial temperament, and averse to heel-taps.

It is scarcely necessary here to do more than state briefly the result of our labors, and the arrangements we finally came to with reference to trade regulations and tariff, more particularly as the details are given at some length in the Blue-Book; there are, however, some points which merit a brief notice.

The general principle upon which the tariff was based, in accordance with the treaty, was the imposition of specific duties of import and export, calculated on an *ad valorem* rate of five per cent. In the case of imports, this principle was adhered to very strictly; in exports, however, it was necessary to apply it with some reserve, as, for instance, in the case of silk, in which the French had a special interest, and where the duty already levied was lower than the five per cent. rate. In consideration of this advantage, certain reasonable concessions were made in other duties.

Our discussions, however, were not limited to a consideration of the export and import trade of China alone; the coasting trade claimed a due share of our attention, and various restrictions which had hitherto operated most prejudicially upon foreigners trading between different ports in the empire were removed. As, however, the native junk traffic was likely to be seriously affected by the new regulations upon this head, it did not seem fair to refuse every concession in its favor; and, in consequence of the urgent representation of the judge Sieh, the export of pulse and bean-cake from the new ports of Teng-chow and New Chwang, under the British flag, was prohibited. This trade is chiefly carried on with Shanghai, some thousands of the sailors engaged in it belonging to that city. An act which should deprive these men of the means of earning their livelihood the Chinese commissioners feared would in all probability create serious riots and local disturbances.

More difficult of arrangement were the details involved in that article of the treaty which provides for the commutation of the transit-dues, and the scope and object of which I have already described. It was finally arranged that this commutation should be limited to a sum not exceeding one half of the tariff-duties, except in the case of the duty-free goods, which should be liable to a transit-duty of $2\frac{1}{2}$ per cent. *ad valorem*. The importance of this regulation, as affecting certain articles, and more especially tea, may be gathered from the fact that a transit-duty, at the rate of nearly 100 per cent., has in some cases been said to have been levied on this commodity. "If I am not misinformed," says Mr. Reed,[*] in a letter to Lord Elgin on the subject, "the transit-duties on tea alone often amount to quite as much as the article itself, and the hope is reasonable that the new treaty will very much reduce them." The present export duty on tea in China is about one tenth of that which we levy on its import into this country, and its transit-due is now reduced to half the former amount.

Involved in the consideration of this most important clause affecting the transit-dues was also the regulation of the conditions under which certificates should be issued, both in the case of exports and imports. These details were often complicated and difficult; the more so, as we had no experience or precedent to guide us in framing them.

---

[*] *Blue-Book*, p. 393.

But perhaps the most important rule in the trade regulations is that which provides for the collection of duties under one system at all the ports, and in which it is stipulated that the high officer appointed by the Chinese government to superintend foreign trade shall be at liberty, of his own choice, and independently of the suggestion or nomination of any British authority, to select any British subject he may see fit to aid him in the administration of the Customs revenue. In pursuance of the plan thus adopted by the Chinese government, they have applied through Mr. Lay for Englishmen to assist him in the important department over which he presides, and twelve gentlemen have already left this country for China to supply the place of Chinese employés in the collection of the foreign customs. Although the recent rupture has prevented this system from coming into operation, there can be no doubt that it will be the one ultimately adopted.

It will readily be conceived that the imperial government would not have consented thus to substitute foreigners for its own subjects, had not a painful experience taught it that it would be impossible, under any other system, to check those malpractices by which the revenue was so extensively defrauded. Unfortunately, the corruption was not confined to Chinese officials alone. Foreign merchants were too often induced to take advantage of the ready unscrupulousness of the Custom-house officers, and a system was in vogue which, if persisted in, would have exercised a most demoralizing influence generally. Doubtless the illegal traffic in opium, so extensively carried on as a notoriously contraband trade, largely contributed to produce the same effect; and so keenly alive was Lord Elgin to the serious nature of the evils produced by the trade in opium, as carried out, that he determined not to shrink from applying the only remedy which appeared to him practicable. The views by which he was actuated in dealing with this question are fully set forth in a correspondence which passed between him and Mr. Reed, the American minister, who came out to China with a strong bias against the opium trade, and with instructions from his government conceived in the same spirit, but who nevertheless became an advocate of the legalization of the trade from witnessing the abuses to which its contraband character gave rise.

In that correspondence, referring to the disinclination which Lord Elgin had evinced to press the matter when at Tientsin,

Mr. Reed observes: "I have more than once understood your excellency to say that you had a strong, if not invincible repugnance, involved as Great Britain already was in hostilities at Canton, and having been compelled in the north to resort to the influence of threatened coercion, to introduce the subject of opium to the consideration of the Chinese authorities. Yet I am confident, unless the initiative is taken by your excellency, things must continue as they are, with all their shame; and I appeal to your excellency's high sense of duty, so often and so strongly expressed to this helpless though perverse people, whether we, the representatives of Western and Christian nations, ought to consider our work done without some attempt to induce or compel an adjustment of the pernicious difficulty. In such an attempt I shall cordially unite." After alluding to the possibility of putting a stop to the growth of opium in India, Mr. Reed goes on to say: "Of effective prohibition, and this mainly through the inveterate appetite of the Chinese, I am not sanguine; and I therefore more confidently, though not more earnestly, call your excellency's attention to the only other course open to us—attempt to persuade the Chinese to put such high duties on the drug as will restrain the supply, regulate the import, and yet not stimulate some other form of smuggling, with or without the connivance of the Chinese. The economical arguments in favor of this course are so fully stated in the accompanying paper that I need not allude to them farther."

In his reply to this communication Lord Elgin states: "I so cordially assent to the views expressed by your excellency in reference to the opium trade, that I do not think it necessary to dwell on this part of your letter. I would only venture to observe, on this head, that when I resolved not to press this matter upon the attention of the Chinese commissioners at Tientsin, I did so, not because I questioned the advantages which would accrue from the legalization of the traffic, but because I could not reconcile it to my sense of right to urge the imperial government to abandon its traditional policy in this respect, under the kind of pressure which we were bringing to bear upon it at Tientsin.

"The circumstances under which this question will come up for discussion in the conferences on the subject of the tariff, which are now being held at this place, are happily different, and I shall not fail to instruct the gentlemen who are acting for me on this occasion to call the attention of the officers of the Chinese government, with whom they are negotiating, to the considerations so ably stated in your letter. I have little doubt but that it will be found that legalization is the only available remedy for the evils which have attracted your excellency's notice, because I am confident that, even if the other difficulties to which you advert could be removed, it would be found practically impossible to suppress the traffic in an article so easily raised and transported, and the demand for which in this country is so great that when the supply, from some cause or another, has fallen short, the price has, I am informed, even within the last few years, risen occasionally to upward of one thousand dollars per chest—a sum exceeding, I should presume, five times the cost of production."

In pursuance of this view, it was represented to the commissioners that many abuses connected with the traffic in opium would be obviated if the drug, which was already practically legalized by the surreptitious levy of a duty upon it by the officers of the government, was placed upon the footing of other imports. The commissioners concurred in this opinion, and opium was inserted in the tariff as liable to a duty of thirty taels per chest. A marked distinction was, however, established between this article and other imports. I have already explained that, by the new regulation, foreigners were empowered to convey their goods into the interior of the country, and that the goods so conveyed were liable to a duty not exceeding $2\frac{1}{2}$ per cent. *ad valorem*. From these advantages the trade in opium was expressly excluded. The Chinese commissioners observed that abuses and collisions with the authorities might arise if foreigners were permitted to carry this drug into the country, and force it into the markets of the interior. Lord Elgin concurred in this opinion; and, farther, deeming an article of this description a very proper subject for taxation, he agreed that the stipulation respecting transit-duties, to which I have referred, should not apply to it. None of the new privileges, therefore, acquired under Lord Elgin's treaty, were extended to opium. It remained on the footing on which general imports stood under the provisions of the Treaty of Nankin. Foreigners could enter it at the open ports upon payment of a duty of thirty taels a chest, but it was then to pass into Chinese hands, and to become subject to such charges as the Chinese government might see fit to impose upon it.

VISIT OF THE COMMISSIONERS.

As affairs were now in an amicable train, it was arranged that the imperial commissioners should pay a grand visit of ceremony to Lord Elgin, and, accordingly, on the 16th of October a large portion of the Shanghai community repaired to the Bund to witness the long uncouth procession, which extended almost from one end of it to the other, and consisted of a most miscellaneous collection of spearmen and banner-men, mounted attendants, and footmen with tall conical red caps, many of them extremely ragged as to costume, regard being apparently had rather to the quantity than the quality of the escort. A great deal of shouting and discordant music heralded the approach of this tattered *cortège*. In the midst of it were the five commissioners in state chairs, preceded and followed by lesser dignitaries in humble chairs.

An interval of nearly four months had elapsed since we had parted with the two senior commissioners, Kweiliang and Hwashana, at Tientsin, so that when Lord Elgin received them at the front door, a cordial greeting, as between old friends, took place.

Although they had never before seen a European house, they manifested an orthodox Chinese indifference at the novel arrangements which now, for the first time, were presented to their view, and, being seated in proper order, the whole party were soon overwhelming each other with the compliments appropriate to the occasion.

We did indeed remark a much greater ease and affability on the part of our guests than had characterized their demeanor at Tientsin; they were evidently actuated by a strong desire to soothe to the uttermost "our uncontrollable fierceness," and took a great apparent interest in Lord Elgin's description of the Transatlantic Telegraph, the news of the success of which had just reached us. The most vivacious of the party was the Governor General Ho: so excited did he become upon a glass of Curaçoa at luncheon, that with a flushed face he began an energetic recital of his functions at Pekin, as the emperor's amanuensis, entering at last into such particulars concerning that high personage, and the etiquette of his court, that his colleagues became alarmed at his garrulous propensities, and my strong-headed friend the judge unceremoniously possessed himself of the next glass which the jovial Ho was about to imbibe, and tossed it down his own throat, with an apologetic remark, tapping his forehead, that Ho was weak in this respect, a statement confirmed by Ho himself, who naïvely informed us that his face was red in consequence of the wine having got into his head.

The judge afterward told me that in all other respects but that of drink Ho's head was strong. At the age of twenty-four he had taken the highest scholastic honors in the empire. His literary labors were as extensive as his imagination was brilliant. He was regarded as one of the finest of Chinese poets, and so skillful in transcribing his thoughts that, before his eyesight had become dimmed from work, he could write a whole poem on a melon seed. At this particular juncture Ho was divided between a desire to conciliate us and chastise the rebels. He evidently considered intoxicating himself at a barbarian meal a master-stroke of policy. In a few days he was to repair to the camp of the imperialist forces and attack the rebels, who were committing some depredations in the neighborhood of Nankin. When Lord Elgin informed the party that he wished to retain a more lasting impression of individuals for whom he had so high a regard than his memory could furnish, and explained to them that Mr. Jocelyn was prepared to take their photographs, they expressed great gratification, and readily took up the required positions, and went through the necessary rigidity of countenance—a simple operation to a Chinaman, who considers it at all times undignified to allow any expression to appear on his face.

On the 18th Lord Elgin returned the visit of the imperial commissioners with a procession of twelve chairs, accompanied by a guard of a hundred marines, and preceded by the band of the Retribution.

An elaborate repast was provided for our entertainment upon this occasion, comprising a more than usual array of Chinese culinary delicacies. The communicative Ho plied Lord Elgin with questions about the government and constitution of England, and showed a greater amount of intelligence and interest in the subject than I had ever before remarked in a Chinaman; even Hwashana, the uncompromising, unbent so far as occasionally to enjoy a joke; while Kweiliang, always anxious to be amiable, constructed pyramids of edibles upon the plates of his neighbors; altogether, our friends seemed gradually to be attaining a better frame of mind, and expressed themselves well pleased with the harmony which characterized our diplomatic intercourse, and full of anxiety for its continuance. There was, however, still one point in reserve, to which the commissioners had not yet alluded, but the importance of which was so great in the eyes of the imperial government that it had led to their special mission to Shanghai. Like the postscript in a lady's letter, however, it had been kept till the last, but the time had now come when the dreaded subject was to be broached, and the effect which their amiability had produced upon the mind of the British plenipotentiary was to be tested.

As this point was none other than that involved in the third article of the Treaty of Tientsin—according to Great Britain the right of a resident minister at Pekin—and as the correspondence which ensued in consequence is especially interesting at the present juncture, I have given it along with the treaty,* in order that the reader may learn the grounds of objection of the Chinese to the enforcement of this treaty-right, and the view which Lord Elgin took in consequence.

The result of this correspondence was, that although the treaty-right was not waived, Lord Elgin promised to submit it as his opinion "that, if her majesty's embassador be properly received at Pekin when the ratifications are exchanged next year, and full effect given in all other particulars to the treaty negotiated at Tientsin, it would certainly be expedient that her majesty's representative in China choose a place of residence elsewhere than at Pekin, and to make his visits to the capital either periodical, or only as frequent as the exigencies of the public service may require."

The commissioners expressed themselves satisfied with this concession, and Lord Elgin determined to take advantage of the temper in which they then were, and their evident desire to satisfy any minor demands in order to gain the one point, to state his determination of proceeding up the Yang-tse-Kiang, "in order that, by personal inspection, he might be the better enabled to judge what ports along its shores it would be most advisable to open, in conformity with the Treaty of Tientsin."

His excellency had long previously determined to make this expedition before leaving China, not merely for the purpose above alluded to, but with the view of creating a wholesome moral impression upon the minds of the people upon its banks, one which should be felt throughout the length and breadth of the empire. He scarcely, however, expected an occasion so opportune as that

* See Appendix.

which now presented itself. So far from making any objection to a proposal which, a few months before, would have caused each particular commissioner's tail to stand on end, they state calmly: "It is our duty to acknowledge this letter, and at the same time to prepare letters, advising the authorities along the lines of your coming. We will also send officers to accompany you with letters, that there may be a satisfactory understanding on both sides."

In the mean time Baron Gros returned from Japan, where he had been equally successful with ourselves. From him we learned, for the first time, the scarcely credible intelligence to which I have already alluded, of the emperor's death six weeks before. The fact had been made public prior to his arrival, and the city of Yedo was mourning profoundly for the departed tycoon during the whole period of his residence in it.

On the 30th of October the commissioners returned Lord Elgin's visit in state, and the project of the Yang-tse-Kiang expedition was discussed. It only remained to obtain the concurrence of Baron Gros and Mr. Reed to the tariff and trade regulations, as agreed upon between the British and Chinese governments, preparatory to their being formally signed.

The harmony which had characterized Lord Elgin's intercourse with both his colleagues throughout was not destined now to be interrupted. They thoroughly assented to the stipulations contained in these important addenda to the Treaty of Tientsin, and on the 8th of November the British and Chinese commissioners met at a temple situated on the outskirts of the city, and affixed their signatures to these documents.

While thus engaged we could see the Furious in the river snorting and pawing like an impatient race-horse, puffing off sharp jets of steam, and lashing the water angrily with her paddles. It was not Lord Elgin's habit to keep her long waiting. We proceeded straight from the temple to our floating home. In a few moments more we were dashing through a maze of shipping in a style peculiar to our gallant ship and its gallant commander, and had proceeded several miles up the broad bosom of the Yang-tse-Kiang before the shades of night compelled us to drop anchor in its little-known waters.

CHAPTER XXXIV.

All the Ships aground.—The Delta of the Yang-tse.—Channel-hunting.—The Kiang-yin Bluffs.—Aspect of the River-banks.—Hard and fast.—Silver Island.—Yang-chow.—A Scene of Desolation.—Chinkiang.—Effects of Rebel Occupation.—Golden Island.—Magnificent View.—Off the Rock.—Tan-too.—Translation of Chinese Names.—Chinese Orthography.—Entrance to the Grand Canal.—Absence of Junk Traffic.—Approach to Nankin.—Action with the Rebels at Nankin.—Its Results.

THE ships which composed the squadron that accompanied Lord Elgin upon his voyage up the Yang-tse-Kiang were the Retribution, Captain Barker, senior officer commanding; the Furious, Captain Sherard Osborn; the Cruiser, Captain Bythesea; the Dove, surveying gun-boat, Commander Ward, and the Lee gun-boat, Lieutenant (now Commander) Jones.

In order to give as clear and detailed account as possible of this most successful and interesting expedition, I shall extract from my journal the daily record of events.

9th November. All our squadron are in sight this morning, but we are dotted about the yellow waters of the Yang-tse in a somewhat irregular fashion. The Cruiser, which had preceded us yesterday, discovered a sand-bank before nightfall, upon which she reposed for many hours, the receding tide leaving her so high and dry that it was found necessary to shore her up, and her officers were enabled to enjoy their exercise in the afternoon by walking round her without wetting their feet. She got off with the high tide, however, and is now at anchor some miles ahead. The Dove and Lee are exploring for a channel; we move on gently in obedience to their signals: the Retribution, drawing more water than any of us, follows cautiously, but nevertheless takes the bottom; the Dove goes to her assistance, and we are left to find our own way, which we don't succeed in doing, but ground hopelessly at the top of high water on hard sand. Before dark the Retribution gets off and comes to our assistance, slowly feeling her way, as a man does on weak ice when he goes to rescue a friend who has tumbled in.

It soon becomes evident that we have no alternative but to

lighten the ship, and all night long the crew are engaged transferring to the Lee the heavy guns and coal, and pumping the water from the boilers.

10*th*. We have already learned to place no reliance on any of the Admiralty charts of the Yang-tse. However accurately the survey may have originally been, the changes which have taken place in the bed of the river since they were made are so great that we have only our instinct for deep water to depend upon. At the spot on which we are now aground nine fathoms are marked in the chart. Meanwhile twenty-four hours of most incessant and arduous exertions on the part of both officers and men have lightened the ship sufficiently to enable the powerful Retribution to drag her off by main force.

The Dove and Lee have found the channel at last, and before nightfall we are all anchored together in the Fairway, under Harvey Point. The breadth of the river is still so great that the opposite shore, which is flat, is not visible.

11*th*. Fortune seems inclined to smile upon us to-day. We move rapidly and freely along, with plenty of water and a fair wind. As we pass the spot marked in the chart as the end of Tsung-ming Island, we observe an unexpected continuation of the shore, which seems to connect this island with the land formerly known as Mason Island, blocking up completely the channel marked in the charts as dividing them. It is not improbable that this important physical change in the delta of the Yang-tse-Kiang may have altered the direction of the current, and diverted a larger portion of it through the northern channel, which may now be found to be the most available for navigation.

Beyond this the river begins to narrow rapidly. At Fooshan, the Hill of Peace, it is not above six miles in breadth. A village and fort are here picturesquely situated on some low hills on the right bank. On the opposite shore a high conical hill is visible, crowned by a pagoda known as Langshan, or Wolf's Hill. We are just congratulating ourselves on our rapid progress, when the gun-boats in advance run up the hated signal, "No Channel," and, splitting off in opposite directions, skirmish cautiously about in search of deep water.

It is a pretty sight to watch these trusty little craft, acting as pioneers to the three large ships which follow carefully in their track some distance astern, ever on the alert to respond to the caution-signal, and placing in them that sort of confidence which a sportsman does in his dogs. Now they are ranging the river far and wide; now they are pointing; we creep up gently, they creep on as gently; the scent seems good: now they are at fault, they throw up their noses, and away again to the right and left, signaling every cast of the lead. We keep under easy steam for a while, reading the flags as they are run up; two fathoms, two and a half, three, two — it is of no use, so we let go the anchor, pipe suppers, and make all snug for the night.

12*th*. This is a busy but unsuccessful day; ship's boats as well as gun-boats are out channel-hunting. There must be a passage somewhere just in front of us—six fathoms are marked on the chart. We pull to the spot, and touch the bottom with a boat-hook; so it is clearly not there. The Dove has harked back and is out of sight; may she bring back good news to-morrow. Meantime we stay where we are.

13*th*. Nothing could be more enjoyable than the temperature at this time of year in the Yang-tse-Kiang; but these lovely days only aggravate us, so long as we are chained to one spot. At night the Dove returned with the welcome intelligence that she has found a channel.

14*th*. Under weigh at daylight. We are compelled to retrace our steps for about six miles; then we cross over to the northern shore, and find a deep broad lead, along which we steam freely for the remainder of the day. The river is still very wide and the shores flat until we reach the Kiang-yin bluffs, behind which is situated the city of the same name. The Cruiser, with her limited horse-power, has not been able to keep up with us, so we anchor here a little before sunset.

15*th*. At the Kiang-yin bluffs the river narrows considerably, and presents scenery of a somewhat picturesque character. Two batteries are built so as to command this pass, but in such a way that their flank might very easily be turned. After rounding the hills, one of which is crowned with a temple, we open up the tall pagoda of Kiang-yin. A great quantity of junks crowded the creek leading to the town. In rear was a range of hills of moderate elevation, between which and the river margin intervened a strip of pleasantly-wooded country. Beyond this the river again expands; the banks once more sink to a dull uniform level, and the only signs of life are people cutting the enormous bulrushes which fringe them.

We observed large flights of wild geese and ducks passing southward. As the wind was ahead and the current strong, we took the Cruiser in tow. The Retribution performed the same kind office for the Dove and Lee, whose tubes wanted cleaning. Our progress to-day was necessarily slow; fortunately, the navigation was comparatively free from difficulty.

16*th*. At seven o'clock this morning the thermometer stood at 37°. Shortly after getting under weigh we passed Keunshan Pagoda, perched upon a hill overhanging the river. At this point the banks become very picturesque—high rocky bluffs rise precipitously from the water's edge, and behind them a range of irregular pointed hills form a complete amphitheatre. On the left bank the shores are wooded and populous, occasionally extensively cultivated, and groups of peasants collect upon the water's edge to look at us, as the five ships progress steadily in line against both wind and stream. Here, too, we remarked extraordinary changes in the course of the river. At one place it divides; one channel, at least half a mile in width, surrounding a populous island, which, at the date of the chart, had been part of the main land.

The sharp exhilarating air, our steady progress, and the increasing interest of the river-banks, all combined to raise our spirits. Presently we sweep round a bold projecting bluff, and Silver Island opens to view, with its quaint temples embowered in autumnal foliage; their white walls are gleaming, and their frowzy priests are basking in the midday sun. Beyond, a noble reach of the river curves beneath the swelling hills which rise from its margin, their summits crowned with the irregular wall of Chinkiang, and their slopes strewn with the debris of that once populous city; while in the distance, as though rising from mid-stream, stands a precipitous rock called Golden Island, with its tall pagoda pointing to the skies.

The scene is one of such surpassing interest and beauty that it rivets our gaze. We are just lamenting that we can not stop for a moment to appreciate more fully its merits, when—crash, our wishes are gratified—the old ship gives a heave and a lurch. It is too late now to "stop her," and go "full speed astern." We are irrevocably pinnacled on the top of a rock; the Cruiser has barely had time to avoid running into us, and shaves cleverly past us as she sheers off. The Retribution, panic-stricken, has let go her anchor. With her gun-boats swinging in mid-stream astern, she looks like a kite with a tail. The current sweeps and eddies past with impetuous velocity, and gradually succeeds in jamming us broadside on to the rock, converting us into a sort of break-water, so that we have quite a little sea on one side, and a dead calm on the other.

We have ceased to enjoy the view now, that pleasure being transferred to our friends the priests, who are apparently much interested in the spectacle. We are within easy hailing distance of them: they afterward told us they were perfectly aware of the danger that awaited us, but they gave us no warning. The whole British fleet, consisting of several ships of the line, besides smaller craft, had passed through this channel fifteen years before without discovering this fatal rock, and sixteen fathoms were marked above it. We were by no means proud of our discovery, but nobody was to blame except the priests, and we were too amiable to quarrel with them, so we landed and paid them a visit. The island had been visited by the rebels at a comparatively recent date. A great part of the very handsome temple had been destroyed, and the idols cast into the river by them. A celebrated vase, reputed to be more than two thousand years old, was kept here; but, on the rumored approach of these iconoclasts, those who were intrusted with the safe-keeping of this precious relic buried it in time to insure its safety, and it had not since been exhumed. A temple, which formerly stood on the highest part of the island, had been burned, more, according to the bonzes, for the purpose of terrifying the neighborhood than from fanaticism.

The island itself was little more than a tumulus rising out of the centre of the Yang-tse to a height of scarce two hundred feet, covered with the richest foliage, at this season of the year a blaze of fiery tints. Its highest point was still crowned with a small edifice, pagoda-shaped, but which contained nothing more interesting than the somewhat unimaginative inscriptions of the British sailor: most of these bore the date of August, 1842. From this elevated position, an extensive panoramic view was obtained over the broad, richly-cultivated plain, which stretches away to the northward, at this particular juncture the scene of rebel depredations. We could see, looming through the distant haze, the pagoda of Yang-chow, reported to be recently taken and still occupied by the rebels. It was to eject them from this city that the energetic Ho had quitted us so abruptly at Shanghai, so that this martial statesman and poet was even now in our immediate proximity. Yang-chow is situated on the Grand Canal, and was formerly reputed to be a city of great wealth and splendor; it has been on three separate occasions in the hands of the insurgents. Mr. Wylie says that a famous imperial library was kept here, of which there were only two duplicates in existence, one at Pekin, and the other at Hang-chow. This valuable collection of books, if not destroyed, is divided and completely dispersed. We could discern the houses of Kwa-chow from the top of Silver Island, well known as the entrance of the Grand Canal into the Yang-tse; and in other directions numerous villages and towns met the eye, dotted over the fertile plains, and giving evidence of a large population.

As in nature the most exquisite flowers are generally inhabited by slimy caterpillars, so in China the most lovely retreats are invariably tenanted by grimy ecclesiastics. We are bound to remember, however, that we are indebted to them for picturesque buildings, which harmonize admirably with the scenes in which they are situated; while the priests themselves, in their long, ash-colored robes, are an agreeable addition, so long as they are kept in the back-ground of the picture. These gentry informed us that the tidal influence extended beyond this point, but was not regular in its operations. They led us to expect, however, a rise of two or three feet, and this, we trusted, would be sufficient to float us off. Meantime, in order to be the better able to take advantage of any favorable change which might occur, we commenced, for the second time, to lighten the ship, divesting her of shot, guns, spars, coal, etc., and working all through the night.

17*th*. Landed on the right bank, and walked to Chinkiang over about two miles of plain, intersected by the remains of rough earth-works. This strip of level ground, which intervenes between a range of hills and the river, was until recently the abode of a thriving and industrious population. Scarce a year has elapsed since it was a scene of violence and bloodshed, the theatre of an action between the rebel and imperialist forces. The devastation is now widespread and complete. A few of the peasantry have crawled back to the desolate spots which they recognize as the sites of their former homes, and, selecting the heaps of rubbish which still belong to them, have commenced to construct out of them wretched abodes—roughly thatching in a gable-end that has escaped the general destruction, or replacing the stones which once composed the walls with strips of matting. Miserable patches of garden were being brought into existence between the crumbling, weed-covered walls; but the destitute appearance of the scanty population served rather to increase than diminish the effect which this abomination of desolation was calculated to produce.

We entered the city by the north gate, and might have imagined ourselves in Pompeii. We walked along deserted streets, between roofless houses, and walls overgrown with rank, tangled weeds; heaps of rubbish blocked up the thoroughfares, but they obstructed nobody. There was something oppressive in the universal stillness, and we almost felt refreshed by a foul odor which greeted our nostrils, and warned us that we had approached an inhabited street.

At a spot where were a few chow-chow shops, and two partially-inhabited streets crossed each other, was the most lively place in the town. We obtained a small share of interest here from a mob of hungry, ragged boys; but the people generally seemed too much depressed even to stare at a barbarian, and we strolled unmolested in any direction our fancy led us.

On our way to a fort which crowned a bluff overhanging the river, we passed under some handsome stone arches, which were still standing conspicuous amid the desolation by which they were surrounded. From our elevated position we commanded an extensive view over the area inclosed by the walls of the city, and which was thickly strewn with its ruins.

Chinkiang was first taken by the insurgents, almost without resistance, on the 1st of April, 1853, and was held by them against a continued imperialist siege up to the commencement of 1857, when it was evacuated in consequence of the failure of supplies. It has been held by the imperialist forces ever since. To judge, however, from the reluctance manifested by its former inhabitants to return to it, confidence is but partially restored. Only the very poorest class of traders and shopkeepers have ventured into its dilapidated streets; and although efforts are being made by the government to give some stimulus to its repopulation, by rebuilding some of the public buildings, such as the government offices, the Confucian Temple, the Drum Tower, etc., the results are by no means encouraging. The rebels have, during their occupation, considerably enlarged the boundaries of the city, having carried a wall over the heights to the east of it, and down nearly to the water's edge on the bank of the river, inclosing a large space beyond the old wall in both directions. The population of Chinkiang was formerly estimated at about 500,000; it does not now probably contain above 500 souls.

18*th*. We have painted a water-line on the rocks, so as to be able to detect the variations of the tide at a glance. As, however, there were no indications of a rise to-day, and the ship seemed immovable, we chartered a small native boat, and started off on an expedition to Golden Island, distant about five miles. As we approached it, we discovered, to our astonishment, that it was no longer an island. Flourishing cabbage-fields now occupied the space marked on the chart as a channel with four fathoms of water in it.

We landed on this recently-formed peninsula, and walked across it to the rock. Climbing up the steps hewn out of the living stone, we reached the base of the pagoda, shorn now of those external decorations which once rendered it celebrated, but still standing, a battered monument of its own departed glory, and of the beauty by which it was surrounded.

Heaps of unsightly ruins marked the spot where once was grouped a picturesque collection of temples and pagodas. The Chinese themselves appreciated its romantic beauty. Sir John Davis thus describes the impression produced upon him by a distant view of it, obtained years before: "The celebrated Kinshan, or Golden Island, which, with its pagoda, and the ornamental roofs of its temples and other buildings, looked like a fairy creation rising out of the waters of the Kiang." "This picturesque place," he remarks, "is celebrated all over China."

Now, with the exception of the dilapidated pagoda, there is not one stone left upon another of the remaining buildings. Though so recently destroyed, a remarkable air of antiquity seems to pervade this sacred spot. The rock-cut steps are worn and crumbling, and the ruins generally look as though centuries had passed since the destroyer's hand had been ruthlessly at work. A line of wall with a few wretched guns in the embrasures, a few wretched soldiers in some mat tents in rear, and a quantity of gay, flaunting flags, indicate that this is a military post. These banners and embrasures are apparent on numerous hill-tops, and surround the city of Chinkiang. If we were to judge by them, the preparations for defense would seem extensive indeed; but it is scarcely too much to assert that there are more flags than embrasures, more embrasures than guns, and more guns than men.

We sat down on the top of the rock to discuss a sandwich and a glass of sherry, and enjoy the view. It was one of melancholy beauty. On our right the skeleton houses of the city clustering up the hill sides, and filling the whole amphitheatre with their ruins—the straggling wall running along the ridges, gay with gaudy banners when all around is sad, and defending, as though in mockery, a dreary waste of rubbish; beyond, the irregular outline of distant hills, with the broad river spreading itself proudly out upon the fertile plains to the north and east; fronting us Silver Island, its bright coloring toned down by distance, and its soft outline contrasting with the precipitous bluffs beside it, all combined to form a picture upon which it was pleasant to gaze in that mild autumnal afternoon.

We could discern the ships anchored in mid-stream: one which was broadside on, and leaning very much over, was a feature in the scene we could have gladly dispensed with. In the situation of Chinkiang, its ruined state and the nature of the surrounding country, I was a good deal reminded of Kertch after its evacuation by the Russians. We walked through it on our way back, and found on our arrival at the ship some excitement existing at the prospect of getting off. The paddle-wheels were revolving violently; hawsers and stream-cables were out in sundry directions; those who were not hauling at something were jumping or rolling the ship. At last a happy and combined effort proved successful, and she seemed literally to tumble off her perch into deep water. The event was signaled by three hearty cheers from all hands, which had no sooner subsided than, to our astonishment, we heard them faintly echoed from the shore. We were wondering whether the Chinamen were mocking us when they were repeated, and we then discovered that Lord Elgin and a small party of walkers were thus heartily testifying their satisfaction. The singular stillness of the evening air rendered sounds audible at a great distance. Two hundred and sixty tons in weight had been removed from the ship before she had been sufficiently lightened to float off the rock.

19*th*. Finding that we should be detained all day in re-embarking our heavy weights, a party of us landed on the right bank to take a stroll with our guns and explore the country. We killed three brace of pheasants in the flat, half-cultivated, half-wild land near the margin of the river, and one of our party had a shot at a deer. We approached, but did not enter the small town of Tantoo. It has been several times in the hands of the rebels, and was the farthest point reached by them in their course seaward. It was in a more flourishing condition than Chinkiang, but prosperous only by contrast. Although it has been in the hands of the imperialists for a much longer time than that city, a large portion of the town still remains in ruins. There has been no attempt to rebuild the temples, and many of the poorer inhabitants are living in straw huts. Mr. Wylie, a gentleman connected with the American mission at Shanghai, and who accompanied the squadron for some distance up the river, told us that formerly it was a place of small but active trade, and at times a scene of busy traffic, from the number of boats passing up and down the creek on which it is situated, this being one of the outlets from the Grand Canal at seasons when the route by Chinkiang is impassable.

20*th*. A little after daylight this morning we bade adieu to our anchorage off Silver Island, or, as it is called by the Chinese, T'seaou Shan, or the Hill of Sorrow—so far as it had concerned us, most appropriately so named. In spite of Mr. Meadows' amusing criticism upon Père Huc's practice of translating Chinese names, in some of which the latter has perhaps given a little too loose a rein to his poetical imagination, I shall indulge with moderation in the same weakness, partly because I find that other sinalogues do not admit the force of Mr. Meadows' objection; while I certainly can not grant the truth of his analogy, upon which alone I am competent to have any opinion.

Mr. Meadows very justly remarks that it would be absurd for any Frenchman talking of "Reading" to translate it by the French word "Lecture," but he surely is not correct when he says that it would be equally absurd to talk of "Bath" as "Bain." It may very properly be doubted whether "Reading" is the English for "Lecture;" but it is, to say the least of it, highly probable that if no "Bains" had existed at Bath, that city would have been endowed with some less significant appellation.

The name of the great river itself upon which we were now

voyaging has usually received an interpretation, which I was assured by Messrs. Wade and Lay was not the correct one. "The Son of the Ocean" is certainly a more poetical rendering of the word Yang-tse-Kiang than "the Son that Spreads;" but the latter is said to be its literal meaning, and this seems the more probable, as it is only applied to the river below Silver Island, where the delta commences, and its waters expand over vast alluvial plains to the sea.

Above this point the river is only known among the natives as the Ta-kiang, or "Great River," which, if it were written as it is pronounced, would be spelt Ta-cheang.

I have, however, in this instance retained the old style of spelling, to avoid confusion. Generally, in giving the names of places upon the river-bank, I have adopted the principle of endeavoring to render with English letters the nearest possible approximation to the sound of the Chinese word. In doing so, I know that I incur the scorn and contempt of even the most amiable of Chinese sinalogues. These gentlemen have attempted, by a copious use of the alphabets of other European languages, and with the assistance of their forms of accentuation and modes of pronunciation, in addition to those contained in our own, to convey to our English ear some idea of the sounds which issue from Chinese throats and noses.

I deny that by any allocation of the letters known to civilized mortals you can impart to them the faintest notion of sounds of which they are totally ignorant. Indeed, the hopelessness of the task is pretty well proved by the fact that every sinalogue sets about it in a different way. Take, for instance, the following word, the name of a city up the river, which, according to the late Mr. Morrison, is spelled Ke-chow; according to Williams, K'í-chau; according to Wade, Ch'i-chou; and according to the Jesuit maps, Khi-tcheou. As one utterly unlearned in Chinese myself, and presuming that my reader is equally ignorant of that euphonious tongue, I would recommend him to sneeze, as the easiest way of making the same sound that a Chinaman would in alluding to the above city. The town at which we afterward left the Retribution was spelt by the above authorities in four different ways, viz., Kew-heen, Kiu-hien, Chiu-hsien, Kieou-sien.

Let us then determine to employ a good, honest Saxon pronunciation in our use of Chinese proper names, and resign the grunts and snorts which properly belong to them to persons who have studied the art of producing those sounds. At Canton we have Anglicized the native word into something attainable by English tongues, nor do we talk of Ning-*poh*; let us not be driven into calling Pekin, Pei-ching, as the latest vocabulary has it, for, even if we did, no Chinaman would understand us.

Henceforth, then, we are to be considered as navigating the mighty waters of the Ta-kiang, and well does it deserve its high-sounding title. A little after passing Golden Island we find ourselves abreast the walled town of Kwa-chow, or the Island of Gourds. At this point the Grand Canal enters the Ta-kiang from the northward, and here formerly a dense crowd of trading junks were at all times collected. It was taken by the rebels the day after they captured Chinkiang, and was only recovered about the end of 1857. It is now a military position, and we observed a considerable body of cavalry picketed among its ruins; not a trading junk was visible on what was formerly the great highway for the internal commerce of the empire.

Lord Elgin thus alludes to the condition in which we found the Grand Canal, as bearing upon his recent policy in the north: "Soon after leaving Silver Island we passed the mouth of the Great Canal, which we found to be entirely deserted save by a few imperialist war-vessels. Captain Osborn informed me that, when he was at the same place in 1842, the grain-junks were so numerous that it was difficult to force a way through them. Your lordship may perhaps remember that when, in April last, I resolved to bring pressure to bear on the emperor by ascending the Peiho River to Tientsin, it was remarked in some quarters that we ought rather to have followed the precedent of the former war, and to have instituted a blockade in the River Yang-tse. I thought at the time that this suggestion was an anachronism, and what I have seen on this trip confirms this opinion.

"We could hardly have done more than the rebels have done to inflict suffering on the population, and render these districts unproductive to government, and yet no effect has been produced by these proceedings on the court of Pekin."*

Proceeding onward from Kwa-chow, we passed the districts of E-ching and Luh-ho, which have frequently been the scene of Tai-ping incursions. Latterly they have been infested by rioters

* *Blue-Book*, p. 443.

of another class, known among the natives by the name Něě-fei, more local, but not less dreaded than the former.

The country now becomes more hilly in character, and at half past four P.M. we pass under Ping-shan Pagoda, situated on the top of a hill, backed by irregular ranges, with valleys in deep shadow, and crests glowing in the afternoon sun. But we were getting too near Nankin to think of any other effects than those which are likely to be produced by the appearance of the Lee in front of its batteries. This gun-boat, with Mr. Wade on board, has been sent ahead to feel the way, and communicate with the rebels, should the latter be so disposed.* We follow, a mile or so astern, the Dove leading the Retribution, the Furious towing the Cruiser.

It may be imagined with what anxious eyes we followed the little craft as she passed battery after battery, apparently unnoticed by their occupants. By this time we were passing through the fleet of imperialist junks, which formed the advanced position of the force then investing Nankin. The crews of these vessels were watching our proceedings with breathless interest. At last, just as the Lee seemed beyond the reach of the farthest battery, the red flag was run up on all the forts, and from the lowest a round-shot was fired, which whistled over the Lee, and caused her

---

* The following is the memorandum which Lord Elgin addressed to Captain Barker upon this occasion, together with the instructions furnished by that officer to Lieutenant Jones, commanding the "Lee:"

Memorandum for Captain Barker's information.

"Collision with the rebels should, if possible, be avoided. If, therefore, the authorities in the vicinity of Nankin evince any desire to communicate, we should be prepared to give them every reasonable assurance that we do not present ourselves with hostile intentions. At the same time, it will be proper that they should be informed that we are proceeding up the river in the exercise of our treaty-rights, and that any attempt to arrest our progress, by whomsoever made, will be resisted.

"Elgin and Kincardine."

Instructions addressed to Lieutenant Jones.

"It is my direction that you proceed with all possible speed toward Nankin, embarking Mr. T. Wade, Chinese Secretary. Should no notice be taken of the Lee, you will proceed past Nankin, and await my joining. Should you see any boat with officials clearly approaching the Lee, you will stop and communicate. Should a shot be fired at or ahead of you, you will hoist a flag of truce, and close the fort for the purpose of communication. Should the flag of truce be fired upon, you will immediately rejoin the squadron, and under no circumstances are you to fire without signal from me.   (Signed),   C. Barker, Captain, Senior Officer."

to run up smartly the flag of truce. So far, however, from this signal producing the desired effect, it had not floated three minutes at the fore before seven shots were fired at it in rapid succession; Lieutenant Jones, true to his orders, not returning the fire until he saw the "engage" signal flying from the mast-head of the Retribution. By this time the Dove had got well within range, and she opened the ball with spirit almost at the same moment that the Lee proceeded to indemnify herself for her forbearance by a vigorous cannonade. The Retribution, Furious, and Cruiser now ranged up as close to the batteries as possible, and, moving very slowly ahead, threw in a pretty hot shower of shot and shell. At this point the river is not above a thousand yards broad, with batteries on both banks, which replied warmly to our fire, and gave abundant occupation to the starboard as well as the port guns.

Lord Elgin had taken up his position on the bridge between the paddle-boxes; but a round-shot cutting through a rope within two feet of his head induced Captain Osborn to exert his authority as commander, and we were all ordered to the deck. Fortunately, although the ship was hulled seven or eight times, two round-shot going into Lord Elgin's cabin, and another smashing his barge, no more serious casualty occurred than a scratch from a splinter.

Meanwhile the Retribution, which was just ahead of us, did not escape so happily. She had one man killed and two wounded severely, one of whom, the signal midshipman, Mr. Birch, lost an arm, and the other a leg. It was now nearly half past five; the action had only lasted thirty-five minutes, and we had passed all the forts. As evening was closing in, it was determined to anchor for the night about two miles above the city. Captain Barker, in consultation with Captain Osborn, then decided that the impertinence of the rebels in offering resistance to our progress up the river in the exercise of our treaty-right, and firing upon a flag of truce, ought not to go unpunished. In this view Lord Elgin fully concurs; and it is accordingly arranged that at daylight to-morrow we drop down abreast of the batteries, and hammer them into ruins and their garrisons into submission.

CHAPTER XXXV.

Renewal of the Action.—A sharp Bombardment.—The Batteries silenced.—An Action between Rebels and Imperialists.—Progress up Stream.—The Rebels receive a Lesson.—We land for Information.—Destitute Peasantry.—Request to aid the Rebels.—Notification in reply.—Enter the province Ngan-Hwui.—A military Procession.—The Eastern and Western Pillar Gates.—Arrival at Woohoo.—A Letter from the Rebel Chief.—We pay him a Visit.—A disorderly Mob.—Variegated Costumes.—An imperialist Spy.—Former Condition of Woohoo.—Its present State.—A Tai-ping Manifesto.

October 21st. Day had not yet dawned when we were all awake and bustling on board the Furious. The vigorous fire kept up last evening, and the readiness evinced by the rebels to commence an engagement, led us to anticipate a sharp action to-day, and we made our preparations accordingly. The morning was chill and biting, but the blood was circulating pretty rapidly in the veins of most of us nevertheless, and we were warmed with the healthy glow arising from the excitement of anticipation. Gradually the two hills, upon the sides and round the base of which Nankin is situated, loomed through the early haze, and then the long line of batteries on the right bank became indistinctly visible.

Opposite, the solitary fort of Poo-kow was appropriated exclusively to the Cruiser; and as we scanned the fair proportions of that handsome craft, we doubted not that her eighteen guns would render a very good account of its batteries. Gradually the details of the scene became wonderfully distinct; the batteries seemed getting suddenly larger; and I for the first time discovered that we were no longer at anchor, but floating silently with the tide into the respective positions allotted to the different ships.

As the Poo-kow battery was the nearest, the Cruiser got first into action, and her gallant commander, Bythesea, seemed determined not to give the garrison any excuse for missing him. He ranged his ship steadily up to within fifty yards of the guns, as though taunting the enemy to begin, and then opened his broadside with telling effect. A few feeble shot were returned in reply; but so rapid and destructive was the Cruiser's fire, that it was evident the fort of Poo-kow was not long destined to be the abiding-place of its brave garrison.

The discharge of our own pivot-gun roused us from the contemplation of the Cruiser's achievements, and the remaining three ships now began, in concert with ourselves, to pour such a storm of shot, shell, grape, and rockets into the batteries, that our fire of the previous evening seemed mere child's play to the bombardment we were now keeping up. It evidently produced its effect in the rebel batteries, for they replied but feebly and at intervals. From the main-top-gallant cross-trees I could look down into the forts, and see the men in bright dresses clustering round the guns, or grouped in sheltered corners, or bolting like rabbits from some spot where a Moorsom shell had just burst, scattering fragments and spreading dismay far and wide.

The one-sided nature of the action may be gathered from the fact that, during the hour and a half that it lasted, we were only hulled once, while no casualties occurred on board any of the ships. It was evident that either our bombardment of the previous evening, or the suddenness with which we opened fire this morning, had thoroughly cowed our opponents. Their fire gradually ceased entirely, and, as an ardent young midshipman lugubriously remarked, "they seemed determined not to show us any sport." So the original intention of landing and spiking the guns was given up, and we withdrew, the less reluctantly as we observed the imperialist fleet through which we had passed the evening before plucking up heart, and, led by a steamer in the service of the Chinese government, commence a fierce action at a three-mile range.

When the rebels saw that we were in no way connected or cooperating with this valiant squadron, they opened fire upon it manfully from some of the batteries which had suffered least from our bombardment; and as we steamed away up the river, we could hear the action still raging furiously, in all probability with very slight consequences to either side.

The Chinese commissioners at Shanghai had appointed a petty mandarin to accompany us, whose presence was intended as a guarantee, to the authorities with whom we might come in contact, of our recognized right to navigate the waters of the Ta-kiang, and who was also expected to assist us in commissariat and other arrangements. This gentleman lived in a boat which we towed astern, and which, upon the morning of the action, was left at anchor in the stream, while its occupants were taken on board the Cruiser for safety, where they remained in a considerable state of alarm until it was over.

We observed the heights in rear of Nankin crowned with the tents and banners of the imperialist forces investing the city, their encampment extending apparently for many miles.

Shortly after, we observed a fleet of junks ahead which we presumed to be rebel, more especially as we saw them firing apparently at the Dove, then our leading gun-boat. Mr. Wade was accordingly sent on in the Lee to investigate, and discovered them to be an imperialist squadron engaging the advanced rebel batteries in this direction.

The action was so feebly maintained that we passed through the midst of it without condescending to notice the fire of either side.

An island about eight miles long extends from Nankin to this point, where the rebel batteries are separated from the imperial position of Hea-san-shan by a narrow creek. This is the only point held by the imperialists on the south bank between Nankin and a post a few miles above Woohoo, or about sixty miles higher up the river.

We now observed ranges of hills, apparently varying between one and two thousand feet in height, on both sides of the river. Those to the north were at a great distance, and only occasionally visible. The southern ranges, however, in some places approach the river, decreasing in elevation, and forming a line of bluffs overhanging the water. The plain which intervened between us and the northern ranges was apparently thinly populated, and, as far as we could discern, an expanse of marshes and moorland. We passed only one insurgent position on the northern bank, that of Too-tse-ke; and in the distance we could distinguish the pagoda of Ho-chow, the chief city of a department of the same name, and now in the hands of the rebels. It is mentioned by Sir John Davis as having been visited by some of Lord Amherst's party on the occasion of their ascent of the river in 1816. When we refer to their account of the traffic upon its waters in those days, it is melancholy to think of the change which the last few years have wrought upon the internal trade of central China. During the whole of this day's steaming we did not observe a single junk upon this magnificent highway of commerce.

We were destined not to close the day, which had commenced

so noisily, without a little more excitement. Upon rounding a bold bluff which projected into the river, we came suddenly upon a small town, built in a recess of the hills, and protected by two or three circular stone redoubts, mounting three or four guns each. These we were inspecting through our telescopes, very much in the spirit in which a Newfoundland would investigate a lapdog, when, to our amazement, a posse of swaggering rebels came trooping down to the water's edge, dressed, as is usual with them, in many-colored garments, flourishing yellow and crimson flags, and led by a horseman in a crimson coat and loose white trowsers, who looked extremely picturesque, caracoling and vaporing in front of his variegated men. He brandished a matchlock in his hand, which he fired defiantly at us, we being about five hundred yards distant at the time; thereupon his followers exploded, in a futile and absurd manner, all their gingalls at us. This they did two or three times, and we slackened speed to watch their humors; but when they all repaired into one of the circular redoubts, and popped off one of their brass guns at us, we considered the joke had gone far enough, and sent a round-shot whistling over their heads. But the flags waved more defiantly than ever; so the Retribution, making splendid practice, dropped a Moorsom right into the centre of the fort, sending the entire construction into the air, and those of its occupants who were still alive skimming along the bare hill side, their panic-stricken leader, now on foot, rolling repeatedly over and over in his headlong flight, and the bright garments of his soldiers streaming in the wind as they ran after him. The sight tickled Jack's fancy so much that he could scarcely stand by his gun for laughing.

The town itself was surrounded by a wall, and perched upon a low hill about fifteen hundred yards distant. A large crowd had collected outside the gate, chiefly composed of rebel soldiers watching the proceedings. We sent them a ten-inch shell, just to give them some idea of our armament. The impression which this little episode produced was most salutary, as we found the same evening, when we anchored a few miles higher up, close to the prefectural city of Tai-ping. The place at which it occurred was called Tsae-shih-ke.

A division of the river into three channels just below Tai-ping baffled us a little before sunset; so we remained there for the night, and I went on shore with Mr. Wade for the purpose of collecting information from some stray peasant near the river-bank with reference to the relative merits of the channels ahead. After the little experience we had just had of their feelings toward us, we were compelled to proceed with caution. As it was not deemed advisable to go out of sight or range of the ships, we landed near a hut a few yards from the river-bank, and walked up alone to reconnoitre it. Not a soul was visible: a harsh-voiced cur, which bayed incessantly at us, was the only sign of life, until at last we dug out a very decrepit old woman, who refused to comprehend Wade's excellent Chinese, till an old man, overhearing his repeated assurances that we should do them no harm, emerged from a place of concealment, but proved very little more intelligent than his better half. His long matted hair only partially concealed the tail that was coiled up beneath it, while his cadaverous countenance and ragged attire proved that he, at all events, had not thriven on rebellion. When we asked him whether he was a rebel, he answered with a shrug, "How could he be otherwise." He told us that he was wretchedly poor, and gave us to understand that he and all his neighbors had been utterly ruined by the "troublesome pests," as they are commonly called by the Loyalists. The aspect of the surrounding country fully confirmed our informant's account of the destitution of its inhabitants; for, in addition to the rural population which properly belonged to it, the fields were dotted with wretched straw huts, the temporary abodes of the townspeople, who had been ejected from their urban domiciles by the rebels, it being the practice of these vagabonds to appropriate to themselves the houses of the unfortunate citizens.

The entire population in districts occupied by rebels allow their hair to grow, long hair being the distinguishing characteristic of the Tai-ping faction. Hence they are commonly called "the long-haired men." Generally, however, from prudential motives, they preserve their tails concealed beneath their flowing locks, so that in the event of their falling into the clutches of the imperialists, they may, by a rapid tonsure, be enabled to assume the aspect of a long-tailed adherent of the imperial cause.

Shortly after our return to the ship a communication arrived from a rebel chief at Tai-ping, inclosed in a yellow envelope, on one side of which was written, "Your younger brother, junior tsien-tien of the navy, Hiung Kwang Ming, respectfully greets your excellencies the foreigners." On the other, the date, "13th day of the 10th moon of the 8th year—viz., the Wu-Wu of the Heavenly Kingdom of Tai-ping," was covered by the official seal of the same Hiung, setting forth his titles as above.

Within he writes, after repeating the greeting written on the cover: "Whereas your younger brother is in chief command of the armed (*lit.*, gun) vessels of the Heavenly Kingdom, and has been several years engaged with the boats of the demons without being able to exterminate them, he earnestly prays your foreign excellencies, with all your heart and might, to assist him in annihilating the rebel vessels; and your younger brother will present a memorial to the Heavenly King, moving him to confer titles and rewards on your foreign excellencies."

The inducements here held out were, unfortunately for the rebels, not sufficiently attractive to tempt Lord Elgin to assist them in the laudable undertaking of exterminating the "Demons," or "Imps," as the imperialists are usually styled by the rebels.

The following notification was returned in reply to the above:

"The Earl of Elgin, embassador of her majesty the Queen of England, issues a notification: Whereas a number of her majesty's ships were on their way to Hankow, it was the particular desire of the embassador that the party in possession of Nankin should understand that these ships were proceeding with no hostile intentions to them. For this purpose, a small vessel was specially detached in advance. A gun was fired on her, to which, in obedience to her instructions, she made no return, but hoisted a flag of truce. The garrison of Nankin, notwithstanding, continued to fire at her. The forts commanding the passage have been, in consequence, taken and demolished, as a warning to all who may be hereafter minded to interfere with the ships of her majesty."

We subsequently learned that news of the punishment which we had inflicted on Nankin this morning had reached Tai-ping by land as quickly as we had by water, and produced exactly the impression which Lord Elgin desired upon the rebel leaders at the forts farther up the river. The importance of securing ourselves from farther molestation by a vigorous display of force at the outset seemed to him to justify the somewhat rough treatment which the Nankin insurgents had experienced at our hands.

A farther evidence of their desire to conciliate was obtained at a late hour of the night. After we had "turned in," some of our party were knocked up to receive a present for Lord Elgin of a number of fowls and two pieces of red cloth.

22*d*. The gun-boats were under weigh early this morning, investigating the respective merits of the channels ahead. At last we hit upon the right one, and, as we passed along it, obtained a good view of Tai-ping-foo. This is a prefectural city of the province of Ngan-hwui, and has been for many years a strong-hold of the insurgents. It was first taken by them on the 7th of March, 1853. They speak of seven or eight thousand troops being quartered there.

We are now in the province of Ngan-hwui, having entered it yesterday, a few miles before arriving at Tai-ping. Ngan-hwui means "Peace and Excellence;" that is, the peaceful and excellent province. It was formerly joined to Kiang-su as one province, under the name of Kiang-nan. Its area is greater than that of Kiang-su, and is computed at from forty to forty-five thousand square miles. The area of these two provinces is about the same as that of the two states of New York and Pennsylvania, and the population of Ngan-hwui was computed, according to the last census, at about thirty-four millions.

We had scarcely cleared the intricate channels leading past Tai-ping when the Retribution took the ground, still within sight of the three pagodas of the city. The whole day was employed in getting her off. Meanwhile the time was not lost to our surveyors, who were actively occupied taking observations and mapping out the river. A party of rebels communicated with Commander Ward while thus engaged; they assured him that the firing upon us at Nankin was quite a mistake; that orders had been given that we should not be fired upon again; and that any description of arms and ammunition, but especially percussion-caps, would be thankfully received. While at anchor at this point, we observed a force, which we estimated at about five thousand men, march out of Tai-ping, apparently in the direction of Woohoo. The stream of soldiers lasted for about three quarters of an hour; they presented a gay and picturesque appearance: officers on horseback, in red, blue, or yellow, and men in many-colored uniforms, while hundreds of gaudy umbrellas and waving flags added to the brilliancy of the procession. Just before sun-down, to our infinite joy, the Retribution was hauled off her bank into deep water; it was too late, however, to shift our position to-night, and sundry anchors have yet to be picked up, involving a little farther delay.

23*d*. Under weigh about eleven. Fourteen miles from Taiping we reached the finest piece of scenery we have yet seen. The river here forces itself through a mighty barrier of rock, the precipitous walls of which rise from its waters; their rugged flanks are scored with zigzag paths and steps hewn out of the living stone, and their projecting ledges are scarped into batteries.

These fine masses of rock are called the Se-leang-shan and Tung-leang-shan, or Eastern and Western Pillar Hills, or, more poetically, the Teen-mun, or Celestial Gate. The Se-leang-shan resembled in shape the Rock of Gibraltar on a small scale. Davis calls it five hundred feet in height; I should not have estimated it at more than three hundred. Half way up he visited a temple in the rock, which is now, in all probability, converted into a guard-house. Crowds of gay soldiers thronged the batteries, their flags flaunting from dizzy pinnacles, and their guns perched on crags where it looked a service of danger to work them. We congratulated ourselves, as we passed through this narrow gorge—for the river was not more than half a mile in width—that the garrison had received orders to confine themselves to staring at us, which they did most eagerly.

This pass is the key to the upper part of the river, and would be impregnable in the hands of a civilized force. As it is, not an imperialist junk can show itself between Woohoo and Nankin; and as all the rebel junks have been destroyed, the river is entirely deserted. At the foot of the Se-leang-shan is a small town, guarded by a battery, and a slip of sand runs out from it into the river, upon which some raking guns might be placed. Immediately on emerging from this defile we reach a bifurcation of the river. We follow the southern branch, which is deep and comparatively narrow, winding under bluffs which form its southern bank; while on the flat island opposite are constructed a series of five forts, admirably neat, and substantially built. The walls were apparently of solid mud. They were loop-holed for muskets, and cut into little embrasures for gingalls. Cannon seemed scarce, and were confined to the angles, which were constructed of stone.

These batteries were placed within half a mile of each other, close to the river margin, and were well garrisoned. Altogether, had our observation of the rebels been limited to the appearance presented by their fortifications and garrisons at this section of the river, we should have been led to form a much more favorable estimate of their power and resources than our subsequent investigations into them justified. The Celestial Gate was undoubtedly the point at which they seemed most formidable, and it will probably be the last strong-hold which will remain in their hands. Report says that a good deal of their treasure is kept there.

About three o'clock in the afternoon we sighted the two pagodas which mark the district city of Woohoo, and soon after came to an anchor before its long white walls. Woohoo is the highest point ever previously reached by a foreign ship, the American steam-frigate Susquehanna having visited it some years ago. Lord Amherst's mission, which ascended the river as far as the Poyang Lake, were conveyed up it in native boats. A large and motley crowd collected on the water's edge as we deliberately dropped our anchors just abreast of the principal gateway, and Mr. Wade was immediately sent on shore to open communication with them, the chief object of his mission being to obtain supplies. Our Chinese official was, of course, invisible on these occasions, as an imperialist in the heart of the rebel country. The bare notion that his presence should be suspected overwhelmed him with dismay.

Mr. Wade, who did not land, returned speedily with the information which he had obtained from a Hoo-peh man, who described himself as an officer of the garrison, that the authorities were anxious to do all in their power to show us civility. A packet for Lord Elgin from How, the commandant at Woohoo, was also handed to him. It contained the original manifesto of Tai-ping-wang, brought down from Nankin in 1853, and the following letter: "How, a Tsiang-tien-yen, the truly loyal and patriotic, by the heavenly command of the heavenly kingdom of Tai-ping, to the younger brethren of Jesus. Whereas, owing to the heavenly bounty of the Heavenly Father, and the heavenly elder brother Jesus, the heavenly dynasty has been recently founded, and our truly Holy Master, the Heavenly King, has been desired to descend on earth, and govern the empire (or the world), he has established his throne in the heavenly capital, and for several years (the people of) the four seas have turned their hearts to him, and the myriad places have felt his civilizing influence. Five foreign ships belonging to you, the brethren of Jesus, have now come to the central kingdom of the heavenly dynasty, and have arrived in the department of Ning (Kiangning, or Nankin). Being in ignorance what propositions you have to make, I have sent a special messenger, Yu-hing-lung, to visit your ships and inquire. If you have any thing to settle, please inform me by letter. The 15th of the 10th moon of the Wu-Wu, or 8th year of the heavenly kingdom of Tai-ping."

As the matter we had to settle merely related to beef and vegetables, Fitzroy and I returned to the shore with Wade, accompanied by Mr. Mainprize, the paymaster of the Furious. Meanwhile Mr. Lay was sent in a gun-boat to communicate with some imperial junks, the streamers of which were visible about three miles higher up the river.

A noisy parti-colored crowd, jostling each other into the water in their anxiety to inspect us, received us as we stepped on shore. We were surrounded by a mob of these long-haired, long-robed ragamuffins as we walked into the fort through the wretched gateway which served as its principal entrance, and, passing along a narrow, half-ruined street, were ushered into a dilapidated yamun in a state of repair. Strains of discordant music announced our approach to the high dignitary within, whom we found seated in solemn state behind a high table or altar, upon which stood two open carved jars like wine-coolers, of silver or imitation silver, which contained long thin slips of wood covered with Chinese characters. The chamber was a small, square apartment, hung with scrolls of yellow silk, covered with texts and mottoes in Chinese, belonging, apparently, as much to Confucianism as to Christianity; and the presiding genius himself was a stout, sensual-looking man, with a keen eye, and an intelligent but bad cast of countenance. He was dressed in a robe of yellow, which fell from his neck to his heels, and was devoid of ornament; round his head was wrapped an orange-colored handkerchief, in the centre of which, above the forehead, was fastened a single piece of jade, mounted in a gold setting. His long hair was collected in a bag, and hung in the nape of his neck, as though in imitation of the fashion prevalent among English young ladies of the present day.

Bowing to us slightly as we entered, How—for so was this

great man called—beckoned us to chairs, the mob by which we had been followed crowding unceremoniously into the small apartment. Not the smallest respect was shown by the insubordinate rabble to their leader, who strove in vain to keep them from pressing round, much to the disparagement of the dignified manner which he evidently desired to maintain in our presence, and by which he hoped to impress us with a due sense of his rank and importance. The odor of garlic which pervaded his undisciplined retainers, their boisterous and noisy manner and filthy aspect, rendered our audience by no means so agreeable as it might otherwise have been. A perfect equality seemed to reign, or rather an absolute confusion of ranks and persons, well dressed and ragged, old and young, thronged impetuously into the little room. It struck me, however, that the young predominated: many of these had been rebels all their lives, and had no tails, but generally the tail was wrapped round the long tangled hair.

How told us that to his functions of commandant and judge he united those of high-priest. The thin slips of wood in the silver vases were inscribed with various punishments, and the form of sentencing consisted in his selecting and throwing to the criminal the punishment to which he was condemned. The building itself was, like its occupant, partly ecclesiastical and partly secular. But we could not obtain from How any very precise description of the form of worship at which he presided. Indeed, we were not tempted to prolong our visit beyond what was necessary, and we gave him a list of our wants, which was rapidly transcribed by his secretary, who stood near him, and concealed the eyes of a countenance which bore a villainous expression with a pair of huge green goggles. His dress consisted of a flowered crimson silk robe, and reached to his heels. Near him stood another scribe, in a bright pea-green tunic and loose red trowsers. Presently appeared another high official, apparently of equal rank with How, for he took a seat next to him, and commenced a deliberate and somewhat insolent survey of our persons. His head was wrapped in an orange handkerchief, like his colleague's, but his robe was of purple, above which he wore a flowered lilac silk tunic. These gay colors looked bright enough when they happened to be new, but those of the crowd were for the most part faded; the material of which their garments were composed was shabby and torn, giving them a tawdry, disreputable appearance, which was not belied by the dissipated, haggard expression of their countenances.

The leaders were Canton men of the worst description. Drunkenness and opium-smoking were prevalent vices, as one of their number, who spoke Canton English, and was evidently a blackguard of the first water, unhesitatingly admitted. In the original code promulgated by Tai-ping, opium-smoking was punishable by death. One of the first questions we were asked by How was, "What have you got to sell?" They were evidently skeptical when we denied that we were traders, and How recurred to the subject before we left him. He had been a merchant in a small way at Canton.

We now proceeded to the exploration of the surrounding streets, and found that we were not in the town, but in a military post, consisting of three separate forts on eminences, with a collection of mean houses round them, and a wall, inclosing the whole within its circumference, extending for some distance along the river margin.

The town of Woohoo we could see about a mile and a half inland. The pagoda was outside the wall, and in order to visit it we passed under a gateway, at which we saw a man chained to the wall by his neck. He was said to be under suspicion of being an imperialist spy. The pagoda consisted of five stories, and was very dilapidated, and the guns on the walls of the forts were very inferior and of small calibre.

We were accompanied on our rambles by a crowd, with the more intelligent of whom Wade got into conversation upon religious subjects; but their theology was of the vaguest description, and did not prevent them from using the foulest language to each other.

We saw very few women, and they were evidently all from the north, probably captured on some of their raids in that direction. It was said that an order had been issued at the commencement of the movement prohibiting wives, and that these had, in consequence, all been taken from their husbands, but subsequently redistributed differently.

We had not time to visit the town of Woohoo, which Davis describes as the largest of its class in China. "The streets," he remarks, "proved, on inspection, to be superior to those of many of the first-class cities, and some were as large and well furnished with handsome shops as at Canton. It is to the great inland commerce carried on by this line that such unusual wealth and prosperity is to be referred." It is interesting to compare the above notice of Woohoo with that of Mr. Wylie, who remained behind with the Retribution, while we were up the river, and visited Woohoo, of which he gives the following account:

"The district city of Woohoo, on the south bank, belongs to Tai-ping-foo, from which city it is distant fifty miles by land, with free communication for the insurgents, who have held it since the 4th of March, 1853. The city stands inland from the river about a mile and a half, on the border of a canal, but little is now left standing of it except the wall, and a part of the two principal streets, extending about half a mile each inside to north and east gates, and nearly as far outside. These contain the stores of the few remaining shopkeepers, who appear to be ill at ease in the pursuit of their avocations.

"The houses are divided among the various companies of fighting men quartered there, most of them having up a placard indicating the officer to whom they belong. Many of the houses have very extensive premises in rear of the shops, where the men and horses find shelter, with the utmost disregard to every thing like order or cleanliness.

"There are two or three official residences in the city, one being that of the medical officer to the army, appointed by imperial commission. Outside the west gate, nearly up to the river, is one vast field of broken bricks and tiles, with nothing but foundations remaining to show what must once have been a very extensive suburb. A walled camp has been built along the river front by the Tai-pings, with a succession of six forts on natural mounds, the approaches to which are defended by stockades, and the rising ground thickly studded with pitfalls. Apart from the commandant, How, the chief officer, who has his yamun in the camp, is Hwang Yuh Ching, 23d, (left hand or) chief minister of state.

"Every fort has its general, with his number attached. They have changed the name of the country about there to Ning-Keang. About eight or ten miles to the south they have a camp, at Hwang-che, where several severe skirmishes have taken place lately. On the opposite side of the river, at Urh-pa, are also several forts which have been taken from the imperialists."

On our return voyage down the river we received at Woohoo a communication purporting to emanate from the rebel Celestial emperor himself, written on a long roll of yellow silk, in red characters, being, in fact, a manifesto addressed to foreigners generally, but endorsed in this instance, "For the jewel glance of his excellency, the Earl Lai, imperial commissioner of Great Britain." I annex a copy of this very singular production, which will convey a better idea than any I could obtain from conversation with the rebels of the nature of their theology, and the amount of their acquaintance with Holy Writ. Of the extent to which they practiced its tenets it was not so difficult to form an opinion:

TRANSLATION OF A MANIFESTO OR DECREE ADDRESSED BY THE HEAD OF THE TAI-PING INSURGENTS TO FOREIGNERS.

The following composition was left at Wu-hu by Lin, a rebel chief of high degree, who, it appears, had been sent thither with it from Nankin, and was found at the former place when the Retribution moved down thither from Kiu-kien. It is written on yellow silk, in red characters—*i. e.*, with the vermilion pencil of majesty, and was inclosed in a yellow paper envelope, on the side of which was written,

"Within [the cover] is presented one document"—the word presented being that which indicates the submission of papers or information to a superior; then the date—viz., the — day of the 11th Moon of the *Wu-Wu*, the 8th year of the Celestial Kingdom of Tai-ping (Universal Peace).

Over the date are two impressions of seals; above, a circular one with some mystic engraving not very clearly defined, with the character *pu*, universal, in the margin, and below, an oblong one, like a Chinese title-page, reading as follows: "Chu Hiung-pang, the loyal and patriotic Pu-T'ien Yen of the Celestial Kingdom of the Tai-ping, appointed to the Board of Works, the officer of the Winter."

It is no doubt this person (who, by his surname Chu, is probably one of those that trace descent from the stock of the Ming Emperors), who employs the character *pin* on the cover, as the letter, or manifesto itself is as from superiors to inferiors.

On the other side of the cover is the address, which, it is understood was written at Wu-hu, "For the jewel glance of his excellency the Earl Lai, Imperial Commissioner of Great Britain."

The writing within is mostly in seven-foot verse, of very small literary pretension, and in indifferent handwriting—singularly indifferent when it is borne in mind how generally the educated Chinese are found to write decently, if not well. Many of the expressions establish it, in the opinion of a well-informed Cantonese, to be the production of one of his fellow-provincials.

The writer uses throughout the imperial pronoun *chén* or *shén*, which we ordinarily translate *we*.

The column is broken, according to Chinese custom, before names of honor: those that refer, apparently, to the first Person of the Trinity rising two places: those indicating the second Person, one place. A character coined to represent the Holy Spirit is also allowed two places. It occurs but once. *T'ien*, heaven, is raised in some lines two places, and is in such cases spelt with a capital letter in the translation.

A TAI-PING MANIFESTO.

1. We proclaim for the information of our foreign younger brethren of the Western Ocean,
2. The things of heaven differ extremely from the things of the world.
3. The Heavenly Father Shang Ti, the Imperial Shang Ti,
4. Is the sacred (or sainted) Father of one and all that heaven overspreads.
5. Our uterine elder brother is Jesus.
6. Our uterine younger brother is Siu-tsing.
7. In the third moon of the year *mo-shin* (1848) Shang Ti descended,
8. And commissioned the King of the East to become a mortal (*lit.*, a world man).
9. In the 9th moon of this year the Redeemer descended,
10. And commissioned the King of the West to manifest divine powers.
11. The Father and the Elder Brother led us to sit on [the throne of] the heavenly kingdom;
12. With great display of authority and might to sit in the hall of heaven;
13. To make the heavenly city our capital, to found the heavenly kingdom;
14. [That] the ministers and people of all (*lit.*, the myriad) nations might do homage to their Father-Emperor.
15. The chapel (or temple) of the True Spirit is within the heavenly court.
16. The chapel of Ki-tu (Christ) is alike glorious forever.
17. In the year *ting yu* (1837) we ascended to heaven.
18. The Father, with words of truth, bestowed on us a volume of verse,
19. Enjoining us to read it well and to regard it as a proof:
20. By the verses to know (or acknowledge) the Father and to keep steady.
21. The Father moreover commanded the Elder Brother to instruct us how to read it.
22. The Father and the Elder Brother did personally instruct us, and laid their injunctions upon us again and again.
23. The Heavenly Father Shang Ti is in the measure of his capacity as the depth of the sea.
24. Up to the thirty-third heaven the demons burst their way.
25. The Father and Elder Brother, taking us with them, drove them away time after time.
26. Supported by the officers and soldiers of heaven on either side of them,
27. They smote on this occasion two thirds of them;
28. From one gate of heaven after another were the demons and goblins repulsed,
29. Until they were all driven down below (or to earth, or under the earth),
30. And but a remnant of them were left. [Thus] was the august Father (or the Father's majesty) made manifest.
31. The Father subsequently (or, then) desired us to return to the world, [promising]
32. In all things to be our support.
33. He enjoined us to set our heart at rest and not to be alarmed;
34. He, the Father, would come forward. His injunctions were repeated twice and again.
35. In the year *wu-shin* (1848), when the King of the South was besieged in Kwei-ping,
36. We besought the Father to come down and manifest his terrors.
37. We had returned from Kwang Si to Kwang Tung;
38. The Heavenly Father did come down to the world, and rescued [the King] of the South.

39. The King of the East redeems from sickness; he is a holy spirit.
40. The Father sent him down with a commission to exterminate the demons.
41. He destroyed goblin-devils without number,
42. And so was enabled to arrive without delay at the capital (Nankin).
43. When the Father descended to the world he made known his holy will.
44. All this we read, and committing it well to memory,
45. We knew the Father's infallibility (or that his power could not fail),
46. And were brought by the Father and the Elder Brother to found the [dynasty of] T'ai P'ing.
47. The Father having deputed the King of the East to redeem from sickness,
48. [On behalf of] the blind, the deaf, and the dumb,
49. He suffered infinite misery.
50. When fighting the demons he was wounded in the neck and fell headlong.
51. The Father had declared by his holy decree,
52. That when our warriors went forth they would have inexpressible affliction;
53. That when they come to the court (Nankin?) they would suffer severely.
54. [The words of] the Father's holy decree were all accomplished.
55. The Elder Brother to ransom sinners gave his life;
56. He became a substitute for myriad myriad thousands of the people of the world.
57. The King of the East, in ransoming the sick, suffered equally with the Elder Brother,
58. And when he fell with the pestilence he returned to [the place of] spirits, to thank the Father for his goodness.
59. Which is the right among the writings of the Father and the Elder Brother it is impossible to know;
60. He who would choose the true must ascend to high heaven.
61. The holy decrees of the Father are numberless.
62. We declare the general purport of one or two.
63. It is some years since the Heavenly Father descended into the world.
64. He was accompanied by the Heavenly Brother, whose distress was as great as formerly.
65. Jesus is your Redeeming Lord,
66. And continues with all his mind to instruct and admonish.
67. The Heavenly Father produced T'siuen to be your ruler.
68. Why are you not loyal to the utmost? why do you willfully (or wrongly) pursue your former course?
69. You have often [been guilty of] serious disobedience of commands.
70. Were we not to issue our decrees your boldness would be great as heaven.
71. For whom was it that the Heavenly Father descended?
72. For whom did Jesus throw away his life?
73. Heaven has sent you down a king to be your true lord.
74. Why are you so troubled, your hearts so unsettled?
75. Let your sons in all parts quit their houses,
76. Leave their homes, resolved to be loyal ministers;
77. Come forward to aid their king, fierce as tigers and leopards;
78. Knowing that now they have a ruler they can be men.
79. If you believe not that the best in the world has appeared in us,
80. Yet bethink you that the Spirit Father errs not in the ruler he establishes (*lit.*, sets up a ruler true).

81. Accept as proof of the independent authority of heaven,
82. That though a thousand surround [us] with valor and daring, they are broken as the dust.
83. The myriad countries, the myriad nations, throng in myriads to [our] court.
84. [Ours are?] the myriad hills, the myriad waters, at infinite distance.
85. For a myriad *li* myriad eyes throng their way up.
86. All (*lit.*, myriad) knowledge, all happiness, all merit [is ours? or, heaven's?]
87. Would [a man] conceal any thing from Heaven, let him not say that Heaven is ignorant of it.
88. Heaven measures as far as the sea in deep; yea, and farther.
89. See now yourselves without courage or resolution.
90. How long will you not be faithful servants?
91. Remember that if in the third watch [of the night] you escape along the dark road,
92. The vengeful demon will blind (or bewilder) you before daylight.
93. Walk each of you, in the true path for our king;
94. Believe the Heavenly Father, and doubt not.
95. Heaven produced the rightful ruler to govern the empire (*lit.*, the hills and streams).

The verses end here for the present; the writer proceeds in prose thus:

When Shang Ti sent down his holy decree (*lit.*, this single sentence of a holy decree), he commanded us to add three sentences. We added [these]:

96. The Heavenly Father, and the Heavenly Elder Brother have great distress of mind (have too much to think of);
97. All authority and power reverts to the Supreme Ruler (*Shang Chu*).
98. How is happiness to be given to the whole empire of Tai-ping?

Shang Ti sent down another holy decree, saying,

99. In the nine-fold heaven let there be one King of the East,
100. To aid the empire as a counsellor long to endure.

When Shang Ti declared his holy pleasure in these two lines, he desired us to add two more. In accordance with the holy pleasure of the Father, we added these two:

101. Ho-nai the teacher, who is at the same time the lord redeemer from disease,
102. Is the great support of all the people in the world.

At a later period Shang Ti made a change, saying,

103. Let there be appointed a pair of phœnixes, one to the east and the other to the west.
104. Let the east, west, north, and south do homage to them (turn to them as the sun).

Shang Ti made another change, saying,

105. Let there be appointed a pair of phœnixes, one to the east and the other to the west,
106. And let them, in gratitude for the bounty of Heaven that has descended on them, do homage together.
107. This purport of the Father's holy pleasure, in general terms,
108. Do we truthfully declare for the information of you, our foreign younger brethren.
109. That the Heavenly Father and the Heavenly Elder Brother really descended on earth,
110. Is proved to be true by the verses of the Father.

111. Their (or His) divine intelligence and authority words can not tell.
112. Come soon to the heavenly temple, and you will be sensible of it.
113. The Chief Elder Brother Jesus is the same (or of the same fashion) with the Father.
114. Not a half sentence of [their] holy decrees shall be changed.
115. Shang Ti, the Heavenly Father, is the true Shang Ti (or is Shang Ti, the Supreme Ruler, indeed).
116. Jesus, the Heavenly Elder Brother, is Heavenly Elder Brother indeed.
117. The Father and the Elder Brother set us to rule the heavenly kingdom;
118. To sweep away and exterminate the devilish spirits; bestowing on us great honor.
119. Foreign younger brethren of the Western Ocean, listen to our words.
120. Join us in doing service to the Father and Elder Brother, and extinguish the stinking reptiles.
121. In all things the Father, the Elder Brother, and ourself are master (or, act independently of any one else).
122. Come, brethren, enthusiastically, and merit all honor.
123. When we were traveling in Kwang-tung some time ago,
124. In the hall of worship (*li pai-t'ang*) we addressed Lo Hiau-tsiuen.
125. We then told him that we had been up to heaven,
126. And that the Heavenly Father and the Heavenly Elder Brother had committed to us great authority.
127. Is Lo Hiau-tsiuen now come hither or not?
128. If he be, let him come to court and speak with us.
129. We are the second son of Shang Ti.
130. The Elder Brother and the King of the East are our uterine brothers.
131. All as one family together adorning the Heavenly Father,
132. There shall be universal peace (*t'ai p'ing*) on earth. It was said long ago,
[*Or it may mean*]. We form one family [above] under the Heavenly Father; on earth we are [the dynasty] T'ai P'ing, as we said long ago (or, as was long ago foretold).
133. The kingdom of heaven is (or was) at hand; now that it is come,
134. Brethren of the Western Ocean, be of good cheer.
135. In former days, when we ascended to heaven, we saw what was destined by the Father,
136. [To wit, that] the myriad nations should aid us to mount the heavenly tower.
137. What the Father destined has now come to pass.
138. Put forth your strength for Heaven; it is a duty, yes, it is a duty.
139. For the Father, and for the Elder Brother, slay the demon goblins,
140. Out of gratitude to the Father for your birth and growth; and when you have conquered in battle, return (or, and you will be victorious in fight).
141. We, the ruler, have given the young ruler, [our son], to be adopted by Jesus;
142. As the adopted of the Elder Brother and ourself to sit in the heavenly capital.
143. The young ruler, as one half the son of Jesus,
144. And one half our son, is the object (or recipient) of the protection of Heaven.
145. [Thus] for generations the young ruler, as the son of Shang Ti,
146. Inherits from the Elder Brother and ourself the whole empire.
147. Brethren of the Western Ocean, adore (or, you adore) the Supreme (*Shang Chu*).

148. It is our wish that the Father and the Elder Brother should cause it so to be.

149. The Chief Elder Brother being in time past nailed on a gallows shaped like the character *shih*, ten, *sc.* the cross,

150. Left it as his sign. In this there is no mistake.

151. The *shih ts'iuen ta kih*, the tenfold [that is, all] perfect, and all fortunate is ourself.

152. In all ways [our course] is that destined by the Father.

153. That the Chief Elder Brother came to life again in three days,

154. And in three days built the temple, is not a vain boast.

155. We were produced by the Father in three days;

156. We built the temple of the Father and Elder Brother, and destroyed the devilish serpents.

157. In our third year *kwei-chau* (1853) we beheaded the devilish serpents.

158. In the year *yih yung* (1855) we exterminated the brutes, by the aid of the Father and the Elder Brother.

159. The serpents and brutes humbled and all exterminated forever,

160. The whole world together sings the song of peace (or, the song of *t'aip'ing*).

161. Foreign brethren of the Western Ocean, you adore Shang Ti; [and it is]

162. The Father and Elder Brother that have brought us to sit on the throne of the empire (the hills and streams).

163. We have now declared to you the truth.

164. Come rejoicing to court, and give thanks to the Father and the Elder Brother.

165. By the memorials of our ministers

166. We have been informed of the coming of the brethren to the heavenly capital.

167. We have desired our ministers to treat you with courtesy.

168. As brethren in one harmonious community, be not doubtful or suspicious.

169. Apprehensive that the brethren might not be aware of [our sentiments],

170. We have issued our manifesto to show our sympathy with you.

171. Foreign brethren of the Western Ocean, worship Shang Ti.

172. Man's blessings, *lit.*, bounty and peace, are in this.

Respect this!

[*In referring to the following notes the reader will be guided by the number of the verse.*]

(1.) Proclaim; the word signifies to address authoritatively as a sovereign.

(3.) Shang Ti, the most honorable among Chinese spirits; the title adopted by many Protestant missionaries to translate the name of God.

(6.) Sîu-tsing is Yang Siu-tsing, the Eastern King, who arrogated to himself among other titles that of the Holy Spirit.

(10.) Or, traces of divinity.

(11.) *Ye*, the Father, and *Ko*, the Elder Brother, as the characters are understood to mean by the native assistant consulted, as a missionary suggests, may be but the adoption in ignorance of the Chinese characters employed to spell Jehovah.

(12.) To be the high-priest?

(13.) Nan-king, the southern capital, is now, to the insurgents, the *tien-king*, heavenly capital.

(15.) The hall of the True Spirit, *chin-shin-tang*, is the title formerly taken by a Protestant missionary chapel at Hong Kong, but subsequently abandoned.

(16.) *Ki-tu* are the characters intended to represent the word Christ in the translation of the Testament.

(18.) Or, did indeed: the expression is Cantonese.

(20.) Keep steady, be saved from upsetting, not the dynasty, but the man in his conduct; also a Canton phrase.

(24.) The thirty-third heaven belongs to fairy tales, and the like.

(31.) Again to descend among the [mortal] community.

(35.) Kwei-ping is a district in Kwang Si.

(43.) Holy will, the words often rendered Decree of this Sacred Majesty, the Placet of the Holy One.

(58.) Pestilence: the word is often used of rebellion. It may have this figurative sense here, in which case Yang must be understood to have fallen in action. He is believed to have been beheaded by Tai-ping Wang's orders.

(58.) Or, returned to his spirit-nature.

(59.) The word rendered writings is ts'au, plants or grass. Draughts of documents are in the running land ts'au tsz', the grass character. That the translation is correct here is uncertain, but no more likely meaning has been suggested.

(67.) Ts'iuin is Hung Siu-ts'iuen, Tai-ping Wang, the leader of the present insurrection.

(68.) Wantonly or extravagantly renew or repair the past.

(78.) Men not devils.

(79.) *Lit.*, the most precious [of the productions] of the hills and streams.

(80.) The Spirit is a newly-coined character not in the Lexicons.

(81.) The text is obscure; it may mean, Relying on the power of heaven to play the chief.

(83.) There is apparently here an allusion to omnipotence and infinity, but whether as the attribute of Tai-ping himself, or the Supreme Being, is not quite clear.

(92.) A proverb much to the same effect as our commonplace *Duro antecedentem scelestum, etc.*

(101.) The characters 禾 *ho* and 乃 *nai*, together make 秀 *siu*. Yang Siu-ts'iuen is here referred to as the great physician.

(102.) The word: a character is used here also which is not authorized, for all together.

(103.) The *fung* is the fabulous bird of China.

(104.) The change, as will be seen, is of the greater part of the 104th verse, of which the 106th is a revision.

(117.) The title Elder Brother preceding his name Yeen is, nevertheless, made one degree less honorable by its place in the column.

(119.) As before, Our words as sovereign.

(122.) *Lit.*, Establish myriad-fold merit.

(124.) Lo, supposed to be the Rev. Issachar Roberts, from whom Hung Siu-ts'iuen is believed to have obtained his first idea of Christianity.

(143). Ten, *shih* ✝, is also the number of completeness in China; ten parts is ten tenths, all.

(151.) There is a play here on *shih*, ten, the crucifix-shaped character meaning also complete, and *ts'iuen*, perfect, which also is part of Hung's name. The expression is common Cantonese; out-and-out good fortune.

(156.) Although the construction does not grammatically warrant it, the intention of the writer is plainly that his building the temple and routing the demons were also three-day operations.

(157.) The two last dates have retained one character of the old Chinese cyclic system, and have altered one.

CHAPTER XXXVI.

A Battle between Rebels and Imperialists.—An Exodus of the Population.—Arrival at Kew-hsien.—The Rebel Position.—Rebel Tactics.—Deserted State of the Country.—Tee-kiang.—Fine Scenery.—Recent Rebel Fortifications.—A wild-boar Hunt.—Description of the Country.—Our Pilot.—Cultivation.—Mandarin Visitors.—Character of the River-banks.—The Imperialist Fleet.—A Visit to the Commodore.—The Legend of the Hen Barrier.—Approach to Ngan-king.—We engage the Forts.—Attack of the Imperialist Troops.—The eight-storied Pagoda.—Tactics of the Imperialists.—Their Treatment of the Peasantry.—Toong-lew.

October 24. We weighed at daylight this morning, and about three miles above Woohoo passed a fleet of twenty imperialist junks, at a village called Loo-kiang. They were under command of a Canton man named Woo, with whom Mr. Lay made acquaintance last evening, and who has politely furnished us with a pilot upon whom he declares we may rely. Eight or ten miles above this we passed a creek, at the mouth of which two imperial junks were stationed. Three or four miles up this creek the insurgents have a camp at the town of Hwang-san-keaou, where they number upward of a thousand fighting men. When we passed, the whole of this army, which had evidently been strongly re-enforced, was hotly engaged with the imperial troops.

It is impossible to conceive any thing more highly picturesque, or theatrical in its effect, than the scene which now lay spread before us. The hills were crowned with the gay flags of the rebels; the rich autumnal tints upon the trees were as bright in their colors as the dresses of the soldiers grouped beneath them; bodies of men were marching in gallant array down the park-like slopes, to meet the foe in the plain beneath. The imperialist position was upon the flat ground upon the river margin. Here they had erected straw screens and temporary earth-works, behind which a few small guns were placed, which were keeping up an apparently harmless fire upon the enemy. Now and then groups of men carrying gingalls would advance from the hostile ranks, and approach to within two or three hundred yards of each other, fire their gingalls, and retire amid a great waving of banners. We could not wait to watch the issue of the battle, which might last forever, if they continued to fight on the same principle.

As we advanced we became still more enchanted with the scenery. Confused masses of wooded hills rose to a height of about two thousand feet, from a plain charmingly diversified by clumps of timber and rich cultivation. It was lamentable to observe that this lovely landscape was being deserted by its inhabitants. It had not before been visited by the pestilent hordes who were now bearing down upon it; and the peasantry, fearful lest they should prove successful in the contest which we had just seen them waging with the imperialists, were now hurrying away, to escape those scenes of rapine and violence which have invariably marked their devastating track. Whole families might thus be seen trudging along the narrow pathways, the men staggering under heavy loads of all their goods and chattels, the women hobbling along on their small feet, their arms filled with babies. Cattle and poultry were being driven or carried by boys and girls. A great exodus was in progress. A few faint wreaths of blue smoke were still curling, probably for the last time, from the cottages and hamlets dotted over the smiling landscape, destined before long to share the fate which had already overtaken the surrounding country, where heaps of blackened cinders and mounds of brickbats alone remained to attest its once populous character.

> "Sunk are thy bowers, in shapeless ruin all,
> And the long grass o'ertops the mouldering wall,
> And, trembling, shrinking from the spoiler's hand,
> Far, far away thy children leave the land."

The principal base of rebel operations, and the head-quarters of their army, was a town called Fan-chang, some twelve or fourteen miles in rear of the range of hills which skirted the south bank of the river. To these hills, which are a debatable ground, separating the insurgents from the imperialists, the latter probably owe their position, as, with the command of the river, they are always able to keep up their communication. Their principal post upon its banks is Kew-hsien, a town we reached at 11 A.M. It was picturesquely situated under the hills. The people crowded to the shore to inspect us. They consisted largely of refugee peasantry. As we were not likely to reach another imperialist town for some time, and the great draught of water of the Retribution rendered her an inconvenient ship with which to pioneer unknown waters, it was decided that she should remain here until our return from Hankow.

This arrangement afforded the officers a good opportunity of exploring the surrounding country in search of game, while Mr. Wylie was enabled to obtain some interesting information with reference to the state of the rebels. We found, on our return, that a red deer, and upward of sixty pheasants, had fallen to the guns of the sportsmen, while the following account was furnished to Lord Elgin by Mr. Wylie as the result of his observation: "Kew-heen" (or hsien, as I have spelt it, as a distinct sibilation was discernible in its pronunciation) "was formerly the site of the district city of Fan-chang, which now stands fourteen miles inland, in a plain surrounded by high hills. This city, which has been in the possession of the rebels for five years, belongs to the prefecture of Tai-ping. The present rebel governor is surnamed 'Wei.'

"Kew-heen has some few vestiges of its former importance, but the place is now half in ruins, from previous visits of the insurgents. A little busy retail traffic is carried on, chiefly dependent on the imperial troops stationed there. These amount to from two to three thousand, under the command of a general named Le. This man was the commander of the besieging force at Kiu-kiang in May, 1853, when three European ships and twenty-five lorchas were engaged in the service. He has now under him companies of Kwang-tung, Che-kiang, and Shan-tung braves. About a dozen junks ordinarily lie there, and some ten gun-boats. This place forms a centre of concourse for the peasantry from the surrounding country, who are driven from their homes by the incursions of the rebels. Many families, with their whole households, are in a continual state of migration, carrying bedding and utensils about wherever they go. These are not beggars, but refugees, who are glad to purchase personal safety by the temporary abandonment of their patrimonial dwellings. A great extent of country adjoining the insurgent territory has thus become depopulated, and hostile encounters between the peasantry who remain, and the rebel invaders, are no uncommon occurrence. It is customary with the latter to make their advances by early dawn; and when they find the peasantry unwilling to enter their service, collisions sometimes ensue, which terminate in the death or disablement of the latter. In such cases the dwellings are reduced to a ruin, and thus for many miles round scarcely any thing is to be found but bare mud walls. The natives who thus involuntarily enter their service are not allowed the same freedom as the old adherents from the south; and on occasion of affrays with the imperialists, it is said they are placed in the front ranks, and fastened together by the tails. The imperialist communication landward between Kew-heen and Loo-keang is cut off by the rebels, but they have an open thoroughfare for their vessels on the river. The channel of the Yang-tse is here divided by three large islands in the centre, two or three miles wide.

"The north bank is all held by the insurgents, who have also the departmental city of Woo-wei, the imperialist magistrate of which, Yeh, now has a temporary office in Kew-heen. There is also a rebel encampment on the north bank, opposite Hih-cha-chow, the island facing Kew-heen."

Mr. Wylie informed me that he had walked to Fan-chang through a hilly wooded country, but did not enter the town. All the hamlets and houses for the last six miles before reaching it were in ruins. From the accounts he gave of their proceedings, we can not wonder at the absence of all sympathy with the rebels on the part of the peasantry. Not only do they harry and *squeeze* these unfortunate people, but press the men by violence into their service, retaining for themselves all the best-looking of their women.

Kew-hsien, as its name implies, was formerly the district city, and its decaying pagoda and ruined temple do indeed impart to it an air of venerable, if not respectable antiquity. I can not say respectable, because the moral character of Kew-hsien is, so to speak, under a cloud. In consequence of a horrible crime having been committed there during the Ming dynasty, it was blotted out from the list of names in the government maps, and Fang-chang was made the district city: this disreputable locality thus became simply Kew-hsien, or "the town that was."

We exchanged our pilot here for a more brilliant-looking individual, and, with three parting cheers to the Retribution, held on our course up the unknown waters of the Ta-kiang.

A little above Kew-hsien a large branch of the river communicates with Lake Chaou-hoo, an extensive sheet of water. On the south we are struck by the romantic beauty of the Pan-tze-chee rock, which rises in a sheer mass from the eddying stream, and is surmounted by the gray, mossy ruins of a temple and pagoda, embowered among trees of many hues.

The hills rise from the water's edge in grassy slopes, partially wooded to a height of from two to three thousand feet, while lovely valleys, richly timbered, open them up in a southerly direction. The range is called Ta-hwa-shan. It trends away to the south and east at the village of Tee-kiang, which, with its three-arched bridge of heavy masonry, and its white but partially ruined houses, clustering up the hill side, or nestling among the trees at its base, reminded me of an Italian rather than a Chinese town. As it is only distant about five miles from Kew-hsien, Mr. Wylie visited and thus describes it: "Te-kiang, which formerly contained about ten thousand inhabitants, is now a deplorable ruin. The few inhabitants that remain in the only existing street are in a constant state of apprehension, always in dread of a visit from the Tai-pings. One such took place by a party of from one to two hundred on the morning of the day on which the writer visited it; but they were beaten off before reaching the town by the imperialists, who have a few junks stationed there, under the direction of the assistant general Tang Kwo-leen. At Hwang-hoo, a small town ten miles up the creek, it is reported there are a thousand or more of the insurgent party; and Shungan, a town a few miles farther up, is also held by them. The whole country seems to be open to them from Fan-chang to Tung-ling, the chief city of the adjoining district westward, which is also in their possession."

The river now abruptly leaves the range, which takes a south-easterly direction, and, expanding into wide reaches, twists and folds itself back like a huge serpent, embracing large flat islands in its coils, but most imposing in breadth and appearance.

We frequently could get no soundings with ten fathoms, and made, in consequence, rapid progress.

We passed on the north bank an imperialist position at Pih-na-tsing, which seemed, however, to be surrounded by rebels in the immediate neighborhood: and, a little before sunset, anchored for the night between rich alluvial banks, extending in a level plain to the base of distant hills.

The scenery through which we have passed to-day is infinitely the finest we have yet seen since entering the river.

25th. Weighed at daylight. We found that our anchorage last night had been upon the outskirts of a rebel position on the north bank. A number of flat, rush-covered islands here split the stream, the southern branch, which Lord Amherst's Embassy followed, passing under the walls of Tung-ling, the chief city of the district, and a strong rebel position.

I made a practice, during my progress up the river, of spending a great part of the day in the top-gallant cross-trees, from which elevated post of observation I could always obtain a good view of the surrounding country. I now looked northward over a vast well-cultivated plain, extending for about ten miles to the base of a range which we estimated at three thousand feet in height. The inhabitants of the islands were gathering the reeds and stacking them, apparently for fuel.

The rebel town of Too-cheaou, on the north bank, presented a very un-Chinese appearance of whitewash and cleanliness. It was situated about a mile from the river, and was surrounded by a white wall, which had evidently been lately built, while the fortifications bore all the appearance of recent construction. To judge by the mass of ruins and debris, which spread from the water's edge to the foot of the wall, the town must formerly have extended to the river.

The next point of interest at which we arrive is the Nang-shan-ke rock, a precipitous bluff on the southern bank, overhanging the stream, in which a rocky path had been scarped, and steps cut, to facilitate the tracking of boats.

The summit was richly wooded, the ruined walls of a temple rising out of the tinted foliage. The stream here forms a broad single sheet of water, but just beyond this it is divided into three branches by two low wooded islands, the largest of which is called Ho-yeh-chow, from a plant like arrow-root which it produces. We again followed the northern branch.

The celebrated mountain of Kew-hwa-shan, famous among other things for the enormous bamboos which it produces, now became visible in the hazy distance, reaching an elevation, probably of from 4000 to 5000 feet. The range of which it forms part approaches the river abruptly, and one of its spurs is the bluff just mentioned. This range, like that behind Kew-hsien, limits the rebel incursions; they hold the country in rear, but the river-banks are here imperialist. The nearer summits were not above 2000 feet in height: their slopes were well timbered, and watered by numerous streams, whose course was marked by fertile valleys. While gazing at this interesting scenery through our glasses, our attention was suddenly distracted by some remarkable evolutions on the part of the Dove. She had begun to pirouette in midstream in a manner quite unaccountable, until we made out the signal "wild pig." We then discovered that she was engaged in an exciting wild-boar hunt. She succeeded in lowering a boat and capturing the grisly monster before he could reach the bank, and hoisted in her prize with great triumph. His long wiry hair, gleaming tusks, and bristling mane were undeniable evidence of his savage character, even had he not shown sufficient ferocity in his endeavors to avenge himself on his pursuers to put the matter beyond a doubt. We afterward found in his head a *pièce de résistance*, which was a most valuable and palatable addition to our larder. No sooner was the boar disposed of than we observed a number of porpoises disporting themselves in the muddy stream. Our time, however, did not admit of our attempting the capture of any of these "river pigs," as they are called by the Chinese.

Looking southward across the island, we observed the houses of Ta-toong, an imperialist position, but closely invested by the rebels, whose flags we could see flying from the hills immediately in rear.

Lord Amherst's party were detained here by contrary winds for four days, and had therefore a good opportunity of exploring the surrounding country. As we were denied any such advantage, I quote a few lines of Mr. Ellis's description of the neighborhood. "I had a delightful walk," he says, "through this truly romantic country. All the valleys are highly cultivated with wheat, rice, cotton, and beans; the houses substantial, and shaded by trees, some of a very large size, in growth resembling the oak. The leaf is forked, and I believe the tree itself is of the maple species. Pudding-stone and sandstone composed the greater part of the hills we crossed to-day. They are all in a rapid state of disintegration. Great varieties of the oak have been observed here. We have called the jagged lofty mountains the Organ Pipes, from their resemblance to those at Rio Janeiro. The soil of the hills is poor and gravelly, adapted for little else but woodland. We have remarked several plantations of the pinaster. We observed great varieties of the fern. The oak plantations are kept very low, the twigs being used for fire-wood; bundles of oak bark were exposed for sale in the market, employed, I believe, as by us, in tanning. The dried broad leaf of the nelumbrium serves as fuel to the lower orders, many of whom we saw returning to their homes with heaps of it."

I observed from the deck some beautiful effects of coloring in the foliage, the dark green of what appeared a species of Scotch fir contrasting charmingly with the varied tints of the maple, or the deep red of the fading leaves of the tallow-tree.

Our pilot proves quite a character, most communicative and anxious to impart information, but how far it is to be relied upon remains a question. He certainly is not to be depended on in the capacity for which we had engaged him; but he made up for his deficiency in this respect by self-sufficiency and quiet impudence, becoming, nevertheless, highly excited whenever we touched the bottom, as upon these occasions he considers that his head is in danger for getting us into a scrape. He has already made friends with sundry sailors, frequents much the stoke-hole upon cold mornings, and appears on deck in a pair of long woolen stockings, which have been served out to him from the ship's stores. Cigars are his especial weakness, and, in order to enjoy them, he perches himself in the chains like a monkey, and smokes in a sybaritic manner, expressive of keen enjoyment. Altogether, he considers that he has performed his functions as a pilot if, after we have got aground, he emerges from some place of concealment, and tells Captain Osborn that at this place the water is not deep, the proper channel being quite in another direction, which he does not venture to specify, but disappears again to finish his cigar, and contemplate the consequences to himself of our unpleasant situation.

This worthy now informs me that the principal staples of cultivation in this district are wheat, cotton, millet, potatoes, rice, and hemp. In the neighborhood of Toong-lew, a city at which we are to arrive to-morrow, they grow tea of an ordinary description, which is sold at tenpence a pound. Tobacco is also grown at a place some distance inland. There is no silk cultivated in this neighborhood. The pilot states that he himself was employed in the junks which transported grain for the annual supply of Pekin prior to the demolition of part of the Grand Canal and the occupation of the river by the rebels. He holds the rebels in supreme aversion and contempt; "not only," he says, "do they not shave the head, but call each other brother and sister, not distinguishing the generations." I remarked that it must be difficult to distinguish between rebels from choice and those who are under compulsion. He said that the length of the hair was a very fair criterion. The imperialists know how long a place had been in rebel occupation, and those people whose hair did not correspond in length to the period of time were generally regarded as old rebels.

As we passed the end of the long island where the Ta-toong branch enters the main stream, we observed two official boats, each decorated with four gaudy flags, and propelled by twelve rowers, standing with their faces to the prow, making toward us. We accordingly eased our speed, and discovered them to be two fifth-grade mandarins (crystal buttons), who came on board. They announced themselves as emissaries of Wang and Le, commanding the imperial troops and fleet at Ta-toong, and who were desirous now of presenting their compliments to the great foreign chief, and of making an offer of their services. We gave them some sherry, which they swallowed with very wry faces. They had evidently never seen a European, much less a four hundred horse-power steam-frigate before, and could scarcely deliver themselves of their message, so rapt were they in contemplation of surrounding objects. The pilot at once commenced expatiating to them on the wonders of the barbarian ship, remarking that he had attained the age of thirty-one, and was only now beginning to have his eyes opened.

Near Ta-toong begins the Meikan Lake, or rather Lagoon, separated from the river by a narrow strip of land, and extending parallel to it for about thirty miles. At Wang-chea-tan, an imperial port, which we passed on the north bank, we observed a creek filled with small junks, and shortly after encountered a large fleet of them. Those whom we hailed told us their cargo consisted of paper. They had emerged from some creek in imperialist occupation on the south shore, and were now on their way up a small tributary into districts not infested by rebels. They were the first trading junks we had seen since entering the river, and the white sails dotted over the broad stream imparted to it an unusual air of animation.

The north bank of the river is more uniformly flat than the south. The range is generally more distant. The intervening country seems thickly, but by no means densely populated: the people collect into small hamlets, each with its clump of willow or other trees.

Before reaching Che-chow the stream again divided, we following, as usual, the northern branch, while Lord Amherst's party took that called Ma Show-ja, leading past Che-chow, which important city was visible in the distance, a handsome seven-storied pagoda indicating its position from afar.

The town itself lies among hills; it is a district city, and one of the strongly-fortified positions of the insurgents, under the command of Wei-che-Suen, one of their high officers.

The view from our airy perch in the cross-trees this afternoon was singularly beautiful. We had exchanged the southern range, which usually skirted the river, for the northern, which now approached it abruptly. In this direction the hills rose in undulating masses, overtopping each other, till a bold, irregular outline of soft dark blue closed the prospect. Small lakes glittered like gems in the hollows; and over the bright foliage of the woods in which they were embosomed the setting sun shed a yet brighter glow—farms, and hamlets, and green fields gave a domestic character to the scenery—and, as we gazed over it, we found it difficult to believe that a country which nature had clothed in such warm and cheerful colors, and invested with so many attractions, should be the theatre which men had chosen for the display of all the worst passions of which human nature is capable. Yet so it proved, and the very accident of war contributed another and most picturesque feature to the scene.

A large imperial fleet was assembled at the mouth of a river, which we could discern winding among the hills, occasionally expanding into a lake, then twisting away like a silver thread.

This fleet was composed of fifty handsome war-junks, filled with soldiers in bright uniforms, and gay with flaunting flags; fluttering above one alone, I counted no fewer than twenty-one flags, all of different colors and devices. Some of the junks were of more than usually quaint construction, elaborately ornamented, carrying six and eight brass guns on a side, and propelled by sweeps. As it was now sundown, we anchored amid this gay throng: when we had furnished the charming landscape with this brilliant and novel foreground, the scene altogether was so fanciful and unreal, that, when the curtain of night shrouded it from our view, we might have imagined that the play was over, and that it only now remained to scramble out of the theatre, call a hansom, and go home to bed.

The absence of beef reminded us of the stern realities of our situation. Messrs. Wade and Lay, therefore, went on board the one from which the greatest number of pennons were flying, and which might not unnaturally be supposed to be the "flag junk," in search of an admiral. They found only a commodore: Admiral Yang, it appeared, who, we understand, was at Ta-toong, had gone on to Nankin to superintend operations against the rebels. The commodore promised beef before daylight without fail. We had no doubt of its existence, as we had observed large herds of cattle at pasture on the north bank. It appeared that the fleet was from the province of Hoopeh; that the river at the mouth of which we were now anchored was called the Tsungyang-ho, and that the town of Tsung-yang was situated among the hills five miles distant.

We thus terminated a long and interesting day. The distance made was satisfactory, the water had been deep, some of the reaches magnificent, and the scenery, on the whole, beyond our expectations.

26th. The beef never made its appearance after all: the early morning hours were too valuable to waste in waiting for it, so we were once more *en route* a little after daylight. I counted altogether anchored on both sides of the river, a little above Tsungyang, two hundred and fifty war-junks, flying defiant flags, and well manned.

We soon pass the Tai-tse-kee rock, rising out of the centre of the river but a very few feet above its waters, upon which, nevertheless, are still visible the ruined walls of an old temple. A few hundred yards beyond it is the 48-chang, or 180-yards' passage. The river is here barred more than half across its width by rocks which rise out of it like stepping-stones. It is called the Lankan-ke, or "Bar-river-hen," and derives its name from the following legend, as graphically narrated to us by our communicative pilot:

"In former days the scenery at this place was very beautiful and romantic, gigantic rocks being strewn over the surface of the country. One day a bonze saw in a dream a quarrel arise between the beneficent spirits of the air and those who resided in the rocks. The presiding spirit of these was a rock in the form of a hen; and the result of the quarrel was, that, to give vent to their spleen, the rock-spirits determined to block up the passage of the river. In pursuance of this ill-natured design, off started the hen-rock, followed by all the rocks in her train, when the priest awoke, and, perceiving what was occurring, with infinite presence of mind commenced crowing like a cock. This so fascinated the leading hen-rock that her progress was arrested in mid-channel, on which the goddess Kwan-yin was invoked; then the people subscribed together, and while the hen-rock was thus enthralled by the well-sustained crowing of the priest, they succeeded in cutting her head off: this effectually checked the progress of herself and attendant rocks, and there they remain to this day."

To avoid this dangerous pass, a cutting has been made on the southern bank through a corner called No-yang-ho. We, however, found deep water, and a safe channel close under the opposite shore. Before reaching Ngan-king the river divides, leaving numerous broad islands, which are flat and extensively cultivated, and well supplied with cattle. We observed green grass spread over the young crops to protect them from the frost. As we heard occasional heavy firing going on ahead, I went up to the cross-trees, and could perceive from them the rebel and imperialist troops skirmishing in the distance. Columns of black smoke rising in various directions proved to us that the work of destruction was progressing, and that houses and villages were being reduced to ashes far and wide. Presently we open Ngan-king, the capital city of Ngan-hwui, with its handsome eight-storied pagoda rising out of a substantially-built isolated stone fort, and massive walls skirting the river, giving the city quite an imposing appearance.

Riding along the shore, and keeping up with us as we steamed against the strong current, was an imperialist officer, apparently of high rank—for he rode a handsome white horse, decorated with gay trappings, and was accompanied by ten or twelve horsemen, well armed and appointed. It seemed that the government troops had received notice of our approach, and had determined to take advantage of it, in order to make a grand attack upon Ngan-king, the advanced rebel position up the river, and strongly garrisoned by them. The mounted mandarin was evidently a general making a reconnoissance, for he did not venture within gunshot of the fort, but galloped back, seemingly well satisfied with his achievement.

The Lee is leading the way, sounding for a channel; we are following cautiously, when puff spurts a little cloud of white smoke from one of the embrasures, and a shot comes singing along over the water, but the elevation is deficient, and it falls into it within twenty yards of its mark. However, the direction was good, and this style of reception demands an immediate rejoinder. It is evident that the news of the Nankin episode has not yet reached Ngan-king; indeed, we knew that it was impossible that it could have done so; and as we anticipated a farther act of folly at this end of the rebel position, our decks were cleared for action, and the men stood ready at their guns. The smoke of the first shot had not cleared away from the muzzle of the gun before the well-known flag which heads the list of British signals was flying from our mast-head, and the Furious, Cruiser, Dove, and Lee had opened in full chorus. The brave garrison just stuck to their guns long enough to fire three times more, and then from my look-out I could see them running like rats out of the fort into the open country in rear of it. Here, however, they found themselves in a dilemma; for the imperialists had descended from the heights behind, and, plucking up courage, were now advancing in light skirmishing order over the open plain, with the evident intention of attacking the fort in rear. They scarcely calculated upon finding the whole garrison out upon the plain to meet them. We could see the rebels hastily running together, and forming under hedgerows, and the imperialists, afraid to advance, waving banners and firing at them at incredible distances with gingalls.

At this time the general effect was in the highest degree exciting and picturesque. The hurrying of bodies of men to and fro over the fields—the waving of flags and firing of gingalls—the thunder of our own heavy guns—the groups of country people hastening across the drawbridge into the city for refuge, staggering under heavy loads, and driving cattle before them—the smoke of their burning homes rising up to the cloudless sky—all combined to form a scene to gaze upon which, as it lay mapped out beneath, must have stirred the heart and sent the blood tingling through the veins of the most unimpassioned nature.

It is so seldom that we experience emotions which unite in themselves at one and the same moment the highest amount of esthetic and animal excitement. When Madame de Staël said, "Pour bien goûter la nature il faut ou l'amour, ou la religion." she had not tried the effect of "la guerre." Our fire only lasted for ten minutes; we did not care to deface the ornamented exterior of the pagoda, or expend our moorsom shells upon empty batteries. Moreover, as the imperialists had not the pluck to run into the deserted fort when we had cleared it for them, they deserved to lose it; so we ceased firing, and steamed gently under the city walls, and before we had passed them saw the fort reoccupied by the original tenants.

Some of Lord Amherst's party visited this pagoda, and describe it as being in good repair, with a handsome marble obelisk in the basement story containing the heart of a celebrated warrior. As a good many of our shot struck the pagoda, the obelisk may have suffered, if the iconoclastic propensities of the rebels have not already led them to regard this monument in the light of a sacred emblem. It was fortunate for us that the effect which our fire, short as it was, had created, prevented the rebels from firing at us from the city walls; for the deep channel led us within fifty or sixty yards of them, and we seemed to look into the muzzles of the guns as we passed before them; but the batteries here, too, were partially deserted, and I could look down upon bare places in the city, where groups were collected, half uncertain as to our intentions; and here and there soldiers ran crouching along the walls, not caring to be seen by us.

Just as we reached the last angle, and were congratulating ourselves upon our good luck, two guns were fired upon us in rapid succession, and at rather close quarters. This was a piece of absurd impertinence, which involved another ten minutes' bombardment as a punishment. It came upon them too hot and strong to admit even of a third shot. The battery was speedily silenced, and, after trying our range at some of the most imposing-looking public buildings in the centre of the town, and bursting a shell or two in the streets by way of a warning, we left Ngan-king behind us, and with it got clear of the last strong-hold of our not very agreeable friends the rebels. On this side of the city, as on the other, country people were running in before the advancing imperialists. These latter are concentrating on this city and on Nankin all their energies, as they are on the extreme right and left of the rebel position, and provincial cities. Though finely situated, and surrounded by a well-built wall, the city is not so extensive or populous in appearance as most towns of its class. I observed, nevertheless, several handsome substantial houses and yamuns.

The suburbs had all been leveled, and presented a lamentable appearance of desolation. Mr. Ellis, who explored the city in 1816. says the shops were not so good as at Woohoo, and the streets were unusually narrow. The best shops were those for the sale of horn lanterns and porcelain. "There would," he remarks, "have been little difficulty in laying out a large sum in curiosities of all kinds, such as necklaces, old china, agate cups, vases, ornaments of corundum and other stones, curious specimens of carved work in wood and metal."

Not long after leaving Ngan-king we passed another imperial fleet of upward of two hundred junks at anchor. We also observed the country people flitting, and upon asking the pilot the reason of this, he said that doubtless the noise of our bombardment had led them to suppose that the city would be captured, and a horde of rebels be let loose upon the country to rob and plunder.

It must not be inferred from this that the insurgents are the only people addicted to these vices. I have already described the country people as flying into Ngan-king before the imperialist troops. The unhappy peasantry are indeed the victims of the lawless propensities of both sides. Indifferent to either, and desiring only peace and quiet, they are pillaged first by one and then the other; and in the case of cities, the imperialists, on driving out the rebels, generally complete the work which these latter have left half finished.

We were now cheered by the sight of occasional trading-junks, and passed several collected at the villages of Hong-tse-kee and Wang-tse-kee, on the south side. At the latter point, red clay bluffs, at the base of which large boulders of rock are strewn, approach the river.

From the cross-trees we saw a vast expanse of water at some distance from the river, on the north bank. This lagoon extends from Ngan-king for a distance of upward of thirty miles parallel with the river, varying in breadth from one to five or six miles. It is known under various names. Behind it high ranges of mountains are visible. In parts the country was park-like, the woods being dotted over it in thick clumps. On the south bank the hills are lower, and wooded, concealing small lakes in their recesses. Altogether, it seemed as though the combination of moor and loch, wood, marsh, and cultivated ground, should afford abundant and varied sport.

The city of Toong-lew is charmingly situated on the south bank. The houses are overtopped by two pagodas. One of eight stories stands close to the river; the other is built on an eminence some distance inland. The town is of no great extent, and is surrounded by a wall which dips and rises over the undulating ground, and finally descends to the water of a lake which half encircles the town, and is fringed with trees. As we looked into it from aloft we saw acres of charred ruins, the traces of rebel occupation: they, however, merely contented themselves with burning a great part of the city, and then evacuated it after holding it for a very short time. A plain half a mile broad separates it from the river. This was soon thickly dotted with human beings, as the people observed us anchor before their city, and came running to the shore to gaze at us. We procured from them some fowls and other minor additions to our stock. Our day's run had exceeded fifty miles, so that we were well pleased with our progress. Some of the reaches along which we had passed, carrying plenty of water, were ten miles in length, and between one and two in breadth, without a bend. We are daily more impressed with the capabilities of this mighty stream.

CHAPTER XXXVII.

A foraging Expedition.—Our Pilot romances.—Grandeur of the Scenery.—The "Little Orphan Rock."—A windy Locality.—Entrance to the Poyang Lake.—Legend of the "Orphan Rocks."—Floods of the Yang-tse.—Method of accounting for them.—Rural Statistics.—Appearance of the Women.—Geographical Features of the Country.—The Valley of the Yang-tse.—Kew-kiang.—A Survey of its Resources.—Villages on the Banks.—Magnificent Scenery.—Depredations of the Nee-fei.—We land at Hwang-shih-kang.—Its commercial Activity.—White Tortoise Island.—Enter the Province of Hoopeh.—The Philosopher Laoutz'.—The "White Tiger Mills."—An unsatisfactory Dialogue.—Approach Hankow.

October 27. Weighed early from Toong-lew. The mountains on the southern bank now increase in height, but we had hardly begun to enjoy the scenery when we went aground on a sandbank. While they were trying to get the ship off we landed on a foraging expedition, and succeeded in procuring four bullocks. The country was flat, and the soil light and sandy. Small farms were dotted about; and carts drawn by buffaloes, ridden instead of driven, creaked across it.

The country people told us that not very long since the rebels had overrun their district, and they had been obliged to fly. They were all armed, and many bore on their breasts the inscription "Valiant," signifying that they were enrolled in the militia. Some of the young men had been kidnapped by the rebels, and one of them, who had escaped from their clutches, was pointed out to us.

We took our pilot ashore with us, which alarmed him greatly, as he supposed that we were going to inflict some description of summary punishment upon him for running us aground. When, however, he discovered that we only required him to bargain for bullocks, he recovered his composure, and was soon imparting, with much animated action, to a group of admiring countrymen, a very highly-embellished narrative of our late action at Ngan-king. With our heroic performances on that occasion he was careful to identify himself. "You should have seen how we gave it to them," he said; "how our shot told, and how big our shot was; why, it would have taken three such blessed old fools as you to lift one of them." This was said to a respectable middle-aged man, who was sucking a pipe and staring incredulously at the narrator. It turned the laugh in his favor.

As some of our party had discovered a lake a short distance inland, we started off to explore it. We found it covered with water-fowl. Pelicans, wild swans, geese, ducks, besides cranes, herons, and a number of feathered bipeds unknown to me, cackled, fluttered, and stalked about, making a great racket. Unfortunately, we were a large and somewhat noisy party, and they were very shy. A rash shot sent them all wheeling into the air with loud cries, and they continued to circle and scream overhead, to see whether we would go away; and, finding us stationary, tailed off in long strings to some more secure retreat.

I prosecuted my explorations with two companions, and, crossing a low ridge, came upon a farm which rejoiced in the descriptive name of Hwa-yuen-chin, or "The Flower-garden Station." It was situated on the margin of a great lagoon, about two miles broad, and of unknown length, called by the natives Ta-hoo, or "The Lake" *par excellence*. Here I shot a brace of fine ducks: one of them, however, was only wounded, and gave us a long chase in a punt, which we opportunely found and appropriated. The water was nowhere more than six or eight feet in depth.

We were told that the light sandy soil retained the heat of the sun in summer, making it almost impossible for the people to work in their fields during the heat of the day. Even now, late in November, the midday sun was formidable, though the nights and mornings were absolutely cold. The ship got off about 4 P. M., but remained at anchor for the night.

28th. Weighed early. The morning was mild at sunrise, but shortly after a regular northeast gale set in, bitterly cold, and very strong. The scenery upon the south shore assumed a character of grandeur, surpassing any thing we had hitherto seen. The mountains came boldly down to the water's edge, projecting into the river in rocky promontories or precipitous bluffs. The most striking of these is the Ma-toong-shan, which, however, as we followed a northern channel, we only saw at a distance. The gale now blew furiously, obscuring the atmosphere with clouds of dust. This haziness, and the general blackness of the weather, invested our approach to the gorge of Seaou-koo-shan with quite an imposing effect. The Cruiser, with top-gallant-masts struck.

lay over to the blast; the two little gun-boats, scarcely visible ahead, seemed plunging into the depths of some infernal region, the gigantic portals of which loomed indistinctly through the mist. Presently we found ourselves forcing our way between two lofty masses of rock, in a channel scarce a quarter of a mile in width, and fifteen or sixteen fathoms deep.

The Seaou-koo-shan, or "Little Orphan Rock," rises precipitously out of the midst of the waves, which were dashing against

The Seaou-koo-shan (Yang-tse-kiang).

it, to a height of near three hundred feet. The mountain opposite called Chin-tse-shan, or the "Mirror Mountain," rises in a sheer mass from the river margin, and is crowned by walls running along the brink of precipices, and towers perched on dizzy pinnacles of rock. Part of this fortification is the work of the rebels. A Buddhist temple has been built, or rather let into the face of the Orphan Rock, like a piece of enamel, about midway between the base and the summit. It is approached by steps hewn out of the rock, and presents a most striking and picturesque aspect. Mr. Ellis, who visited this temple, says that a paper was brought to him by the priests stating that the temple had been endowed by the emperor's mother. Junks usually stop here to make offerings to propitiate the local deity. We observed an inscription upon a smooth part of the rock, conspicuously placed, and which Mr. Wade imagined to be a quotation. It was as follows:

"Green hill by the river,
From the extremity of its bend, one beholds thee."

This pass marks the boundary between the provinces of Ngan-hwui and Kiang-si.

We now enter this latter province, described in the Chinese Repository as one spacious valley, comprising an area of 72,176 square miles, or about equal to the State of Virginia, with a population of more than twenty-three million of souls. The first place on it at which we arrive is Pang-tse, picturesquely situated among the hills. The few buildings that remain of a town, never very extensive, are surrounded by a wall, which incloses as well a vast area of barren hill and valley. The object of those who planned the wall seems to have been to carry it to the top of the highest hills, and over ridges so steep that they were of themselves a defense.

As the wind increased almost to a hurricane this afternoon, we came to an anchor at 2 P.M. at a spot where a very disagreeable bar of sand rendered caution necessary. We were led to believe that gales such as the one we were now experiencing were common in this locality, from the numerous sand dunes which we observed upon the southern bank, and which presented a remarkable contrast to the green knolls and wooded mountains which usually rose from it.

29th. The thermometer early this morning fell for the first time to two degrees below freezing. It was found necessary to buoy the channel ahead, and the wind having moderated, we weighed, and carried three fathoms of water across the bar. The gale of yesterday seems to have cleared the air, for the day is beautiful, and enables us to appreciate the magnificent scenery which opens upon us as we approach the entry to the Poyang Lake. The channel connecting this extensive sheet of water with the great river is about three miles long and one broad. On its eastern shore, at the point of junction, Hoo-kow, the "City of the Lake's Mouth," is perched upon the precipitous rock called Tsa-chee, or the "Jagged Head," opposite to which the majestic Lew-shan, or "Mule" Mountain, rears its imposing crest to a height of 5000 feet. Rising out of the waters of the lake in solitary grandeur, we could discern in the distance the Takoo-shan,

Entrance to the Poyang Lake.

or Great Orphan Rock. These romantic scenes, and the associations connected with them, have rendered them the frequent subjects of poetic celebration among the people.

Our pilot, who is a great legend-monger, gave us the following account of the origin of the Takoo-shan: A fisherman once dropped his anchor under Seaou-koo-shan, or the Little Orphan Rock, and could not find it again, so he applied to a priest to help him. The priest gave him an invocation, which he was to place upon his forehead, and then dive for his anchor. The spell succeeded to a miracle; not only did he discover his lost anchor, but a charming river-nymph as well, who had chosen it for her couch. At first he stood entranced at so fair a vision; then, regaining his presence of mind, he determined on preserving a memento of it, and gently abstracting a tiny shoe from the fascinating crushed foot of this Chinese Naiad, he ascended to the surface with his anchor. But the lady, probably roused by finding herself dispossessed of her iron bedstead, discovered the loss of her shoe, and instantly started in pursuit. Notwithstanding that a stern chase is usually a long chase, the fisherman was rapidly losing ground, when he bethought himself of altering the position of the sails, so as to mislead his fair pursuer as to the direction he was taking, the stem and stern of his junk being alike. This device, however, though it originated an entirely new rig upon the river, failed, and he was ultimately so hard pressed that he was obliged to throw the shoe overboard at the mouth of the Poyang Lake: and on the spot arose the solitary rock called Takoo-shan, or sometimes Sheae-koo-shan, or the Shoe Hill, ever after.

The navigation at this point was in the highest degree intricate: the mass of water pouring out of the lake, and meeting the swift current of the river, formed whirlpools and eddies, known in China as "chow-chow" water, and, what we dreaded more, shoals and bars in every direction.

We had not advanced ten miles from our last night's anchorage before we found ourselves hard and fast upon one of these provoking impediments. Not that delays of this character were to be altogether regretted, as they gave us opportunities of landing and exploring the country. The ship had not been on shore ten minutes before we followed its example, and were straggling far and wide, some of us in search of game, others of information, and others, again, of bullocks and fowls.

We had landed on the north bank, and the country stretched away, in one unbroken level, to a range of hills just visible in the distance. Herds of buffaloes were grazing upon the pastures, numbers of them bestridden by urchins, who, seated upon the backs of these ungainly animals, tended the herd, presenting, as they did so, a most singular appearance. A *levée* extended along the river-bank to keep its waters from overflowing the country in rear, and upon it the peasantry had built an almost continuous row of mean cottages, the roofs and walls of which were of reeds. Here and there a stone building had been erected as a rebel post, or as a house of entertainment by some enterprising speculator. A dread of floods operated as the chief inducement to putting up tenements of so unsubstantial a character, many of the owners having farms on the hills, to which they repaired during the rains. They asserted that the river occasionally rose a hundred feet. We were contented to believe, however, our own observation, and the marks we perceived convinced us that fifty feet above its then level was a low estimate for its summer rise. Here the current had evidently rushed violently over the face of the country, devastating an immense area of cultivated or pasture land by depositing upon it great quantities of sand.

It would appear that ultimately the waters only partially recede, leaving vast tracts covered with those lagoons and marshes which we continued to observe on both banks of the river. During the dry season a considerable subsidence takes place, and the channels by which their surplus waters were discharged into the river dry up. The consequence is, that, after partial rains, all those mountain torrents which would, under other circumstances, go to swell the waters of the parent stream, get absorbed in the lakes at the base of the hills, and, unless the rain is of sufficient duration to overflow them, the river receives no additional supply. Meantime the great evaporation which must take place from so large a surface of water renders the rise of the lakes comparatively slow. This would appear the only way of accounting for the fact that, although partial rises do occur in the river, they are not so common as the humidity of the climate would lead one to anticipate. In all probability, it will be found, however, that these rises occur more frequently below the Poyang Lake than above it. This may be presumed from the fact that the waters which supply the Poyang, rising in lower latitudes, are not subject to those frosts, and are more readily thawed than the upper tributaries of the river, and that, consequently, the volume of water discharged from the lake varies in amount to a much greater extent than that which flows down to meet it.

But the violence of the river was not more dreaded by the unhappy peasantry than that of the rebels: when they were not flooded out by the one, they were burnt out by the other. But a few months had elapsed since the "pests" had scoured this district, and had burnt all the houses for fuel. As one of the peasantry pathetically remarked when he told us of it—"Ah! those were sad times!"

We entered a small brick cottage, on the door-post of which the owner had signified that it was a house of entertainment for travelers, and found that it was divided into two small rooms and one large one. In the latter were straw beds on the ground, in which eight or ten travelers might have been closely packed. The owner informed us that he possessed three acres of land, producing various descriptions of pulse and grain, which he showed us, and for which he paid government a ground-rent of 3s. 6d. He exported his produce to the neighboring districts.

Close to the inn was a village school, in which there were only eight pupils. The schoolmaster told us that he got eight strings of cash, or about nine shillings a year, per pupil, but that many of the country people were too poor to avail themselves of the privilege, and sent their children to tend cattle instead.

Passing another cottage, we detected the fumes of opium, and on entering found two men smoking tobacco; but a light gleaming through a crevice from an inner compartment betrayed the secret occupation of the inmate, and on looking in, we found him stretched comfortably on his side, frizzling the opium through a flame into his pipe in the most approved manner. So absorbed was he in the enjoyment of "kief" that he scarcely condescended to notice us, though we must have presented a very unexpected and startling apparition. His comrades asked us what we had to sell, evidently inferring, from the interest we displayed in the consumption of the "drug," that we had some of it to dispose of.

We did not see many women; those who did favor us with a sight of their countenances might certainly have spared us that treat. I think I never saw the fair sex under a less attractive exterior.

It was at this point that Lord Amherst's mission left the Great River, taking the route to Canton by way of the Poyang Lake, which gave rise to the following parting reflection, to be found in Mr. Ellis's *Journal:* "In vain will the patriot look for kindred feelings—in vain will the man of honor look for a friend, and still more in vain would amiable woman look for a companion on the banks of the Yang-tse-kiang." So far as our experience went, this latter sentiment was as true of "amiable" man.

The village we had been exploring was called Pa-le-kiang, or the Eight-le-river, and is the spot from which travelers journeying south usually cross the Ta-kiang. Père Huc, who traveled overland from Woochang, struck it at this point, and crossed to Hookow.

In a geographical point of view, the section of the river which traverses this corner of Kiang-si is perhaps the most interesting. We had now ascended the Ta-kiang for a distance of four hundred and fifty miles, and had only just reached its first real affluent; for, with the exception of the Tsung-yang River, all those tributaries marked as such in the map turned out to be ditches almost dry in the winter time. But here the great river meets a feeder worthy of it. In a single deep rolling tide the Poyang Lake discharges into it the whole drainage of the vast province of Kiang-si. Surrounded on all sides by lofty ranges, the northern barrier of this lake must at some former period have proved the feeblest, and given egress to the accumulated waters through this gorge.

As though to meet this important accession, the Ta-kiang takes that southern bend which forms one of the most marked features of its course. In forming this curve it has been compelled to force its passage through the Ma-tze-shan, or "Horse's Spine" range, which forms part of the western boundary of Kiang-si, dividing that province from Hoopeh. These mountains cross the river at Woo-such, and under another name trend away to the northeast, marking the frontier of the province in that direction, and leaving a small strip of it inclosed between them and the northern bank of the Ta-kiang. After having thus fulfilled its mission by dipping into Kiang-si and carrying off the surplus waters of the Poyang, the great river leaves the province by the romantic pass of the Seaou-koo-shan, or "Orphan Rock," already described.

The mountain system of this part of China may be better understood by supposing that, with those ranges, along the base of which the river forms its southern curve, a northern range is connected, forming, as it were, a loop upon it, and opposing barriers which the river has burst to obtain ingress and egress. At the same time, it is to be borne in mind that the mountains composing this loop are not the only mountains to the north of the river. As repeatedly observed, high ranges were constantly visible in that direction, though they rarely approached the river. In fact, throughout the whole length of our voyage, the great valley of the Yang-tse, or Ta-kiang, has maintained the same general character, which may be described in a few words. Its breadth varied exceedingly, and may have ranged from ten to fifty miles. The river invariably hugged the southern range, which seldom reached more than four or five miles from its banks, leaving a strip of alluvial plain, while numerous lakes washed the base of the hills or lay embosomed among them. To the north, plain and lake sometimes extended far as the eye could reach; but generally mountains, more or less distant, closed the prospect.

30*th*. We found, to our disgust, that we had followed the wrong passage; we were therefore obliged to retrace our steps over the bar, and, rounding the island opposite the entrance to the lake, look for a channel in that direction. This we were at last fortunate enough to discover, but not without crossing another very difficult bar. At 2 o'clock P.M. we were opposite Kew-kiang. As we had letters to the authorities of this important "foo" city, the first one of its class belonging to the imperialists we had reached since leaving Chin-kiang-foo, we remained here for the remainder of the day, and went on shore to investigate its present condition. We found it to the last degree deplorable. A single dilapidated street, composed only of a few mean shops, was all that existed of this once-thriving and populous city; the remainder of the vast area, comprised within walls five or six miles in circumference, contained nothing but ruins, weeds, and kitchen-gardens. The inhabitants declare that this is partly owing to the five years' occupation of the town by the rebels, and partly to the destructive propensities of the imperialist troops, who retook it from them only last April, or seven months ago. Its present garrison consisted of four thousand men, while its population scarce amounted to as many hundreds. They seemed, all of them, following in our train, their faces expressive of intense astonishment, mingled with some alarm.

In the centre of the city was an eminence covered with ruins, which commanded an extensive and remarkable view. Beneath us lay a dreary waste of brickbats; behind us rose the magnificent peaks of the precipitous Lew-shan; before us a chain of lakes extended into the dim distance, until they were merged in the fiery haze of the setting sun; while, sweeping under the walls, the mighty Ta-kiang poured its yellow volume seaward. The only bright object in Kew-kiang was a Confucian temple, which had just been built by the emperor; it contained a tablet inscribed by a celebrated minister of state to the memory of his friend, a Tartar general, who had fallen at the capture of the city.

In the suburb there was a more substantial street and better shops: one of them was devoted to the sale of foreign fabrics; in it I observed Manchester calicoes and a species of red serge which was imported from Russia. We visited an apothecary's shop, and saw him prescribe crushed spiders, ginseng, and sundry roots and reptiles, to anxious patients; also a baker's establishment, where we found that some of the flour used came all the way from the province of Shantung. We nibbled sweetmeats at a grocer's, inspected cottons at a haberdasher's, and searched in vain for old china in a crockery-shop. Kew-kiang boasts two pagodas—one outside and one inside the city: the latter partially destroyed.

December 1. In consequence of the difficulties of the navigation yesterday, the Lee was sent on this morning to explore the river ahead; on her returning with a favorable report, we weighed, and proceeded prosperously for about twenty miles, when we were brought up suddenly by a bar, across which it was necessary to buoy a channel. We ultimately scraped over, with about three inches to spare under the keel. At this point the village of Loong-ping is situated on the north bank, and on the opposite side some red clay bluffs are a conspicuous feature.

Looking in a southerly direction, we could see from the crosstrees a large lake dotted with high wooded islands, upon which, in the distance, the white sails of numerous junks that were' navigating it were visible.

To the north, an extensive lake, also covered with junks, stretched away to the base of a distant range. I here observed, for the first time, wood-rafts, each with a small population of its own, who lived in huts constructed upon them. The country was flat and well cultivated, maintaining a large and apparently more thriving population than we had observed at any previous section of the river. A much-frequented road traversed the plain, along which numerous travelers journeyed in wheel-barrows, protecting themselves from the sun's rays with bright-colored umbrellas.

A few miles farther we pass, on the northern bank, the flourishing market-town of Woo-sueh, the whole population of which turned out to stare at us; and on the south the pretty village of Ma-kow, charmingly situated in a wooded valley. The Ma-tze-shan, or Horse's Spine Mountains, now approach the river, rising abruptly from its waters to a height of 1500 or 2000 feet. We are delighted to observe that the northern chain seems to bar our progress ahead, as through them we shall have to force our way to-morrow; and, to judge from the mountainous nature of the country, we may depend upon fine scenery. Meantime our voyage of to-day has been invested with an interest peculiar to itself. Never before had these waters been explored by a foreigner, unless mayhap some stray Jesuit in disguise, who has given us no account of his wanderings, may have traversed them in the course of his missionary labors. We could now, therefore, look forward to indulging for some days in that rare but delightful excitement of gazing for the first time upon scenes heretofore unvisited.

2*d*. We were on deck earlier than usual this morning, determined not to miss any of the unknown beauties of the river. Shortly after weighing, we entered the gorge from which the river emerges into the province of Kiang-si. Mountains overhang it on both sides, and as it winds between them it assumes all the appearance of a highland loch. The valleys are wooded with dark-green firs; the gray rocks are crowned with purple heather, and wild crags force themselves into bold and picturesque relief.

The most striking spot is at the precipitous bluff of Pwan-pien-shan, opposite to which the surface of the limestone cliff is quarried out, and on a projecting point a temple is left standing. With almost every revolution of the paddle-wheels a new point of view opened upon us, displaying unexpected attractions of peak and pinnacle in the foreground, and the abrupt outlines of lofty ranges in the distance. To one of these, in consequence of a singular depression in its outline, we gave the name of the "Devil's Bite Range."

Passing the towns of Sha-wootze and Tien-shia-chin, we reached at 11 A.M. the sub-prefectural city of Ke-chow, its walls crowning a bluff which overhangs the river. Rising from the midst of the stream is a circular stone fort. We remained here a short time to receive a mandarin, who came on board to present to Lord Elgin the compliments of the Governor General of Hoo-Kwang, into whose jurisdiction we had now entered. The river was crowded with small junks, all going in one direction, and foot-passengers thronged the roads along its margin. We learned from our visitor, on asking him the cause of this commotion, that the rebels were at Kwang-tse, a city lying thirty or forty miles distant to the northeast, and mentioned by Huc as having been visited by him.

These were probably not the Tai-ping rebels, but some of the Nĕĕ-fei, who had taken advantage of the insecure state of the country to commit depredations which were driving the country people from their homes. Some of the provincial authorities were now in the city, endeavoring to restore confidence; to assist them, a large body of imperial cavalry, numbered at 10,000 by our informant, had just arrived, and were then encamped in the neighborhood. Ke-chow had been partially destroyed by the Tai-pings, who held it off and on until they were finally driven away about a year ago.

A little beyond the city we passed the scene of a bloody fight between the rebels and imperialists in 1854, of which our pilot gave us a most animated description; according to him, the former were beaten, forced into the river, and upward of 20,000 drowned or otherwise destroyed.

In the afternoon we passed the precipitous bluff Taou-tse-fuh, rising in an unbroken wall to the height of 500 feet out of the water. Behind it, a magnificent mountain range displayed scenes of great grandeur and picturesque beauty. A Chin-chai, or mandarin of high degree, followed by a train of boats, passed us in the largest river-junk I have yet seen, handsomely decorated, and with the usual display of gongs, umbrellas, and banners. He was probably on his way "to restore confidence." We reached the important market-town of Hwang-shih-kang, or "Yellow Stone" —probably so called from the quarries in the neighborhood—in time to explore it before dark. A splendid river-wall of sandstone, surmounted by a handsome balustrade, gave the place a most imposing appearance. The water was so deep that we were compelled to anchor close to the junks, which were made fast to the shore. A dense crowd came pouring out of the gate, and down to the water's edge, as the huge triton took up its position among the minnows, and commenced blowing off steam in a manner calculated to confirm the impression that we had arrived direct from the infernal regions.

It was almost impossible to step on shore out of the boats, so closely had the people packed themselves into the river itself. On entering the town, we were surprised at the universal cleanliness of the streets, and the superiority of the shops, generally, over any we had yet discovered at other towns on the river. The numerous junks moored before it gave evidence of a high degree of commercial activity: this general air of prosperity and opulence was the more striking, as it was quite unexpected, and contrasted so strongly with all that had previously come within the range of our observation. The surrounding country produces great quantities of cotton; as much as 800,000 taels worth of this article, unmanufactured, is transported annually to Chang-sha, the capital of Hoonan. Indigo is also largely grown in the neighborhood; and we inspected the process of rolling the newly-dyed cotton with gigantic stone rollers, worked partly by the feet and partly by machinery. The raw cotton, of which I got some specimens, seemed short in the staple. Superior hemp is imported from Hing-kwoh, a town not many miles distant, while coal is procured from a mine only five miles off. Neither tea nor silk were cultivated here, but a considerable trade is carried on in grain. I saw in the shops some gray Manchester calicoes and Dutch velveteens. The process of investigation in a Chinese city is never very agreeable; but here, although the crowd was respectful, it was so highly perfumed, and so pressing in its attentions, that we were glad to get down to our boats once more, and breathe fresh air.

The immunity which Hwang-shih-kang has enjoyed from rebel violence is probably due chiefly to the absence of any wall or fortification, which could render it a valuable position in a military point of view.

3d. In consequence of the intricacy of the navigation, our progress to-day was slow. Lakes were visible on both sides, and pretty broken country to the south, with occasional bluffs, and distant ranges. The river still averages upward of a mile in breadth. In the afternoon we passed Woo-chang-hsien, a walled town with two seven-storied pagodas, a lake at the back, some fine ranges beyond, two very picturesque gates, and a great crowd staring at us from the bank. The town itself seems in good preservation, probably because the rebels evacuated it, and made Hwang-chow their military position. A rock rising out of the stream here is called Peh-kwei, or White Tortoise Island. The name is derived from a fable, to the effect that a soldier was once pursued by his enemies to this island, and to escape them leaped into the river, when one of the huge tortoises lying near the shore took him upon his spacious back and carried him safely to the opposite bank.

About two miles higher up is situated the district city of Hwang-chow. It boasts the finest pagoda on the river, which, in spite of rebel occupation, remains in a state of excellent preservation. An imperialist army was encamped under the walls, and a fleet of war-junks moored to the shore. The appearance of this combined land and river force was most picturesque. The white tents and bright flags; the horses picketed in groups, and the men clustering into masses in rude parade; the gay junks, each with its special device, formed a striking scene. Here is a gorgeous barge bearing on its flag, "The Leader of the Hoonan Braves;" and here another, "The Commissary General of the Flying Camps of Hoopeh."

The walls of Hwang-chow inclose the usual howling waste. The city was abandoned by the rebels about two years ago.

We ran our nose upon a sand-bank a few miles above Hwang-chow, and occupied the whole of the remainder of the day in fruitless efforts to find a channel.

4th. We spent almost the whole of to-day at anchor in one spot, the gun-boats channel-hunting. The difficulties in the navigation are now so numerous that we almost despair of forcing the old ship another hundred miles up the river.

It is, however, some satisfaction to feel that we have reached Hoopeh, one of the central provinces of the empire. "This province," says the *Chinese Repository*, "enjoys so many advantages of temperature, climate, fertile soil, navigable rivers, and beautiful lake and mountain scenery, that it is called the granary of the empire." Our own experience fully confirms the latter part of this description. Since entering the province, some lake or other had always been visible from the cross-trees.

The Liang-tze, which we saw yesterday, is connected with the Ax Lake by a conduit forming a communication across the bend of the Ta-kiang at this place. The population of Hoopeh is estimated at 27,000,000; its area is double that of England without Wales. The signification of the term Hoopeh is "North of the Lakes." Père Huc describes it as being in many respects inferior to Sz-chuen. The soil is somewhat sterile, though covered with numbers of lagoons and marshes, from which the Chinese, in spite of their patient industry, can extract but little utility; the villages, in consequence, present an appearance of misery and suffering. The vegetable productions are bread-stuffs, silk, cotton, tea, and timber; it possesses extensive mineral resources, and produces gold, silver, tin, iron, mica, copperas, crystal, marble, argillate, etc. Its manufactures are bamboo paper, wax-cloth, crystal and other ornaments, which are famed throughout the empire.

Hoopeh is also celebrated as the province which gave birth to Laoutz', a philosopher of scarcely less repute than Confucius. He was born fifty-four years before Confucius, and is believed to have had white hair and eyebrows at his birth, and to have been carried in the womb eighty years, whence he was called Laoutz', or "The Old Boy," and afterward Lankiun, or "The Venerable Prince." He was the founder of the sect of the Rationalists, or Tau-kia, and is the author of *Tau-tih-king*, or a "Memoir on Reason and Virtue," which is the text-book of his disciples.

Late in the afternoon we discovered a narrow and intricate passage behind a low island covered with long grass. We scraped so close under the high river-bank that the groups of peasantry, collected upon it to see us pass, might almost have jumped upon our decks. I landed with Wade on the island in search of game, when he succeeded in bringing down a fine wild goose out of a flock which was sailing overhead.

5*th.* We had only one serious difficulty to-day, and made good progress. The country did not seem so thickly inhabited or well peopled as the district through which we had just passed: in parts, the northern bank was well wooded and level, with occasional lakes; to the south it was more broken; but there were no hills of any elevation. The "White Tiger Hills," which are the most remarkable in form, jut out into the river, but are not above 500 feet above it. In summer large tracts of country, now pasture-land, must be under water. The weather is getting sensibly colder. It hailed last night, and this morning I observed specks of sleet.

Though nearly five hundred miles from the sea, we saw porpoises again to-day, called by the Chinese "Cheang-choo-tsze." They use the oil as silk dye. Junks and rafts are more numerous than formerly, and our terrific aspect creates invariably so great a sensation as almost to stupefy the crews. Not only must our appearance, but our ignorance, astonish them. We bawl out for information about lakes, mountains, and cities, to them well known, but of the names of which our pilot is as ignorant as ourselves. He makes up for this, however, by the energy with which he shouts his queries upon all sorts of subjects to the passers-by. Thus he begins:

"Hi, on the raft there—Ho, father!" The only response is a vacant stare.

Pilot again, more energetically: "Hi! Ho! Ah! Great uncle!" This more remote term of relationship elicits not only a stare, but a prolonged "a-a-a-a," not unlike the bleating of an asthmatic sheep.

Pilot, getting slightly indignant, becomes even less affectionate, and puts his question: "Much-honored relation, do you hear, what place is this?"

Answer from the much-honored relation: "Ah-ah-ah," in a different cadence from before.

Pilot, angrily: "Venerable party, I ask you what place this is?"

Venerable party, roused at last, shouts, and points up the river. He says, "It's all right; go on."

Pilot, now thoroughly exasperated, suddenly substitutes abusive for polite epithets; he rolls these out with great volubility, working up the last syllable to a high key, and dwelling upon it long, with great vigor and bitterness of expression, thus: "Oh, you old addle-pated, thick-skulled, noodle-oodle oodle-o-o-o-o-o, I did not ask you whether it was all right, but the name."

Answer: "Oh-ah-oh, the name of the town—the name of the town—oh-ah-oh, the name of the town you want to know? The town's name is—"

Pilot: "And what is the name of the lake?"

Answer: "There is no lake."

Pilot: "I tell you there is a lake."

Answer: "A lake, you said; oh-ah-oh, is there a lake? no-oh-no, there is no lake." And so on, till we steam ahead again in despair. The river is the big river or the old river, and the mountain has no name, and never had one. Occasionally, when we are at anchor, some of these boats approach us, to stare more closely at our huge bulk; then the pilot becomes friendly and communicative. "Come up," he says, "and see a little of the world." We never can gather from these visitors any idea of our distance from Han-kow. The nearer we approach it, the greater the number of "le" invariably becomes, which are still to be traversed.

6*th*. The Dove was sent on yesterday, to reach Han-kow if possible. We hoped to do the same, but our departure has been delayed by a dense fog. When this cleared off, we saw from the cross-trees a vast arable plain, extending in a northerly direction to a large lake, upon which we could distinguish through the haze the sails of distant junks. To the south the plain was intersected by a low irregular range, apparently densely populated; an extensive lake also bounded the prospect in this direction.

The well-cultivated and well-peopled aspect of the country leads us to hope that we are approaching a large town. Gradually the houses line the banks, and kitchen-gardens, neatly fenced, separate them from each other. Then we see a dense mass of houses, and a hill crowned with a wall, and the masts of many junks; among them the white funnel of the Dove, and we know that the goal is reached at last, and that the toils and anxieties of a month's river navigation are crowned with success.

CHAPTER XXXVIII.

First Impressions of Han-kow.—Its Resemblance to Nijni Novgorod.—Our first Landing.—An orderly Crowd.—Plan of Han-kow.—View of Wo-chang and Han-yang.—Population of these Cities.—Manufacture of Bamboo Cables.—Price of Manchester Cottons.—Insect-wax.—The Mode of its Production.—Recent Demolition of Han-kow.—Its mixed Population.—Mandarinic Diplomacy.—Commercial Investigations.—Difficulty of obtaining Information.—A Dialogue.—Commerce of Han-kow.—The Tea-producing Districts.—A Visit to Han-yang.—Statements of Père Huc.

THE general appearance of the celebrated and far-famed mercantile emporium of Han-kow, as seen from the cross-trees of the Furious, was eminently disappointing. We had heard so much of the congeries of cities that are situated at the junction of the Han and the Yang-tse—of their extent, population, and commercial activity—we had longed so eagerly to reach them—had doubted so frequently whether we should ever thus be gratified—that we had formed grander expectations, and anticipated a nobler reward after all our anxieties and exertions. Still it was pleasant, after having seen nothing but ruins and heaps of brickbats, as supplying the places of populous cities, once more to look upon teeming streets and an animated river, even though on a smaller scale than we had been led to suppose.

In the situation of Han-kow and the topographical features of the surrounding country I was strongly reminded of Nijni Novgorod. Han-kow occupies the angle formed by the Han and Great River, which meet at right angles. On the opposite or right bank of the Han is a precipitous range of hills, crowned with the fortifications of the now ruined city of Han-yang. These correspond to the Kremlin of Nijni, while Han-kow answers to the fair. On the opposite side of the Yang-tse is the important provincial city of Wo-chang, which has no equivalent on the banks of the Volga. The shape of Han-kow is an acute-angled triangle, the base of which, resting on the Yang-tse, is a mile long, while it extends for about two miles and a half along the banks of the Han, dwindling away almost to a point. Being a purely commercial city, it is not surrounded by walls or any semblance of fortification.

The Han, which is the first important tributary that the Yang-tse receives (ascending the river), varies in breadth from a hundred to a hundred and fifty yards, and is a much less imposing stream than was to have been expected from its long course, and the amount of traffic which is carried on upon its waters. Numerous ferries supply the place of any bridge. For about half a mile from its point of junction with the parent stream, the Han is as densely crowded with junks as it is possible to pack them: very few, however, remain moored in the Yang-tse. This noble river is three quarters of a mile wide at this point; and immediately off the town we were anchored in thirteen fathoms of water, and this at a distance of nearly six hundred miles from the sea. Meantime, while we were engaged in making these observations, the crowd became denser, the river more alive with boats: the air resounded with the voices of thousands of persons gazing eagerly at us, and expressing their wonder in confused and audible murmurs. Presently boat-loads of minor officials were observed sculling about among the aquatic spectators, apparently to keep order. These crammed themselves close to the ship, under her bows, stern, and quarters, peering in at the port-holes, and feeling her sides, as though to see what she was made of.

We now determined to land, and thus still farther to gratify their curiosity; accordingly, we steered our way with no little difficulty through a maze of boats of all sorts and sizes, and filled with all classes and conditions of sight-seers, to a landing-place from which a flight of steps led up into the town, but which was now so crowded with human beings that it seemed a problem how we should ever succeed in forcing our way through them. We no sooner stepped ashore than a lane was somewhat precipitately opened, and the people fell back almost as if alarmed. We found the streets as thronged as the steps, but every where the crowd made way respectfully; indeed, it was rather a curious illustration of the moral influence exercised by the presence of four foreign ships in the very heart of the empire, that we should traverse the streets of a populous city not only unhindered and unmolested, but obliged in a friendly voice to exclaim constantly, "Puh, pao! puh, pao!" "Don't be afraid! don't be afraid!" a most condescending piece of advice for a handful of strangers to give to a million of people.

The streets themselves were superior to any I had seen in any other city of the empire. They were well paved, and roofed over with mats as they are in Persian or Egyptian cities, but still broad enough to be bright and cheerful. The shops were well stocked, and upon a much grander and handsomer scale than those at Canton or any of the open ports. Foot-passengers, wheelbarrows, loaded either with merchandise or people, and gentlemen of substance in chairs, crowded the thoroughfares. We observed that one chair followed us pertinaciously, and discovered that it contained a petty mandarin, who had either assumed, or was instructed to perform, the office of spy. When we objected to his surveillance, he assured us that he followed us purely out of regard for our safety, and for the purpose of keeping the crowd in order. Indeed, he soon began to display an amount of vigor in the performance of this duty which we by no means approved, getting out of his chair whenever we entered a shop, and dispersing the crowd which naturally collected round the doorway with violent blows of his whip. As this was a mode of procedure calculated to make us unpopular with the people, who were only manifesting a most natural and harmless curiosity, we remonstrated, and ultimately succeeded in shaking off our officious attendant; but we had reason to suspect that his conduct was in accordance with instructions received from the supreme authority of the province. We were soon after confirmed in this view by the request which our attendant official, Wang, who had accompanied us from Shanghai, made the same day, that Lord Elgin would not press the point of entering the provincial city of Wochang, or of calling upon the governor general.

We observed proclamations posted up in various parts of the town, informing the people of the intended visit of foreigners to their city, but assuring them that their stay was to be a short one, and not for commercial purposes. Nevertheless, the commonest query among those of the crowd who were bold enough to address us was, "What have you got to sell, and when are you coming to trade?"

The plan of Han-kow is very simple. Two principal arteries intersect it in parallel lines, while across them run a number of curved streets about equidistant from each other. After we had taken a cursory view of the town and its shops—the latter we proposed to investigate more thoroughly—we crossed the Han, and proceeded to scramble up the hill on its opposite bank. The tower at its summit was probably about three hundred feet above the plain, and afforded a magnificent and extensive prospect. The hill itself was called Ta-pieh, or "The Great Dividing Mount."

At our feet the mighty Yang-tse rolled its yellow tide seaward, above this point a well-navigated and useful stream, but henceforward to flow through a devastated country, and bear upon its bosom the wreck and debris of those populous cities whose active commerce once gave life and animation to its now deserted waters. We looked down upon the decks of our own ships, riding proudly at anchor where foreign ships had never lain before, towering above the black mass of boats that crowded round them; nor was it possible to help feeling a thrill of exultation as we watched the British ensign fluttering for the first time in the very heart of the empire.

Facing us as we gazed across the stream, and nobly situated on swelling hills, rose from the water's edge Wo-chang, the capital of Hoopeh, and worthy of being called the queen of Yang-tse. Its hills, terraced with houses and crowned with pagodas, and its

Wo-chang.

double wall lining the margin of the river with towers, gateways, and bastions, all combine to give it an imposing and majestic appearance. It was not until we entered its streets that the delusion vanished. Now it was a charming feature in the view. Beneath us, on our right, hemmed in by two steep ridges, along which ran its turreted walls, is the departmental city of Han-yang. We looked down upon its deserted streets, its roofless houses, crumbling walls, and grass-grown courts. Never a city of any great extent, it has suffered severely from rebel occupation, and forms a melancholy but not unpicturesque feature in the view.

On the left, in strong contrast to this scene of desolation, the crowded mart of Han-kow lay spread upon the plain at our feet, while the Han, teeming with its boat population, was lost in the distance, its winding course marked by the sails of numerous junks. A setting sun shed a warm glow over the lakes which were dotted over the country to the northward, and beyond them swelling hills closed this magnificent and most interesting panorama.

The point at which we now stood enabled us to see at a glance the extent of the area occupied by the three cities of Wo-chang, Han-yang, and Han-kow, and to form a very fair estimate of their present populations. Huc, who merely passed through the two latter cities, and does not seem to have had very good opportunities of judging, calculates the population at eight millions. With every possible allowance for the faculty which the Chinese possess of packing closely, I do not think that it was practicable to have compressed into the area beneath us a population considerably greater than that of the whole of Ireland. We thought that we made a very liberal calculation when we put the entire population then inhabiting these three cities at one million; but we saw them, doubtless, under a very great disadvantage; the area strewn with ruins was about as great as that inhabited, so that in Huc's time these cities probably contained more than twice their present number of inhabitants: perhaps their united populations may have equaled that of London, but certainly never exceeded it.

Meantime a number of Chinese had discovered the group of foreigners at the top of the hill, and were crowding up it; so we thought it time to descend from our exalted position, more especially as we could not help out our calculations by information derived from the by-standers; for when we asked what was the number of persons inhabiting the cities, they gave us the usual Chinese answer on such occasions, "Many myriads."

7th. The petty mandarin, Wang, who had accompanied us from Shanghai, and had yesterday expressed the hope that Lord Elgin would not visit the governor general in Wo-chang, was this morning dispatched to that city with a note to his excellency, informing him of Lord Elgin's intention to visit him to-morrow. Some officers from some of the ships also went off on an exploratory expedition to Wo-chang. I accompanied Lord Elgin on a voyage of discovery to the left bank, with a view of making more minute investigations into the contents of the shops, and the resources of Han-kow generally.

We had been struck, when on board the ship, by a number of high stages like watch-towers erected along the river margin. On closer inspection these proved to be bamboo-cable manufactories. The split bamboo is collected upon a stage raised thirty or forty feet from the ground. This stage is of very small dimensions—merely affording accommodation to a single man, who is sheltered by a mat roof. The process of plaiting the cable takes place here, and it is coiled on the ground below, the object of the contrivance being apparently to enable one man unassisted to coil and dispose comfortably of so unwieldy an article as a six-inch bamboo cable. At first sight, the appearance of these stages, with a long rope depending from them, was most mysterious and puzzling.

It was Lord Elgin's habit, when in China, to lose no opportunity of entering into personal communication with the people, and upon this occasion we got upon intimate terms with sundry intelligent artisans and shopkeepers. The first person we observed whose occupation arrested our attention was a man whose arms were a brilliant blue as far as his elbows, and who was engaged in spreading upon the grass cloths of the same hue. We found, upon a closer inspection, that these were Manchester cottons. He told us they cost him 700 cash a chang.* The process of dyeing them cost 200 cash a chang; so that the entire cost of Manchester cotton, dyed blue in China for clothing, was 900 cash a chang, or about ninepence halfpenny a yard. Cotton used for the same purpose, of Chinese manufacture, of one third the width, was worth 200 cash a chang, making it, after estimating the difference in width, 100 cash cheaper than British.

The indigo, which was the dye used, is grown in large quantities in the immediate neighborhood. It is also extensively cultivated in Kwei-chau. Some of the cotton was being dyed green. This is a cheaper dye than indigo, and prepared from two kinds

* 4 yards = one chang; 288 cash = one shilling.

of bark. We entered the house, and saw the boiling process going on. One species of bark is called Tung-leu, and is grown in Chang-teh; the other, Shwing-chin. The cloth is washed in a mixed infusion of these twice a day—in the case of native cotton, for five days, and in that of long cloths, for ten days.

We also inspected the manufacture of a species of native cotton velvet. The cotton cloth is stretched and scraped with a horse-hair brush into a sort of long plush; it is then prepared with a peculiar leaf, an infusion of which poured over it gives it a curly woolen appearance.

The most interesting subject of our investigations, however, was the Peh-lah, or insect-wax, of which we saw large quantities exposed for sale in the tallow-chandlers' shops. It is usually sold in blocks shaped like cheeses, and, when broken, presents a flaky, crystalline appearance not unlike spermaceti. When we went into the tallow-chandler's back shop, or rather candle manufactory, we discovered one of its principal uses. The vegetable tallow of which candles are usually made melts with great facility; in order, therefore, to prevent them from running, they are coated with a thin crust of finest wax: this is extremely hard, and slow to melt, so that it retains the vegetable tallow in a liquid state, and is a clean and economical ingredient.

While we were in vain endeavoring to extract some precise data from the shopkeeper as to the source of supply of this singular production, a man in the crowd volunteered the information. It was, he said, the article in which he traded. The province in which it was produced was Sz'-chuen; but, singular to state, although the peculiar tree necessary to the sustenance of the insect would thrive there, it was found necessary to keep up the supply of insects by the constant importation of eggs from beyond the western frontier of the province. He had constantly been engaged in these expeditions. He described the insect as being about an inch in length, and of a pale gray color. The tree on which, according to our authority, it feeds exclusively, is called the Peh-lah-shuh. One insect is considered to have performed his part creditably if he exudes one ounce of wax in the season. This lasts only during the summer months. The insect is not affected by rain or weather, but when the leaves fall it dies. The wax is then collected, and melted in a cloth over boiling water. It is of the purest white. On the large cakes hanging in the grocers' and tallow-chandlers' shops at Han-kow we often observed the inscription written, "It mocks at the frost, and rivals the snow." The price was forty dollars a picul, or about fifteen pence a pound.

We were gratified on observing, in some of the shops, well-known British stamps, proving that the manufactures of our own country were at last beginning to find their way into the empire. We asked the price of some ladies' superfine habit-cloth, and found it five taels and a half a chang,* or about six shillings a yard.

It is worthy of remark that native-grown opium was freely exposed for sale in the streets.

The fur-shops of Han-kow were numerous and well-stocked. The winter supply had evidently just come in, and some of the most expensive and rare furs from the province of Shansi and the Thibetian frontier were to be procured here at the usual fabulous prices. Our searches for old china, bronzes, and curiosities proved vain. Han-kow was apparently too practical a place to offer attractions to dilettanti; and there was a stir and movement in the streets which betokened great mercantile activity. We could scarcely credit the fact that only two years and four months ago this bustling city had been leveled to the ground. Many of the townspeople, whom we questioned on the subject, assured us that not a stone had been left standing upon another, so completely had the rebels demolished the shops and houses, after having rifled them of their contents.

No stronger proof could be afforded of the vitality of trade at this point, and of its importance as a commercial centre, than the marvelous resuscitation of Han-kow. In every direction houses were being built and new shops opened. An additional stimulus was doubtless afforded by the stagnation of the past two years, the unavoidable result of rebel proximity. Now, however, those "troublesome pests" were removed to a greater distance, and the chances of their revisiting Han-kow were sufficiently remote to encourage the people to re-establish themselves, though a marked disinclination was always evinced to allude to the "long-haired men," as the rebels were invariably called. Whenever they were mentioned, the cautious Chinaman was always on his guard against saying any thing which might be hereafter brought up against him as an evidence of hostility to the revolutionary cause. It

---

* 1200 to 1400 cash = one tael.

was remarkable that at Han-kow all the little shrines in the private houses and verandas were empty. Generally, in a Chinese town, the Lares and Penates of the householder are in these recesses, and joss-sticks burn before small images. Now there was not one to be seen, in deference, doubtless, to the iconoclastic propensities of the "long-haired men." The only sacred edifice which we observed in process of restoration at Han-kow was the Temple of Longevity, in which the emperor's birthday is celebrated.

Like great marts which partake in some measure of the nature of fairs, the population of Han-kow is both varied and fluctuating. At certain seasons of the year traders from Ili, Kobdo, and other parts of Thibet visit Han-kow, their marked Tartar features and turbaned heads distinguishing them from the Chinese. In no other city of the empire have I seen so great a variety of type of feature. There is, of course, the general character which distinguishes the Mongol in them all; but, though flat noses and oblique eyes are universal, yet it is scarcely conceivable how many distinct varieties of flat noses and oblique eyes there may be. Then, besides this, the shades of complexion, though they are all of a copper tinge, are very different. Han-kow, being simply a mercantile emporium, comprises in its population a much larger proportion of males to females than is to be found in Chinese cities generally. This is easily accounted for by the fact of so many of its inhabitants being merely visitors.

We were unable to make any purchases to-day, as the officials, with a view of discouraging, as much as possible, our supposed trading propensities, had forbidden the people to take our money. To such an extent was this carried, that all the dollars which had been expended for ships' stores, and which had been readily taken by the people before the order was issued, were brought on board by the authorities this afternoon, who wished to return them. Lord Elgin, however, steadily declined to accept any thing without paying for it, and refused sheep, cattle, etc., which were pressed upon him, unless allowed to give their full value in return. It was not difficult to see through the shallow diplomacy of the mandarins, and to perceive that their object was to prevent, as much as possible, all intercourse with the people, who were only too anxious to be upon the most intimate terms with us.

We had a still stronger proof of this determination in the afternoon, when the party returned from Wo-chang after an ineffectual attempt to enter the city. They had been refused entrance by the guards at the gate with some rudeness, and altogether treated in a manner somewhat at variance with the tone which the commissioners at Shanghai had manifested during our intercourse, and which was at that time supposed to be the tone of the government generally.

8*th*. Although the authorities were by no means in that frame of mind to which it was desirable they should be brought, the governor general scarcely ventured to refuse to see Lord Elgin. Wang therefore returned late last night with a message from the governor general to the effect that he would be prepared to receive a visit from the British plenipotentiary, and this morning a special messenger arrived to make arrangements for the ceremony, which is to take place to-morrow at two o'clock. Meantime I went with Mr. Lay on another tour of commercial investigation, but upon this occasion we confined ourselves to the waters of the Han.

The junks were moored side by side to each bank of the river as closely as it was possible to pack them, leaving only a narrow fairway down the centre of the stream. You could walk for hundreds of yards from the deck of one to that of another, inspecting the cargo of each, and cross-examining her owner or captain as you did so.

The construction of these junks varied according to the district to which they belonged. Many of them had descended the Yang-tse-Kiang, or some of its tributaries, for upward of a thousand miles. Some were long narrow craft, pointed both at stem and stern; others were turned up in the bows like a Turkish slipper, or built like an old Dutch lugger with a swelling bosom. Many of them were handsomely fitted up with cabins, apparently for the accommodation of passengers as well as cargo; others were filthily dirty, and afforded shelter only to a greasy skipper and still more greasy crew.

It is a melancholy admission to be obliged to make, that after all our trouble we did not succeed in obtaining any very reliable information. Had we been contented to believe what the first glib Chinaman chose to tell us, we might have returned well supplied with facts; but, unfortunately, the more we prosecuted our researches, the more difficult did it become to know what to believe, as we never succeeded in getting two people to agree upon any one point, however simple, and, one should suppose, unsusceptible of dispute. This did not arise from any desire to mislead; on the contrary, the people invariably manifested the utmost willingness to impart all the information in their power; they seemed highly gratified at the interest we took in the subject, and were evidently most anxious that we should be induced to come and trade with them. The great difficulty was to prevent them from all speaking at once, and induce them to give direct or intelligible answers to very plain questions.

For instance, it was hopeless to expect them to comprehend any inquiry which presupposed any premises whatever. You could not begin by asking where silk was grown. The introduction necessary to arrive at this result is the incontrovertible statement, "There is such a thing as silk."

Chinaman repeats eagerly, "There is such a thing as silk; oh yes; ah! there is such a thing as silk."

"Silk grows in some provinces; in some it does not."

Chinaman repeats, thoughtfully, "Yes, silk grows in some provinces; in some it does not."

By-standers, who have taken up the idea with greater rapidity, remark to one another, "Ah! true; in some provinces silk does not grow."

"Does this province produce silk?"

"Yes."

"Does Sz'chuen produce silk?"

"No."

"Then do you carry silk to Sz'chuen?"

"No."

"What do you carry to Sz'chuen?"

Chinaman repeats, puzzled, "What do I carry to Sz'chuen?"

By-standers all repeat, vivaciously, "What do you carry to Sz'chuen?"

Chinaman: "Sometimes I carry silk to Sz'chuen, and sometimes I carry cotton."

"Does cotton grow in Sz'chuen?"

"Yes."

"And yet you carry cotton to Sz'chuen?"

"Oh! sometimes I bring cotton here from Sz'chuen."

By-standers, unanimously: "Sometimes he brings cotton here from Sz'chuen."

And so on until one's patience is fairly exhausted, and one wonders wherein the indisputable intelligence of a Chinaman consists, and how it happens that, notwithstanding his utter inability to stand cross-examination upon the subject with which he is most familiar, he excels every other nation in his instincts for developing the internal traffic in his vast and productive country.

Fortunately, most of these junks had their cargoes on board, so we could judge for ourselves. Those laden with coal formed a large proportion of the fleet then at anchor in the river, which were principally from Hoonan. We shipped coal, some of a good and some of a very inferior quality, at £2 9s. 3d. a ton. The best coal comes from a place called Ching-Leang. Hoonan also sends to Han-kow quantities of oil and charcoal; also hemp, beans, rice, and grain. In fact, Hoonan seemed to produce almost every thing but cotton. This is the principal production of Hoopeh, and it forms the bulk of the cargoes to Hoonan and Sz'chuen. We arrived at very different conclusions with reference both to Hoonan and Hoopeh from the accounts given in the *Chinese Repository*. According to that very trustworthy authority, the external traffic of Hoonan is trifling, but our observation led us to believe that it formed the principal share of that at Han-kow; so the description of Hoopeh in the *Repository* would give one to understand that it produced almost every thing, whereas, except cotton and tea, we found it difficult to induce our junk friends to name a product; but that may have been from a want of imagination on their part.

Silk seems to be grown in the Lotien district, and some of a yellow description in Ma-ching, which also produces gypsum and some indigo. Shang-teh produces indigo of a very superior description.

Sz'chuen is the great mineral-producing province. Tin, lead, and copper come from the capital, Ching-tu. The best sugar is also grown in Sz'chuen; and indigo, tobacco, and drugs find their way down the Yang-tse from the same province.

Tin and iron of a superior quality are found at Paouching.

The trade from Kwei-chau and Hoonan did not seem to be very extensive; the latter was described as a great grazing province, exporting cattle and hides. Kiang-si sends its quota of grain and sugar, but is more especially famous for its porcelain.

Last, but not least, we come to that most important product, tea. The province of Hoopeh, in which we now were, is supposed to produce the finest description of Congo. This is known in Canton and the ports as Oopak tea, Oopak being the Canton pronunciation of Hoopeh; but it does not seem necessarily to come from this province. These teas are also grown in the mountainous province of Kwei-chau, and in Hoonan. The best Oopak tea, however, was said to be grown in the district of Toong-shan, in the department of the Wo-chang.

The yellow teas, commonly stated to be exported to Russia from Hoopeh, appear to be grown in Ngan-hwui, the adjoining province.

A bitter tea, somewhat resembling our own strong black tea, which we tasted afterward on the occasion of our visit to the governor general, and which was served immediately after dinner, instead of coffee, as a digestive, is grown only at a place called Pu-urh, a department in the province of Yunan, on the Laos frontier and Meikon River. This tea is made up in large or small circular cakes, according to its quality. It is very expensive, and considered the most *recherché* thing in the way of tea which can be imbibed. I only once tasted it during my residence in China. There are two descriptions of Hoopeh tea, which are made up into bricks tightly pressed, and present somewhat the appearance, when cut transversely, of a cake of cavendish tobacco. I bought these at a little more than two shillings a brick. There can be no doubt, however, that the finest teas grown in China are those of Fukhien and Cheh-kiang, which already compose the principal share of the tea exported to this country.

I trust that the above very prosaic description of the trade of Han-kow will have been skipped by those of my readers who are not interested in our commerce with China. Those who are must remember the uncertain sources from which it was derived, and not give it more credit than it deserves; the chief portion of it was obtained on board a very handsome junk, used as a grain-store and agency. The heads of the firm happened to be on board at the period of our visit, and regaled us with tea and pipes. A considerable crowd collected before we had been there many minutes, and when, after a long mercantile discussion, we rose to go away, and bade them adieu, hoping that when they next saw Europeans it would be to trade, the intimation was received with a noisy acclamation, as nearly approaching a cheer as could be expected of a Chinaman. I have inserted in the Appendix a list of prices procured by Captain Osborn at Han-kow, with which he has kindly furnished me.

We occupied the afternoon in exploring Han-kow to its farther extremity, reaching, after a walk of about two miles, the open country. There we impressed our visit upon the memories of a noisy rabble of urchins who followed by giving them a scramble for cash, under cover of which we effected our escape into a ferry-boat, and crossed the Han with a view of visiting the interior of the city of Han-yang. It is surrounded by a massive, well-built wall in good repair, and has evidently been a compact, handsome city of small dimensions, probably not above two miles in circumference. It was apparently an aristocratic, quiet place, chiefly inhabited by officials and their retainers, and containing all the departmental public buildings. The ruins of these were extensive. Fragments of lions and dragons, carved in granite or marble, lay strewn about the well-paved streets. Here and there, a handsome carved granite archway still spanned the principal thoroughfares; but they were more often prostrate and overgrown with weeds. Some were undergoing the process of restoration, and many of the authorities were inhabiting temporary abodes.

The scene of desolation was as complete here as elsewhere after rebel occupation, and presented the most melancholy traces of its former grandeur. Of the street connecting Han-yang with Han-kow, and which must be upward of two miles in length, scarcely a house was left standing. M. Huc says that he took an hour to traverse the long streets of Han-yang. This is probably the street to which he refers, as there is no street inside the walls of Han-yang upward of half a mile long; but the Jesuit missionary is not always scrupulously accurate in his statements. He describes the Yang-tse-Kiang as presenting the appearance of an arm of the sea, and dangerous to cross, though wherein the danger consists we were at a loss to discover.

Again, apparently ignorant of the existence of any such river as the Han, M. Huc describes Han-kow as situated on a river falling into the Yang-tse almost under the walls of Wo-chang, and translates the Chinese name Han-kow by "Bouche de Commerce" instead of "Bouche de Han," a rendering which, if it has not the merit of being a translation, is at least descriptive of the character of this great mercantile emporium.

CHAPTER XXXIX.

First Appearance of Strangers.—Snipe-shooting near Han-kow.—A Visit to the Governor General.—External Aspect of Wo-chang.—Reception by the Governor General.—A magnificent Repast.—The return Visit.—A brilliant Scene.—Inspection of Midshipmen.—The Brave Army.—Their singular Uniform.—Panoramic View of Wo-chang.—Reasons for our Return.—Subsidence of the River.—A "Squeeze."—Civility of the rural Population.—The Lee in Trouble.—Lime-quarries.—Wild Scenery.—Deep Water.

December 9. Lord Elgin having still reason to be dissatisfied with the tone maintained by the officials, and the determination apparently evinced by them to prevent our making purchases of the most trifling character, sent Messrs. Wade and Lay over to Wo-chang in the Cruiser with a rather tart message, postponing his visit to that high functionary.

The Cruiser consequently shifted her berth, and took up a position immediately facing the principal entrance to the city. This demonstration produced the desired effect. Messrs. Wade and Lay were received with the utmost politeness, and the restrictions of which we complained were at once removed.

In the afternoon I had an opportunity of testing the good dispositions of the peasantry toward foreigners. In company with Lieutenant Nott, of the Royal Marine Artillery, I walked to a distance of four or five miles from the ships to a charming lake which we discovered lying embosomed among the hills in the distance. The rumor that barbarian ships were at Han-kow may have reached the little village lying in this secluded spot, but certainly no specimen of the mysterious race that navigated them had ever before appeared among its simple inhabitants. Children ran crying at the hideous apparition to the maternal wing, and doubtless to this day are frightened into being good by threats of our reappearance. Laborers suspended, for a longer interval than is usual with an industrious Chinaman, their avocations, to gaze and wonder at the two curiously-clad bipeds who seemed to prefer paddling along the margin of the lake up to their knees in water to walking on the dry land. Fishermen in boats coasted near us, staring, criticising, and marveling at our conduct, which, to persons innocent of the existence of such an amusement as snipe-shooting, seemed unaccountable; but when a bird fell dead into the water near them, their astonishment and delight were complete, and they willingly performed the office of retrievers without an idea of remuneration. Their good-nature and desire to be useful were unbounded, and we had no difficulty in getting ferried about the lake in any direction our fancy prompted.

We only succeeded in bagging four couple of snipe and a hare, yet we were well repaid for the expedition by the beauty of the scenery and the civility of the people. Though it was late before we turned our steps homeward, and we were five miles from the ships, and quite alone among this race, popularly supposed to be so inveterately hostile to foreigners, so reassuring was the manner of the people that we were under no alarm, and plodded back in the dark as confidently as if we were coming home from the moors.

On our homeward voyage I was constantly out shooting, occasionally at a considerable distance from the river, and invariably found the same good-will prevailing on the part of the country people. Wherever it does not exist the influence of the mandarins may always be distinctly traced.

10*th*. We started on our visit to the governor general to-day at 1 P.M. Our party was a large one, consisting of thirty officers in uniform, besides the members of the mission. Forty marines and thirty blue-jackets formed the guard of honor. As the Lee got under weigh with the embassador on board, the heavy guns of the Furious and Cruiser thundered out such a salute as had never before resounded through the crowded streets of Han-kow, or shaken the frame-works of its wooden houses. A dense crowd, which had collected on the water's edge to see the party embark on board the Lee, incontinently tumbled over one another in their alarm and confusion, and haste to escape; nor was it till some moments had elapsed that they became assured of the harmless character of our fire, and, laughing at their own fears, returned to their old position.

We were soon ferried across the river in the Lee, and found a number of chairs waiting to convey us through the streets, and a Chinese guard of honor drawn up at the landing-place. As we passed through the city gates, we observed another still stronger guard on duty there. We traversed Wo-chang for at least a mile and a half before we reached the yamun of the governor general. The main street was the handsomest I had yet seen in China. Probably the best streets in Soochow equal it, but those along which I passed on the occasion of my visit to that city were certainly inferior to the principal thoroughfare in Wo-chang. As our procession of chairs, marines, and blue-jackets filed along it, the crowds drawn up on each side were quiet and respectful, though intensely curious, gazing fixedly into each chair as it passed, as though determined that the lineaments of its occupant should be photographed upon their minds.

A hill terraced with houses intersects the city. The main street, however, tunnels under this, and the shops continue through the tunnel: indeed, the finest part of the street is at the entry to this interesting specimen of Chinese engineering. The shops here are better supplied, and there is a life and gayety which the rest of the town does not present: indeed, it is slowly recovering from the effects of prolonged rebel occupation. We crossed large areas of desolation on our way to the yamun, but we had better opportunities of judging of their extent upon a future occasion.

The yamun itself seems to have been spared by the insurgents, for it was a handsome edifice, in good repair. We were received, on entering, with the usual salutes and discordant music, and found the governor general standing at the door of the inner court, surrounded by a brilliant staff, waiting to receive Lord Elgin. I had never before seen such a splendid gathering of Chinese mandarins. Usually they do not think it worth while to receive barbarians in their official costume, and are scrupulously plain in their attire. Now, however, as the governor general took care to inform Lord Elgin, all the provincial, civic, and military authorities were present in full dress, their silks, satins, and furs of the handsomest material, and their breasts emblazoned with dragons and other devices, elaborately embroidered. The spacious audience-hall contained at one end the usual raised seat, upon which Lord Elgin and the governor general took their places. On each side, a long row of chairs and little tea-tables afforded accommodation for a British officer and a Chinese mandarin alternately; though, beyond hobnobbing over hot tea, it was difficult to interchange civility, much less ideas.

Kwan, Governor General of Hoopeh and Hoouan, is a Tartar. He stands high in imperial favor, having been very successful in his campaigns against the rebels, whom he has succeeded in expelling from his government. He professed great knowledge of foreigners, from the circumstance of his having, at a former period of his life, served in Canton as second in command of the Tartar garrison of that city. He had, therefore, had opportunities of seeing the barbarian occasionally at a distance.

After a short conversation upon general subjects, our host led the way to another apartment, in which a magnificent banquet was prepared upon a scale infinitely superior to any similar entertainment at which we had assisted in China. Four sets of tables, sufficient to accommodate the whole party, were loaded with all the delicacies of the season, tastefully arranged in pyramidal and globular structures. Nor was this merely the cold collation common to official visits. A great variety of hot dishes made their appearance in rapid succession, generally somewhat greasy in their nature, but occasionally very palatable to persons of a confiding temperament, and who did not care minutely to investigate the materials of which these various entrées were composed.

Sundry descriptions of hot wines were also pressed upon us, and afterward the excellent Pu-uhr tea, to which I have already alluded. It was not merely from a desire to soothe our "uncontrollable fierceness" that we were thus magnificently entertained. Our host was evidently a bon-vivant, and a man of hospitable tendencies. He delighted in piling delicacies on his own plate as well as the plates of his neighbors, and took a manifest pride in the excellence of his cuisine, and completeness of his arrangements generally. We afterward learned that the escort of seventy men had also been provided with refreshment. At last, after having done thorough justice to his feast, we bade adieu to our sybaritic entertainer, who accompanied Lord Elgin, as usual, to his chair, with many expressions of regret at being obliged to part with him, and assurances that, in the mean time, his only consolation would be in the prospect of returning the visit on the following day.

We were followed by a considerable crowd on our way back to the river-bank, and re-embarked under a Chinese salute, well satisfied with the day's experiences, our entire enjoyment being alloyed only by a vague feeling of uneasiness and apprehension at the possible consequences of our gastronomic indulgences, with which we were not unnaturally haunted for the succeeding twenty-four hours.

11*th*. The bright, clear autumn days in which we have been reveling are most propitious to the interchange of official civilities, which involved so much open-air display. At eleven this morning, the Prefect of Wo-chang, and several other mandarins of rank, came on board to prepare the way for the great man. As the ceremony was to be invested with much pomp and circumstance, the news had spread far and wide, and the surface of the great river was literally alive with boats full of pleasure-parties and sight-seers, who turned out as freely as if our gun-boats had been in Southampton water instead of the Yang-tse-Kiang, and they had come down express to see the great naval review.

We could discern with our glasses the troops, both cavalry and infantry, lining the opposite bank, and make out the state junk. After the usual amount of suspense and watching, three puffs of smoke indicated the arrival of the governor general; then the unwieldy craft got under weigh, and the excitement became intense. Official boats, with flags fluttering from stem and stern, darted about, ordering, directing, and clearing the way; the hum of many voices filled the air; the river brink presented a dense mass of heads, whose owners were all squeezing, staring, and gabbling.

Meantime the huge state junk, covered with flags, and towed by six twenty-oared boats in line, all similarly decorated, was sweeping at a slow and dignified pace across the stream, surrounded by crowds of boats containing minor officials and spectators. As she approached, we added our own collection to the dragons and other Celestial devices which were already waving in the breeze. Suddenly the ships were dressed, and a suppressed "Ay, yah!" of astonishment was uttered by the crowd. Meantime mandarins of all ranks were arriving, and pouring in upon our deck; and the ship was surrounded by boats full of soldiers in red jackets, with spears, bows, matchlocks, and tridents, with other quaint and fantastic weapons.

Among these the executioners were the most conspicuous, with their conical bloodstained hats, truculent countenances, and plaited thongs for castigation—the badges of their office. Then the great junk was made fast alongside, and all the ships manned yards, and belched out a noisy welcome to the exalted visitor as he stepped on board; and the flags waved, and the gongs beat, and the crowd murmured their satisfaction, while the bright sun shone gloriously upon a scene as exciting and novel as it was ever my good fortune to witness.

The governor general and suite were now taken over the ship, and looked for the first time upon the wonderful mechanism of a

The Governor General of Hoo-kwang, with his Suite.

400-horse-power steam-engine without betraying any astonishment. When, however, the 95-hundred-weight pivot gun was worked for their edification, a gleam of dignified surprise might be detected by an acute observer lighting up all their countenances. After a luncheon, which could scarcely equal in its proportions that of the governor general, but to which he did full justice, he was "posed" for his photograph upon the deck. The result, which may be seen in the annexed wood-cut, charmed his excellency, and he extorted the most solemn promises from Mr. Jocelyn that he should be furnished with a supply of prints to be sent to him from Shanghai.

Our distinguished guest was particularly struck with the youthful warriors by whom he found himself surrounded. Midshipmen are always a source of astonishment to Chinamen, who are accustomed to treat boys with a kindness almost amounting to respect, and can in no degree comprehend the system which induces us to expose them at so early an age to the perils and dangers which are involved in the service of their country. Kwan requested a collection of these young gentlemen to be brought to him for inspection, and informed them, with an approving smile, that he discovered, in the expression of their countenances, a very high order of talent. At last the great man took his leave, protesting with a vehement and energetic fervor the satisfaction he had derived from the visit, and professing, in affectionate terms, sentiments of eternal respect and amity. Then, under the thunder of more salutes, he stepped on board his gay barge. That ponderous and singular specimen of naval architecture once more swung slowly into the stream, and, like an elephant drawn by an army of rats, followed its fleet of many-oared boats to the opposite shore.

As we were desirous of a closer inspection of the brave troops drawn up in gallant array under the walls of Wo-chang, and had not yet sufficiently satisfied our curiosity with respect to that city, a party of us pulled across, and reached the opposite bank almost as soon as the governor general himself. We found from fifteen hundred to two thousand men drawn up in a line upon the river margin.

The cavalry were mounted on rough ponies, thirteen or fourteen hands high. A red jacket of coarse cloth, and a remarkable description of lappet, falling over the outside of the thigh over their trowsers, composed the uniform. The men were all armed with matchlocks swung behind their backs, and the officers had swords, and quivers full of arrows. The bows were not visible. But the costume of the infantry was far more grotesque and fantastic. Attached to each regiment were a score or more of men dressed in a complete flesh-colored suit, fitting tightly to the skin, and which reached from the hood that covered their heads down to their ankles. Each man held over the middle of his person a circular straw shield, upon which hideous ogre faces were painted. At a distance these men looked as though they were naked, with nothing on but their shields. On approaching nearer, however, they assume rather the appearance of harlequins, for then we could discern that the yellow skin which covered them was ornamented with little black twirligigs like tadpoles. Altogether, their aspect was most absurd and ludicrous; and as they seemed to have no weapon of defense, they are probably expected to strike terror into an enemy by their personal appearance. Next in order to this squad of tom-fools was a small body of men in black, armed with matchlocks, the fuses wound round the stock of the gun. Then came the main body of the regiment in red, armed with spears, bows and arrows, and swords. Four or five such regiments, besides the cavalry, were drawn up to receive the governor general, and a portion of them accompanied him as a guard of honor through the town. We managed to avoid the procession, and, escaping into some by-streets, reached the ridge to which I have already alluded as being tunneled through by the principal street.

From the summit of this hill, which divides the city into two equal parts, a good panoramic view of it is obtained. The area of ground inclosed by the walls of Wo-chang is probably larger than that occupied by Canton; but not more than a third of this space is built upon and inhabited, so that the relative proportion of its population with that of the latter city is materially altered.

We estimated the population of Wo-chang at from three to four hundred thousand. The walls are dilapidated, in some parts out of repair, and mount no guns. Large tracts of ground are strewn with ruins and the debris of houses destroyed by the rebels. Some idea of the deserted character of portions of the city may be formed from the fact that, while walking down the centre of it, we put up two brace of pheasants. So solitary was the spot that the crowd did not discover us for some time, and then only collected in small numbers. From the highest point we commanded a bird's-eye view of all the public buildings left standing. Of these the principal were the hall of examination, the yamun of the Governor General Kwan, that of the governor of the city, and a handsome pagoda. A body of troops was encamped in tents at our feet, and parade was actually going on.

Altogether the military display at Wo-chang was more complete and extensive than any thing I had yet seen in China.

Beyond the walls the country was broken and undulating; numerous lakes lay glittering beneath the rays of the setting sun, whose ruddy disk, almost touching the level horizon of the plains in a westerly direction, warned us that we had not allowed ourselves more time than was necessary to regain the bank, and cross the wide river to our faithful ship among the junks at Han-kow.

12*th*. We had now spent six days at Han-kow; but five weeks had elapsed since our departure from Shanghai, and we began to give our friends credit for feeling some anxiety on our account. Knowing the fertility of the Chinese brain in inventing improbable stories, and the readiness of the British public to believe them, it became incumbent on us to commence, without unnecessary delay, our return journey. Nor was there any very valid excuse for pushing farther up the river. Han-kow was the extreme point at which we were to be allowed a port by treaty, and, except for purposes of exploration, we had no public reason for prolonging our voyage.

Never before, in the annals of British naval enterprise, had one of her majesty's frigates accomplished so many miles of river exploration; and it was with the utmost reluctance that we now exposed the stern instead of the bows of our good ship to the force of that current which she had so bravely breasted. We had at one time been sanguine enough to indulge the hope of reaching the Toong-ting Lake, the largest sheet of water in China, and from which we were scarce a hundred miles distant; this probably would be the extreme limit to which a ship drawing sixteen feet of water could ascend, under the most favorable circumstances; beyond that are the rapids of Kwei, as to the exact character of which obstruction we are not yet informed, but it is not impossible, from the vague accounts which have reached us, that river-steamers drawing little water, and with plenty of power, might ascend them.

During the whole period of our stay the people had never ceased collecting opposite the ships and staring at them; and, doubtless, many years hence, when there are steamers plowing the waters of the Yang-tse as freely as they do now those of the Mississippi, old men will tell their wondering progeny, who are probably stokers, that they remember the day when foreign ships, then supposed to be under demoniacal influence, suddenly appeared for the first time among the now obsolete craft, formerly known as junks, at Han-kow, and, after remaining a week, as suddenly vanished; and how, for some time afterward, until barbarians again reached Han-kow and built a magnificent city upon its river-banks, it was popularly supposed that the apparition had been supernatural.

We reached the "*Squeeze*," above Hwang-chow, in time to buoy it out for to-morrow, but found, to our dismay, that since we had last crossed it the water had fallen five feet, and was still subsiding rapidly. The information, therefore, which we received on our way up, that the water had already been at its lowest, was entirely false and erroneous.

13*th*. The day was spent in looking in vain for a passage over a bar a little below Hwang-chow. Things begin to look serious; every moment of delay renders our chance of getting over the several bars ahead more remote. The Dove and Lee are indefatigable in their efforts to find a channel. Some of our party consoled themselves by landing on a sand-bank in pursuit of wild geese, and were fortunate enough to bag three.

14*th*. Dove on shore, and our channel-hunters completely nonplused. Gloomy spirits indulge in the most depressing speculations as to the future, and visions of wintering up the Yang-tse are somewhat forcibly presented to the imagination. By way of testing the resources of the neighborhood in the event of such a contingency, parties of us landed, and shot and explored in all directions. We found an extensive plain stretching from the villages and cultivation which line the bank to the blue distance where trees were faintly discernible.

This plain is a lake in summer, and we crossed to where some of its waters still remained. It is traversed by a mere muddy ditch, which is a tributary to an inconsiderable stream called the Paho, which enters the Yang-tse-Kiang at this point. The short green herbage affords grazing to numerous flocks of unapproachable wild geese. Storks, cranes, herons, and all sorts of monster water-fowl stalk about the grass, so shortly cropped that it would not afford shelter for a mouse, and loom in the distant haze like ostriches. Distorted pigs, and buffaloes ridden by boys, share the pasturage with these birds.

Many of these water-fowl were of a description entirely new to me. Besides wild duck there were grebe of many varieties, more interesting to the ornithologist than to the sportsman. Teal and widgeon were abundant, and I had no difficulty in killing four brace; but in the absence of a retriever, fishing them out of the water afterward was a less agreeable pastime. Fortunately, I found the peasantry here, as elsewhere, delighted to be of use; and one man abandoned entirely his agricultural operations, and devoted himself to swimming in after the birds, or plunging vigorously into the tenacious mud, stripping each time to his work.

We were frequently invited to refresh ourselves, as we plodded through the fields, with the hot tea which the laborers always keep ready boiling to comfort them during their midday toil; a few charges of powder, or a dozen lucifer matches, were more highly appreciated than handfuls of cash: the matches especially were handed about, and treasured as miracles of pyrotechnic skill. In many instances the peasantry declined any pecuniary remuneration, and would only receive these curiosities at our hands.

Lord Elgin had in the mean time visited the town of Paho, and described it as a compact little place, substantially built of red sandstone. While I was engaged in ingratiating myself into the affections of the rural population, I suddenly observed the recall signal flying at the mast-head of the Furious, and reached her just in time to share in the excitement of charging a fourteen-feet bar.

The deepest channel that could be found gave us eighteen inches less water than we were drawing. However, as the only alternative was to remain where we were, Captain Osborn felt justified in putting the old ship at it, and it must be admitted that she took her fence in a most creditable style. At one moment she canted over a good deal, and we were in doubt whether the bottom was soft enough and the current strong enough to carry her over. It was with no little satisfaction that we dropped anchor at last in deep water, on the right side of this formidable obstacle.

15*th*. Our hopes of last night have proved as false and shifting as the bed of this most treacherous river. No sooner had we congratulated ourselves upon the success of our late achievement than the Lee was brought up in ten fathoms upon a pinnacle of rock, upon which she began gracefully pirouetting, as though in mockery of our despair. While her zealous commander, Lieutenant Jones, was engaged in laying out hawsers and stream-cables, and backing astern, and going ahead, and rolling and jumping, and ultimately lightening her, we, who were now familiar with every process to be resorted to with a gun-boat in difficulties, again took advantage of the delay to land and explore some interesting quarries we had observed on our voyage up.

A precipitous range of limestone cliffs, from 1500 to 2000 feet in height, overhung the river at this point; at its base the village of Shih-wa-yaou, inhabited principally by quarrymen, was picturesquely situated, while its rugged sides were deeply scored and undermined by the long-prosecuted labor of men. The limestone is hewn out of the hill side with pickaxe and cold chisel, the process of blasting being apparently unknown. The kilns were situated at the base of the hill. The fuel used was coal, principally procured from the neighborhood of Hing-kwoh, its price at this place being 18s. a ton. The coal is mixed in the furnaces with red clay. This clay, after it is burnt, is used for building purposes, and is placed together with unburnt brick in thick layers of lime. All the houses of which the town is composed are constructed in this manner. I did not understand the object of mixing the clay with the coal in the first instance. As scoriæ, it seemed a convenient building material.

The quick-lime is stacked in huge wicker frames, thirty or forty feet in height, thatched at the roof, so that they present the appearance of enormous baskets turned topsy-turvy, the shape being that of an inverted truncated cone. The quick-lime is sold at the rate of 18s. a ton, while the slack-lime is used as manure.

It appeared that the quarries were free to all comers, any man being entitled to purchase the privilege of working them by the payment of a rent of 1000 cash, or about four shillings, for six months, to a company who farm the quarries from the government.

We were unable to discover the total amount paid by this company to the government, nor could we obtain any accurate information as to the quantity of lime annually produced. The atrocious dialect in which our informants spoke rendered the task of acquiring any precise knowledge of the subject more than usually difficult. One piece of intelligence they gave us, however, which was by no means encouraging, and this was, that the river was still likely to fall some feet, as the rock on which the Lee was now perched was distinctly visible at low water.

We ascended the hill to an elevation of 700 or 800 feet above the river, and reveled in the prospect which was spread out before us. The flourishing town of Hwang-shih-kang, presenting a favorable contrast to the demolished cities in its neighborhood, lay basking in the sun a few miles distant—broad blue lakes and grassy plains extended northward to a purple range in the dim distance; while behind us were wooded valleys, and wild rugged hills, with spurs jutting into the great river, and rising in abrupt wild crags from its yellow waters. We descended into a valley where some excavations into the hill side, with blackened edges, gave promise of coal. None of the pits into which we entered were deep. The people said that they had not been worked for fifty years, but that, previous to that period, coal had been extracted from them.

We were cheered, on our return to the ship, to find that the Lee had been rescued from her perilous position, though not without injury to her bottom; still, we had every reason to congratulate ourselves that the rock had been discovered by her instead of by the Furious. With her greater draught of water and superior momentum, that excellent old tub, had she struck it, would in all probability have prematurely terminated her existence in the cause of diplomatic exploration.

Projecting into the river a few miles below us is the remarkable bluff of Ke-tow, or the Cock's Head. The Dove has just returned from sounding beneath this stupendous rock, and reports thirty-three fathoms of water.

CHAPTER XL.

Exploration of a Lake.—An educated Peasant.—Charging the Bar.—Intricate Navigation.—Good Sport.—We abandon the Furious.—Christmas-day.—Close Stowage in the Lee.—Approach Ngan-king.—Mr. Wade's Visit to the Rebels.—His Report of it.—Arrival at Woohoo.—A Rebel Communication.—We land at Nankin.—A Visit to a Rebel Chief.—Report of the Interview.—Our Interview with Le.—The real State of the Case.—Morals of the Rebels.—Strength of the Garrison.—The Rebel Theology.

December 16. Our day's voyage led us through the gorge of Pwan, undoubtedly the finest piece of scenery on the river. A small river enters the Yang-tse-Kiang from the south, dividing Hoopeh from Kiang-si. At a place called Toong-sha, on this river, the finest tea of Hoopeh is said to be produced. Coal and cotton are two most important productions of this district.

The downward voyage involved many more difficulties of navigation than we had experienced on our way up. We had then grounded frequently; now there was five feet less water, and a strong tide sweeping us down on unknown dangers. The incidents of a voyage down the Volga were forcibly recalled to my mind, but the "pericartes" (or sand-banks) of that noble stream were nothing to the shoals and rocks of the Yang-tse.

17*th.* The gun-boats have been employed all day looking for a passage over the bar at the Red Bluffs—a serious obstacle on our way up, and now apparently a hopeless one. We can scarcely regret these constant delays except for the sake of the ship's bottom, as they afford us admirable opportunities of becoming acquainted with the rural population, and the general features of the country.

After a walk of between two and three miles from the ship across the plain, we reached an extensive lake, the shores of which rose in swelling undulations from its glassy surface. Wooded promontories projected half way across, forming deep bays where cottages were clustered and boats were moored, and cotton-fields terraced the hill sides.

Water-fowl of many varieties paddled and fluttered upon the margin of this vast sheet of water, for we could not see its whole extent from any one point; and a small river, meandering through the plain, watered the meadows, where flocks and herds were grazing. Sometimes the great river itself overflows this rich expanse. We were informed that this catastrophe had not occurred since 1849, when immense damage had been done, and miles of cultivated land were overlaid with five or six feet of sand. We observed many barren spots, where pits had been dug down to the rich loam that had been thus buried.

Over one of the cottages in a small village Lord Elgin observed a tablet, which, on being interpreted, was found to be a notice to the effect that one of the members of the family then inhabiting it had taken a high scholastic degree, and, though the son of a peasant, had achieved an important grade of mandarinic dignity. The brother was the present occupant of the humble abode, also a man of literary tastes and tendencies; and, though only the proprietor of three acres of land, he had paid a hundred and eight taels for one degree, but had unfortunately been plucked at all his succeeding attempts, so that he was reduced to the humiliating alternative of being obliged to wait until he should attain the age of sixty, when he would be entitled to an *ad eundem*. In the back of the cottage was a curiously constructed press filled with cotton-seed: this was subjected to the blows of a huge beam, swung like a catapult; and the oil thus extracted, we were informed, was used for culinary purposes.

In whatever direction the different exploring parties wandered, they all met with the same uniform civility from the country people, into whose cottages we never hesitated to enter. This day was memorable to us as the anniversary of our first embarkation on board the Furious. A year's residence in that ship had sufficed to attach us to our floating home, though we already begun to suspect that a tender and somewhat abrupt parting was in prospect.

18*th*. The only incident of the day was the determination at which Captain Osborn arrived of charging the bar to-morrow.

19*th*. The Cruiser, drawing a few inches less than fourteen feet, crossed without touching. We, drawing eighteen inches more, knew what to expect, and went at it full speed. It was a pleasure to see the gallant way in which the old ship was handled in this cross country work, and how splendidly she behaved; how beautifully she was kept together as she approached her fences, how obedient to the slightest touch of the reins. The captain on one paddle-box, the master on the other, four men at the wheel, hands by the jib-halliards and spanker out-haul, men by bow and stern anchors, engineers alert in the engine-room; then, with a swinging tide, "full speed ahead!" we rush at the second cutter, anchored on one bank to starboard, in a manner calculated to lead the young gentleman in the boat to suppose that we are bent on his destruction; then, shaving him by a miracle, steer clear of a buoy on the port side by an eighth of an inch, then run out the spanker and haul down the jib in the twinkling of an eye. It is of no use: the ship is perfectly in hand; we keep the channel to a nicety; but, unhappily, it surpasses even the capabilities of the Furious to float in fourteen feet of water when she is drawing fifteen. There is a scrape and a lurch; the paddles revolve helplessly; the order, "Stop her!" is reluctantly given, and the next process of hawsers, stream-cables, and anchors, in all sorts of directions, is vigorously entered upon. By dint of dexterously bringing the ship broadside on to the current, she was converted into a species of dredging-machine, and, during upward of twelve hours, we dragged steadily through the mud, shifting our anchors whenever our altered position rendered this operation necessary.

19*th*. At four o'clock this morning, when we were all profoundly indifferent as to our possible fate, the good ship had been forced by the current through the mud, and was anchored immediately beyond the bar. When day broke we found our position scarcely improved; we were moored with our nose up stream, in a channel so narrow that it seemed impossible to turn, and equally difficult to find our way, stern first, along the tortuous channel ahead. The manœuvre was most cleverly effected at last by running the ship's stern actually upon the shore, so as seriously to imperil the toes of some Chinamen standing staring at the water's edge; then the current and the jibs together took her bows round, and we once more found ourselves triumphantly sweeping down the turbid waters of the great river.

As we passed Loong-ping we observed the tents of an imperialist force, a number of man-of-war junks, and some troops apparently on the march. We augured from this that the rebels were in close proximity.

We were met just before dark by the Dove, bringing us the painful intelligence that the deepest water to be found on a bar ahead was eleven feet. This, if true, was absolute annihilation to all idea of reaching the sea in the Furious. However, we still hoped for the best, and anchored for the night a little below the city of Kew-kiang.

20th and 21st. While the Lee and Dove are away channel-hunting, we, as usual, are engaged in a less important but more amusing sport. We rambled for miles over the charming country which intervenes between the river and the Poyang Lake. We explored in all directions the hills wooded with stunted oak and pine, cultivated with cotton, flax, and corn, of different varieties, inhabited by a simple population, whose snug houses nestle in the recesses of secluded valleys: these, not being subject to inundation, are more substantially built than those in the plains. Charming lakes are embosomed among the hills, and that most extensive and celebrated of all, the Poyang, lays away to the far south, like an ocean with a horizon of silver. We bag numerous pheasants, magnificent birds with gorgeous plumage, in these woods, wild duck and snipe on the borders of the lakes; and one of our party was fortunate enough to bring home a fine roe-deer as the result of his day's sport.

22d. We made a good bag to-day, but it was not enough to console us for the melancholy intelligence we received on our return to the ships of the non-existence of any channel, and the still more melancholy determination that had been arrived at, in consequence, of deserting the Furious and Cruiser, and proceeding to Shanghai in the Dove and Lee.

23d. This day was spent in condoling with our shipmates of the last year on the gloomy prospect in store for them of a winter in the heart of China, for there seemed no hope of a rise in the river before spring. It was a day of sighs and lamentation, bustle and confusion—the rapid transfer of the accumulated effects of a year to the limited capacities of a gun-boat—the abandonment of much in despair—the packing, condensing, and the breakage and ejaculations incidental thereto; lastly, the final meeting of a spasmodically jovial character, protracted until a late hour of the evening, when pathetic songs, extemporized for the occasion, were sung, and the memories of scenes of interest and adventure were recalled for the last time.

We all turned in with heavy hearts for the last night, as we supposed, on board the Furious.

24th. The sky was weeping in unison with our feelings this morning. It seemed almost shabby to desert Captain Osborn after his unwearied exertions and splendid achievements, and to abandon our old home, with all its kind and friendly occupants; but the necessity was inevitable; so we resigned ourselves to the inexorable decrees of fate, and made the Lee as comfortable as her accommodation would permit. Then, when all was ready, Lord Elgin addressed Captain Osborn, the officers and ship's company of the Furious, in a few stirring words, expressive of the regret he felt on being now compelled to leave them; and we parted with many good wishes from our naval companions, with every one of whom, during our long residence on board, we had been upon terms of the utmost intimacy and good-fellowship. Adverting to this incident in his dispatch to the Secretary of State, Lord Elgin says: "On personal grounds, I left the Furious with great regret. For upward of a year I had had my home on board of her, during the whole of which period I never once heard that it was difficult for the Furious to go any where or to do any thing that the interests of the public service rendered it in my judgment desirable to attempt."* Then came the final salute, and then we cheered each other as long as we could respectively be heard, to the intense astonishment of a body of imperial troops, who were apparently occupied in "matchlock drill" on the north bank of the river.

25th. Our Christmas-day was of the most lugubrious and doleful description. Notwithstanding the praiseworthy efforts of our most attentive host, Lieutenant (now Commander) Jones, it was impossible to be very lively. A storm of sleet and snow swept over the exposed deck of our tiny craft, and reduced us to the condition of amphibious animals whenever we emerged from the cabin. Unfortunately, the alternative of remaining there was scarcely to be preferred. It is most probable that no one of my readers, except those who composed the party on that occasion, knows what it is to form one of twelve first-class passengers in a gun-boat's cabin. Mr. Jones, to whom the problem first presented itself of how to stow away this invasion of barbarians, made an elaborate diagram of his guests as he intended they should appear in bed. Each man was allowed an inch less than his height, and the smallest of the party was put upon a book-shelf, and formed

* *Blue-Book,* p. 446.

an admirable substitute for the light reading which it usually contained. Two men were in cots swung over the only table, two more occupied the said only table; and two more, stretched underneath, used the same article of furniture as a four-poster. When we were not all asleep, some of us were washing and dressing, and the remainder waiting in the rain on deck for their turn. When all the toilettes had been performed, the meals were begun; and when the meals were over, the fumes of cavendish pervaded the atmosphere until it was bedtime, and we all fitted into one another again like herrings in a barrel.

By the time eight days and nights had been thus profitably and sociably employed, we could readily appreciate the merits of a description of craft which are a credit to the British navy. "As I think," says Lord Elgin, in the dispatch above alluded to, "that these useful vessels (gun-boats) are not always sufficiently appreciated, I would beg leave to call your lordships' attention to the fact that the Lee, with the aid of a junk, which she towed part of the way, and eventually discarded, conveyed safely the whole mission, servants included, from Kew-kiang to Shanghai, a distance of some 450 miles, through an intricate navigation, and a country equivocally disposed toward us. It rained incessantly, and we were rather closely packed; but the obliging attentions of Lieutenant Jones enabled us to bear with these trifling inconveniences."* Poor little Lee! bravely did she do her part wherever there was work to be done; nor did she in her last hour disgrace the flag that still remained flying at her mast-head. After riding out a typhoon on the coast of Japan, running the gauntlet of the batteries at Nankin, and escaping the dangers of the Yang-tse-Kiang, the Lee left her bones at last on the mud-banks of the Peiho, where, riddled and shattered by shot, and with seventeen out of her small crew killed and wounded on her deck, she sank beneath the feet of her gallant commander.

We anchored for the night within sight of the batteries of Ngan-king.

26*th*. I can best describe the proceedings of the earlier part of this day by quoting from the Blue-Book a few lines from Lord Elgin's dispatch and Mr. Wade's report.

"The course," says his excellency, "to be taken in passing Ngan-king was a matter which required consideration, as I have

* *Blue-Book*, p. 446.

already mentioned. We were fired at when we reached it on our way up; and the nature of the channel compelled us, on our return, to steer so immediately under the city walls that our decks could easily have been swept from them by gingalls. When attacked in passing it previously, the gun-boats were accompanied by two large vessels. They were alone and unsupported when we arrived before it on our route downward. It was, moreover, important to insure a safe passage, not only for ourselves, but for such other vessels as might be sent up from time to time to communicate with the Furious and Cruiser.

"In order to attain these objects, I thought it necessary to take a pretty high tone with the rebel authorities.

"Mr. Wade was accordingly sent on shore at an early hour on the 26th of December to deliver a message, the nature and satisfactory result of which are described in his report. To menace with capture by two small gun-boats a great city, walled and garrisoned, might have been bad taste elsewhere, but in China it was the proper thing to do."

The following is Mr. Wade's report of the result of his mission to the rebels at Ngan-king:

"On the evening of the 26th of December, as the gun-boats approached Ngan-king, by desire of his excellency the Earl of Elgin, I proceeded in the Dove to communicate with the insurgent garrison who had fired upon our squadron on its way up. Night set in very suddenly, and running on in the darkness, we found ourselves but a few hundred yards from the walls. It seemed to us that we were seen. Lights were visible here and there along the walls, and junks appeared to be moving across the channel ahead of us. Having had no opportunity of testing the disposition of the garrison since we exchanged shots with them on the 26th of November, I did not think it advisable to discharge my mission without being able to see my way, and accordingly returned to the Lee. On the following morning, about 8 o'clock, Lieutenant Bullock, of the Actæon, called for me. It was raining heavily, and red umbrellas multiplied along the shore as the boat approached the city. The bearers were dressed in the gaudy blue and red, which gave the rebel forces a picturesque appearance. A large red flag was waved, probably to direct our course, which, however, lay toward the point it indicated, namely, the upper or southwestern angle of the walled position. In advance of this, a rude chevaux-de-frise of some yards' width protected the slope, and the inner batteries, which are of a yellow stone, apparently easy to work, were finished with some neatness. Three or four of the crowd detached themselves to receive us. One, almost a boy, carried a large red flag on the usual spear-staff; but, with this exception, I saw no signs of arms in the hands of any one, and, except some wretched-looking guns in the embrasures, nothing of the character of hostile preparation. Being informed by one of these people that the chiefs were all Cantonese, I desired to speak with one, and a young man came forward from the mass assembled under a gate through which the path led from the point off which the boat was lying. He was, I found, a native of Kwang-si, but speaking very good Cantonese. He afterward stated himself to be the third in authority. I told him I was directed to inquire why the garrison had, without any provocation, fired on her majesty's ships bound up the river. The chief said it was a mistake due to the ignorance of some of the provincials in their garrison, not Canton or Kwang-si men. The latter were unaware of the circumstance until the ships were some way past the city. They then recognized the English flag ('Ta Ying Ki'). The thing would never happen again. I recommended him to be careful. We had no wish to begin a quarrel with any who did not interfere with us, and I had purposely been sent because it was the British minister's desire not to take life without occasion; but that our vessels would be going up and down, perhaps next month, perhaps the month after; and, although we had no desire to side with either party in the civil war now waging, if any one attacked us we should resent it as we had done at Nankin, where the garrison had fired on us as we were passing, and we had, in consequence, destroyed their forts.

"'Oh yes,' said the chief, 'we have heard of what happened at Nankin;' and then repeated his excuses in even more apologetic phrase than before, for the mistake of his own people. He said they would send a present of oxen and other provisions to our great man. This I of course declined. He also invited me, as had one or two of the others, to land, and pay the principal chief, a Cantonese, a visit. This I also declined, saying that I was sent to deliver the message which I had given, and which I now once more repeated, adding that they no doubt knew how simple a matter it would be for us to sweep them away utterly, were we provoked to do it. To this he assented, with the same evidence of conviction he had given when I mentioned Nankin. As I pushed off he used the common Cantonese salutation, 'Go well!' 'Good luck!' etc.

"The crowd generally seemed to me in better case than the Woohoo rebels, more healthy-looking, and better dressed. One of them, who was much the reverse, however, had pushed himself forward, and addressed me in Cantonese English. He volunteered the information that he came from Whampoa, and bore other marks, besides his acquaintance with our language, of subjection to our influences. He looked, what I have no doubt he was, an opium-smoking coolie. The majority seemed to me to hold back, and but a small number came to the boat's side."*

Passing the rebel batteries unmolested, we made a long day's run, and anchored for the night at Toongling.

27*th*. We just succeeded in reaching the Retribution at Woohoo before the light failed us. Captain Barker kindly placed his accommodation at the disposal of the mission; but, as we were quite unconscious of feeling crowded, and enjoyed each other's animal heat in the cold weather, we remained in possession of the cabin of the Lee.

Captain Barker had, since his arrival at Woohoo, received an apologetic note relative to the affair which had occurred near Taiping on our way up. It was probably intended for Lord Elgin, and ran as follows: "Some time since, when your excellency honored our humble place with a visit, certain ignorant people in our central station (or barrier) fired upon you by mistake, on which our Heavenly King, Hung-siu-tsuen, decapitated all these ignorant scoundrels. Your ships being still in movement, Hung-siu-tsuen could not catch them to make his apologies, and therefore sent instructions to us, your younger brethren, to transmit his decree; but as your honored vessels continued on their way, we failed to overtake them; and as there were demon vessels (imperialist) also barring the way, we confined ourselves for the time to making a report to the Heavenly King, and waited here for the return of your honored vessel, to pay our respects to you in person, and to receive from your own mouth your commands, on

* *Blue-Book*, p. 448.

which we will make our report to the Heavenly King. We accordingly send a person in advance to welcome your excellency."

28th. This day was a somewhat anxious one, as we were uncertain whether the Retribution would clear the bar below Tai-ping; fortunately, she went over, with one inch to spare.

29th. Reached Nankin about midday. The extremely apologetic tone of the communication above quoted seemed to Lord Elgin to open the door to farther intercourse with the rebels at Nankin. He therefore sent Messrs. Wade, Lay, Wylie, and myself on shore, to pay a visit to the authorities and pick up information.

We landed on the south bank, at one of the forts which had been most pertinacious in its fire on our way up. All was silent now, and we felt some slight hesitation in stepping on shore, with such slender knowledge of the dispositions of the brave garrison toward us. Presently a few ragged soldiers emerged from a gateway, as little prepossessed by our looks as we were by theirs. However, our object was to reach the city, and we now found that the nearest part of the suburb was at least a mile distant. Thither we determined on proceeding, and traversed on foot a muddy plain under a pitiless snow-storm. A boy, whom we pressed into service as a guide, led us through some narrow lanes to an official residence of inferior description, where the officer in command of the troops of this division had his head-quarters. As our last communication with this gentleman had been in the shape of a cannon ball, and no formal interchange of amicable sentiments had passed since, we felt a little uncertain as to the view he would take of this unceremonious visit on the part of four of his late enemies. We soon discovered that his intention was to detain us by polite speeches, and send for instructions. As this did not suit our views, and we found four very nice ponies tethered in his court-yard belonging to some of his staff, we decided on appropriating them, and pursuing our way into the city. Finding all remonstrances useless as we speedily untied and mounted them, the general—for such we found to be his rank —furnished us with a guide, and soon after a courier passed us at full speed, doubtless conveying to the authorities within the walls the intelligence of our approach.

We skirted the city walls for upward of six miles before we found the gate at which we were intended to enter; on our way we passed the spot on which stood formerly the Porcelain Tower, but not a fragment is left to mark the site of this once celebrated monument.

Entering the city through a massive gateway furnished with a portcullis, we traversed for upward of a mile its deserted streets before we reached the residence of one of the rebel chiefs named Le. This dignitary met us at the door, and conducted us to his audience-chamber. Here donning an elaborately embroidered head-dress, which was a combination of a bishop's mitre and a fool's-cap, he seated himself in his chair of state, and solemnly awaited our statement. This high functionary was dressed in a somewhat similar costume to his colleague at Woohoo: a robe of yellow reached from his neck to his heels. The only ornamental portions of his dress were his shoes and his cap: the former were of a most brilliant pattern; the latter was covered with dragons, and, Mr. Wylie alleged, was an imitation of the cap of office worn during the Ming dynasty.

As the conversation was carried on between Le and Mr. Wade, I will give this gentleman's report of what passed in his own words: "We stated the object of our visit, which was to inform the garrison that we had received the explanation forwarded to Woohoo of the mistake they had made in firing upon her majesty's ships, and that, as we had ships now up the river, others would be probably going and returning, interference with which would oblige us to resent it as before. Le was apologetic, but without servility. He seemed more anxious to take us on the religious side, beginning again and again that we were brothers of one family as Christians, but this in a constrained way, without impressiveness or enthusiasm. He said that Hung-siu-tsuen was still Taiping-wang, and had not been, as we had understood, succeeded by his son.

"We asked for the Eastern King, who, it was long since reported, had been slain in a fray. This was an embarrassing question; but, after a moment's hesitation, he replied that Yang was in heaven; and to a farther question, that he was succeeded in his honors and functions by his son. The number of his own force he put at several hundreds of thousands. He himself was Governor General of Kiang-nan, and, as we afterward heard, chief executive authority in Nankin. He called himself an officer or noble of the third degree, and wore on his high cap the badge, Yih-tien-fuh. The last character appears to mark his degree of nobility, though it properly means happiness or blessings. The two first mean to advantage heaven. We asked for any new books he might have, but the few he could produce were almost all the same with those brought down from Nankin in 1853 by Sir George Bonham. In one, a calendar for the coming year, Yang still figures as the Eastern King. Le promised us more books if we would stay the night; we could then visit the court of the Heavenly Kingdom. We had already requested permission to do this, but Le declared that, unless bidden thither, he could not present himself. One of his attendants, an intelligent-looking bonze-like personage, appeared rather amused at our eagerness about the books. He and the rest of the Chinese present, who were not very numerous, crowded in with as little restraint as at Woohoo, and sat where they pleased.

"We asked to see their place of worship; but, though one of them at first seemed to say that there was one at no great distance, Le interfered to observe that the brethren celebrated their worship every day in their own houses, and assembled on the Sabbath at the Yu-tai (Jewish?) temple in the king's court. This led to some inquiry regarding their days in the week, but we failed to ascertain whether they keep their Sabbath on the first or the seventh day, inasmuch as they certainly were at issue as to the place of the Wednesday we were then passing with them. So much of the day had been consumed by our long ride, that we were unable to stay more than a quarter of an hour with Le. Before our departure we again referred to the question of our ships. He begged that, if we were coming by, we would let the garrison know, in which case there would be no chance of collision. In accordance with our instructions, we told him that steps should be taken to this end, and, declining refreshment, we departed."

We had determined to return to the river through the city instead of skirting its walls, and therefore, despite the usual remonstrances at our independent behavior, started off on foot in the direction we wished to go, for we could not depend upon a guide; but, after effectually losing ourselves under our own guidance, we ultimately got back to the yamun, and Le, finding us obstinate, ordered a good-natured-looking man, of small military rank, to conduct us to the river-gate. By this time it had got dusk, and we had still a walk of five or six miles before us. The night was thick and sleety, and in the course of that long, dreary trudge we became quite intimate with our guide. At first, and while his companions were within earshot, he declared that the resources of the rebels were abundant, and spoke in Mandarin; but during our solitary walk through the wooded park-like country which is inclosed within the walls of the city of Nankin, he relapsed into the Canton dialect, and confided to us a very different state of matters. The rebels, he said, were reduced to great extremities for supplies; and he was confirmed in this assertion by the proclamations of Le, which we saw on the walls, calling on the people to subscribe.

Our guide also asked Mr. Wade if he could not take him on board one of the English ships to escape. This, he was told, was impossible, on which he expressed his desire to trade in opium or small-arms. He himself smoked, and so, he said, did one third of the people of Nankin; not openly, however, for indulgence in the drug is forbidden by law, nor is it publicly sold. He said that, although there were not many men in Nankin, there were four large rebel forces in existence—one in the Kwang provinces, one in Fuh-kien, one in Cheh-kiang, and one in Ngan-hwui: the last was very numerous. He spoke of the imperialists, not as the rebels usually affect to do, as demons or imps, but as the troops of government. They always fled, he said, when the rebels attacked them; but he admitted that the rebels, when attacked, also fled, so that the war was likely to last long enough. He also told us that polygamy was the order of the day. The Heavenly King had 300 wives, and he himself admitted to having had a very pretty bride allotted to him recently. The captured women are distributed among the soldiers; and we observed some pleasing female faces as we passed along the streets.

The captured men are pressed into the service, and tied together, and put into the front rank when they go into action.

The only form of prayer that our guide knew was a short grace said before meals, which he repeated. Sometimes they knelt, and the teacher prayed, but they never understood what he said. Three officers and twenty men had, he said, been killed by the fire of our ships on the way up the river.

The city of Nankin was occupied exclusively by rebel forces. We did not observe a single shop, nor was there any person engaged in trade. Many of the streets were entirely deserted, and the houses unoccupied. A vast portion of the area within the walls has never been built upon, while yamuns and public buildings still exist to attest its former magnificence. The most remarkable of these was the Choong-koo-low, or Central Drum Tower, under which we passed.

The present strength of the rebel garrison is estimated at from 10,000 to 15,000 men; that of the besieging force at double that number. The only hope of the latter seems to be to starve out the insurgents, for which end they have stopped up all thoroughfare by the three sides landward, and merely left open the side toward the river, which the rebels have secured by forts on both sides of the Yang-tse, thus retaining to themselves liberty of egress at pleasure. Six out of the thirteen gates which formerly gave access to the city are open, the rest are bricked up.

The centre of authority is evidently within the city, but there are circumstances which throw a doubt over the existence of Hung-siu-tsuen, although his followers all speak of him as still living, and edicts are issued under his name, with the title "Teĕn-wang" (Celestial prince). The evidence is more complete as to the death of the four secondary princes — North, South, East, and West. Two of these were killed in battle, and the others, who held their courts at Nankin, became the victims of internal feuds. Successors are said to have been appointed to the East, West, and South princes—all minors. Besides the prime minister Tsin, who, it is whispered, personates the prince, the resident executive chiefs seem to be four men, named Chin, Le, Mung, and Sin, and these have their offices within the city. The assistant prince, Shih Ta-kac, was reported to be at the head of the army in Fuh-kien, on the east of Kiang-si.

There are twenty-four chief, and the same number of secondary ministers of state, who are distributed in various parts of the insurgent territory. Most of the offices of trust are held by members of the original confederation, the majority being Kwang-tung or Kwang-si men.

It will be seen that our intercourse with the rebels, though more extensive than that of any foreigners hitherto, has not been of a character to enable us to acquire any very minute details with reference to their religious tenets. Mr. Wylie, who had for some years watched with interest the progress of the rebellion, was of opinion that the religious eccentricities which began to appear soon after its commencement are now assuming such prominence as to threaten the extinction of the vital truths of Christianity. The supremacy of their chief, Hung-siu-tsuen, they seem disposed to insist on, exalting him to divine honors as the third in rank, below whom all believers in Jesus are junior brethren. Whether any large number of them believe in the divine mission of Hung is, Mr. Wylie thinks, questionable; and it is to be feared that skepticism is equally prevalent regarding the better parts of their professed creed. The destruction of temples and idols is still insisted on, as we saw by the fragments of images which strewed the streets; and proclamations were posted up, urging the extirpation of idolatry in every form. This does not extend to the ancestral temples, however, these being universally respected, which implies that the worship there is in harmony with their profession.

The doctrines of their religion, in so far as they are expounded in their public documents, appear to consist of an extraordinary jumble of Jewish polity, Christian theology, and Chinese philosophy. The result, as tested by our observation, was very much what might have been expected from so incongruous a compound. We found the rebels making war like Jews, living like the worst description of professing Christians, and believing like—Chinamen!

CHAPTER XLI.

The Yang-tse-Kiang commercially considered.—Sensation on our Arrival.—Sudden Appearance of the Furious.—The secret Edict.—Correspondence with the Commissioners.—The Affairs of Canton.—Result of the Correspondence.—Decree published in the "Pekin Gazette."—Departure from Shanghai.—Military Promenades near Canton.—Expedition to Fayune.—A Voyage to Hainan.—Adieu to China.—Arrival at Malta.

As Lord Elgin was anxious to reach Shanghai in time for the mail, we pushed on in the Lee, leaving the Dove to pilot the Retribution through the more intricate navigation. We performed the voyage from Kew-kiang to the mouth of the Shanghai River in a week. When we remember that this was at the dryest season of the year, and our gun-boat drew eight feet of water, we are forced to admit the capabilities of the great river of China for purposes of navigation. When, however, steamers built expressly for the purpose begin to ply on this great channel of internal communication, they will find that their success depends, not upon the depth of water, but upon the nature of the competition with which they will have to contend. If river-tugs can tow flats at a cheaper rate than the Chinese can work barges upon the canals and inner waters of the country, then the Yang-tse-Kiang will become the highway for British commerce. In any other country in the world, machinery, whether applied to steam-ships or cotton-mills, will beat manual labor. In China, where a man's work is not worth a farthing a day, his labor takes a higher place in competition with steam-power. We have failed to substitute to any extent in China cotton manufactured by machinery for that manufactured by the hand; let us hope that, at all events, we may succeed in replacing junks by steamers.

Where valuable cargoes, such as opium, are concerned, there is no doubt that steamers will be preferred to the water-conveyances of the country; but in teas and heavier cargoes the question is more problematical.

If we fail, we shall probably console ourselves by attributing it to the influence of the government in some incomprehensible way. Doubtless the Chinese government has much to answer for, but it can not, and does not, affect the fundamental principles of political economy. Lord Elgin, in referring to our commercial prospects in the markets of the interior, thus alludes to this popular delusion: "My general impression is, that British manufacturers will have to exert themselves to the utmost if they intend to supplant, to any considerable extent in the native market, the fabrics produced in their leisure hours, and at intervals of rest from agricultural labor, by this industrious, frugal, and sober population. It is a pleasing but pernicious fallacy to imagine that the influence of an intriguing mandarin is to be presumed whenever a buyer shows a preference for native over foreign calico."* This will be equally true if he shows a preference for native over foreign river-craft.

At the same time, this problem—if problem it be—can not be solved until the rebels are dispossessed of their position for a hundred and fifty miles upon the banks of the Yang-tse-Kiang. We can not expect the Chinese government to permit us to trade with the insurgents. Nor, if the river is once opened to the commercial enterprise of foreigners, is it easy to devise a system by which all intercourse shall be confined to those who are well disposed toward the constituted authorities of the country.

The result, then, of our six weeks' exploration of the great river of China had been most satisfactory as regards its navigable capabilities, and tolerably so in a commercial point of view, if all political difficulties were removed; but, unfortunately, these latter were of a nature calculated, in a great measure, to neutralize all other advantages. Let us hope that an opportunity may now be afforded, which did not present itself during the period of our diplomatic experience in China, of removing those obstacles, and opening this magnificent highway to the merchants of the world.

We steamed up to Shanghai, and cast anchor among the shipping that crowded the river, under the pleasing consciousness that we were creating a sensation. A squadron of five ships had left the port six weeks ago; all that returned of it was a solitary gunboat, with Lord Elgin's flag flying at the main. The public of Shanghai were completely at fault. It had been reported that Lord Elgin, and the rest of the mission, had been captured and sent in cages to Pekin, and that most of the ships had been sunk, and that the Furious alone survived to tell the tale. That was

* *Blue-Book.* p. 446.

only to be expected; but now it appeared that Lord Elgin had returned without the Furious. This was a much more startling and unnatural phenomenon. We were received most cordially by a knot of inquirers, who greeted us as we landed on the bund, and all derived thorough satisfaction from the intelligence of two British ships being fixed for the winter in the heart of China. Could any method have been devised by which the country would be more inevitably opened up? What prodigies of exploration might not two such enterprising leaders as Captain Osborn and Bythesea, with their officers, perform during a residence of four or five months in the far interior? Poor fellows, they would need mental and bodily comforts of all kinds. The Dove, about to return with supplies, was consequently loaded with light literature and Bass's beer, woolen stockings, No. 4 shot, cavendish tobacco, wading-boots, and every luxury or necessary that the kind-hearted community could contribute, to console them for an existence which, we all devoutly hoped, for the good of commerce generally, might continue over many months.

Our astonishment may be imagined when, before we had been in Shanghai a week, we were startled about midnight by the unexpected appearance of Captain Osborn himself. It seemed that he had taken advantage of a sudden rise of the river, after heavy rains, to make a flying leap over the bar, and had come down at a slashing pace with our good old ship, whose well-known proportions were visible next morning just off the consulate windows.

We found the imperial commissioners in a most amiable mood on the occasion of a visit of congratulation which they hastened to pay Lord Elgin on his safe return from the perils of the recent river navigation.

About this time intelligence reached us from Canton, and gave rise to a correspondence too important not to be noticed. A body of British troops, exercising in the neighborhood of Canton, were unexpectedly attacked by a strong force of braves, and though, fortunately, no serious loss was inflicted, they were compelled to retreat with some haste to the city. This wanton act of hostility, at a time when the imperial government was professing, through its commissioners at Shanghai, sentiments of the most affectionate and conciliatory nature, called for prompt punishment; and an expedition was consequently organized against the small town of Shek-tsing, about seven miles distant from Canton, known as the head-quarters of a large body of the local militia. This operation was executed with great spirit and success. With a loss of four men wounded, we succeeded in destroying Shek-tsing, driving out the braves, who dispersed in great confusion, and capturing some of the private papers of the commissioners appointed by the government to organize militia against barbarians, and popularly known as the Fayune commissioners.

At the same time, a document of a remarkable character, which had fallen into the hands of Mr. Parkes, was forwarded by that gentleman to Lord Elgin. It purported to be an edict secretly issued by the government, inciting the braves to hostile action, and indicating a policy so infamous and treacherous that Lord Elgin forwarded it to the commissioners, with the remark that his excellency "refrains from any comment upon this paper, in the sincere hope that the commissioners will be enabled to assure him that its authors, in imputing to the emperor the insidiously hostile policy which it declares, have unwarrantably abused his majesty's name." The commissioners, in reply, unhesitatingly affirm this to have been the case. "As regards the document," they say, "to which your letter refers, and of which you have sent us a copy, we have the honor to assure you most positively that, after examining it together, we entertain no doubt that it is a forgery.

"The commissioner Twan has been in the council (by which they are prepared and transmitted) so many years, that he is certainly qualified to pronounce upon that point, and an inspection of the document has thoroughly satisfied him that it is a spurious composition."

Notwithstanding this assurance, Lord Elgin was so ill pleased with the state of matters in the south that he determined to adopt a tone in his correspondence which should oblige the commissioners to aid him in remedying the evil; he therefore recurred to, and insisted upon, his original demand, that they should procure from the emperor the dismissal of Hwang, the Governor General of Kwang-tung, and the dissolution of the committee of gentry, whose functions were to organize braves ostensibly for the protection of the country against rebels, but really to disturb us in our occupation of Canton.

It will be remembered that when the commissioners arrived at Shanghai at the commencement of October, Lord Elgin called their attention to the unsatisfactory position of affairs at Canton, and informed them that he declined to enter into negotiations with them until he should receive from them the assurance that Hwang, the Governor General of Kwang-tung, as well as the chiefs of the Fayune committee, should be removed from office.

Their excellencies undertook to memorialize the emperor for the removal from office of the persons above named, and to furnish Lord Elgin with a copy of the decree which the emperor might issue, giving effect to the prayer of their memorial.

On the faith of these assurances the embassador entered into negotiations with the commissioners on various matters, which it was important to settle definitively, with a view to the establishment of peace, and a good understanding between Great Britain and China.

On our return to Shanghai after an interval of three months, when Lord Elgin applied to the commissioners for the copy of the imperial decree which he had been promised, he was furnished with an imperial decree which, so far from removing Hwang and dismissing the Fayune chiefs from office, informs the commissioners that the emperor declines to be guided in this matter by their advice. At the same time, intelligence is received from Canton to the effect that our troops have been fired upon. Under these circumstances, Lord Elgin informed the commissioners that he had come to the following resolutions:

First. "To hold no farther communication with the imperial commissioners on the subject of Canton, as they clearly have no sufficient authority from the emperor to deal with this matter."

Second. "To urge the military and naval commanders of the British forces at Canton to move their troops freely about the province, and to punish severely any braves or others who may have the temerity to molest them."

Lord Elgin concludes by saying that "when the undersigned (or his successor) proceeds to Pekin for the exchange of the ratifications of the Treaty of Tientsin, he will ascertain whether the occurrences at Canton, of which he complains, have or have not the sanction of the emperor, and will act accordingly."

This missive had the desired effect. We had reason to believe that a copy of it was forwarded to Pekin at the rate of 600 le a day; and it provoked from the commissioners a reply, in which a positive assurance was given that Hwang and the committee should be removed, and the conduct of the braves was denounced in the strongest possible terms. Before leaving China, Lord Elgin had the satisfaction of receiving from the commissioners a communication inclosing a copy of an imperial decree, transferring to Ho, the enlightened Governor General of the Two Kiangs, the seal of the imperial commissioner hitherto held by Hwang. As this decree was promulgated avowedly in consequence of Lord Elgin's representation above quoted, there can be little doubt that the allusion to his proceeding to Pekin operated strongly upon the imperial mind.

The last official communication which Lord Elgin received from China, when on his way to England, was a notification that this same decree, removing Hwang and denouncing the secret edict as a forgery, had been published as a spontaneous act on the part of the Chinese government in the *Pekin Gazette*. It runs as follows:

IMPERIAL EDICT.
(*From the Pekin Gazette, 31st January.*)

"We have this day received a memorial from Kweiliang and his colleagues to the effect that they have received, with the letters from the British, a false imperial edict of the kind dispatched directly from the imperial court, and which, they were informed, had been obtained by an Englishman in Kwang-tung."

"On perusing this, OUR surprise was extreme. From all time China has held fast by principles of the highest justice in her benevolent measure for tranquillizing the various nations: she has never laid plans for secretly injuring them."

"Subsequently to the failure of Yeh-mingshin, WE appointed Hwang-tsung-han to be Governor General of the Two Kwang, and gave him the seal of imperial commissioner of OUR territories. As to Vice-President Lo-tun-yen and his colleagues, they, stimulated by patriotic ardor, enrolled braves for the defense of their country—a perfectly rightful occupation for local gentry."

"Recently, however, the amicable negotiations of Kweiliang and his colleagues at Tientsin having been finished, Hwang-tsung-han had to busy himself with internal military affairs only, while Lo-tun-yen and his colleagues had, in obedience to OUR commands, to deal solely with native bandits. It was not in contemplation that they should engage in hostilities with the British and French. Although these nations have not yet redelivered the capital of Kwang-tung, yet if they maintain proper order among their troops, causing no annoyance to the inhabitants, they may live together in peace, free from all troubles."

"A court dispatch has, however, been fabricated, giving cause to difficulties between Lo-tun-yen with his colleagues on the one side, and these two nations on the other, and producing doubt and suspicion in the mind of the British. We now therefore command Hwang-tsung-han to take strict measures for the seizure of the lawless fabricators, and to punish them with the utmost rigor of the law. Thus may all nations know that China transacts her affairs in an open, rightful, and liberal spirit, and that, when once a settlement is arrived at, suspicions and doubts may be given up, and so no room be left for the instigation of false mischief-makers.

"As Shanghai, where the arrangements connected with the general trade are at present being made, lies at a considerable distance from Kwang-tung, WE hereby appoint the Governor General of the Two Keang, Ho-kwei-tsing, to be imperial commissioner of foreign affairs, and WE hereby command Kwang-tsung-han to send a special officer to deliver to him the seal of imperial commissioner now in use. Respect this."

When it is remembered that the *Pekin Gazette* is published purely for the information of the Chinese population, and is not supposed to be read or seen by foreigners, we could not but regard the official promulgation of such conciliatory sentiments as a hopeful symptom of the future.

Meantime, Lord Elgin was of opinion that his presence at Canton would tend to facilitate the settlement of matters in that troubled locality: he had already urged upon General Straubenzee the expediency of vigorously following up his successful operations on Shek-tsing. "I think it very important," says his excellency, "that advantage should be taken of this cool season to accustom the rural inhabitants of the vicinity of Canton to the presence of our troops, and to punish severely braves or others who may venture to attack or resist them—every security, of course, being given that the peaceful inhabitants shall not in any way be molested."

Lord Elgin now announced to the commissioners his determination to proceed to Canton, stating as he did so that it was his intention to return to Shanghai, to discuss with them various questions, the settlement of which was still pending. He was ultimately prevented from carrying this arrangement into effect by learning on his arrival at Canton that Mr. Bruce, who had been appointed to relieve him, was expected immediately. The mercantile community, believing that the special mission was about to bid a final adieu to Shanghai, presented his excellency with an address, congratulating him upon the large measure of success with which his diplomatic efforts, both in China and Japan, had been crowned.

On the 25th of January Lord Elgin gave a farewell ball at the Consulate, immediately after which we once more turned into our familiar cots on board the Furious, and slept till an advanced hour of the following day, when Shanghai was twenty miles astern, and the turbid waters of the Yang-tse-Kiang were for the last time sweeping us rapidly out to sea.

Early in February, 1859, the Furious took up her berth in the Canton River, at the same anchorage at which I had left her precisely a year before. How great a change had been wrought in Canton during the interval! Then the troops were camped on the walls, or roughly barracked in yamuns; the streets were crowded with people leaving the city under the influence of fear; many of the shops were shut; and numbers of houses were uninhabited and in ruins.

Now a well-organized system of government had produced order out of chaos. A body of efficient police patrolled the streets, which were cleaner than those of any other town in China. The gambling-booths were all closed. Vacant spaces had been cleared of rubbish and turned into parade-grounds. Officers and men occupied comfortable quarters, and the streets might be traversed in any direction with perfect security. Trading was flourishing; the merchants, for the most part, occupying temporary abodes on Honan Island (on the opposite side of the river) until the site for the new British factory should be definitively decided upon.

The numerical strength of the police force which kept order in Canton during a year's occupation only amounted to one hundred and fifty men. Captain Pim, who commanded this body of men, informed me that, out of the number, he had lost four men killed and twelve wounded in the execution of their duty. These outrages had been committed during the summer, when braves were in the habit of secretly entering the city, and assassinating solitary Europeans. The townspeople, however, so far from sympathizing in the proceedings of these ruffians, used frequently to point them out to our men.

The success of the Shek-tsing expedition, and the wholesome moral effect which had been already produced upon the rural population of the district adjoining Canton, suggested the idea of military promenades on a more extensive scale. One was accordingly undertaken to Fat-shan, and another to Taileck, the principal village of the confederation known as the "Ninety-six Villages," both passing off peaceably, and producing, so far as we were enabled to judge, the most salutary effect upon the population. The notorious town of Fayune, however, situated between thirty and forty miles to the north of Canton, had still to be visited, and thither General Straubenzee proposed to march with a force of a thousand men. I was permitted to accompany the troops upon this expedition, which proved, in fact, a most interesting and agreeable five days' excursion, and partook rather of the character of a picnic than a military reconnoissance. As, however, it was fully described at the time, and was invested with no immediate interest beyond that which must necessarily attach to a march through a little-known country, I shall not enter upon any description of it. The political results of this, as of the other military promenades of the same nature which were undertaken about this period, were in the highest degree satisfactory. The country people, whose feeling toward foreigners are naturally amiable, became accustomed to our presence, and less than ever disposed to subscribe for the support of the disreputable rabble that had collected in the neighborhood of Canton from other parts of the country, and called themselves "Braves."

The "Braves" themselves found their prestige destroyed by the Shek-tsing affair, and now, for the first time, became aware that barbarians could undertake military movements unsupported by "devil ships," and that no retreat in the vicinity of Canton was secure from the visits of a foreign force. The dissolution of the Committee of Fayune by imperial edict, and the encampment for twenty-four hours of a thousand men under the walls of that town, effectually extinguished the warlike spirit of the militia, and it will be our own fault if we ever allow it to break forth again.

As, by the mail due in China at the end of February, we expected to receive definite intelligence of the movements of Mr. Bruce, as well as the views of the home government upon a question of policy which might render it necessary for Lord Elgin to return to Shanghai, he determined to occupy the interval by a voyage of discovery and exploration to the new port opened by the Treaty of Tientsin in the island of Hainan.

Unfortunately, as we approached that little-known and unsurveyed coast, it came on to blow a gale of wind. On our lee bow was a low, sandy, treacherous-looking shore, with a high conical mountain inland; on our quarter, the precipitous Taya Islands loomed dangerously through the haze; round us the waves foamed and chopped in an unpleasant manner, suggestive of strong currents and hidden reefs. Still the cry of the leadsman, anxiously waited for as we crept cautiously along, was "No bottom:" suddenly there came a sharp short "Seven fathoms." Our leadsmen were too well trained to waste the time in musical cadences on these occasions. In a second the helm was hard down, and the shoaling of the water, as the ship turned almost in her own length, proved how near had been the danger. The sea was running too high to make channel-hunting among the coral reefs, without a gun-boat, either an agreeable or safe amusement. So we turned our backs in disgust upon the inhospitable shores of Hainan, and ran for shelter and comfort into a pretty little port on the main land, where a snug pirate village nestled among woods, in a nook so secluded that we only stumbled on it by accident, and found a cutthroat population living in considerable comfort upon no apparent resources beyond what a certain number of well-armed junks could provide them with. After touching at the island of St. John's, and fruitlessly exploring one of its bays in search of the tomb of François Xavier, we once more anchored in Hong Kong harbor, as we devoutly trusted, "positively for the last time."

The arrival of the mail with scarcely any letters for the mission decided the question. It was evident that we were supposed in England to be on our way home, for both private and official correspondence had all but stopped. As Mr. Bruce had been charged to exchange the ratifications, and the admiral had been instructed to have a ship waiting for him at Singapore at the end of February, there was nothing to be gained by lingering longer amid the scenes of our protracted diplomatic labors.

On the 4th of March we watched with inexpressible delight the rugged coast of China sink behind the horizon, and a week afterward landed at Singapore. It was not, however, until we reached Ceylon that we met Mr. Bruce, whose departure from England had been delayed until a somewhat later period than had been anticipated.

The Furious, more faithful to us than we had been to her in the Yang-tse-Kiang, conveyed us in safety to Suez, where we had the satisfaction of being the first passengers who had ever breakfasted in the Red Sea, and dined the same afternoon in the Mediterranean. A very faint idea of our anxiety to get home may be gathered from this circumstance.

We entered the harbor of Valetta upon the anniversary of the day on which, two years before, we had steamed out of it on our way to the East. Since then India and China had successively occupied the public mind; and now it was absorbed in watching the destinies of Italy. Unhappily, events have again occurred in the Celestial Empire as unforeseen as they have been unfortunate. Whether our labors during two years in that country have been wasted, and the Treaty of Tientsin becomes at last a reality or a fiction, must depend upon the skill of our diplomacy no less than on the force of our arms.

APPENDIX.

No. I.
TREATY OF TIENTSIN.
INCLOSURE IN No. 181.

Treaty between Her Majesty and the Emperor of China. Signed in the English and Chinese languages, at Tientsin, June 26, 1858.

Her majesty the Queen of the United Kingdom of Great Britain and Ireland, and his majesty the Emperor of China, being desirous to put an end to the existing misunderstanding between the two countries, and to place their relations on a more satisfactory footing in future, have resolved to proceed to a revision and improvement of the treaties existing between them, and for that purpose have named as their plenipotentiaries, that is to say:

Her majesty the Queen of Great Britain and Ireland, the Right Honorable the Earl of Elgin and Kincardine, a Peer of the United Kingdom, and Knight of the Most Ancient and Most Noble Order of the Thistle;

And his majesty the Emperor of China, the High Commissioner Kweiliang, a Senior Chief Secretary of State, styled of the East Cabinet, Captain General of the Plain White Banner of the Manchu Banner Force, Superintendent General of the administration of Criminal Law; and Hwashana, one of his imperial majesty's Expositors of the Classics, Manchu President of the Office for the regulation of the Civil Establishment, Captain General of the Bordered Blue Banner of the Chinese Banner Force, and Visitor of the Office of Interpretation;

Who, after having communicated to each other their respective full powers, and found them to be in good and due form, have agreed upon and concluded the following Articles:

ARTICLE I.

The Treaty of Peace and Amity between the two nations, signed at Nankin on the twenty-ninth day of August, in the year one thousand eight hundred and forty-two, is hereby renewed and confirmed.

The Supplementary Treaty and General Regulations of Trade having been amended and improved, and the substance of their provisions having been incorporated in this treaty, the said Supplementary Treaty and General Regulations of Trade are hereby abrogated.

ARTICLE II.

For the better preservation of harmony in future, her majesty the Queen of Great Britain and his majesty the Emperor of China mutually agree that, in accordance with the universal practice of great and friendly nations, her majesty the queen may, if she see fit, appoint embassadors, ministers, or other diplomatic agents to the court of Pekin; and his majesty the Emperor of China may, in like manner, if he see fit, appoint embassadors, ministers, or other diplomatic agents to the court of St. James'.

ARTICLE III.

His majesty the Emperor of China hereby agrees that the embassador, minister, or other diplomatic agent, so appointed by her majesty the Queen of Great Britain, may reside with his family and establishment, permanently at the capital, or may visit it occasionally, at the option of the British government. He shall not be called upon to perform any ceremony derogatory to him as representing the sovereign of an independent nation on a footing of equality with that of China. On the other hand, he shall use the same forms of ceremony and respect to his majesty the emperor as are employed by the embassadors, ministers, or diplomatic agents of her majesty toward the sovereigns of independent and equal European nations.

It is farther agreed that her majesty's government may acquire at Pekin a site for building, or may hire houses for the accommodation of her majesty's mission, and that the Chinese government will assist it in so doing.

Her majesty's representative shall be at liberty to choose his own servants and attendants, who shall not be subjected to any kind of molestation whatever.

Any person guilty of disrespect or violence to her majesty's representative, or to any member of his family or establishment, in deed or word, shall be severely punished.

ARTICLE IV.

It is farther agreed that no obstacle or difficulty shall be made to the free movements of her majesty's representative, and that he, and the persons of his suite, may come and go, and travel at their pleasure. He shall, moreover, have full liberty to send and receive his correspondence to and from any point on the sea-coast that he may select; and his letters and effects shall be held sacred and inviolable. He may employ, for their transmission, special couriers, who shall meet with the same protection and facilities for traveling as the persons employed in carrying dispatches for the imperial government; and, generally, he shall enjoy the same privileges as are accorded to officers of the same rank by the usage and consent of Western nations.

All expenses attending the diplomatic mission of Great Britain shall be borne by the British government.

ARTICLE V.

His majesty the Emperor of China agrees to nominate one of the secretaries of state, or a president of one of the boards, as the high officer with whom the embassador, minister, or other diplomatic agent of her majesty the queen shall transact business, either personally or in writing, on a footing of perfect equality.

ARTICLE VI.

Her majesty the Queen of Great Britain agrees that the privileges hereby secured shall be enjoyed in her dominions by the embassadors, ministers, or diplomatic agents of the Emperor of China accredited to the court of her majesty.

ARTICLE VII.

Her majesty the queen may appoint one or more consuls in the dominions of the Emperor of China; and such consul or consuls shall be at liberty to reside in any of the open ports or cities of China, as her majesty the queen may consider most expedient for the interests of British commerce. They shall be treated with due respect by the Chinese authorities, and enjoy the same privileges and immunities as the consular officers of the most favored nation.

Consuls and vice-consuls in charge shall rank with intendants of circuits; vice-consuls, acting vice-consuls, and interpreters, with prefects. They shall have access to the official residences of these officers, and communicate with them, either personally or in writing, on a footing of equality, as the interests of the public service may require.

ARTICLE VIII.

The Christian religion, as professed by Protestants or Roman Catholics, inculcates the practice of virtue, and teaches man to do as he would be done by. Persons teaching it or professing it, therefore, shall alike be entitled to the protection of the Chinese authorities; nor shall any such, peaceably pursuing their calling, and not offending against the laws, be persecuted or interfered with.

ARTICLE IX.

British subjects are hereby authorized to travel, for their pleasure or for purposes of trade, to all parts of the interior, under passports which will be issued by their consuls, and countersigned by the local authorities. These passports, if demanded, must be produced for examination in the localities passed through. If the passport be not irregular, the bearer will be allowed to proceed, and no opposition shall be offered to his hiring persons, or hiring vessels for the carriage of his baggage or merchandise. If he be without a passport, or if he commit any offense against the law, he shall be handed over to the nearest consul for punishment, but he must not be subjected to any ill usage in excess of necessary restraint. No passport need be applied for by persons going on excursions from the ports open to trade to a distance not exceeding 100 li, and for a period not exceeding five days.

The provisions of this article do not apply to crews of ships, for the due restraint of whom regulations will be drawn up by the consul and the local authorities.

To Nankin, and other cities disturbed by persons in arms against the government, no pass shall be given until they shall have been recaptured.

ARTICLE X.

British merchant-ships shall have authority to trade upon the Great River (Yang-tsz). The Upper and Lower Valley of the river being, however, disturbed by outlaws, no port shall be for the present opened to trade, with the exception of Chin-kiang, which shall be opened in a year from the date of the signing of this treaty.

So soon as peace shall have been restored, British vessels shall also be admitted to trade at such ports as far as Hankow, not exceeding three in number, as the British minister, after consultation with the Chinese Secretary of State, may determine shall be ports of entry and discharge.

ARTICLE XI.

In addition to the cities and towns of Canton, Amoy, Foo-chow, Ningpo, and Shanghae, opened by the Treaty of Nankin, it is agreed that British subjects may frequent the cities and ports of New-Chwang, Tang-Chow, Tai-Wan (Formosa), Chau-Chow (Swatoa), and Kiung-Chow (Hainan).

They are permitted to carry on trade with whomsoever they please, and to proceed to and fro at pleasure with their vessels and merchandise.

They shall enjoy the same privileges, advantages, and immunities at the said towns and ports as they enjoy at the ports already opened to trade, including the right of residence, of buying or renting houses, of leasing land therein, and of building churches, hospitals, and cemeteries.

ARTICLE XII.

British subjects, whether at the ports or at other places, desiring to build or open houses, warehouses, churches, hospitals, or burial-grounds, shall make their agreement for the land or buildings they require at the rates prevailing among the people, equitably, and without exaction on either side.

ARTICLE XIII.

The Chinese government will place no restrictions whatever upon the employment, by British subjects, of Chinese subjects in any lawful capacity.

ARTICLE XIV.

British subjects may hire whatever boats they please for the transport of goods or passengers, and the sum to be paid for such boats shall be settled between the parties themselves, without the interference of the Chinese government. The number of these boats shall not be limited, nor shall a monopoly in respect either of the boats, or of the porters or coolies engaged in carrying the goods, be granted to any parties. If any smuggling takes place in them, the offenders will, of course, be punished according to law.

ARTICLE XV.

All questions in regard to rights, whether of property or person, arising between British subjects, shall be subject to the jurisdiction of the British authorities.

ARTICLE XVI.

Chinese subjects who may be guilty of any criminal act toward British subjects shall be arrested and punished by the Chinese authorities, according to the laws of China.

British subjects who may commit any crime in China shall be tried and punished by the consul, or other public functionary authorized thereto, according to the laws of Great Britain.

Justice shall be equitably and impartially administered on both sides.

ARTICLE XVII.

A British subject having reason to complain of a Chinese must proceed to the consulate and state his grievance. The consul will inquire into the merits of the case, and do his utmost to arrange it amicably. In like manner, if a Chinese have reason to complain of a British subject, the consul shall no less listen to his complaint, and endeavor to settle it in a friendly manner. If disputes take place of such a nature that the consul can not arrange them amicably, then he shall request the assistance of the Chinese authorities, that they may together examine into the merits of the case, and decide it equitably.

ARTICLE XVIII.

The Chinese authorities shall at all times afford the fullest protection to the persons and property of British subjects whenever these shall have been subjected to insult or violence. In all cases of incendiarism or robbery, the local authorities shall at once take the necessary steps for the recovery of the stolen property, the suppression of disorder, and the arrest of the guilty parties, whom they will punish according to law.

ARTICLE XIX.

If any British merchant-vessel, while within Chinese waters, be plundered by robbers or pirates, it shall be the duty of the Chinese authorities to use every endeavor to capture and punish the said robbers or pirates, and to recover the stolen property, that it may be handed over to the consul for restoration to the owner.

ARTICLE XX.

If any British vessel be at any time wrecked or stranded on the coast of China, or be compelled to take refuge in any port within the dominions of the Emperor of China, the Chinese authorities, on being apprised of the fact, shall immediately adopt measures for its relief and security; the persons on board shall receive friendly treatment, and shall be furnished, if necessary, with the means of conveyance to the nearest consular station.

ARTICLE XXI.

If criminals, subjects of China, shall take refuge in Hong Kong, or on board the British ships there, they shall, upon due requisition by the Chinese authorities, be searched for, and, on proof of their guilt, be delivered up.

In like manner, if Chinese offenders take refuge in the houses or on board the vessels of British subjects at the open ports, they shall not be harbored or concealed, but shall be delivered up, on due requisition by the Chinese authorities, addressed to the British consul.

ARTICLE XXII.

Should any Chinese subject fail to discharge debts incurred to a British subject, or should he fraudulently abscond, the Chinese authorities will do their utmost to effect his arrest, and enforce recovery of the debts. The British authorities will likewise do their utmost to bring to justice any British subject fraudulently absconding or failing to discharge debts incurred by him to a Chinese subject.

ARTICLE XXIII.

Should natives of China who may repair to Hong Kong to trade incur debts there, the recovery of such debts must be arranged for by the English courts of justice on the spot; but should the Chinese debtor abscond, and be known to have property, real or personal, within the Chinese territory, it shall be the duty of the Chinese authorities, on application by, and in concert with, the British consul, to do their utmost to see justice done between the parties.

ARTICLE XXIV.

It is agreed that British subjects shall pay, on all merchandise imported or exported by them, the duties prescribed by the tariff; but in no case shall they be called upon to pay other or higher duties than are required of the subjects of any other foreign nation.

ARTICLE XXV.

Import duties shall be considered payable on the landing of the goods, and duties of export on the shipment of the same.

ARTICLE XXVI.

Whereas the tariff fixed by Article X. of the Treaty of Nankin, and which was estimated so as to impose on imports and exports a duty at about the rate of five per cent. *ad valorem*, has been found, by reason of the fall in value of various articles of merchandise therein enumerated, to impose a duty upon these considerably in excess of the rate originally assumed as above to be a fair rate, it is agreed that the said tariff shall be revised, and that, as soon as the treaty shall have been signed, application shall be made to the Emperor of China to depute a high officer of the Board of Revenue to meet at Shanghai officers to be deputed on behalf of the British government, to consider its revision together, so that the tariff, as revised, may come into operation immediately after the ratification of this treaty.

ARTICLE XXVII.

It is agreed that either of the high contracting parties to this treaty may demand a farther revision of the tariff, and of the commercial articles of this treaty, at the end of ten years; but if no demand be made on either side within six months after the end of the first ten years, then the tariff shall remain in force for ten years more, reckoned from the end of the preceding ten years; and so it shall be at the end of each successive ten years.

ARTICLE XXVIII.

Whereas it was agreed in Article X. of the Treaty of Nankin that British imports, having paid the tariff duties, should be conveyed into the interior free of all farther charges, except a transit duty, the amount whereof was not to exceed a certain percentage on tariff value; and whereas, no accurate information having been furnished of the amount of such duty, British merchants have constantly complained that charges are suddenly and arbitrarily imposed by the provincial authorities as transit duties upon produce on its way to the foreign market, and on imports on their way into the interior, to the detriment of trade; it is agreed that within four months from the signing of this treaty, at all ports now open to British trade, and within a similar period at all ports that may hereafter be opened, the authority appointed to superintend the collection of duties shall be obliged, upon application of the consul, to declare the amount of duties leviable on produce between the place of production and the port of shipment, and upon imports between the consular port in question and the inland markets named by the consul; and that a notification thereof shall be published in English and Chinese for general information.

But it shall be at the option of any British subject, desiring to convey produce purchased inland to a port, or to convey imports from a port to an inland market, to clear his goods of all transit duties, by payment of a single charge. The amount of this charge shall be leviable on exports at the first barrier they may have to pass, or, on imports, at the port at which they are landed; and on payment thereof, a certificate shall be issued, which shall exempt the goods from all farther inland charges whatsoever.

It is farther agreed that the amount of this charge shall be calculated as nearly as possible, at the rate of two and a half per cent. *ad valorem*, and that it shall be fixed for each article at the conference to be held at Shanghai for the revision of the tariff.

It is distinctly understood that the payment of transit dues, by commutation or otherwise, shall in no way affect the tariff duties on imports or exports, which will continue to be levied separately and in full.

ARTICLE XXIX.

British merchant-vessels of more than one hundred and fifty tuns burden shall be charged tonnage dues at the rate of four mace per ton; if of one hundred and fifty tons and under, they shall be charged at the rate of one mace per ton.

Any vessel clearing from any of the open ports of China for any other of the open ports or for Hong Kong, shall be entitled, on application of the master, to a special certificate from the Customs, on exhibition of which she shall be exempted from all farther payment of tonnage dues in any open port of China for a period of four months, to be reckoned from the date of her port clearance.

ARTICLE XXX.

The master of any British merchant-vessel may, within forty-eight hours after the arrival of his vessel, but not later, decide to depart without breaking bulk, in which case he will not be subject to pay tonnage dues. But tonnage dues shall be held due after the expiration of the said forty-eight hours. No other fees or charges upon entry or departure shall be levied.

ARTICLE XXXI.

No tonnage dues shall be payable on boats employed by British subjects in the conveyance of passengers, baggage, letters, articles of provision, or other articles not subject to duty, between any of the open ports. All cargo-boats, however, conveying merchandise subject to duty shall pay tonnage dues once in six months, at the rate of four mace per register ton.

ARTICLE XXXII.

The consuls and superintendents of customs shall consult together regarding the erection of beacons or light-houses, and the distribution of buoys and light-ships, as occasion may demand.

ARTICLE XXXIII.

Duties shall be paid to the bankers authorized by the Chinese government to receive the same in its behalf, either in sycee or in foreign money, according to the assay made at Canton, on the thirteenth of July, one thousand eight hundred and forty-three.

ARTICLE XXXIV.

Sets of standard weights and measures, prepared according to the standard issued to the Canton Custom-house by the Board of Revenue, shall be delivered by the Superintendent of Customs to the consul at each port, to secure uniformity and prevent confusion.

ARTICLE XXXV.

Any British merchant-vessel arriving at one of the open ports shall be at liberty to engage the services of a pilot to take her into port. In like manner, after she has discharged all legal dues and duties, and is ready to take her departure, she shall be allowed to select a pilot to conduct her out of port.

ARTICLE XXXVI.

Whenever a British merchant-vessel shall arrive off one of the open ports, the Superintendent of Customs shall depute one or more Customs officers to guard the ship. They shall either live in a boat of their own, or stay on board the ship, as may best suit their convenience. Their food and expenses shall be supplied them from the Custom-house, and they shall not be entitled to any fees whatever from the master or consignee. Should they violate this regulation, they shall be punished proportionately to the amount exacted.

ARTICLE XXXVII.

Within twenty-four hours after arrival, the ship's papers, bills of lading, etc., shall be lodged in the hands of the consul, who will, within a farther period of twenty-four hours, report to the Superintendent of Customs the name of the ship, her register tonnage, and the nature of her cargo. If, owing to neglect on the part of the master, the above rule is not complied with within forty-eight hours after the ship's arrival, he shall be liable to a fine of fifty taels for every day's delay: the total amount of penalty, however, shall not exceed two hundred taels.

The master will be responsible for the correctness of the manifest, which shall contain a full and true account of the particulars of the cargo on board. For presenting a false manifest, he will subject himself to a fine of five hundred taels; but he will be allowed to correct, within twenty-four hours after delivery of it to the Customs officers, any mistake he may discover in his manifest, without incurring this penalty.

ARTICLE XXXVIII.

After receiving from the consul the report in due form, the Superintendent of Customs shall grant the vessel a permit to open hatches. If the master shall open hatches and begin to discharge any goods without such permission, he shall be fined five hundred taels, and the goods discharged shall be confiscated wholly.

ARTICLE XXXIX.

Any British merchant who has cargo to land or ship, must apply to the Superintendent of Customs for a special permit. Cargo landed or shipped without such permit will be liable to confiscation.

ARTICLE XL.

No transhipment from one vessel to another can be made without special permission, under pain of confiscation of the goods so transhipped.

ARTICLE XLI.

When all dues and duties shall have been paid, the Superintendent of Customs shall give a port clearance, and the consul shall then return the ship's papers, so that she may depart on her voyage.

ARTICLE XLII.

With respect to articles subject, according to the tariff, to an *ad valorem* duty, if the British merchant can not agree with the Chinese officer in affixing a value, then each party shall call two or three merchants to look at the goods, and the highest price at which any of these merchants would be willing to purchase them shall be assumed as the value of the goods.

ARTICLE XLIII.

Duties shall be charged upon the net weight of each article, making a deduction for the tare weight of congee, etc. To fix the tare on any article, such as tea, if the British merchant can not agree with the Custom-house officer, then each party shall choose so many chests out of every hundred, which being first weighed in gross, shall afterward be tared, and the average tare upon these chests shall be assumed as the tare upon the whole, and upon this principle shall the tare be fixed upon all other goods and packages. If there should be any other points in dispute which can not be settled, the British merchant may appeal to his consul, who will communicate the particulars of the case to the Superintendent of Customs, that it may be equitably arranged. But the appeal must be made within twenty-four hours, or it will not be attended to. While such points are still unsettled, the Superintendent of Customs shall postpone the insertion of the same in his books.

ARTICLE XLIV.

Upon all damaged goods a fair reduction of duty shall be allowed, proportionate to their deterioration. If any disputes arise, they shall be settled in the manner pointed out in the clause of this treaty having reference to articles which pay duty *ad valorem*.

ARTICLE XLV.

British merchants who may have imported merchandise into any of the open ports and paid the duty thereon, if they desire to re-export the same, shall be entitled to make application to the Superintendent of Customs, who, in order to prevent fraud on the revenue, shall cause examination to be made by suitable officers, to see that the duties paid on such goods, as entered in the Custom-house books, correspond with the representation made, and that the goods remain with their original marks unchanged. He shall then make a memorandum on the port-clearance of the goods and of the amount of duties paid, and deliver the same to the merchant; and shall also certify the facts to the officers of Customs of the other ports. All which being done, on the arrival in port of the vessel in which the goods are laden, every thing being found on examination there to correspond, she shall be permitted to break bulk, and land the said goods, without being subject to the payment of any additional duty thereon. But if, on such examination, the Superintendent of Customs shall detect any fraud on the revenue in the case, then the goods shall be subject to confiscation by the Chinese government.

British merchants desiring to re-export duty-paid imports to a foreign country shall be entitled, on complying with the same conditions as in the case of re-exportation to another port in China, to a drawback certificate, which shall be a valid tender to the Customs in payment of import or export duties.

Foreign grain brought into any port of China in a British ship, if no part thereof has been landed, may be re-exported without hinderance.

ARTICLE XLVI.

The Chinese authorities at such port shall adopt the means they may judge most proper to prevent the revenue suffering from fraud or smuggling.

ARTICLE XLVII.

British merchant-vessels are not entitled to resort to other than the ports of trade declared open by this treaty. They are not unlawfully to enter other ports in China, or to carry on clandestine trade along the coasts thereof. Any vessel violating this provision shall, with her cargo, be subject to confiscation by the Chinese government.

ARTICLE XLVIII.

If any British merchant-vessel be concerned in smuggling, the goods, whatever their value or nature, shall be subject to confiscation by the Chinese authorities, and the ship may be prohibited from trading farther and sent away, as soon as her accounts shall have been adjusted and paid.

ARTICLE XLIX.

All penalties enforced, or confiscations made under this treaty, shall belong and be appropriated to the public service of the government of China.

ARTICLE L.

All official communications addressed by the diplomatic and consular agents of her majesty the queen to the Chinese authorities shall henceforth be written in English. They will, for the present, be accompanied by a Chinese version; but it is understood that, in the event of there being any difference of meaning between the English and Chinese text, the English government will hold the sense as expressed in the English text to be the correct sense. This provision is to apply to the treaty now negotiated, the Chinese text of which has been carefully corrected by the English original.

ARTICLE LI.

It is agreed that henceforward the character "I" 夷 (barbarian) shall not be applied to the government or subjects of her Britannic majesty in any Chinese official document issued by the Chinese authorities, either in the capital or in the provinces.

ARTICLE LII.

British ships of war coming for no hostile purpose, or being engaged in the pursuit of pirates, shall be at liberty to visit all ports within the dominions of the Emperor of China, and shall receive every facility for the purchase of provisions, procuring water, and, if occasion require, for the making of repairs. The commanders of such ships shall hold intercourse with the Chinese authorities on terms of equality and courtesy.

ARTICLE LIII.

In consideration of the injury sustained by native and foreign commerce from the prevalence of piracy in the seas of China, the high contracting parties agree to concert measures for its suppression.

ARTICLE LIV.

The British government and its subjects are hereby confirmed in all privileges, immunities, and advantages conferred on them by previous treaties; and it is hereby expressly stipulated that the British government and its subjects will be allowed free and equal participation in all privileges, immunities, and advantages that may have been, or may be hereafter, granted by his majesty the Emperor of China to the government or subjects of any other nation.

APPENDIX.

ARTICLE LV.

In evidence of her desire for the continuance of a friendly understanding, her majesty the Queen of Great Britain consents to include in a separate article, which shall be in every respect of equal validity with the articles of this treaty, the conditions affecting indemnity for expenses incurred and losses sustained in the matter of the Canton question.

ARTICLE LVI.

The ratifications of this treaty, under the hand of her majesty the Queen of Great Britain and Ireland, and his majesty the Emperor of China respectively, shall be exchanged at Pekin within a year from this day of signature.

In token whereof, the respective plenipotentiaries have signed and sealed this treaty.

Done at Tientsin, this twenty-sixth day of June, in the year of our Lord one thousand eight hundred and fifty-eight; corresponding with the Chinese date, the sixteenth day, fifth moon, of the eighth year of Hien Fung.

(L. S.)   ELGIN AND KINCARDINE.

[Signature of First Chinese Plenipotentiary.]

[Signature of Second Chinese Plenipotentiary.]

[Seal of the Chinese Plenipotentiaries.]

Separate Article annexed to the Treaty concluded between Great Britain and China on the twenty-sixth day of June, in the year one thousand eight hundred and fifty-eight.

It is hereby agreed that a sum of two millions of taels, on account of the losses sustained by British subjects through the misconduct of the Chinese authorities at Canton, and a farther sum of two millions of taels on account of the military expenses of the expedition which her majesty the queen has been compelled to send out for the purpose of obtaining redress, and of enforcing the due observance of treaty provisions, shall be paid to her majesty's representatives in China by the authorities of the Kwang-tung province.

The necessary arrangements with respect to the time and mode of effecting these payments shall be determined by her majesty's representative, in concert with the Chinese authorities of Kwang-tung.

When the above amount shall have been discharged in full, the British forces will be withdrawn from Canton.

Done at Tientsin, this twenty-sixth day of June, in the year of our Lord one thousand eight hundred and fifty-eight; corresponding with the Chinese date, the sixteenth day, fifth moon, of the eighth year of Hien Fung.

(L.S.)   ELGIN AND KINCARDINE.

[Signature of First Chinese Plenipotentiary.]

[Signature of Second Chinese Plenipotentiary.]

[Seal of the Chinese Plenipotentiaries.]

No. II.

CORRESPONDENCE RELATIVE TO A RESIDENT MINISTER AT PEKIN.

No. 216.

The Earl of Elgin to the Earl of Malmesbury. (*Received December* 29.)

(Extract.) Shanghai, November 5, 1858.

In my dispatch of the 22d ultimo I inclosed a précis of a very important letter which I had just then received from the Chinese imperial commissioners. I informed your lordship that it was very becoming in its tone, but that it expressed a very strong hope that her majesty would exercise the option conferred on her by Article III. of the Treaty of Tientsin, by directing her minister to visit Pekin occasionally, instead of residing there permanently, and I requested you not to come to any final decision on this point until you should have heard from me again. I have now the honor to transmit herewith a translation of the letter in question, and of the correspondence to which it has led.

In order that your lordship may correctly apprehend the drift of this correspondence, it is necessary that I should state at the outset that the Chinese authorities contemplate the permanent residence of foreign ministers at the capital with more aversion and apprehension than any of the other innovations introduced by the Treaty of Tientsin.

In reply to the representations which I have been able, through private channels, to make to them in favor of this arrangement as the best means of obviating international disputes, and of preventing them, when they chance to arise, from assuming undue proportions, they are wont to urge, in the first place, of course, the traditional policy of the empire, and, then, the difficulties in which, if he were constantly resident at the capital, the idiosyncracies of an individual foreign functionary, of violent temper and overbearing demeanor, might involve them. As regards this latter point (I refer now to communications which have passed between us through official channels), they are in the habit of illustrating their meaning by examples. "If we were quite sure," say they, "that you would always send to us men thoroughly wise, discreet, and considerate, it might be different; but if, for instance, so and so were appointed to represent a foreign government at Pekin (and the right, if exercised by you, would, of course, be claimed by all other governments), a month would not elapse before something would occur which would place our highest officers in the dilemma of having either to risk a quarrel or submit to some indignity which would lower the Chinese government in the eyes of its own subjects." No doubt such apprehensions are to some extent chimerical; but I am bound to admit that I do not consider them to be altogether so. The doctrine that every Chinaman is a knave, and manageable only by bullying and bravado, like the kindred doctrine that every trading junk carries guns and is piratical, is, I venture with all deference to think, sometimes pushed a little too far in our dealings with this people. Be this, however, as it may, I advert to the point now only because I wish your lordship to understand that I believe that the objections to the permanent residence of foreign ministers at Pekin, which the Chinese authorities urge on this head, are sincerely entertained by them, and not entirely groundless.

Again, we know from the "Pekin Gazette" that the emperor has issued orders for the reconstruction of the forts which we knocked down at the mouth of the Peiho, and for the erection of other works to protect Pekin. It would hardly, I think, be reasonable on our part to require that the Emperor of China should leave his capital undefended for the express purpose of enabling us, whenever we see fit so to do, to attack him there. Nor do I, on the other hand, think that any works which he is likely to raise will prevent us from reaching it if we resolve to go thither in pursuance of a treaty-right. At the same time, it may be a question whether it would be expedient to exercise the option conferred on her majesty by Article III. of the Treaty of Tientsin in such a manner as would force the emperor to choose between a desperate attempt at resistance and passive acquiescence in what he and his advisers believe to be the greatest calamity which can befall the empire.

Short, however, of the extreme measure of a forcible resistance to the invasion of the capital by foreign ministers, with their wives and establishments (these latter being, it appears, in the eyes of the Chinese, more formidable than the ministers themselves), there is a risk which I feel myself bound, under present circumstances, not to pass over without notice.

Your lordship may perhaps remember that, on the eve of the day on which the Treaty of Tientsin was signed, I received a representation to the effect that the Chinese commissioners would certainly lose their heads if they conceded the articles in my treaty providing for the residence of a British minister at Pekin, and empowering British subjects to travel through the country for trading purposes.

This representation caused me a good deal of anxiety at the time, but I resolved to disregard it, and to act on the hypothesis that, being in the vicinity of Pekin with an armed force, I might so demean myself as to make the emperor think that he was under an obligation to his plenipotentiaries for having made peace with me even on the terms objected to.

The result justified this calculation. Kweiliang and Hwashana, the commissioners who negotiated with me the Treaty of Tientsin, are now here, and seem still to enjoy the imperial confidence and favor. Moreover, if they entertained before they arrived here any hope of being able to call in question the concessions secured to foreigners by that treaty, they have been induced since their arrival entirely to abandon it, partly by the peremptory language which I held to them respecting affairs at Canton, and partly by the assurance which has been unofficially conveyed to them, that, if they act toward me in perfect good faith, they will find me reasonable and considerate. If, however, after having, in terms so ample and language so respectful, acceded to my requirements, they are compelled to report to the emperor that they have failed to obtain from me any consideration whatever for the representations urged by them on behalf of their sovereign, I fear that their degradation and punishment will be inevitable, and I need hardly say that an occurrence of this nature would tend much to unsettle the Chinese mind, and to beget doubts as to the emperor's intentions with respect to the new treaty.

Moreover, the treaty-right to navigate the Yang-tze, and to resort to ports upon that river for purposes of trade, was also made contingent on the re-establishment of the imperial authority in the ports in question; because, as we have seen fit to affect neutrality between the Emperor of China and the rebels, we could not, of course, without absurdity, require him to give us rights and protection in places actually occupied by a power which we treat with the same respect as his own.

Nevertheless, it is important that it should be known to Chinese and foreigners that the emperor has conceded in principle the opening up of the river; and I have long thought that if I could contrive to go up it in person, with the consent of the imperial government, with the plea of selecting the ports which would be most suitable for foreign trade, it would be a very effectual way of tendering to the public the required assurance on this point.

It is only, however, by conciliating the good-will of the imperial commissioners that this result can be brought about; for, until the Treaty of Tientsin is ratified, I have clearly no title to go up the river as a matter of right.

I might refer to other important subjects that fall within the category of matters which, although they are beyond the strict provisions of the treaty, it is desirable, if possible, to settle amicably at the present time; but I think it unnecessary to swell this dispatch by enumerating them.

Under these circumstances, it became necessarily my duty to consider whether I might not, by a different mode of proceeding, turn the disposition of the imperial commissioners to better account.

I find, on inquiry, that by adopting a more conciliating tone in reference to the subject which they have brought under my notice, I can secure the following objects:

Firstly, I can obtain from them, in the fullest terms, a recognition of the rights accruing to her majesty and to British subjects, under the Treaty of Tientsin, including that very right of the permanent establishment of a minister at Pekin which forms the subject of discussion;

Secondly, I can induce them to take at once all the steps for giving effect to the treaty which they can be properly required to take previously to its ratification;

Thirdly, I can farther induce them to accede to my wishes in reference to certain other matters not covered by the treaty, but to which I attach, nevertheless, considerable importance.

Fourthly, I can contrive so to meet their proposal as to leave in the hands of her majesty's government, to be wielded at its will, a moral lever of the most powerful description, to secure the faithful observance of the treaty by the Chinese government in all time to come.

As, in a transaction of so much delicacy, the choice of each word is important, I must refer your lordship to the inclosed correspondence for a full exposition of the method which I have pursued in furtherance of these ends. The upshot of it all is this: that after reserving, in the most unqualified terms, her majesty's right to exercise as she may see fit the option conferred on her by Article III. of the Treaty of Tientsin, I have undertaken to communicate to her majesty's government the representations that have been made to me on the subject by the Chinese imperial commissioners, and humbly to submit it as my opinion that if her majesty's embassador be properly received at Pekin when the ratifications are exchanged next year, and full effect given in all other particulars to the treaty negotiated at Tientsin, it will be expedient that her majesty's representative in China be instructed to choose a place of residence elsewhere than at Pekin, and to make his visits to the capital either periodically, or as frequently as the exigencies of the public service may require.

In pursuance of the above pledge, I address to your lordship the present communication, and respectfully request for it your favorable consideration.

In conclusion, I would beg leave to remind your lordship that it is only in the British treaty that the right to appoint a minister to reside permanently at Pekin is provided for. Any other nation desiring to exercise this privilege must borrow it from that treaty under the most favored nation clause; and if such a claim on the part of any other power were admitted, of course the objection to the residence of a British minister at the capital would be at once, by that fact, removed.

And, farther, although I adhere to every opinion I have formerly expressed with regard to the importance of the establishment of direct diplomatic relations with the court of Pekin, I am bound to admit that the position of a British minister at the capital during the winter months, when the thermometer, if Humboldt is to be believed, falls to 40° below zero, the River Tientsin is frozen, and the Gulf of Pechelee hardly navigable, would not be altogether a pleasant one; and that it is even possible that, under such circumstances, his actual presence might be to the mandarin mind less awe-inspiring than the knowledge of the fact that he had the power to take up his abode there whenever the conduct of the Chinese government gave occasion for complaint.

Inclosure 1 in No. 216.

Commissioners Kweiliang, Hwashana, etc., to the Earl of Elgin.

(*Translation.*)

Kwei, a Chief Secretary; Hwa, President, etc.; Ho, Governor General of the Two Kiang; Ming, an officer of the Household; and Twan, a titulary President, etc., Imperial Commissioners, make a communication.

The proper end of treaty negotiations is the maintenance of peace between two nations, with such an interchange of good offices that neither side is advantaged to the prejudice of the other; it will continue long in operation, its benefit unmixed.

This is the object really belonging to treating of peace and to improvement of relations.

When the Commissioners Kwei and Hwa negotiated a treaty with your excellency at Tientsin, British vessels of war were lying at that port; there was the pressure of an armed force, a state of excitement and alarm;* and the treaty had to be signed at once, without a moment's delay. Deliberation was out of the question; the commissioners had no alternative but to accept the conditions forced upon them.† Among these were some of real injury to China, (to waive which) would have been of no disadvantage to your excellency's government; but in the hurry of the moment, the commissioners had no opportunity of offering your excellency a frank explanation of these.

On their return to the capital, accordingly, his majesty the emperor issued a special commission to us all to come to Shanghai to consult together, and earnestly to press a matter which will be to the common advantage of both parties.

The sincerity of our desire for a lasting continuance of friendly relations is plain to the clear sight of your excellency; and it is naturally our duty, acting toward you in a spirit of honesty, and with no intention to deceive, to set forth with all truth the matter which is the most irksome to China.

In Article III. of the treaty it is laid down that "the embassador, or other such high officer of her majesty the Queen of England, may reside permanently at the capital, or may visit it occasionally, at the option of the British government." (The employment of) the word "or" expressing, as it undoubtedly does, the absence of a decision, is evidence enough of the sense and reasonableness of your excellency, who would not precipitately decide upon an arbitrary course toward any one.

Now the majority of the inhabitants of the capital are Banner-men,‡ who, never

---

* *Lit.*, weapons of war were constraining, there was a state of crackling fire and of rushing water.

† *Lit.*, could only bend and give consent. The word rendered "bend" generally implies the employment of undue violence.

‡ Banner-men: the Manchus, Mongols, and Chinese, enrolled on the same footing, are formed into eight banners, under an establishment part civil, part military.

having been beyond its walls, or in intercourse with other people, are quite ignorant of the feelings of men or the ways of the world outside. The business the officials, high and low, have to transact in the capital, again, is entirely metropolitan.

They have had no personal experience of the popular feeling on public affairs of provinces, and know nothing whatever about them. Then the habits and dispositions of the people of the capital are different from those of the eastern and southern provinces. If foreigners reside in Pekin, it will certainly come to pass that in their movements something will create misgiving and surprise on the part of the multitude; any slight misunderstanding will be sure to beget a quarrel; and great, indeed, would be the injury to our country were some trifling cause of difference to attain serious dimensions.* China, too, is at the present moment in a crisis of great difficulty, and should the people, as it is to be apprehended they might, be misled by idle words upon this point, they would commence some trouble in addition (to those already on our hands). It would never do, surely, to bring China to such a pass.

Peace being now to endure to perpetuity between China and your excellency's country, the grand object of both must be their common interest, a community of weal and woe.

The fairness with which your excellency proceeds in business is well known to us: you would be reluctant to impose a task of difficulty upon a friendly state; nor surely can there be less reluctance on the part of her majesty, the sovereign of your excellency's country, illustrious for well-doing and justice, equitable in her administration, to employ the wealth of her realm and the power of her arm in inflicting this injury upon our country, in disregard of the amicable dispositions of China.

Besides, by every article of the treaty, several times ten in number, your country is a gainer, and to no slight extent.

The assent of his majesty the emperor to every proposition really showed an extraordinary desire to accommodate a large abundance of kindly feeling.

The condition of residence at Pekin is very irksome to China, and as the French and Americans have not this privilege (*lit.*, article), and it is only your nation that has, we beg your excellency to consider what compromise may be effected, and to dispense with its peremptory (enforcement).

Should such an arrangement be agreed on as is proposed, the emperor will still specially depute, on the part of China, a chief secretary of state, or president of a board, to reside in the provinces, at whatever point the high officer sent by your excellency's government may see fit to choose for his residence. When Nankin is retaken, he may, if it suit him, reside at Nankin.

The several provisions of the treaty recently concluded are, without doubt, to be observed (or will be sure to be observed) from this time forth for evermore. On the violation of any of them, it will be open (to the minister) to establish himself permanently at the capital.

In making this request we have not the smallest intention of violating the treaty. We write to propose that the point be reconsidered in our behalf simply because the words "either" and "or" leave it undecided, and we trust your excellency will yield it.

If there be any thing else which may be to the advantage of your country, without doing injury to ours, it will be similarly for us to consider the means of accommodating you.

A necessary communication addressed to the Earl of Elgin, etc.

Hien-fung, 8th year, 9th moon, 10th day (October 22, 1858).

* *Lit.*, because of some little thing, agitation, or ferment, should grow to great hurt.

Inclosure 2 in No. 216.

The Earl of Elgin to Commissioners Kweiliang, Hwashana, etc.

The undersigned has the honor to acknowledge the receipt of the imperial commissioner's letter of the 22d instant.

The commissioners express a hope that the undersigned will consent to the establishment of her majesty's minister in China at some other place than Pekin. They base their appeal to the undersigned upon the wording of Article III. of the Treaty of Tientsin, which they quote.

It is the duty of the undersigned at once to declare emphatically that it is not in his power to alter or modify the conditions of the treaty signed at Tientsin. It must rest with her Britannic majesty alone to decide which of the two courses left open by treaty to her majesty is the more expedient—the permanent residence of her representative at the capital, or his occasional appearance there. The undersigned would, moreover, impress upon the commissioners that, in insisting on the insertion of the article in question in the treaty, he was actuated by no intention to do injury to China, but by an earnest desire to obtain the best possible security for the preservation of peace between the two countries.

It is the usage of England, France, America, Russia, and every other power in the Western world, to maintain representatives at each other's capitals. These being in direct communication with high officers specially appointed to administer foreign affairs, the contingency of serious differences has been found to be, in a great measure, averted.

It has been the custom with China to intrust the administration of foreign affairs to an imperial commissioner at a great distance from the capital.

The result has been a succession of misunderstandings between that officer and the representatives of foreign nations. The court of Pekin has persisted in ignoring all complaints against this functionary, whose reports to it, on the other hand, have not been either complete or exact.

Hence all that has happened of hostility; and it was to secure such a guarantee as the practice of Western nations has shown to be of some avail against the recurrence of wars, to ward off the necessity for farther capture of cities and destruction of forts, that the undersigned, under the instruction of her majesty's government, demanded access for her majesty's representative to the capital.

The right of that officer to reside at Pekin, if her majesty shall see fit, being determined by treaty, the undersigned begs to repeat that no act or word of his can restrict its exercise as the commissioners propose; nor, indeed, will he lightly undertake, the great object of the treaty concession considered, to recommend its restriction.

That object has been clearly stated to the commissioners, and the undersigned really fears that it will not be in the power of their excellencies to offer any guarantee for the good faith of the imperial government, and for the maintenance of peace between the countries, equivalent to that which would be furnished by the permanent residence of a British minister at Pekin.

Shanghai, October 25, 1858.

(Signed), ELGIN AND KINCARDINE.

Inclosure 3 in No. 216.

Commissioners Kweiliang, Hwashana, etc., to the Earl of Elgin.

(*Translation.*)

Kwei, a Chief Secretary, etc.; Hwa, President of the Board of Civil Office; Ho, Governor General of the Two Kiang; Ming, a high officer of the Household; Twan, a titulary President, Imperial Commissioners, make a communication in reply.

We are in receipt of your excellency's letter of the (25th October), to the effect that when you insisted in Article III. of the Treaty of Tientsin that her Britannic majesty's representatives should either reside in permanence at the capital, or visit it from time to time, you were actuated by no unfriendly feeling toward China, but, on the contrary, by a sincere desire for the continuance of peace between the two countries, and that, the importance considered of the condition regarding the permanent residence of the British minister at Pekin, viewed as a guarantee of good faith on the part of China, and uninterruptedness of friendly relations between our two countries, it will be difficult for us, you fear, to substitute any guarantee of equal value.

Inasmuch as in the Treaty of Peace concluded between our two nations, it is laid down that the British minister shall either reside in permanence at the capital or visit it occasionally, at the option of the British government, such being the plain language of the article, it must doubtless be abided by; and if it be the fixed purpose of your excellency's government that the residence (of the minister) shall be permanent, China can not, of course, gainsay this.

The established reputation of your excellency for justice and straightforwardness, for kind intentions and friendly feeling, make us place the fullest confidence in your assurance that when you exacted the condition referred to, you were actuated by no desire whatever to do injury to China. The permanent residence of foreign ministers at the capital would, notwithstanding, be an injury to China in many more ways than we can find words to express. In sum, in the present critical and troublous state of our country, this incident would generate, we fear, a loss of respect for their government in the eyes of her people; and that this would indeed be no slight evil, it will not be necessary, we assume, to explain to your excellency, with greater detail.

It is for this reason that we specially address you a second letter on this subject, and we trust that your excellency will represent for us to her majesty your sovereign the great inconvenience you feel (the exercise of the right would be) to our country, and beseech her not to decide in favor of the permanent residence at Pekin.

When we bethink us of the lustre shed by the well-doing and justice of her majesty, we feel assured that she would not wish, by being peremptory in a matter so hurtful to our country, to involve it in embarrassment; and our country will not fail to be impressed with gratitude.

We are ourselves in perfect good faith, and if there be any method of proceeding by adopting which we demonstrate our sincerity, we beg your excellency to state it frankly; there is no satisfactory arrangement we are not ready to make.

It is our earnest hope the present feeling may be constantly observed on both sides, and that our two countries, evermore at peace with one another, may continue in the enjoyment of comfort and advantage.

A necessary communication, etc.

Hien-fung, 8th year, 9th moon, 22d day (October 28, 1858).

Inclosure 4 in No. 216.

The Earl of Elgin to Commissioners Kweiliang, Hwashana, etc.

The undersigned has the honor to acknowledge the imperial commissioners' letter of the 28th instant.

The imperial commissioners observe that if, in accordance with the plain language of the treaty-stipulations, her majesty's government shall determine to place the British minister in permanence at Pekin, it is impossible for China to gainsay this determination. This is doubtless a correct appreciation of the inviolability of the conditions by treaty agreed to.

Their excellencies admit, at the same time, their faith in the undersigned's assurance that this treaty-right was not insisted on by the undersigned with any intention to do injury to China, but, on the contrary, in a sincere desire to secure a continuance of peace between the two countries. Their excellencies, he begs to assure them, do no more than justice to the intentions of the undersigned.

The exercise of the treaty-right in question, their letter proceeds to urge, is, notwithstanding, of serious prejudice to China, mainly because, in her present crisis of domestic troubles, it would tend to cause a loss of respect for their government in the minds of her subjects; and their excellencies accordingly request the undersigned to beseech her majesty, to whom the treaty undoubtedly leaves it to determine whether or not her representatives shall permanently reside at the capital, or occasionally visit it, to decide in favor of the latter course.

Their proposal has been attentively considered by the undersigned; and he now begs to state that, although he is resolved by no act or word to abate one tittle of the rights secured to his government by treaty, it is his wish, so far as such a course is consistent with his duty, to endeavor to reconcile due consideration of the feelings of the Chinese government with the satisfaction of the rights of his own. He is prepared, consequently, on viewing the whole of the circumstances before him, at once to communicate to her majesty's government the representations that have been addressed to him by their excellencies the imperial commissioners upon this important question, and humbly to submit it as his opinion that if her majesty's embassador be properly received at Pekin when the ratifications are exchanged next year, and full effect given in all other particulars to the treaty negotiated at Tientsin, it would certainly be expedient that her majesty's representative in China should be instructed to choose a place of residence elsewhere than at Pekin, and to make his visits to the capital either periodical, or only as frequent as the exigencies of the public service may require.

Her majesty's treaty-right will, of course, in any case, remain intact; but the undersigned will take on himself so to express his conviction that, so long as the imperial government adheres with fidelity to its obligations toward England, China will have no cause to complain of a want of consideration on the part of the government of her Britannic majesty.

The anxiety expressed by their excellencies for an enduring continuance of peace is not stronger than the desire of the undersigned for an improvement of the friendly relations which he trusts from this time forth are now established between the two countries; and, with a view to the removal of all doubts and misgivings, he begs to add that if, in the opinion of the commissioners, the discussion of any proposition of common interest would be rendered easier or more advantageous by personal explanation, the undersigned is willing to confer with their excellencies whenever an interview may be convenient to them. (Signed), ELGIN AND KINCARDINE.

No. III.

THE TREATY OF YEDO.

INCLOSURE IN No. 200.

Treaty of Peace, Friendship, and Commerce, between Her Majesty and the Tycoon of Japan. Signed in the English, Japanese, and Dutch languages, at Yedo, August 26, 1858.

Her majesty the Queen of the United Kingdom of Great Britain and Ireland, and his majesty the Tycoon of Japan, being desirous to place the relations between the two countries on a permanent and friendly footing, and to facilitate commercial intercourse between their respective subjects, and having for that purpose resolved to enter into a treaty of Peace, Amity, and Commerce, have named as their plenipotentiaries, that is to say:

Her majesty the Queen of Great Britain and Ireland, the Right Honorable the Earl of Elgin and Kincardine, a Peer of the United Kingdom, and Knight of the Most Ancient and Most Noble Order of the Thistle:

And his majesty the Tycoon of Japan, Midzno Tsikfogono Kami; Nagai Gembano Kami; Inouwye Sinano no Kami; Hori Oribeno Kami: Iwase Higono Kami; and Tsuda Hanzabro;

Who, after having communicated to each other their respective full powers, and found them to be in good and due form, have agreed upon and concluded the following articles:

ARTICLE I.

There shall be perpetual peace and friendship between her majesty the Queen of the United Kingdom of Great Britain and Ireland, her heirs and successors, and his majesty the Tycoon of Japan, and between their respective dominions and subjects.

ARTICLE II.

Her majesty the Queen of Great Britain and Ireland may appoint a diplomatic agent to reside at the city of Yedo, and consuls or consular agents to reside at any or all the ports of Japan which are opened for British commerce by this treaty.

The diplomatic agent and consul general of Great Britain shall have the right to travel freely to any part of the empire of Japan.

His majesty the Tycoon of Japan may appoint a diplomatic agent to reside in London, and consuls, or consular agents, at any or all the ports of Great Britain.

The diplomatic agent and consul general of Japan shall have the right to travel freely to any part of Great Britain.

ARTICLE III.

The ports and towns of Hakodadi, Kanagawa, and Nagasaki shall be opened to British subjects on the first of July, one thousand eight hundred and fifty-nine. In addition to which, the following ports and towns shall be opened to them at the dates hereinafter specified:

Nee-e-gata, or, if Nee-e-gata be found to be unsuitable as a harbor, another convenient port on the west coast of Nipon, on the first day of January, one thousand eight hundred and sixty.

Hiogo, on the first day of January, one thousand eight hundred and sixty-three.

In all the foregoing ports and towns British subjects may permanently reside. They shall have the right to lease ground, and purchase the buildings thereon, and may erect dwelling and warehouses; but no fortification, or place of military strength, shall be erected under pretense of building dwelling or warehouses: and to see that this article is observed, the Japanese authorities shall have the right to inspect, from time to time, any buildings which are being erected, altered, or repaired.

The place which British subjects shall occupy for their buildings, and the harbor regulations, shall be arranged by the British consul and the Japanese authorities of each place, and, if they can not agree, the matter shall be referred to and settled by the British diplomatic agent and the Japanese government. No wall, fence, or gate shall be erected by the Japanese around the place where British subjects reside, or any thing done which may prevent a free egress or ingress to the same.

British subjects shall be free to go where they please, within the following limits, at the opened ports of Japan.

At Kanagawa to the River Logo (which empties into the bay of Yedo, between Kawasaki and Sinagowa), and ten *ri* in any direction.

At Hakodadi, ten *ri* in any direction.

At Hiogo, ten *ri* in any direction, that of Kioto excepted, which city shall not be approached nearer than ten *ri*. The crews of vessels resorting to Hiogo shall not cross the river Euagawa, which empties into the bay between Hiogo and Osaca.

The distance shall be measured by land from the goyoso, or town-hall, of each of the foregoing ports, the *ri* being equal to four thousand two hundred and seventy-five yards English measure.

At Nagasaki, British subjects may go into any part of the imperial domain in its vicinity.

The boundaries of Nee-e-gata, or the place that may be substituted for it, shall be settled by the British diplomatic agent and the government of Japan.

From the first day of January, one thousand eight hundred and sixty-two, British subjects shall be allowed to reside in the city of Yedo, and from the first day of January, one thousand eight hundred and sixty-three, in the city of Osaca, for the purposes of trade only. In each of these two cities a suitable place, within which they may hire houses, and the distance they may go, shall be arranged by the British diplomatic agent and the government of Japan.

ARTICLE IV.

All questions in regard to rights, whether of property or person, arising between British subjects in the dominions of his majesty the Tycoon of Japan, shall be subject to the jurisdiction of the British authorities.

ARTICLE V.

Japanese subjects, who may be guilty of any criminal act toward British subjects, shall be arrested and punished by the Japanese authorities, according to the laws of Japan.

British subjects, who may commit any crime against Japanese subjects, or the subjects or citizens of any other country, shall be tried and punished by the consul, or other public functionary authorized thereto, according to the laws of Great Britain.

Justice shall be equitably and impartially administered on both sides.

ARTICLE VI.

A British subject having reason to complain of a Japanese, must proceed to the consulate and state his grievance.

The consul will inquire into the merits of the case, and do his utmost to arrange it amicably. In like manner, if a Japanese have reason to complain of a British subject, the consul shall no less listen to his complaint, and endeavor to settle it in a friendly manner. If disputes take place of such a nature that the consul can not arrange them amicably, then he shall request the assistance of the Japanese authorities, that they may together examine into the merits of the case, and decide it equitably.

ARTICLE VII.

Should any Japanese subject fail to discharge debts incurred to a British subject, or should he fraudulently abscond, the Japanese authorities will do their utmost to bring him to justice, and to enforce recovery of the debts; and should any British subject fraudulently abscond or fail to discharge debts incurrred by him to a Japanese subject, the British authorities will, in like manner, do their utmost to bring him to justice, and to enforce the recovery of the debts.

Neither the British or Japanese governments are to be held responsible for the payment of any debts contracted by British or Japanese subjects.

ARTICLE VIII.

The Japanese government will place no restrictions whatever upon the employment, by British subjects, of Japanese in any lawful capacity.

ARTICLE IX.

British subjects in Japan shall be allowed the free exercise of their religion, and for this purpose shall have the right to erect suitable places of worship.

ARTICLE X.

All foreign coin shall be current in Japan, and shall pass for its corresponding weight in Japanese coin of the same description.

British and Japanese subjects may freely use foreign or Japanese coin in making payments to each other.

As some time will elapse before the Japanese will become acquainted with the value of foreign coin, the Japanese government will, for the period of one year after the opening of each port, furnish British subjects with Japanese coin in exchange for theirs, equal weights being given, and no discount taken for recoinage.

Coin of all description (with the exception of Japanese copper coin), as well as foreign gold and silver uncoined, may be exported from Japan.

ARTICLE XI.

Supplies for the use of the British navy may be landed at Kanagawa, Hakodadi, and Nagasaki, and stored in warehouses, in the custody of an officer of the British government, without the payment of any duty; but if any such supplies are sold in Japan, the purchaser shall pay the proper duty to the Japanese authorities.

ARTICLE XII.

If any British vessel be at any time wrecked or stranded on the coasts of Japan, or be compelled to take refuge in any port within the dominions of the Tycoon of

Japan, the Japanese authorities, on being apprised of the fact, shall immediately render all the assistance in their power; the persons on board shall receive friendly treatment, and be furnished, if necessary, with the means of conveyance to the nearest consular station.

ARTICLE XIII.

Any British merchant-vessel arriving off one of the open ports of Japan shall be at liberty to hire a pilot to take her into port. In like manner, after she has discharged all legal dues and duties, and is ready to take her departure, she shall be allowed to hire a pilot to conduct her out of port.

ARTICLE XIV.

At each of the ports open to trade, British subjects shall be at full liberty to import from their own or any other ports, and sell there, and purchase therein, and export to their own or any other ports, all manner of merchandise, not contraband, paying the duties thereon, as laid down in the tariff annexed to the present treaty, and no other charges whatsoever.

With the exception of munitions of war, which shall only be sold to the Japanese government and foreigners, they may freely buy from Japanese, and sell to them, any articles that either may have for sale, without the intervention of any Japanese officers in such purchase or sale, or in making or receiving payments for the same; and all classes of Japanese may purchase, sell, keep, or use any articles sold to them by British subjects.

ARTICLE XV.

If the Japanese Custom-house officers are dissatisfied with the value placed on any goods by the owner, they may place a value thereon, and offer to take the goods at that valuation. If the owner refuses to accept the offer, he shall pay duty on such valuation. If the offer be accepted by the owner, the purchase-money shall be paid to him without delay, and without any abatement or discount.

ARTICLE XVI.

All goods imported into Japan by British subjects, and which have paid the duty fixed by this treaty, may be transported by the Japanese into any part of the empire without the payment of any tax, excise, or transit-duty whatever.

ARTICLE XVII.

British merchants who may have imported merchandise into any open port in Japan, and paid duty thereon, shall be entitled, on obtaining from the Japanese Custom-house authorities a certificate stating that such payment has been made, to re-export the same, and land it in any other of the open ports without the payment of any additional duty whatever.

ARTICLE XVIII.

The Japanese authorities at each port will adopt the means that they may judge most proper for the prevention of fraud or smuggling.

ARTICLE XIX.

All penalties enforced, or confiscations made under this treaty, shall belong to, and be appropriated by, the government of his majesty the Tycoon of Japan.

ARTICLE XX.

The articles for the regulation of trade which are appended to this treaty shall be considered as forming part of the same, and shall be equally binding on both the contracting parties to this treaty and on their subjects.

The diplomatic agent of Great Britain in Japan, in conjunction with such person or persons as may be appointed for that purpose by the Japanese government, shall have power to make such rules as may be required to carry into full and complete effect the provisions of this treaty, and the provisions of the articles regulating trade appended thereto.

ARTICLE XXI.

This treaty being written in the English, Japanese, and Dutch languages, and all the versions having the same meaning and intention, the Dutch version shall be considered the original; but it is understood that all official communications addressed by the diplomatic and consular agents of her majesty the Queen of Great Britain to the Japanese authorities shall henceforward be written in English. In order, however, to facilitate the transaction of business, they will, for a period of five years from the signature of this treaty, be accompanied by a Dutch or Japanese version.

ARTICLE XXII.

It is agreed that either of the high contracting parties to this treaty, on giving one year's previous notice to the other, may demand a revision thereof, on or after the first of July, one thousand eight hundred and seventy-two, with a view to the insertion therein of such amendments as experience shall prove to be desirable.

ARTICLE XXIII.

It is hereby expressly stipulated that the British government and its subjects will be allowed free and equal participation in all privileges, immunities, and advantages that may have been, or may be hereafter, granted by his majesty the Tycoon of Japan to the government or subjects of any other nation.

ARTICLE XXIV.

The ratification of this treaty, under the hand of her majesty the Queen of Great Britain and Ireland, and under the name and seal of his majesty the Tycoon of Japan, respectively, shall be exchanged at Yedo within a year from this day of signature.

In token whereof, the respective plenipotentiaries have signed and sealed this treaty.

Done at Yedo, this twenty-sixth day of August, one thousand eight hundred and fifty-eight, corresponding to the Japanese date, the eighteenth day of the seventh month of the fifth year of Ansei Tsut sinonye mma.

(Signed), ELGIN AND KINCARDINE.
MIDZNO TSIKFOGONO KAMI.
NAGAI GEMBANO KAMI.
INOUWTE SINANO NO KAMI.
HORI ORIBENO KAMI.
IWASE HIGONO KAMI.
TSUDA HANZABRO.

No. IV.
TRADE RETURNS BETWEEN SHANGHAI AND JAPAN.

IMPORTS FROM JAPAN FROM 11TH NOV. TO 31ST DEC., 1858.

Dried fish	150 peculs.	Seaweed	30 peculs.
Ginseng	18,474 catties.	Shark-fins	24 —
Mussels	35 peculs.	Vegetable wax	1206 —
Rice	1200 —		

FROM 1ST JANUARY TO 30TH JUNE, 1859.

Beeswax	54 peculs.	Isinglass (Kanting)	1551 peculs.
Bicho de Mar	377 —	Medicines	108 —
Brooms	1000 pieces.	Mushrooms	226 —
Candles	60 peculs.	Mussels	28 —
Camphor	97 —	Nut-galls	1050 —
Cassia	77 —	Oil, vegetable	4786 —
Copper wire	5 —	Paper	180 —
Cotton manufactures	3200 pieces.	Peas and beans	4180 —
Coal	4955 tons.	Rice	13,546 —
Dried fish	2335 peculs.	Raw silk	366.42 peculs.
Flax	4 —	Seaweed, all kinds	61,561 peculs.
Flour	130 —	Shark-fins	1051 —
Fungus	9 —	Silk piece-goods	70.28 peculs.
Ginger	3 —	Soy	562 peculs.
Ginseng	36,746 catties.	Vermicelli	459 —
Hemp cloth	589 pieces.	Wax, vegetable	3469 —
Imitation leather ware	4 peculs.	Wheat	5537 —
Japan root	75 —		

RE-IMPORTS.

Alum	625 peculs.	Muslins	100 pieces.
Cambrics	200 pieces.	Iron wire	33 peculs.
Cochineal	360 catties.	Pepper, black	8 —
Cottons, dyed	274 pieces.	Quicksilver	50 flasks.
" fancy	400 —	Rhubarb	109 peculs.
" printed	8338 —	Sugar	5094 —
Dates	34 peculs.	Tin	32 —
Goats' horns	2 —	" plates	379 boxes.
Handkerchiefs	6296 dozen.	Tortoise-shell	2 peculs.
Long ells	40 pieces.	Velvets and velveteens	420 pieces.
Medicines	111 peculs.	Window-glass	15 boxes.
Lead	704 —	Spanish stripes	48 pieces.
Iron	1352 —	Woolen and cotton mixtures	528 —
Indigo	50 —		

EXPORTS TO JAPAN FROM 27TH NOV. TO 31ST DEC., 1858.

Cotton, printed	1500 pieces.	Betelnut	292 peculs.
Camlets	120 —	Cloves	200 —
Cottons, dyed	300 —	Cutch	250 —
Handkerchiefs	2506 dozen.	Gamboge	1 —
Long cloths, gray	2850 pieces.	Indigo	75 —
Long ells	220 —	Liquorice	27 peculs.
Muslins	100 —	Mangrove bark	50 —
Spanish stripes	228 —	Medicines	19 —
Spelter	500 peculs.	Matting	5 bundles.
Tin	325 —	Paper, native	2 peculs.
" plates	450 boxes.	Redwood	300 —

EXPORTS TO JAPAN FROM 27TH NOV. TO 31ST DEC., 1858—*continued*.

Rosewood	500 peculs.		Tortoise-shell	2 peculs.
Rhubarb	132 —		Turmeric	1 —
Sapanwood	2736 —		Window-glass	6 boxes.

FROM 1ST JANUARY TO 30TH JUNE, 1859.

Broadcloths	280 pieces.		Ebony	350 peculs.
Cambrics	400 —		Eggs, preserved	1500 pieces.
Camlets	395 —		Fans	467 —
Cottons, dyed	7680 —		Galangal	185 peculs.
" fancy	3843 —		Gamboge	18 —
" printed	11,793 —		Garroo-wood	30 —
Damasks	1405 —		Ginseng	13.20 peculs.
Dimities	200 —		Goats' hair	34 peculs.
Drills, gray	420 —		Gold thread	4 cases.
Handkerchiefs	19,005 dozen.		Gum, dragons' blood	1.68 peculs.
Lastings	46 pieces.		" myrrh	2.50 —
Long cloths, gray	15,198 —		" olibanum	103 peculs.
" white	3600 —		Gypsum	1886 —
Long ells	140 —		Hartall	156 —
Muslins	625 —		Indigo	252 —
Spanish stripes	103 —		Ink, India	7 —
Twills, gray	300 —		Joss-sticks	5 —
Velvets and velveteens	3448 —		Laka-wood	13 —
Woolen and cotton mixtures	867 —		Lamp-wicks	10 —
			Liquorice	771 —
Window-glass	21 boxes.		Medicines	2748 —
Iron, nail, rod, and bar	1352 peculs.		Mangrove bark	1914 —
Iron wire	33 —		Matting	2058 bundles.
Lead	824 —		Nankeen towels	200 pieces.
Quicksilver	78 —		Nutmegs	19 peculs.
Spelter	852 —		Orange peel	3 —
Steel	55 —		Paper	142 —
Tin plates	184 boxes.		Pepper, black	120 —
Tin	60 peculs.		Putchuck	66 —
Amber	15 —		Ratans	1706 —
Aniseed	276 —		Redwood	720 —
Alum	1875 —		Red and yellow lead	90 —
Betelnut	1255 —		Rhinoceros horns	3 —
" husk	39 —		Rhubarb	425 —
Birds' nests	6 —		Sandalwood	137 —
Buffalo horns	17 —		Sapanwood	2076 —
Camphor, native	2 —		Seaweed	70 —
Cardamum	32 —		Shark-skins	53 —
Carpets	2800 pieces.		Sheep-skins	4272 pieces.
Cassia buds	5 peculs.		Silk piece-goods	14 peculs.
Chestnut	97 —		Sugar	10,507 —
China root	25 —		" candy	1257 —
" pencils	43,000 pieces.		Sticklac	30 —
Cinnamon	2 peculs.		Straw shoes	586 pairs.
Cloves	782 —		Tortoise-shell	5 peculs.
Clamp shells	14 —		Tinfoil	4 —
Cocoanut husk	14 —		Turmeric	388 —
Colors	8 —		Vermilion	135 —
Copperfoil	5 —		Woodware	2 —
Cutch	218 —		Leather cushions	183 pieces.
Dates	213 —		Liquorice	771 peculs.
Dye stuff	68 —		Lucraban seed	487 —
Earthenware	540 pieces.			

APPENDIX. 687

No. V.

List of Articles generally sold, and of Staples found in the Shops at Han-kow, when visited by H. M. Steam-ship "Furious," Dec., 1858.

District Number	Nature	Of Piece. Length.			Of Piece. Breadth.			Price. Of Piece.	Price. Per Yard, Foot, etc.	Remarks
		Yds	Feet	In.	Yds	Feet	In.			
1	Native Linen	6	0	9	0	0	10½	260 cash*	2s each per yard	*These remarks were made at Shanghai.*
2	do.	5	0	9	0	0	10½	220 do.	2s do. do.	Assorted chintz (7 Pundrelas), 2¾ by 2⅜, val. 1 dol. 40c., lately 2 dol. 50c.
3	Native Cotton	4.5	0	6	0	0	11	450 do.	60 do. do.	Assorted brocade, 40 by 36 in., value 3 dollars 1 cent to 4 taels.
4	do.	5	1	0	0	0	11	240 do.	43 do. do.	Do.
5	do.	5	1	0	0	0	10	220 do.	43 do. do.	Dyed twills—usually 28 inches broad, lengths vary 40 yards to 36 yards.
6	do.	5	2	6	0	0	10	220 do.	40 do. do.	64-reed gray sheeting, 38¼ yds. by 39 in., val. in Shanghai, 2 dol. per piece.
7	do.	5	2	3	0	0	11	205 do.	46 do. do.	
8	do.	5	1	0	0	0	10½	240 do.	43 do. do.	
9	Foreign Manufacture	2	0	0	0	0	3	800 cash per chang†	213 do. do.	This iron comes from the province of Honan, and town or district of Chang-sdm.
10	do.	3	2	0	1	0	3	900 do.	240 do. do.	£4.—The 1st quality was severely tested by engineers at Shanghai—found to be as good as the best Swedish.
11	do.	1	2	0	0	2	3	800 do.	213 do. do.	
12	do.	2	2	3	0	0	5	750 do.	200 do. do.	
13	do.	3	2	0	1	0	3	420 do.	132 do. do.	
	Bar Iron, 1st quality	Pied of 150 catties						4400 each per picul 2400 to 2800 do.	3l·07 each per cwt. 2016 to 2352 each per cwt.	
	do. 2d do.	" 100 "								
	Copper, 1st quality	(From Yunan and Kwei-chang)						560 each per catty	42l·12 each per cwt.	
	do. 2d do.	province						300 do. do.	25·56 do. do.	
	Insect Wax, 1st quality	In large quantities, 400 each per catty						440 do. do.	250 each per lb., avoirdu.	
	Raw silk, 1st quality	The tael is equal to 6s. 8d. sterling						200 taels per picul.	5609 do.	
	Woolen Cloth (Foreign)	Very coarse and rough, no gloss, but strong; said to come from the North (Russia). The Chinese foot is equal to 14.3 inches English.						1300 each per Chinese foot	3342 each per yard	This is grown about Han-kow, and used for making linen as well as rope. At Ningpo the same flax costs respectively 164 and 140 cash per catty.
	Flax, 1st quality							80 each per catty	6·39 each per cwt.	
	do. 2d do.							70 do. do.	5·36 do. do.	

* 1000 cash are equal to the dollar at 59 pence English.   † A chang is equal to 3 yards 2 feet 3 inches English.

SHERARD OSBORN, *Captain.*

No. VI.
NOTE ON PROSTITUTION.

Though the "social evil" is never an agreeable subject to treat of, it enters into the manners and customs of the people in a manner so singular, and at the same time so prominent, that no account of Japan would be complete without some allusion to it. The same order which governs all the other institutions of the country is applied to this one. There is nothing slovenly in the mode of administration. Vice itself is systematized. Thus courtesans are divided into four classes, and are held in various degrees of estimation according to their rank in the social scale. Two distinct quarters of this vast city of Yedo are set apart for purposes of debauchery. The eastern suburb, which seems to be frequented by the middle and lower classes, contains persons of the second and third class, and is simply a den of infamy where the poor creatures flaunt about the streets, as they do in our own large cities.

Sinagawa, however, is the resort of the aristocracy. Hither noblemen repair with their wives and families, to pass an hour or two in the society of women who are considered the most highly accomplished of their sex. Not only are they expert in music, singing, painting, dancing, and embroidery, but it is said that they are highly educated, and charm by reason of their conversational powers.

Although it is usual to visit such resorts "nayboen," it is considered no disgrace for the master of the house to be accompanied by the female members of his family. Nor is it any uncommon thing for a man of rank to choose his wife from an establishment of this description. That a woman should have been brought up in one of them operates in no way unfavorably against her in a social point of view; nor after her eyebrows are pulled out, and her teeth blackened, is she less likely to make a good wife than any one else. It would, indeed, be somewhat unfair upon her if she suffered for this accident of her early life, for she is bought as a mere child by the degraded men who speculate in this trade, of indigent parents, who are unable to maintain a family of girls, and at the age of seven or eight enters the establishment. Her first years are spent in her education, and after she is grown up her master is ready to part with her whenever he receives a fair offer.

As it was just at the gayest hour of the festive day that we rode through Sinagawa, every house contributed its swarms of gazers; on each side their faces, painted in pink and white, rose in tiers above each other. I could not judge of the numbers, but they were to be estimated by thousands rather than hundreds. The houses were handsomer than any I had seen in Yedo, except the residences of the princes. We could generally see through them into court-yards, where fountains played in cool gardens.

It would seem that the government not only sanctions by license these establishments, but lends itself to the still farther disgrace of deriving a direct revenue from this infamous source.

Mr. Loch obtained upon good authority the following curious information upon the subject, with which he has kindly furnished me:

"Prostitution is supported and protected by the government, large districts being set apart for the residence of the females, who are kept under strict surveillance. Parents who are unable, or disinclined to bring up their female children, can sell them to government between the ages of six and ten. Until they are fourteen they remain as servants, and are educated in various domestic duties, such as cooking, housekeeping, etc. At that age they come on the regular establishment, are open to the public, and are obliged to serve in this capacity for ten years. Should any man, before that period elapses, wish to marry any one of them, he must pay the government a sum of money for permission to do so; her name, however, being still retained on the books. Should no such offer be made, at the expiry of the ten years she is returned to her parents or friends, with a small sum of money, and having been taught some employment. No disgrace attaches to women who have been brought up in this manner, and they generally make good marriages; but should she be guilty, after marriage, of any indiscretion, it is in her case (as in that of every Japanese wife) punishable by death."

No. VII.
THERMOMETRICAL REGISTER KEPT BY DR. SAUNDERS, R.N.,
From April 1, 1858, to March 31, 1859.

Date, 1858.	Position.	Ther. in Shade, 7 A.M.	Ther. in Shade, 4 P.M.	Extreme Heat.	Extreme Cold.	Wind.	Weather.
April 1	At Shanghai	60	..	70	58	W.	Showery.
2	do.	50	..	67	50	N.W.	Fine.
3	do.	46	..	54	46	S.	Fine.
Sund. 4	do.	46	..	57	46	N.E.	Fine.
5	do.	52	..	55	45	E.	Rainy.
6	do.	51	..	57	50	E.	Rainy.
7	do.	51	..	55	50	S.E.	Rainy.
8	do.	51	..	54	51	E.	Fine.
9	do.	51	..	55	51	E.	Fine.
10	At Woosung	54	..	64	54	N.	Fine.
Sund. 11	Lat. 33° 16′ N., Long. 122° 55′ E.	55	..	60	54	E.	Fine.
12	35° 47′ N., 123° 13′ E.	50	..	54	49	N.E.	Fine.
13	37° 19′ N., 121° 38′ E.	45	..	62	44	N.	Fine.
14	In Gulf of Pechelee	49	..	53	46	N.E.	Fine.
15	do.	50	..	54	48	N.E.	Fine.
16	do.	55	..	61	48	N.E.	Fine.
17	do.	53	..	59	53	W.	Fine.
Sund. 18	do.	50	..	62	49	S.W.	Rainy, and squally.
19	do.	58	..	65	49	S.W.	Fine, squally.
20	do.	53	..	66	52	N.	Fine.
21	do.	49	..	65	50	S.W.	Fine, squally.
22	do.	54	..	62	48	E.	Fine.
23	do.	47	..	58	42	E.	Foggy, squally.
24	do.	53	..	61	53	N.W.	Fine.
Sund. 25	do.	55	..	58	53	S.W.	Fine, strong breeze.
26	do.	51	..	60	51	S.E.	Rainy.
27	do.	50	..	59	50	N.W.	Foggy, fine.
28	do.	50	..	62	48	N.W.	Fine, gale.
29	do.	56	..	62	51	N.W.	Fine, strong breeze.
30	do.	60	..	74	60	W.	Foggy.
May 1	do.	60	..	68	60	S.W.	Foggy, fine.
Sund. 2	do.	58	..	66	58	N.E.	Rainy, squally.
3	do.	57	..	64	57	W.	Fine.
4	do.	57	..	67	57	N.W.	Fine.
5	do.	59	..	61	55	S.W.	Fine.
6	do.	58	..	64	58	S.	Rainy.
7	do.	57	..	64	57	S.W.	Fine.
8	do.	61	..	67	54	S.	Fine, squally.
Sund. 9	do.	61	..	61	59	S.E.	Showery, thun., etc.
10	do.	54	..	65	54	N.	Showery, squally.
11	do.	58	..	59	58	N.	Fine, strong breeze.
12	do.	60	..	60	59	S.W.	Fine, strong breeze.
13	do.	59	..	60	57	S.W.	Fine, strong breeze.
14	do.	60	..	68	60	S.	Fine.
15	do.	60	..	68	60	S.W.	Fine.
Sund. 16	do.	60	..	66	60	S.	Showery.
17	do.	57	..	65	63	N.	Showery.
18	do.	59	..	64	56	N.W.	Fine.
19	do.	63	..	63	53	W.	Fine.
20	do.	63	..	63	58	W.	Fine.
21	do.	64	..	64	55	S.W.	Fine.
22	do.	65	..	65	60	S.W.	Fine.
Sund. 23	do.	64	..	65	60	W.	Fine.
24	do.	66	..	70	62	S.W.	Fine.

APPENDIX. 641

Date. 1858.	Position.	Ther. in Shade, 8 A.M	Ther. in Shade, 4 P.M	Extreme Heat	Extreme Cold	Wind.	Weather.
May 25	In Gulf of Pechelee	67				S.	Fine.
26	do.	64				E.	Cloudy, strong br.
27	do.	64				N.	Fine.
28	do.	68	72			S.W.	Fine.
29	do.	69	73	79	69	S.W.	Fine.
Sund. 30	do.	68	71	71	68	S.E.	Fine.
31	do.	71	71	75	67	S.W.	Showery, squally.
June 1	do.	67	71	76	65	S.E.	Fine.
2	do.	71	80	85	68	S.	Showery.
3	do.	69	76	79	69	S.	Showery, thunder.
4	do.	72	82	82	71	S.W.	Fine.
5	In Peiho River	78	88	88	74	S.W.	Showery.
Sund. 6	At Tientsin	76	79	79	70	N.E.	Fine.
7	do.	72	75	82	65	N.W.	Showery, squally.
8	do.	62	72	72	62	N.W.	Showery, squally.
9	do.	65	74	74	63	N.W.	Fine, squally.
10	do.	65	76	76	62	N.E.	Fine.
11	do.	61	79	79	64	S.E.	Fine.
12	do.	68	75	77	67	E.	Fine.
Sund. 13	do.	67	71	73	67	E.	Showery.
14	do.	66	80	80	66	N.W.	Fine.
15	do.	72	83	84	72	S.W.	Showery, thun., etc.
16	do.	73	82	82	72	E.	Fine, squally.
17	do.	72	81	82	72	E.	Fine.
18	do.	75	83	86	73	N.	Showery, thun., etc.
19	do.	69	82	82	69	N.W.	Fine.
Sund. 20	do.	73	83	83	73	S.E.	Fine.
21	do.	73	70	74	70	N.E.	Rainy.
22	do.	68	77	77	68	E.	Fine.
23	do.	71	78	78	70	S.E.	Cloudy, thunder, etc.
24	do.	71	81	81	71	S.W.	Fine.
25	do.	71	83	83	71	S.E.	Fine.
26	do.	71	82	84	71	S.E.	Fine.
Sund. 27	do.	72	83	83	72	S.E.	Fine, thunder, etc.
28	do.	71	71	76	71	S.E.	Rainy, thunder, etc.
29	do.	69	76	77	69	S.E.	Fine.
30	do.	71	84	83	71	W.	Fine.
July 1	do.	71	82	83	71	S.	Fine.
2	do.	73	84	83	73	S.	Fine.
3	do.	79	91	91	78	S.W.	Fine.
Sund. 4	do.	81	92	96	80	W.	Fine.
5	do.	83	92	92	82	S.W.	Fine.
6	Steaming down Peiho River	81		92	81	S.E.	Fine.
7	In Gulf of Pechelee		83		83	S.E.	Fine.
8	Lat. 59° 56′ N., Long. 129° 5′ E.	78	80	80	78	N.	Rainy.
9	37° 49′ N., 122° 7′ E.	72	82	82	72	S.E.	Fine.
10	35° 15′ N., 122° 47′ E.	75	81	81	75	S.	Showery.
Sund. 11	32° 18′ N., 122° 50′ E.	81	83	83	80	S.W.	Fine.
12	At Shanghai	82	86	86	82	S.W.	Fine, lightning.
13	do.	85	91	91	83	S.	Fine, lightning.
14	do.	86	94	94	86	S.	Fine.
15	do.	86	92	92	86	Calm.	Fine.
16	do.	86	91			Calm.	Fine.
17	do.	86	93			Calm.	Fine.
Sund. 18	do.	87	93			Calm.	Cloudy, thunder, etc.
19	do.	81	86			Calm.	Showery.
20	do.	83	82			S.	Showery, thun., etc.
21	do.	83					Showery, thun., etc.
22	do.	81	81				Showery, thun., etc.
23	do.	79	83				Showery, thun., etc.
24	do.	79	86				Fine.

Date, 1858.	Position.	Ther. in Shade, 7 A.M.	Ther. in Shade, 4 P.M.	Extreme Heat.	Extreme Cold.	Wind.	Weather.
July, Sund. 25	At Shanghai	81	87	..	..	..	Fine.
26	do.	83	85	..	..	..	Fine.
27	do.	83	87	..	..	..	Squally, thun., etc.
28	do.	81	82	..	..	..	Showery, thun., etc.
29	do.	80	86	..	..	..	Fine.
30	do.	80	85	..	..	..	Fine.
31	Steaming down river	84	85	..	..	..	Fine.
Aug., Sund. 1	Lat. 31° 33′ N., Long. 125° 0′ E.	83	83	..	..	..	Showery.
2	31° 51′ N., 127° 38′ E.	83	84	..	..	..	Fine.
3	At Nagasaki, Japan	82	84	..	..	..	Showery.
4	do.	84	86	..	..	..	Fine.
5	32° 44′ N. do. 129° 52′ E.	83	87	..	..	..	Fine.
6	31° 0′ N. do. 130° 20′ E.	84	83	..	..	..	Showery.
7	Near Cape Chichacoff	84	84	..	..	S.W.	Showery, gale.
Sund. 8	Lat. 31° 21′ N., Long. 132° 5′ E.	84	85	..	..	S.W.	Showery, gale.
9	31° 51′ N., 136° 49′ E.	83	83	..	..	S.W.	Fine, strong breeze.
10	At Simoda, Japan	78	84	..	..	W.	Fine, strong breeze.
11	do.	80	84	..	..	W.	Fine.
12	At Yedo, Japan	78	84	..	..	W.	Fine, squally.
13	do.	82	80	..	..	S.W.	Showery, squally.
14	do.	73	76	..	..	E.	Rainy.
Sund. 15	do.	71	78	..	..	Calm.	Fine.
16	do.	73	72	..	..	N.E.	Showery.
17	do.	72	78	..	..	N.	Fine.
18	do.	73	77	..	..	..	Fine.
19	do.	71	76	..	..	..	Cloudy.
20	do.	68	..	..	..	..	Fine.
21	do.	75	81	..	..	..	Showery.
Sund. 22	do.	75	79	..	..	..	Rainy.
23	do.	77	80	..	..	..	Showery, strong br.
24	do.	76	85	..	..	..	Fine.
25	do.	75	84	..	..	..	Fine.
26	do.	73	..	..	..	..	Fine.
27	Steaming out of Yedo River	75	78	..	..	..	Fine.
28	Lat. 32° 54′ N., Long. 135° 33′ E.	81	82	..	..	..	Showery.
Sund. 29	31° 57′ N., 131° 51′ E.	83	80	..	..	..	Rainy, gale.
30	Cape Chichacoff	80	82	..	..	..	Showery, squally.
31	Lat. 31° 2′ N., Long. 125° 31′ E.	79	76	..	..	..	Showery, gale.
Sept. 1	30° 33′ N., 123° 53′ E.	74	79	82	70	N.W.	Showery, strong br.
2	In Woosung River	77	78	80	70	N.W.	Showery.
3	At Shanghai	74	81	..	..	N.W.	Fine, strong breeze.
4	do.	71	83	83	70	N.	Fine.
Sund. 5	do.	71	79	82	69	N.	Fine, strong breeze.
6	do.	73	82	84	68	S.E.	Fine.
7	do.	74	80	80	73	S.E.	Fine, squally.
8	do.	76	80	80	73	E.	Fine.
9	do.	78	85	85	74	S.E.	Fine.
10	do.	79	82	85	74	S.E.	Fine.
11	do.	79	80	80	75	E.	Showery, strong br.
Sund. 12	do.	79	80	80	76	E.	Cloudy, strong br.
13	do.	79	80	82	76	S.E.	Showery, strong br.
14	do.	79	81	81	75	S.E.	Showery.
15	do.	79	87	87	75	S.	Showery, lightning.
16	do.	78	77	82	72	N.W.	Rainy.
17	do.	76	78	80	70	S.E.	Showery.
18	do.	75	78	78	69	S.E.	Fine, strong breeze.
Sund. 19	do.	74	82	82	74	S.E.	Fine.
20	do.	78	83	85	69	S.	Fine.
21	do.	73	77	78	70	N.E.	Fine, strong breeze.
22	do.	75	77	79	69	S.E.	Fine.

APPENDIX. 643

Date, 1858.	Position.	Ther. in Shade, 7 A.M.	Ther. in Shade, 4 P.M.	Extreme Heat	Extreme Cold	Wind.	Weather.
Sept. 23	At Shanghai	75	75	75	66	N.	Rainy, squally.
24	do.	69	71	71	65	N.	Rainy, squally.
25	do.	68	73	74	63	N.W.	Fine.
Sund. 26	do.	67	75	77	65	E.	Fine.
27	do.	69	75	77	65	E.	Fine.
28	do.	71	75	77	66	E.	Fine.
29	do.	73	77	79	69	S.E.	Fine.
30	do.	73	80	81	70	S.	Showery.
Oct. 1	do.	70	65	71	61	N.	Cloudy, squally.
2	do.	64	71	72	60	N.W.	Fine.
Sund. 3	do.	65	74	74	64	N.E.	Fine.
4	do.	67	71	74	64	N.E.	Cloudy.
5	do.	67	72	73	60	E.	Fine.
6	do.	64	71	73	62	E.	Fine.
7	do.	63	72	72	62	S.E.	Fine.
8	do.	66	73	73	64	S.E.	Fine.
9	do.	65	73	73	64	S.E.	Fine.
Sund. 10	do.	65	70	71	64	E.	Rainy.
11	do.	66	72	73	60	N.E.	Fine.
12	do.	65	72	72	59	E.	Fine.
13	do.	63	72	73	61	E.	Fine.
14	do.	66	69	71	55	N.E.	Fine.
15	do.	57	69	69	57	E.	Fine.
16	do.	64	65	69	57	N.	Cloudy.
Sund. 17	do.	62	67	69	56	N.E.	Fine.
18	do.	59	67	69	56	N.E.	Fine.
19	do.	62	67	68	54	N.E.	Fine.
20	do.	56	67	68	54	N.	Fine.
21	do.	64	67	69	61	E.	Cloudy.
22	do.	63	69	69	53	S.E.	Fine.
23	do.	55	64	64	49	N.W.	Fine.
Sund. 24	do.	52	67	67	52	W.	Fine.
25	do.	52	68	68	52	E.	Fine.
26	do.	60	70	70	51	S.E.	Fine.
27	do.	53	70	70	52	W.	Fine.
28	do.	55	67	67	55	E.	Fine.
29	do.	60	71	71	56	S.E.	Fine.
30	do.	55	62	64	45	N.W.	Fine.
Sund. 31	do.	48	66	66	47	W.	Fine.
Nov. 1	do.	49	69	70	48	S.W.	Fine.
2	do.	50	69	70	49	W.	Fine.
3	do.	47	68	69	47	N.W.	Foggy, fine.
4	do.	53	62	63	48	N.E.	Fine.
5	do.	51	63	63	48	E.	Fine.
6	do.	55	67	67	46	W.	Fine.
Sund. 7	do.	50	66	69	42	N.W.	Fine.
8	Steaming down river	46	62	66	41	N.W.	Fine.
9	In Yang-tse-Keang	58	68	69	50	S.	Fine.
10	do.	57	67	71	47	W.	Fine.
11	Off Fooshan	55	66	66	43	N.W.	Fine.
12	do.	53	67	69	44	W.	Fine.
13	do.	56	67	73	51	W.	Fine.
Sund. 14	Between Fooshan and Kiang-yin	57	66	68	46	E.	Fine.
15	Near Kiang-yin	54	57	60	42	N.E.	Fine, strong breeze.
16	Silver Island Rock	37	53	55	36	E.	Fine.
17	do.	42	62	62	42	S.E.	Fine.
18	do.	49	?	66	47	N.E.	Fine.
19	do.	50	?	65	48		Fine.
20	Between Chin-kiang and Nanking	48	65	67	48	S.W.	Fine.
Sund. 21	Between Nenkin and Taiping	48	62	64	40	N.E.	Fine.
22	Off Taiping	46	61	61	45	S.E.	Fine.

Date, 1858.	Position.	Ther. in shade, 3 A.M.	Ther. in shade, 4 P.M.	Extreme Heat	Extreme Cold	Wind.	Weather.
Nov. 23	Between Taiping and Wuhu	45	65	65	45	W.	Fine.
24	Off Kewheen	50	62	62	42	W.	Fine.
25	Between Kewheen and Tsung-yang	46	63	63	44	N.W.	Fine.
26	Off Nganking-foo	49	62	62	45	N.	Fine.
27	Above Tungliu	48	65	65	48	N.	Fine.
Sund. 28	Near Pangtseh-hien	53	52	58	48	N.E.	Fine, strong breeze.
29	Off Hukau	31	48	48	28	N.E.	Fine.
30	Off Kiukiang-foo	39	?	44	31	E.	Fine.
Dec. 1	Between Kewkeang and Keehow	38	51	51	34	Calm.	Fine.
2	Passing Keehow	49	55	55	42	N.E.	Cloudy.
3	Between Keehow and Hwanchow	48	54	54	37	N.W.	Cloudy.
4	Above Hwanchow	43	53	53	37	E.	Showery.
Sund. 5	Between Hwanchow and Yanglo	47	48	50	43	E.	Rainy.
6	Between Yanglo and Hankow	36	?	48	36	E.	Foggy, fine.
7	At anchor off Hankow	43	57	57	39	N.E.	Fine.
8	do.	47	63	63	42	Calm.	Fine.
9	do.	52	54	57	48	N.E.	Rainy.
10	do.	45	57	57	39	N.E.	Fine.
11	do.	54	58	58	44	E.	Fine.
Sund. 12	Between Hankow and Hwanchow	50	?	59	47	E.	Foggy, showery.
13	Betw. Hwanchow and Woochang	35	56	56	35	N.	Fine.
14	Between Hwanchow and Paho	43	?	50	32	N.	Fine.
15	Between Paho and Shihwayu	37	51	51	31	S.E.	Fine.
16	Between Shihwayu and Wooseuh	43	43	52	43	S.E.	Rainy, hail.
17	Between Wooseuh and Kew-keang	44	45	53	44	S.E.	Rainy, squally.
18	do.	44	?	54	42	E.	Rainy, squally.
Sund. 19	do.	44	44	49	41	N.	Rainy.
20	Near Kew-keang	42	46	51	42	E.	Rainy.
21	At anchor below Kew-keang	47	?	57	42	W.	Rainy.
22	do.	43	46	54	43	E.	Rainy.
23	do.	43	?	49	39	W.	Rainy.
24	Between Kew-keang and Tungliu	44	46	50	42	N.E.	Rainy, strong breeze.
25	Between Tungliu and Nganking	43	45	47	41	N.E.	Rainy.
Sund. 26	Between Nganking and Toonglu	39	41	46	39	N.E.	Rain, snow.
27	Between Tookeaow and Woohoo	43	46	49	43	N.E.	Rainy.
28	Between Woohoo and Taiping	41	45	46	40	N.	Rainy.
29	Between Taiping and Nanking	39	39	44	37	N.E.	Snow.
30	Between Nanking and Chosan	34	38	46	34	N.E.	Snow.
31	Between Chosan and Plover P.	34	41	43	34	N.E.	Cloudy.
1859. Jan. 1	At Shanghai	36	47	47	33	W.	Fine.
Sund. 2	do.	32	33	37	28	N.W.	Fine.
3	do.	29	34	40	27	N.W.	Fine.
4	do.	23	38	40	23	S.W.	Fine.
5	do.	30	39	45	30	N.W.	Fine.
6	do.	26	43	47	26	N.W.	Fine.
7	do.	30	?	41	30	N.W.	Fine.
8	do.	29	41	45	29	E.	Fine.
Sund. 9	do.	36	51	54	36	S.	Fine.
10	do.	37	55	53	34	W.	Fine.
11	do.	31	45	52	31	N.W.	Fine.
12	do.	33	47	53	33	E.	Fine.
13	do.	36	53	56	36	W.	Fine.
14	do.	42	42	47	33	N.E.	Rainy, squally.
15	do.	29	37	49	28	N.W.	Fine.
Sund. 16	do.	27	39	44	27	W.	Fine.
17	do.	29	37	44	25	N.W.	Fine, squally.
18	do.	21	40	40	21	S.	Fine.
19	do.	35	55	55	35	S.	Fine.
20	do.	41	49	52	41	N.E.	Foggy.
21	do.	44	45	47	39	N.E.	Rainy.

APPENDIX.

Date, 1859.	Position.	Ther. in Shade, 4 A.M.	Ther. in Shade, 4 P.M.	Extreme Heat	Extreme Cold	Wind.	Weather.
Jan. 22	At Shanghai	39	42			N.	Rainy
Sund. 23	do.	37	34			N.W.	Rain, snow.
24	do.	34	41			N.	Cloudy.
25	do.	39	?			N.E.	Rainy.
26	Steaming down river	42	41		27	N.E.	Cloudy.
27	Anchor at Woosung	30	31		27	N.E.	Fine.
28	Steaming down river	34	43		26	N.N.E.	Fine.
29	Between Woosung and Hong Kong	49	50			N.N.E.	Cloudy.
Sund. 30	do.	54	54			N.N.E.	Misty rain.
31	do.	56	58			N.E.	Cloudy.
Feb. 1	Pedro Blanca in sight	59	66			³ N.	Fine.
2	Anchor at Hong Kong	56	57			² N.W.	Showery.
3	Canton River	53	54			³ N.	Cloudy.
4	do.	45	46			² N.W.	Rainy.
5	do.	44	?			² N.	Showery.
Sund. 6	do.	46	51			³ N.W.	Cloudy.
7	do.	48	55			² N.W.	Cloudy.
8	do.	46	61			¹ S.E.	Fine.
9	do.	54	64			¹ S.E.	Misty rain.
10	do.	59	69			Calm.	Fine.
11	do.	59	68			¹ N.W.	Fine.
12	do.	59	68			² W.	Fine.
Sund. 13	do.	54	69			² N.W.	Fine.
14	do.	52	69			² S.E.	Fine.
15	do.	59	71			Calm.	Fine.
16	Anchor at Macao	64	67			Calm.	Fine.
17	Between Macao and Hainan	58	63			N.E.	Fine.
18	Hainan	70	73			N.E.	Fine.
19	Hoilangshan	64	68		..	E.	Fine.
Sund. 20	St. John's	62	65		..	E.N.E.	Fine.
21	Between St. John's and C. R.	57	58		..	N.E.	Cloudy.
22	Hong Kong	53	60		..	N.	Fine.
23	do.	53	66		..	E.	Fine.
24	do.	53	60		..	E.	Showery.
25	do.	59	64		..	E.	Showery.
26	do.	65	73		..	¹ N.E.	Cloudy.
Sund. 27	do.	69	75		..	Calm.	Misty rain.
28	do.	73	73		..	Calm.	Cloudy.
Mar. 1	do.	73	74		..	Calm.	Showery.
2	Canton River	69	74		..	S.E.	Thund., lightg., etc.
3	do.	65	60		..	E.	Rainy.
4	Steaming out of river	51	56		..	N.E.	Cloudy.
5	Lat. N., Long. E.	71	74		..	E.	Fine.
Sund. 6		77	70		..	E.	Fine.
7	12° 40′ N., E.	80	82		..	E.	Fine.
8	10° 7′ N., E.	80	82		..	E.	Fine.
9	7° 23′ N., E.	80	82		..	S.E.	Fine.
10	4° 20′ N., E.	82	83		..	S.E.	Showery.
11	Pedro Blanca	79	76		..	N.W.	Showery.
12	At Singapore	76	82		..	N.E.	Showery.
Sund. 13	Left Singapore 2 P.M.	82	83		..	W.	Fine.
14	M. Straits of Malacca	79	84		..	W.	Fine.
15	At Penang	82	85		..	N.W.	Fine.
16	Left Penang 8 A.M.	80	85		..	E.	Fine.
17	Lat. Long.	84			..	N.	Fine.
18–31							

THE END.

Fresh Books of Travel and Adventure,

PUBLISHED BY

HARPER & BROTHERS, NEW YORK.

HARPER & BROTHERS will send either of the following Works by Mail, postage paid (for any distance in the United States under 3000 miles), on receipt of the Money.

Lord Elgin's Mission to China, &c. Narrative of Lord Elgin's Mission to China and Japan in 1857, '58, '59. By LAURENCE OLIPHANT, Secretary to Lord Elgin. Illustrations. 8vo, Muslin, $2 75.

Life in Spain. Past and Present. By WALTER THORNBURY, Author of "Every Man his own Trumpeter," "Art and Nature," "Songs of the Cavaliers and Roundheads," &c. With Illustrations. 12mo, Muslin, $1 00.

The Prairie Traveller. A Hand-Book for Overland Emigrants. With Maps, Illustrations, and Itineraries of the Principal Routes between the Mississippi and the Pacific. By RANDOLPH B. MARCY, U. S. Army. Published by Authority of the War Department. 16mo, Muslin, $1 00.

Ellis's Madagascar. Three Visits to Madagascar, during the Years 1853–1854–1856. Including a Journey to the Capital, with Notices of the Natural History of the Country and of the Present Civilization of the People. By the Rev. WILLIAM ELLIS, F.H.S., Author of "Polynesian Researches." Illustrated by a Map and Wood-cuts from Photographs, &c. 8vo, Muslin, $2 50.

Fankwei; or, The San Jacinto in the Seas of India, China, and Japan. By WILLIAM MAXWELL WOOD, M.D., U.S.N., late Surgeon of the Fleet to the United States East India Squadron, Author of "Wandering Sketches in South America, Polynesia," &c., &c. 12mo, Muslin, $1 25.

Page's La Plata. La Plata: The Argentine Confederation, and Paraguay. Being a Narrative of the Exploration of the Tributaries of the River La Plata and Adjacent Countries, during the Years 1853, '54, '55, and '56, under the orders of the United States Government. By THOMAS J. PAGE, U.S.N., Commander of the Expedition. With Maps and numerous Engravings. 8vo, Muslin, $3 00; Half Calf, $4 00.

The Land and the Book; or, Biblical Illustrations drawn from the Manners and Customs, the Scenes and the Scenery of the Holy Land. By W. M. THOMSON, D.D., Twenty-five Years a Missionary of the A.B.C.F.M. in Syria and Palestine. With two elaborate Maps of Palestine, an Accurate Plan of Jerusalem, and *several Hundred Engravings*, representing the Scenery, Topography, and Productions of the Holy Land, and the Costumes, Manners, and Habits of the People. Two elegant Large 12mo Volumes, Muslin, $3 50; Half Calf, $5 20; Half Calf extra, $5 50; Half Morocco extra, $5 00.

Fred Markham in Russia; or, The Boy Travellers in the Land of the Czar. By W. H. G. KINGSTON, Esq., Author of "Salt Water," "Peter the Whaler," "Mark Seaworth," "Manco," &c. Profusely and elegantly Illustrated. Small 4to, Muslin gilt, 75 cents.

South Africa. Missionary Travels and Researches in South Africa; including a Sketch of Sixteen Years' Residence in the Interior of Africa, and a Journey from the Cape of Good Hope to Loando on the West Coast; thence across the Continent, down the River Zambesi, to the Eastern Ocean. By DAVID LIVINGSTONE, LL.D., D.C.L. With Portrait, Maps by ARROWSMITH, and numerous Illustrations. 8vo, Muslin, $3 00.

North and Central Africa. Travels and Discoveries in North and Central Africa. Being a Journal of an Expedition undertaken under the Auspices of H.B.M.'s Government, in the Years 1849–1855. By HENRY BARTH, Ph.D., D.C.L., Fellow of the Royal Geographical and Asiatic Societies, &c., &c. Profusely and elegantly Illustrated. Complete in 3 vols. 8vo, Muslin, $7 50; sheep, $8 25; Half Calf, $10 50.

Western Africa: Its History, Condition, and Prospects. By Rev. J. LEIGHTON WILSON, Eighteen Years a Missionary, and now one of the Secretaries of the Presbyterian Board of Foreign Missions. With numerous Engravings. 12mo, Muslin, $1 55.

Southwestern Africa. Lake Ngami; or, Explorations and Discoveries during Four Years' Residence in the Wilds of Southwestern Africa. By CHARLES JOHN ANDERSSON. With numerous Illustrations, representing Sporting Adventures, Subjects of Natural History, Devices for Destroying Wild Animals, &c. New Edition. 12mo, Muslin, 75 cents.

A Hunter's Life in the Interior of Africa. Five Years of a Hunter's Life in the Far Interior of South Africa. With Notices of the Native Tribes, and Anecdotes of the Chase of the Lion, Elephant, Hippopotamus, Giraffe, Rhinoceros, &c. A new Edition. With Illustrations. 2 vols. 12mo, Muslin, $1 75.

Boat Life in Egypt. By WILLIAM C. PRIME, Author of "The Old House by the River" and "Later Years." Illustrations. 12mo, Muslin, $1 25.

Tent Life in the Holy Land. By WILLIAM C. PRIME, Author of "The Old House by the River," "Later Years," &c. Illustrations. 12mo, Muslin, $1 25.

Atkinson's Siberia. Oriental and Western Siberia: A Narrative of Seven Years' Explorations and Adventures in Siberia, Mongolia, the Kirghis Steppes, Chinese Tartary, and part of Central Asia. By THOMAS WITLAM ATKINSON. With a Map and numerous spirited Illustrations from Drawings by the Author. 8vo (uniform with Livingstone's Travels), Muslin, $3 00.

European Acquaintance: Being Sketches of People in Europe. By J. W. DE FOREST. 12mo, Muslin, 75 cents.

Washington Territory and the Northwest Coast. Three Years' Residence in Washington Territory. By JAMES G. SWAN. Map and numerous Illustrations. 12mo, Muslin, $1 25.

Virginia Illustrated: containing a Visit to the Virginian Canaan, and the Adventures of Porte Crayon and his Cousins. Illustrated from Drawings by Porte Crayon. 8vo, Muslin, $2 50; Half Calf antique, $3 50; Half Calf extra gilt, $4 00.

Random Sketches and Notes of European Travel in 1856. By Rev. JOHN E. EDWARDS, A.M. 12mo, Muslin, $1 00.

Explorations and Adventures in Honduras, comprising Sketches of Travel in the Gold Regions of Olancho, and a Review of the History and General Resources of Central America. With Original Maps and numerous Illustrations. By WILLIAM V. WELLS. 8vo, Muslin, $2 00.

Stories of the Island World. By CHARLES NORDHOFF, Author of "Man-of-War Life," "The Merchant Vessel," "Whaling and Fishing," &c. Illustrations. 16mo, Muslin, 75 cents.

El Gringo; or, New Mexico and her People. By W. W. H. DAVIS, late United States Attorney. 12mo, Muslin, $1 25.

Dore. By A STROLLER IN EUROPE. 12mo, Muslin, $1 00.

New Granada: Twenty Months in the Andes. By I. F. HOLTON. With between 20 and 40 Illustrations, Maps, and a Copious Index. 8vo, Muslin, $2 00; Half Calf, $3 00.

The Araucanians; or, Notes of a Tour among the Indian Tribes of Southern Chili. By EDMOND REUEL SMITH, of the U.S.N. Astronomical Expedition in Chili. 12mo, Muslin, $1 00.

A Journey through the Chinese Empire. By M. HUC, Author of "Recollections of a Journey through Tartary and Thibet." With a new and beautiful Map. 2 vols. 12mo, Muslin, $2 00.

Jarves's Parisian Sights, First Series. Parisian Sights and French Principles seen through American Spectacles. By JAMES JACKSON JARVES. With Illustrations. 12mo, Muslin, $1 00.

Jarves's Parisian Sights, Second Series. Parisian Sights and French Principles seen through American Spectacles. Second series. By JAMES JACKSON JARVES. Numerous Illustrations. 12mo, Muslin, $1 00.

Jarves's Italian Sights. Italian Sights and Papal Principles seen through American Spectacles. By JAMES JACKSON JARVES. Numerous Illustrations. 12mo, Muslin, $1 00.

Ida Pfeiffer's Journey Round the World. A Lady's Second Journey Round the World; from London to the Cape of Good Hope, Borneo, Java, Sumatra, Celebes, Ceram, the Moluccas, &c., California, Panama, Peru, Ecuador, and the United States. By IDA PFEIFFER, Authoress of the "Lady's Journey Round the World," &c. 12mo, Muslin, $1 25.

Beckwourth's Life and Adventures. The Life and Adventures of JAMES P. BECKWOURTH, Mountaineer, Scout, and Pioneer, and Chief of the Crow Nation of Indians. Written from his own Dictation. By T. D. BONNER. Illustrations. 12mo, Muslin, $1 25.

Baird's Modern Greece. Modern Greece: A Narrative of a Residence and Travels in that Country. With Observations on its Antiquities, Literature, Language, Politics, and Religion. By HENRY M. BAIRD, M.A. Illustrated by about 60 Engravings. 12mo, Muslin, $1 25.

www.ingramcontent.com/pod-product-compliance
Lightning Source LLC
Chambersburg PA
CBHW021221300426
44111CB00007B/389